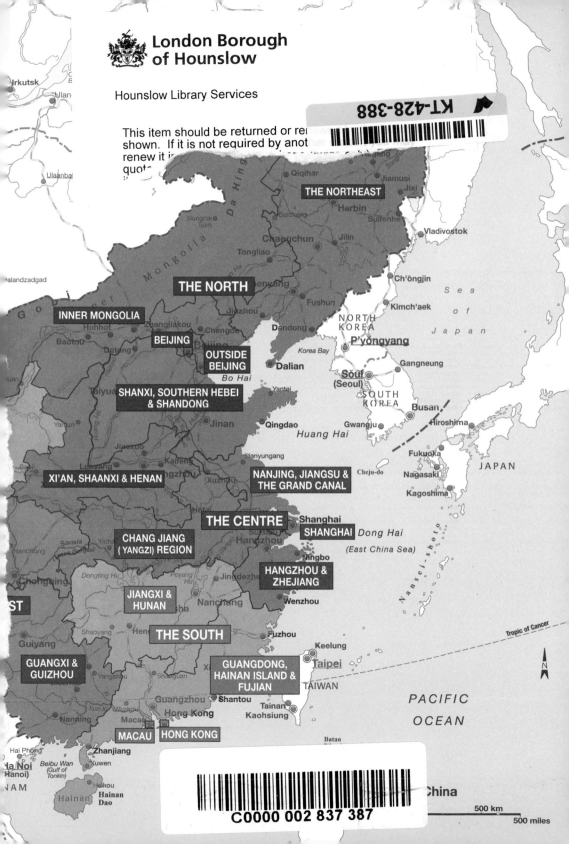

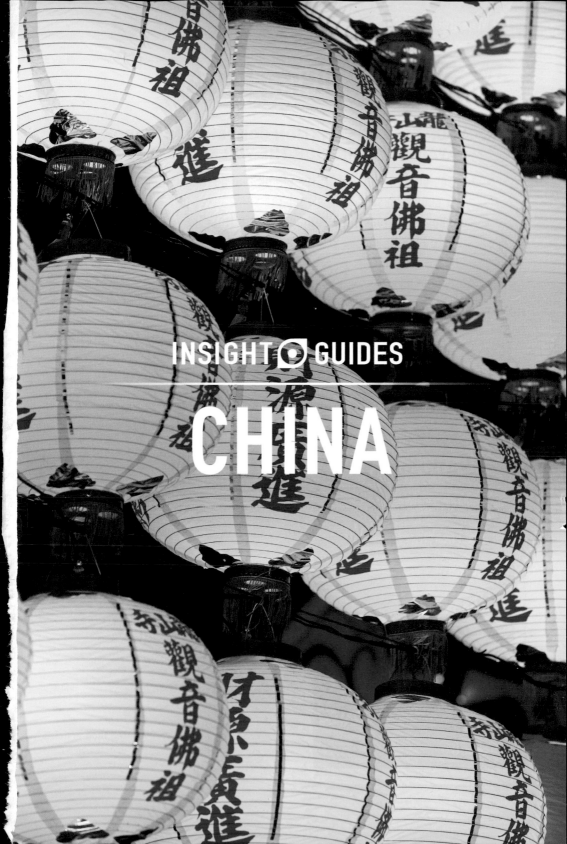

INSIGHT ◉ GUIDES

CHINA

⊙ Walking Eye App

YOUR FREE DESTINATION CONTENT AND EBOOK AVAILABLE THROUGH THE WALKING EYE APP

Your guide now includes a free eBook and destination content for your chosen destination, all for the same great price as before. Simply download the Walking Eye App from the App Store or Google Play to access your free eBook and destination content.

HOW THE WALKING EYE APP WORKS

Through the Walking Eye App, you can purchase a range of eBooks and destination content. However, when you buy this book, you can download the corresponding eBook and destination content for free. Just see below in the grey panels where to find your free content and then scan the QR code at the bottom of this page.

Destinations: Download your corresponding essential destination content from here, featuring recommended sights and attractions, restaurants, hotels and an A–Z of practical information, all for free. Other destinations are available for purchase.

Ships: Interested in ship reviews? Find independent reviews of river and ocean ships in this section, all available for purchase.

eBooks: You can download your free accompanying digital version of this guide here. You will also find a whole range of other eBooks, all available for purchase.

Free access to travel-related blog articles about different destinations, updated on a daily basis.

HOW THE DESTINATION CONTENT WORKS

Each destination includes a short introduction, an A–Z of practical information and recommended points of interest, split into 4 different categories:

- Highlights
- Accommodation
- Eating out
- What to do

You can view the location of every point of interest and save it by adding it to your Favourites. In the 'Around Me' section you can view all the points of interest within 5km.

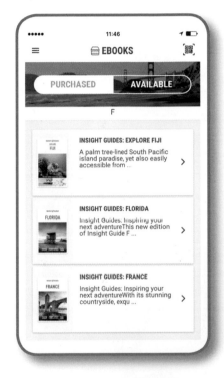

HOW THE EBOOKS WORK

The eBooks are provided in EPUB file format. Please note that you will need an eBook reader installed on your device to open the file. Many devices come with this as standard, but you may still need to install one manually from Google Play.

The eBook content is identical to the content in the printed guide.

HOW TO DOWNLOAD THE WALKING EYE APP

1. Download the Walking Eye App from the App Store or Google Play.
2. Open the app and select the scanning function from the main menu.
3. Scan the QR code on this page – you will then be asked a security question to verify ownership of the book.
4. Once this has been verified, you will see your eBook and destination content in the purchased ebook and destination sections, where you will be able to download them.

Other destination apps and eBooks are available for purchase separately or are free with the purchase of the Insight Guide book.

CONTENTS

LEGEND
♀ Insight on
◙ Photo Story

THE BEST OF CHINA: TOP ATTRACTIONS

The must-see sights of this vast country range from awe-inspiring ancient treasures to futuristic city skylines, timeless landscapes and fascinating old towns.

▷ **The Great Wall.** Built to keep the northern barbarians out of the Middle Kingdom, this is a true wonder of the world, extending more than 6,400km (4,000 miles) across northern China from the east coast to the Gobi Desert. The section of Great Wall north of Beijing is both accessible and spectacular, writhing its way across a dramatic hilly landscape. See page 150.

▷ **Lijiang.** In the mountainous northwest of Yunnan province, the old town of **Lijiang** is one of the most popular destinations in China, with excellent tourist facilities, a relaxed atmosphere and superb scenery on its doorstep. See page 380.

◁ **Shanghai.** The skyline with its glittering array of buildings, including the iconic Pearl Oriental TV Tower, is the most compelling visual evidence of China's contemporary prosperity. The city is bursting with life, and this, combined with its unique history and architecture, makes it a fascinating place to spend a few days. See page 213.

△ **The Silk Road.** Follow this ancient route through the wide-open spaces of the northwest to experience a completely different side of China. Oasis towns strung along this conduit of trade and cultural exchange – such as Turpan and Kashi – have retained their exotic Central Asian flavour and are full of interest. See page 415.

◁ **Terracotta Warriors**. One of the world's most extraordinary historical sights, only discovered in the 1970s. Three large underground vaults house over 8,000 life-sized figures. See page 202.

△ **Guilin landscapes**. The magnificent scenery around the city of Guilin, which has inspired countless Chinese scroll paintings, comes to life along the Li River south of the city. Dreamlike rock spires tower above lush riverine scenery to stunning effect. See page 345.

▽ **Huang Shan. A** fabulously scenic mountain in central China with all the attributes of a classic Chinese peak: rocky crags, twisted pines and ethereal views over a sea of clouds. See page 270.

▷ **Guizhou province minority groups**. The Miao and Dong people are known for their spectacular festivals, impressive drum towers and unique wind-and-rain bridges. Rural life has changed little in this remote region, making it a fascinating place to visit. See pages 351 and 356.

▽ **Yangzi Gorges**. Take a river cruise along China's longest river and marvel at the scenery. See page 262.

▽ **The Temple of Heaven, Beijing**. Perhaps the most accessible and beautiful of the country's heritage sights. Set in a large park, the highlight is the circular Hall of Prayer for Good Harvests. See page 137.

THE BEST OF CHINA: EDITOR'S CHOICE

Unique attractions, colourful festivals, urban highlights, fabulous landscapes, quiet backwaters, river cruises ... here are our recommendations for the must-sees on your trip to China.

TOP CITIES

Beijing. The great hub of power in China, past and present, with an array of unmissable sights. See page 131.

Shanghai. China's frenzied commercial capital, an extraordinary blend of old and new. See page 213.

Guangzhou. One of the best cities in China for eating out, this is a fast-paced boom town. See page 307.

Nanjing. With its broad avenues and placid canals, Nanjing is an attractive and relaxed city. See page 232.

Chengdu. The 2,000-year-old capital of Sichuan has kept some of its traditional feel, with colourful streets lined with tiny shops and teahouses. See page 360.

Kunming. Capital of China's most diverse province, Yunnan,

Kunming has an easy-going charm and a delightful climate. See page 372.

Qingdao. This northern port has a smattering of Teutonic architecture and sandy beaches. See page 179.

Xiamen. A port facing traffic-free Gulangyu island, full of eccentric European buildings. See page 320.

Xi'an. China's ancient capital has some major sights and the Terracotta Warriors nearby. See page 188.

Lhasa. At a dizzying altitude, the Tibetan capital is a fascinating city, home to many of the holiest sights of Tibetan Buddhism. See page 397.

Hong Kong. Unique, vibrant and full of things to see and do, a perfect introduction to the Chinese world. See page 281.

Classical Chinese garden, Suzhou.

BEAUTIFUL TOWNS

Fenghuang. A visit to this beguiling riverside town in Hunan province is a rare chance to see the old China, its wooden buildings and narrow streets representative of how much of the country looked in days gone by. See page 332.

Dali. With its splendid setting between towering green mountains and a peaceful lake, laid-back Dali is one of the most relaxing places in China. See page 376

Pingyao. A wonderfully preserved small town in Shanxi province enclosed

within Ming-dynasty walls. See page 178.

Chaozhou. Retaining the atmosphere and architecture of an ancient city, this is a southern Chinese gem. See page 317.

Quanzhou. This pleasant city on the sub-tropical southeast coast was once the world's busiest port. See page 323.

Kaifeng. One of the best-preserved old centres anywhere in China. See page 200.

Turpan. A Silk Road oasis deep in Central Asia, full of interest. See page 424.

Wilderness landscape in western Sichuan.

MAGNIFICENT SCENERY

The rice terraces at Longsheng, Guangxi.

Guilin region. The famous limestone scenery along the Li River south of Guilin is one of China's most memorable sights. See page 342.

Huang Shan. This lofty peak in central China has an ethereal beauty. See page 270.

Longsheng rice terraces, Guangxi. The "Dragon's Back" terraces wind in huge layers 800 metres (2,600ft) up the sides of a steep valley. The rice terraces of southern Yunnan are similarly spectacular. See page 348.

Northern and western Sichuan. Magical, sparklingly coloured lakes at Jiuzhaigou, and the panda reserve at Ya'an Bifengxia Base. Further north are expanses of wild grassland. See page 368.

Xishuangbanna, Yunnan. This tropical region, home to rare birds, elephants and the Buddhist Dao people, has more in common

with neighbouring Laos and Burma than the rest of China. See page 384.

The Three Parallel Rivers, Yunnan. Mighty gorges along the remote headwaters of three great rivers – the Nu Jiang, the Mekong and the Yangzi. See page 382.

Southern Hainan beaches. The white sands of Dadonghai and Yalong Wan are as close as China comes to a tropical paradise. See page 318.

Emei Shan. The Holy Mountain of Sichuan, with many Buddhist temples spread around its thickly forested slopes. See page 365.

Tai Shan. A sacred peak, with stupendous views across the northern plains. See page 181

Tian Chi (Lake of Heaven). A dazzling lake ringed by the snow-capped Tian Shan. See page 428.

Wulingyuan Scenic Reserve. A magical landscape of limestone spires and forest. See page 331.

Miao festival finery, Guizhou.

Detail from a "nine-dragon screen" at Beijing's Forbidden City.

OFF THE BEATEN TRACK

Guizhou province. Home to over 30 minority groups, each with its special culture – such as the Dong, builders of covered bridges, or the Miao, famed for colourful festivals. See page 350.

Beihai, Guangxi. A pleasantly relaxed port city near the Vietnamese border, with beaches and characterful old buildings from its days as a trading centre. See page 349.

Lushan, Jiangxi. This hill town above the Yangzi plain was used as a summer retreat by western missionaries and, later, by Mao Zedong. See page 327.

Kashi (Kashgar), Xinjiang. China's westernmost city, a Silk Road caravanserai surrounded by deserts and high mountains. See page 429.

Lanzhou, Gansu. Few tourists stay in this dusty city: there is little

to see in terms of conventional sights and the air quality is notoriously bad. Yet Lanzhou is unique: ranged along a Yellow River gorge, this long, narrow city has a Central Asian feel and some great food. See page 415.

Inner Mongolian grasslands. A seemingly infinite expanse of grass and steppe, interrupted by a few lonely Buddhist stupas. See page 171.

Karakoram Highway. One of the world's most spectacular roads, between awe-inspiring peaks into Pakistan. See page 432.

The Siberian far north. Vast pine forests and reed lakes – the habitat of many rare birds – along the border with Russia. See page 167.

Southwest Fujian. Yongding County features numerous Hakka round-houses. See page 324.

The Hall of Benevolence and Longevity at the Summer Palace, Beijing.

Martial arts training at Shaolin.

CLASSICAL CHINA

West Lake, Hangzhou. Celebrated by poets, this misty lake is ringed by woods and pagodas – the quintessential Chinese beauty spot. See page 250.

The Grand Canal. The ancient 1,800-km (1,100 miles) waterway, extended over 1,000 years, links a series of picturesque towns. See page 245.

The Summer Palace, Beijing. One of the most complete classical Chinese gardens, with lotus pools between lakeside pagodas. See page 146.

Suzhou. Historically prosperous Suzhou is famous for exquisite gardens and silk. See page 238.

Yangzi River cruise. The amazing scenery of the Yangzi Gorges makes a cruise on China's great river a memorable experience. See pages 261, 445.

Li River cruise. A placid trip through a spellbinding landscape. See page 348.

Dayan Ta (Great Wild Goose Pagoda), Xi'an. One of China's most striking pagodas, dating from the 7th century AD. See page 190.

TEMPLES AND MONASTERIES

Wong Tai Sin Temple, Hong Kong. The "Fortune-tellers' Temple" is one of the most bustling, and most colourful of China's Daoist shrines. See page 292.

Lama Temple, Beijing. A beautiful Lamaist temple in the heart of Beijing. See page 141.

Xuankong Si Temple. This "hanging temple" clings to the cliff face on Heng Shan, one of China's sacred Daoist peaks. See page 176.

Putuo Shan Island. A Buddhist holy mountain on a tranquil island near Shanghai, presided over by the Goddess of Compassion, Guanyin. See page 256.

Shaolin. Famous worldwide as the great centre of Chinese martial arts. See page 196.

Labrang Monastery, Xiahe. The largest Lamaist monastery outside Tibet, with over 2,000 monks. See page 418.

Baima Si Temple. The oldest Buddhist temple in China, founded in AD 68. See page 195.

Qiongzhu Si Temple. Surreal sculptures of Buddhist saints in the hills above Kunming. See page 374.

Confucius Temple (Kong Miao), Qufu. China's most important Confucian temple. See page 184.

A peaceful scene in Suzhou.

MAJOR HISTORICAL SIGHTS

Terracotta Warriors. This awe-inspiring sight is a must-see on any China itinerary. See page 202.

Forbidden City, Beijing. History on a grand scale right in the heart of the capital, the emperors' city is a must-see. See page 132.

Longmen Caves. Amazing Buddhist carvings spread across a series of grottoes. See page 195.

Leshan Buddha. This colossal 71-metre (230ft) statue of Buddha was built to protect river traffic. See page 367.

Mogao Caves. Over 490 caves lived in, carved and painted over 1,000 years

The Big Buddha at Leshan.

by Buddhist monks, inside a mountain on the edge of the Gobi Desert. See page 422.

Potala Palace, Lhasa. Symbol of Tibet, the immense 1,000-room palace of the Dalai Lamas dominates the city of Lhasa. See page 398.

Shaoshan. Mao's birth-place in Hunan province is now a museum-village, with his childhood home carefully preserved. See page 329.

Tiananmen Square, Beijing. This vast square at the gates of the Forbidden City has witnessed momentous historical events. See page 135.

The Terracotta Warriors near Xi'an.

FESTIVALS AND EVENTS

Chinese New Year. A special time, with dragon dances, parades and temple fairs. See page 389.

Mid-Autumn Festival. Moon cakes and lanterns make this a picturesque occasion. See pages 388.

National Day. Marked with parades and floral displays; as at Chinese New Year, most shops and businesses close for a week. It's a bad time to travel. See page 450.

Ice-sculpture Festival, Harbin. Spectacular ice-carving festival in the depths of the north-eastern winter. See page 167.

Dragon Boat Festival. An exciting event held all over eastern and southern China, with fiercely competitive races and plenty of noise. See pages 388 and 450.

Miao and Dong Festivals. These festivities in Guizhou province are some of the most colourful spec-tacles in the country. See page 354.

Tin Hau Festival. The birthday of the Goddess of the Sea (also known as Matsu and A-Ma), is marked in southern coastal regions with firecrackers and parades. See page 322.

TRAVELLERS' TIPS

Tourist information Most CTS (China Travel Service) and CITS (China International Travel Service) offices exist to sell tours – rather than to impart free information to tourists. All CTS/CITS offices should be able to assist with tickets for air and rail travel.

Buying rail tickets For overnight journeys, you should purchase your tickets 2–5 days in advance (10 days is usually the maximum), as they often sell out – more of a problem if you are joining the train a long way into its journey. The choice is either hard-sleeper or the noticeably more comfortable soft-sleeper. If you are told there are none left, it may still be possible to buy from a travel agent such as CTS. Rail-way stations in large cities usually have a dedicated ticket window for foreigners, with little queuing invol-ved. See page 441.

Buses Some long-distance buses (mostly between smaller cities) only set off once every inch of space is occupied. Tickets are usually easy to buy at bus stations on the day of travel. Express buses are a reasonable alternative to trains, particularly now that the coun-try's road network is vastly improved.

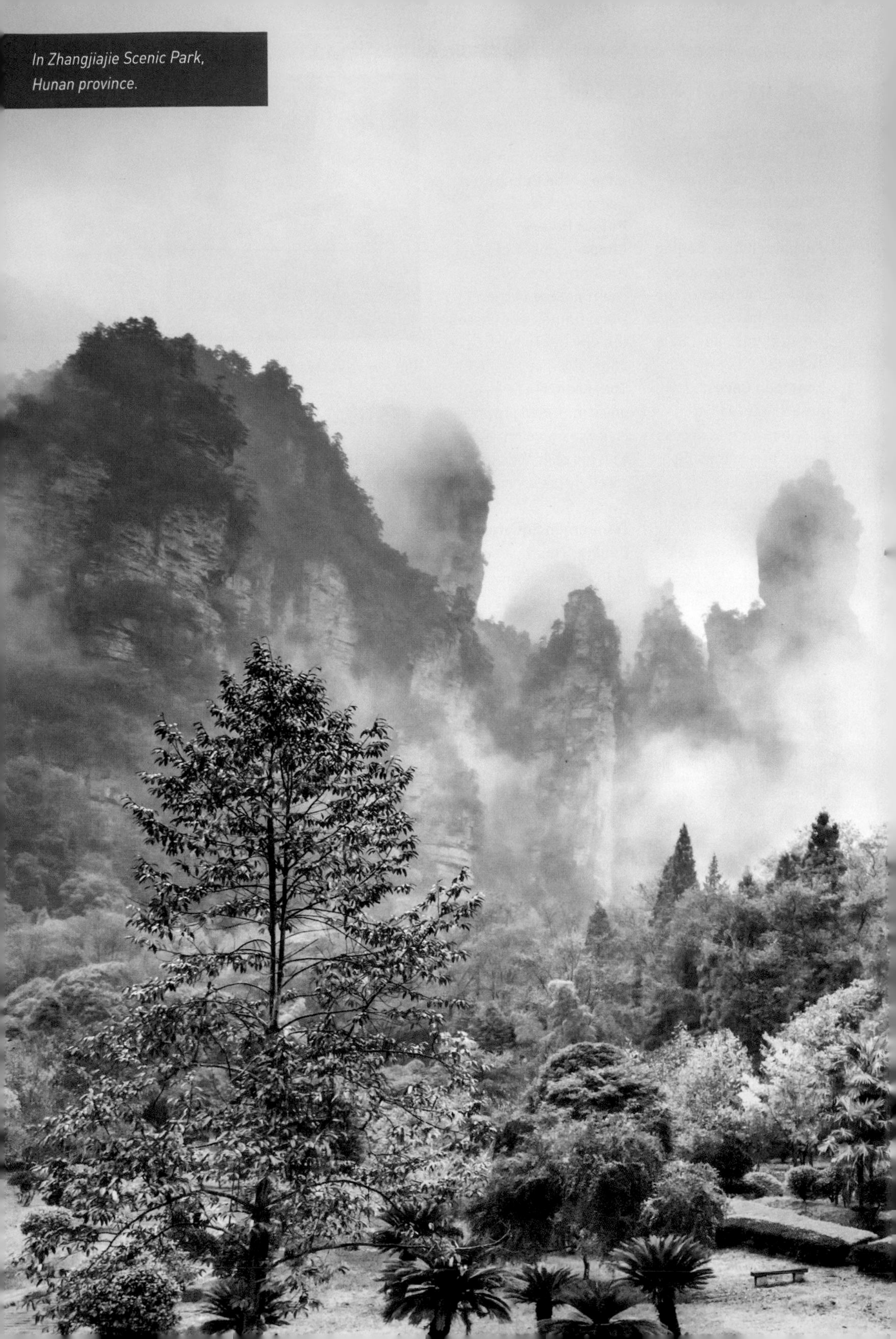

In Zhangjiajie Scenic Park, Hunan province.

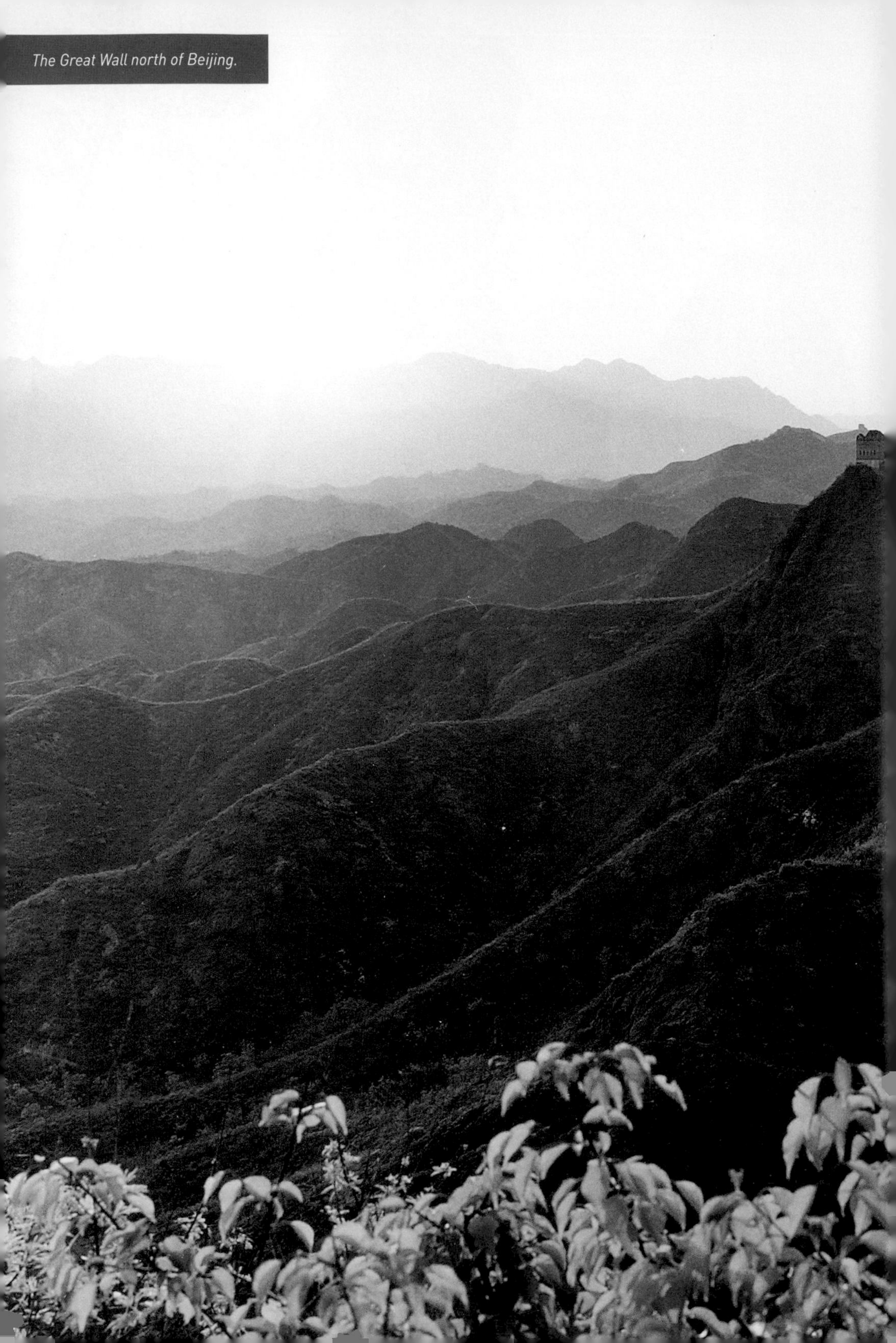

The Great Wall north of Beijing.

Rice terraces in southern Yunnan province.

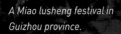

THE NEW SUPERPOWER

After 40 centuries of introspection, China is now helping to define the world's future, whether we're ready or not.

Buyi minority women in Yunnan province.

China is a land of superlatives. The most populous country on earth with the second-largest economy, it claims the world's longest continuously recorded history: the precociously advanced civilisations of its distant past have given humanity some of its most significant scientific and technological inventions. After an extended period of decline and turmoil, China has risen to become an economic superpower at dizzying speed, hosting a successful Olympic Games and weathering a global economic crisis along the way. Challenging to interpret, impossible to ignore – China has arrived on the global stage and invites you to marvel at its achievements.

The name China, as used in the West, can be traced back to the Qin dynasty (221–206 BC), when the concept of a unified China became reality. The land was variously known as Tschin, Tschina or Tzinistan, and later Cathay, in the Indo-Germanic languages, while to the Chinese themselves it has always been, simply, Zhongguo – the Middle Kingdom.

In Beijing's Temple of Heaven a marble altar signifies the centre of the known ancient world, a place that only the emperor was allowed to enter. According to the world-view of ancient China, the Middle Kingdom lay precisely below the centre of the firmament. The further one was from the emperor's throne, the lower one was in the cosmic hierarchy. The unfortunate people and cultures living on the dark peripheries of the earth, especially to the gloomy north and the arid west, and to Europe beyond, were considered barbaric.

Buddhist monks at Wutai Shan, one of China's sacred peaks.

For centuries, Europeans similarly regarded China as near the edge of the known world; admittedly the Middle Kingdom was an empire of magnificence and cultural interest, but of little importance to the world scheme. Much later, Western analysts and pundits referred to China as a sleeping giant, or more lyrically, a sleeping tiger or dragon. Modern China, now wide-awake, is a global power helping to shape the new millennium.

Yet this role is not something with which the country is comfortable or experienced: for most of its existence China has turned its back on the world and focused inward, like a tai chi student seeking a centred stability. China may be learning fast, but the nation's emergence onto the world stage has not been without its difficulties.

Since the end of World War II, the country's population has more than doubled to 1.38 billion people. Although only approximately 7 percent of China's land is suitable for agriculture, a fifth of the world's people must subsist on it. Finding employment for such a large section of humanity is a further headache: with the boom in the Chinese economy in recent years, the government has to do all it can to sustain employment levels in the new industries.

Travellers to China's large cities will see the results of accommodating the explosive demographic, and economic, growth: monochromatic, concrete cities veiled with the smoke of pollution, and legions of men from the countryside looking for work. Travellers will also see increasing affluence as the growth of the consumer society continues to eradicate the austerity of the past. The standard of living has improved exponentially for many in recent years, particularly in the prosperous coastal cities. The ruling Communist Party – the social and economic system is, of course, far from communist these days, yet the one-party state remains – is intolerant of political diversity or dissent.

Economics and politics aside, it is the land and peoples of China that enthral. A baffling hotchpotch of dialects unified by a common script, China is a fantastic and unique journey. From the mountain vastness of Tibet in the west to the affluent eastern coastline, from the dry northern heartlands to the

A cultural performance in Suzhou, one of China's most popular tourist resorts.

resourceful and fertile south, China is a constantly engaging and challenging destination. "Seeing is easy, learning is hard" goes an old Chinese proverb. The insightful traveller must necessarily realise and acknowledge that China simply is China.

NOTES ABOUT SPELLINGS AND LANGUAGE

The romanisation system used in this book is *pinyin*, the modern standard and the official system used within the People's Republic. What was Peking is now Beijing, and it is now Nanjing, not Nanking. The founder of the Communist Party used to be Mao Tse-tung; now it's Mao Zedong. Most *pinyin* transliterations are straightforward and simple to pronounce – the main exceptions are the letters *q* (pronounced *ch*) and *x* (pronounced *sh*).

Cycling past a traditional building in Chaozhou, Guangdong province.

Mandarin uses suffixes to indicate many proper nouns, such as river (*-jiang or -he*), temple (*-si or -ta*), mountain (*-shan*), or street (*-lu or -jie*). In romanised or *pinyin* form, the suffix is sometimes integral with the root, sometimes not. We have chosen to separate the suffix to clearly identify the subject. Thus, the Tian Mountains are referred to as "Tian Shan". For the majority of temples and parks, we use the Chinese *pinyin* as the primary reference in bold type, followed by Chinese characters and English in parentheses. However, where a sight is more usefully identified in English – as in the case of most museums, or with well-known sights with a familiar English name such as the Great Wall or Moon Hill – we have used the English in bold followed by Chinese characters and *pinyin*.

Xiangqi, also known as
Chinese chess.

THE LANDS OF CHINA

China's vast territory extends from subarctic north to tropical south, from barren deserts and mountains in the west to intensive cultivation on the coastal plains.

For many centuries, China's imposing geographical barriers created a natural border that both protected and isolated the Chinese from foreign contact. To the east and southeast is a coastline of about 18,000km (11,000 miles), and to the west are the Himalayas and the Tibetan plateau. In the north, contact with "barbarians" from Mongolia spurred the Chinese to build a series of walls over the centuries, collectively called the Great Wall.

China covers an area of 9,560,900 sq km (3,691,500 sq miles), with a border of 20,000km (12,500 miles). Its neighbouring countries are North Korea, Mongolia, Russia, Kazakhstan, Kyrgyzstan, Tajikistan, Afghanistan, Pakistan, India, Nepal, Bhutan, Burma (Myanmar), Laos and Vietnam. The distance from the northernmost town of Mohe, located on the northeastern border with Russia, to the south coast of Hainan Island on the South China Sea, is 4,000km (2,500 miles). East to west from the westernmost extremity in the

Winter scene at the Great Wall, near Mutianyu.

China is either the third or fourth largest country in the world: it's close enough in size to the US that territorial disputes tip the balance.

Pamir Mountains to the easternmost point – the confluence of the Heilong Jiang and the Wusuli Jiang – measures 5,200km (3,200 miles).

On Hainan Island in the far south, winter is warm, while at the same time the northeast is paralysed by Siberian frosts and icy winds. Some parts of Tibet endure perpetual frost, while crops grow year-round in Guangdong and southern Yunnan.

CLIMATE

Given China's size, it is not surprising to find a variety of climatic conditions. The varying elevation from the western mountain ranges to the eastern flatlands has an effect, but the main determining factor of China's weather is the country's position at the edge of the Asian continent next to the Pacific Ocean. In winter, frigid air masses form high-pressure zones in the heart of the continent which then move southwards over China; this results in dry winters. An unpleasant aspect of this is the high dust content in northern China as the air blows the loess in from the Gobi Desert. In the summer, low pressure sucks in air from the Pacific bringing the rains from the ocean, with a rainy season lasting from May until September. (See Travel Tips, page 447.)

TOPOGRAPHY

Two-thirds of China's territory is mountainous, hilly or high plateau. The terrain falls into three main regions, which can be thought of as topographical terraces.

The highest terrace is the Tibet-Qinghai Plateau, which rises 4,000 metres (13,000ft) above sea level and consists of Tibet, Qinghai and western Sichuan. Although the area is about a

rivers. It rarely rises more than 500 metres (1,600ft) above sea level and runs along the east coast from the north of China down to the south. More than two-thirds of the population lives along this coastal stretch, and it is China's agricultural and industrial heartland.

This terraced structure is the result of massive tectonic movements beneath the Chinese land mass, which remain unsettled. Earthquakes continue to strike in many regions of China, particularly the northwest, southwest and northeast. The 1976 earthquake in

Fertile rice fields in northern Guangxi.

quarter of China's total land mass, it is home to less than one percent of the nation's population. All the major rivers of China and Southeast Asia start in the Tibet-Qinghai Plateau. The Huang He (Yellow River) flows eastwards from the remote wastes of Qinghai province, while the Chang Jiang (Yangzi) heads south and then east to bisect the country. The Nu Jiang (Salween) and Lancang (Mekong) flow south through Yunnan province, before coursing their way into Burma and Laos.

The second terrace is formed by plateaux with heights averaging between 1,000 and 2,000 metres (3,000–6,500ft) in central and northwest China. The third terrace is formed by the plains and lowlands on the lower reaches of the large

⊘ TERMS OF GEOGRAPHY

In Chinese, a suffix usually follows a name. In this book, most suffixes are separated from the proper name to make recognition easier. For example, we use Huang He (Huang River) rather than Huanghe.

shan, feng: 山, 峰: hill, mountain(s), peak

he, jiang: 河, 江: river

pendi: 盆地: basin

hu, chi: 湖, 池: lake

hai: 海: sea

wan: 湾: bay

xia: 峡: gorge

wenquan: 温泉: spring

bei: 北: north

nan: 南: south

dong: 东: east

xi: 西: west

shi: 市: city, municipality

xian: 县: county

sheng: 省: province

zizhiqu: 自治区: autonomous region

> *The Himalayan range is nearly 2,400 km (1,500 miles) long and includes over 100 mountains that exceed 7,200 metres (23,620ft) in height.*

Tangshan, 145km (90 miles) east of Beijing, claimed an estimated 250,000 to 665,000 lives. In May 2008, another massive earthquake hit Sichuan province and the neighbouring region, claiming 70,000 lives.

the Taklamakan. On the other side of the Tibetan Plateau are the Hengduan mountains running through eastern Tibet, western Sichuan and Yunnan. These remote ranges have, even in modern times, formed a largely insurmountable barrier between China and the lands lying to the west.

In the northeast, the relatively low Greater Xingan range forms a natural border between the Manchurian lowland and the Mongolian steppe. This is also China's largest wooded area and thus an important watershed, with considerable influence on the climate. A similarly important cli-

Black-headed gulls at Bird Island, Qinghai Lake.

Rising above these terraces are the mountains. China has many of the highest peaks in the world. The Himalaya range, forming the southwest border of the country, is one of the youngest mountain ranges on the planet. On the border with Nepal is Mount Everest, the world's highest point at 8,850 metres (29,035ft).

Running parallel to the Himalaya range further north are the Kunlun mountains. In summer, the rivers that spring from the Qinghai Plateau are fed with frigid water from its melting glaciers.

Still further north and again extending from west to east is the 4,000-metre (13,000ft) high Tian Shan range which, together with the Kunlun mountains, encloses China's largest desert,

matic divide is the Qinling range, which reaches from the Gansu-Qinghai border all the way to Henan in central China. In summer, the Qinling acts as a barrier to the heavy masses of humid air brought by the monsoon: lands to the north are noticeably drier. In winter, the range effectively reduces the impact of the freezing winds streaming down from the Siberian steppes.

GREAT RIVERS

In historical terms, Huang He, the Yellow River, is undoubtedly the most important waterway in China. The region around the confluence of the Huang He and Wei rivers formed the cradle of Chinese civilisation. Yet, throughout the centuries, the river has also been known as "China's

Sorrow". Given to radical shifts in its course and frequent flooding (a result of irregular rainfall upstream and heavy silt deposits), the Huang He has been a source of anxiety to generations of peasants living by the river.

Rising in the western province of Qinghai, the Huang He makes a sharp bend to the north near Lanzhou and then further on, near Baotou in Mongolia, it turns south again, forming the famous Huang He knee. Only as it passes through the central Chinese loess plateau does it fill up with the yellow earth that has suggested the river's name.

The lower channel of the Huang He has radically changed course several times. Between 602 BC and AD 1194, it flowed to the north of its present-day path into the Yellow Sea. From 1194 to 1853, it shifted south so that it entered the East China Sea, south of Shandong Peninsula. After some flooding, it shifted its course to flow north of the peninsula. In 1938, Nationalist troops smashed the dykes in Henan to divert the river and slow the advance of Japanese troops. An estimated 900,000 civilian lives were lost as a result. In recent years, however, the lower

Climbing Everest.

Due to early deforestation, the land erodes very easily. The Huang He transports more than 1 billion tons of sediment into its lower reaches every year. In fact, the water level in the estuary is so low that there is no shipping route to the sea. As the riverbed widens in the lowland plain, the river deposits more than 4 million tons of silt.

Attempts to control the river go back almost as far as Chinese history itself. In 220 BC, Qin Shi Huangdi ordered dykes built and deepened the river's course. Over the centuries, peasants have built elaborate systems of dykes and levees that require constant maintenance because a breach in even one of the dykes can cause flooding for hundreds of kilometres around.

reaches of the river have repeatedly been dry.

The longest river in China, and third-longest in the world, is the 6,300km (3,900-mile) Chang Jiang, which rises in the Tanggula mountains of Qinghai province. Chang Jiang is the name commonly used for the middle reaches of the river, while the locals call the lower reaches, from Yangzhou to the estuary, the Yangzi. This is the name missionaries and colonialists became familiar with, and thus became established in Europe.

The Chang Jiang has also caused considerable flood damage over past centuries. The most notable in recent history is the flood of 1931, in which 3 million people died. In 2003, the Three Gorges Dam, designed to control and subdue the mighty river, as well as generating electricity, began operating. Completed three years later, it is the largest in the world at 180 metres (600ft) high and 2.25km (1.5 miles) long, and behind it there is a reservoir that is over 640km (400 miles) long. A ship elevator that can lift vessels of up to 3,000 tonnes entered service in 2016. It is the largest ship lift in the world. Critics of the dam point to its high financial and social costs (about 1.4 million people have been relocated) and warn of an ecological disaster in the making (for more on the dam, see page 266).

Ambitious, and some say unsustainable, plans

South China Sea – a situation which has brought a long-running dispute with Vietnam and other Southeast Asian lands that also claim the territory. China is also the world's largest producer of rare earths – a group of metals used in devices such as smart phones and electric car batteries. Demand for rare earths is growing globally and critics of China's trading practices say the country is limiting exports to unfairly support their own high-tech industry.

Fertile soil is found in the south and east of the country. Despite being the world's largest

Tiger Leaping Gorge, Yunnan.

Crops suffering in a recent drought, Hubei province.

to exploit hydroelectric power along the Chiang Jiang and its tributaries include blueprints for a chain of a dozen dams on the river's upper reaches that would have twice the capacity of even the colossal Three Gorges Dam.

RESOURCES

China is rich in natural resources. Coal exists in abundance, and China is among the world's top producers of gold, tin, mercury, aluminium, tungsten and barite. There are limited oil reserves in the northeast (wastefully exploited during the Mao era), Shaanxi and a few other places. China is now the world's largest importer of oil, and desperate to exploit potential oil (and gas) fields around the Spratly and Paracel islands in the

producer of rice and wheat, feeding a population of 1.38 billion is one of China's greatest challenges. Only 40 percent of the country can be used for agriculture or forestry, with only 12 percent of the total land suitable for farming. Deforestation and desertification are now two of China's biggest problems. In the past two decades, China has planted over 35 billion trees, increasing the area of forested land from 12 to 17 percent.

In 2002, an ambitious plan to divert water from the Yangzi Basin to the arid north via Huang He was given the go-ahead. The eastern route was expected to start operating in 2013. However, water pollution and construction delays have affected the viability of this project.

○ ENVIRONMENTAL ISSUES

China is facing increased pressure from home and abroad to combat widespread pollution and environmental damage caused by rampant economic growth.

China's overcrowded land has long been under intense pressure, with its forests, rivers and other natural resources heavily exploited for centuries to meet the needs of its vast population. More recently, there has been a reckless disregard for the environmental consequences of industrialisation, particularly during the Mao years but also with gargantuan schemes such as the Three Gorges Dam. Poaching, logging and soil erosion have jeopardised wildlife habitats. Air and water pollution are perennial problems and unrestrained consumption of water supplies has made North China increasingly arid in recent decades.

POLLUTION HOTSPOTS

Despite the efforts of the State Environmental Protection Agency and various high-profile international agencies, the primary focus inevitably remains on economic development. This isn't to say that efforts have not been made, but all too often inadequate regulation of factories and other, often state-owned, polluters makes the task almost impossible. China's notorious corruption means it is all too easy to bend the rules: companies simply ignore expensive anti-pollution measures.

Rural areas are often the worst affected, as China's hunger for resources seeks out even the slimmest pickings. Away from the central government's gaze, "cancer villages" blot the countryside as powerful interests pollute poor areas without conscience or consequence – though an increase in reporting transparency is bringing these deadly hotspots to public attention.

Of course, as China's economic growth poisons its population – particularly visible is the air pollution that leads to shocking levels of respiratory disease – there are protests. Organised demonstrations – some peaceful, some not – have led to the successful scrapping of plans for factories and other polluting projects.

GLOBAL CONCERN

China's environmental problems are very much of global importance. Now the world's biggest emitter of carbon dioxide in an era when climate change dominates the headlines, it is hard for Western nations to continue to allow China to be the world's workshop without taking into account its environ-

Many of China's cities are shrouded in a polluted haze.

mental practices. Unfortunately, the Chinese Communist Party refuses to be pressurised on internal issues by foreign governments and any change will be entirely on their own terms. Understandably enough, China also resents what is seen as the hypocrisy of Western nations that preach green policies but, at the time of their own industrialisation, gave no thought to the environment whatsoever.

Thankfully, China does have a few tricks up its sleeve owing to an increasingly high-tech manufacturing capability: it is soon to become the world leader on solar energy and electric car production. The government is also setting ambitious targets for renewable energy use and developing more sustainable models for economic growth through eco-cities.

Though it's hard to imagine China will struggle less than any other country in tackling the global ecological woes, it's certain not just to provide problems, but also some solutions.

For more on wildlife and conservation, see page 334.

THE CHINESE

More than 1.38 billion people – almost one-fifth of the planet's population – live in China, and most are crowded into just one-fifth of the country's land area.

The notion of being Chinese – that is, Han Chinese – is to some degree a cultural rather than an ethnic concept, an acceptance of Chinese values. Although over 90 percent of Chinese are considered ethnically Han, the distinction between them and other racial groups is not always clear cut. The Han Chinese are, of course, derived from a distinctive racial background, but over the many centuries, their gradual migration southwards from their original homelands around the Huang He (Yellow River) has seen the absorption of numerous racial minorities.

The Han – the name relates to the Han dynasty (206 BC–AD 220), a pivotal period in Chinese history – have traditionally populated the eastern part of the country, leaving the empty west and north to the minority ethnic groups. But overpopulation in the east, coupled with the government's desire to bring minority areas in line with the rest of the country, along with financial incentives, has encouraged ever greater numbers of Han migrants to move to far-flung places like Xinjiang and Tibet. Only in Tibet does the indigenous group remain in the majority, despite frequent reports of population transfers that would seem to suggest the contrary.

The Chinese today have more opportunities than they have ever had: more freedom to move around and travel overseas, more opportunities to seek better jobs and better education, and more chances to work and save money for a better future. The outlook has never been so good for so many people.

But at the same time, inevitably, huge problems exist. A wide gap separates rich from poor, and the gap is growing. In the cities, many people make relatively good money, but the cost of

A Shanghai migrant worker.

education, medicine and housing, as well as other services which were taken for granted a generation ago, has risen exponentially as China's Brave New World of market economics replaces the socialist past. Many of China's poor struggle just to survive. Farmers suffer from inflation and low prices for their crops, and widespread land grabs have seen many pushed off their land by developers.

POPULATION HEADACHES

Ninety percent of China's population lives on one-fifth of its land, mostly in the east and south. In contrast, the vast empty areas in the north and west are sparsely populated and often barely habitable.

China's population was counted for the first time about 2,000 years ago, in AD 4. By AD 742, during the Tang dynasty, the population was just over 50 million people. At the time of the invasion of Genghis Khan and the Mongols, the 100 million mark was probably exceeded for the first time. By the middle of the 18th century, the number had doubled; a century later, in 1850, the population had reached 400 million.

Shortly after World War II, there were half a billion people in China. Between the mid-1960s and the early 1980s, the population increased by over 300 million, more than the total population of either the United States or the former Soviet Union. According to official statistics, in 2015 China was home to almost 1.38 billion people, nearly 20 percent of the world's total population.

The governing and administrative challenges of such a huge population are mind-boggling. Gathering statistics for over 1 billion people, much less analysing it, defies the imagination. Still, statistics reveal much about China's options. The numbers are startling, considering that less than 10 percent of the world's agrarian

China's controversial one-child policy had limited success in rural areas.

⊘ TOO MANY PEOPLE, TOO FEW SURNAMES

When Genghis Khan was asked how he would conquer northern China, he replied: "I will kill everybody called Wang, Li, Zhang and Liu. The rest will be no problem."

With a population of well over 1 billion, it might be assumed that there would be plenty of surnames to go around in China. Yet of the 12,000 surnames that once existed in the nation, there remain today just 3,000. Nearly one-third of the population shares just five family names. In fact, nearly 90 percent of Chinese use just 100 surnames (the phrase *lao bai xing*, "old 100 names", is used to refer to the masses), with 90 million sharing the name Li, becoming by default the world's most common surname. In the US, by comparison, there are only 2.4

million people with the name Smith, the most common family name in the English-speaking world.

It is not surprising, then, that literally thousands of people in China can share the same full name, leading to many frustrating cases of mistaken identity. The possibility of a bureaucratic meltdown over the confusion caused by such a limited number of names is not far-fetched.

Much of the problem concerning the shortage of surnames began centuries ago when non-Han Chinese, seeking to blend quietly into the dominant culture, adopted the common names of the Han Chinese.

In China it is usual to address someone using their surname rather than first name, as a mark of respect.

China's vast population brings major advantages and disadvantages. A seemingly endless supply of cheap labour ensures a booming economy, but intense demand for food, fuel and other resources leaves the countryside exhausted and increasingly reliant on imports.

areas are in China. For every 1,000 people, there are 21 births but just six deaths.

In 1979, the government began a one-child-per-family programme to slow the population growth rate and combat fears of overpopulation; the programme lasted until 2015, with a new 'two-child' policy officially introduced in 2016. In urban areas, the one-child programme was mostly successful, but in rural areas, where traditions die hard and larger families were needed for farming, it had limited success. Exceptions were granted in various cases, such as for rural families where a son was considered necessary for farming, and for specific groups or provinces. Indeed, by the time the policy was revised, there were around two dozen different exemptions in place.

Skewing all population statistics was the traditional preference for male heirs. In China, family lines are passed on through the male child. Partly because of this, and because male offspring are more likely to support ageing parents, especially in rural areas, sons are preferred to daughters. Sex-selective abortions have long been an open secret throughout China and female infants in the countryside have even fallen victim to infanticide. From 1953 to 1964, the sex ratios at birth were within normal margins at a little under 105 males for every 100 female infants. Ultrasound scanners, which allow the determination of the sex of foetuses, were first introduced to China in 1979. As their use became widespread, especially among the middle and upper classes, the ratio climbed to 120 males to 100 females in 2008 and in certain areas it was as high as 135. The government looked to crack down on sex-selective abortions, but had to admit that China was projected to have some 24 million more men than women by 2020. Problems such as social discontent and human trafficking are feared will follow the trend.

The eventual change in the policy, formally allowing married couples to have two children as of the start of 2016, was ultimately driven by concerns about replacement demographics. As in many developed economies, there are fears over a smaller working-age population and a large aging population. Time will tell if the revised law impacts the birth rate in the way the economy – and sex ratio – demands. Although the one-child policy's original targets have proved excessively optimistic (as of 2011, the birth rate in China was closer to 1.4 per

Construction workers in Beijing.

woman) it has greatly reduced the rate of population increase. According to a recent estimate, the policy had prevented 400 million births by 2011, although thirty percent of births are not planned, despite widespread use of condoms, and sex education is still a taboo topic, especially in conservative rural areas where the grandmother educates her grandchildren according to her own beliefs. In the cities, on the other hand, it is possible that families might actually prefer to continue having only one child, as living space is restricted and women's career choices are better. Because living space in Shanghai or Beijing averages only 3.5 sq metres (38 sq ft), population-control measures are more accepted – and the impact of years of government insistence that small families are a good thing is unlikely to be undone quickly.

MIGRANT WORKERS

Contemporary China is the scene of a huge population movement, as tens of millions of migrant workers, lured by the sudden promise of wealth, have abandoned the still-poor villages and towns of their home provinces in China's interior and western regions and headed for the coastal cities in search of opportunities.

Communal exercise in a Beijing park.

And what have they found? Better lives, mostly. Many are content living in dorms, working long hours, saving money. Most of the successful migrant workers are young, and often single. When conditions are favourable – reasonable hours, comfortable dorm rooms, decent working conditions and prompt payment of wages – this can be a good life. And the money they send home does a great deal to support the rural countryside, especially in the poorest provinces.

But the less fortunate migrants have found only struggle and hardship. The Chinese have a phrase, *chi ku*, meaning to eat bitterness, that describes the lives of these unlucky ones. Many of them are men, often with families far away, who work in dangerous, dirty factory jobs, or on

dangerous, dirty construction sites. They are everywhere in China, in the railway stations, on the streets, in the factories and on the building sites, always without helmets or safety goggles. With their dirty clothes, unkempt hair and ceaseless energy, they are easy to spot.

Like itinerant workers everywhere, the migrants of China face discrimination. With their provincial dialects – many don't speak *putonghua* (Mandarin), the national language – and grinding poverty, they make easy targets. Migrants are often blamed for crime, and, indeed, they are guilty of many muggings, purse-snatchings and pickpocketings (bigger crimes, such as extortion, kidnapping and drug-smuggling, are usually the work of resident local gangs).

Profit margins for the factory owners and construction companies employing migrant workers are often paper-thin, as huge retail chains like Walmart and Target, with their massive economies of scale, beat down prices to the last fraction of a penny. As wages rise throughout China – a trend that began in 2004 and has been accelerating ever since – margins are further squeezed.

Perhaps the most serious problem for the migrant workers is non-payment of wages. Pursuing a case requires time and money and lacking the means or awareness of their legal rights, most workers have little choice but to accept whatever deal their employers offer. Declining export demand and labour reforms saw sudden factories closures flare up in 2008 and again in 2011, with tens of thousands of unpaid workers in the Pearl River Delta taking part in rioting. Further protests and riots have continued to take place in the years since.

CHANGE TO THE SYSTEM

In the old days, before market reforms and the lure of wealth changed everything, China was a place where lifetime employment was largely guaranteed, and people tended to remain in the same town or village for life. This stability was underpinned by the *hukou* system, whereby everyone in the country was registered at a particular address and which subsequently restricted movement as this required permission from the *danwei* (work unit). This has been breaking down since the 1990s, a process which has made it far easier for people to move around the country seeking work, though not necessarily settle down in first-tier cities with the same rights as locals.

Accompanying this freedom of movement, however, was a growing lack of security. Migrant workers have rarely been eligible for national health insurance, could not afford private insurance, and their employers seldom provide it. With hospitals routinely turning away those who can't afford treatment, an injury can mean the end of employment, or the end of a life. However, reforms to the *hukou* system are underway: crucially, the ability for migrant workers to change their status from rural to urban residents after residing in their new homes for six months, provided they are employed, which will grant urban residence permits and accompanying rights to 100 million migrants by 2020. The right to *hukou* will allow migrants and their families to access local healthcare and schooling. The government is intending a slow transition, with continuing greater restrictions on cities such as Shanghai and Beijing, to avoid overwhelming the existing services and infrastructure. This admission of rights is a big development, although for the forseeable future, the change will only affect just over a third of China's migrant population.

It is important to stress that it is not just the migrant workers who have suffered from the collapse of the state welfare system in matters of health, education and housing. Party workers benefit from free healthcare and schooling, but this is not the case for much of China these days. For most, free housing is no longer provided, and for good medical treatment or schooling, payment is essential. These services are increasingly privatised, a process at the heart of a profound transition as China switches from a centrally controlled socialist system to a market economy.

THE URBAN-RURAL DIVIDE

Farmers, who live far from media centres and big-city spotlights, are China's forgotten demographic. The migration from countryside to city is the largest movement in human history and it is hollowing out the rural heartland. Many rural dwellers are lonely: ageing parents with sons and daughters working far away, families with absentee fathers, wives living without their husbands. Even in the richer areas of Beijing, Shanghai and its hinterland, Guangdong, Fujian, Zhejiang and Jiangsu, the farmers have their

problems. As farmland gives way to industry and urban sprawl, they are often removed from their land. Compensation is supposed to be mandatory, but the amounts can vary according to the whims of local officials.

Farmers and poor rural residents have been fighting back, often by gathering in huge, hard-to-ignore protests. Sometimes the protests get violent, and sometimes, too, they get the attention of the rulers in Beijing, who generally side with the peasants. But the central government has limited power in the rural areas of China.

Ploughing the fields in rural Guizhou province.

Given the fact that farmers officially lease their land from the government (see page 74), this is a major political issue. Provincial, city and local officials all have much to gain by luring big-money projects to their fiefdoms, often in defiance of directives from Beijing. The tug-of-war between low-level officials and central government has become one of China's defining issues, with those in the middle – the rural poor – awaiting the outcome.

The once-peaceful village of Wukan in Southern China became an unlikely testing ground for a quasi-democratic uprising in late 2011 after village leaders attempted an extremely profitable land grab. Organised protesters clashed with officials and police, eventually deposing the village committee, obtaining compensation and electing a new party leader. Under the watchful eye of social networks such as Weibo, other protests, such as a mass demonstration against a huge chemical plant in Sichuan province's Shifang on environmental grounds in 2012, have proved successful.

THE URBAN MIDDLE CLASS

In China, the middle class is clearly on the rise, growing in both numbers and general prosperity. These are the men and women who commute to

FAMILY VALUES

The Communist Revolution of 1949 and some of the movements that followed it – notably the Cultural Revolution, an assault on all Chinese traditions – along with the country's heady modernisation over the past two decades, have had a serious impact on the primacy of the family in Chinese society. Moreover, the one-child policy, which was introduced in 1979 and ran until 2015, has changed the traditional Chinese family structure – prior to the 1970s, families are thought to have averaged five children.

Commuter traffic, Shanghai.

work in the cities, the secretaries, salespeople, accountants and other service-sector workers. They tend to be educated, computer literate and sometimes English-speaking. They have disposable income and leisure time, they watch films and go to restaurants, buy tailored suits, mobile phones, cars and flat-screen TVs. They travel, too, to domestic hot-spots like Hainan Island and Guilin, and overseas. Some are now seasoned travellers, and have visited cities in Europe and the US. On the negative side, the collapse of the state welfare system is a burden, and the rich cities on the eastern coast are starting to experience problems familiar to many in the West: high property prices, crowded commutes and rising crime.

⊘ INFLATING PRICES

When the Chinese character for "price rise" was voted word of 2010 on popular internet forum *Tianya*, few were surprised. Inflation, speculation and the hoarding of everything from property to food staples has led to costs soaring above even China's spectacular 10 percent economic growth rate. Unwilling to burst the housing bubble or introduce price controls, the government watches carefully as resentment grows amid a widening wealth gap. While unemployment has fortunately remained stable, the enormous challenge of graduate employment in the new economy could potentially spell disaster for China's social stability.

It was harder to implement the one-child policy in the countryside, where family ties remain strong. In villages, common surnames traditionally identify membership of the extended family clan.

Even if the one-child policy has not been as effective as many outsiders imagine (see page 31), some estimates indicate that the policy has resulted in as many as 400 million fewer births nationwide by 2011, and combined with a swelling tide of urban migration, the outcome is a shortage of farmhands in rural China, where once the crops were tended by extended families. The policy is thought to have allowed a greater integration of women into the workforce, but on the downside it has put enormous strains on traditional family expectations. In times past, children were expected to support parents and grandparents in their old age, and as a result of the one-child policy, a vast number of young Chinese face the burden of providing for two parents and four grandparents.

Problems such as these are being compounded by a generational fracturing. Young people speak the national language, *putonghua* (Mandarin), and sometimes even English, while their parents often speak only a local dialect. The older generation also knows nothing of the obsessions of China's youth: mobile phones, gaming, designer clothes, comic books and foreign fashions.

Thirty or 40 years ago, a city dweller's ticket to security was a job for life – the so-called "iron rice" bowl – with the Communist Party. On the farm, it was even simpler: plant the crops, work the fields and hope the elements were on your side. However, the new ticket to success is a university degree, proficiency in English and, more than anything else, youth. China's youth are drawn to the bright lights of China's coastal cities and don't want to work on the farms, and many of those for whom the bright lights are out of reach take jobs far away from home in the factories of the Pearl River Delta and the Shanghai hinterland. This has resulted in a generational gap unprecedented in China's history, with many young people feeling they have nothing to learn from their parents, and the parents themselves often feeling like they have nothing to teach. After all, the older generation was raised on a diet of Communist dogma that has very little place in China's freewheeling and effectively capitalist society, where money rules.

Women's status has improved immensely in recent years. Between 1990 and 2000 the number of women in the workforce rose from 280 million to 330 million, and they now account for around 49 percent of the total. Eight of the top 20 wealthiest self-made women in the world in 2016 were Chinese, proving that, despite facing discrimination in the workforce, the glass ceiling can still be resoundingly shattered.

A stroll in a Chengdu park.

SOCIAL LIFE

The Chinese are far more communal than Westerners and like to eat and travel in groups, and group activities start young for the Chinese. Before their lessons begin, schoolchildren often exercise together. Taped music and a voice blare out from speakers as they dance or perform callisthenics.

Morning streets are crowded with commuters, and the armadas of cyclists that once poured through the streets have been replaced by motorbikes and private cars. Buses are always packed – people push their way on into the throng, stand crushed against their neighbours, watch in case a seat becomes free, then push their way out when they reach their destinations. Queuing is an introduced and foreign concept.

As their rich and varied cuisine reflects, the Chinese love to eat, and China's rise in living standards is apparent at mealtimes. City residents, to whom even pork was once a treat, now regularly consume beef, fish and shrimp. While meals in the home may be relatively simple affairs with a small selection of dishes from which to choose, restaurant meals can be veritable banquets.

This is especially the case if the meal is charged to entertainment expenses, or is being paid for by a businessman who wants to impress – the Chinese very rarely split the tab. For a banquet really to impress, it should include rare delicacies such as exotic fungi or, sadly and illegally, endangered wildlife. But whatever the offering, there should always be more food than the diners can eat, otherwise the host loses face. Dinner is the chief evening event, though with China's explosion of nightlife options in recent years, the younger generation is likely to move on to bars and clubs later.

China's national and regional television stations are improving, and news reports in particular – while politically conservative – have become more daring. The production values in domestically produced sagas have improved greatly and they sometimes rival foreign soap operas and dramas in popularity. Satellite dishes and cable TV bring MTV, the Disney Channel and Star TV into Chinese homes (BBC and CNN can only be accessed in top hotels), and with China's profusion of internet access, more and more Chinese are downloading films and TV shows from abroad.

One indisputable phenomenon that can be attributed to China's new media is a sharp rise in the visibility of nationalist sentiment countrywide. In the lead up to the Beijing Olympics anti-foreign sentiment was running at a high that had not been seen in decades. The main reason was a media blitz against perceived Western bias, occasioned by reports of protests in Tibet, and by news of the Tibet support groups disrupting the Olympic torch relay around the world. Anti-Philippine sentiment has boiled up amid sabre rattling over sovereignty of what China calls Huangyan Island. The US, a mediator in South China Sea disputes, has not remained unscathed in public opinion.

3-D glasses at a Bai festival, Dali.

⊘ MEDIA AND POPULAR CULTURE IN TODAY'S CHINA

In their leisure time, the Chinese middle classes do what their counterparts do the world over: they watch TV. As Hong Kong industrialist Gordon Wu famously pronounced in the early 1990s: the people of China don't care about politics, what they want is to watch television in air-conditioned comfort. On one channel is basketball, or a football match from England. On other channels are politically-safe historical costume dramas, or stiff news programmes, foreign films or TV shows from Japan, Korea or the US. By far the most popular programmes are reality shows matching couples and churning out pop stars.

The internet is also immensely popular with China's over 700 million users who, like their Western counterparts, seek out news, social interaction, games and pornography. Censorship is a constant presence, however, with the "great firewall of China" routinely blocking sites that might organise and inform dissidents and barring search results for dozens of hot topics. A oasis of comparative freedom is microblogging site *Weibo*, where the tech savvy seek out unofficial news and discuss social topics.

In 2010, a government white paper even recognised the internet as a legitimate social watchdog. Though China's Communist Party strives to use the technology for control and to spread propaganda, when it comes to the free-flow of information, the internet genie is well and truly out of the bottle.

The result is a new mood in China: one of extreme pride in the nation's achievements and any criticism from home or abroad is often deemed anti-Chinese.

MINORITY GROUPS

There are over 50 officially recognised minority groups living in China today, including those in Tibet and Xinjiang. Most of these minority groups live along China's strategic, sometimes troubled and usually sparsely populated international borders. Thus, when one of the minority groups needles Beijing, such as happens with Tibetans and Uighurs, the central government takes such deviations quite seriously. Riots in Ürümqi in 2009 that caused 200 deaths resulted in a complete blackout of the internet across Xinjiang that lasted 10 months. A wave of self-immolations in Tibetan-occupied areas which peaked in 2012 led to media blackouts and increased restrictions for foreign tourists.

In 2000, the central government announced its "Go West" campaign, aimed at opening up western China, especially to foreign investment, improving the infrastructure and, it can be surmised, trying to keep any separatism in check. It also encourages ever more Han Chinese to relocate to these areas.

The defining elements of a minority are language, homeland and social values. Around 8 percent of China's population is part of a minority group, with the largest being the 16-million-strong Zhuang, in southwestern China.

FREEDOM OF LANGUAGE

The constitution guarantees minorities certain rights and privileges. One of the most important is the right to use their own language. To grant these minorities the right to live according to their own beliefs and traditions is, in the eyes of the Chinese, a sign of goodwill, and the renunciation of the expansionism of the old regime. However, spoken and written fluency in standard Mandarin is the only way to become educated and improve social status. Schools for members of national minorities are rare, and universities teaching a minority language hardly exist. In reality, the slow expansion of the Chinese nation from its original heartland around the Huang He is linked to an equally slow assimilation of non-Chinese peoples into the Han Chinese society, considered culturally and technically more advanced than the surrounding cultures.

In the autonomous region of Xinjiang in north-western China, Uighurs remain the largest existing ethnic group, but these days make up only 46 percent of the population. Only when grouped together with the Kazakhs, Kirghiz and others do Uighurs constitute an Islamic, Turkic-speaking majority. In the 1950s, 80 percent of the population fulfilled these criteria. But now, all the large cities (except for Kashi) have a majority of Han Chinese. Ürümqi, a city with over 1 million peo-

Hui Muslims in Lingxia, Gansu province.

ple, is now more than 72 percent Han Chinese.

The Muslim Hui make up only one-third of the population in their autonomous region of Ningxia, and they usually live in the economically less privileged areas. Most Hui can only satisfy the criteria used to classify a Hui (Chinese-speaking Muslim) with great difficulty.

In Inner Mongolia, the Han have predominated for decades and now represent 80 percent of the population. Yet, surprisingly, more Mongolians live in this region than in the neighbouring country to the north – Mongolia. It is mainly the nomadic population who are Mongolian; almost all the settled farmers and people living in the towns are Han Chinese whose families have emigrated here from eastern China.

DECISIVE DATES

The Terracotta Warriors date from the 3rd century BC.

THE EARLY EMPIRE

c.21st–16th century BC
Xia dynasty. Some scholars question whether this dynasty existed.

c.16th–11th century BC
Shang dynasty, the first recorded dynasty. Ancestor worship is ritualised.

c.11th century–256 BC
Zhou dynasty. Capital established at Chang'an (now Xi'an), later at Luoyang.

770–476 BC
Spring and Autumn Period. Consolidation of aristocratic family-states. Confucius (551–479 BC) stresses moral responsibility of ruler.

403–221 BC
Warring States Period.

QIN DYNASTY (221–206 BC)

221 BC
Qin Shi Huangdi unifies China to found the first imperial dynasty. Weights and measures, currency and writing are standardised. Qin Shi Huangdi builds an immense underground tomb, including an army of thousands of terracotta warriors.

HAN DYNASTY (206 BC–AD 220)

206 BC
Han dynasty founded, with Chang'an (modern-day Xi'an) as its capital.

180 BC
Eunuchs are employed at the imperial court to look after the emperor's wives and concubines.

165 BC
Civil service examinations instituted.

AD 25
Capital moved to Luoyang.

105
Traditional date for the invention of paper. Paper may have already been in use for two centuries. Commerce

Wei-dynasty tomb guardian.

between China and Asia/Europe thrives.

2nd century
First Buddhist establishments are founded in China.

220
Abdication of the last Han emperor. Wei, Jin, and Northern and Southern dynasties divide China.

SUI DYNASTY (581–618)

581
Following nearly four centuries of division, Sui dynasty

Much of the Great Wall was built in the Ming dynasty.

reunifies China. New legal code established.

589–610
Repairs of early parts of the Great Wall. Construction of a system of canals linking northern and southern China.

TANG DYNASTY (618–907)

618
Sui dynasty collapses; Tang dynasty proclaimed. Government increasingly bureaucratised. Buddhism influences all sectors of society. Chang'an (Xi'an) grows into one of the world's largest cities by the end of the Tang dynasty.

Xi'an, China's ancient capital.

690–705
Empress Wu (627–705) governs China as its first female ruler. Writing of poetry becomes a requisite in civil service examinations.

907–960
Fall of Tang dynasty. Five Dynasties and Ten Kingdoms partition China. Anarchy in much of China.

SONG DYNASTY (960–1279)

960
Northern Song dynasty reunites China; capital established at Kaifeng.

1040
Invention of movable type, but not as efficient for printing pages of Chinese characters as woodblock printing. Development of Neo-Confucianism during 11th and 12th centuries.

1127
Beginning of the Southern Song dynasty, as invaders take over northern China and the Song capital is moved to Hangzhou, near Shanghai.

YUAN DYNASTY (1279–1368)

1279
After nearly half a century of trying, Mongols led by Kublai Khan, grandson of Ghengis Khan, rout the Song court. Tibet is added to the empire. Trade along the Silk Road flourishes. Beijing is made the capital.

MING DYNASTY (1368–1644)

1368
Founding of the Ming dynasty after Han Chinese overthrow the Mongols.

Emperor Kangxi.

1405–33
During the reign of Emperor Yongle, Muslim eunuch Zheng He (1371–c.1433) commands seven overseas expeditions to Southeast Asia, India and East Africa. Maritime trade is later abruptly curtailed as China turns inwards.

1514
The first Portuguese ships anchor off Guangzhou (Canton).

1553
Macau becomes a Portuguese trading port, and the first European settlement in China.

QING DYNASTY (1644–1911)

1644
A non-Han Chinese people, the Manchu, seize Beijing, beginning the Qing dynasty.

1661–1722
Reign of Emperor Kangxi

1735–96
Reign of Emperor Qianlong.

An opium den in the late 19th century.

1800
First edict prohibiting the importation and local production of opium.

1838
Lin Zexu, a court official, suspends all trade in opium. The following year, the Qing court terminates all trade between Britain and China.

1839–42
British forces gather off China's coast. Fighting begins in 1841 in the First Opium War.

1842
Treaty of Nanjing signed. More Chinese ports are forced open to foreign trade, and Hong Kong Island is surrendered to Great Britain "in perpetuity".

1851–64
Anti-Manchu Taiping Rebellion devastates large areas and results in tens of millions of deaths.

1855–75
Muslim rebellions.

1858
Conflicts arise between European powers, mainly France and Britain, and China. Treaties of Tianjin signed, opening more ports to foreigners.

1860
British and French troops burn the Summer Palace in Beijing; Kowloon Peninsula ceded to Britain.

1894–5
Sino-Japanese War, which China loses.

1900
Boxer Rebellion seeks to remove foreign influences from China. Rebels take Europeans hostage.

1911
Republican Revolution: representatives from 17 provinces gather in Nanjing to establish a provisional republican government. Sun Yatsen is chosen president, but soon steps down.

1912
Forced abdication of the last emperor, Puyi.

POST-IMPERIAL CHINA

1912–20
Warlord Yuan Shikhai nominally rules much of China, but several provinces declare independence. After his death in 1916 China falls apart. Civil war among various warlords.

1919
On 4 May in Beijing, a large demonstration demands measures to restore China's sovereignty, thus beginning a nationalist movement.

1921
Founding of the Communist Party (CCP) in Shanghai.

Sun Yatsen, founder of modern China.

1925
Sun Yatsen dies.

1927
Chiang Kaishek's Nationalist forces attack the Communists in Shanghai, take Beijing from warlord control and establish their capital at Nanjing.

1934–6
The Long March: Communists forced by Nationalists to abandon their stronghold in southern China.

1937–45
Following the Japanese invasion and the Nanjing Massacre in 1937, the Communists and Nationalists fight the Japanese – mostly separately – with American and British assistance.

1945
Japan defeated in World War II; full-scale civil war ensues in China.

PEOPLE'S REPUBLIC OF CHINA

1949
Mao Zedong declares People's Republic in Beijing on 1 October; Nationalist army flees to Taiwan.

1950–53
Chinese troops support North Korea in the Korean War.

1958–61
Great Leap Forward results in a mass famine.

1960
Split between China and the Soviet Union.

1966–76
Cultural Revolution brings chaos, destruction and death across China.

1976
Zhou Enlai and Mao Zedong die; the Cultural Revolution ends. Tangshan earthquake kills over 240,000.

1978
Deng Xiaoping becomes leader, instituting a policy of economic reform and opening China to the West.

1989
Tiananmen Square demonstrations; military crackdown ends with hundreds of deaths.

1997
Deng Xiaoping dies in February; Hong Kong reverts to Chinese sovereignty on 1 July.

2001
China joins the World Trade Organisation.

2003
Shenzhou-V manned space mission. SARS epidemic.

2008
Beijing hosts the 29th Summer Olympic Games. A huge earthquake in Sichuan kills 70,000 people.

2009
60th anniversary of the founding of the People's Republic.

2010
China overtakes Japan to become the world's second biggest economy.

2013
Xi Jinping becomes President of the People's Republic of China, having succeeded Hu Jintao as General Secretary of the Chinese Communist Party in 2012.

2016
China's economy growth falls to 6.7 percent, the lowest rate in 25 years.

2017
In autumn, the 19th Communist Party Congress is scheduled to elect the new leader of the party.

2022
Beijing will host the 24th Winter Olympic Games.

Revolutionary imagery.

The Terracotta Warriors, a vivid insight into China's ancient past.

IMPERIAL CHINA

From the ancient Xia dynasty to the demise of the Qing in 1911, China's imperial history extends back over a period of 4,000 years.

Historical legends remain a powerful symbol of the endurance and unity of Chinese cultural values. During imperial times, emperors claimed to follow the sage kings' examples as rulers; more recently, China's leaders have glorified the length of their history and its early achievements – even while condemning other aspects of the past – to foster unity and nationalism among the people.

Archaeological findings indicate that primitive people lived in the territory of today's China half a million years ago. In the early decades of the 20th century, archaeologists excavated a series of caves, one nearly the size of a football field, near a village just southwest of Beijing. Skulls, teeth and bones of more than 40 *Homo erectus* were uncovered, along with tens of thousands of stone tools dating from 200,000 to 400,000 years ago. Peking Man and Woman were hunter-fishergatherers who lit fires for warmth and for cooking animals like bear, hyena, sabre-toothed tiger and water buffalo.

Later discoveries indicate that early Chinese civilisation developed in a number of areas and possessed distinctive local characteristics as well as common features. Neolithic China (12,000–2000 BC) was characterised by the spread of agricultural communities, although people also hunted and fished for food; they raised pigs and dogs, and grew hemp to use for fabric. Silk was also discovered in this period, possibly as far back as 6000 BC. Clustered dwellings suggest kinship units, and pottery designs featured clan or lineage symbols, as well as pictures and images of animals and plants.

Of the early legendary dynasties – Xia, Shang and Zhou – the actual existence of the Xia remains in doubt for some. However, excavations in 1959 at Erlitou (near present-day Luoyang, in

Government officials, 1901.

Henan province) unearthed palaces believed to have been of a Xia dynasty capital.

Over the centuries the Chinese population migrated further south from their northern homelands, displacing the indigenous Austronesian aboriginals (related to similar groups in the Philippines and Indonesia) as they did so. Large parts of present-day Zhejiang, Jiangxi and Fujian provinces retained these communities well into historic times, and they still survive in parts of Taiwan. Other ethnic groups, such as the Miao peoples of the southwest, retreated into the hills.

SHANG DYNASTY (16TH–11TH C. BC)

In 1899, scholars noticed pharmacists selling bones inscribed with archaic characters. By the late 1920s, these oracle bones had been traced to Anyang, in Henan province, where the last Shang capital was excavated. Shamans, serving the Shang kings, made divinations by applying a hot point to the shoulder-blade bones of animals to create cracks, which were then interpreted and the results etched onto the bone. Over 100,000 such oracle bones have been collected.

Oracle bones and inscriptions on bronze work, the excavation sites themselves, and the written records of the subsequent Zhou dynasty describe the Shang as a remarkably stratified society. The

A bronze wine vessel from the Shang dynasty.

elite hunted for sport and fought in horse-drawn chariots, while the peasantry lived in semi-subterranean dwellings. Ancestor worship was ritualised, and royal tombs contained valuable objects as well as animal and even human sacrifices. The mobilisation of mass labour for public works like city walls attested to the authority and power of the Shang aristocracy.

ZHOU DYNASTY (11TH C.–256 BC)

The primary structure of the Chinese state is considered to have emerged during the Zhou dynasty. The Zhou clan had long been vassals of the Shang, but eventually grew strong enough to defeat them in warfare in the 11th century. Their capital was built at Chang'an (now called Xi'an),

and the sons of Zhou rulers were despatched to preside over vassal states in a feudal-like system. A belief in heaven's mandate established a new basis for the legitimacy of rule. The idea of the mandate of heaven held that a leader's right to rule was based on his ability to maintain harmony between heaven and earth, himself and his officials, and the officials and the people.

The beginning of the Eastern Zhou period was marked by the eastward movement of its capital to Luoyang, in 771 BC. In the chaotic Spring and Autumn period (770–476 BC), aris-

> *Early Chinese civilisations emphasised labour-intensive food production, which required a large population and a strict, hierarchical political system to build and control irrigation networks and maximise harvests.*

tocratic family-states formed shifting alliances and fought or absorbed each other until there were only seven large states remaining by the Warring States era (403–221 BC). Despite such political strife, social and economic advances included the introduction of iron, the development of infantry armies, currency circulation, the emergence of private land ownership, urban expansion and the breakdown of class barriers.

The foremost thinkers of the time were Confucius (551–479 BC) and his followers Mencius (c.370–300 BC) and Xunzi (c.310–215 BC). Perhaps in response to the anarchic times in which he lived, Confucius stressed the maintenance of tradition and the cultivation of personal morality and the moral accountability of the ruler towards the people. Peace and abundance were guaranteed if the ruler ruled fairly, preserved proper relationships in society and cultivated his own moral values.

QIN DYNASTY (221–206 BC)

The Qin state emerged as the most powerful state during the Warring States Period. Ruling by strict laws that supported agriculture and strengthened the state, it finally conquered the other states in 221 BC. The first emperor of the Qin dynasty, Qin Shi Huangdi, is considered to be the first ruler of a united China.

Weights and measures, currency and, most importantly, writing were standardised. Highways were constructed, and waterways and canals were dug in the south to facilitate water transport. The archives of defeated states were burnt and hundreds of scholars critical of Qin rule were murdered. The immensity of the emperor's power and ego is illustrated by the discovery near Xi'an of over 7,000 life-sized terracotta warriors created to protect his elaborate tomb. Walls were built during these times, but the legend that the Great Wall was built by Qin Shi Huangdi is incorrect. While many dynasties built extensive walls for protection, the Great Wall visible today was mostly built by the Ming dynasty during the 16th century.

Qin Shi Huangdi's ruthless and perennial exploitation exhausted both the populace and China's financial resources, and his empire rapidly fell apart after his death in 210 BC.

HAN DYNASTY (206 BC–AD 220)

While repudiating the harsh rule of the Qin, the Han rulers built upon the established centralised bureaucracy. The important difference, however, was the way in which Han officials were drafted into service. By the 1st century BC, it was generally accepted that officials should be men trained in the Confucian classical texts, meaning they now had to reconcile their positions serving the emperor and state with the Confucian values of proper behaviour and personal integrity. It was during the Han dynasty that Confucianism became indelibly ingrained into Chinese politics, society and culture.

The stability of the Han period enabled China's population to grow to more than 50 million. Trade and industry developed, and communication and transportation systems improved, all of which fostered closer ties among China's far-flung and diverse regions. Cities attracted the educated and the wealthy from all over the country, becoming important cultural centres. People elsewhere, especially in areas of hardship, migrated to locations that afforded more opportunity.

In 180 BC, a new social class appeared at the imperial court for the first time: palace eunuchs, who were to maintain an important role all the way through until 1911. Originally hired to look after the emperors' wives and concubines, eunuchs soon became advisers,

playing a significant part in palace intrigues and power struggles.

The Han dynasty reached its prime under the rule of Han Wudi (140–87 BC). The Chinese empire had long sought to control the troublesome nomadic tribes in the north and the west, and Wudi succeeded in defeating the Huns, a group that had established a strong empire in the north. Following this success, the empire stretched all the way west to what is now Xinjiang. This expansion encouraged numerous contacts with other cultures through traders from

The Yellow Emperor, Qin Shi Huangdi.

⊙ DYNASTY PRIMER

Xia 21st–16th centuries BC
Shang 16th–11th centuries BC
Zhou 11th century–256 BC, Spring and Autumn Period 770–476 BC, Warring States Period 403–221 BC
Qin 221–206 BC
Han 206 BC–AD 220, Three Kingdoms Period 220–581
Sui 581–618
Tang 618–907
Song 960–1279
Yuan 1279–1368
Ming 1368–1644
Qing 1644–1911

distant lands. From the 1st century BC, caravans had travelled along the Silk Road, bringing horses and gold in exchange for silk.

Buddhism was introduced to China from India during the late Han period; while Confucianism waned, Buddhist teachings and art made a lasting impression on Chinese culture in the north and the south. Buddhism was permitted to flourish by non-Chinese rulers of northern China, in part because it too came from outside the Chinese establishment that they were subsuming themselves.

Wei-dynasty Buddhist rock carvings at the Longmen Caves.

DIVISION AND REUNIFICATION

Regionalism and class distinctions grew after the fall of the Han dynasty around 220, as China split into the three rival states of Wei, Wu and Shu – a time known as the Three Kingdoms Period. Reunification and economic advance were achieved under the vigorous but short-lived Sui dynasty (581–618).

When the founder of the Sui took power, he rapidly established a new legal code, organised local governments and continued several institutions initiated by earlier kingdoms. Despite the unification and strengthening of the state, the depletion of the country's resources under the grand visions of the second Sui emperor led to the dynasty's downfall.

TANG DYNASTY (618–907)

The founders of the Tang dynasty – considered to have been something of a golden age – inherited the accomplishments of the Sui, including the large capital at Chang'an, now Xi'an. The Chinese bureaucracy continued to develop. During the Sui Tang era, seven ministries were established – personnel, administration, finance, rites, army, justice and public works – as was a censorate, an agency responsible for inspecting and reporting on official and even imperial conduct.

Under the second emperor, Tang armies expanded east into Korea, south into northern Vietnam and west into Central Asia. This was the great era of the Silk Road, and as trade expanded along this route, contacts with the people and cultures of Central and West Asia increased and Chang'an developed into a great international metropolis. Between AD 600 and 900, no city in the world could compare in size and grandeur. People from Japan, Korea, Vietnam, Persia and West Asia seeking trade, Buddhist enlightenment or simply adventure injected their energy into Tang urban life.

The Tang dynasty is regarded as a golden age in Chinese history, with the arts – notably poetry and scroll painting – reaching new heights. The capital, Chang'an (Xi'an), was the largest city in the world, with a population of around 2 million.

The strength of the Tang nurtured a vigorous literary and artistic creativity. Later periods looked to Tang poetry in particular as a model of excellence. That the writing of poetry became a requisite in the civil service exams for higher qualifications and promotion can be credited to China's only female ruler, Empress Wu Zetian, who reigned from around 690 to 705.

The growing importance of the examinations in the late Tang period served to weaken powerful, aristocratic families of the north and presented greater opportunities for those from other areas to enter government. Scholar officials – those who earned their rank through success in the examinations – started to become a minor elite within the imperial bureaucracy. The influence of great families became linked to the position of family members in high office; a powerful family could rapidly fall apart if two or three generations passed without a member attaining a high government position.

The height of Tang-dynasty splendour was reached under Emperor Xuanzong, who reigned from 713 until 755. Nevertheless, failings accumulated: military campaigns became overextended and expensive; powerful generals meddled in court politics; officials became involved in factional infighting, and the emperor increasingly turned to court eunuchs for support.

SONG DYNASTY (960–1279)

Anarchy reigned during the final half century of Tang rule, but eventually regional states emerged out of the political and social chaos – called the Five Dynasties and Ten Kingdoms.

The Song dynasty was founded by the palace-guard commander of the last of the Five Dynasties in northern China, and is considered one of China's most creative and artistic eras. It is divided into two halves; the Northern Song (960–1127) and the Southern Song (1127–1279), the latter referring to the period after invaders took

A silk tapestry from the 12th century.

In his old age, Xuanzong let his control deteriorate when he fell for a beautiful concubine.

A military rebellion weakened the throne but was put down; Tang rule was restored but its power never fully recovered. In 845, the emperor Wuzong ordered the repression of Buddhist monasteries that, by this time, had acquired large, tax-exempt estates with glorious temples housing thousands of monks. Thousands of monasteries were shut down, and Buddhism's decline was accelerated by the court's issuing of ordination certificates for monks. Subsequently, Confucianism experienced something of a revival, while Daoism also began to emerge. By this time, the population of the Tang empire had reached 80 million.

over northern China (to found the Jin dynasty there) when the imperial capital was moved from Kaifeng to Hangzhou.

Population growth promoted urbanisation, particularly in the capital. Coal and iron industries developed, and foreign trade was a large source of government revenue in the latter Song era, not to be matched again until the 19th century. Foreign trade decreased land tax and increased the use of paper money, a practice initiated in the late Tang period. China led the world in nautical expertise. Chinese ships could carry 500 men on as many as four decks, powered by a dozen sails on four or six masts.

The Song was the first society with books (paper had been invented in the 1st or 2nd century BC), key to the era's educational development. The government initially tried to control printing, but by the 11th century it was granting land and books to encourage the establishment of schools. The civil service examination system became a huge and elaborate institution crucial to upper-class life, until the structure's abolition in 1905. A majority of officials still gained office through nepotism, but the Song bureaucracy was staffed by more exam graduates than ever before. In theory, nearly any male could take the exams, but

Mongolian women at Genghis Khan's Mausoleum.

in reality it was generally only the wealthier families who could afford the time and money on tutors.

The expanding educational system revived the study of Confucianism and fostered its reinterpretation by a number of scholars, characterised by a Buddhism-inspired focus on individual self-cultivation.

YUAN DYNASTY (1279–1368)

The emperors of the Yuan dynasty were the descendants of Mongol leader Ghengis Khan, who had conquered most of Central Asia and parts of Eastern Europe in the early 1200s. By 1215, a part of northern China was under Mongol control, and in 1279 the Song dynasty finally

fell to Ghengis's grandson Kublai Khan, who ruled China from 1271 until 1294.

Yuan officials set up a form of military administration that was soon dominating the Chinese-style bureaucracy. Most important posts throughout the empire were filled by Mongols or their non-Chinese allies; few Chinese rose to positions of authority except in cultural affairs. The Mongols were tolerant, however, of differing religions, reflecting the diversity of their multiethnic empire. During their rule, Tibet and Yunnan became part of China.

Trade along the Silk Road flourished. The Grand Canal between northern and southern China was repaired, as the new capital in Beijing (called Dadu) depended upon grains from the south. Domestic trade flourished, as did maritime trade from West Asia and India.

MING DYNASTY (1368–1644)

After a long period of insurrections, the Mongols were overthrown by Han Chinese troops under Zhu Yuanzhang (Hongwu), who became the first emperor of the Ming dynasty in 1368.

Sponsored by Emperor Yongle (r. 1402–24) and under the command of the Muslim eunuch Zheng He, the Ming naval fleet made seven expeditions between 1405 and 1433 to Southeast Asia, India, the Persian Gulf and the east coast of Africa. Although some trade was conducted, the missions were mainly of a diplomatic nature, intended to foster the tribute system whereby China granted large gifts to tributary states who in turn acknowledged China's supremacy and offered tribute (usually smaller gifts than they received from China). After Yongle's death in 1424, state support of overseas trade and diplomacy ceased, and the fleets of immense ships – larger than any European – were dismantled (see page 52).

During the rule of the Ming, the first Christian missionaries came to China with the arrival at Guangzhou (Canton), in 1514, of Portuguese ships. The danger to the Ming emperors' rule, however, continued to come from Northern and Central Asia. The Great Wall was once again reinforced to protect China from the nomads, and the wars against the Mongols lasted into the 16th century.

Towards the end of the Ming period, intrigues of the palace eunuchs paralysed the court and sometimes its foreign policy, and the secret police suppressed even the slightest signs of opposition.

THE COMING OF THE EUROPEANS

The first recorded account of Europeans in China appears to have been a visit of Northern European traders to Kublai Khan's court in 1261. Marco Polo is said to have travelled in China in the 1270s and 1280s, though some scholars now doubt he ever made it (he never mentioned the Great Wall, for example), suggesting he fabricated his writings from other sources. In any

China's early encounter with Jesuits, however, was positive, as these were educated men who could relate to Chinese scholar-officials on intellectual terms. While the Jesuits condemned Buddhism, they accepted most Confucian precepts, even conceding that the veneration of ancestors was a secular ritual.

Chinese scholars displayed interest in Jesuit expertise in astronomy, cartography, European clockworks and other sciences. The Italian Jesuit Matteo Ricci, who arrived in Macau in 1582, was probably the most important figure in Jesuit

A Dutch engraving from 1665 showing Chinese peasants at work in the fields.

case, his narrative in *The Travels* introduced the splendours of China to medieval Europe, particularly the sophistication of its urban life.

Early Catholic missionaries made their way to China during the Yuan dynasty (1279–1368), but large-scale commercial contact between China and Europe did not occur until the 1500s. Portuguese ships dropped anchor off Guangzhou in 1514, but the unruly behaviour of the crew onshore offended Chinese officials, who decided to contain them by leasing Macau to Portugal in 1553 as a trading base, from which the Portuguese could conduct business. In the early 1600s, Dutch and English ships also arrived on China's south coast, reproducing the discourteous behaviour of the Portuguese.

missionary activity. In 1598 he was introduced at court in Beijing, and a few years later was granted permission to live there on an imperial stipend as a Western scholar.

Rival groups of Catholic missionaries in China, opposed to the Jesuits, regarded Confucian rites of ancestor worship as incompatible with the Christian faith and appealed to the Vatican for a decision. The papal authorities duly obliged, and from this time relations between Beijing and all missionaries deteriorated.

QING DYNASTY (1644–1911)

In 1644 the Manchus, a non-Han Chinese people from Manchuria (the area of northeast China now known as Dongbei), continued the long

INVENTIONS AND TECHNOLOGY

China failed to capitalise on its early inventive genius; today it relies heavily on technology borrowed from the West.

The Chinese invented the magnetic compass.

The Chinese were once world leaders in technology; monumental inventions such as paper and moveable-type printing, magnetic compasses, gunpowder and irrigation were familiar to them hundreds of years before they were developed in Europe.

The belief that the emperor was the Son of Heaven led to the very early development of astronomical observation in China: Halley's Comet was first recorded in 467 BC, and a calendar of 360 days was in use by the 3rd century BC. By the 13th century there was a total of 17 different astronomical instruments at the Beijing Observatory, and Chinese astronomers had fixed the length of the year as 365.2424 days, very close to modern calculations.

The Chinese first made paper around AD 200, while printing evolved around eight centuries later – albeit with carved stamps rather than movable type.

Imperial geographers were busy with the deviation of magnetic north from true north before Europeans were even aware that the earth had a magnetic field. More than a millennium ago iron foundries in China were producing quantities of iron and steel unmatched in Europe until the 18th century. Irrigation was in use by the 1st century AD, and the waterwheel 400 years later, again well ahead of Europe. In the 9th century, Daoist monks, searching for the elixir of life, mixed charcoal, saltpetre and sulphur and accidentally made gunpowder. The mixture was later used for fireworks and in bombs and grenades. The creation of porcelain is a famous example of Chinese technological superiority: fine glazed ceramics were being crafted in China from around AD 100, and later became highly prized in Europe (where it was, and is, known as "china"). It was not until 1708 that Europeans hit upon the elusive secret of its manufacture.

THE DECLINE OF CHINESE TECHNOLOGY

Yet for all their precocious ingenuity, the Chinese inventions were the exclusive preserve of the uppermost echelons of society. This had the effect of restricting the further development of existing technologies, in sharp contrast with what was happening in Europe in the later Middle Ages.

The Chinese world was, above all, an insular one. Just when the rich and powerful Ming dynasty was poised to reach outwards and develop trade with Southeast Asia and beyond, an imperial edict – essentially the result of nothing more than a court squabble – banned foreign voyages by the Ming fleet, and at a stroke changed the course of Chinese history. Within 100 years, the first European adventurers were guiding their ships, equipped with guns developed from Chinese gunpowder technology, into the region, eventually to devastating effect. Before long, China was being subjugated and humiliated by the European colonial powers.

These days China is once again pursuing technology, this time with unprecedented rapidity and government investment. However, modern Chinese technology in fields such as the electronics and auto industries is in large part a result of copying technical expertise from the West.

The island of Taiwan was of little interest to the mainland Chinese until the 17th century, when it was used by the Ming loyalist Koxinga as a base to fight the new Qing dynasty. The rebels' defeat in 1683 brought Taiwan into the Chinese empire.

tradition of attacking imperial China from the north and sacked the Ming capital at Beijing. The Qing dynasty was founded.

The Manchus had long been in contact with the Chinese and the Mongols. Although they were foreign conquerors, their rule did not break with Chinese traditions, unlike that of the Mongols in the Yuan dynasty. Instead, they adopted the terms, structure and ideology of Confucianism to support their political authority, promoting the veneration of ancestors and the study of the traditional Chinese classics, and accepting the Confucian theory that rulers ruled by virtue of their moral uprightness. The Manchu used a system of dual appointments in their civil administration, having both Han Chinese and Manchu in important positions and relying on civil service examinations. While the Manchu attempted to maintain their own identity and customs, they also promoted many Chinese traditions. The arts flourished, as did scholarship, and basic literacy was relatively high, even in rural areas.

Under the Qing, the Chinese empire would reach its greatest extent, controlling not just the whole of "classical" China, but also a vast area to the west encompassing Tibet, Xinjiang, all of Mongolia and a large slice of what is now Kazakhstan and Kyrgyzstan. In the mould of the later stages of its predecessor, however, it would develop as and remain very much a continental, land-based power, exercising little influence at sea.

MARITIME CHALLENGES

While the Manchu carefully managed the inner frontiers, Western maritime powers were expanding and continuing to make their way towards East Asia. In China, all legitimate Western trade from 1760 to 1842 was regulated by what was called the Canton system, stipulating that Western traders must conduct all business in Guangzhou (Canton) under the supervision of Chinese merchants belonging to a guild called

the Cohong. Western merchants were restricted to the city's riverbank area, but had to withdraw to the Portuguese settlement on Macau during the offseason. They were discouraged from learning Chinese, and they could not speak directly with government officials, but instead had to communicate through the Cohong.

The British and Dutch East India companies, established around 1600, were commissioned by their home governments to manage territories overseas and monopolise trade, essentially acting as the counterpart to the Chinese Cohong.

The Ming Tombs outside Beijing.

The British bought large amounts of tea, silk and porcelain from China, but the Chinese did not buy much more than woollen textiles from Britain, and China's low demand for imported goods eventually created a trade imbalance that forced the British to pay for goods in silver, rather than barter.

The British East India Company despatched James Flint, a Chinese-speaking trader, in 1759 to present complaints to the Qing court about restrictions on trade and corruption in Guangzhou. Emperor Qianlong at first seemed receptive, agreeing to send a commission of investigation to Guangzhou. Then, changing his mind, he had Flint apprehended and imprisoned for three years, charging him with violating regulations, improperly presenting petitions and learning Chinese.

In 1792, Lord Macartney was sent by Great Britain's King George III to China as a special ambassador to the Qing court. Macartney arrived in Guangzhou in the summer of 1793, and was allowed to continue to Tianjin because he claimed to be honouring Qianlong's 80th birthday. He was accompanied by an entourage of nearly 100, and two escort vessels loaded with gifts meant to display British manufacturing technology. The gifts were deemed "tribute from England" and once ashore, he was escorted without delay to Beijing.

Lord Macartney requested the abolition of

French troops in action during the Taiping Rebellion.

the Canton system, the right to establish a British diplomatic residence in Beijing, the opening of new ports for trade, and fixed tariffs. Qianlong dismissed all of the requests, writing the famous letter to King George in which he praised the British king for inclining himself "towards civilisation", but informed him that "we have never valued ingenious articles, nor do we have the slightest need of your country's manufactures... You, O King, should simply act in conformity with our wishes by strengthening your loyalty and swearing perpetual obedience". Despite this unequivocal rebuff, a growing number of foreign traders continued to arrive in Guangzhou, and the Qing continued to enforce their previously established rules.

Emperor Qianlong's private life inspired many romantic stories. With two main wives and countless concubines and serving maids he sired 17 sons and 10 daughters.

British traders, in particular, were becoming exasperated by the trade deficits that compelled them to make huge payments in silver for Chinese tea and luxuries. This trade imbalance motivated the British to ship opium from India to southern Chinese ports.

Despite the growing threat from outside, the Qing empire was at its peak during the reign of Emperor Qianlong (r. 1735–96), ruling virtually unchallenged over an area in excess of 13 million sq km (5 million sq miles), an area almost 40 percent larger than that currently ruled by the People's Republic.

THE OPIUM WARS AND THE TAIPING REBELLION

As the Chinese consumption of opium grew, so did the outflow of silver from China, to the exasperation of the Qing rulers. In 1838, a respected court official, Lin Zexu, recommended the strict suppression of the opium trade and the rehabilitation of addicts. He was dispatched to the south, and upon arrival in Guangzhou immediately demanded that the foreign merchants hand over all the opium in their possession. In addition, he announced that all foreign merchants would be required to sign a bond promising never again to import opium. When the foreigners failed to take Lin seriously, he suspended all trade, blockaded foreign factories, and held 350 foreigners hostage, including the British Superintendent of Trade, Captain Charles Elliot.

Elliot commanded all British traders to surrender their opium to him, issuing receipts and taking responsibility on behalf of the British government. Elliot then handed over the opium to Lin, who publicly destroyed it. Lin lifted the blockade, permitted the resumption of trade and released the hostages.

Elliot and the entire British community left Guangzhou, and a Qing imperial edict was issued in 1839 that terminated trade between China and Britain. The British government decided that the only recourse to the termination of trade was war. Despite some attempts at negotiation, fighting began around Guangzhou in mid-1841, and after the British captured several coastal cities, the Qing agreed to binding negotiations.

The Treaty of Nanjing was signed in 1842. Its provisions included an indemnity to be paid by China to Britain, "equal relations" between China and Britain, four more ports opened to foreign trade with consuls and foreign residency, abolition of the Cohong monopoly, fixed tariffs and the surrender of Hong Kong to Britain in perpetuity. It was a devastating blow to Chinese integrity and independence.

By this time the Qing dynasty was in dire straits. A long, steady decline had set in from the early years of the 19th century, with poverty and official corruption sparking a series of increasingly violent uprisings across China. In 1851 a rising broke out at Jintian (today's Guiping) in Guangxi, when a 10,000-strong rebel force led by Hong Xiuquan defeated the Qing garrison forces. This was the beginning of the great Taiping Rebellion (1851–64), an uprising that would strafe southern and central China, causing at least 20 million deaths, and up to 50 million according to some estimates – the bloodiest conflict in the history of the world up to this time, and since superseded only by World War II. Several other rural rebellions across 19th-century China resulted in the deaths of millions more.

At the same time, tensions continued between the foreign communities in China and the beleaguered Qing government. Minor incidents swelled into large-scale conflicts, which led to foreign intervention. Guangzhou was soon overrun by Anglo-French forces, who proceeded north to Tianjin. The Qing court yielded and the Treaties of Tianjin were signed in 1858. Ten new ports were opened, indemnities specified, and diplomatic residences established in Beijing.

Insisting on finalising the treaties in Beijing instead of Shanghai, as the Chinese wanted, the British occupied Beijing, then moved to the Summer Palace and razed it, forcing the emperor into exile.

The treaty was then reaffirmed, indemnities increased, and the Kowloon Peninsula ceded to Britain. Its terms effectively rendered parts of China into European colonies, especially with the provision of extraterritoriality under which foreigners were liable to foreign, not Chinese, law.

THE BOXER REBELLION

The Boxer Rebellion was a popular protest movement brought about by the combination of Qing misrule and foreign intrusion. In the plains of Shandong province, where the movement originated, years of floods and drought had left the people desperate. Germany's seizure of Qingdao in 1898 heightened anti-foreign sentiment and unrest. To protect their interests, Shandong peas-

US troops in Beijing after the Boxer Rebellion, 1901.

ants turned to secret societies such as the Boxers.

The Qing court initially backed the Boxer movement in the hope that it might succeed in expelling the foreigners. The rebels made their way to Beijing, where they killed a number of Christians and held missionaries, diplomats and other foreigners hostage in the Beijing legation quarter for eight weeks until an army marched on the capital.

The Qing court retreated as the foreign troops approached, but soon arranged an agreement with the foreign powers, who had an interest in maintaining Qing rule – stability was good for foreign trade. The government was, nevertheless, compelled to pay a huge indemnity. The dynasty, and China's imperial tradition, was to survive for just one decade.

END OF EMPIRE TO MODERN TIMES

Much of China's 20th century was marked by civil war and political intrigue, the turbulence and unrest culminating in Mao's disastrous Cultural Revolution. A change to pragmatic policies since then has brought ever-increasing prosperity – to the point that China is now a global economic power.

When Westerners first began to intrude on China's sovereignty in the mid-1800s, China's rulers had to confront outsiders who would not conform to the Chinese view of the world. How to respond to the challenge and make China stronger became a top priority.

By 1901, the Qing court had realised reform was unavoidable. It dispatched two official missions abroad in 1906 to study constitutionalism in England, France, Germany, the United States and Japan. The delegates returned recommending that a constitution, civil liberties and public discussion could in fact strengthen the emperor's position, as long as he retained supreme power.

THE REVOLUTION OF 1911

Although institutional changes were moving rapidly, dissatisfaction grew more intense, driving the forces of revolution. Anti-Qing activists came from many quarters. There were Sun Yatsen's anti-Manchu Revolutionary Alliance, secret societies, disaffected military personnel, provincial leaders in government and business and intellectuals who wavered between advocating a constitutional monarchy and revolution.

In November 1911, representatives from 17 provinces gathered in Nanjing to establish the Provisional Republic Government under Sun Yatsen and a local military commander. To guarantee Manchu abdication, Sun was soon compelled to step down in favour of military strongman Yuan Shikai.

In 1912 Puyi, who had taken the emperor's throne after the death of Cixi in 1908, was forced to sign a declaration of abdication. Puyi continued to live in the Imperial Palace in Beijing until 1924, but the rule of the Sons of Heaven on the

Sun Yatsen in Shanghai, 1912.

Dragon Throne, which had begun 4,000 years earlier, had come to an end.

A number of political parties formed and attempted to make an effective parliamentary system, but they were poorly organised and Yuan Shikai was intolerant of their criticism. He periodically dissolved the parliament and had the constitution rewritten, even attempting to make himself emperor in 1915. Yuan died the next year, but the violent opposition he incited helped create the conditions for the warlord period of 1916 to 1928.

POLITICAL AWARENESS

A seminal event in the rise of Chinese nationalism, and still commemorated today, the May

Fourth Movement was a major student protest that took place on 4 May 1919 in response to China's treatment in the Treaty of Versailles, following the end of World War I. China had been told by the Allies that, upon Germany's defeat in the war, German territorial possessions in Shandong province would be returned. However, during the war, Japan had taken control of these territories (principally Qingdao) and, due to the Allies' inability forcibly to counter Japan at that time, the Japanese were not dislodged. The Versailles decision not to honour their promise was

initiated workers' organisations in the cities. Support for Chiang Kaishek's Nationalist Party was revived and an interest in Marxism developed.

CIVIL WAR

China's increasingly politicised intellectuals were attracted to Marxist theory largely because it provided an explanation for China's hardships – imperialism and exploitation by the upper classes – and prescribed a way to order society that they believed could strengthen the nation. This led to the Chinese Communist Party (CCP)

Zhou Enlai addresses the troops at Zunyi during the Long March.

Chiang Kaishek at a Nationalist rally

a major affront to Chinese national pride.

The events of 4 May served to broaden political awareness. The demonstrations of 1919 widened further the belief that protest is an honourable expression of people's concern with political events. It also reinvigorated the discussion of new ideas, as disillusionment with the leaders' ability to govern effectively led to further questioning of political progress.

Between 1917 and 1923, political and social change, and the conception of modernisation, took on new dimensions. Young intellectuals denounced Confucianism and started socialist study groups, created political journals, travelled to the countryside to educate farmers, and

being founded in Shanghai in 1921. The Nationalist Party (Guomindang; also spelt "Kuomindang"), which under Sun Yatsen had ruled China in the immediate post-imperial period, was the Communists' main rival for power. In the 1920s, both parties were in contact with the leaders of the Soviet Union.

Following Sun Yatsen's untimely death in 1925, Chiang Kaishek took over control of the Nationalists. With warlords still in control in the north, a long-planned "Northern Expedition" to unite China under Guomindang control was launched, with the support of the CCP – but this did not last long. Chiang Kaishek, who distrusted his allies, seized an opportunity to use his criminal connections in Shanghai to attack

POST-IMPERIAL LEADERS

Since the fall of the empire in 1911, China's leaders have overseen a series of turbulent and, at times, tragic events.

Sun Yatsen is admired by both Communists and Nationalists.

Honoured as the father of modern China in both the PRC and Taiwan, **Dr Sun Yatsen** (in Mandarin, Sun Zhongshan) was born in 1866 near Macau in southern Guangdong province. Influenced by Christian and Western ideas, Sun plotted the overthrow of the emperor and founded the republican Guomindang (Nationalist Party). With China divided, he set up a government in Guangzhou in 1920 that was to rival the military powers in the north, then reorganised the Guomindang with the Soviet Union's help. Sun died, aged 58, in 1925.

Chiang Kaishek (in Mandarin, Jiang Jieshi) was Sun's successor. Born in 1887, he underwent military training, then joined the Guomindang. After defeat by the Communists in the civil war, he fled to Taiwan, where his government was able to boost the economy with the help of the US. He died in 1975 without achieving his ambition of overthrowing the Communists and recapturing the mainland.

Chiang Kaishek's great adversary was **Mao Zedong**. No other figure had such an influence on 20th-century China. Born to a peasant family in Hunan province in 1893, Mao became co-founder of the Chinese Communist Party in 1921. During the Long March, he established himself as its leader, a position he retained until his death in 1976. Mao led the country out of its post-war economic misery, only to let it sink into chaos during the Great Leap Forward and the Cultural Revolution.

Next in importance was **Zhou Enlai** (1898–1976), Mao's closest ally. Born in Huai'an, Jiangsu province, in 1898, Zhou was the son of a wealthy family. After studying in Europe, Zhou took a leading role in the Communist movement. His special skill, diplomacy, soon became apparent, and he used his influence to curb some of Mao's worst excesses. Zhou's achievements in foreign policy are particularly significant – China emerged from isolation to become a member of the United Nations in 1971.

Deng Xiaoping (1904–97), was Zhou Enlai's right-hand man and close friend. Hailing from a peasant family in Sichuan, Deng studied in France, took part in the Long March and became a prominent politician. In 1973, he was appointed by Zhou Enlai as deputy prime minister, and was responsible for opening China's economy to the world as China's president. Despite some setbacks – notably the suppression of the Tiananmen Square democracy movement in 1989 – Deng displayed finesse by steering China back into the global community.

Deng's protégé, **Jiang Zemin**, became General Secretary of the Party during the demonstrations of 1989, and State President in 1993. He maintained Deng's policies of economic reform, oversaw the return of Hong Kong and Macau to China, and China's entry into the World Trade Organisation. Jiang was succeeded as party General Secretary in 2002 and later as State President in 2003 by **Hu Jintao**, a native of Anhui province who studied engineering at Beijing's prestigious Tsinghua University. Hu was known for his "Eight Honours and Eight Shames", a set of moral codes for Party cadres to follow as an example to all Chinese. Hu's premier **Wen Jiabao** became a well-like populist. Hu Jintao was succeeded by **Xi Jinping** in 2012. Since 2013 he has also been the State President.

Once in control of the Guomindang, Chiang Kaishek was able to consolidate his power by marrying Soong May-ling, the sister of Sun Yatsen's widow.

the Communists, whose power base was in the city. A brutal campaign, the White Terror, led to thousands of Communists and sympathisers being rounded up and executed.

The Guomindang forces continued northwards and took Beijing in 1927, ending the period of warlord rule. Chiang Kaishek established his capital at Nanjing and became the diplomatically recognised leader of the Chinese Republic.

Meanwhile, the CCP retreated to a remote stronghold in the hills of Jiangxi province, but under sustained Nationalist attack, its troops were forced out in 1934 and embarked on the legendary Long March. This epic journey lasted three years and involved marching to a new northern base at Yan'an in Shaanxi province. Of the 100,000 who set out, fewer than one-fifth survived the 10,000km (6,200-mile) ordeal. During this period, Mao emerged as the leader of the party.

JAPAN AND WORLD WAR

As early as 1931, Japan had annexed parts of northeastern China, where it founded a puppet state, Manchukuo, headed by Puyi, the last Manchu emperor, who had abdicated the imperial throne in 1912. The Japanese planned further conquests in China. Faced by this threat, Chiang Kaishek was unable to use his troops against the Communists. Also, those wishing to end the civil war and join forces with the Communists against the common Japanese threat were expressing criticism within his own party. They even "persuaded" Chiang to agree to an unlikely renewed alliance with the Communists.

By 1937, China and Japan were officially at war. Shanghai was bombarded and captured by the invaders, who are thought to have killed over 200,000 civilians in the brutal Nanjing Massacre. Chiang Kaishek retreated to Chongqing, in Sichuan province. The Communists fought a guerrilla war from their bases in the north, while Chiang's troops resisted the Japanese in the

south. The two forces eventually stopped the Japanese advance. In part because of the drain on Japanese resources caused by the war in China, the Allies were able to gain military superiority over the Japanese in the Pacific after 1942.

The civil war began again in earnest following Japan's surrender in 1945. Chiang Kaishek, backed by the Americans, fought against Mao Zedong's Red Army, which was fighting mostly on its own and with minimal Soviet support. The resumed four-year civil war was, for the most part, an easy victory for the Communists: the

British troops in southwestern China during World War II.

Guomindang was weakened when it demobilised large numbers of soldiers after 1945. Another decisive factor was that the Communists rapidly won the support of the Chinese people, exhausted by war and suffering from the Nationalists' mismanagement of the already extremely fragile economy.

After several campaigns, there was a decisive battle on the Yangzi, and Nationalist troops were so weakened that they were forced to retreat to the island of Taiwan, along with nearly 2 million refugees and most of China's gold reserves. The civil war was finally over. On 1 October 1949 Mao Zedong stood on Tiananmen and proclaimed the founding of the People's Republic of China. And thus, a new nation was born.

THE PEOPLE'S REPUBLIC

The initial public reaction after 1949 was one of euphoria. The CCP army was disciplined and polite, unlike the looting and raping Nationalist troops. Industries were nationalised and government administration taken over.

Land distribution had already taken place in many rural areas in the north before 1949; now it continued in the south. Mao's implementation of class struggle began in the countryside. After individual class status was determined, people were encouraged to "speak bitterness"

Mao accompanies the Soviet First Secretary, Voroshilov, on a state visit, Beijing, 1957.

against their former landlords. Up to 1 million landlords were dispossessed of their land, and many were killed.

A new marriage law made women equal to men and divorce possible. The liberation of women, in theory, seemed like true progress, but in reality women had to hold full-time jobs in addition to maintaining the home as before.

By the mid-1950s, Premier Zhou Enlai noted that political pressures had demoralised China's intellectuals and scientists. This led to the Hundred Flowers Movement: christened after the adage "Let 100 flowers bloom and 100 schools of thought contend", it was devised to allow open criticism of the party. For several months

> *In 1960 relations with the Soviet Union, in trouble for some years, were terminated. Soviet advisers were expelled, to the detriment of Chinese industry and development, and Mao pursued increasingly isolationist policies.*

in 1957, people were encouraged by statements from Mao and others to criticise the government and its policies. After some hesitation, many vented their dissatisfactions, with calls for more freedom of speech, independence of the judiciary and freer trade unions. Perhaps shocked by the level of discontent, the CCP reversed its policy and the Anti-Rightist campaign ensued (some believe Mao's motive for encouraging criticism was to search for enemies, but evidence is unclear). Limits to free discussion were now specified: any talk and debate must unite the people, benefit socialism and strengthen the Communist state. Thousands of intellectuals were persecuted and imprisoned and creativity was quenched, if not eliminated altogether.

THE GREAT LEAP FORWARD

Mao believed that China could be industrialised rapidly, fuelled by ideological motivation and the reorganisation of production. Rural and urban communities were encouraged to use their surplus labour and resources for heavy industries, especially steel production. Communes were established to increase the scale of production, while private enterprise was eliminated. "Backyard furnaces" were built to produce steel, but because of a lack of expertise, it turned out to be unusable – a perfect illustration of the period's misguided zeal. Agricultural production was expected to increase, and so local leaders falsely reported astronomical growth to advance their careers and avoid being labelled politically uncommitted or incorrect.

Between 1958 and 1961, the failure of the policies of the Great Leap Forward, combined with three years of bad weather, led to a famine in which up to 40 million Chinese died.

THE CULTURAL REVOLUTION

The final, bloody chapter of the period, the Cultural Revolution was an attempt by Mao – who had withdrawn into the background following the disaster of the Great Leap Forward – to prevent bureaucratic stagnation and to purge the party of what he saw as corrupt elements. He also wanted to consolidate his own power base.

Mao wanted to replace older leaders with younger ones, whose revolutionary zeal would be amplified by the act of toppling the establishment. He saw students as his activists and encouraged them first to turn on their teachers. The most chaotic phase lasted from May 1966 to late 1967. Students organised "Red Guard" units

was called in to restore order, and millions of Red Guards were sent to the countryside to "learn from the peasants".

TRANSITION TO A NEW ERA

The chaos could not continue, and following Mao's death, the last two decades of the 20th century witnessed dramatic changes in the tempo and direction of Chinese society, government and economy. The convulsions of the Cultural Revolution spent, China set about rebuilding itself, and economic development,

Mao figurines and other "maomorabilia", on sale all over China.

Red Guards in Shanghai, 1973

all over the country. Mao's slogan that "It is right to rebel" propelled their campaigns to destroy remnants of the old society. Brandishing Mao's "Little Red Book" of quotations, they destroyed temples and historic sites, and broke into private homes to smash and burn books, jewellery and art. Party leaders and other "counter-revolutionary" forces were denounced and subjected to mass trials.

Many died at the hands of the Red Guard, or, humiliated, committed suicide. Liu Shaoqi, Mao's chosen successor, was one of the first political victims. By 1968 there was widespread street fighting and virtual anarchy as rival Red Guard factions turned on each other. The army

not political struggle, defined the era.

Zhou Enlai's death in 1976 went unmarked by the Chinese leadership; he had been under indirect criticism from party radicals since 1973, but his death caused widespread grief among the people. The Monument to the People's Heroes in the centre of Tiananmen Square was adorned with thousands of wreaths and poems in his honour, but overnight all of the wreaths were removed, sparking the first genuinely spontaneous demonstration since the founding of the People's Republic. The crowd of 100,000 clashed with police throughout the day, until the square was cleared early that evening. Deng Xiaoping, perceived to be siding with the less radical faction of the party, was dismissed from his posts two days later, and Hua Guofeng became premier and first deputy chairman of the party.

When Mao Zedong died on 9 September of that same year, Hua Guofeng succeeded him in key government and party positions.

DENG'S NEW DIRECTION

The post-Mao era was the epoch of Deng Xiaoping, right up until his death in 1997. Although Deng was purged twice during the Cultural Revolution, he made a final comeback in 1978, acquiring positions and real power to set the

national defence, and science and technology – for Chinese development, first proposed by Zhou Enlai some years earlier. Mao had considered politics the key to China's progress. Deng defined China's modernisation to emphasise economic development.

Earlier, during autumn 1978, posters had appeared in Beijing calling for a fifth modernisation: democracy. The posters criticised the authoritarianism of Mao's time and appealed for free speech and institutional reforms. Initially tolerated by the leadership, the so-called

US President Gerald Ford and Deng Xiaoping, China's then-vice-President, at a state banquet in 1975.

political agenda. Deng began establishing his legitimacy by restoring the good reputations of many of those who had been politically persecuted during the 1950s and 1960s and during the Cultural Revolution.

Within the party and government bureaucracy, many who held prominent and powerful positions had acquired them by demonstrating revolutionary zeal during the Cultural Revolution, rather than on merit through knowledge or ability. Reversing the pattern, Deng began promoting education and professionalism in government and party ranks.

In December 1978, Deng inaugurated what he called a "second revolution". He reiterated the "Four Modernisations" – in agriculture, industry,

Democracy Wall Movement was forcibly halted in the spring of 1979.

Relations with the United States were normalised in 1979 (although President Nixon's visit to China in 1972 had started the process). Deng travelled to the US a few months later, when he met President Carter and congressional and business leaders. Deng's policy of "opening" China to the outside was recognition that China needed technological expertise and capital from elsewhere. The Chinese political system, however, was not to be influenced by Western political systems or culture.

To modernise agriculture, Deng disbanded Mao's disastrous communes. Farmers could now sell excess vegetables, fruit, fish or poultry in private markets and keep the extra profits. Consequently, rural agricultural production rapidly increased in the 1980s, far outpacing population increase. Deng began reforming industry by upgrading outdated technology and managerial systems, implementing price reforms, advocating foreign trade and investment, revamping the banking system and encouraging private business. Promises of private profit for entrepreneurs and other non-government workers led to dramatic and sustainable production increases. It was a chaotic time, and

> *Deng Xiaoping was unable, or unwilling, to denounce Mao: to do so would have meant discrediting China's Communist Revolution. The solution was to divide Mao's rule into a "good" early phase and a "bad" latter phase.*

it is a mistake to think that Deng had carefully planned every stage. There were still serious impediments to economic development. But he deserves credit for allowing private enterprise, stifled for so long, to flourish.

The Maoist emphasis on heavy industry shifted to light industrial goods for export. A new responsibility system in industry authorised managers, not party committees as in days past, to make decisions. The opening of foreign trade and investment led to the build-up of coastal cities formerly engaged in foreign trade, especially in the south. Special Economic Zones (SEZ) were set up, beginning with Shenzhen, right on the border with Hong Kong.

PROTEST AND DEMONSTRATIONS

Despite the establishment of SEZs, for many Chinese – particularly the young educated elite – the opening up of the economy was not happening fast enough, and frustration at the tardiness of change was compounded by other issues such as official corruption and inflation. In April 1989, these problems came to a head and Tiananmen Square became the focus of the world's media as university students, later joined by workers, aired their grievances against the government in the largest demonstrations since 1949. The protests, which were prompted

by the death of Hu Yaobang – one of the few high-ranking officials who offered the hope of political liberalisation – quickly developed into demands for democratic reform.

The protests gained momentum until, on 19 May, martial law was imposed. After several attempts to persuade the protesters to leave, the party lost patience. Through the evening of 3 June, soldiers and civilians clashed at various points in Beijing, and in the early hours of 4 June the student protesters were forced out of Tiananmen Square by tanks and guns. The

Promoting family planning.

soldiers were under express orders not to fire on anyone in the square itself, but several students were killed after exiting the square (most deaths occurred in Muxidi, west of Tiananmen Square, and at Liubukou). At least 300 people are believed to have died, although the government has never given a full account of what happened, and some witnesses and exiled leaders claim the number of deaths exceeded 2,000. In the following days, similar protests across the country petered out, most peacefully.

A nationwide hunt for the demonstration leaders – Wu'erkaixi, Wang Dan, Chai Ling and Han Dongfang – ensued. Thousands of demonstrators were arrested and some executed, but many dissidents somehow managed to flee the country. Zhao Ziyang, reformist general secretary of the Communist Party, was ousted from office (immediately replaced by Jiang Zemin), and other reformers met similar fates.

A far-reaching consequence of the events of 4 June 1989 (known as *liusi* in Chinese) was to cripple the dissident movement. China's internal critics ended up in prison, went into exile abroad or were silenced. Meanwhile, the party became ever more vigilant in its campaign against dissent. The nascent China Democracy Party was rapidly demolished and its organis-

Members of China's military police force.

ers jailed in the late 1990s as part of President Jiang Zemin's policy of quickly suppressing any organised opposition before it had time to grow. The quasi-Buddhist Falun Gong movement was outlawed in July 1999 after members demonstrated outside Zhongnanhai, Beijing's political nerve centre. Periodic Falun Gong protests were staged in Tiananmen Square, but the movement has been rigorously suppressed.

Not all protests are banned. After the NATO bombing of the Chinese embassy in Belgrade, police did little to prevent protesters stoning the US embassy in retaliation, and similarly allowed the populace to vent their anger against Japan in the Diaoyu islands dispute in 2012: the government is prepared to allow some public release

of pent-up frustration as long as the target is not the Chinese Communist Party itself. Another factor is that patriotic and nationalistic sentiments are encouraged.

China has managed to become part of the modern economic world without commensurate political evolution. Access to information remains highly controlled, with the internet filtered for any undesirable content (eg BBC news online in Chinese), leaving Chinese citizens disengaged and disadvantaged. However, in recent years, the proliferation of blogs and social networking sites has alleviated the situation somewhat.

INTERNATIONAL ISSUES

After Tiananmen, China was lambasted over its human rights record, particularly with regard to political prisoners and the situation in Tibet. Yet it soon became evident that Beijing cared little about world opinion of its internal affairs. As the economy continued to grow through the 1990s, and with the potential of the vast Chinese market rapidly becoming economic reality, foreign agents were increasingly likely to do business regardless.

China's most important relationship – with the United States of America – is fraught with distrust, but is not outwardly hostile. The US has frequently railed against China's human rights abuses, but China always shrugs off the criticism. China desires good relations with the US so that it can continue to develop and modernise in peace and security; America views China's growing power and prestige as a threat to its influence in the Far East, but both countries value their trade with each other. Taiwan – which the US has pledged to defend against a Chinese invasion – remains a particularly sharp thorn in relations.

Attempting to limit the supremacy of the US, China adopts a passive policy of fostering strategic alliances with countries such as Russia and Pakistan. Sino-US ties improved markedly, however, after the 9/11 terror attacks on New York and Washington in 2001. With the War on Terror dominating the agenda, China seized the opportunity to crack down harder on "splittist tendencies" amongst the Muslim Uighurs of Xinjiang Autonomous Region. It remains to be seen how the 2016 election of Donald Trump as president of the US will impact US-China relations, given his vocal renunciation of politics as usual, including international diplomacy, and avowed intent to pursue a more isolationist strategy for the US.

Relations with Japan remain tricky, largely due to Japan's bloody occupation of China and the refusal of the Japanese prime minister to offer a full apology for its imperial conquest. Among the common people *(laobaixing)*, it is not rare to hear anti-Japanese remarks. In 2012 a potentially dangerous row erupted with Japan over the sovereignty of the Diaoyu islands (Senkaku to the Japanese) in the East China Sea, with widespread anti-Japanese protests across the country. Japan,

Having weathered the Asian financial crisis of the late 1990s, it is China, rather than Japan, that is seen by many as Asia's economic stabiliser in the 21st century. Whatever this century holds for Asia, China has a major part to play.

RELATIONS WITH TAIWAN

Since 1949, a consistent aim of the Chinese Communist Party has been to reunite Taiwan and China. The Nationalists in Taiwan have carried the same banner, but with differing terms. With the issue of Hong Kong and Macau (returned by Por-

Anti-Japanese protesters in Hong Kong wave Chinese and Taiwanese flags during the Diaoyu islands dispute in 2012.

however, remains a major investor in China and Beijing seeks to maintain the cash flow.

China's power in the Far East has made its neighbours increasingly anxious. China claims territorial sovereignty, for example, over islands far from its borders and closer to Vietnam, the Philippines and Indonesia. It offered two arguments: "historical" rights from centuries ago, when imperial ships sailed the South China Sea, and territorial rights, in fact applicable under international law only to true archipelagos like Indonesia and the Philippines. The islands involved – the Paracels and Spratlys, among others – sit on extensive petroleum reserves at a time when China is importing more and more oil to fuel its economic growth.

tugal in 1999) resolved, China has focused on Taiwan, which it claims is a renegade province, not an independent state. The clumsy attempt to influence Taiwan's first direct presidential elections in 1996 – by conducting "missile tests" directly into Taiwan's two primary shipping lanes – cost Beijing considerable political capital. Afterwards, Taiwan's political and commercial contacts increased with several foreign governments.

Beijing has long expressed its determination to reunite Taiwan and China peacefully, while reserving the right to use force if necessary. China's avowed ambition is to adopt the "one country, two systems" structure to Taiwan in the same way that it has been applied to Hong Kong and Macau. With each successive government in Taipei, Taiwan's approach to handling the delicate situation has changed back and forth from a clear independence agenda to a closer relationship. Ma Ying-jeou, president of Taiwan from 2008–16, provided a stage for China and Taiwan to return to their former status quo – with Taiwan neither asserting its independence nor moving towards reunification with China, with openness to business opportunities provided by the economic powerhouse across the straits. During Ma's first term, a landmark trade deal was approved, cutting tariffs on a raft of goods, making China Taiwan's major trading

propaganda following the arrangement made clear Beijing's position that enabling the breakaway island to defend itself against possible military action was grossly unfair. Its anti-secession stance, ratified by a law in March 2005, authorising the use of "non-peaceful means" if Taiwan formally declares statehood, seems unlikely to soften. Sabre-rattling aside, the status quo suits the three major players well enough for the time being, although President Trump's break from diplomatic protocol by speaking with President Tsai directly (the first such phone call since the

Collecting scrap metal from a rubbish tip in Shanghai. China's huge appetite for raw materials has caused global scrap prices to rise.

partner, soaking up more than 40 percent of its exports. However, at home Ma was seen by many as an appeaser, too feebly defending Taiwan's interests in the international arena and 2016 saw the opposition come into power, with Tsai Ing-wen becoming president, the first woman to hold the office. Thus, the official line towards mainland China has shifted yet again, from working with the PRC's 'One China' policy to stating firmly that Taiwan is a *de facto* independent state.

The present détente takes place against a backdrop of military build-up. The US pledge to help defend Taiwan in the event of an invasion has been accompanied by billions of dollars' worth of arms sales. A wave of anti-US

US formally severed ties with Taiwan at China's behest in 1979) following his win of the 2016 US election, has concerned Beijing. Trump has publicly questioned the 'One China' policy, as well as stated resistence to China's territory incursions in the South China Sea.

CHANGING IDEOLOGY

During the industrialisation of China in the 1950s and 1960s, the Communist Party was the paramount touchstone in work and society, not only assuring ideological consistency among workers, but dictating industrial policy itself. Yet China's blossoming market economy (officially a "socialist market economy with Chinese characteristics")

China is keenly pursuing economic cooperation in the Arab region. It has been criticised by western nations, however, for vetoing UN resolutions to address the civil war in Syria, maintaining its principle of non-interference in the internal affairs of sovereign countries.

discourages intellectual conformity and rigid industrial policy. And the expanding sector dominated by non-industrial entities – securities and trading firms – is increasingly free of party influence (although the big four state banks are organs of the party). Those working in these areas are young, urban and increasingly as affluent as their counterparts in Japan and the West.

Ideology has been influenced by economic developments, and in March 1999 the NPC enshrined "Deng Xiaoping thought" in the constitution, giving Deng a status equal to Mao. The party publishes collections of his speeches and promotes slogans used by him. Deng's policies largely continued under President Jiang Zemin and his successor, Hu Jintao.

In November 2002, the 16th Party Congress marked a symbolic shift away from communist ideology, with significant changes to the wording of the constitution and membership of the party available to all, not just the "working class", while the 2007 National People's Congress saw the passing of the long-disputed property law, a significant step towards guaranteeing the right to the ownership of private property.

SOCIAL TENSION

"Social disorder" is the biggest fear of the party, which is determined never to allow a repeat of the 1989 Tiananmen demonstrations. Anniversaries of the Tiananmen massacre have passed with little incident. Other issues have come to the fore, however. Large-scale interest in the prescriptions of Falun Gong practice (see page 85) pointed to the spiritual hollowness of contemporary life in China, after decades of Marxism were swiftly overturned by decades of mass consumerism. The Communist Party remains fearful of mass religious movements, perhaps recalling the devastating effects of rebellions such as the Taiping in the 19th century.

With the exponential rise of personal wealth and the expansion of consumerism in China, crime has mushroomed since the early 1980s, although it remains low by international standards. Corruption is a serious problem, and the root cause of a rapid growth in the number of riots and demonstrations across the country. Government officials, from local mayors and cadres to senior party members, have been frequently implicated in a series of profiteering scandals, from the infamous case of melamine-tainted baby milk powder in 2008 to the expulsion of China's top railway

The artist Ai Weiwei, outspoken critic of the government, at a press conference.

minister on charges of mass corruption within the troubled high-speed railway network.

Minority groups continue to present Beijing with issues that challenge its rule of this immense country. Buddhists in Inner Mongolia and Muslims in Xinjiang, as well as Tibetans, remain under close scrutiny following the rise in ethnic tensions in western China. During the lead-up to the 2008 Beijing Olympics, pro-Tibet activists interrupted the Olympic torch relay and Tibetans took to the streets in Lhasa. Of even more concern to Beijing were the violent riots that exploded on the streets of Ürümqi and Kashi in Xinjiang in the summer of 2009. Uighur lynch mobs went on the rampage, killing dozens of Han Chinese, who in turn retaliated. The situation has remained tense.

A further threat to stability is regional imbalance. China has achieved staggering economic growth over the past 25 years, but the fruits of reform have been unevenly distributed. The east and southern coastal cities grow rich while the rural areas of the interior lag ever further behind.

21ST-CENTURY CHINA

China entered the 21st century on an optimistic note. In 2001 it joined the World Trade Organisa-

successful launch and return of the mission, and astronaut Yang Liwei. A first space walk followed in 2008. Like the costly Olympic Games, China's exploration of space is largely a vanity project intended to appeal to the population's patriotism. If Chinese people feel their country is competing and winning on the world stage, they are unlikely to seriously question the legitimacy of the government, goes the thinking. Unfortunately, the wealth gap is widening, house prices are sky high and cracks are even starting to appear in the Party itself. And in the 2016 Olympic Games, China only

The Shanghai World Financial Centre, the Jinmao Tower and the Shanghai Central Tower.

tion – a hugely significant event that opened the world's markets to Chinese manufactured goods and the vast Chinese domestic market to foreign companies. Later in the same year Beijing succeeded in its bid to hold the 2008 Olympic Games. International companies continued to beat a path to China's door, and internal anti-government dissent had been effectively smothered. In 2002, Jiang Zemin handed over leadership of the Party to his deputy, Hu Jintao. Together with Wen Jiabao (who replaced Zhu Rongji as premier), Hu tended to favour greater transparency and democracy.

Technological developments also proceed apace. As well as the Three Gorges Dam project (see page 266), China became the third nation to achieve manned space flight in 2003, with the

came third in the medal table with their smallest haul of gold medals in two decades.

In the run-up to the National Congress and leadership change in 2012 that saw Hu Jintao step down to be succeeded by Xi Jinping, political infighting intensified to the point that, unfounded rumours even circulated that a coup had taken place at Zhongnanhai. What did occur was the downfall of a rising star of the political elite, Bo Xilai, and the unfolding of the extraordinary cloak-and-dagger tale of the former Chongqing Communist Party leader – his gang-busting, "red revival" policy and his wife's conviction for the murder of a British businessman. Intrigue aside, the demise of such a high-ranking Communist leader threw into question the legitimacy of the regime.

A major concern within the government is the widespread corruption that has proved so difficult to stem. President Xi Jinping initiated a far-reaching anti-corruption campaign that resulted in arrests of many high-ranking officials and a considerable number of investigations. Another is the question of liberal reform – something that has, to date, not progressed under Xi as some had hoped. Following 2012's National People's Congress, Wen Jiabao broke with protocol to call for a move towards reforms that would include grass-

and their opponents, generally paid bureaucrats who work for the Chinese Communist Party, promoting the government's policies and shoring up support in times of crisis. Once dubbed the "Fifty Cent Party" after the micro-wage the government allegedly paid workers for a single pro-communist internet post, the propaganda has become more sophisticated in recent years. Likewise, the Western perception of modern China is also divided. Pro-China commentators feel the West has much to learn from an economic model that survived the global economic

President Xi Jinping at a news conference.

roots democracy, if not universal suffrage. Previously, Wen had been censored by official media for talking about political reform, one of the few shifts towards a more Western style society that has never been seriously undertaken. Meanwhile, vocal dissidents such as artist Ai Weiwei have drawn attention internationally and admiration from intellectual circles for their outspoken criticism of China's social wrongs – gained at the risk of a lengthy police detention, however, as happened to Ai for two months in 2011 and dozens of other activists while popular uprisings were sweeping the Middle East and North Africa.

The internet, the de facto platform for public debate, is now broadly divided into two factions: the liberals who envy the freedoms of the west

crisis and continues to grow at one of the fastest rates in the world along with India, even if this rate has slowed in recent years. Others continue to anticipate, almost ghoulishly, China's impending collapse and the threat an undemocratic, unchecked power presents to the world.

The Communist Party of China holds its Congresses every five years, with the next scheduled for autumn 2017, when it's expected to elect the new leadership of the party. Many of the Central Politburo members may step down, yet the incumbent General Secretary (and President) Xi Jinping will most probably continue for another term.

For more on the economy, see The New China, page 70.

THE NEW CHINA

China's extraordinary economic transformation has brought unprecedented prosperity to millions. Yet growing inequality between rich and poor, environmental pressures and other issues present serious challenges.

In 1992, Deng Xiaoping, who had gradually emerged as de facto leader of China after Mao's death in 1976, embarked on a tour of southern China, visiting Guangzhou and the two special economic zones (SEZs) of Shenzhen and Zhuhai. In the aftermath of the Tiananmen protests of 1989, leftist forces had been pressing to rein in the limited reforms of the 1980s and put China back on a more solidly centralised track. Deng's tour was, then, a deliberate intervention, and he took it as an opportunity to repeat the rallying cry with which he had jump-started rural reforms in 1982, "To get rich is glorious." Chinese needed to go into business "even more boldly" and "more quickly" to create a socialist market economy with Chinese characteristics, said Deng.

Deng's power had been greatly diminished since the Tiananmen protests, and his tour had little initial impact. Nevertheless, a series of articles he published in Shanghai's *Liberation*

Urban planning exhibition, Beijing.

A large proportion of China's new business elite emerged during the chaotic years of the 1980s. Many of these people had been imprisoned under Mao but, following their release, seized the new opportunities created by Deng's reforms.

Daily under a pen-name won over local elites, and before long the calls for economic liberalisation began to become orthodoxy nationwide.

The result has been an explosion of economic growth unparalleled in human history. China's GDP growth was averaging more than 9 percent in the years following Deng's tour, although in 2012 the GDP growth began to fall and in

2016, it was only 6.7 percent, the lowest level in 25 years. Nevertheless, it is now the country with the world's second-largest economy. In 1985, foreign direct investment (FDI) inflows amounted to around US\$2 billion, but by 2016 they had exploded to around US\$118 billion.

Meanwhile, China has become the world's leading exporter, with a share of global exports at almost 14 percent as of 2015. Significantly, it has also risen to become the world's second largest importer, with Chinese imports seen as important enough to the US economy to warrant near-constant pressure on Beijing to revalue its currency, which the US has long considered undervalued (thus damaging US exports by making them unfavourably expensive compared to China's), although the International Monetary Fund (IMF) stated in 2015 that they no longer considered this to be the case.

Since the start of its opening and reform policy, China has carried out innumerable reforms that have collectively transformed its economy – and the restructure continues. The country's membership of the World Trade Organisation since 2001 has had a major impact, effectively opening up the country to foreign trade, and the world's markets to Chinese manufactures.

Whatever the risks ahead, two decades of

families were permitted to establish businesses with up to seven employees. At the same time the government began to allow foreign investment, in the form of joint ventures, with the opening of 14 coastal cities to outsiders, and – between 1980 and 1988 – the establishment of Special Economic Zones (SEZs) in Shenzhen and other places.

The SEZs were all essentially harbour interfaces with the outside world, which had long been kept at bay by the political Great Wall of the Mao era. Shenzhen was to become the most

The bright lights of Nanjing Road, Shanghai.

reforms have turned China into an economic powerhouse, with pundits variously predicting it will become the world's largest economy anywhere between 2018 and 2031 – giving it some room to deal with the occasional and inevitable setback.

REFORM BEGINNINGS

China first started to turn its back on the collectivised economy it had practised since the Communist Revolution of 1949 when it began to dismantle the agricultural commune system in the 1970s, allowing "village enterprises" to be established. In the early 1980s, it became possible for individuals to set up one-person enterprises, or *getihu*, while by the mid-80s

successful due to its proximity to that bastion of free trade and then British colony, Hong Kong.

Between 1978 and 1997, Hong Kong's manufacturing businesses relocated over the border into the so-called Pearl River Delta (PRD) region. Hong Kong's – and later Taiwan's – investment in the PRD is such that it has become common to call the delta "the world's workshop", though in recent years Shanghai and the Yangzi River Delta (YRD) have been catching up.

For the first 10 years of China's reforms, the PRD led China into the global economic order via foreign-invested firms in Shenzhen, Dongguan and Guangzhou, and is today a leading global source for electronics, electrical and electronic components, textiles and garments, shoes, toys, watches and clocks, and everything from clothes hangers to cocktail mixers. Accounting for just 0.4 percent of China's total land area, the PRD is responsible for around 35 percent of the nation's total trade (imports and exports).

REGIONAL COMPETITION

The PRD may have spearheaded China's economic rise, but in recent years it has been overtaken by competition from Shanghai and its Yangzi River Delta (YRD) hinterland, and also faces competition from the so-called Bohai Sea

Many observers have called the relationship between China and the United States as the most important in the world. Inextricably linked, and incredibly powerful, the uneasy union is sometimes dubbed "G2" – the Group of Two.

in China's factories as of 2017, in recent years there have been consistent reports of labour shortages, leading to rising labour costs.

A Guangzhou internet café.

Economic Zone, which includes the municipalities of Beijing and Tianjin, and the city of Qingdao in Shandong province. Exports from the YRD have grown at an average of 41 percent per year since the beginning of the new millennium, and it now accounts for 34 percent of China's total exports.

With annual GDP growth of 6.9 percent in 2015, it is calculated that Shanghai will overtake Hong Kong (GDP growth of 6.2 percent in 2015) before 2020. However, the rise of the YRD and other regional economies is placing a strain on the availability of the migrant workers – the low-cost labour pool that has powered China's growth over the past decade. Despite the fact that more than 277 million migrant workers have left their fields in the countryside to work

Recognising that growth has been overwhelmingly concentrated in four southeastern Chinese provinces – Guangdong, Fujian, Zhejiang and Jiangsu – in 2000 China adopted a Go West policy. The government has since spent more than Rmb 1 trillion on infrastructure development in the interior, including the 1,140km (710-mile) railway to Tibet and a vast network of fast, efficient roads. Growth rates have fared better than the national average since, though foreign firms have yet to show much enthusiasm for investing in these less advanced regions. For many manufacturers, despite massive government investment in transport infrastructure, much of China's interior – home to some 700 million of the country's population – is simply too far from any port to run an economically viable business. This discrepancy in growth between the coastal areas and the hinterland is just one of many tensions that often bubble over into serious social unrest, a problem that the central government is extremely concerned about, and which has led to a nationwide campaign for "social harmony".

THE DIRTY WORK

Rising labour costs and the appreciation of the Chinese yuan against the US dollar gradually began to erode China's price competitiveness as

some point in recent years, although these are generally not reported in China for fear of inciting similar action elsewhere.

Those who do find work can hardly be said to enjoy a workers' paradise. Taiwanese-owned manufacturer Foxconn garnered grisly headlines for its working conditions in 2010 when it was reported that 14 of its workers had committed suicide. Tight margins demanded of China-based electronics manufacturers from global corporations such as Apple, Dell and Sony contribute to unpaid overtime and other abuses of

Five-year-old Angelina works on her golf swing.

Lunchtime for office workers.

a source for cheap manufactured goods towards the end of the 21st century's first decade. China's key exporting provinces reacted to this by shifting gears towards the production of higher-value products, such as cars, electronics and computer chips. In the meantime, manufacturers of the products that made the PRD rich have tended to relocate to Vietnam and India rather than China's relatively undeveloped inland hinterland.

Since the world financial crisis bit in 2008, waves of factory closures have hit, with many owners simply fleeing without paying workers due wages. The problem of non-payment of wages, as well as lay-offs and falling wages in some cases, has resulted in intermittant strikes and labour protests in every region of China at

workers who are unaware of their rights or too desperate for employment to complain.

PROTESTS IN A DIVIDED NATION

In 2005, Beijing estimated there were nationwide some 87,000 "mass incidents", a loose term to describe protests and uprisings comprising more than 15 people. Since then, official figures have stopped being published but few deny that the numbers have continued to rise. Such uprisings are not happening in the relatively affluent areas that the vast majority of foreign tourists travel through, but in the huge swathes of rural China where as many as 80 percent of the population live and watch on as a small minority profit from China's juggernaut acceleration towards economic superpower status. Triggering these protests are a host of factors, but chief among them are land and environmental issues.

Land is a particularly contentious issue in modern China because it is still state-owned, and in the countryside farmers have leases of 30–70 years. With real-estate speculation rife throughout the nation, this provides ample opportunity for corrupt officials to cooperate with developers, evicting rural dwellers from their properties with minimal compensation and allowing business to make handsome prof-

relatively leafy, park-endowed Hong Kong has to endure. The explosion of manufacturing in the PRD has led to a situation where, on a bad day, visibility can be so poor it is barely possible to see across the harbour.

But if Hong Kong bemoans its environmental woes, the situation elsewhere in China is far worse. According to the World Health Organisation (WHO), China is the world's deadliest country for outdoor air pollution, with more than a million people dying from dirty air in 2012. The air, water and soil across much of China are

Living the high life, supercars and all, in Hong Kong.

its from housing developments, hotels, factories and, in some cases, infrastructure build-outs.

With the value of land skyrocketing, it's not surprising that most mass incidents are caused by land grabs. Those affected have little choice but to appeal to higher authorities, thus risking being arrested for disturbing social order. Travelling to petitioning offices in Beijing is a common pilgrimage for the rural victims of official corruption, complicated by the risk of being kidnapped at transport hubs and landed in illegal "black jails" to be detained without trial.

The environment is another source of conflict, as China's race to the future has largely been run at the expense of massive environmental degradation. This is a problem that even

heavily polluted by its industry. The food chain is threatened by heavy metals from factories and also overuse of pesticides and fertilisers by farmers. Pollution is a concern not only of the central government, which has to pick up a sizeable bill for environmental damage, but also those directly affected. The city of Shifang in western Sichuan province became a testing ground for environmental protest in 2012 when tens of thousands of residents took to the streets to voice their disapproval over the construction of a huge copper-smelting complex. After photographs of protestors clashing with police were released online, public opinion swayed against the city government and plans for the complex were scrapped.

21ST-CENTURY CHALLENGES

The reality is that, for all the talk of the coming China century, the rise of the world's most populous nation is a far more complex phenomenon than many commentators give credit to. A visitor who touches down in cosmopolitan, spectacularly affluent Hong Kong, and travels on to any of the innumerable five-star hotels in Beijing or Shanghai, could be forgiven for thinking China has "arrived". But lurking in the wings of China's success story is a host of problems that mostly impact on those who have not prospered from the past two decades of meteoric growth.

Land and environmental issues usually top the lists of China's woes, but access to water, and the health and educational systems, also deserve a mention. Healthcare reforms mean 95 percent of the population now have access to some basic healthcare, but the coverage of this varies widely, as does the cost the individual must cover. The quality of care is also variable, depending on where you are – major cities have Western standards while poorer, rural areas do not. Similarly, although a minimum of nine years of education is theoretically funded by the government, in reality many parents – again, depending on their province – are expected to also pay tuition fees to supplement the education system, with the result that paying for their children's education puts an enormous strain on the poor.

A focus on science, technology and education has proved a double-edged sword for China's ruling party. Some 50 percent of the population now has access to the internet and it's not just for the privileged – by 2016, there were around 200 million internet users in rural areas. A public gaffe can now signal the end of a political career for a careless official, but of more concern is the internet's incredible effectiveness in organising and coordinating mass social movements. Inevitably, the government will have to move from a draconian to a more placatory approach in dealing with an informed population.

Added to these highly complicated social issues is the Communist Party's ability to maintain growth and continue to improve the prosperity of its people as the world is buffeted by economic woes. More than 600 million Chinese people have been lifted out of poverty since economic reforms began in 1978, perhaps the Party's greatest achievement and claim to legitimacy. China's economy is highly dependent on global conditions, however, and the world financial crisis that began in 2008 saw its exports and FDI inflow decline significantly. Accustomed to taking bold measures in the face of crises, Beijing responded with a massive US$586 billion stimulus package to increase bank lending and boost domestic consumption. The move worked to avoid a hard landing in the manner of many other countries around the world, but financial wobbles since then have periodically made the markets edgy.

Migrant workers flock to China's booming cities.

There are signs of rot in China's finances, too. In 2012, the National Audit Office announced there were irregularities totalling US$84 billion in local government debt. Away from Beijing's watchful eye, provincial and city governments had been playing fast and loose with the figures. Moreover, many of the massive infrastructure and construction projects across China funded by the stimulus package remain largely unused. The government sought to impose fiscal discipline on local governments, but as of 2016, this seemed to once again be slipping.

China's extraordinary rise has been led by extraordinary ambition. But the reckless greed that has accompanied that ambition could well be China's downfall.

Shoppers in the Xujiahui district of Shanghai.

BELIEFS AND RELIGION

As diverse as the land and people, the beliefs and philosophies found in China reflect a historical depth and breadth existing nowhere else in the world.

The "three teachings" of Confucianism, Daoism (Taoism) and Buddhism have traditionally dominated China's spiritual life. Of the two indigenous systems, Confucianism developed as a moral form of philosophy that taught ethical and pragmatic standards of behaviour, while Daoism had a religious as well as a philosophical dimension. Buddhism was imported from India in the 1st century AD, gradually evolving into a uniquely Chinese form as it was influenced by Daoism and Confucianism.

When the Communists came to power religion was deemed "counter-revolutionary", and during the Cultural Revolution there was widespread destruction of temples, mosques and churches. After Mao's death things became less repressive, and in 1982, freedom of religious belief was guaranteed by law – although what are deemed to be "cults", such as the Falun Gong movement, are seen as subversive and remain illegal (see page 64).

A woman praying at Shanghai's Jade Buddha Temple.

ANCIENT BELIEFS

Apart from the fusion of Confucianism, Daoism and Buddhism that lies at the heart of Chinese religious belief, Islam is also practised, especially in the northwestern parts of China, and a small, but growing, Christian minority worships nationwide. Beyond philosophy or theology, the age-old traditions of lucky numbers, fortune-telling and geomancy naturally survive.

FORTUNE-TELLING AND FENG SHUI

Many Chinese take superstition, as distinct from organised religion, seriously. The idea of fate started in the feudal society, when it was believed that "the god" – that is, the emperor – decided one's destiny. With the Tang (618–907) and Song (960–1279) dynasties, society became more complicated, people were more concerned about fate, and fortune-telling became popular.

Following a fortune-teller's advice can mean shaving your head to appease the fortune god, or wearing a bright-red belt irrespective of your outfit. Carrying gold images around may bring good fortune, as may removing mirrors from the bedroom, or eating more mutton or less beef in the Lunar New Year period.

Fortune-tellers make predictions by reading faces and palms, or doing complicated calculations based on a person's name or the time and date of birth. The Chinese zodiac of 12 animal signs – rat, bull, tiger, rabbit, dragon, snake, horse, goat, monkey, chicken, dog and

The concept of lucky numbers played its part in the 2008 Beijing Olympics. The number 8 is considered auspicious and in view of this, the Games' opening ceremony kicked off at 8.08pm on the date 8.08.08.

pig – was created during the Han dynasty (206 BC–AD 220). It divides people into the 12 categories according to the year they are born, and also tells their fortune and future by combining philosophy and numbers. At the end of every year, dozens of fortune-telling books are published.

Feng shui (wind and water) is a set of traditional spiritual laws, or geomancy, used to attract the best luck and prevent bad fortune. Those who take feng shui seriously consult a geomancer – a master of feng shui – to advise on designs of buildings, dates of important decisions, and layout of one's home and office. The most important tool in a feng shui master's bag is a compass-like device, which has eight ancient trigrams *(bagua)* representing nature, its elements and eight animals – horse, goat, pheasant, dragon, fowl, swine, dog and ox.

Feng shui theories are based mainly on the principle of *qi* – life's spirit or breath – divided into *yin* and *yang*, the female-passive and male-active elements of life. The concept of *wuxing* also has a prominent standing in Chinese philosophy, medicine, astrology and superstition. The term translates as "five elements", in which the five types of energy dominate the universe at different times. Water dominates in winter, wood in spring, fire in summer, metal in autumn, and earth is a transitional period between seasons.

Modern corporations in China often take feng shui extremely seriously. In Hong Kong's Central District, the angular design of the Bank of China tower is said to fling bad feng shui at just about every competing bank. The Hongkong and Shanghai Bank building, designed by Norman Foster, is supported on a series of giant pillars, making it possible to walk underneath the building. This satisfies the feng shui principle that the centre of power on the island (Government House) should be directly accessible from the main point of arrival (the Star Ferry).

LUCKY (AND UNLUCKY) NUMBERS

Even though most mainland Chinese – unlike their Cantonese neighbours in Hong Kong – tend to be somewhat dismissive of the idea that some numbers are more auspicious than others, the connection between the pronunciation of Chinese numbers and possible bad- and good-luck associations with other Chinese words runs deep in Chinese culture. Chinese hotels and

Candles lit in offering at Man Mo Temple in Hong Kong.

buildings of any sort, for example, often do not have a fourth floor, because the pronunciation – *si* – is a homonym for "death".

"Two" is generally considered a positive number because good things come in pairs, and for the Cantonese "two" has a particular resonance because it is pronounced *yat*, a homonym for "easy" – as in easy money. "Six" is not a major auspicious number, but it is liked by Chinese because *liu* is a homonym for "to flow", and triple-six – the Number of the Beast in the West – is considered auspicious in China. "Eight" is the most auspicious of numbers, as it sounds similar to *fa*, or "to prosper", as in *facai*. "Nine" is regarded well by Chinese because it is a homonym for "long-lasting" – both are pronounced *jiu*.

ANCESTOR WORSHIP

Although the origins of ancestor worship are very ancient, Confucian notions of filial piety extending into the afterlife no doubt later conditioned it. By making offerings to the departed in the afterlife, the living show their respect and ensure that their ancestors will continue to take an interest in the fortunes of their descendants. One of the many superstitions that the revolutionary-era Communist Party attempted to banish from China, it is still a force in rural China, and Mao Zedong himself is subject to a

Incense coils at Tai Ping Shan temple in Hong Kong.

form of ancestor worship – as the father of modern China – in public portraits and icons hanging over the dashboards of taxis and buses.

Ancestor worship has dwindled in importance in contemporary China. By contrast, it thrives in the Chinese communities of Hong Kong, Taiwan and even Singapore – communities that are in many ways more traditional than those of the mainland. Yet, even if it might seem to have no bearing on the lives of China's educated urban elite, it is not unusual to see photographs of departed family members on the walls of rural family homes. Some Chinese still make a small shrine with offerings of fruit and burning incense for ancestors. In the traditional clan culture of rural China, ancestors could be traced back

many, many generations, their names inscribed on plaques in clan temples where offerings could be made and ceremonies conducted.

Ancestor worship also manifests itself in popular holidays such as Qingming, known in English as the Grave-Sweeping Festival, when traditional Chinese families go to the tombs of their ancestors, clean them up and make offerings of fruit, light incense and, particularly in Hong Kong and Taiwan, burn paper money.

DAOISM (TAOISM)

A central concept of Daoism is the *dao*, which means the way or path, but also has a secondary meaning of method and principle (by which the universe operates). Another important premise is *wuwei*, which is sometimes simply defined as passivity, or "swimming with the stream". The Chinese martial art of *taijiquan (tai chi)* is inspired by this concept. The notion of *de* (virtue) is another central tenet, as virtue that manifests itself in daily life when *dao* is put into practice.

Daoism perceives the course of events in the world to be determined by the forces *yin* and *yang*. The feminine, weak, dark and passive elements are considered to be *yin* forces; masculinity, brightness, activity and heaven are seen as *yang* forces.

Laozi was the founder of Daoism, living at a time of crises and upheavals. He is traditionally thought to have been born in Henan province in 604 BC, into a distinguished family. Laozi was a contemporary of Confucius and ancient chronicles record that the two met. For a time, he held the office of archivist in Luoyang, which was then the capital, but later retreated into solitude and died in his village in 517 BC. According to a famous legend, he wanted to leave China on an ox when he foresaw the decline of the empire. Experts today still argue about Laozi's historical existence and legends swarm around his name. One of them, for instance, says that he was conceived by a beam of light, and that his mother was pregnant with him for 72 years and then gave birth to him through her left armpit. His hair was white when he was born and he prolonged his life with magic.

The earliest, and also most significant, followers of Laozi were Liezi and Zhuangzi. Liezi (5th century BC) was particularly concerned with the relativity of experiences, and he strived to comprehend the *dao* with the help of meditation.

Zhuangzi (4th century BC) is especially noted, if not famous, for his poetic allegories. The Daoists were opposed to feudal society, yet they did not fight actively for a new social structure, preferring instead to live in a pre-feudalistic tribal society.

Ordinary people were not particularly attracted by the abstract concepts and metaphysical reflections of Daoism. Yet even at the beginning of the Han period in the 3rd century BC, there were signs of both a popular and religious Daoism. As Buddhism also became more and more popular, it borrowed ideas from Daoism, and vice versa, to the point where one might speak of a fusion between the two.

Both Daoists and Buddhists believed that the great paradise was in the far west of China, hence the name, Western Paradise. It was believed to be governed by the queen mother of the west, Xiwangmu, and her husband, the royal count of the east, Dongwanggong.

Religious Daoism developed in various directions and schools. The ascetics retreated to the mountains and devoted all their time to meditation, or else they lived together in monasteries. In the Daoist world, priests had important functions as medicine men and interpreters of oracles. They carried out exorcisms and funeral rites, and read special services for the dead or for sacrificial offerings.

The classic work of Daoism is the *Daodejing* (also written as *Tao Te Ching*), the "Way of Power". Although attributed to Laozi, it now seems certain that this work was not written by a single author.

CONFUCIANISM

While Laozi was active in the south of China, Kong Fuzi, known in the West as Confucius, lived in the north. For Confucius, too, *dao* and *de* were central concepts. For more than 2,000 years, the ideas of Confucius (551–479 BC) have profoundly influenced Chinese culture, which in turn coloured the world-view of neighbouring lands such as Korea, Japan and Southeast Asia. It is debatable whether Confucianism is a religious philosophy in the strictest sense, rather than a moral code for society. But Confucius was worshipped as a deity, although he was only officially made equal to the heavenly god by an imperial edict in 1906. (Up until 1927, many Chinese offered him sacrifices.)

Mencius, a Confucian scholar, describes the poverty at the time Confucius was born: "There are no wise rulers, the lords of the states are driven by their desires. In their farms are fat animals, in their royal stables fat horses, but the people look hungry and on their fields there are people who are dying of starvation."

Confucius himself came from an impoverished family of the nobility who lived in the state of Lu (near the village of Qufu, in the west of Shandong province (see page 183). For years he tried to gain office with many of the feudal

In Man Mo Temple, Hong Kong.

lords, but was repeatedly dismissed, so he travelled around with his disciples and instructed them in his ideas. All in all, Confucius is said to have had 3,000 disciples, 72 of them highly gifted individuals who are still worshipped today.

Confucius taught mainly traditional literature, rites and music, and is thus regarded as the founder of scholarly life in China. The Chinese word *ru*, which as a rule is translated as Confucian, actually means "someone of a gentle nature" – a trait that was attributed to a cultured person. Confucius did not publish his philosophical thinking in a book, but his thoughts were recorded and collected together in the *Lunyu* (Analects) by his loyal disciples. The classic Confucianism canon also includes: *Shijing*, the book of songs; *Shujing*, the book of charters; *Liji*, the book of rites; *Chunqiu*, the spring and autumn annals; and *Yijing (I Ching)*, the book of changes.

Confucianism is, in a sense, a creed of law and order. Just as the universe is dictated by the world order, and the sun, moon and stars move according to the laws of nature, so a person, too, should live within the framework of world order. This idea, in turn, is based upon the assumption that people can be educated.

Ethical principles were turned into central issues. Confucius was a very conservative

A statue of Confucius.

reformer, yet he significantly reinterpreted the idea of the *junzi*, a nobleman, to that of a noble man, whose life is morally sound and who is, therefore, legitimately entitled to reign. Confucius believed that he would create an ideal social order if he reinstated the culture and rites of the early Zhou period (11th century–256 BC). Humanity *(ren)* was a central concept at the time, its basis being the love of children and brotherly love. Accordingly, the rulers would meet success if they governed the whole of society according to these principles. Confucius defined the social positions and hierarchies very precisely. Only if and when every member of society took full responsibility for his or her position would society function smoothly.

Family and social ties, and hierarchy, were considered to be of fundamental importance: between father and son (son must obey father without reservations), man and woman, older brother and younger brother, and a ruler and subject.

In the 12th century, Zhu Xi (1130–1200) succeeded in combining the metaphysical tendencies of Buddhism and Daoism with the pragmatism of Confucianism. His systematic work includes teachings about the creation of the microcosm and macrocosm, as well as the metaphysical basis of Chinese ethics.

This system, known as Neo-Confucianism, reached canonical status in imperial China; it formed the basis of all state civil service examinations, a determining factor for Chinese officialdom until the 19th century.

BUDDHISM

Today, there are Buddhists among the Han Chinese, Mongols, Tibetans, Manchus, Tu, Qiang and Dai (Hinayana Buddhists) peoples.

The Chinese initially encountered Buddhism at the beginning of the 1st century AD, when merchants and monks came to China using the Silk Road. The prevalent type of Buddhism in China today is the Mahayana (Great Wheel), which – as opposed to Hinayana (Small Wheel) – promises all creatures redemption through the so-called Bodhisattva (redemption deities).

Two aspects particularly appealed to the Chinese: the teachings of karma provided a better explanation for individual misfortune, and there was a hopeful promise for existence after death. Nevertheless, there was considerable opposition to Buddhism, which contrasted sharply with Confucian ethics and ancestor worship.

Buddhism was most influential in Chinese history during the Tang dynasty (618–907). Several emperors officially supported the religion; the Tang empress Wu Zetian, in particular, surrounded herself with Buddhist advisers. Late in the dynasty, however, for three years Chinese Buddhists experienced the most severe persecutions in their entire history: a total of 40,000 temples and monasteries were destroyed, and Buddhism was blamed for the dynasty's economic decline and moral decay.

In the course of time, 10 Chinese schools of Buddhism emerged, eight of which were essentially philosophical and did not influence popular religion. Only two schools have remained: Chan, or Zen Buddhism (associated with the Shaolin Temple – see page 196), and Amitabha-Buddhism, or Pure Land. The more influential is the Zen school, developed during the Tang dynasty, which preaches redemption through Buddhahood, which anyone can attain. It denounces knowledge gained from books or dogmas. The masters of Zen consider meditation to be the only path to knowledge.

In the 7th century AD, another type of Buddhism, called Tantric Buddhism or Lamaism, was the incarnation of the Bodhisattva of mercy (Avalokiteshvara; Guanyin to the Chinese), who is also worshipped as the patron god of Tibet. The Panchen Lama is higher in the hierarchy of the gods and is the embodiment of Buddha Amitabha. The present 14th Dalai Lama, who was enthroned in 1940, fled to India from Tibet after an uprising in 1959, and has been living in exile since. The identity of the successor to the 10th Panchen Lama, who died in 1989, remains under dispute, and is a divisive political issue. The boy named as the successor by the Dalai

Buddhist monks and nuns.

introduced into Tibet from India. With the influence of the monk Padmasambhava (also known as Guru Rinpoche), it replaced the indigenous Shaman Bon religion, while absorbing some of its elements. Tibetan monasteries developed into centres of intellectual and worldly power, yet there were recurring arguments. Only the reformer Tsongkhapa (1357–1419) succeeded in rectifying conditions that had become chaotic. He founded the sect of virtue (Gelugpa), which declared absolute celibacy to be a condition and reintroduced strict rules of order. Because the followers of this sect wear yellow caps, this order came to be known as Yellow Hat Buddhism.

The Gelugpas are led by the Dalai Lama and the Panchen Lama. The Dalai Lama represents

⊘ CONFUCIAN THOUGHTS

It is a pleasure to have friends come to visit you from afar. It is these things that cause me concern: failure to cultivate virtue, failure to go deeply into what I have learned, inability to move up to what I have heard to be right, and inability to reform myself when I have defects.

A man of humanity, wishing to establish himself, also establishes others, and wishing to enlarge himself, also enlarges others.

He is the sort of man who forgets to eat when he engages himself in vigorous pursuit of learning, who is so full of joy that he forgets his worries, and who does not notice that old age is coming on. (Describing himself.)

Lama was removed by the Chinese authorities and is being held in Beijing. The Chinese government's choice was installed at Tashilhunpo monastery in 1995, but the majority of Tibetans do not recognise him as the new incarnation.

In Lamaism, a complex pantheon exists; apart from the Buddhist deities, there are numerous figures from the Brahman and Hindu world of gods and the old Bon religion. Magic, repetitive prayers, movements, formulae, symbols and sacrificial rituals are all means for achieving redemption.

Hui Muslims outside Xi'an's Great Mosque.

ISLAM

Ten of the 56 recognised nationalities in China define themselves as Muslim: Hui, Uzbek, Uighur, Karach, Kyrgyz, Tatar, Shi'ite Tajik, Dongxiang, Sala and Bao'an – an estimated total of around 20 million people. The Hui are the only group who enjoy the special status of a recognised minority solely because of their religion: they are mostly Han Chinese, and adhere to the teachings of the Koran less than most other Muslims.

Islam came to China via two different routes: one was the famous Silk Road, the other from across the sea to the southeastern coast of China. During the Yuan dynasty (1279–1368), the religion became permanently established in China.

Many of the policies of the Qing dynasty (1644–1911) were hostile to Muslims. In the 18th century, for example, the slaughtering of animals in accordance with Islamic rites was forbidden, and the building of new mosques and pilgrimages to Mecca were not allowed. Marriages between Chinese and Muslims were declared illegal, and relations between the two groups were made increasingly difficult.

The Cultural Revolution led to terrible persecution of Chinese Muslims, but by the 1980s Beijing's attitude to religions – particularly among the country's minorities – softened, and a more tolerant approach was adopted. Today, government figures indicate there are more than 35,000 mosques in China, and the religion has seen a resurgence, with Chinese Muslims taking the annual pilgrimage – or Hajj – to Mecca in increasing numbers – reportedly more than 10,000 in 2007. The events of September 11 in 2001, and the subsequent US War on Terror has, however, had negative effects for followers of Islam in China. Beijing has, in particular, cracked down on Xinjiang's population of Uighurs, who resent Chinese control of the province (and the large-scale influx of Han settlers) and harbour ambitions of independence.

CHRISTIANITY

Christianity was first brought to China by the Nestorians, in 635, who disseminated their teachings with the help of a Persian called Alopen, who was their first missionary.

For a period, in spite of religious persecution, the religion spread to all the regions of the empire, and survived in some parts of the country until the end of the Mongol Yuan dynasty. At the same time, contacts were made between China and the Roman Catholic Church. The first Catholic church in China was probably built by a Franciscan monk from Italy, who arrived in Beijing in 1295. During the Ming period, Catholic missionaries began to be very active in China. A leading figure among the Jesuit missionaries, who played an important role, was an Italian, Matteo Ricci. When he died, there were 3,000 Christians in China.

The Jesuits used their knowledge of Western sciences to forge links with Chinese scholars, but other Catholic orders were more dogmatic and caused tension. The Chinese emperors, fed

> *The Chinese tend to have a flexible approach to religion which is reflected in the long-running osmosis between Daoist and Buddhist faiths, as well as interaction with ancestor worship and more general superstitions.*

up with the squabbling, persecuted them all. In the early 1800s, Protestants began missionary activities using methods to convert people that were not always scrupulous.

The Vatican took a strong anti-Communist stance after World War II, and post-revolutionary China ordered Chinese Catholics to be no longer accountable to Rome. There has been a thaw in relations between the two in recent years – 2016, China and the Vatican have been holding talks about reopening diplomatic ties – but the oft-predicted switch in relations from Taiwan to China has not yet materialised, with the Vatican maintaining its position that there is insufficient religious freedom in China to justify abandoning politically and religiously free Taiwan.

RELIGION IN CONTEMPORARY CHINA

Despite the Vatican's views, there has been a significant loosening of control over people's right to worship in China, and among the increasingly affluent and educated elite a resurgence of interest in spiritual matters. Nevertheless, the Chinese Communist Party remains suspicious of organised religions, unless it can have a controlling hand in their appointments of clergy. This can be seen in Tibet, where there are deep divisions over Beijing-approved lamas and those approved by the Tibetan government in exile, and in the Catholic Church, which is divided between a Beijing-sanctioned order and an underground Church – the major sticking point in ongoing negotiations to normalise relations with the Vatican.

It can also be seen very clearly in Beijing's dealings with followers of the Falun Gong movement, a form of spiritual practice introduced to China in 1992 by Li Hongzhi. Based on meditative practices, Falun Gong aims to improve the characters of its followers through the principles of Truthfulness, Compassion and Forbearance. In 1998 the Chinese government estimated that

the movement had attracted as many as 70 million followers (the movement itself claims 100 million worldwide). Fearing it could become the kind of subversive millennial cult that plagued the closing years of the Qing dynasty, the Chinese government banned it in 1999. Since then there have been routine reports of followers being imprisoned and tortured.

In the meantime, however, Buddhist and Daoist temples have been renovated nationwide – and, in some cases, new temples constructed – partly to cater for China's fast growing tour-

Fuhu Si, one of many Buddhist temples on the slopes of Emei Shan.

ism industry. But the proliferation of places of traditional worship in China has also resulted in a resurgence of religious practice among ordinary Chinese unseen since the Communist Revolution. Increasingly, also, China's educated elite – particularly the creative elite – are turning to China's traditional faiths of Buddhism and Daoism, and in some cases Tibetan Buddhism, which is enjoying a resurgence of interest throughout China despite Beijing's opposition to the Dalai Lama.

Many Chinese remain broadly atheistic, however, a spiritual vacuum that is filled with a firm belief in the path of scientific progress, the joys of materialism and the destined rise of their nation.

📷 A GUIDE TO CHINESE TEMPLES

China's Buddhist, Daoist and Confucian temples are repositories of culture, and share many characteristics.

By far the largest number of temples in China are Buddhist. As with all temples, halls are arranged on a north-south axis, with the main door facing south, and opening onto a courtyard. A so-called spirit wall may exist at the front entrance, barring evil spirits from entering. The first hall is where you usually encounter Maitreya, the rotund Laughing Buddha. Standing behind him is Weituo, protector of the Buddhist faith, often portrayed with a sword lying across his arms. The altar in the main hall supports three golden statues: the Buddha Sakyamuni (historical Buddha) flanked by the Buddhas of the present and the future. To the back of the main hall is a statue of Guanyin, the multi-limbed goddess of compassion, who often appears holding a small child.

Daoist temples share a similar layout to Buddhist temples, but can generally be distinguished by their black pillars (Buddhist temples normally use red), *bagua* symbols, and prevalence of animal statues. The main hall is usually dedicated to Daoism's own holy trinity: Laozi, its founder; the Jade Emperor (Yuhuang Dadi); and the Yellow Emperor (Huangdi). Tianhou (Tin Hau), goddess of seafarers, and black-bearded Guandi, god of war, are also often celebrated. In parts of China, particularly in the south, Daoism and Buddhism fuse together, and some temples feature deities from both pantheons.

Confucian temples are fewer in number, and neither as colourful nor as vibrant as Daoist and Buddhist shrines. The main courtyard generally contains steles commemorating scholars, sometimes supported on the backs of *bixi*, mythical turtle-like dragons. Confucius himself is honoured with a statue at the entrance or by an effigy in the main hall, flanked by his disciples.

The Jade Buddha Temple (Yufuo Si) in Shanghai features a pair of exquisite jade Buddhas from Burma.

Prayers written on small scraps of paper hang from a tree at a Confucius Temple, Qufu.

A temple guardian figure outside Dali's San Ta Si (Three Pagodas).

Tortoises represent longevity.

Mythological creatures

Traditional Chinese buildings are home to a veritable zoo of mythological animals. A pair of stone lions is often seen guarding the gates to temples and other buildings. On the left, the male is identified by a ball under his paw, symbolising control of the empire; to the right, the female has her paw on a cub, indicating offspring and continuation of empire. Not native to China, lions are associated with power and prestige, and the use of this beast was reserved for the court and officials of high rank.

Even more revered than the lion is the dragon, which reigns supreme over all animals. Dragons are believed to rise into the skies in the spring, and later plunge into the waters in autumn. As a creature between heaven and earth and symbolising the *yang* (male) energy, the dragon came to be identified with the emperor, thought to be the son of heaven. Together with the mythological phoenix, which represents the *yin* (female) force and is associated with the empress, the dragon appears frequently in decorative designs of imperial buildings. In combination, the dragon and phoenix can also stand for matrimonial harmony.

Other creatures include tortoises and cranes, which both represent longevity, and various beasts from the Daoist pantheon and the Chinese zodiac. Stylised fish on temple roofs (mainly in southern coastal regions) represent harmony and prosperity.

Statues at the City Temple of Shanghai (formerly the Temple of the Town God). Each city in China once had its own "town god" temple.

A clay and wood sculpture of the "thousand-armed" Guanyin at Shuanglin Si, Shanxi province.

Stylised lions flank temple entrances.

TRADITIONAL MEDICINE

For millennia, the old-fashioned Chinese methods of caring for and treating the body have worked just fine. Can a billion people be wrong?

The mention of traditional Chinese medicine often conjures up images of the near mystical application of needles, aromatic herbs and strange animal parts. Yet, despite its exotic stereotype, traditional Chinese medicine has increasingly gained respect from both scientists and the general public in the West.

In China, scepticism and debate arose as to the value of traditional medicine during the first half of the 20th century. Intellectual and political groups, such as the Nationalists and Marxists, were particularly disapproving, and the medical establishment suffered greatly at their hands. After the founding of the People's Republic of China, competition between Western and Chinese medicine was eradicated for practical as well as ideological reasons, with an attempt to integrate the two systems.

This approach has persisted, and today medical care in China often consists of a mixture of both Western and traditional Chinese medicine, although Western-style medicine, or *xiyi*, tends to be dominant. Large public hospitals *(renmin yiyuan)* in cities across the country offer both traditional Chinese and Western approaches to medical treatment. Hospitals dealing exclusively with traditional Chinese medicine, or *zhongyi*, tend to be smaller, less well equipped and harder to find.

The Chinese will usually visit a doctor trained in Western medicine if they feel that they are seriously ill and need to be treated quickly. If the problem is not too serious or urgent, the patient will most likely seek out a traditional doctor, who will attempt to restore harmony to the body.

HISTORICAL ROOTS

Traditional Chinese medicine, as practised today and in past centuries, is based upon an array of theories and practices from both foreign and native

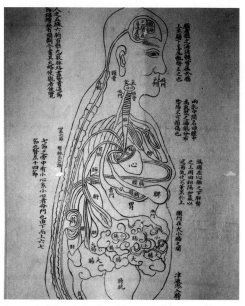

Anatomical illustration for Chinese medicine practitioners.

Yin-yang philosophy and the theory of five elements form a system of categories that explain the complex relationships between parts of the body and the environment.

sources. Some argue that Chinese medicine can trace its roots back as far as 5,000 years to the time of Shennong, a divine farmer credited with the discovery of medicinal herbs. Historical writer Liu Shu reported that "Shennong tasted hundreds of herbs himself... some days as many as 70 poisonous herbs in one day". The validity of that statement is surely one to be debated, but *Shennong*

Bencaojing (Shennong's Classic on Materia Medica) describes the medicinal effects of some 365 herbs and is the earliest known text of its kind.

Another early text, which continues to be a cornerstone in the Chinese medical canon, is *Huangdi Neijing* (The Yellow Emperor's Canon of Interior Medicine). While authorship is unknown, its present-day version is believed to have been compiled between the 2nd century BC and 8th century AD, and later revised during the Song dynasty (960–1279). Over the centuries, volumes upon volumes of commentary have been written about this ancient text. Its influence remains important, as the main principles of Chinese medicine are still based on theories first set forth by it.

KEY PRINCIPLES

Several main concepts are essential to understanding traditional Chinese medicine. Holism, or the concept that parts of a human body form an integral, connected and inseparable whole, is one of the main distinguishing features of traditional Chinese medicine. Whereas Western medicine tends to treat symptoms in a direct fashion, traditional Chinese medicine examines illnesses in the context of a whole.

The *yin-yang* philosophy is at the heart of Chinese medicinal practice. *Yin* and *yang* represent two opposite sides in nature such as hot and cold, or light and dark. Each of the different organs is said to have *yin* or *yang* characteristics. Balance between the two is vital for maintaining health. The five elements – earth, fire, water, metal and wood – are categories of characteristics into which all known phenomena can be classified. For example, just as water subdues fire, phenomena associated with water are said to control those classified under fire.

THE PHARMACY

A traditional Chinese apothecary has a unique smell made up of thousands of scents emanating from jars and cabinets stocked full of dried plants, seeds, animal parts and minerals. Among them are the well-known ginseng roots, dried or immersed in alcohol. You will also recognise the acupuncture needles and the cupping glasses made of glass or bamboo.

One of the most famous Chinese apothecaries is the legendary Tongrentang pharmacy, in an old part of Beijing, which has been in business for over 300 years. It was once a royal dispensary during the Qing dynasty and still produces all the pills and secret concoctions once used by royalty. The size of this pharmacy is overwhelming, as is the selection of remedies: small and large eggs, snakes coiled in spirals, dried monkeys, toads, tortoises, grasshoppers, fish, octopuses, stag antlers, rhinoceros horns and the genitalia of various unfortunate – and sometimes endangered – animals. And then there are the myriad kinds of dried and preserved herbs, blossoms, roots, berries, mushrooms and fruits.

A traditional pharmacy.

ACUPUNCTURE

The popularity of acupuncture outside China has made it nearly synonymous for many Westerners with all traditional Chinese medicine. Not meant as a cure for everything, acupuncture has nonetheless enjoyed renewed interest in recent decades, and is especially effective in controlling pain.

The practice of acupuncture is based on a theory of channels or meridians by which "influences" flow through the body. The flow of positive influences through the body is vital in maintaining health. Unhealthy symptoms are, in fact, manifestations of improper *qi*, the essence of life. The *Huangdi Neijing* describes 365 sensitive points used in acupuncture, in addition to 12 main conduits in the human body. Executed properly, acupuncture should be relatively painless. Many countries are still somewhat reluctant to accept acupuncture as part of an alternative approach to medicine. However, it is increasingly accepted as a treatment by many Western physicians, particularly for pain relief. While Westerners may rely on drugs to moderate physical pain, the Chinese go to the acupuncturist. Chronic problems, however, require a longer healing process.

There is also a system of ear acupuncture, performed without needles. Small, round seed kernels are stuck onto certain points of the ear

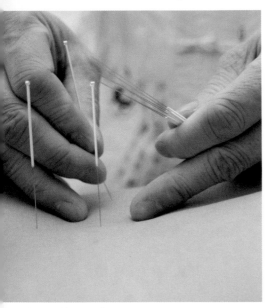

Acupuncture needles.

> *The Western medical community may still remain sceptical about the effectiveness of Chinese medicine, but over a billion people, including increasing numbers in the West, find that it works for them.*

and massaged by the patient every so often. This method is not only very successful in the treatment of pain, but is also said to relieve some allergies, such as hay fever.

An acupuncture clinic often smells similar to a pharmacy. This is the typical smell of the *moxa* herb, or mugwort. It is considered especially helpful in the treatment of illnesses that, in Chinese medical terminology, are classified as "cold"; for example, stomach and digestive complaints without fever, certain rheumatic illnesses, chronic pains in the back, and cramped shoulders and neck. The mugwort is formed into small cones and placed on slices of fresh ginger; then it is allowed to grow slowly. The plant is then placed onto the acupuncture point and burnt in a process known as moxibustion.

EXERCISE

On any early morning in China, millions of people, most of them elderly, gather in parks to exercise. There are several types of traditional exercise that are regarded not only as ways to take care of one's body, but also as therapy.

The most common type of exercise is tai chi (*taijiquan*), which translates as 'Supreme Ultimate Boxing'. Another, perhaps less familiar to Westerners, is *qigong*, which is often translated as "breath skill". *Qigong* plays a large part in the practice of tai chi. With certain exercises, which may or may not involve conscious breathing, the patient learns to control *qi* – a person's vital energy. It is claimed that those who have mastered *qigong* can walk outdoors in sub-zero temperatures without sufficient clothing and remain oblivious to the cold.

During the Cultural Revolution, *qigong* (along with many martial arts) was forbidden because it too closely resembled "superstitious" practices. Yet, in the 1980s, new *qigong* groups sprang up throughout the country. Today, an estimated 70 million people in China practise *qigong* daily, and the therapy is also followed in the West.

⊘ MEDICINAL FOODS

Diet is fundamental to the philosophy of traditional medicine. China's herbalists attribute medicinal value to various foods; indeed, the distinction between food and treatment is often blurred. Consider three traditional delicacies: shark's fin, abalone and bird's nest. These are exquisite parts of an extensive cuisine, eaten in part for their sensory delights. Yet each is claimed to have medicinal value. Shark's fin, for example, is said to benefit internal organs, including the heart and kidneys. Abalone calms internal organs; moreover, it regulates the liver and reduces dizziness and high blood pressure. Bird's nest, usually taken as a soup, cleanses the blood and assures a clear complexion.

THE ANIMAL TRADE

Across the globe, respect for and patronage of Chinese medicine continues to spread, yet this growing interest has a darker side.

The use of animal parts for medicine is not new. The Chinese have been using them for well over 1,000 years. The practice spread from China to other countries such as Korea and Japan, and to other parts of the world with significant East Asian populations.

The result is that some species, already suffering from the loss of habitat due to the intensive industrial and economic growth of many Asian countries, none more so than China itself, are now being pushed to the brink of extinction by the increased demand for their body parts.

The demand for tiger parts, for example, threatens the survival of the world's five remaining sub-species of this magnificent feline. Various parts of the tiger are employed in traditional medicine: eyeballs are used to treat epilepsy; the tail for various skin diseases; the bile for convulsions in children; whiskers for toothaches; and the brain for laziness and pimples. Yet of all tiger parts, it is the bones that are most valued; they are often used to treat rheumatism, weakness, stiffness or paralysis. Tigers have vanished from many of their natural habitats in Asia and, without radical intervention, they may disappear completely from the wild in less than a decade.

Tigers aren't the only victims of the trade in animal parts. Rhinoceros, bear and even shark populations are also rapidly shrinking. Rhinoceros horn has a reputation for being an aphrodisiac, and the number of rhinoceros in the wild is falling. Without assistance, they too could be extinct within a decade or two. Bears from Asia and North America are also under threat, since their paws are believed to have medicinal value.

Shark's fin, though not used exclusively for medicine, is a highly sought-after delicacy. Served most commonly as shark's fin soup, this broth is believed to benefit the internal organs. The shark has become an unlikely poster boy for conservationists, however,

and a lengthy campaign has finally seen the government ban the dish from official banquets.

SUSTAINABLE ALTERNATIVES

Human populations and disposable incomes have increased dramatically in East Asia in general, and in China in particular, along with a resurgence of

Demand for tiger body parts threatens the survival of the species.

interest in traditional cures. Use of certain traditional medicines is often seen as a status symbol, and as a way of holding on to traditional customs amid the whirlwind of social and economic changes.

The health benefits of the active ingredients present in many Chinese prescriptions are often disputed, however, and components such as bear bile can be synthesised in a laboratory. As endangered animal populations continue to decline to the point of extinction, the use of their parts to feed an ever-growing demand is no longer sustainable. What is clear is that the trade in endangered animal parts for medicine must stop. This means finding an alternative to alternative medicine.

CHINESE LITERATURE

The complexities of Chinese literature, beginning with the thoughts of Confucius in the 5th century BC, are challenging and inspiring. That is to be expected after 25 centuries of creativity.

China has a long and venerable tradition in the written word. While it is true that vernacular literature did not fully take shape as an art form until the 14th-century Yuan dynasty, the history of literature in the Middle Kingdom goes back to far earlier times, and sophisticated poetry was in evidence by the early Tang period (7th century AD). Perhaps the most famous of these ancient works are the thoughts of Confucius (551–479 BC), collected by his disciples into his famous *Lunyu* (Analects), a work that underpins the Confucian moral code – a long-lasting pillar of Chinese society.

POETRY

The earliest existing collection of poems is the *Shijing* (a book of odes). It is said that more than 3,000 songs were collected, of which Confucius selected 300, cutting out the saucier entries; he then compiled them in the *Shijing*. The contents of the odes are wide-ranging: love songs, songs

A Confucian prayer.

> The writings of Confucius have profoundly influenced Chinese culture. Confucianism is more a moral code for society than a religious philosophy, though Confucius is sometimes worshipped as a deity.

about the land and songs glorifying outstanding personalities or personal qualities.

Poems in the lyrical or epic style play an extremely important part in Chinese literature. To be able to read and write poetry was part of the elementary education of the higher social classes. Students and civil servants of any rank or age were expected to be able to write a poem for any occasion. Girls and women who knew how to recite poems graciously were ensured the admiration of the opposite sex. The *Chuci*, another collection of songs, comes from the south of China: its creation is attributed to the poet Qu Yuan (c. 322–295 BC).

The Tang dynasty (618–907) marked the golden age of Chinese poetry. No other period in history has produced such a great number of poets and epic works. *Quan Tangshi*, the vast collection of Tang poetry, contains nearly 50,000 compositions by 2,200 poets. One of the most famous wordsmiths of the time was Li Bai (699–762), who is said to have written his best-known poems in a state of total inebriation. The poet Du Fu (712–70) was a friend of Li Bai's, though his style is very different. He held office at the court for just a short time and was forced to flee due to political upheavals. He then led an unsettled, wandering life for a long time, eventually settling in Chengdu, where one can still visit the straw hut, Du Fu Caotang, that served as his home (see page 359).

It is hard to say which of the two poets has better survived the passage of time. Li Bai was a natural talent, humorous, devoted to nature and close to the Daoists. Du Fu became a poet mainly through diligence. Bold and serious, his concerns about social issues were closely linked to Confucian ideas.

FICTIONAL CLASSICS

Every child in China knows the novel *Journey to the West* (*Xiyouji* in pinyin) and its famous heroes: the monkey king Sun Wukong; a pig, Zhu Bajie; the river demon, Sha; and the Buddhist pilgrim and monk, Xuanzang. The novel recounts the adventures of the monkey king, who, together with the other characters, accompanies Xuanzang on a pilgrimage to India, in order to collect Buddhist scriptures. The story is closely tied in with Chinese popular religion, and includes Daoist and Buddhist deities. Its popularity can be explained by this familiarity and the fact that it combines exciting adventure with the themes of morality and spiritual purpose.

The *Shuihuzhuan* (*The Water Margin*, also known as *Outlaws of the Marsh*), whose origins are unclear, is a novel about thieves dating from the Ming period. The story is partly based upon historical facts about the robber Song Jiang and his companions, who wandered through what is now the province of Shandong around the end of the Northern Song dynasty (960–1127). Just like Robin Hood and his merry men, Song Jiang and his followers fought injustices according to their code of honour. They finally submitted to the imperial doctrine and fought against rebels who were threatening the state system.

The Water Margin is said to have been Mao Zedong's favourite book, although during the time of the Cultural Revolution, it was considered a negative illustration of capitulation.

GENRE NOVELS

The epitome of the genre novel is *Jinpingmei* (*The Plum Blossom in a Golden Vase*), written in the Ming dynasty. *Jinpingmei* portrays people as individual characters, realistically describing the many amorous adventures of its hero, Ximen. This novel conveys a very precise portrayal of social conditions in the 16th century. In 1687, Emperor Kangxi banned the book, yet it continued to be read, and in 1708 it was even translated into Manchurian. It was again censored in 1789 and once more in 1949.

Hongloumeng (*Dream of the Red Mansions*), written by Cao Xueqin in the 18th century, is considered to be the most complete genre novel. Its central character is Jia Baoyu, the amorous and sentimental son of a high-ranking official. The novel relates the rise and fall of the house of Jia, a distinguished Manchu family, in intricate detail.

An operatic performance of the classic Journey to the West.

⊘ A LI BAI SAMPLER

Li Bai was the Tang dynasty's most beloved poet.
Moonlight gleams before my bed,
Like frost on the floor.
Lifting my head I see the bright moon,
Lowering my head I think of my old home.
At Yellow Crane Tower, I said goodbye to an old friend.
It was the third month, the season of flowers, when you went down to Yangzhou.
Your solitary sail has become a distant blue dot, and all I saw was the Yangzi flowing into the sky.
We are but travellers on the world's horizons.
Meeting thus in a common fate, what does acquaintance matter?

POST-IMPERIAL LITERATURE

The political and cultural May Fourth Movement of 1919 heralded drastic social changes. Among other things, it aimed at reforming the use of classical language in literature, and prose literature became increasingly regarded as a means for social change. The leading proponent of this new vernacular prose was the writer Lu Xun, who believed China needed to modernise through revolution. His satirical novella *The True Story of Ah Q* is considered to be a masterpiece of modern Chinese literature. Ding Ling was one of a large group of women writ-

> *The oldest Chinese books were written on strips of bamboo, fixed together like a roller blind. This helps to explain why traditional writing runs from top to bottom and from right to left.*

The annual Hong Kong book fair.

ers that emerged during the May Fourth Movement. In *Miss Sophia's Diary*, she evokes the lifestyle of her female contemporaries through the observations of an unhappy young woman.

The 1920s and 1930s were a period of literary productivity in China. One of the most prominent writers of the time was Ba Jin. His best-known work, *The Family*, written in the tradition of *Hongloumeng*, relates the decline of a civil servant's family at the beginning of the 20th century.

Another key figure to emerge during the period was Guo Moruo (1892–1978), one of the founders of the Creation Society, which championed a romantic style of writing. A dedicated Marxist, Guo went on to become an influential figure in the rise of communism in China – he was one of many writers of the early 20th century sympathetic to the cause. Their literature became increasingly politicised, dealing with real rather than imagined events and glorifying communism. After Mao Zedong's speech on art and literature, in Yan'an in 1942, Social Realism was established as the only legitimate art form.

In 1956, during the Hundred Flowers Movement (see page 60), liberalist writers and intellectuals expressed dissatisfaction with the policies of the Communist Party, protesting in particular against the lack of artistic freedom. They were branded as rightists, and their works labelled as "poisonous weeds". In the following decade the Cultural Revolution brought all literary endeavours to a halt: for a time, Chinese Opera was deemed the only acceptable form of cultural expression.

A NEW AGE

The end of the Maoist era in 1976 marked a resurgence of writing, focusing on the traumas caused by the Cultural Revolution. Lu Xinghua's work *Scar* gave the term "literature of the wounded" to this new literary form, itself part of the so-called New Realism, which typically looked at society's imperfections and the abuses of power. The 1980s saw a burst of literary creativity in new writing techniques. Around 2,000 novels were published between 1979 and the early 1990s (compared with a total of 320 between 1949 and 1966).

Today, popular genres include officialdom novels that give a behind-the-doors glimpse at the life of cadres, *chuanye*, in which a protagonist travels back to past dynasties – often for romantic encounters – and science fiction works in which China has risen to global dominance. Censorship is still stifling, however, and many publishers prefer conservative fare to topics that could land them in hot water with the authorities – notably politics, horror and sex. Many of the Chinese writers best known in the West now live in self-imposed exile, a literary diaspora.

CINEMA IN CHINA

Over the past three decades, Chinese cinema has captured the imagination of film buffs around the world.

Film – literally "electric shadow play" in Chinese – appeared in China in the early 20th century. The first silent movies, including the first "kung fu" films, were made in Shanghai, the centre of Chinese cinema. When the Communists took over, all films, apart from Socialist Realist propaganda, were banned. Then the Cultural Revolution brought film-making to a standstill, apart from a few socialist "model operas".

It wasn't until 1978 that the Beijing Film Academy reopened its doors to students. A new generation of film-makers, known as the Fifth Generation, developed individual forms of expression, moulded by the experiences of forced labour and political terror. Chen Kaige's debut *Yellow Earth* (1984) portrays the failure of those who rebel against authority and laments the failure of China's liberation through Communism. Other Fifth Generation films examined the destructive forces of power and tradition with landmark films like Zhang Yimou's *Judou* (1989) and *Raise the Red Lantern* (1991), and Chen Kaige's *Farewell My Concubine* (1993).

The subsequent Sixth Generation of film-makers have produced grittier, more realistic films, dwelling on urban desolation and the negative impact of China's economic growth. One of the movement's pioneers, Zhang Yuan, dealt with such taboo themes as homosexuality (*East Palace West Palace*, 1996), and he later achieved commercial success with the poignant *Little Red Flowers* in 2006. Other leading directors of this genre, often likened to Italian neo-realism, are Wang Xiaoshuai (*Beijing Bicycle*, 2001), Li Yang (*Blind Mountain*, 2007) and Jia Zhangke (*The World*, 2004 and *Still Life* – winner of the 2006 Golden Lion in Venice).

Chinese-language films are increasingly reaching mainstream audiences abroad. After the success of *Sense and Sensibility* (1995), Taiwanese director Ang Lee went on to make *Crouching Tiger, Hidden Dragon* (2001), which was a big box-office hit around the world – despite being received rather poorly in China itself. His spy thriller *Lust, Caution* (2007) won him a second Golden Lion award and for his dramas *Brokeback Mountain* (2005) and *Life of Pi* (2012), he won Best Director Academy Awards, becoming the first Asian to win this accolade.

Another dazzling martial-arts epic (the genre is known as *wuxia*), Zhang Yimou's *Hero* (2002) was met with rave reviews in the West. He followed it up two years later with *House of the Flying Daggers*. Most recently Yimou directed the most expensive movie in Chinese history, *The Flowers of War* (2011), staring Christian Bale as an American caught up in the Japanese invasion of Nanjing. Possibly inspired by the

Chow Yun Fat in the third "Pirates of the Caribbean" film.

successful casting of such a Hollywood A-lister, Feng Xiaogang bagged performances from Oscar winners Tim Robbins and Adrien Brody in his own World War II epic, *Remembering 1942* (2012).

Hong Kong cinema is known for its hard-man actors such as Chow Yun Fat and Jackie Chan, a household name the world over, and superstar Maggie Cheung. Apart from fast-action and martial-arts films, independent productions such as Wong Karwai's tender and violent *Chungking Express*, set in Hong Kong and starring Faye Wong, have found an international audience.

In 2016, the Chinese-Hong Kong science-fantasy-romantic-comedy *The Mermaid,* directed and produced by Stephen Chow, became the highest-grossing Chinese film of all time.

CHINESE OPERA

The emphasis in Chinese opera is on Confucian ethics and morality. Stories invariably have endings in which goodness is upheld and evil is punished.

Although Chinese theatre in the form of skits, vaudeville, puppet shows and shadow plays has existed since the Tang dynasty (618–907), formal music-drama had its origins in the Yuan period (1279–1368), when scholars who were displaced from their government positions by the foreign Mongols turned to writing dramas in which songs often alternated with dialogue.

Since then, opera has evolved into one of the most popular forms of folk entertainment in China, and although there are reckoned to be more than 300 different styles, all share some general character-istics. Plots are based on legends or folklore with which audiences are familiar, and performances are a composite of different art forms – such as litera-ture, song, dance and mime, as well as the martial arts. Costumes and make-up are symbolic, helping the audience to understand the various roles and personalities of the cast. Time is marked with the aid of a redwood clapper that produces a high-pitched clicking sound when struck. The flute, with its wide-ranging melodies, is the primary instrument.

Styles of regional opera include *chaozhou* (Teo-chew) opera, the puppet operas of Fujian, and the *bangzi xi* (clapper operas), which are popular in Shaanxi and the northern part of China, and which feature as their main accompaniment a datewood clapper struck with a stick.

By far the most popular Chinese opera, however, is the highly stylised *jingxi* (Beijing or Peking opera), which dates from the 1800s. The accom-panying musical instrument in Bei-jing opera is usually the *huqin*, a Chinese fiddle, although cymbals are sometimes, but not always, employed in action scenes.

Opera masks are often sold as souvenirs.

The elaborate costumes are based on those of the court of the Han, Tang, Song and Ming dynasties, although they are symbolic rather than realistic. All actors must hone the fine body movements that are an essential part of every style of opera.

Whether in soliloquies, spoken verse, songs or dialogue, the words used in Beijing opera are almost always colloquial – its intended audience has always been the common people. Performances often took place on streets and in market places and were a useful way for people to learn about life beyond their day-to-day existence.

The epic tales of the Monkey King are one of Chinese opera's classic works. The adventures of the cunning, boisterous hero are brought to life with a dazzling display of acrobatics, music, puppetry and vibrant costumes.

Visiting the opera

A visit to the Chinese opera is a relaxed though occasionally quite noisy experience; formal dress is not the norm. Be warned, however, that this exotic art form doesn't appeal to everyone: once you've got over the visual spectacle of the elaborate costumes and startling make-up, you might find the strangled singing style, the atonal music and the complex plot too much to take for a whole performance – and performances can be long. Of course, a good grasp of the language enhances the experience (although some theatres provide subtitles in English).

Colours are highly symbolic. Red make-up on a male character indicates bravery and loyalty, while white denotes a powerful villain. Clowns have their own special make-up, often with a white patch on the tip of the nose to indicate wit or playfulness. The female role (dan) is usually played by a man wearing white make-up with various shades of carmine.

To get the most out of Chinese opera, it helps to know something of its conventions. Changes in time and place are evoked through speech, action and ritualised use of props. Walking in a circle symbolises a journey; circling the stage with a whip indicates riding a horse. English subtitles are provided in some theatres in Beijing and Shanghai.

ARTS AND CRAFTS

With its long history and inward-looking tradition, China has developed and refined a resplendent catalogue of fine arts and exquisite crafts.

From very early times, Chinese artisans dazzled the world with technical brilliance and innovation, and today, Chinese arts and crafts are renowned the world over. Since the 1950s, China has attempted to revive the traditional and native arts. Research institutes were established in craft centres to continue the tradition of the crafts, as well as to make further technical advancements. Promising young talent is recruited from around the country for training in specialised schools.

PAINTING AND CALLIGRAPHY

There has always been a close connection between Chinese painting and calligraphy. Ancient Chinese words started as pictograms, and while each has developed in a separate direction, there have nonetheless remained inextricable ties between the two. As a rule, classical Chinese painters have extensive training in calligraphy, while calligraphers have experience in

A traditional calligrapher at Fenghuang.

Calligraphy has always been important to the Chinese as a marker of an individual's intelligence and social status. Mastery of the art form has always been closely linked to the attainment of knowledge.

painting. Both forms are created with the same brushes and are often present together in one piece of work.

In fact, what separated and elevated the status of painting from other crafts was its similarity to calligraphy. Both calligraphy and painting are considered scholarly pursuits and have grand and esteemed traditions, but calligraphy has

been held in higher regard. Literati painters, for example, judged works by their combination of painting, poetry and calligraphy. Success in all three areas deemed paintings to be art. According to such standards, paintings and other art forms that lacked calligraphy were merely crafts, regardless of their level of technical brilliance.

For the Chinese, the written word is the carrier of culture, and the difficulty of learning written Chinese ensured the high social status of the scholar-gentry class. Mastery of writing and calligraphy was highly esteemed. Furthermore, despite the numerous spoken dialects in China, Chinese writing has maintained its single standard and style (apart from the presence of traditional, or full-form, Chinese characters in Hong

Kong and Macau). This nationwide unifying and historically continuous script was therefore always more important than the spoken language.

CLASSICAL CHINESE PAINTING

Painting is learnt in much the same way as writing: by copying old masters or textbooks. Once developed, a particular painting style is rarely lost or abandoned, and is preserved in the painting canon.

Classical Chinese paintings can be grouped into six general categories: landscapes, portraits, flowers and birds, bamboo and stone, animals, and palaces or other buildings. Art connoisseurs later added four more groups: religious paintings, barbarians and foreign tribes, dragons and fish, and vegetables and fruits.

One of the most favoured painting forms in China since the Tang dynasty (618–907) is landscape painting. Called "mountain water paintings" in Chinese, this style features mountains and water most prominently, accented with clouds, mist and trees. By contrast, human figures are small specks in the landscape and lack

Calligraphy brushes.

A typical classic painting.

⊘ TOOLS FOR THE JOB: THE FOUR TREASURES OF THE STUDY

Writing and painting utensils are referred to in China as the Four Treasures of the Study. They consist of the brush, ink, rubbing stone (or ink stone), and paper – tools held in high esteem by poets, scholars and painters.

Brushes are made with bamboo and various kinds of animal hair such as rabbit's fur, horsehair and even mouse whiskers, and come in a wide variety of sizes. Some brush tips are treated with glue to stiffen them.

Ink was traditionally made from the soot of coniferous resin with the addition of glue. Ink in solid form, pressed into the shape of slabs, bars or prisms, is used both for writing and painting, and although liquid ink is now available, its use removes one of the more contemplative and ritualistic aspects of traditional Chinese painting, in which one first drips water onto a rubbing stone, then rubs the ink stick on it. The resulting ink is an intense black, but can be diluted to the lightest of greys as necessary. Ink of good quality has perfume added – musk in former days, but cloves are now commonly used.

Silk was once the standard of professional and court painters, as it gave better control over ink and washes, but scholar-painters preferred paper for its immediate response to the brush. Itself another ancient Chinese invention, developed by Cai Lun and used from the 2nd century AD onwards – paper is now produced in different qualities, offering varying absorption and texture.

the detail lavished on the vegetation, water and mountain. These proportions reflect Chinese philosophies on the relationship between individuals and the outside world. Unlike Western paintings, in which humans are central subjects and natural environments are rendered as backdrops, Chinese paintings show people as subservient to or a small part of their surroundings.

Chinese paintings are abstract and do not aim for realism. The best paintings successfully capture the spirit or essence of a subject. Further-

Antique porcelain commands high prices.

more, a painter is considered a master of his art when the necessary brush strokes for a bird, chrysanthemum or waterfall flow effortlessly from his hand. Chinese painting values quick execution. Indeed, the nature of the materials and brush techniques do not allow for careful sketching or repainting; mistakes cannot be hidden or painted over.

This strong emphasis on perfection quickly leads to specialisation by painters on particular subjects. In this way, for instance, Xu Beihong (1895–1953) became known as the painter of horses, just as Qi Baishi (1862–1957) was famous for his shrimps.

A feature of the presentation of paintings is the scroll. After being painted on silk or paper,

the painting is backed with stronger paper and mounted on a long roll of silk or brocade. Then a wooden stick is attached at the lower end (or left end, if the scroll is to be displayed horizontally). Typically, the picture was stored away rolled up and brought out only on special occasions, to be slowly unfurled and revealing only parts of a scene that were pieced together in the mind of the observer, subtly drawing him into the picture. Whether vertically or horizontally, pictures were rarely displayed for long.

CRAFTS

Calligraphy, painting, poetry and music are regarded in China as noble arts, the knowledge of which was required of any scholar. By contrast, applied arts such as silk and carving are considered merely honourable crafts, performed by craftsmen and gentlewomen. All the same, in the West these skilled crafts have always held a special fascination.

SILK

The cultivation of the silkworm is said to go back to the 3rd century BC. The planting of mulberry trees and raising of silkworms is credited to Fuxi, a legendary figure of prehistoric China. For centuries, silk held the place of currency: civil servants and officers as well as foreign envoys were frequently paid or presented with bales of silk. The precious material was transported to the Middle East and the Roman empire, mostly via the Silk Road.

The Chinese maintained a monopoly on silk until about 200 BC, when the secret of its manufacture became known in Korea and Japan. In the West – in this case the Byzantine empire – such knowledge was acquired only in the 6th century AD. The Chinese had long prohibited the export of silkworm eggs and the dissemination of knowledge of their cultivation, but a monk is said to have succeeded in smuggling – an offence punishable by death – some of the prized quarry to the West.

Today's centres of silk production are concentrated around the cities of Hangzhou, Suzhou and Wuxi, where silk can be bought at a lower price. Hangzhou has the largest silk industry in the People's Republic, while in Suzhou, silk embroidery has been brought to the highest artistic level.

PORCELAIN

The Chinese invented porcelain sometime in the 7th century. The history of Chinese ceramics, however, goes back to Neolithic times. Along the Huang He (Yellow River) and Chang Jiang (Yangzi), 7,000- to 8,000-year-old ceramic vessels – red and even black clay with comb and rope patterns – have been found. The Yangshao and Longshan cultures of the 5th to 2nd millennium BC developed new types of vessels in a diversity of patterns in red, black, and brown. Quasi-human masks, stylised fish, of the Tang period in the shape of horses, camels, guardians in animal or human form, ladies of the court, and officials. The Song-period celadons – ranging in colour from pale or moss green, pale blue or pale grey to brown tones – were also technically excellent. As early as the Yuan period, a technique from the Near East was used for underglaze painting in cobalt blue, commonly known as Ming porcelain (*Qinghua* in Chinese). Some common themes seen throughout the Ming period were figures, landscapes and theatrical scenes. At the beginning of the

Silk embroidery.

and hard, thin-walled stoneware, with kaolin and lime feldspar glazes, were created. Later, light-grey stoneware with green glazes, known as *yue* ware – named after the kilns of the town of Yuezhou – were designs of the Han period (206 BC–AD 220). During the Tang dynasty, Chinese porcelain was known in Europe and the Middle East.

The most widespread form of ancient Chinese porcelain was celadon, the product of a blending of iron oxide with the glaze that resulted, during firing, in a green tone. *Sancai* ceramics, with three-colour glazes from the Tang dynasty, became world-famous. The colours were mostly strong green, yellow and brown. *Sancai* ceramics were also found among the tomb figurines

Qing dynasty, blue-and-white porcelain attained its highest level of quality.

Once patronised by imperial courts, Jingdezhen (Jiangxi province) has been the centre of porcelain manufacture since the 14th century. Today, however, relatively inexpensive porcelain can be bought throughout China. Antique pieces are still hard to come by, as the sale of articles predating the Opium Wars is prohibited by the Chinese government.

JADE

Jade is China's most precious stone and one of the earliest art forms to reach a superior level of achievement. According to a Chinese creation myth, when the god Pan Gu died, his breath became the wind and clouds, his muscles became soil, and the marrow of his bones jade and pearls. Chinese valued the stone for its beauty as well as for attributed magical powers. In early times, jade was used for ritual and religious purposes, but later it came to be used for ornamentation and other aesthetic purposes.

The oldest jades so far discovered come from the Neolithic Hemadu culture about 7,000 years ago. The finds are presumed to be ritual objects. Many small circular plates called *bi*, given to the dead to take with them, have been found. These round discs represent the harmony between heaven and earth. Even today, many Chinese wear these types of discs.

Jade was believed to have preserving powers and, consequently, burial suits were made with the precious stone. The Han dynasty probably saw an early peak in jade carving. During this time, the corpses of high-ranking officials were clothed in suits made of more than 1,000 thin slivers of jade sewn together with gold wire (see page 204). The Hebei Provincial Museum in Shijiazhuang displays the jade suits of Prince Liu Sheng and his wife. It is said that jade glows with the vitality of the owner. If the owner became ill, for example, the jade would become tarnished. Jade ornaments were believed to impart good health, luck, and offer protection.

Jade is not a precise mineralogical entity, but rather comprises two minerals, jadeite and nephrite. The former is more valuable because of its translucence and hardness, as well as its rarity. Nephrite is similar to jadeite, but not quite as hard. Colours vary from white to green, but also black, brown and red. The Chinese value a clear, emerald-green stone most highly. Jade is an especially difficult material to shape due to its hardness.

In the jade-carving workshops of present-day China, there are thought to be as many as 30 kinds of jade in use. Famous among the jade workshops are those in Khotan (also called Hetian; Xinjiang), Shoushan (Fujian) and Luoyang (Hunan).

In government shops, jade can be trusted to be genuine. On the open market and in private shops, however, caution is advised. Genuine jade always feels cool and cannot be scratched with a knife. Quality depends on the feel of the stone, its colour, transparency, pattern, and other factors. (If in doubt, a reputable expert should be consulted.)

Jade ornaments on sale in Shanghai.

⊘ BUYING ANTIQUES IN CHINA

It is fairly standard practice to bargain when purchasing antiques in China, although don't try it in the state-owned stores. It is essential to check that the official red seal of the shop is on the item, which allows it to be exported (most antiques that date from before 1911 cannot be taken out of the country).

Beware of fakes, as the fabrication of new "antiques" – and the official red seal – is a thriving industry. Avoid buying anything made from ivory or other illegal animal products. Apart from the moral issues, most Western countries ban imports.

LACQUERWARE

The oldest finds of lacquered objects date back to the Warring States Period (403–221 BC). At that time, lacquerware was an everyday material: bowls, tins, boxes, vases and furniture made of various materials (wood, bamboo, wicker, leather, metal, clay, textiles, paper) were often coated with a skin of lacquer. Emperor Qianlong (1735–96) had a special liking for carved lacquerware; he was buried in a coffin carved and preserved using this technique.

The glossy sheen of lacquerware is not only attractive but also strong and lightweight. The bark of the lacquer tree, which grows in central and southern China, exudes a milky sap when cut, which solidifies in moist air, then dries and turns brown. This dry layer of lacquer is impervious to moisture, acid and scratches, and is therefore ideal protection for materials such as wood or bamboo.

To make lacquerware, a base coat is applied to a core material, followed by extremely thin layers of the finest lacquer that, after drying in

pandering to Western tastes with their Cultural Revolution themes. Wang Guangyi and his highly recognisable style of Chinese "Political Pop" – juxtaposing Red Guards and Western corporate logos is a typical trope – has been particularly derided as clichéd.

Thanks to a maturing market, and plenty of cynical speculation, the native art market is now heating up and private collectors and institutions are keeping some of China's top works on home soil. Fang Lijun's *1993 No. 4*, a fine example of cynical realism, was returned from Europe in

3-D artwork at an exhibition in Hangzhou.

dust-free moist air, are smoothed and polished. If soot or vinegar-soaked iron filings are added to the lacquer, it will dry into a black colour; cinnabar turns it red.

THE CONTEMPORARY ART SCENE

The development of Chinese art in the 21st century caught many off guard. Suddenly "discovered" by western collectors, once poverty-stricken artists woke to find their works selling on the international market for millions of dollars. Zhang Xiaogang caught the world's attention when one of his signature disquieting portraits *A Big Family* fetched US$1.5 million at a 2006 Christie's auction in London. Artists such as the Gao Brothers were even criticised for

2012 by a Chinese buyer for a cool US$3.67 million. Converted factories, such as the 798 Art District in Beijing and 50 Moganshan Lu in Shanghai, are now popular sites for domestic tourism.

Dissenting political themes are unsurprisingly off-limits, though activist and iconoclast Ai Weiwei remains a hero in some circles. Despite being criticised in the crackdown following the Tiananmen Square massacre, Xu Bing has worked as a vice-president at the Central Academy of Fine Arts and produces some iconic installation pieces. Creativity runs high in the comparative freedom of contemporary art. Chinese people can now enjoy challenging works from a legion of artists, both broadening their horizons and leading them to question the world around them.

ARCHITECTURE

In imperial China, architectural principles were dictated by the cosmology defining heaven and earth. Across the country, temples, palaces and pagodas are imbued with these principles to create a harmonious architectural legacy.

The principles of traditional Chinese architecture reflect the twin philosophies of order and authority. Careful layout applies not only to residences and ceremonial buildings, but to entire cities. The longevity and universal application of this approach also mean that classical buildings across the length and breadth of China, be they temples, pagodas or imperial palaces, tend to exhibit similar characteristics.

COMMON FEATURES

Feng shui ("wind and water"), the traditional Chinese practice of placement to achieve harmony with the environment, has been a significant factor in the construction of buildings since records began. The preferred orientation is north–south, with the most important structures facing south, towards the sun. A sheltered position, facing the water and away from a hillside, is also considered auspicious.

Guilin's Riyue Shuangta (Sun and Moon Pagodas).

Much of China's historic architecture was lost during the vandalism of the Cultural Revolution. Most of what has survived – the old clan houses, ancient pagodas and traditional temples – is classical Chinese.

One of the most characteristic aspects of Chinese architecture is the use of curving roofs – more marked in the south of China than the north – with ceramic tiles and circular end tiles, a style dating back to the Warring States Period (403–221 BC). Overhanging eaves offered shelter from the rain as well as keeping out the sun in summer, and allowing it in during winter. Simple homes had plain gabled roofs.

Surrounding and enclosing classical Chinese residences, temples and palaces, is a wall. Walls are very important to the Chinese; not only do they provide protection and privacy, but they symbolise the containment and group mentality that are such important aspects of Chinese society. Cities were also surrounded by walls, their entrance gates surmounted by watchtowers. Drum and bell towers would announce the opening and closing of the city gates.

From the earliest days, wood was favoured as a building material as it was easily transported and practical – although increasingly hard to come by in most parts of China in more recent centuries. Residences were designed to be rebuilt, not to be permanent monuments. Brick and stone were only used for important buildings intended to withstand the elements for a prolonged period, such as imperial palaces, tombs, temples, ceremonial structures and, occasionally, bridges.

IMPERIAL ARCHITECTURE

Imperial buildings, mainly royal palaces and temples, can be identified by the use of yellow-glazed tiles on their roofs. Yellow was not only reminiscent of the Huang He (Yellow River), where Chinese civilisation is believed to have originated, but it also represented the element of earth that lay at the centre of the universe. In large palace complexes, the splendid Nine Dragon walls fulfilled the same function as spirit walls (a non-structural wall built behind or in front of entrances to bar the entry of evil spirits), while many pagodas, teahouses and other structures were approached by nine-cornered bridges – another anti-evil-spirit measure.

Chinese court architecture reached its apotheosis with the Forbidden City in Beijing, designed during the Ming dynasty. As with imperial buildings throughout China, its construction follows the fundamental principles of classical Chinese architecture, but on a very grand and opulent scale. The precise, geometric layout reflects the strict, hierarchical structure of imperial society, its fixed and ordered harmony an expression of cosmic order (for more about the Forbidden City and its layout, see page 132).

PAGODAS AND TEMPLES

Majestic and ornate, pagodas are an integral part of any romantic image of the Far East, and yet they are not indigenous to China. The concept originated in India where brick-built monuments, known as stupas, were used to enshrine sacred objects. During the first centuries AD, Buddhist missionaries from India preached the teachings of Buddha in China. Many Chinese monks later travelled the same route back to India, and in this way, reports of burial rites, religious art and impressive monastic and temple architecture filtered into China. Through the centuries, Chinese pagodas lost their religious associations and incorporated traditional Chinese architectural styles.

The oldest surviving pagoda, the Songyue Pagoda, stands near the old imperial city of Luoyang. Built in AD 523, this 40-metre (130ft)-high, 12-sided structure has withstood the ravages of weather, natural disasters and revolutions for over 1,400 years. At the nearby Shaolin Monastery, another rare sight is the Forest of Pagodas, a cemetery containing more than 200 stone funerary pagodas and the last resting place of monks.

Possibly the best-known pagodas in China are the two Wild Goose pagodas in Xi'an. Dayan

Qiongzhu Si (Bamboo Temple) outside Kunming.

Ta, the Great Wild Goose Pagoda, was designed by the monk Xuanzang, who, in the 7th century AD, undertook a long pilgrimage to northern India to collect Buddhist scriptures: the journey is the subject of the Chinese literary classic *Journey to the West*. After his return to China, he had a pagoda constructed to store the manuscripts he brought back with him. The Xiaoyan Ta, or Little Wild Goose Pagoda, is smaller and more graceful than its monumental and somewhat clumsy counterpart.

Best-known for the Forbidden City, Beijing also contains many fine examples of Buddhist-inspired architecture. Rising majestically to the west of the imperial city, the White Dagoba is a massive bell-shaped structure set on a square base in the style of a Tibetan stupa (chorten). It was built in 1651 to commemorate the first visit of the Dalai Lama.

Chinese temples, be they Buddhist, Daoist or Confucian, share the same design features, and are built to the same principles as palaces and wealthy traditional Chinese homes – laid out on a central north–south axis, with entrances facing the auspicious south and protected by a spirit wall. The main differences between them lie in decorative details such as colour – the pillars of Buddhist temples are

Old wooden houses line the banks of the Tuo River, Fenghuang.

bright red, while Daoists use black – and the carvings of animals and deities. One of the most outstanding examples of temple architecture is the Temple of Heaven in Beijing, whose magnificent centrepiece is the Hall of Prayer for Good Harvests, with its highly unusual circular form. For more on Chinese temples, see page 86.

RESIDENTIAL ARCHITECTURE

Chinese households traditionally centre around courtyards; the higher the rank of the occupant, the greater the number of courtyards. An important official might live in a large residence along with numerous relatives and servants. The home

of the head family is situated in the north of the compound, and faces south. The side buildings facing the central courtyard might belong to sisters and brothers, while more distant relatives might live around courtyards further south. In more modest homes, a similar layout prevails, with parents living in the main northern quarters facing south and children occupying the side quarters facing the courtyard.

Traditional timber-frame buildings were laid on elevated platforms made of beaten earth, brick or stone; the roof was supported by heavy wooden columns set in stone bases, often embellished with decorative carving. Inside, partition walls were made of light materials. In summer, the panels between the load-bearing columns could be easily removed. Colour and construction styles varied according to the significance of the building and social status of the owner.

Certain areas are characterised by more individual buildings inhabited by ethnic groups such as the distinctive Hakka roundhouses found in western Fujian and eastern Guangdong provinces, designed to house an entire clan. Set in a circle around a central courtyard, the three- or four-storey structures were made of an innovative mix of clay, sand, lime, sticky rice and sugar, reinforced with wood or bamboo.

The Dong minority areas of Guizhou province are famous for their unusual drum towers and wind-and-rain bridges (so called because they are covered), lovingly decorated by master carpenters. The Chengyang Wind-and-Rain Bridge in Sanjiang county is one of the best examples. Elsewhere in China, local architectural styles include the whitewashed, trapezoid buildings of Tibet, the ornate Buddhist temples of Xihuangbanna in southern Yunnan, the cave dwellings of the loess plateau in Shaanxi, and various forms of Islamic architecture in the northwest.

COLONIAL RELICS

It may be considered a shameful episode in China's history, but the colonial period did produce a scattering of architectural gems in the various Treaty Ports that provide welcome relief from the pervasive blandness of the modern urban landscape. The most notable concentrations are in Shanghai, Macau, Xiamen, Guangzhou (Shamian Island), Beihai and Qingdao, with a few remaining in Hong Kong, Shantou, Tianjin and Haikou on Hainan Island.

Shanghai has done a good job of preserving its architectural past, even if the famous buildings along the Bund are solid rather than elegant. In the former French Concession areas numerous English-style residences, complete with the occasional mock-Tudor building, create an unusual effect.

Despite the recent boom in casino-building, Macau has managed to preserve many of its colonial-era charms. Many of its Portuguese structures were the first of their kind on Chinese soil.

Xiamen, in Fujian province, was one of the busiest colonial enclaves in China in the late 1800s and early 1900s. Gulangyu Island, five minutes by ferry from the city, is home to dozens of examples of the large, graceful colonial-era structures that once served as consulates, residences and offices. Amid the colonial buildings are some equally well-preserved Chinese courtyard mansions.

Fifteen Western-style buildings in Beihai, on the coast of Guangxi, were recently included on a list for top state protection. The one-time German colony of Qingdao, further north on the Shandong coast, features a uniquely Teutonic city centre.

MODERN ARCHITECTURE

Much of modern China is architecturally undistinguished, to put it mildly: a mass of residential towers and office blocks, mostly ugly and built on the cheap. Even many so-called "heritage" schemes have a dubious value. The Xintiandi area of Shanghai was flattened and rebuilt in a faux "old style" – but many other municipalities consider it a model for "cultural renovation". Tong Mingkang, president of the International Council on Monuments and Sites (ICOMOS) China and former deputy director of cultural heritage, commented that "it is like tearing up an invaluable painting and replacing it with a cheap print". Nonetheless, there are a few noteworthy modern architectural projects, mainly in Shanghai.

The view from the Jin Mao Tower, Shanghai.

⊘ GARDENS OF PHILOSOPHY AND EMPIRES

Classical Chinese gardens strive for a delicate balance between natural and artificial elements, reflecting the core Daoist principles of striving for harmony with nature. Philosophical concepts such as *yin-yang*, as well as literary and painterly themes, were used as the bases of garden design. The art of gardens flourished during the Ming and Qing dynasties. Emperors – and the rich and powerful of the times – invested huge amounts of money and labour to build elaborate private gardens and retreats.

Two main types of gardens dominate: the imperial park and the scholar-official's private retreat. The best-known gardens of the first type are the Summer Palace and Yuanming Yuan (the Old Summer Palace), as well as Chengde (Jehol). Imperial parks were meant to suggest the riches and diversity of the empire. Chengde, the massive imperial park built by Emperor Qianlong northeast of Beijing, contains Tibetan Buddhist-inspired architecture that was meant to assert the diversity of China.

Further south, in what is an historically prosperous region, the cities of Suzhou and Hangzhou offer numerous attractive examples of the scholar-officials' private garden hideaways, which sought to stir emotions by creating an intense microcosm of the natural world.

CUISINES OF CHINA

From the hot spicy dishes of Hunan and Sichuan to the more delicate flavours of the Yangzi region and the distinctive northern school, there is plenty to explore and enjoy on China's brimming dining tables.

Few people in the world have a more passionate relationship with food than the Chinese. Food shortages over many centuries have forced the Chinese to be creative in order to utilise and conserve their relatively scant food supplies. The elite, meanwhile, have traditionally used a flamboyant approach to food as a way to flaunt their status. China's great geographical variety offers a wealth of different produce.

The Chinese preoccupation with food is reflected in China's philosophy and literature. Indeed, as depicted in numerous historical, literary and philosophical writings, more often than not scholars were also gourmands. Laozi, the founder of Daoism, said, "Handle a large country with as gentle a touch as you would cook a small fish." Another Daoist sage, Zhuang Zi, wrote a poem in which he advises an emperor to watch his cook: "A good cook needs a new chopper once a year – he cuts. A bad cook needs a new one every month – he hacks." Few will dispute the old saying that "appetite for food and sex is nature". This recognition of the importance of food has helped nurture a variety of healthy and delicious cuisines.

The old traditions are alive and well in Chinese cooking, yet – inevitably in a country as fast-changing as China – there are various new trends in evidence, too. Over the past two decades there has been a revolution in terms of dining options: scores of upmarket restaurants, the increasing popularity of Western cuisine in the cities, the arrival of fast-food chains, hotpot chains, Korean barbecue and Japanese restaurants. And Chinese food itself is undergoing changes: restaurants are experimenting with fusion cuisines and paying greater attention to health issues – using less oil and natural flavours in favour of the once near-universal monosodium glutamate (MSG).

Preparing food in a Beijing restaurant.

A traditional greeting amongst Chinese is "ni chi fan le mei you?", which translates literally as "have you eaten yet?", emphasising the central importance of food in Chinese culture.

TECHNIQUE

It is said that the four essentials in a Chinese kitchen are a cutting board, knife, wok and spoon. Historical fuel shortages made a reduced cooking time an early priority, and the proper preparation of ingredients is an important first step. Rapid, even chopping is a required trademark of any good cook. Faithful students of Confucius recorded that "he would not eat meat that was not cut properly, nor that which was served without its proper sauce". His pickiness made sense, since meat and vegetables cut to varying proportions result in unevenly cooked food.

The majority of Chinese dishes – generically known in Chinese as *xiao chao*, or "little fries" – are **stir-fried** fast and at a very high temperature in a wok. This not only saves fuel but also cooks meat thoroughly, while ensuring that vegetables have a crisp texture and retain their vitamins. **Steaming** is a technique used more in southern

flavours and colours within a meal, and few dishes feature any one ingredient exclusively. The harmonious blending of ingredients and balance in seasoning is important; common seasonings are soy sauce, ginger, garlic, vinegar, sesame oil, soybean paste and spring onions.

Rice is the staple food for most Chinese, although those living in the north traditionally eat food created from wheat flour, including noodles, dumplings and various steamed, deep-fried or griddle-fried breads. Soybean curd, both fresh and dried in either sheets or twists, provides important

Dim sum in Hong Kong.

China than elsewhere – particularly for vegetables and fish – but it is used nationwide for cooking buns and dumplings. **Braising** is used throughout China, often for cooking pork and beef in stew-like dishes seasoned with aniseed and peppers. Very few Chinese homes – or restaurants for that matter – have ovens, and **roasting** is reserved for only a few speciality dishes, such as the famous Beijing Duck. Deep-frying is very rarely used in Chinese cuisine. **Hotpot**, in which meats and vegetables are placed in a simmering broth, is a Sichuan dish that has become enormously popular throughout China.

INGREDIENTS

Chinese cuisines seek a balance of textures,

protein in a country where the majority of available land is given over to crops rather than grazing.

Cows and sheep, which require pasture lands, are not as common as poultry and the ubiquitous pig. Without doubt, pork is the most popular meat. In addition, both fresh- and saltwater fish are highly prized and usually well prepared.

Vegetables are of supreme importance, but are rarely eaten raw. This stems partly from hygienic considerations, as the traditional fertiliser was human waste. The range of vegetables cultivated in China is vast, particularly in the warmer south, and includes not only those known in the West, but other delights such as a huge range of leafy greens, bamboo shoots, water chestnuts, taro and lotus root. Some common vegetables such as cabbage and white radish are also salted or dried and used as seasoning, especially during the bitter winter months in the frozen north.

The use of monosodium glutamate (MSG) has had a significant effect on Chinese cooking, although it is a little less prevalent now than in the past. Called *wei jing* in Chinese, this miracle powder was introduced by the Japanese in the 1940s. Cooks discovered that it instantly added a meaty sweetness to the food, which could otherwise only be achieved by simmering stock for hours. Travellers who have an intolerance to monosodium glutamate can request that it not be used by saying *Bu yao fang wei jing*.

THE REGIONAL CUISINES OF CHINA

With its vast range of climates and terrain, it is not surprising that distinct regional cuisines have developed in different parts of China. Experts argue endlessly over just how many exist, but it is generally agreed that there are four major styles. These include Cantonese, the food found in the southern province of Guangdong (and in neighbouring Hong Kong); the pungent, spicy food of the Sichuan Basin in western central China, particularly of the cities of Chengdu and Chongqing; the delicate flavours of Shanghai, Jiangsu and Zhejiang in eastern China, collectively known as Huaiyang cuisine; and northern cuisine, centred in Beijing but largely inspired by the province of Shandong, whose chefs monopolised Beijing's restaurants in the 19th century.

Increasingly considered a fifth major form of Chinese regional cuisine is the hot spicy food from Hunan province in central southern China. Somewhat similar to Sichuan cuisine, and sometimes even spicier, it is known in Chinese as *Xiangcai* and has become extremely popular across the country, partly due to the fact it is the home cuisine of Mao: Hunan restaurants often feature a portrait of the former Chairman.

CANTONESE CUISINE

Thanks to the large-scale emigration of Chinese from the southern province of Guangdong to the four corners of the Earth, Cantonese is by far

A market in central Kunming.

⊙ COMMON ITEMS ON THE MENU

English *pinyin* Chinese characters
Steamed rice *mifan* 米饭
Fried rice *chao fan* 炒饭
Noodles *miantiao* 面条
Meat *rou* 肉
Pork *zhu rou* 猪肉
Chicken *ji rou* 鸡肉
Duck *ya rou* 鸭肉
Beef *niu rou* 牛肉
Lamb *yang rou* 羊肉
Fish *yu* 鱼
Seafood *haixian* 海鲜
Vegetables *shucai* 蔬菜

Soup *tang* 汤
Egg *jidan* 鸡蛋
Pancakes *bǐng* 饼
Chopsticks *kuàizi* 筷子
Mineral water *kuangquanshui* 矿泉水
Tea *chashui* 茶水
Coffee *kafei* 咖啡
Beer *pijiu* 啤酒
Alcoholic drink *jiu* 酒
Soft drinks *yǐnliào* 饮料
May we have the bill/check, please Qing jie zhang/ maidan 请结帐/买单
For more menu items, see page 462.

China's best-known cuisine. Many claim that it is also the finest, and there's no doubt that the fertile south benefits from a benign climate and the widest selection of fresh produce anywhere in China.

Cantonese food is characterised by its great variety, and its delicate seasoning and freshness of ingredients. Cantonese chefs are renowned for their creativity and willingness to incorporate foreign ingredients. Chefs make abundant use of fruit and many types of vegetables, as well as seafood such as prawn, abalone, squid and crab.

Cantonese cooking methods are lacquer roasting, very quick stir-frying and steaming. Cantonese roasted chicken and pork are justifiably renowned. Seafood is typically seasoned first and stir-fried in hot oil, or else steamed.

The famous Cantonese array of titbits known as dim sum (or, in Mandarin, *dian xin*) is often served as brunch or a snack. Dim sum portions are usually dainty. Among the great variety of treats are dumplings of pork or seafood wrapped in transparent rice-dough wrappers; stuffed mushrooms or chilli peppers; deep-fried yam balls; and tiny spring rolls. Self-serve trolleys arranged with small plates are wheeled through restaurants and teahouses. Although the Chinese do not normally eat dessert, two common offerings at a dim sum spread are custard tarts and cubes of almond-milk jelly.

SICHUAN CUISINE

After Cantonese, the cuisine of the southwestern province of Sichuan (formerly spelled as Szechuan) is perhaps the best-known to Westerners and the most emphatically flavoured in all of China.

Much of this emphasis comes from chillies, which appear in many guises: dried and fried in chunks, together with other ingredients; ground into a paste with a touch of added oil; as chilli oil; and crushed to a powder. Other ingredients important to Sichuanese cuisine are Sichuan "pepper" (the dried berry of the prickly ash or fagara), garlic, ginger and fermented soybean. The combination of chillies and the Sichuan pepper – known in Chinese as *huajiao* – produces a flavour unique to Sichuan cuisine: *mala*, or, literally, "hot numb". Some writers claim that the Sichuan love of spicy, pungent food can be attributed to the humid climate, with its sticky summers and cold, clammy winters.

There are many superb Sichuan dishes, including duck smoked over a mixture of camphor and tea leaves, then deep-fried, and beancurd scrambled with minced pork and spicy seasonings. One of the best-known Chinese dishes, *mapo tofu* (or *doufu*), comes from Sichuan. Translated as "the pockmarked woman's tofu", the rather prosaic story relates how Mrs Chen, a pockmarked woman, created a spicy beancurd dish in the tavern she owned in the 19th century.

A now-famous Sichuan eating experience originated on the wharfs of Chongqing, where poor riverside workers prepared meals by tossing whatever they had available to eat into pots

A dish featuring braised pork and spring onions (scallions).

of boiling river water. More refined these days, when eating hotpot, or *huo guo*, diners sit around a table with a pot of seasoned broth heated by a gas fire (charcoal was used in the past). Each diner adds bits and pieces of prepared vegetable, meat, fish and beancurd. The food cooks very quickly and can be fished out of the broth using chopsticks or a special strainer, then dipped in sesame oil, peanut sauce or a beaten egg. Hotpot chains are now ubiquitous in cities across China.

HUNAN CUISINE

Hunan cuisine, the hottest of all Chinese regional styles, is something of a fusion of Sichuan and northern styles of cooking, although it also has some Muslim influences, which can be seen in skewers of lamb seasoned with cumin. Cumin is also used in another popular dish, *pingguo rou*, or "flat pot meat", in which the meat simmers on a bed of onion and vegetables over a low flame on the table where the diners sit.

Other popular Hunan dishes include Mao's favourite, red-cooked fatty pork, now usually referred to as *Maojia* or *Maoshi*, *hongshao rou* – Mao home or Mao clan red-cooked pork – often served with a dish of peanuts, and fish head cooked in a bright sea of chopped chilli peppers.

Street food can be outlandish in appearance.

HUAIYANG CUISINE

The cuisine of the lower reaches of the Yangzi River, especially around Huaian and Yangzhou, gave rise to the term *huaiyang* to describe the food of China's eastern seaboard (it is also known as Jiangzhe cuisine, reflecting its origin in the north of Jiangxi and Zhejiang provinces, and sometimes as Shanghai cuisine). This fertile area, known as "the land of rice and fish", produces a wide range of crops as well as abundant fish, prawns and crabs. These aquatic foods are cooked simply, bringing out natural flavours. Huaiyang cooks often steam or gently simmer their food, rather than using the faster deep-frying style. Signature dishes include pork steamed in lotus leaves, Duck with Eight Ingredients, and

> *Chaozhou (Chiu Chow) cuisine is considered to be a branch of Cantonese. Centred on the city of Shantou in eastern Guangdong, it is best-known for its steamed crab, shrimp balls and steamed pork.*

Lion's Head Meatballs, all of which should be found in any good restaurant around Shanghai. Huaiyang cuisine places emphasis on soups, which come with every meal. In addition, "red cooking" (stewing meat in stock with soy sauce, star anise and other flavourings) and the heavy use of peanut oil and lard are characteristic.

NORTHERN CUISINE

The cuisine of northern China tends to be a rustic, home-style cooking that makes abundant use of onions and garlic, but is lacking in the variety of vegetables characterising the cuisines of China's more fertile regions.

Northerners eat wheat-based foods as a staple, not the rice found elsewhere in China. Indeed, one can find a wide variety of noodles; dumplings that are steamed, pan-fried or boiled; breads (once again, fried or steamed); and deep-fried lengths of dough, which are excellent with a bowl of sweet or salty soybean milk.

Most northern cuisine stems from Shandong province, but with some influences from Mongolian and Hebei cooking. Braised meat and poultry cooked in brown sauce, which form the base of much northern cuisine, are some of the most common dishes.

Although the indigenous food is relatively simple, Beijing benefited from its status as imperial capital. The emperors sought out the best chefs in the land, and the first among them could count on being given the rank of minister.

It was during these days that the most refined and complex dishes such as Peking Duck, Mandarin Fish, Phoenix in the Nest and Thousand-Layer Cake were created. Today, the ordinary citizen of Beijing (and, of course, visiting foreigners) can sample these palace dishes in special, but often expensive, restaurants.

No visitor should leave without a meal of Peking Duck. After the duck is slaughtered, air is pumped between the skin and the flesh of the duck, and then the skin painted with a mixture of honey, water and vinegar. The duck is dried, and then roasted in a special oven. The succulent, crisp skin is tucked into fine wheat-flour pancakes, painted with sweet black sauce and enlivened with spring onions. After this course, diners might enjoy the meat of the duck and complete the experience with a finale of duck soup.

THE PHILOSOPHY OF FOOD

For centuries, Chinese have regarded food as curative or preventative medicine: tradi-

A variety of street food is served on skewers.

tionally, food should not only be filling, but it should also have a healing effect. A Chinese meal is based on balance, even at the largest and most extravagant of banquets. Indeed, at times the relationship between food and medicine can seem quite blurred. In fact, the word for recipe, *fang*, is the same as for prescription.

When planning a menu, the chef will want to consider the physical conditions of the diners and external conditions such as the weather. One of the most basic theories behind a balanced Chinese diet is that of "hot" and "cool" foods. Certain foods are believed to be either *yin* (cooling) or *yang* (warming); the ideal is to seek a balance between the two.

Internal heat is caused by eating "hot" elements such as coffee, meat and spicy food. Excess internal heat can cause unpleasant symptoms such as heartburn, rashes, cold sores and bad breath. Not surprisingly, "hot" foods are popular in cold weather. Snake meat, for example, is considered to be fortifying and is therefore a popular winter dish in some parts of the country. On the other hand, "cooling" foods combat excess internal heat. Low-calorie, bland vegetables such as watercress, bitter melon and white radish, as well as most fruits, are considered "cooling".

The preparation of Peking Duck is a lengthy and complicated business.

SYMBOLISM AND FESTIVALS

For all the attention and significance lavished on food by the Chinese, it is not surprising that Chinese food "language" developed to a level probably unparalleled by any other cuisine. Food can be endowed with symbolic meaning, and special occasions such as holidays or birthdays are observed with specific foods.

Chinese New Year is a particularly significant food event. As the most important holiday of the year, much care, planning and money is spent on celebrating this event with as sumptuous a feast as possible. Oranges and tangerines keep the sweetness of life, ducks represent fidelity and joy, and fish represent prosperity, wealth and regeneration.

Birthdays are often observed by the serving of noodles, because the lengthy strands are said to represent long life. Another favourite is steamed buns shaped and coloured to look like peaches, as peaches also represent longevity. During the mid-autumn festival, also known as the moon festival, people eat heavy, round-shaped pastries called mooncakes. Round like the full moon, these cakes are usually filled with sweet paste and sometimes an egg yolk in the centre.

During the dragon-boat festival, people eat fragrant sticky rice wrapped in bamboo leaves or

> *The Chinese typically cherish a boisterous atmosphere when eating, filled with toasts and jokes and conversation. This is called re nao – hot and noisy – and is considered the hallmark of a good meal.*

different in the south, where social life continues until the late evening. Chinese meals are best eaten in a group, with diners sharing a variety

Street food in Hohhot, Inner Mongolia.

reeds, a treat called *zong zi*. The tradition commemorates the death of the poet and statesman Qu Yuan, author of the *Chuci*, who threw himself into a river and drowned. Townspeople threw *zong zi* into the river to feed the fish so that they would be distracted from eating Qu Yuan's body.

EVERYDAY EATING IN CHINA: WHAT TO EXPECT

Everyday meals are simple affairs. The Chinese tend to eat quite early, and lunch is often served in Chinese restaurants from 11am. (Hotels and restaurants catering for foreigners have, of course, adjusted to their preferences.) Away from the main centres you won't easily find a meal after 8pm, though this is somewhat

of different dishes; Chinese restaurants are, on the whole, not well suited to individual diners.

Breakfast might consist of a bowl of rice, *baozi* steamed buns, or, in the south, with *zhou* (rice porridge) which comes with pickled vegetables and bits of meat, or perhaps hot soy milk and deep-fried dough sticks (*youtiao*). For **lunch**, a noodle soup (*tangmian*) or a plate of rice with some meat and vegetables is common. A proper family **dinner** will normally consist of the staple rice or noodles, soup, and three or four freshly prepared hot dishes. The soup is generally served at the end of a meal, except in Guangdong, where it is sipped throughout the meal. Although Chinese do not generally finish their meals with desserts, they will often – when it is available – eat fruit at the end of a meal, and in many restaurants, slices of watermelon or orange will be served.

DRINKS

The Chinese almost always eat to the accompaniment of cups of tea. In regular downscale restaurants, this will be served as a matter of course, and will generally be an inexpensive green tea. In more expensive establishments, however, diners are usually asked to choose from a selection of teas, the most popular being

without first toasting one of the other diners, and if you are toasted – and as a foreigner you will be, repeatedly – you are expected to down your drink in one go: the meaning of the Chinese toast, *ganbei*, is "empty glass". If you are not particularly keen on drinking, or simply don't want to be inebriated at 7pm, it is sometimes possible to ward off the incessant toasts by declaring *suiyi* (which roughly translates as "drink as much as you want"); this gives you the freedom to respond to toasts with small sips rather than an empty glass.

Mooncakes are eaten at the mid-autumn festival.

Tea is an essential accompaniment to a Chinese meal.

the semi-fermented varieties of Wulong and Tieguanyin, unfermented green tea, or *lücha*, and sometimes the popular Cantonese jasmine tea – *molihua*. If the tea is served in a pot, the correct etiquette when it's empty and you want it refilled with hot water is to leave the lid ajar.

When dining in groups, Chinese invariably also accompany their meals with alcoholic drinks. Sometimes this is simply beer (Tsingtao is the best-known brand internationally), but often it will be one of China's very potent rice, sorghum or barley wines – *baijiu* and *damaijiu*, though there are countless varieties. Several foreign joint-venture wineries now produce a variety of drinkable red and white table wines. It is impolite to take a sip of an alcoholic beverage

⦿ ETIQUETTE PRIMER

Chinese table manners are quite different from those of the West. The Chinese slurp their soup (to cool it), keep their elbows on the table, and lift their bowls. The usual way to eat a bowl of rice is to hold the bowl up with one hand and shovel the rice into the mouth with chopsticks – although you are unlikely to see people doing this in a top-class restaurant. Similarly, soup can be either sipped directly from the bowl or with a soup spoon. Bills are rarely split and it is good form to put up a spirited attempt to pay for a meal and claim the honour of playing host. Piling the more expensive dishes onto your guests' plates shows consideration and overrides their polite reticence to eat them.

Xian's city wall and watchtower.

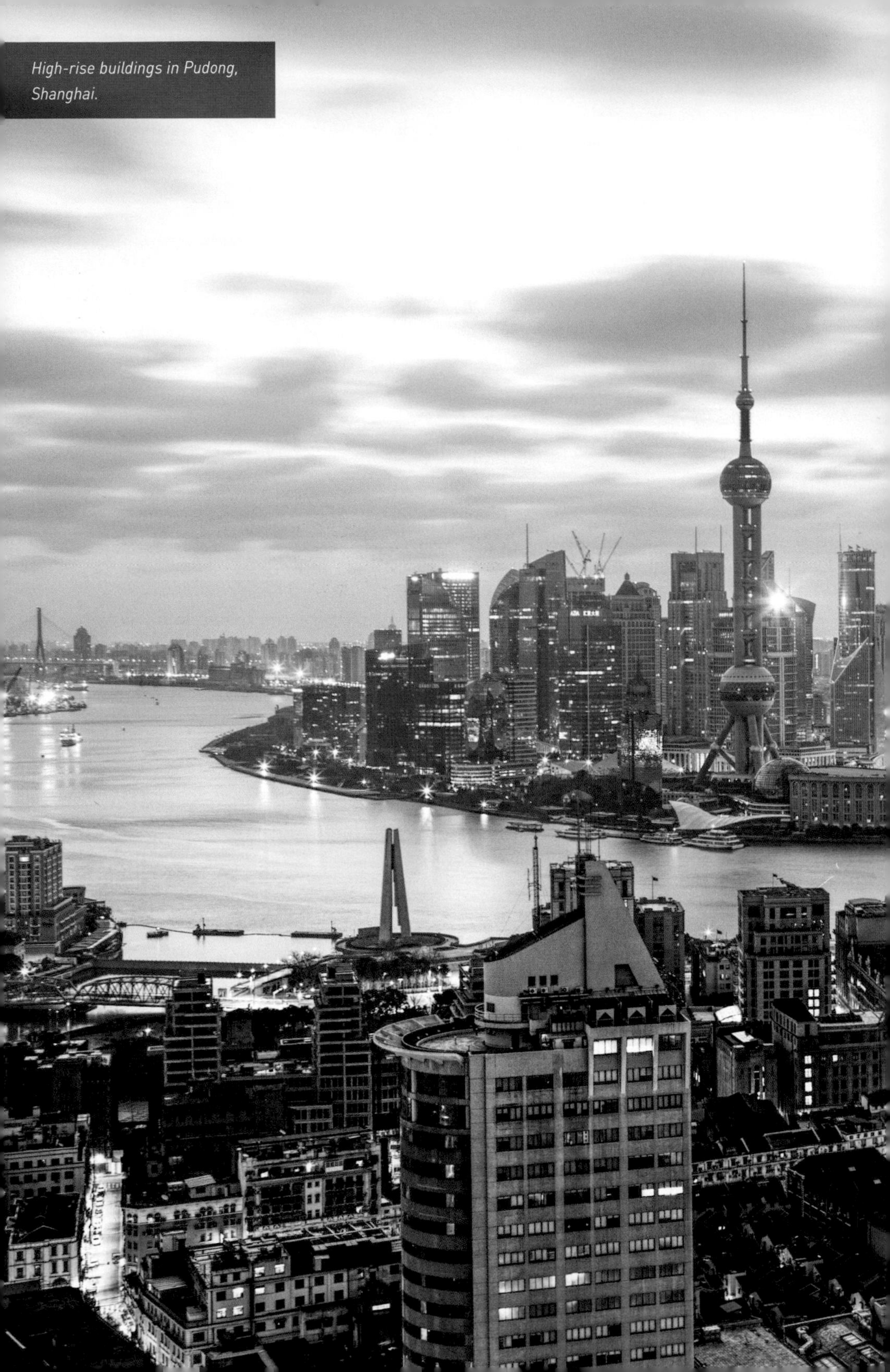

High-rise buildings in Pudong, Shanghai.

Beijing's Imperial City north gate.

INTRODUCTION

A detailed guide to the entire country, with principal sites clearly cross-referenced by number to the maps.

Festival attire in a Beijing park.

On early maps of China, only the scale of the coastline is correct; the further they extend into the interior, the more distorted becomes the cartography, or else it remains blank. One might have said the same about European understanding of China as a whole. Today the understanding has improved, but there is still a great deal of mystery and confusion about China and its people. And as before, the further one travels into the interior the more exotic and remote the landscapes and cultures become. Contemporary travellers will readily see that China is no monolithic culture. The influence of the Han Chinese may seem ubiquitous, but the rich Turkic culture of Xinjiang, the lively colours of Yunnan, or the lofty mantras of Tibet are also, often controversially, a part of China. Travellers may also come to recognise northern and southern differences among the Han themselves.

The northern part of China extends from Dongbei in the northeast – known to Westerners as Manchuria – across Inner Mongolia to the dusty lands around the Huang He (Yellow River), the cradle of Chinese civilisation. The terrain is often dry and infertile, freezing in winter, stifling in summer; yet the imperial capitals of China – Xi'an, Luoyang and Beijing – are all here, with a dazzling array of ancient sights.

The central belt of China follows the grandest of rivers, the Chang Jiang, or Yangzi to Westerners. This river divides China north and south before emptying into the sea close to Shanghai, China's brash, booming megalopolis.

Wulingyuan Scenic Reserve, Hunan province.

Along the coast of southern China are the feisty, entrepreneurial regions centred around Guangzhou and Hong Kong, while parts of the inland south are home to colourful minority peoples and some beautiful scenery – notably around Guilin in Guangxi province. Yunnan province, in the country's southwestern corner, is an intoxicating mix of high mountains, tropical lowlands and ancient cities. The west of China is a land apart, and travelling to the remote landscapes and vivid cultures of Tibet and the Silk Road region of Xinjiang remains a rare adventure.

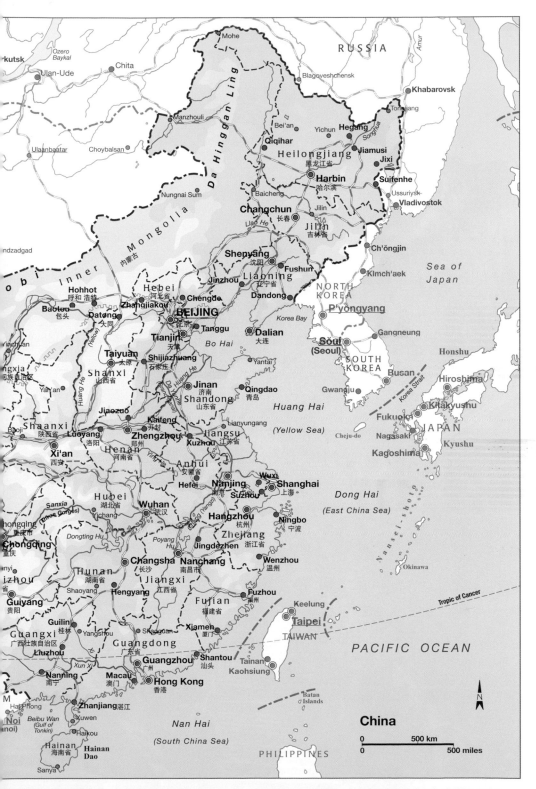

China

0   500 km

0   500 miles

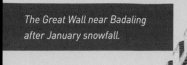
The Great Wall near Badaling after January snowfall.

THE NORTH

The north may be inauspicious in Chinese cosmology, but it was by the Huang He – the Yellow River – that flows through the northern plains, that Chinese civilisation took root and flourished.

The amazing Terracotta Warriors.

Taking such a huge chunk of China and calling it "the North" leads to the suggestion of homogeneity, but this is emphatically not the case – the region is, after all, bisected by the Great Wall, emphatic dividing line between the civilised and the barbarian. Anchored by the great imperial cities of Beijing and Xi'an, this vast swathe of land stretches for thousands of miles across the wide open spaces of the northeast and Inner Mongolia to the dusty heartlands of ancient China around the Huang He (Yellow River).

Beijing has risen as a global city, Olympic host and economic powerhouse but remains a fascinating jumble of ancient and modern, its 21st-century glass towers and gigantic 1950s architecture contrasting dramatically with the narrow *hutong* alleyways, imperial parks and classical Chinese buildings from an earlier time. Beyond the city, snaking westwards over the rocky hills and mountains, is the magnificent Great Wall. On the other side of the Wall is Dongbei – literally, East-North, but better known to the world as Manchuria – while reaching all the way west to Gansu and the Silk Road are the empty grasslands and deserts of Inner Mongolia.

Rock carvings at Yungang Shiku, Datong.

To the southwest of Beijing are the regions where Chinese civilisation first flowered, and other ancient capitals: Xi'an, Luoyang, Anyang and Kaifeng. The silt-laden Huang He river loops through the Mongolian steppes and then heads south, flowing close to Xi'an, where the first emperor of a unified China, Qin Shi Huangdi, made ancient history. The starting point of the ancient Silk Road, Xi'an is famous today for the army of terracotta warriors discovered nearby.

Further east, the Daoist mount of Hua Shan invites pilgrims to attempt its slopes. In its lower reaches, the Huang He cuts through Shanxi – home of the Buddhist Yungang caves before traversing Henan, home to the awesome Longmen caves near Luoyang and globally renowned Shaolin Temple. Before emptying into the sea, the river passes through Shandong, home of Confucius, peerless Tai Shan and breezy Qingdao, the former German enclave on the shores of the Yellow Sea.

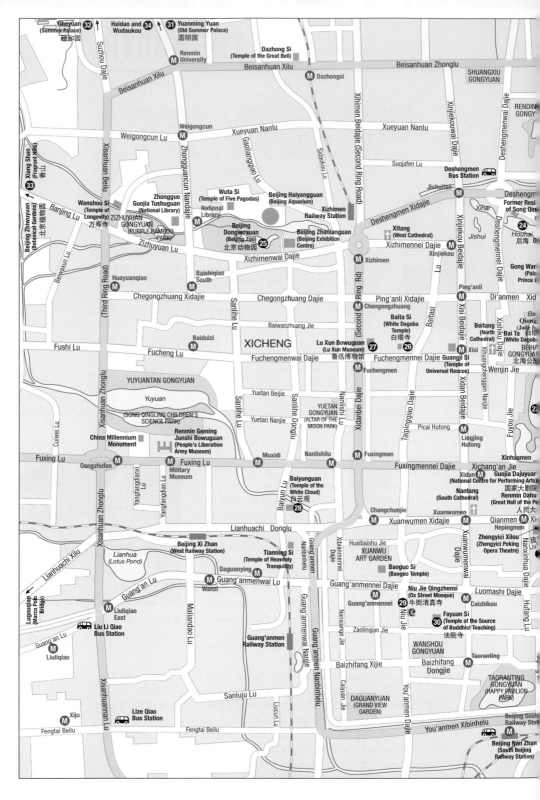

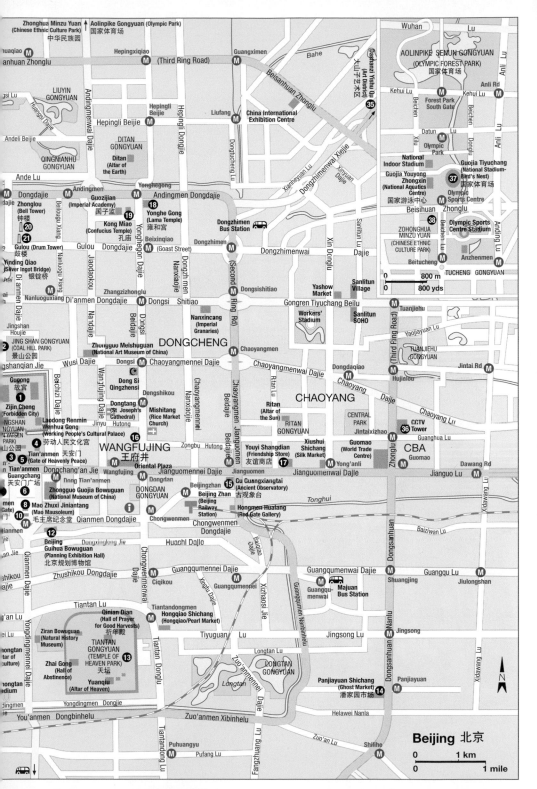

Beijing 北京

Qinian Dian (the Hall of Prayer for Good Harvests) at the Temple of Heaven.

BEIJING

Laid out in a grid according to feng shui principles, the Northern Capital and seat of political power is now a vast modern metropolis with an array of spectacular sights.

Over the past 1,000 years, **Beijing** (北京) has served as the primary residence for three major dynasties. Under the rule of Kublai Khan in the 13th century, the city was known as Khanbaliq – the City of the Khan – and it was a magnificent winter residence for the Yuan-dynasty emperor. During the Ming dynasty, which replaced the Yuan, the Imperial Palace (Forbidden City) was built and Beijing acquired the layout that survives today. The Qing emperors surveyed their realm from the palace until the dynasty collapsed in 1911.

Traditional Chinese thought perceived the world not as the Ptolemaic disc of the West, but as a square. It was believed that a city, especially a capital city, should reflect this cosmic order and adhere to its geometrical definition, with a north–south and east–west orientation of roads and buildings. In no other Chinese city was this idea fulfilled as completely as in ancient Beijing. But the history of the area around the capital goes back much further: the discovery of the skull of *Sinanthropus pekinensis* (Peking Man), southwest of Beijing, proved that prehistoric humans settled here more than half a million years ago. Yet little more is known until 5,000 years ago, by which time Neolithic agricultural villages had been established.

The much-admired Bird's Nest Stadium.

THE CHANGING CITY

Beijing today is a mass of tower blocks, gargantuan flyovers and expressways. Construction sites are everywhere. Bicycles still throng the streets, but a huge knot of taxis, cars and buses brings traffic to a crawl. The successful bid for the 2008 Olympics propelled the Beijing authorities to start an ambitious regeneration plan. Massive investment in the subway and road networks, together with a beautification programme, changed the face of the city from that of Shanghai's unrefined

Main Attractions

Forbidden City
Tiananmen Square
Temple of Heaven (Tiantan)
Lama Temple (Yonghe Gong)
Houhai/Back Lakes area
Hutong Alleyways
New Summer Palace (Yiheyuan)

Maps on pages 128, 133, 147

and provincial cousin to a sharp and ambitious world player. Overall the effects have been beneficial, although some question the exorbitant cost (estimated at a staggering US$44 billion) while others bemoan the fate of the historic and unique *hutong* – most of which have fallen prey to road-widening schemes and gentrification.

Beijing's identity crisis is further exacerbated by a constant flood of migrant workers and the government frequently vacillates between relaxing and tightening rules for foreigners and non-resident nationals alike. Meanwhile, an interest in "old Beijing" grows as many true Beijingers strive to keep at least some of their traditions alive against the onslaught of modernisation.

Beijing's harsh northern climate brings long, hot summers and cold, dry winters. When sandstorms swirl through the city in spring, the fine dust forces its way through cracks and crevices in poorly insulated homes. Vehicle exhaust fumes, dust from construction projects, coal smoke and industrial emissions add to the long-term unresolved problem of air pollution and pervasive greyness.

Despite the rapid modernisation there remains plenty of history, including the unmissable Forbidden City and some of China's most spectacular temples and palaces, often set in beautiful gardens. To experience a more intimate side of the city, walk through its few remaining *hutong*, alleys usually flanked by the gates and walls of traditional courtyard houses. By way of contrast, wandering around the vast spaces of Tiananmen Square surrounded by monumental buildings, or along the grand avenue of Chang'an Jie, gives a keen sense of recent history and centralised power.

THE FORBIDDEN CITY

At the heart of the teeming metropolis of modern Beijing, and unmissable on any city map at the centrepoint of the capital's grid layout, the **Forbidden City ❶** [故宫; Gugong [Imperial Palace]; http://en.dpm.org.cn; Tue–Sun Apr–Oct 8.30am–5pm, Nov–Mar 8.30am–4.30pm, ticket office closes an hour earlier) is simply breathtaking. It is one of the world's best-preserved, and largest, historical sites – a vast labyrinth of interconnected halls, chambers and courtyards.

Following 17 years of construction, the Ming emperor Yongle moved into the new palace in 1421. It was to remain the imperial residence and centre of the Middle Kingdom for almost 500 years through the reigns of a total of 24 emperors, until the founding of the Chinese Republic in 1911.

Entrance was denied to ordinary mortals. Behind walls more than 10 metres (33ft) high enclosed within the 50 metre (165-ft) -broad moat, life was dictated by the complex rules and rituals of the imperial court. The mandarins would arrive in their litters for the morning audience with the emperor, each shown to his place – arranged according to rank – where they listened

---

⊘ GEOMANTIC DESIGN

The third Ming emperor, Yongle, is credited with the planning of the city. In 1421, he moved his government from Nanjing to Beiping (Northern Peace) and renamed it Beijing (Northern Capital). His plans followed the principles of geomancy, the traditional doctrine of feng shui that strives to attain harmony between human life and nature. Beijing lies on a plain that opens to the south, an auspicious direction, as it is towards the south that the generosity and warmth of *yang* is thought to reside. All important buildings in the Old City face south *(nan)*, protected from harmful *yin* influences from the north *(bei)* – whether winter Siberian winds or enemies from the steppes.

A north-south axis centred on the Forbidden City divided the city, with important buildings and city features laid out as mirror images on either side. Ritan (Altar of the Sun), for example, has its equivalent in Yuetan (Altar of the Moon). Equally complementary were the eastern *(dong)* and western *(xi)* commercial quarters of Xidan and Dongdan. In the middle was the heart of ancient China and the centre of the physical world, the Dragon Throne, from which the emperor governed as the ritual mediator between heaven and earth. Outside it was the imperial city, again square, and crowded around this was a sea of mainly single-storey houses. This part of Beijing is still considered to be the inner city, or Old City.

to the emperor in respectful silence. Within the palace were more than 8,700 rooms in which some 8,000–10,000 people lived, including 3,000 eunuchs, as well as maids and concubines.

Preserved as a museum since the 1920s, and a Unesco World Heritage Site since 1987, the Forbidden City is usually entered from the south. From Tiananmen Square proceed through Tiananmen Gate (under the Mao portrait) and walk across the large courtyard, divided by another gate (Duanmen), to reach the 35 metre (117-ft) -high **Wumen A** (午门; Meridian Gate), where the ticket office is located. Shenwumen, the northern gate, also has a ticket office but at the time of publishing can only be used as an exit.

Once beyond Wumen, one encounters the three great halls and courtyards of the outer area. The first and most impressive of these is the **Taihe Dian B** (太和殿; Hall of Supreme Harmony), the largest building in the palace and fronted by an immense courtyard that could hold 90,000 spectators. In its centre is the ornately carved, golden **Dragon Throne** (龙椅), from which the emperor ruled. The most solemn ceremonies, such as the New Year rites or the enthronement of a new emperor, were held here. Behind Taihe Dian are **Zhonghe Dian** (中和殿; Hall of Complete Harmony) and **Baohe Dian C** (保和殿; Hall of Preserving Harmony), completing a trinity that reflects the Three Buddhas and the Three Pure Ones of Daoism.

To the east of Baohe Dian is the splendid **Jiulongbi D** (九龙壁; Nine Dragon Screen), representing the emperor as the indisputable son of heaven. On the other side of the Outer Court, to the north and separated from it by **Qianqingmen** (乾清门; Gate of Heavenly Purity), lies a labyrinth of gates, doors, pavilions, gardens and palaces. This is **Qianqing Gong E** (乾清宫; Palace of Heavenly Purity), the residence of the imperial family, almost exclusively female as the emperor and eunuchs were the only men permitted to enter. The centre of this private section is formed by three rear halls called the **Housan Gong** (后三宫). The

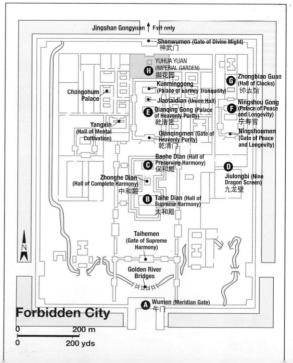

Posing for the camera at the Forbidden City's Dragon Gate.

Jingshan Gongyuan ↑ Exit only

Shenwumen (Gate of Divine Might)
神武门

YUHUA YUAN
(IMPERIAL GARDEN)
H 御花园

Kunminggong
(Palace of Earthly Tranquility)

Jiaotaidian (Union Hall)

E Qianqing Gong (Palace of Heavenly Purity)
乾清宫

Qianqingmen (Gate of Heavenly Purity)
乾清门

Baohe Dian (Hall of Preserving Harmony)
C 保和殿

Zhonghe Dian
(Hall of Complete Harmony)
中和殿

B Taihe Dian (Hall of Supreme Harmony)
太和殿

Taihemen
(Gate of Supreme Harmony)

Golden River Bridges

A Wumen (Meridian Gate)
午门

Chongohum Palace

Yangxin
(Hall of Mental Cultivation)

G Zhongbiao Guan
(Hall of Clocks)
钟表馆

F Ningshou Gong
(Palace of Peace and Longevity)
宁寿宫

Ningshoumen
(Gate of Peace and Longevity)

D Jiulongbi (Nine Dragon Screen)
九龙壁

N

Forbidden City

0 ———— 200 m
0 ———— 200 yds

politics of state business took place in the interlinked rooms to the left and right, where the scene was set for plots and intrigues as the more influential eunuchs and concubines vied for power and influence within the court.

The well in the northeast, just behind **Ningshou Gong ⑤** (宁寿宫; Palace of Peace and Longevity), was the place of one such grisly episode. In 1900, a concubine of Emperor Guangxu dared to oppose the fearsome Empress Dowager Cixi. As punishment, the concubine was rolled up in a carpet and thrown down into the shaft of the well by the palace eunuchs.

In the smaller halls to the east and west of the main halls are the exhibitions of the **Imperial Palace Museum** (故宫博 物院; Gugong Bowuguan). One highlight here is the **Zhongbiao Guan ⑥** (钟表馆; Hall of Clocks), where the exhibits include water clocks and various intricate, richly decorated European and Chinese mechanical timepieces.

At the end of the Forbidden City is **Yuhua Yuan ⑪** (御花园; Imperial Garden), composed of flower beds, cypress trees and mosaic walkways, before the northern exit, **Shenwumen** (神武门; Gate of Divine Might).

OUTSIDE THE FORBIDDEN CITY

Across the street from Shenwumen, on land that was formerly part of the palace grounds, is **Jing Shan Gongyuan ②** (景山公园; Coal Hill Park; daily Apr–Oct 6am–9pm, Nov–Mar 6.30am–8pm), the ideal place from which to view the palace complex. This artificial, pavilion-crowned hill was built with the earth dug from the palace moats in the early 15th century. The last Ming emperor, Chongzhen, hanged himself from a tree here in 1644, after killing his family and fleeing the besieged palace during a peasant uprising; the tree survives.

Back at the southern end of the Forbidden City between Tiananmen Gate and the ticket office at Wumen Gate are two areas of parkland. The western half, **Zhongshan Gongyuan ③** (中山公园; Sun Yatsen Park; daily June–Aug 6am–10pm, Apr–May and Sept–Oct 6am–9pm, Nov–Mar 6.30am–8pm), is a very relaxing landscaped park

Mao's portrait dominates Tiananmen Gate.

occupying the site of an old temple honouring the gods of the earth and of fertility. It was renamed after Sun Yatsen (1866–1925), revered founder of the Chinese republican movement.

To the east is **Tai Miao**, the former shrine of the imperial ancestors, now called **Laodong Renmin Wenhua Gong ❹** (劳动人民文化宫; Working People's Cultural Palace; daily summer 6.30am–8.30pm, winter 6.30am–7.30pm). The three imposing temple halls date from the Ming dynasty and housed the ancestral tablets of the imperial forebears, which the emperor was required to honour.

TIANANMEN SQUARE

On 1 October 1949, Mao Zedong, chairman of the Communist Party, proclaimed the founding of the People's Republic of China from the balcony of **Tiananmen Gate ❺** (天安门; Gate of Heavenly Peace; daily Mar–Oct 8.30am–5pm, Nov–Feb until 4.30pm). The present structure dates from 1651, and was preceded by a wooden gate built in the early 15th century.

When emperors left the Forbidden City to celebrate the New Year rites at the Temple of Heaven, they made their first offerings here.

Mao's giant image faces south across the expansive boulevard of Chang'an Jie to **Tiananmen Square ❻** (天安门广场; Tiananmen Guangchang). Quadrupled in size during the 1960s so that it could hold up to a million people, the square has been the venue

The Great Hall of the People.

Tiananmen Gate is lit up in the evening.

⊙ Tip

For entry to the Temple of Heaven and Summer Palace, it's best to buy an all-inclusive ticket (tao piao), otherwise you have to pay for entry to each building. However, the standard ticket for the Forbidden City gives access to all except a couple of galleries of the Palace Museum.

for numerous political dramas, from Red Guards' rallies during the Cultural Revolution to the 1989 student demonstrations and subsequent bloodshed. In the centre of the square stands the **Monument to the People's Heroes** (人民英雄纪念碑: Renmin Yingxiong Jinianbei), an obelisk unveiled in 1958. Immediately west of the square, **The Great Hall of the People ⑦** (人民大会堂; Renmin Dahuitang; daily except when in session July–Aug 7.30am–4pm, variable hours rest of the year) is an imposing building in the Soviet neoclassical monumental style, where meetings of the People's Congress take place.

In 1977, a year after Mao's death, the **Chairman Mao Mausoleum ⑧** (毛主席 纪念堂; Mao Zhuxi Jiniantang; Tue–Sun July–Aug 7–11am, rest of year 8am–noon; free) was completed at the southern end of the square. People still come to pay their respects, filing past his embalmed body in its rose-hued glass enclosure. Queues can be lengthy for this dubious pleasure so it's advisable to arrive before 8am.

⊙ TRANSPORT

Getting around Beijing

Public buses are complicated to use without Chinese and crowded during rush hours. If you can copy and paste Chinese addresses, website www.bjbus.com can help plan bus trips.

Taxis are unfortunately not as plentiful as they once were. The meter starts at Rmb 13 and goes up Rmb 2.3 per km after the first three. Again, as drivers usually cannot speak much English, it is a good idea to have your destination and the name and address of your hotel written down in Chinese before setting off. (Hotel name cards in Chinese are very useful for this.)

Walking or cycling between some sights is feasible, but be sure to check distances on a map as Beijing is vast. The city is laid out as a grid, so carrying a compass or paying attention to north (北; bei), south (南; nan), east (东; dong) and west (西; xi) – as well as centre/middle (中; zhong) – marked on street signs makes navigation quite easy.

The ever-expanding metro system (www.bjsubway.com) is easy to use and can take you directly to centrally located major sites. Electronic tickets cost from Rmb 3 and have to be bought for each single-way journey on the day of travel. Having some Rmb 1 coins ready for automated ticket machines is advisable.

Behind the Great Hall of the People is the city's most controversial building, the incongruous **National Centre for the Performing Arts ⑨** (中国国家大剧院; Zhongguo Guojia Dajuyuan; exhibition area Tue–Sun 9am–5pm), a giant glass-and-titanium dome rising out of a tranquil moat. Unaffectionately nicknamed "The Egg" by locals, the Paul Andreu design breaks Beijing's age-old tradition of feng shui, and its proximity to the capital's heartland brought howls of consternation from conservatives. The top-notch facilities inside cannot fail to impress, and you can wander around the interior for the price of an entrance ticket as well as enjoy displays in the exhibition area.

Opposite the eastern side of the square, the **National Museum of China** (中国国家博物; Zhongguo Guojia Bowuguan; http://en.chnmuseum.cn; Tue–Sun 9am–5pm; free) was reopened in 2011 as one of the biggest museums in the world. A cavernous main hall is flanked by two wings covering 65,000 sq metres (699,660 sq ft) of exhibition space – one third of the entire floor area. Permanent exhibitions focus on Chinese arts, culture and, particularly, history.

At the southern end of Tiananmen Square, the **Qianmen Gate ⑩** (前门) was once the southern entrance into the old Inner (Chinese) City from the Outer (Tartar) City and dates from 1421 during the reign of Yongle. The gate comprises two separate structures: the stone Arrow Tower (Jianlou), which burnt down in 1900 and was reconstructed in 1903; and the main gate, the wooden Gate Facing the Sun (Zhengyangmen), just to the north, to which the city wall itself was connected. Just looking at the breadth of this gate gives you an idea of how thick the former wall once was.

SOUTH OF TIANANMEN

The old neighbourhood south of Qianmen Gate has undergone a controversial transformation as part of Beijing's modernising facelift. What was once a traditional and characterful collection of restaurants, opera houses, shops and brothels dating back to the Ming dynasty has become a modern retail development. Family homes and their occupants have been replaced by more than 300 shops with faux 1930s facades hawking international brands such as Adidas and Apple.

Nearby **Liulichang** ⓫ (琉璃厂) owes its name to a Yuan-dynasty workshop that produced the distinctive glazed tiles for the city's palaces and temples. It is now a renovated "culture street" featuring numerous shops for art supplies, calligraphy, trinkets and antiques, mostly reproductions, as well as a large amount of kitsch. It's still a good point from which to explore the maze of surrounding *hutong*.

To take in the vast sprawling grid of Beijing's urban construction all at once, the **Beijing Planning Exhibition Hall** ⓬ (北京规划博物馆; Beijing Guihua Bowuguan; 20 Qianmen Dongdajie; www.bjghzl.com.cn/language/2/; Tue–Sun 9am–5pm) is an extravagant pat on the back

for the city's planning and includes an eye-popping scale model of central Beijing that covers an entire floor.

THE TEMPLE OF HEAVEN

Twice a year during imperial times, the emperor and a magnificent procession of some 1,000 eunuchs, courtiers and ministers would leave Gugong, the Forbidden City, for the **Temple of Heaven** ⓭ (天坛; Tiantan; http://en.tiantanpark. com; buildings: daily Mar–June 8am–5.30pm, July–Oct until 6pm, Nov–Feb until 5pm, park: 6am–10pm) 3km (2 miles) to the southeast of the Imperial Palace. Each time he would spend

The National Grand Theatre is Beijing's first unorthodox modern building. It has been a welcome addition to the city's cultural scene.

The Hall of Preserving Harmony in the Forbidden City.

🔍 HUTONG

For anyone keen to gain a sense of Beijing's past, a stroll through one of the city's old *hutong* neighbourhoods is essential.

In a region formerly protected by the Great Wall, Beijing was also once hidden behind its own city walls. And within the city walls were its citizens, each with a wall built around their own homes and courtyards, or *siheyuan*.

Today, ring roads and walls of high-rise buildings have taken over the function of the city wall, itself a victim of town planning. In the city centre, a dwindling labyrinthine inner core of crumbling old grey alleyways date back several centuries. These are the *hutong*, now disappearing to make way for roads, business parks and high-rises.

In Beijing's traditional hutong.

Old Beijing is a Mongol city. The nomadic conquerors who made it their capital brought their way of life and language with them. Horses were part of their lifestyle. Wells were dug and horse-troughs, *hut* or *hot* in Mongolian (as in Hohhot, the capital of the province of Inner Mongolia), were set up. The people of Beijing turned these Mongol wells into the Chinese *hutong*.

Mongols or no Mongols, Beijingers could hardly leave their houses and homes lying unprotected amid the horse-troughs. All they had to do was close up the small spaces between the houses with a wall and privacy was restored. It was even simpler to build on to the wall of their neighbours, although no one was allowed to build so as to block another householder's route to water. In this way, the tangle of *hutong* grew, with space just wide enough to let a rider through.

The houses and courtyards, hidden away and boxed in, are themselves closed off with wooden gates that often have carved characters intended to bring good fortune to the house owner and to his trade. There will be a few trees, flowers and cacti. Three or four single-storey buildings overlook the courtyard. In the *siheyuan* of more affluent families, a second and third courtyard may adjoin the first.

The name of each *hutong* tells its story by describing the life it contains. Some indicate professions or crafts: Bowstring Makers' Lane, Cloth Lane, Hat Lane. Some lanes, if mostly populated by a single family, are named after that family.

WHERE TO SEE HUTONG

The most popular, and therefore crowded, area is around **Houhai Lake**, though most of the pleasant lanes are regularly punctured by major roads. Nearby **Nanluoguxiang** (南锣鼓巷) is Beijing's most famous *hutong*. Dozens of winding paths lead off this vertical axis that are often commercial in nature but worthwhile in their own right. A large area of residential *hutong* remains east and southeast of the **Drum and Bell towers** and are still full of communal life. **Baita Si** (White Pagoda Temple) fronts a warren of ancient alleyways including shady **Qingfeng hutong** (庆丰胡同). A maze of rarely visited traditional lanes surrounds the **Lu Xun Museum**.

a night of fasting and celibacy in **Zhai Gong** (Hall of Abstinence) prior to the sacrificial rites the next morning. At the winter solstice, he expressed thanks for the previous harvest, and on the 15th day of the first month of the lunar year he begged the gods of sun and moon, clouds and rain, and thunder and lightning to bless the coming harvest.

Set in the middle of a park of 270 hectares (670 acres), the buildings in the Temple of Heaven complex form an outstanding ensemble of Ming-dynasty architecture. The park grounds are square, although the northern edge follows a curve, a symbolic expression of the fact that the emperor, in offering his sacrifices, had to leave the square-shaped earth for the round-roofed heaven.

The buildings are divided into two main groups: northern and southern, with the former centred around the **Qinian Dian** (祈年殿; Hall of Prayer for Good Harvests), one of the most famous sights in China. An exquisite example of Chinese wooden architecture and constructed without the use of a single nail, the round, 40-metre (130ft) tower has three levels covered with deep-blue tiles that symbolise the colour of heaven. The roof is supported by 28 pillars: the four largest ones in the centre represent the four seasons, and the double ring of 12 pillars represents the 12 months, as well as the traditional divisions of the Chinese day, each comprising two hours. The hall has been destroyed several times, and was last rebuilt in 1890.

The southern group of buildings includes a white, circular marble terrace, **Yuanqiu** (Altar of Heaven), the most spectacular of the city's imperial altars, comprising a stone terrace of three levels surrounded by two walls – an inner round one and an outer square one. The lowest level symbolises the earth, the second, the world of human beings, and the last, heaven.

The nearby **Echo Wall** is famous for its acoustics – sound is transmitted along its length with remarkable clarity. The **Echo Stones** on the other side of Yuanqiu produce another peculiar effect: if you stand on the first slab and

Musician in the park at the Temple of Heaven.

Qinian Dian (the Hall of Prayer for Good Harvests) is surrounded by a broad terrace.

Wangfujing is Beijing's most prestigious shopping street.

Food stalls off Wangfujing.

clap your hands, you will hear a single echo. On the second step you will hear a double echo, and on the third, a triple. The secret behind this ingenious phenomenon has to do with the different distances at which each stone slab is placed from the wall.

The surrounding park is one of the best places in Beijing to watch early-morning enthusiasts of *taijiquan*, *gongfu*, calligraphy, ballroom dancing and badminton. Senior citizens gather to perform, and to listen to, Chinese music on traditional zithers and other instruments.

About 4km (2.5 miles) to the east, past Longtan Park and close to the Third Ring Road, is **Panjiayuan Shichang** ⓮ (潘家园市场; Ghost Market; Huawei Lu Dajie), also sometimes known as the Dirt Market. It's a good place to buy reproduction antiques and souvenirs.

EAST OF THE FORBIDDEN CITY

Head east from Tiananmen along Chang'an and Jianguomennei Dajie to reach the **Ancient Observatory** ⓯ (古观象台; Gu Guangxiangtai; http://eng.bjp.org.cn; Wed–Fri 9.30am–3.30pm, Sat–Sun 9.30am–4.30pm, during summer and winter holidays until 5pm). Chinese emperors were keen patrons of astronomy. An observatory was first built here in 1442, on what was then a tower in the city wall of the imperial capital. Jesuit Ferdinand Verbiest supervised the construction of Western measuring instruments, some of which remain on the Ancient Observatory's high plinth. In total there are eight bronze devices with complex applications and fascinating names such as the elliptical armilla and azimuth theodolite. Exhibition rooms, set around a quiet garden, house historical records and explanations of the instruments.

A short walk south, immediately to the east of Beijing Railway Station is **Red Gate Gallery** (红门画廊; Hongmen Hualang; www.redgategallery.com; daily 9am–5pm), located in an ancient and magnificent Ming dynasty watchtower. Regular exhibitions here promote established domestic artists.

About 1km (0.6 mile) east of Tiananmen lies **Wangfujing** ⓰ (王府井), Beijing's premier shopping district, crowned by the glittering Oriental Plaza, a vast and impressive retail complex. Partly pedestrianised Wangfujing has a commercial history of several hundred years, and many long-standing brands can still be found such as Quanjude roast duck,

Yongantang traditional medicine and Wuyutai tea. Set back off the northern part of Wangfujing is **Dongtang** (东堂; East Cathedral or St Joseph's; access for worship only), rebuilt after a fire in 1900, and one of the city's most prominent churches.

Further east again along Jianguomenwai Dajie, beyond the Second Ring Road, is the souvenir-laden **Friendship Store** ⑰ (友谊商店; Youyi Shangdian; daily 9.30am–8.30pm). Its notorious neighbour the **Silk Market** (秀水市场; 8 Xiushui Dongjie) deals in a selection of clothing, pearls, souvenirs and electronics, and is perennially tied up in international lawsuits over fake brand-name items. Sellers are used to dealing aggressively with foreign shoppers, so be prepared for hard bargaining.

NORTH OF THE FORBIDDEN CITY

The most elaborately restored sacred building in Beijing is the **Lama Temple** ⑱ (雍和宫; Yonghe Gong; daily Apr–Oct 9am–4.30pm, Nov–Mar until 4pm), a

Lamaist (ie Tibetan Buddhist) temple in the northeast of the Old City, most easily reached by taking an underground train to the Yonghegong stop. Originally the private residence of Prince Yong, it was converted into a monastery when Yong became emperor in 1723. According to ancient Chinese custom, the former residence of a Son of Heaven had to be dedicated to religious purposes once he left.

From the mid-1700s, this was a centre of Lamaist religion and art, which at the same time offered the central imperial power welcome opportunities for influencing and controlling Tibetan

The Lama Temple.

Guozijian (the Imperial Academy) at the Confucius Temple.

Nine Dragon Screen at the Forbidden City.

and Mongolian subjects. The temple belongs, nominally at least, to the Yellow Hat sect, whose spiritual leader is the Dalai Lama – but given the ongoing tension between Tibetans and Chinese, it can hardly be considered a genuine working religious centre. Soaring aloft in the three-storeyed central section of Wanfuge (Pavilion of Ten Thousand Happinesses) is a 26-metre (85ft) statue of the Maitreya, or Future, Buddha carved from a single piece of sandalwood.

Opposite the Lama Temple, across Yonghegong Dajie, are the **Confucius Temple** ⑲ (孔庙; Kong Miao) and **Imperial Academy** (国子监; Guozijian; both daily May–Oct 8.30am–6pm, Nov–Apr until 5pm), tranquil and now largely ignored former centres of scholarship. In its glorious past, the Confucius Temple was where emperors came to offer sacrifices to Confucius for guidance in ruling the empire. Built in 1306 during the Yuan dynasty, the temple's prize possession is a collection of 198 stelae inscribed with records of ancient civil service examinations. It is the second-largest Confucian temple in China, after that in Confucius's hometown, Qufu (see page 184).

Now the Capital Library, the Imperial Academy was the highest educational institution in the country. Thousands of students and scholars came here to prepare for the imperial examinations, held once a year. A set of stelae commissioned by Emperor Qianlong records 13 Confucian classics. A total of 800,000 characters were engraved by a single scholar over a period of 12 years.

To the west of the Confucius Temple, the **Bell Tower** ⑳ (钟楼; Zhonglou) and **Drum Tower** ㉑ (鼓楼; Gulou; both daily 9am–5pm) date from the Yuan-dynasty rule of Kublai Khan. The Drum Tower faces towards the Imperial Palace, 3km (2 miles) due south, and the Bell Tower is immediately north of the Drum Tower. They once marked the northern edge of Beijing, but were in the centre of the Yuan-dynasty city. Last rebuilt in 1747, the Bell Tower stands 47.9 metres (157ft) high. The Drum Tower once held 24 giant drums that were struck to mark the closing of the city gates and the passing

of the night watches. There is a great view from the top over the surrounding area of traditional *siheyuan* courtyard houses which extends east to Houhai Lake, though the area is under the constant threat of renovation.

BEIHAI PARK

The area to the immediate northwest of the Forbidden City, in the grounds of today's **Beihai Park** ㉒ (Beihai Gongyuan; 北海公园; park daily Apr–Oct 6.30am–9pm, Nov–Mar until 8pm; buildings 8am–5pm), was the winter residence of the Mongol emperor Kublai Khan. Now, only legends remain of his former palace on Qiongdao (Jade Island), the site of the **White Dagoba** (白塔; Bai Ta). A Buddhist shrine from 1651, the distinctive structure is 35 metres (115ft) high, and was built in Tibetan style to commemorate the first visit to Beijing by a Dalai Lama. Other temples congregate on the northern shore of the lake, including the impressive Xitian Fanjing, not far from which is a spirit wall (designed to protect buildings from bad spirits), the glazed **Nine Dragon Screen**. Tuancheng (Round Town), in the southern part of the grounds, was once the administrative centre of the Mongol Yuan dynasty.

Zhongnanhai ㉓ (中南海; South and Central lakes), the site of the Politburo and State Council offices and grounds to the south, is known by many as the "New Forbidden City" and is strictly closed to the public. Mao Zedong and Zhou Enlai both lived and worked at Zhongnanhai. Its entrance is rather elegant, complete with a spirit wall.

HOUHAI LAKE

Snaking north from Beihai Park (and just west of the Bell and Drum towers) are three man-made lakes – Qianhai, Xihai and **Houhai** ㉔ (后海) – which once served as the terminus of the city's canal network. The area was a gentrified locale during the Yuan dynasty and contains some impressive courtyard houses and **former residences**, including those of Sun Yatsen's wife **Song Qingling** (宋庆龄故居; 46 Houhai Beiyan; daily 9am–5.30pm) and Puyi's father **Prince Gong** (恭王府; 24 Liuyin Jie; daily Apr–Oct 8am–5pm, Nov–Mar 9am–4pm). As tourists flock to the decreasing number of traditional *hutong* and Beijingers' thirst for nightlife grows, so Houhai has exploded into a frenetic, and profitable, free-for-all. Rickshaw drivers, masseurs and bombastic bar staff all jostle for your custom, and chartering a vessel for some calming boating on the lakes may be the best escape. **Nanluoguxiang** (南锣鼓巷), around 10 minutes walk east of Houhai, is a long renovated *hutong* packed with varied cafés, restaurants, backpacker hostels and some quirky and implausibly small shops.

The picturesque little bridge of **Yinding Qiao** (银锭桥; Silver Ingot Bridge), at the eastern end of Houhai, once marked the terminus of China's Grand Canal – the main artery between north and south (see page 245). Here traders from as far as Hangzhou would unload huge shipments of grain for trading.

◔ **Fact**

One of six ancient capitals in China, Greater Beijing today encompasses 16,800 sq km (6,500 sq miles) and is divided into 16 county-level districts. Every day in Beijing – China's second largest city after Shanghai – an average of 265 babies are born, 219 people die, 9.2 million people go to work and 3.5 million cars hit the roads.

Bai Ta, the White Dagoba, at Beihai Park is a city landmark.

The Aquarium at Beijing Zoo.

WESTERN DISTRICTS

Known as Wanshengyuan (Ten Thousand Animals Garden) when it was the personal menagerie of Empress Dowager Cixi, **Beijing Zoo** ㉕ (北京动物园; Beijing Dongwuyuan; daily Apr–Oct 7.30am–6pm, Nov–Mar until 5pm) is located between the Second and Third ring roads, 7km (4 miles) west of Houhai. The animals' living conditions are often squalid, but the pandas remain a popular attraction and the aquarium (daily Apr–Oct 9am–5.30pm, Nov–Mar 10am–4.30pm) is impressive.

On Suzhou Jie, west of the zoo, **Wanshou Si** (万寿寺; Temple of Longevity; Tue–Sun 8.30am–4.30pm) dates from the 16th century and was originally built to store Buddhist sutras. The temple features a museum collection, with a fascinating array of Buddhist statues and effigies displayed within the side halls of the complex.

Baita Si ㉖ (白塔寺; White Dagoba Temple; daily 9am–4.30pm) is 3km (2 miles) southeast of the zoo. Established in 1096 and extensively rebuilt in Lamaist style in 1271, the temple

Bathing in Beihai Park.

is noteworthy for its fine collection of Tibetan Buddhist statuary, its collection of 18 ancient Luohan (*arhat*) terracotta figures and its white dagoba, a Tibetan stupa similar to that in nearby Beihai Park. To the west, close to the Second Ring Road, is the **Lu Xun Museum** ㉗ (鲁迅博物馆; Lu Xun Bowuguan; Tue–Sun 9am–4pm; free), and adjacent former residence, displaying personal effects of the "father of modern Chinese literature". The area between the museum and Baita Si retains a sizeable proportion of its original *hutong*.

Southwest of Baita Si, not far from Beijing West Railway Station, lies **Baiyunguan** ㉘ (白云观; White Cloud Temple; daily May–Sept 8.30am–4.30pm, Oct–Apr 8.30am–4pm), once the greatest Daoist centre of northern China. This former imperial palace was given by Genghis Khan as the headquarters of Qiu Chang Chun, a Daoist leader who had promised that "if the conqueror respects Daoism, the Chinese will submit". Today, a small group of monks live here, operating the headquarters of the China Daoist

Association onsite, and helping superstitious visitors pray for luck at various sacred icons and statues.

Islam reached China during the Tang dynasty (618–907), and Muslims now live throughout the country. The **Ox Street Mosque** ㉙ (牛街清真寺; Niu Jie Qingzhensi; daily 8am–4pm) was built in 966 and, although it has all the usual features of mosques found elsewhere in the world – minaret, prayer hall facing Mecca, Arabic inscriptions – the buildings themselves are distinctly Chinese. The neighbourhood surrounding the mosque is one of the main concentrations of Hui Muslims in the capital, although many have moved elsewhere as the area has been redeveloped. It remains Beijing's largest and oldest mosque.

A five-minute walk east is **Fayuan Si** ㉚ (法院寺; Temple of the Source of Buddhist Teaching; daily 8.30am–4pm), completed in 696 during the Tang dynasty to honour soldiers killed in battle. It is the oldest surviving temple in the city, though the current buildings are all from the 18th century. Today, the

temple houses the Buddhist Academy, formed in 1956 and devoted to teaching Buddhist novices. The pleasant grounds are dotted with friendly monks and make a more authentic alternative to the major tourist stop-off that is the Lama Temple.

The Marble Boat cost a fortune to construct.

SUMMER PALACES

The great aesthete Emperor Qianlong, who ruled from 1736 to 1795, fashioned a huge masterpiece of landscaping and architecture 16km (10 miles) northwest of the city centre: **Yuanming Yuan** ㉛

Foxiangge Pagoda at the Summer Palace, with Kunming Lake beyond.

The Long Corridor at the Summer Palace.

Beijing's Botanical Gardens.

(圆明园; daily May–Aug 7am–7pm, Apr, Sept–Oct until 6pm, Jan–Mar and Nov–Dec until 5.30pm), now better-known to Westerners as the **Old Summer Palace.** Construction followed the most lavish European styles, according to plans by the Italian Jesuit missionary and artist Giuseppe Castiglione and based upon models such as the palace at Versailles. During the Second Opium War (1856–60), the Western powers, led by British and French troops, pillaged the palace and reduced it to rubble. Amid the picturesque ruins – crowned by the sublime ruins of the Great Waterworks – is a restored brick maze with a central pavilion.

A replacement for the devastated Yuanming Yuan was built nearby in the grounds laid out by Qianlong as a place of retirement for his mother. This new summer residence is associated with the notorious Empress Dowager Cixi, who fulfilled a wonderful, if rather expensive, dream in 1888. Using money intended for the building of a naval fleet, she constructed the **New Summer Palace** 32 (颐和园; Yiheyuan; daily park Apr–Oct 6.30am–6pm, Nov–Mar 7am–5pm, buildings 8.30am–5pm and 9am–4pm, respectively), west of the Old Summer Palace.

As in every classical Chinese garden, water and mountains (usually represented by rocks) determine the landscape. **Kunming Lake** (昆明湖; Kunming Hu) covers three-quarters of the total area; on its shore is **Wanshou Shan Ⓐ** (万寿山; Hill of Longevity). Accessible via a series of bridges, stairs, gates and halls is the massive **Foxiangge Ⓑ** (佛香阁; Pagoda of the Incense of Buddha), which crowns the peak of Wanshou Shan. In the eastern corner is a jewel of classical Chinese garden design, **Xiequ Yuan Ⓒ** (谐趣园; Garden of Joy and Harmony), a picturesque copy of a lotus pool from the old city of Wuxi.

To make it more difficult for strangers to spy into the grounds, **Renshou Dian Ⓓ** (仁寿殿; Hall of Benevolence and Longevity) was built right next to the eastern gate, **Dongmen Ⓔ** (东门), now the main gate. Behind it lay the private apartments of Cixi, which today

house a theatrical museum. Here, Cixi used to enjoy operatic performances by her 384-strong ensemble of eunuchs. Of light wooden construction and decorated with countless painted scenes from Chinese mythology, the impressive 728-metre (2,388ft) **Changlang** **F** (长廊; Long Corridor) runs parallel to the northern shore of the lake, linking the scattered palace buildings. It ends near **Qingyanfang** **G** (清晏舫; Marble Boat), an expensive folly in which Cixi took tea.

As with its predecessor, the Summer Palace was damaged by foreign troops, who were in China to fight the Boxer rebellion in 1900. Cixi had fled to Xi'an, and was said to have become apoplectic with rage when she heard that her throne had been flung into Kunming Lake. When she returned, some buildings were restored before her death in 1908.

XIANG SHAN (FRAGRANT HILLS)

One of the most popular destinations for Beijing's day-trippers, particularly when splashed with brilliant autumn colours, is **Xiang Shan** ㉝ (香山; Fragrant Hills; daily Apr–June, Sept–mid-Nov 6am–6.30pm, July–Aug until 7pm, mid-Nov–Mar, Nov–Dec until 6pm), 8km (5 miles) west of the Summer Palace. Clamber up the steps or jump aboard the cable car for views from the summit of Incense Burner Peak. **Biyun Si** (碧云寺; Temple of the Azure Clouds), near the North Gate, is well worth a visit. Among its several halls are the Hall of Arhats, containing 500 statues of Luohan (among which are two Qing emperors, Kangxi and Qianlong, represented as Luohan) and the Vajra Throne Pagoda, a stupa at the rear where the body of Republican leader Sun Yatsen was briefly interred.

To the east of Xiang Shan, the **Botanical Gardens** (北京植物园; Zhiwuyuan; www.beijingbg.com; daily 7am–5pm) contain a large conservatory (daily 8.30am–4.30pm) and pleasant grounds – best visited in May to catch the blossoming fruit trees. In the north of the gardens, **Wofu Si** (卧

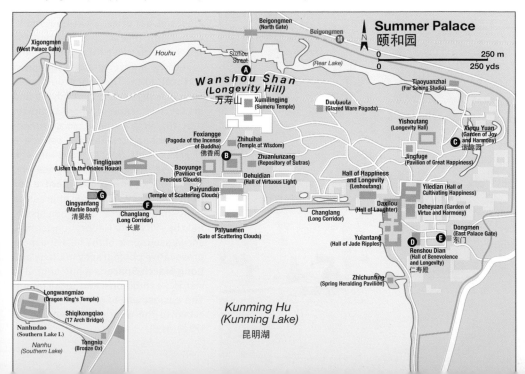

⊙ Tip

The best way to get to Xiang Shan on public transport is to take bus 112 from Pingguoyuan (at the western end of subway line 1). Bus 360 from Beijing Zoo is another possibility. Bus 696 runs between Xiang Shan and the Old Summer Palace. All will drop you at a car park 10 minutes' walk from the park entrance.

佛寺; Sleeping Buddha Temple; daily 8.30am–4.30pm) is chiefly notable for its 54-ton reclining effigy of Sakyamuni (Buddha).

HAIDIAN DISTRICT

Though seldom on tourist itineraries, **Haidian** ㉞, Beijing's high-tech and university district, offers some cultural sites and an engaging look into the future of the capital. The campuses of Beijing's two most prestigious educational institutions, **Peking University** (北京大学; Beijing Daxue) and **Tsinghua University** (清华大学; Qinghua Daxue), date back over 100 years and are attractions in themselves. Rarely visited, **Lidai Diwang Miao** (历代帝王庙; Temple of Emperors of Successive Dynasties; Fuchengmennei Dajie; Wed–Sun 9am–4pm) was built in 1530 during the reign of Jiajing as a place to pay homage to past rulers. Several huge buildings matching the imperial majesty of the Forbidden City are inside.

Wudaokou (五道口) has become a shorthand for Beijing's student bar

The 798 art gallery.

area. Over-25s will probably feel old going out here, but there are lots of cheap restaurants around as well as shops stocking suitable gifts for younger relatives. A short walk northwest from the Wudaokou subway station leads to the prestigious **Tsinghua University** (清华大学), as famous for a picturesque campus as for its numerous high-flying alumni. The former Qing-dynasty garden has retained many traditional Chinese elements such as sculpted lakes and imperial residences.

Zhongguancun (中关村) is China's answer to Silicon Valley, a major technology hub and home to several bustling electronics markets.

DASHANZI ART DISTRICT

In the far northeast of Beijing, beyond the Fourth Ring Road and also known as just "798" after the German-built former arms factory-turned-gallery that serves as its symbolic heart, the **Dashanzi Art District** ㉟ (大山子艺术区; Dashanzi Yishu Qu, galleries closed Mon) is a thriving community of contemporary artists, shops, studios and galleries great and small. Under the threat of demolition for years, the district's future now seems secure as a government-sanctioned cultural zone. The numerous cafés are packed with big-shot buyers and art tourists, some of whom complain that the area is now too commercial. Dashanzi remains a collective of grass-roots talents, however, who still have the ability to surprise and even shock. The **Ullens Centre for Contemporary Art** is an impressive multi-million-dollar exhibition space, nearby 798 Photo Gallery consistently showcases some of the best and most provocative photography in China and **Long March Space** is a hub of quality visiting exhibitions and local talent. The easiest way to get here is to take a taxi to the west of **Jiuxianqiao Lu** (酒仙桥路).

CCTV TOWER

Across the Third Ring Road from the green expanse of Yuyuantan Park, the headquarters of state-run China Central Television, the **CCTV Tower** ㊱ is emblematic of Beijing's post-bid status as a playground for pioneering architects. Rem Koolhaas's US$750 million masterpiece is an implausible Möbius loop design, which creates a huge open space beneath the gravity-defying overhang viewable from a public observation deck.

THE OLYMPIC SITES

Out beyond the Third Ring Road in the north of the city are the amazing stadia created for the 2008 Olympic Games. The main **National Stadium** ㊲ (国家体育场; Guojia Tiyuchang), known as the Bird's Nest, is flanked by the **National Aquatics Centre** (国家游泳中心; Guojia Youyong Zhongxin). The Aquatics Centre enjoys moderate popularity as a water park while the National Stadium is now rarely used except as a curiosity for sightseers. North of the sports facilities is the **Olympic Forest Park** (奥林匹克森林公园; Aolinpike Senlin Gongyuan), Beijing's largest green space. The Forest Park subway station abuts the verdant southern section, a decent walk leads to the northern part: a bird reserve.

The stadia built for the 2008 Summer Olympics will be used again during the 24th Winter Olympic Games, scheduled to be hosted by Beijing in February 2022. When Beijing won the Olympic bid in 2015, it made them the first city in the world to host both the Summer and Winter Olympics. The only new venue due to be constructed in Beijing is the Capital Indoor Stadium, which will host the speed skating events, while the skiing and snowboarding events will be held in towns across the neighbouring Hebei province.

Located just to the south, the **Chinese Ethnic Culture Park** ㊳ (中华民族园; Zhonghua Minzu Yuan; daily 8am–6pm) is a cultural theme park featuring a large number of reconstructions of buildings from around China, as well as song and dance performances that the cynic might consider somewhat inauthentic or cheesy.

En route to the airport, Dashanzi or "798" art district is an interesting area to look around.

Inside the Bird's Nest (Olympic) Stadium.

OUTSIDE BEIJING

One of the wonders of the world, the Great Wall is an essential part of any Chinese itinerary. Further afield, the imperial summer residence of Chengde is a rewarding excursion.

◎ Main Attractions
Great Wall at Badaling
Great Wall at Mutianyu
Great Wall at Simatai
Ming Tombs
Chengde
Beidaihe
Shanhaiguan

Map on page 155

The area surrounding Beijing is dotted with arresting sights that attract visitors hoping to escape the daily chaos of the capital. Transport by train or bus is possible, though for shorter trips such as the Great Wall at Badaling and the Ming Tombs, a pre-arranged tour or taxi is easiest; there are also regular tourist buses to Badaling from Qianmen in central Beijing.

THE GREAT WALL

Punctuated by strategically located towers, the **Great Wall** (万里长城; Wanli Changcheng), winds its way for some 6,400km (4,000 miles) like an endless, slender dragon from Shanhaiguan on the Yellow Sea through five provinces, two autonomous regions, and deep into the Gobi Desert. It is a structure of overwhelming physical presence; a vast wall of earth, brick and stone topped by an endless procession of stout towers, rolling over craggy peaks and across deep ravines and barren deserts. It is massively symbolic of the tyranny of imperial rule, the application of mass labour,

the ingenuity of engineers commissioned to work on the grandest scale, and the human desire to build for immortality.

The Wall receives upwards of 10 million visitors a year. Badaling, the section that nearly all foreign tourists, and many Chinese, choose to visit is easily reached as a day trip from Beijing; other sections are also possible as a day trip.

BADALING

The most accessible and developed of all the Wall sites is at **Badaling ❶** (八达岭; daily Apr–Oct 6.30am–7pm, Nov–Mar 7am–6pm), just 60km (38 miles) northwest of Beijing, which attracts an avalanche of visitors who stream past the tacky souvenir stalls before surging up the Wall. Despite the crowds, the views are breathtaking from the vantage points, where the mighty barrier climbs and descends across a fascinating mountain landscape.

The Wall here was strategically important and heavily fortified by the Ming emperors, the towers solidly built with high arrow slits. The way up on both sides of the valley leads to high beacon towers, from which you can see the northern plain and the Wall snaking across faraway hills. The western side is a steeper climb.

The majority of tourists visit Badaling as part of a tour, often taking in the Ming Tombs en route and sometimes also stopping at **Juyongguan Fortress ❷** (居庸关堡垒; daily Apr–Oct 8am– 5pm, Nov–Mar 8.30am–4pm), built to guard the narrow, 20km (13-mile) -long valley, and Beijing, against invading armies from the north. The Wall climbs steeply on both sides from the fortress.

OTHER WALL SITES

The scenery at **Mutianyu ❸** (慕田峪; daily Apr–Oct 8am–5pm, Nov–Mar 8.30am–4.30pm) is similarly imposing, but located some 90km (55 miles) north of Beijing, this section of wall is far less touristy. A long section of restored Wall follows a high ridge, giving views over wooded ravine, and some sections remain as they were

Souvenirs at Mutianyu.

The Great Wall snakes across the hills north of Beijing.

⊙ Fact

Although Beijing has been the capital for five dynasties, only the Ming Tombs are nearby. The Qing Tombs are 125km (78 miles) to the east, and as the Mongol rulers of the Yuan dynasty did not have burial rites, no Yuan tombs survive.

The Great Wall near Badaling.

– not rebuilt – so visitors get a more authentic feel, although the walk is tiring and quite tricky in places. Cable cars take visitors from the bottom of the hills almost to the Wall itself, though some may prefer to hike up the 1,000 steps.

The hike is even more strenuous at **Simatai** ④ (司马台; daily Apr–Oct 8am–7pm, Nov–Mar 8am–5pm), 110km (68 miles) northeast of Beijing, as the renovated section quickly turns into steep, dilapidated climbs. For the reasonably fit, the area makes for great hiking and camping, with panoramic mountain views.

A cable car is at hand at the east side of the reservoir. You can take this to a point 20 to 30 minutes' walk below the Wall, or make a longer excursion on foot. If you opt for the latter, from the car park you will see a small reservoir between two steep sections of Wall. Go through the entrance gate and take the path to the right (east) leading to the higher section of Wall. This is the most spectacular stretch.

Jinshanling (金山岭; daily 8am–5pm), 10km (6 miles) to the west of Simatai, has been restored and is a bit kinder and easier to climb.

Once one of the main garrison areas guarding the capital, **Huanghuacheng** ❺ (黄花城; daily Apr–Oct 8.30am–5pm, Nov–Mar 8.30am–4.30pm) lies 60km (38 miles) north of Beijing, the closest the Wall gets to the city. Sporadic renovation has taken away some of its charm, but there's a great view of a section of wall from a small reservoir to the east of the road. Exploring the wall as it wends south is worthwhile, but you may be charged entrance to parts that cross private farmland.

A relatively tourist-free section of the Great Wall, **Huangyaguan** (黄崖关; Huangya Pass; daily 7.30am–6.30pm), lies east of Beijing, close to the Eastern Qing Tombs and 30km (17 miles) north of Jixian town. This was an important section of the Wall during the Qing dynasty.

Popular with more serious hikers is the **Jiankou** (箭扣; daily 8am–5pm) section, named after a watchtower

⊙ TRANSPORT

Getting to the Great Wall

Tours: There are dozens of tours to sections of the Great Wall on offer by car, bus or bicycle. Most big hotels and tour companies in Beijing run their own excursions.

By bus: Public buses leave from Dongzhimen bus station in Beijing to termini near different sections of the Wall. Tourist buses leave from around Tiananmen Square taking passengers to entrances of some sections, but may try to overcharge.

Elsewhere in the region

Tianjin: Super-fast bullet trains ("D" trains) run to Tianjin West Station from Beijing (1 hour), Qingdao (5 hours) and Nanjing (7 hours).

Chengde: Trains run from Beijing (5 hours), though buses (5 hours) are more frequent. Qinhuangdao (near Shanhaiguan) takes 5 hours by bus from Beijing.

Beidaihe: Trains to/from Beijing are plentiful and take around 2.5 hours. Frequent trains and buses run from Beidaihe to Shanhaiguan (1 hour).

that lies a good five-hour hike along a pleasingly unrestored and picturesque section of wall. From a car park at **Xizhazi Village**, a short trail leads to the Wall and eventually the Jiankou watchtower from where you can descend to the road for a short walk back to the car park.

THE MING TOMBS

A visit to the Great Wall is normally combined with a trip to the **Ming Tombs** ❻ (十三陵; Shisanling; daily Apr–Oct 8am–5.30pm, Nov–Mar 8.30am–5pm). Protected by an auspicious range of hills to the north, east and west, the tombs of 13 of the 16 Ming emperors lie in this geomantically favourable spot. Entry from the south on the valley floor passes through numerous gates of honour along the 7-km (4-mile)-long **Shendao** (神道; Spirit Way), flanked with imposing stone figures of animals and officials.

Of the 13 tombs themselves, only three tombs are open to the public at present, and Chang Ling and Ding Ling are most often visited. **Chang Ling** (长

陵) is the final resting place of Emperor Yongle (died 1424), the third emperor of the Ming dynasty. Historians often look at Yongle's reign as ushering in a second phase of the Ming dynasty, as he made significant adjustments to the institutional forms of the state established by the founder of the Ming dynasty, his father Zhu Yuanzhang. Yongle usurped power from the chosen successor, his nephew, and moved the capital city from Nanjing to Beijing after reconstructing the city.

It was Yongle who chose the site of the tombs, and as he was the first to be buried here, his tomb is the largest and the most centrally located. Moreover, his tomb has served as the model for the other tombs that followed. The mound of the tomb has not been excavated, and the emperor and the empress still lie within the underground vaults today. Above are magnificent courtyards and ceremonial halls.

Ding Ling (定陵), the tomb of the 13th emperor, Zhu Yijun (died 1620), is the only Ming tomb to have been excavated. Take the wide staircase

Stone elephant along the Shendao (Spirit Way) at the Ming Tombs.

The Great Wall winds its way across northern China for some 6,400 km (4,000 miles).

⊘ FACT VS FICTION

A number of myths surround the Great Wall, perhaps unsurprisingly for such a remarkable, improbable structure. Contrary to popular belief, the Wall is not visible to the human eye from space, or even from a low orbit, unlike numerous other man-made structures such as bridges and dams. Nor is it filled with the bodies of dead labourers, as such material would prove structurally unstable. For some, the Wall represents a monumental folly, but historian David Spindler says it is wrong to say that it was ultimately ineffective – as, after all, it helped the Ming army to maintain its sprawling territory for hundreds of years. Spindler cites two major instances of the Mongol hordes from the north being kept at bay: in 1554 at the Jinshanling section and in 1561 at Badaling.

Stone guardian at the Ming Tombs.

The Tianjin Eye.

down to the entrance of the vaults, the underground palace, located 30 metres (100ft) below. The emperor's primary wife and one concubine were buried with him, although all you can see down there nowadays are some decorative chests and two stone thrones, placed for the sake of tourists.

The underground palace was sealed with a specially designed lock. The locking stone, which is still on display inside the entrance, fell automatically into place inside the vault when the doors were closed, making it nearly impossible to open them again. Unfortunately, grave robbers managed to gain access, and when the tombs were finally opened the vaults were nearly empty. The underground palace consists of three main halls. Two exhibition rooms above the vaults showcase rare relics belonging to the royals, although most have been moved to the museum at Chang Ling.

TIANJIN

Some 140km (90 miles) southeast of Beijing and easily reached by train or bus, **Tianjin ❼** (天津), with a population of over 10 million, is the largest port city in northern China. A walk around town (by far the best thing to do in Tianjin) tells much about its history. If some of the city's colonial architecture and layout is suggestive of Shanghai, this is because Tianjin had a prosperous international community during the late 1800s. In 1860, Western powers, wanting to expand trade with China, turned it into a treaty port by landing troops in the city and forcing Beijing to parcel out the city to the various Western interests.

There are more than 200 concession-area buildings on **Diwu Dajie** (Fifth Avenue) alone, with French architecture prominent – especially on Chifeng Lu, which now serves as Tianjin's fashion district. Despite recent renovation lessening its authenticity, **Gu Wenhua Jie** (古文化街; Ancient Culture Street) in central Tianjin is a good place to look for books, porcelain, carpets, crafts and food, including the local speciality, *goubuli baozi* (steamed buns). It is also the location of the fine Daoist **Tianhou Gong** (天后宫; Tianhou Temple; 9am–4.30pm), dedicated to Mazu, Goddess of the Sea.

Around 1km (0.6 mile) to the north is the Buddhist **Dabeichan Yuan** (大悲禅院; Dabei Monastery; 40 Tianwei Lu; Tue–Sun 9am–4.30pm), containing several impressive statues to Guanyin, the Goddess of Mercy. **Zhongxin Park** (中心公园; Zhongxin Gongyuan) is an attractive place to take in the ambience, and a stroll from here to Binjiang Dao via Chifeng Lu is one of Tianjin's most rewarding.

The impressive, Japanese-designed **Tianjin Museum** (天津博物馆; Tianjin Bowuguan; 31 Youyi Lu; Tue–Sun 9am–4.30pm; free) houses priceless cultural relics including ancient calligraphy, paintings and ceramics – many from the imperial collections of Beijing and Chengde. Also worth seeing

are the displays of local history on the top floor. For views across the sprawling city, the **Tianjin Zhi Yan** (天津之眼; Tianjin Eye; Yongle Qiao; daily) is a 110-metre (360ft) -diameter observation wheel on Yongle Bridge; on a clear day, it can provide views of up to 40km (25 miles).

Yangliuqing (杨柳青) is a pleasant old town situated about 15km (9 miles) west of the city, and known throughout China for its traditional Lunar New Year pictures made with woodblock printing.

CHENGDE, IMPERIAL RETREAT

Chengde ⑧ (承德), formerly known as Jehol, was the summer residence of the Qing emperors. A five-hour train ride 250km (150 miles) northeast of Beijing, it has retreated once again into the sleepy town it was before Qing-dynasty emperor Kangxi built his new summer palace in 1703. Summer temperatures are pleasantly cool compared with those of Beijing, and even though Chengde now has the ugly

buildings and busy roads found everywhere in China, it has kept the feel of a summer resort.

For over 100 years, the emperors and their retinues passed the summer months here, spending their time on hunting excursions, equestrian games and other diversions, as well as on state business. Yet after 1820, when a bolt of lightning killed Emperor Jiaqing here, the resort was abandoned. Fearing that fate might deal them a second blow, the court stayed away, and the buildings and gardens fell into ruin.

What remains is the largest imperial residence in China that has survived in its original condition. The palace complex, the **Bishu Shanzhuang** (避暑山庄; Imperial Summer Villa; daily Apr–Oct 7am–6pm, Nov–Mar 8am–5.30pm), is close to modern town of Chengde; its main hall, **Zhenggong**, built with valuable *nanmu* hardwood from Yunnan province, was where Emperor Xianfeng reluctantly signed the agreement with the British and French in 1860 which opened China to foreign trade. The

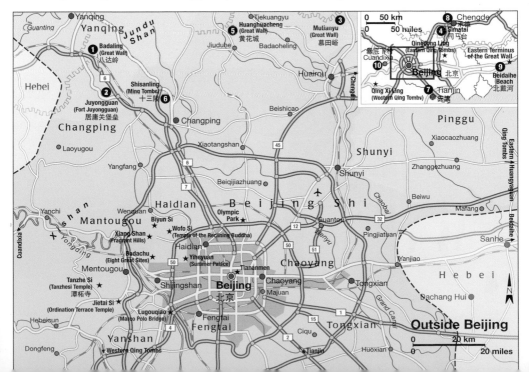

main attraction, however, is the spacious grounds which extend north from the palace and are home to elegantly situated pagodas, halls and pavilions.

Outside the palace grounds, to the north and east, a total of 11 temples – mostly in the Tibetan style (a sign of the favour shown to the Lamaist religion by the Qing emperors) – were built. The **Waiba Miao** (外八庙; Eight Outer Temples; daily Apr–Oct 7am–6pm, Nov–Mar 8am–5.30pm) are of greatest interest, and the largest and most impressive of these is the dramatic, red-walled **Putuozongcheng** (普陀宗乘之庙; Shizigou Lu), dating from 1771 and based on the Potala Palace in Lhasa, Tibet – indeed the temple served as a residence for high Tibetan dignitaries when they stayed at the Chinese imperial court. It is usually possible to access the roof for panoramic views across the entire complex.

Next door to the east is **Xumifushou** (须弥福寿之庙), which was built in 1780 in honour of the sixth Panchen Lama's visit to Chengde for Qianlong's 70th birthday. It exhibits a blend of Han Chinese and Tibetan architecture. The Temple of Universal Peace, or **Puning Si** (普宁寺; Puning Temple) houses a magnificent statue of the thousand-armed (actually there are only 42 arms) Guanyin, carved from five different types of wood and towering 22 metres (72ft) high.

There are several peaks in the immediate surroundings of Chengde, offering pleasant hiking opportunities in the summer and early autumn.

SEASIDE ATTRACTIONS

On the coast to the east of Beijing, **Beidaihe** ❾ (北戴河) is a favourite summer destination for high-level party officials and several million tourists every year. The town has sandy beaches, some old Western-style villas, great seafood, and bicycles can be hired in the summer months to explore the surrounding area.

East along the railway line from Beidaihe, the small, walled town of **Shanhaiguan** (山海关) marks the Great Wall's eastern boundary with the sea. Formerly an old garrison town,

Shanhaiguan Lao Long Tou.

Shanhaiguan is crisscrossed with small, manageable streets similar to Beijing's *hutong*. The official highlight here is the **Tianxia Diyiguan** (天下第一关; First Pass Under Heaven; May–Oct 7am–6pm, Nov–Apr 7.30am–5pm), a stretch of battlements bombarded by music blaring from loudspeakers. Far more serene and impressive is the section of Wall at **Jiao Shan**, 3km (2 miles) north of town, where the Wall mounts its first range of hills. It may be tiring, but walking along the Wall is well worth the effort (there is also a cable car), and some fine walks are possible into the hills beyond. The potentially momentous **Lao Long Tou** (老龙头; Old Dragon Head), where the Great Wall meets the sea 4km (2.5miles) south of town, is actually an overpriced anticlimax, but access to the beaches on either side affords the same view for free.

INTO THE RURAL PAST

A tantalising glimpse of old-world China can be found at the village of **Cuandixia** ⓿ (爨底下村), 90km (55 miles) west of Beijing. Set in a valley not far from Zhaitang town, it is an enchanting jumble of traditional dwellings climbing the hillside. In total, there are over 70 courtyard houses dating from the Ming and Qing dynasties. The village is also notable for its collection of Maoist political slogans from the Cultural Revolution, which have been touched up and preserved.

Reaching Cuandixia by public transport is not easy; the best bet is to take the subway to Beijing's westernmost stop (Pingguoyuan) and then to take a taxi the rest of the way. Residents of the village also offer very cheap, simple accommodation for those who wish to stay overnight.

Either visited as you return from Cuandixia, or as a separate excursion, **Tanzhe Si** (潭柘寺; Menglougou District; daily 8am–5pm, until 4.30pm in winter) is a vast Buddhist temple 45km (28 miles) west of Beijing that purportedly predates the city itself. The temple halls are arranged up the hillside in a glorious setting, and there is a sublime collection of stupas within the attached temple of **Talin Si** (塔林寺).

☉ Tip

One of the area's most spectacular winter sights is the annual ice and snow festival at Longqing Gorge (80km/50 miles northwest of Beijing). The extravagant and kitschy ice sculptures are illuminated by neon lights during the evening and rate second only to the similar world-famous festival at Harbin. Held in January and February.

Cuandixia in winter sunlight.

BUILDING THE WALL

This astonishing project, conceived as the ultimate defence, took nearly 20 centuries to complete and involved millions of conscripted labourers.

The Great Wall dates back more than two millennia, when a series of shorter walls were systematically linked during the Qin dynasty (221–206 BC) to protect China's northern borders. Centuries of gradual decline, and occasional repair, ensued before officials of the Ming court – fearing attack from the north – decided to rebuild the Wall into a formidable barrier, the "Ten Thousand Li Great Wall". The gargantuan project took over 100 years, but singularly failed to prevent the invasion of China by the Manchus in the mid-17th century.

The Ming-dynasty wall averages 8 metres (26ft) high and 7 metres (21ft) wide. Some sections are broad enough to allow five or six soldiers to ride side by side. Surveyors planned the route so that, where possible, the outer (generally north-facing) wall was higher. Countless parallel walls, fortified towers, beacon towers, moats, fortifications and garrisons completed a complex system. Local military units supervised construction. In a simple contract, officers and engineers detailed the time, materials and work required.

Many sections of the wall around Beijing were built on granite blocks, with some foundation stones weighing more than one ton. Elaborate wooden scaffolding, hoists and pulleys, and occasionally iron girders aided the builders. To speed up the construction process, prefabricated stone parts were used for beacon towers, including lintels, gate blocks and gullies.

Construction of the Wall varied according to the terrain and the perceived level of threat. To maximise defence, surveyors often chose routes across near-vertical hillsides.

The Wall was built sufficiently broad to allow five or six horsemen to ride side by side.

The Wall follows a ridge near Huanghuacheng.

The view from one of the thousands of watchtowers along the wall.

A guard's life

From their small rooftop sentry boxes, Great Wall guards, though they kept their weapons and torches primed, saw no enemies for months on end. If an assault came, the guards' main function was not to defend the wall but to alert the nearest garrison using a complex system of torch signals.

Most guards lived in remote watchtowers shared with five to ten others. During the day, those not on lookout duty tilled small patches of farmland on the hillside, collected firewood and dried wolf and cattle dung, and sometimes hunted. They ground wheat flour in stone mortars and carried out minor repairs to the wall and towers. To supplement food supplies brought by road, migration of farmers was encouraged or enforced, and guards helped them construct irrigation canals and farmhouses.

The guards' crowded living quarters also served as storage for grain and weapons. Doors and windows had heavy wooden shutters to keep out the winter cold – the areas through which the wall passes regularly experience temperatures below –20°C (4°F) – and often guards shared a kang, a heated brick bed.

The 7 metre (23-ft) -thick wall was constructed of an outer layer of brick and stone enclosing an inner core of earth, rubble and, legend has it, the bones of conscript labourers.

Patriotic tourists on the Wall.

Towers in remote areas were built close enough together to enable a beacon warning system to function. When trouble was spotted, guards burned dried wolf dung to create smoke signals.

Harbin's restored cathedral.

THE NORTHEAST

China's rugged northeast, known to the West as Manchuria and to the Chinese as Dongbei, has been shaped by conflict between China and neighbouring Japan, Korea and Russia.

Northeast of Beijing lie the three provinces of Liaoning, Jilin and Heilongjiang, collectively known as **Dongbei**, literally "East-North". The old name of Manchuria, still in use outside China, goes back to the fact that this was once the territory of the Manchu *(manzu)*, rulers of the Qing dynasty. With a blend of Chinese, Korean and Russian influences, this far-flung region has an unusual cultural identity. It was brutally occupied by the Japanese in the 1930s, and has long been the focus of conflict and power struggle. Recent fortunes have been mixed: the closure of state-controlled enterprises has caused difficulties in Dongbei's industrial heartlands – particularly in Jilin province – but some cities, notably Dalian, have thrived with the booming Chinese economy.

The Manchu rulers prohibited the settlement of Han Chinese in the region until the middle of the 19th century, when the pressure of an expanding population and the dislocations of the Taiping Rebellion forced them to change their policy. During the 1930s, the Japanese attempted to separate the northeast from China by setting up the puppet state of Manchukuo, under the rule of the former, and last, Chinese emperor, Puyi. The region was rapidly industrialised in the early Communist years, and the Manchu population became completely assimilated

Zhongshan Square, Dalian.

with the Han Chinese; in recent years, however, the special customs and traditions of the Manchu are once more being emphasised.

SHENYANG

A busy transport junction and capital of Liaoning province, **Shenyang ①** (沈阳) is one of the most important industrial cities in China. Formerly known by its Manchurian name of Mukden, it did not gain significance until the Song dynasty, when it became a centre of trade for nomadic livestock breeders.

⊙ Main Attractions

Imperial Palace, Shenyang
Dalian Beaches
Changbai Shan Nature
  Reserve
Harbin
The Far North

Map on page 163

Shenyang's rise in status came during the Qing dynasty, when Liaoning was the home of the Manchu, the Qing emperors. Today, more than half of the Manchu (manzu) ethnic minority lives here. Formerly called the Jurchen, they constitute the most populous non-Han minority in the northeast, and are also found scattered through Inner Mongolia. Now virtually indistinguishable from the Han Chinese, the Manchu once spoke an Altaic language unrelated to Chinese and used a separate writing system in existence since the 17th century. Today's Manchu population speak Mandarin and the Manchu tongue appears to have died out.

Shenyang's main tourist attraction is its **Imperial Palace** (故宫; Shenyang Gugong; 171 Shenyang Lu; http://en.sypm.org.cn; daily mid-Apr–mid-Oct 8.30am–5.30pm, mid-Oct–mid-Apr 9.30am–4.30pm), China's largest and most complete palace complex after the Forbidden City in Beijing. It was built in 1625, after the Manchu had declared Shenyang to be their capital, and it contains more than 300 buildings

Dalian's Xinghai beach.

in an area covering more than 60,000 sq metres (650,000 sq ft). The palace was the residence of Nurhachi, the founder of the Qing dynasty, and his successor Abahai (Huang Taiji in Chinese), and it was maintained after the Qing emperors moved to the capital of Beijing. The main buildings – an amalgamation of Chinese, Manchu and Mongol architecture – are Chongzheng, Qingning Palace, Dazheng and Wensu Pavilion. Qing weaponry and banners of the Manchu army are on display.

Of the three imperial Qing tombs in Liaoning province, two are in Shenyang. The Northern Imperial Tomb, **Bei Ling** (北陵; 12 Taishan Lu; daily 8am–5pm), was built in 1643 for Nurhachi's son Abahai and is now in the centre of Beiling Park in the north of the city. The Eastern Imperial Tomb, **Dong Ling** (东陵; 210 Dongling Jie; daily 8am–5pm), also known as Fuling, is the final resting place of Nurhachi and is 8km (5 miles) outside the city on a hill covered by ancient, weathered pines.

For those interested in the Japanese occupation of Manchuria, the

⊘ TRANSPORT

Getting to Dongbei

Flights: Harbin has a small international airport receiving domestic flights from most major cities in China. Dalian and Shenyang also have airports.

By train and bus: Shenyang is a major transport hub, with extensive rail links and long-distance buses from cities across the northeast.

By boat: Dalian has a passenger ferry terminal with connections to Inchon in South Korea, also Shanghai (37 hours), Tianjin (13 hours) and Yantai (5–7 hours).

Getting around Dongbei

Shenyang: The fastest trains go to Dandong (4 hours), Dalian (4 hours) and Jilin (5 hours).

Changchun: Frequent trains to Harbin (2 hours) and Shenyang (2 hours) make Changchun a useful rail hub. Bus journeys are an alternative, such as to Jilin (1.5 hours).

Changbai Shan: Yanji International Airport has infrequent flights to/from Dalian and Beijing. Erdao Baihe town has rail connections to Shenyang (13 hours via Tonghua).

9.18 History Museum (九一八历史博物馆; Qinhua Rijun Di 731 Budui Yizhi; 46 Wanghua Nanjie; daily 8.30am–4.30pm; free) gruesomely details the period and China's eventual successful resistance. The museum takes its name from the date the Japanese arrived in Shenyang – 18 September 1931. Public buses run to tourist spots from **Government Square** (市府广场), and Shenyang's two train stations are also centrally located.

BOOM TOWN OF THE NORTHEAST

Anshan (鞍山) is a nondescript city 80km (50 miles) south of Shenyang, and the point of access for a pleasant visit to the scenic mountain of **Qian Shan** (千山国家公园), blanketed with ancient pines, pavilions, temples and monasteries dating from the Ming and Qing periods.

South from Anshan, the railway line passes broad fields of millet and soybeans to the tip of the Liaodong Peninsula and the dynamic city of **Dalian** ② (大连). This is an economic success story dubbed the "Hong Kong of the North", and one of the most attractive cities in north China. The ice-free harbour is the northeast's largest, a fact reflected in its repeated conquest: first by Japan in 1895 after the Sino-Japanese War, then for a short time by the Russians, until the Japanese regained control in 1905; they hung onto Dalian until it fell into the hands of the Soviet Union in 1945 before finally returning to China in the 1950s.

The main impression of Dalian is of a busy port with broad streets and large squares planted with greenery. The period of foreign occupancy bequeathed the city an attractive array of European architecture, with the best examples ringing central Zhongshan Square – have a look at the Dalian Hotel and the old Bank of China Building. The city is also renowned for its mild climate, excellent seafood restaurants and beaches that are worth visiting but unlikely to become world famous.

Sections of the coastline offer dizzy views of plunging cliffs, especially at **Laohu Tan** (老虎滩; Tiger Beach).

Tip

For a closer look at North Korea, take one of the daily boats from Dandong that goes out onto the Yalu River, the international border, and comes within 20 metres/yards of the North Korean side.

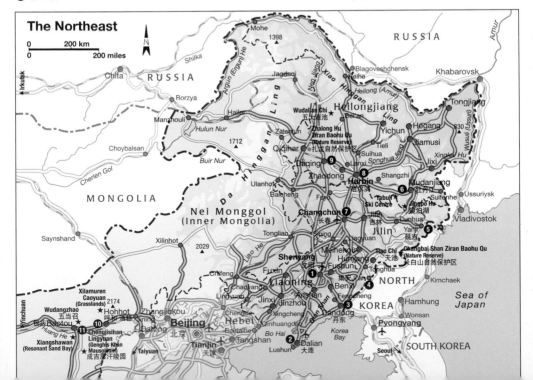

The Northeast

Dongbei is one of China's best areas for birdwatching, with several species of crane, including the red-crowned crane (also known as the Japanese or Siberian crane).

Lake Tian Chi in Changbai Shan straddles the North Korean border.

There is pleasant scenery and a sandy beach at **Bangchuidao Jingqu** (棒棰岛景区; Bangchuidao Scenic Area; Binhai Lu), 5km (3 miles) southeast of the city centre. The sand-and-pebble beach at **Fujiazhuang** (府家庄; Xigang District; daily 6am–11pm) is probably the best spot to swim or sunbathe away from the crowds. Using public buses is not particularly straightforward, but taxis are plentiful.

KOREAN BORDERLANDS

Southeast from Shenyang, or northeast from Dalian, is the city of **Dandong** ❸ (丹东) and the mountainous vistas of **Dagu Shan** (大孤山), right on the North Korean border. From Dandong, the railway carries on into North Korea as far as its capital, Pyongyang. For those who want to say they've nearly set foot in North Korea, boats carry visitors to within only a few metres of the North Korean side on the Yalu Jiang River. Alternatively you can walk along the original bridge that linked China with North Korea until you reach the twisted wreckage created by American

bombers and carefully preserved since by Chinese authorities.

East of Shenyang, the main road runs to the nearby industrial town of **Fushun** (抚顺), where the last emperor, Puyi, was imprisoned from 1950 until 1959. Still further east is **Tonghua** (通化), a wine-producing town in the southeast of Jilin province. Accessible by train or bus from Tonghua, **Ji'an** ❹ (集安) lies on the Chinese-Korean border, on the upper course of the Yalu Jiang. The numerous tombs in the vicinity (not all are open to the public) testify to the fact that Ji'an was once the capital of the Korean kingdom of Koguryo. Today it lies in the middle of an autonomous region of China's Korean minority (there are about 2 million ethnic Koreans living in China, and more than 60 percent live in this region). The Yalu Jiang, separating China and North Korea, is only 30 metres (100ft) wide here, and in the summer months, women chat across the border while doing their laundry and children from both sides swim in the river together

– although swimming to the opposite bank is not officially permitted.

The capital of this autonomous region is **Yanji** ⑤ (延吉), where the Koreans also have their own university. The Korean influence is not restricted to this area alone. Some parts of Shenyang, Changchun, Jilin city and Mudanjiang, too, feel unmistakably Korean – people wear Korean clothing, signs are written in Korean, and Korean is the primary language of commerce. (In Shenyang, there is a cemetery dedicated to the memory of the Chinese who died in the Korean War.)

Between Tonghua and Yanji, the **Changbai Shan Nature Reserve** (长白山自然保护区; Changbai Shan Ziran Baohu Qu) follows the mountains along the China–North Korea border, one of the most diverse mountain-forest ecosystems in Asia and sanctuary for many endangered animals – leopards, Siberian tigers and bears amongst them. The easiest way to explore is to head to the **Changbai Shan Scenic Area** (长白山风景区; Changbai Shan Fengjing Qu; daily 8am–4pm), which includes the Underground Forest and the Changbai Waterfall, or arrange a tour with CITS or a big hotel in Jilin. A highlight of this wild reserve is the beautiful **Tian Chi** (天池; Lake of Heaven), a volcanic crater lake high up in the mountains. Measuring 15km (9 miles) in circumference, the lake makes for a rewarding trip, but is only accessible between June and September; for the rest of the year the road is iced over and treacherous. Note that the lake straddles the North Korean border (which is not clearly marked), so don't walk all the way round. A creature akin to the Loch Ness monster has allegedly been spotted lurking beneath the waters; the last sighting was in 1981. Water from the lake descends in an impressive waterfall, source of the Songhua Jiang River.

Surrounded by beautiful scenery north of Yanji, in Heilongjiang province, is the town of **Mudanjiang** ⑥ (牡丹江). The main attraction in these parts is **Jingpo Hu** (镜泊湖), a lakeside resort area surrounded by miles of virgin forest.

TO THE NORTH

Connected to Yanji by road and rail, **Jilin City** (吉林) in central Jilin province is most famous for its winter display of ice-rimmed trees along the banks of the Songhua Jiang River. Other sights include the impressive functioning **Catholic Church** (天主教堂; 3 Songjiang Lu; daily 8am–6pm; free) and the **Wen Miao** (文庙; Wen Miao Hutong; daily Nov–Apr 8.30am–4pm, May–Oct until 5pm), a temple built for imperial examination hopefuls to pay homage to Confucius.

The large provincial capital of Jilin, **Changchun** ⑦ (长春), did not become an important city until the end of the 19th century, when it was the terminus of the Manchurian railway (built by skilled Russian labour). In 1932, the town, then known as Hsinking, became the seat of the government of the Japanese puppet state of Manchukuo.

Young children learning traffic policing skills.

A Siberian tiger.

Winter wonderland: ice sculptures are a feature of Harbin's freezing winters.

Nowadays, the town still shows signs of Japanese urban planning in its ruler-straight boulevards. This industrial university city of around 7.5 million people is also well known in China for its car-manufacturing works, and because of its large parks, it is sometimes known as the "town of woodland". At the **Weihuang Gong** (伪皇宫; Puppet Emperor's Palace; 5 Guangfu Lu; daily May–Nov 8.30am–5.20pm, Oct–Apr until 4.50pm), you can peruse Puyi's living quarters and mementoes from the bizarre life of China's last emperor. Much of what's on display are replicas but the overall effect is impressive.

WHERE CHINA MEETS RUSSIA

From Changchun, the journey continues north to **Harbin** ❽ (哈尔滨), the capital of Heilongjiang province, situated almost 1,400km (900 miles), and 13 hours by train, from Beijing. The city lies along the Songhua Jiang, which joins the Heilong Jiang, the river that defines China's border with Russia to the north (where it is known as the Amur). Harbin has its industrial areas and newly built apartment blocks, which stand in stark contrast to some of the older, European-looking architecture of Central Street (Zhongyang Dajie) downtown.

Russians first arrived in Harbin at the end of the 19th century with the railway, which passed through the city on its way from Vladivostok to Dalian. Large numbers of refugees followed after the Russian Revolution of 1917, and although most returned to the homeland after World War II, the city has retained the feel of a Russian outpost. The central **Daoli District** (道里区), in particular, has onion-domed churches, Russian restaurants and, following improved relations and easier travel between the two countries since the mid-1990s, increasing numbers of Russian traders and tourists, too. There are over a dozen Orthodox Christian churches, many of them built in neo-Gothic style, culminating in the restored **Cathedral**, formerly known as St Sofia's (圣索菲亚教堂; corner of Zhaolin Jie and Toulong Jie; 8.30am–5pm), which houses exhibitions on local architecture. The district also offers some upmarket restaurants and hotels.

In the village of Pingfang, 30km (20 miles) south of Harbin, **Unit 731 Japanese Germ Warfare Experimental Base** was the site of the Japanese army's gruesome and inhumane medical experiments during the 1930s and 40s. The site is now open to the public as a **museum** (侵华日军地731部队遗址; Xinjiang Dajie; www.unit731.org; Tue–Sun 9–11.30am and 1–4pm). Denied by the Japanese government for decades after World War II, its existence eventually came to light after a Japanese scholar uncovered documented proof. Over 4,000 prisoners of war – Chinese and Allies – died from "medical" experiments involving cold, heat, chemicals, injections of viruses and plague, and live dissection.

Harbin is close to Siberia, and winters are extremely cold; temperatures regularly fall below –30°C (–22°F). The need for warm clothing cannot be

exaggerated, especially considering the unmissable outdoor sights displayed every winter during the famous **Ice Lantern Festival** (冰灯节; Bingdeng Jie). The festival starts on 5 January and lasts for one month (though frozen sculptures often remain longer) and centres on **Zhaolin Park** (兆麟公园; Zhaolin Gongyuan; 5am–9pm, from 10am during the festival; free, charge only during festival), which becomes home to dozens of extraordinary ice sculptures, including animals, plants, mythical figures and famous buildings lit up from inside by coloured lights. On the north bank of the Songhua Jiang, **Ice and Snow World** (冰雪大世界; Bingxue Da Shijie; 11am–10pm) is a huge exhibition featuring the larger works. **Taiyang Dao** (太阳岛; Sun Island Park; Dec 8am–5pm, Jan–early Mar until 8pm) mainly displays incredible snow carvings whose detail and sheer size defy belief.

Several ski resorts can be reached by bus from Harbin, including **Yabuli** (亚布 力滑雪旅游度假区; Xiangzhi City; Nov–Apr), China's best-equipped and largest ski centre, 200km (120 miles) southeast of the city.

The train from Harbin runs on to the northwest, towards the border with Inner Mongolia, passing through the oil town of **Daqing** . About 30km (20 miles) before the industrial sprawl of Qiqihar, the railway passes close to the **Lake Zhalong Nature Reserve** (扎龙自然保护区; daily 8am–4pm), where the swampy terrain is home to rare redcrowned and white-naped cranes. The reserve can be reached by public buses leaving from Qiqihar's Number One Department Store or by tours organised by the CITS office. To the north, near Bei'an, is the volcanic area of **Wudalian Chi** (五大连池), with numerous hot springs and therapeutic mud baths.

In summer months, it is possible to journey north into "Chinese Siberia", a vast and remote region of endless birch and pine forests extending to the Heilong Jiang River (Amur to the Russians). It is theoretically possible to cross into Russia from the town of **Heihe**, although a permit may be required from the Public Security Bureau (gonganju).

Fact

Excellent ski facilities at Changchun play host to the annual Chinese Vasaloppet cross-country skiing competition.

Early 20th century buildings in the Daoliqu "Russian" area of Harbin, along Zhongyang Dajie.

INNER MONGOLIA

The wide open spaces of Inner Mongolia are China's big-sky country: remote, empty and inaccessible. The southern edge is more populated, with some unusual attractions.

Map on page 163

A vast, crescent-shaped swathe of northern China from the Siberian borderlands to the Gobi Desert, **Inner Mongolia** (内蒙古; Nei Monggol) is one of the world's emptiest places, a continuation of the endless grasslands and deserts of the independent Republic of Mongolia to the north.

Although the name Mongolia conjures up visions of Genghis Khan's horse-bound hordes and their phenomenal 13th-century military conquests – from a stunned imperial China right through the gates of eastern

Europe – the cultural landscape of today is rather more subdued. As part of the People's Republic of China, the indigenous culture of Inner Mongolia has long been diluted by waves of Han Chinese settlers, with less than 15 percent of the population considering themselves ethnically Mongolian. But while Beijing's Sinification efforts are viewed as a model for more unruly regions such as Tibet and Xinjiang, far-flung pockets of traditional Mongolian life still flourish, and with a modicum of time and effort it is still possible for travellers to absorb some of these timeless nomadic rhythms. The industrialised population centred along the southern fringes may resemble that of most other large Chinese cities at first glance, but closer inspection reveals an undercurrent of Mongolian influence, whether through cuisine or custom. Finally, the mesmerising landscapes – from the sprawling grasslands in the northeast to the golden sand dunes of the southwest – represent a world-class attraction in their own right.

HOHHOT

The most accessible part of Inner Mongolia is around the main cities of Baotou and Hohhot, where the Huang He (Yellow River) meanders through the dusty plains. Most visitors use **Hohhot** ❿ (呼和 浩特), the autonomous region's

Mongolian women outside their yurt.

capital, as a base for organising summer trips to the well-trammelled grasslands within 80km (50 miles) of the city, but the town itself has several significant sights and is the most convenient place in which to get orientated. It's largely a Han Chinese conurbation, although there is a palpable Mongolian presence in the old quarter as well as a visible and vibrant Hui (Chinese Muslim) community nearby. A good, if somewhat overwhelming, venue for getting acquainted with the official Chinese version of Inner Mongolian history, culture and geography is the enormous **Inner Mongolia Museum** (内蒙古博 物馆; Nei Menggu Bowuguan; Tue–Sun, 9.30am–5pm; free), housed in a capacious, multi-storey building. The museum, 15 minutes away by taxi in the eastern suburbs, tells the region's story from its prehistoric woolly mammoths to recent space-shuttle launches.

BUDDHIST LAMASERIES

In the old Mongolian enclave in Hohhot's southwest corner is a cluster of Buddhist lamaseries, heavily Tibetan in both style and substance, and clear reminders of the historic importance of Lamaist Buddhism to Mongolia. In their courtyards, young Tibetan and Mongolian monks mingle, keeping strong a special religious bond the cultures have shared for centuries – local lamas can often be spotted determinedly but clumsily reciting *sutras* in stilted Tibetan.

The largest and most active site is the Ming-dynasty **Dazhao** (大召; daily 8am–6pm), on the west side of Danan Jie. First built in 1579, the original temple was itself a symbol of Mongolia's acceptance of Lamaist Buddhism, as it was founded by Altan Khan, who converted to Tibetan Buddhism after paying an official visit to Sonam Gyatso (who later became known as the third Dalai Lama) in Qinghai. It has been restored numerous times, including recently, but is still an active centre of Buddhist practice, and the lamas' daily routines can be enjoyed with discretion.

A short walk to the northeast across Danan Jie is another historic lamasery,

Hohhot's Wuta Si is an unusual Indian-style temple. There are a total of 1,563 Buddha reliefs on the walls, as well as script and various arcane charts.

Tibetan-style stupa at Xilituzhao lamasery in Hohhot.

⊘ TRANSPORT

Getting to Inner Mongolia

Flights: Hohhot's Baita Airport, located about 14km (9 miles) east of the city centre, has connections with 28 Chinese cities, with daily flights to/from Beijing, Xi'an, Xilinhot and Hailaer, and frequent connections to Guangzhou and Shanghai. The only regularly scheduled international flight is from Ulaan Baatar.

By train and bus: Both Hohhot and Baotou are well connected by train to major northern Chinese cities, with daily services from Beijing, Datong, Taiyuan, Yinchuan and Lanzhou. The Trans-Manchurian and Trans-Mongolian railway lines running through Inner Mongolia make train travel from Russia and Mongolia possible. There is a daily bus service from Beijing and Datong to Hohhot, and there are daily buses from Yulin and Yan'an to Baotou.

Getting around Inner Mongolia

Hohhot: There are regular daily express trains to Baotou (2 hours), while buses depart every 30 minutes for Baotou (2 hours) and Dongsheng (3 hours).

Baotou: There are regular daily express trains to Hohhot (2 hours), with buses leaving every 30 minutes for Hohhot (2 hours) and Dongsheng (1 hour).

comprising five pagodas. Originally built in 1727 as part of a larger complex, its walls are adorned with remarkably well-preserved reliefs of Buddhas, as well as an engraving of *sutras* in Sanskrit, Tibetan and Mongolian that extends the length of its perimeter. Inside the structure and around the back some intriguing Mongolian cosmological charts are etched into the stone walls.

Back onto Danan Jie and around 1km (2/3 mile) to the north, the **Qingzhen Dasi** (清真大寺; Great Mosque; daily 8.30am–6pm), with its mixture of Chinese and Arabic styles, is the main place of worship for Hohhot's sizeable Hui population. In the surrounding alleys are several Muslim noodle and kebab restaurants.

BAOTOU AND WUDANGZHAO

The industrial town of **Baotou**  (包头), shrouded in smog from its numerous furnaces, lies two hours by train to the west of Hohhot. Though there is little to see in the city itself, it is the staging point for excursions to the handful of nearby attractions. The area's most historically significant sight is the captivating Tibetan-style lamasery of **Wudangzhao** (五当召; daily 8am–5pm), about 70km (43 miles) northeast of Baotou. By far the largest and best-preserved lamasery in Inner Mongolia, the complex of white-washed temples and prayer halls stretches up the side of a hill and still houses numerous lamas. Founded in 1749, the lamasery was dedicated to the Yellow Hat Sect of Tibetan Buddhism, and its adherents still cling to the sect's tenets.

GENGHIS KHAN MAUSOLEUM

The **Genghis Khan Mausoleum** (成吉思汗陵园; Chengjisihan Lingyuan; daily 8am–6pm), outside the coal-stained city of Dongsheng, about 110km (68 miles) south of Baotou, is very much revered by Mongolians from Inner and

Prayer flags at Hohhot's Xilituzhao lamasery.

Endless grasslands.

the **Xilituzhao** (席里图召; daily 8.30am–6pm), built in 1586 following a reciprocal visit to Hohhot by Sonam Gyatso. Sutras are chanted each morning in the main prayer hall, which is heavily decorated in Tibetan Buddhist style inside and out.

A 15-minute walk southeast of Xilituzhao is Hohhot's most intact example of historic architecture, the **Wuta Si** (五塔寺; Five Tower Temple; daily 9am–5pm), a compact and rather unusual Indian-style stone structure

Outer Mongolia alike, and is one of the primary icons of their cultural identity.

Within the three distinctive cement buildings, constructed by the Chinese in the 1950s and representing Mongolian yurts, lie what are reputedly artefacts from the 13th century. While most experts do not believe the Great Khan was ever actually interred here, this does not deter thousands of ethnic Mongolians from converging on the grounds during the impressive sacrificial ceremonies that are held four times each year. During these times, entire families of Mongolians (who travel great distances from across both Inner and Outer Mongolia), clad in colourful traditional dress, come to pay homage to their most influential historic figure. The main statue of the chieftain stands tall in the principal chamber of the three-domed mausoleum.

RESONANT SAND BAY

Encroaching on the steppe about 45km (28 miles) south of Baotou is the spectacular **Xiangshawan** (响沙湾; Resonant Sand Bay), a sprawling sea of shifting sand dunes on the northern fringe of the Kubuqi Desert. The golden dunes, the highest of which are 110 metres (360ft), are an arresting sight, swallowing whole the surrounding patches of sparse grassland (it is in fact an illustration of one of the many serious environmental problems facing China – desertification as the Gobi Desert spreads southwards). A windswept section of the dunes has been made into a mini amusement park (open daily 8am–6pm) – accessible by cable car and offering camel rides and a sand slide – but a short walk will take you away from the tacky development and into a Sahara-esque dreamscape.

The entrance is 3km (2 miles) down a turn-off branching west from Highway 210, about halfway between Baotou and Dongsheng. Buses running between the two cities will let you alight at the turn-off, but from there you would need to walk to the dunes. Alternatively, CITS in Baotou offers day tours.

> **⊘ Tip**
>
> Tours regularly depart from Hohhot to the grasslands beyond; many travellers find the tour-group atmosphere and paraphernalia intrusive, while others manage to appreciate the huge prairie to its full. Most visit the Xilamuren grasslands 80km (50 miles) to the north; other grassland tours (which typically last three to four days) head further afield to Huitengxile and Gegentala.

Lines of docile camels ferry a group of tourists within the Xiangshawan desert park.

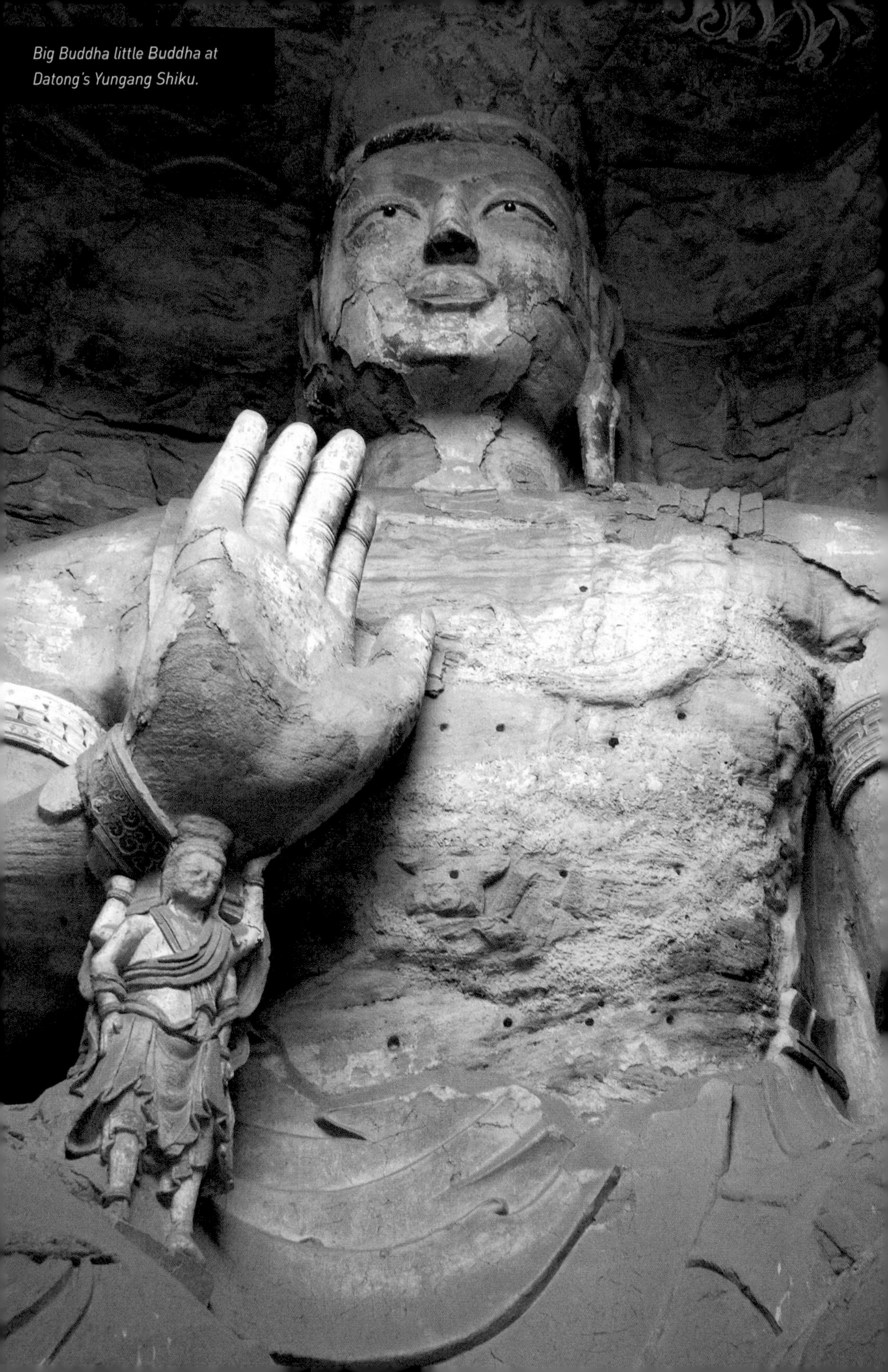

Big Buddha little Buddha at Datong's Yungang Shiku.

SHANXI, SOUTHERN HEBEI AND SHANDONG

The flood plains of the Huang He (Yellow River) nurtured the birth of Chinese civilisation, and the ancient sites strewn across the region bear witness to five millennia of history.

In a country famed for its rich cultural heritage, the northern heartlands encompassed by the modern provinces of Shanxi, the southern part of Hebei and Shandong (as well as Henan, covered in the following chapter) are home to some of the greatest historical and religious sites – as well as being the homeland of three of the most revered philosophers of ancient China: Confucius, Laozi and Mencius. These lands around the lower stretches of the **Huang He** (黄河; Yellow River) have been cultivated for at least 5,000 years, and several of China's earliest states arose in this region. The great river and its tributaries irrigated the soil, but regular floods and changes of course forced people to work in close cooperation. Over the centuries, the Huang He has changed course numerous times, disrupting life and agriculture and earning the sobriquet "China's sorrow". Not until 1933 did it find its present outflow to the ocean.

East of the river's long loop south from the barren wastes of Inner Mongolia, **Shanxi** (山西) province boasts a rich cultural heritage with the Buddhist caves at Yungang, the extraordinary temple of Xuankong Si on the Daoist peak of Heng Shan, and the sacred Buddhist range of Wutai Shan. A picturesque relic from a more recent era, the

Pingyao street scene.

town of Pingyao is a veritable museum of Ming- and Qing-dynasty buildings.

The sights of **Hebei** (河北) largely congregate in the north of the province within reach of Beijing (see Outside Beijing, page 150). The main attraction in southern Hebei, which extends down towards the Huang He, is the ancient town of Zhengding, dotted with impressive temple architecture.

The final stretch of the Huang He passes through **Shandong** (山东). The holy Daoist peak of Tai Shan, along with Qufu, hometown of China's beloved

Main Attractions

Yungang Shiku Caves, Datong
Wutai Shan
Pingyao
Qingdao
Tai Shan
Qufu

Map on pages 175, 180

Kong Fuzi (Confucius), are a big draw for visitors, while the former German colony of Qingdao on the peninsular coast is a further trump card with its picturesque streets, beaches and excellent seafood.

SHANXI PROVINCE: DATONG

A seven-hour train ride west of Beijing, the brutal industrial sprawl of **Datong** ❶ (大同) doubles as a tourism centre due to the diverse array of ancient religious structures and statuary left over from the succession of non-Han Chinese peoples who made it the seat of their dynasties. The precursor to the modern city first gained prominence when the Turkic Toba people moved the capital of their Northern Wei dynasty here in AD 386, and the sublime cave sculpture – China's oldest and best-preserved collection of Buddhist cave carvings – created by these devout Buddhists is the main reason to visit.

The sculptures are located 16km (10 miles) west of town at **Yungang Shiku** (云岗石窟; Cloud Ridge Grottoes; http://tour.yungang.org/en; daily Apr–mid-Oct

Buddhist statuary at Yungang Shiku.

8.30am–5.30pm, mid-Oct–Mar until 5pm), a series of several dozen man-made caves forged into the side of a sandstone cliff and stretching for about 1km (0.6 mile). The grottoes, a Unesco World Heritage Site, are an impressive testament to the Buddhist fervour that began to grip the Northern Wei in the 5th century, and represent an intriguing blend of South and Central Asian Buddhist art with traditional Chinese styles. The caves were constructed from AD 453–525 by tens of thousands of labourers and artisans, many of them freshly returned from pilgrimages to western neighbours such as Afghanistan. Duly inspired, they frequently incorporated Indian and Central Asian characteristics into the smooth carvings that line the cave walls – this is particularly evident in the faces of the enormous Buddhas at the western caves (nos. 16–20), noteworthy for their sheer size and sharp facial features. The 14 metre (45-ft)-high Buddha at cave 20, in modern times exposed to the elements, is easily photographed and has become the

complex's most iconic figure. Among the other highlights are the 17-metre (56ft) painted Buddha in cave five and the central sandstone pillar in cave six, replete with ornately carved Buddhas and Bodhisattvas.

Within Datong itself are a few historically significant sites, including the two temples that comprise the **Huayan Si** (华严寺; both daily 9am–5pm), among the oldest remnants of the Mongol Khitan people's Liao dynasty which made the city its capital in 907. The more architecturally impressive **Upper Huayan Si** (上华严寺), first built in 1062, is distinguished by the roof of its main hall crowned by "horns" that, on closer inspection, are a pair of ornate lions. Inside are five Buddhas representing the four compass points plus a centre, ie omnipresence. The most noteworthy feature of the **Lower Huayan Si** (下华严寺) is its main hall, Datong's oldest building and one of China's best examples of Liao-period architecture. Originally built in AD 1038, the hall's walls are lined with an exquisitely carved wooden cabinet used

for storing Buddhist scriptures. A few minutes' walk east of here is the **Jiu-longbi** (九龙壁; Nine Dragon Screen; daily 9am–5pm), a 45-metre (148ft) wall covered in colourfully glazed tiles depicting nine whirling dragons that is much larger, but otherwise almost identical, to one in the Forbidden City.

HENG SHAN

Heng Shan ② (恒山), 70km (45 miles) south of Datong, is the most northerly of China's five sacred Daoist mountains

Xuankong Si, the famous Hanging Temple clinging to the sides of Heng Shan, draws the crowds in the summer months – avoid if you suffer from claustrophobia and/or vertigo.

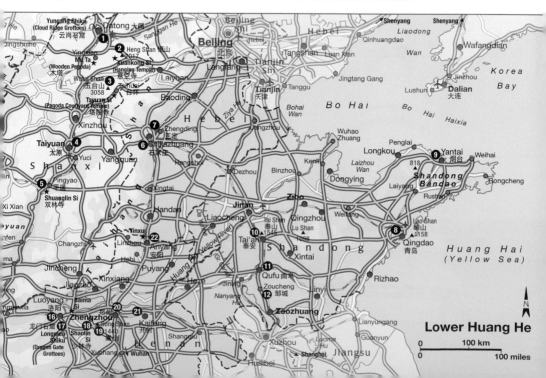

Lower Huang He

Fried dough sticks (youtiao), fried pancakes (youbing) and other doughy delights on sale in Pingyao.

(and not to be confused with the other Heng Shan, also Daoist but far to the south in Hunan province – see page 330). The hilly area is dotted with historic temples, hinting at its importance as a spiritual retreat as long as 2,000 years ago. Though devout Daoists still flock here to worship at the temples and climb the highest peak (2,000 metres/6,560ft), the vast majority of visitors come to see the picture-postcard **Xuankong Si** (悬空寺; Hanging Temple; daily 9am–5pm). Perched just off Provincial Highway 203, 1km (0.6 mile) from Heng Shen, is a gravity-defying former monastery high on a cliff face and supported only by wooden beams embedded into the rock. Originally constructed during the Northern Wei dynasty, the structure has been repeatedly rebuilt at successively higher locations after being swept away during flooding of the river that used to flow below it. Those with a head for heights can shuffle along the wooden walkways connecting the temple's main halls, which house shrines to Buddha and Confucius, as well as Laozi.

Tayuan Si stupa at Wutai Shan.

The elegant **Mu Ta** (木塔; Wooden Pagoda; daily 8.30am–6pm) towers over the town of **Yingxian**, 30km (20 miles) west of Heng Shan, a solemn reminder of the architectural heights reached during the Liao dynasty. Built in 1056, and topping out at a lofty 67 metres (220ft), it is both the oldest and tallest fully wooden pagoda in China. Originally constructed without any metal nails, its support beams are connected by clever interlocking wooden brackets that have helped the pagoda to survive numerous earthquakes.

WUTAI SHAN

South of Heng Shan, and a five-hour bus ride from Datong, lies **Wutai Shan** ❸ (五台山; Five Terrace Mountain; daily 8am–8pm), one of China's four sacred Buddhist mountains and a major point of pilgrimage for Chinese and Tibetan Buddhists, who come in droves to worship at the three dozen or so temples that dot the hillsides. The five rounded peaks after which the area is named are believed by Chinese Buddhists to be the earthly domain of

Manjusri ("Wenshu" in Chinese), the *Bodhisattva* associated with wisdom who is typically portrayed riding a lion and holding a manuscript. By the time of the Tang dynasty, there were over 200 temples in the Wutai Shan area; although many have not survived, a large concentration can be found in the tourist village of **Taihuai** (台怀), nestled in a valley encircled by the mountains. The village has a cluster of small hotels and restaurants, frequent daytime bus connections to Datong (and Taiyuan to the south), and is only a short walk from some of the most revered temples.

Standing out from the rest is the **Tayuan Si** (塔院寺; Pagoda Courtyard Temple), named after the whitewashed Tibetan-style stupa that crowns its central courtyard. From here, a climb up a series of steps to the temple at **Pusa Ding** (菩萨顶; Bodhisattva Summit) will yield sweeping views over the valley. About an hour's walk into the hills south of Taihuai is the **Nanshan Si** (南山寺; Southern Mountain Temple), a sizeable complex first built in the Yuan dynasty and affording splendid views of the mountain tops to the north.

Clam dishes at a Qufu restaurant.

sanctuary renowned for its collection of *sutras* printed in the Song, Jin, Yuan, Ming and Qing dynasties. Some of these, including a few in Tibetan, are on display inside the main hall. The "twin" pagodas of the **Shuangta Si** (双塔寺; Twin Pagoda Temple; daily 8.30am–5.30pm), built in the early 17th century, are both just under 55 metres (178ft) in height. The 13 storeys of the slightly taller **Xuanwen Ta** can be climbed via a

Meditation at Wutai Shan.

TAIYUAN

The capital of Shanxi province, **Taiyuan** ❹ (太原) is an industrial city whose origins as a settlement hark back to the 5th century BC. A convenient transport hub, most tourists use Taiyuan as a base from which to explore Wutai Shan and Pingyao just to the south, but the city itself has a handful of worthwhile sights including a provincial museum.

Sitting on the west bank of the river, the **Shanxi Museum** (山西博物馆; Shanxi Bowuguan; Tue–Sun mid-Mar–mid-Nov 8.30am–6pm, mid-Nov–mid-Mar 9am–5.30pm) celebrates the region's formative role in the birth of Chinese civilisation.

Chongshan Si (崇善寺; Honouring Kindness Temple; daily 9am–5.30pm) is a peaceful Ming-dynasty Buddhist

While leisurely strolls along the town's myriad side lanes are a delight, it's possible to enter many of Pingyao's temples and traditional family homes.

narrow, spiral stone staircase for outstanding views of the city.

Approximately 40km (25 miles) south of Taiyuan, on the right side of the road to Pingyao, is the **Qiao Jia Dayuan** (乔家大院; Qiao Family Compound; daily 9am–5pm), the lavish Qing-dynasty courtyard house that film director Zhang Yimou used as the setting for his tragic masterpiece *Raise the Red Lantern*. The residence consists of six main courtyards with more than 300 rooms.

PINGYAO

On the Beijing-Xi'an railway line around 100km (60 miles) south of Taiyuan, the picturesque town of **Pingyao** ❺ (平遥) is perhaps China's best-preserved ancient walled city and a highlight of many tourists' visit to the country. Although it has a 1,200-year history, Pingyao is mostly renowned for its largely intact Ming- and Qing-dynasty architecture, a result of its prominence as one of China's first banking centres and a subsequent decline that managed to protect it from the ravages of modernisation. A Unesco World

Heritage Site, the town is surrounded by a 6km (4-mile) Ming-dynasty city wall (which you can walk around) complete with gates, enclosing the quaint streets in a grid-like pattern.

Though the entire town is filled with surprises, some of the best-kept architecture lies on **Mingqing Jie** (明清街; Mingqing Street) and **Nan Dajie** (南大街; South Avenue), both filled with souvenir shops, restaurants and hotels. Many of the old buildings have been converted into atmospheric guesthouses with lovely courtyards and period furnishings. Established in 1824, **Rishengchang** (日升昌; daily Apr–Oct 8am–6.30pm, Nov–Mar 8.30am–6pm) is a small museum on the site of one of China's first banks that claims to be the birthplace of written cheques. You gain admittance to various attractions in Pingyao and the city wall by purchasing an all-inclusive ticket *(tao piao)*, valid for two days.

About 6km (4 miles) to the southwest of town, the rarely visited **Shuanglin Si** (双林寺; Twin Forest Temple; daily 8am–7pm) houses a large collection of original Buddhist wood-and-clay statuary, each hall brimming with fantastic coloured figures – many of them crumbling, but retaining their original paintwork – dating as far back as the Song dynasty.

SHIJIAZHUANG AND ZHENGDING

Shijiazhuang ❻ (石家庄), Hebei's capital, is a modern creation, built on the back of the railways and only making it onto the map in the early 20th century as a major junction town. The city's main attraction is the **Hebei Provincial Museum** (河北省博物馆; Hebei Sheng Bowuguan; Tue–Sun 9am–5pm, no entrance after 3.30pm; free), which has some excellent exhibits, including the Han-dynasty jade burial suits of Prince Liu Sheng and his wife Douwan. There is also a reproduction Han-dynasty chariot and an extensive accumulation of funerary objects excavated in the region.

⊘ TRANSPORT

Getting to Shanxi

Flights: Taiyuan's Wusu Airport, 15km (9 miles) south of the centre, has regular connections from Beijing, Chongqing, Shanghai and Xi'an. Datong also has a tiny airport with daily flights to/from Beijing, three weekly to Guangzhou. **By train and bus:** Taiyuan's railway station is conveniently located and provides frequent connections to other points in Shanxi as well as long-distance services from other cities. There are daily buses to/from Beijing, Luoyang, Xi'an and Zhengzhou.

Getting around Shanxi

Taiyuan: Buses are the most useful form of transport within Shanxi. There are regular buses from Taiyuan to Pingyao (1.5 hours), Datong (4 hours) and the tourist village of Taihuai in Wutai Shan (5 hours). There are several trains daily to Datong (5.5 hours) and Pingyao (2 hours), though for the latter these are often standing-room only unless you book well in advance. **Datong:** There are frequent buses to Taiyuan (4 hours) and Wutai Shan (5 hours). Trains to Taiyuan take about 5 hours. An overnight train leaves each night for Pingyao (9 hours). **Pingyao:** Buses go throughout the day to Taiyuan (1.5 hours), as do trains to Taiyuan (2 hours). There are daily trains to Linfen (3 hours) to the south, for the Hukou Falls. **Wutai Shan (Taihuai):** Buses leave each day for Datong (5 hours) and Taiyuan (5 hours).

A short trip by bus or taxi 16km (10 miles) northeast of Shijiazhuang is the historic walled town of **Zhengding** ⑦ (正定), with its rich complement of religious architecture. The most important shrine is the **Dafo Si** (大佛寺; Big Buddha Temple, also called Longxing Si; daily 8am–5pm), with its 21 metre (69ft) Song-dynasty bronze effigy of Guanyin in the **Dabei Ge** (大悲阁; Great Mercy Pavilion).

SHANDONG PROVINCE: QINGDAO

At the end of the 19th century, an ambitious Germany was looking for a place in China to plant its colonial aspirations. After two German Catholic priests were killed by Boxer rebels in 1897, German troops were sent in to establish a presence at **Qingdao** ⑧ (青岛). In true imperial style, the Chinese were quickly forced into an agreement to lease the surrounding Bay of Jiaozhou to Germany.

Before the first frigate moored in the bay, Qingdao had been a quiet fishing village. But German officers, sailors and traders were soon promenading up and down the Kaiser Wilhelm Ufer and dining in the seafront Prinz Heinrich Hotel. They drank beer from the Germania brewery, which later achieved fame in many parts of the world under the name Tsingtao (the old Wade-Giles system of spelling Qingdao).

The success of the **Tsingtao Brewery** ④ (青岛啤酒厂; 56 Dengzhou Lu; daily 8.30am–4.30pm), guides tell visitors, is due not only to German expertise but also to the spring water collected from nearby Lao Shan. This is one of China's oldest and most successful export businesses, and Tsingtao is possibly its most famous global brand. The museum and visitor centre have an idiosyncratic "Willy Wonka" charm adorned with boozing cartoon animals and beer-bottle-shaped fountains.

Aside from beer, Qingdao is perhaps most famous for its beaches, although the city itself is also appealing with relics of the colonial past, including many 19th-century, **German-style buildings** whose red-tiled roofs, half-timbered facades, sloping gables and triangular

⊘ Where

Qingdao boasts the world's longest bridge over water. The T-shaped Jiaozhou Bay Bridge, constructed in 2011, has the imposing aggregate length of 41.58km (25.8 miles) and is supported by over 5,200 concrete pillars. The bridge links central Qingdao with the Huangdao district, cutting the road distance between them by 30km (19 miles).

Pingyao is one of the best-preserved old towns in China.

Tip

At the Tsingtao Brewery you can view the factory floor, where six bottles of beer fly off the line every second, and free samples are handed out. There is a good bar and restaurant street immediately opposite.

attic windows lend the centre of town a unique Teutonic flavour. Most striking of all are the tall towers of **St Michael's Catholic Church** Ⓑ (天主教堂; Tianzhu Jiaotang; Zhongshan Lu; daily 8.30am–5pm), the **Protestant Church** Ⓒ (基督教堂; Jidu Jiaotang; 15 Jiangsu Lu; daily 8.30am–5pm) and the **former governor's residence** Ⓓ (迎并管; Ying Bingguan; 26 Longshan Lu; daily 8.30am–5.30pm), which has the air of a Prussian hunting lodge. St Michael's holds regular Sunday services, and some of the features have captions in English. The German presence lasted until 1914 – the beginning of World War I – when Japan conquered the colony. Liberated by the Chinese in 1922, Qingdao was reoccupied briefly by the Japanese in 1938.

There are a number of free parks dotted throughout the city including the coastal **May Fourth Square** Ⓔ (五四广场; Wusi Guangchang; 35 Donghai Xilu; daily 24 hrs; free), named after the nationwide anti-imperialist protest movement of 1919 that followed the ceding of Qingdao to Japan. **Zhongshan Park** Ⓕ (中山公园; Zhongshan Gongyuan; daily 7am–6pm; free) is a huge green space that includes the city zoo. Taiping Shan Park, its northeastern section, is crisscrossed by numerous paths and a hill atop which a TV tower offers unparalleled views of the city.

Most of Qingdao's visitors come for the **white sand beaches** or to take part in water sports that have spiked in popularity since the city hosted the 2008 Olympic sailing events. Fushan Bay shelters the Olympic Sailing Centre (Aofan Zhongxin), which is open to the public without charge when sailing events are not taking place. Entrepreneurial sailors offer various water-based activities depending on the season. The No 1 Bathing Beach is also home to the Qingdao International Sailing Club where boats can be hired with or without sailing lessons. The No 6 Bathing Beach features a pier that extends some 350 metres (1,150ft) into the ocean and ends at the Huilian Pavilion with bracing sea views. The No 2 Bathing Beach requires a charge and is somewhat quieter and cleaner.

The best beach near the city centre is **Old Stone Man** (Shi Laoren), a long sandy strip named after a prominent rock outcropping said to resemble an old fisherman. Lao Shan Beach is located at the entrance to Lao Shan Park and has impressive views of the mountain range.

Lao Shan (崂山), a mountainous region 40km (25 miles) east along the coast from Qingdao, is famed for its Daoist fables and the spring water that finds its way into Tsingtao beer. The area is very scenic, with waterfalls, caves and (mostly ruined) Daoist temples. There are several winding routes up the mountain, as well as a cable car. **Taiqing Gong** (太清宫; Palace of Great Purity; Laoshan Lu; daily 24 hrs) comprises three pavilions. The **Sanqing Pavilion** (三清殿) houses a statue of Laozi, regarded as the founder of Taoism.

YANTAI

Yantai ❾ (烟台) is a port city sitting on the northern coast of the Shandong Peninsula, a quieter version of Qingdao with beaches and some colonial architecture. The **Yantai Museum** (烟台 博物馆; Yantai Bowuguan; 257 Nan Dajie; daily 8am–5pm) is housed in the largest of the city's former guildhalls. The train and bus stations and passenger ferry terminal are all in the northwestern part of town.

The **Penglai Pavilion** (蓬莱阁; www.travelchinaguide.com; daily 7am–5.30pm) is an attractive and unusual temple 70km (44 miles) west of the city. The legend of the Eight Immortals Crossing the Sea supposedly took place here, and the place is famous for the "Penglai mirage", an optical illusion which appears every few decades.

TAI SHAN

Considered to be China's most sacred Daoist mountain, **Tai Shan ❿** (泰山) lies 300km (190 miles) west of Qingdao and 80km (50 miles) south of Jinan. Popular Chinese religion treats mountains as living beings: as well as creating clouds and rain, their stabilising power perpetuates the cosmic order. In ancient Chinese mythology,

The Germanic architecture of Qingdao is striking: St Michael's Church is one of the best examples.

Ascending Tai Shan.

god of Tai Shan. This temple complex of more than 600 buildings was the venue for elaborate sacrifices and provided quarters for the emperor before he ascended Tai Shan. **Tiankuang Dian** (天贶殿; Hall of Heavenly Gifts), one of the largest classical temple halls in China, contains a fresco more than 60 metres (200ft) long.

A few hundred metres/yards north of the temple, **Daizong Fang** (岱宗坊; Gate of the God) marks the starting point of a stone stairway to the 1,545 metre (5,070-ft) -high summit. In earlier years, emperors and mandarins were carried up the 6,293 steps in litters. Modern pilgrims and travellers need a whole day for the round trip, or they can ride to a halfway point by minibus, then ascend by cable car almost as far as the summit. Of course, those who take the quick way miss the splendid variety of this open-air museum: temples, pavilions, shrines, stone stelae, inscriptions and waterfalls.

A little way off the main path, the text of a *sutra* has been engraved in a huge block of stone. The 1,050 characters, each 50cm (20ins) high, are considered a masterpiece of calligraphy. A more recent addition to the mountain's calligraphic works is Mao's "The most creative people are the people now", penned in 1969.

Once past **Zhongtianmen** (中天门; Middle Gate of Heaven), the ascent becomes steeper. Passing **Wudaifu Song** (五大夫松; Pines of the Fifth Order of Officials), which, according to legend, were given this title by Qin Shi Huangdi after they sheltered the emperor from a thunderstorm, the path leads to **Nantianmen** (南天门; Southern Gate of Heaven). This is the entrance to the "realm of the immortals" on the summit, but first one must negotiate the earthly delights of **Tian Jie** (天街; Heaven Street), a Qing-dynasty parade of shops and restaurants. You can stay overnight here

Tai Shan is said to have risen from the head of Pangu, the creator of the world. Shamans, and later emperors, have performed sacred rituals here for four millennia.

At the foot of the mountain, in the centre of the quiet tourist town of **Tai'an** (泰安), stands the magnificent **Dai Miao** (岱庙; www.travelchinaguide.com; daily 8am–5pm), honouring the

⊘ TRANSPORT

Getting to Shandong

Flights: Qingdao has a modern airport with domestic flights from major cities and international flights from nearby Asian countries. Jinan Airport offers some domestic flights.

By boat: Qingdao has ferry connections to Japan and South Korea, also Dalian and Shanghai (seasonal). Yantai has ferry connections to South Korea and Dalian.

By train and bus: Jinan is the major rail hub. Shandong is well serviced by buses.

Getting around Shandong

Qingdao: Super-fast bullet trains ("D" trains) go to Beijing (6 hours) and Shanghai (10 hours). Long-distance buses leave from south of the train station regularly to Yantai (3.5 hours), Qufu (5 hours) and Jinan (4.5 hours).

Yantai: Yantai has limited rail connections to Qingdao (4 hours) and Jinan (7–8 hours), a likely interchange station. Buses run from the train station and Qingnian Lu's long-distance bus station to all major cities.

Jinan: Regular bullet trains go to Qingdao (3 hours) and all major cities. There are several bus stations; the one opposite the main train station has services to Qufu (2.5 hours), Yantai (5 hours) and Qingdao (4.5 hours).

if you wish to join others in catching the famous Tai Shan sunrise: in clear weather the panorama can extend nearly 200km (125 miles) to the Yellow Sea.

QUFU

In 1919, Kong Linyu, a descendant of China's greatest philosopher, Kong Fuzi (Master Kong in English, Confucius in its Latinised form), died at the age of 76 during a visit to Beijing. According to tradition, Kong Linyu's two daughters could not continue the family line. All was not lost, as his concubine was in the fifth month of her pregnancy. Rival factions of the Kong clan posted guards outside the chamber of the pregnant woman, but the doors of the house remained open, to make it easier for the "wise ancestor" to find his way back for rebirth. In February 1920, Kong Decheng was born, representing the 77th generation after Confucius. Succession was assured, and the "first family under heaven" celebrated. But 17 days later, Kong Linyu's first – and childless – wife poisoned her rival, the mother of the heir.

The scene of this family drama was **Kong Fu**, or **Kong Family Mansion** (孔府; www.travelchinaguide.com; daily 7.30am–4.30pm), in **Qufu ⑪** (曲阜), the hometown of Confucius (551–479 BC), located 140km (90 miles) south of Tai Shan. Confucian ideology was given imperial status in the Han dynasty by Emperor Wudi, and subsequent emperors granted the great sage's descendants lavish titles and property. Originally built in the 16th century during the Ming dynasty, the family mansion was home to the Kongs until 1948, when, with the Communist victory imminent, the last of the line left for exile in Taiwan. The outside of the residence looks rather plain, but it has around 500 rooms. Towards the end of the 19th century, the head of the Kong family was one of the wealthiest property owners in the country, presiding over his own judicial system and a private army. Inside, many rooms are valuable works of art, calligraphy, articles of clothing and extensive archival material.

Confucius forest in QuFu, Konglin, is a graveyard of Chinese scholars.

The entrance to the Confucius Temple (Kong Miao), Qufu.

Confucius himself was buried under a simple grass-covered mound in the **Confucius Forest** (孔林; Kong Lin; daily 7.30am–sunset), the Kong family cemetery a short distance north of town. The way to the mound is lined with human and animal figures in stone, a custom otherwise reserved for emperors. The whole forest has been planted with hundreds of varieties of trees, attracting large numbers of song birds, and is well worth exploring for a few hours.

Reflecting the glory of China's great sage is the size and splendour of the **Confucius Temple** (孔庙; Kong Miao; daily 7.30am–4.30pm) in the centre of Qufu. A temple is supposed to have been built on this site as early as 478 BC, one year after the death of Confucius. The view on the walk north, past ancient cypress trees and stone stelae, is dominated by the triple-roofed, 23 metre (75-ft) -high Kuiwenge (Pavilion of the Constellation of Scholars), first built in the 11th century. Passing the 13 pavilions in which stelae with imperial inscriptions are kept,

the path leads to the 18th-century Dacheng Dian (Hall of Great Achievements), the main hall of the temple and once the venue for sacrificial rites in honour of Confucius. The 28 stone pillars supporting the roof of the hall have a total of 1,296 dragons carved on them. The yellow roof on the main hall – yellow was a colour reserved for temples and imperial buildings – again emphasises the traditional importance of the great philosopher.

Outside Qufu are several other noteworthy sites. **Zoucheng** ⑫ (邹城), 25km (16 miles) to the south, was home of the most famous follower of Confucius, Mengzi (or Mencius), and is where you can find the Meng Fu (the Meng family home), Meng Lin (Mencius Forest) and Meng Miao (Mencius Temple). **Shao Hao Ling** (少昊陵) is an unusual 6-metre (20ft) pyramid-shaped tomb faced with grey stone, situated 4km (2.5 miles) east of Qufu. It is said to be the burial place of a legendary emperor, Shao Hao, who ruled this part of China around 4,000 years ago.

⊘ CONFUCIAN THOUGHTS

Although Confucius was vilified during the Mao years as a symbol of backward conservatism, he has enjoyed something of a renaissance in modern times with a state-backed film featuring superstar Chow Yun-fat as the great sage, which garnered moderate critical and popular acclaim in 2010. Author and television lecturer Yu Dan also broke sales records for interpretations of the Analects that recast the ancient wisdom as lessons for a fulfilling modern life. Meanwhile, students of the zither – a seven-stringed instrument – learn songs written by Confucius some 2,500 years ago to stimulate philosophical contemplation among those aspiring to improve their education and moral character.

Finely carved marble dragon-coiled columns at Confucius Temple in Qufu.

The massed ranks of the Terracotta Warriors.

XI'AN, SHAANXI AND HENAN

Its ancestry traceable back to the foundations of the Chinese state, Xi'an's supreme attraction is its awesome Army of Terracotta Warriors. Close to Luoyang to the east are the spectacular Longmen Caves and the legendary monastery of Shaolin.

Xi'an, southern **Shaanxi** (勉县) province and neighbouring **Henan** (河南) form the heartlands of early Chinese civilisation, germinated by the abundant waters of the **Huang He** (黄河; Yellow River), which nourished the soil and encouraged the seminal settlements to which the Han Chinese trace their roots. As such, the entire region is brimming with antiquities – some excavated but the vast majority still doubtless underground – putting it on a par with the richest archaeological zones of ancient Mesopotamia, Egypt and Greece.

The capital of the Zhou dynasty, dating from the 11th century BC, was situated close to present-day Xi'an. It was here, too, that the state of Qin was founded, the first to unify the land and from whose name the English word for China is believed to have derived. The Silk Road, linking China to Central Asia and Europe, began here, attracting other cultures whose religions and art changed China forever. And the Huang He's perennial volatility – frequently flooding and changing course – forced people to work in close cooperation.

Southern Shaanxi's brilliant past has bequeathed some truly spectacular sights. The dusty floodplains surrounding Xi'an are covered with imperial tombs, though none are as celebrated as that of Qin Shi Huangdi, with its underground Army of Terracotta

Warriors. Bolstering the ample archaeological attractions is a formidable crop of museums and historic temples, further illuminating the region's long history. And within easy reach of Xi'an are several other worthwhile destinations, including the venerated Buddhist temple of Famen Si, the revolutionary pilgrimage site of Yan'an and the sacred Daoist peaks of Hua Shan.

Far less famous than Shaanxi, Henan province to the east can nevertheless claim a history that rivals its neighbour in both scale and substance. Though

Main Attractions

Dayan Ta (Great Wild Goose Pagoda), Xi'an
Terracotta Warriors
Hua Shan
Yan'an
Longmen Caves
Song Shan
Kaifeng

Maps on pages 175, 189

An old street in Xi'an.

Night view of downtown Xi'an from Zhonglou (Bell Tower).

Xi'an has a large Hui Muslim population.

White Horse Temple near Luoyang, considered by many to be China's oldest Buddhist sanctuary. Some of the world's most revered Buddhist statuary is carved into the cliff-side caves of the Longmen Shiku near Luoyang.

XI'AN

Xi'an ⑬ (西安), capital of Shaanxi province, lies in the protected valley of the Wei River, some 160km (100 miles) west of its confluence with the Huang He. It was from this irrigated valley that the emperor Qin Shi Huangdi unified China for the first time. Xi'an, then known as Chang'an (Everlasting Peace), served as the capital for more than 1,100 years and 13 imperial dynasties. During the Tang years (618–907) it enjoyed unsurpassed prestige as the largest city in the world and the destination of thousands of foreign Silk Road traders. Following the demise of the Tang dynasty, Xi'an's importance began to fade.

now considered by many Chinese to be a rural backwater, for centuries Henan was the centre of the Chinese universe, its fertile plains sustaining a sizeable population and its cities serving a succession of dynastic capitals.

Religion flourished here, and the area was a major portal in the spread of Buddhism throughout China. As such, Henan has many of the country's oldest Buddhist sites, including the world-renowned Shaolin Temple – the original home of Chan (Zen) Buddhism and Shaolin boxing – and the

THE CITY CENTRE

While Xi'an's centre retains its Tang layout, it is largely overwhelmed by

⊘ TRANSPORT

Getting to Shaanxi

Flights: Xi'an's airport is near the town of Xianyang, about 40km (25 miles) northwest of the city centre. It is well connected, with regular flights from all major domestic destinations as well as a few international ones.

By train and bus: Xi'an's railway station is one of China's busiest, with frequent connections to most major cities, including express services to/from Beijing and Shanghai. There are bus links to cities in neighbouring provinces, but most tourists choose to arrive and depart by train.

Getting around Shaanxi

Xi'an: The tourist sites to the east and west of Xi'an make for good day trips on dedicated tourist buses. Private buses to Hua Shan (2 hours) leave throughout the day from in front of the train station. To Yan'an, buses (6 hours) run all day, while there are two overnight trains (8–10 hours) daily.

Hua Shan: There are daily bus and train connections to Xi'an as well as destinations to the east such as Pingyao and Taiyuan in Shanxi province and Henan province's Luoyang and Zhengzhou. **Yan'an:** Fast trains take less than 4 hours to Xi'an. There are daily buses (6 hours) and trains (8–10 hours) to Xi'an, as well as one daily bus each to Ningxia's Yinchuan (8 hours) and Taiyuan (3 hours) in Shanxi province. A couple of buses run each day to Yichuan (4 hours), the staging point for the Hukou Falls.

modern buildings and heavy traffic. The Tang city stretched over 9km (6 miles) from east to west and nearly 8km (5 miles) north to south. All roads in the town itself were laid out in a classic Chinese grid pattern, running straight north–south and east–west, meeting at right angles. While the layout remains today, the plan of the ancient city is not identical to the modern one. Although the walls built during the Tang dynasty no longer exist, 14km (9 miles) of the Ming wall still surrounds the centre, and much of its length has been restored. Visitors can buy a ticket to climb up onto the wall for a stroll or bicycle tour, and in places such as **Nanmen** (南门; South Gate), it is possible to climb on top of the 12 metre (40-ft) -thick ramparts. The moat outside the wall has also been reconstructed and integrated within a park.

In the heart of the city centre, where two main roads intersect, is the **Zhonglou A** (钟楼; Bell Tower; daily late Oct–Mar 8.30am–6pm, Apr–late Oct 8.30am–9.30pm). This renovated 36-metre (118ft) tower dating from

1384 was moved to its present site in 1582 and today is encircled by Xi'an's main shopping and commercial centre. East from Zhonglou runs Dong Dajie, with many shops and restaurants. Dong Dajie intersects with Jiefang Lu, which runs to the north and leads to the railway station.

A few minutes' walk to the northwest from Zhonglou is the not dissimilar **Gulou B** (鼓楼; Drum Tower; daily late Oct–Mar 8.30am–6pm, Apr–late Oct 8.30am–9.30pm), also dating from the 14th century – although rebuilt after 1949. More than 60,000 Hui Muslims live in Xi'an, and the Drum Tower highlights the Muslim quarter to the west. Lined with souvenir shops, alleys winding through the Hui neighbourhoods lead to **Qingzhen Dasi C** (清真大寺; Great Mosque; daily 8am–7.30pm), a Ming-dynasty structure that has been skilfully renovated several times. As with other Chinese mosques, its halls and inner

A lion statue outside the Xiaoyan Ta (Little Wild Goose Pagoda) in Xi'an. The irregularity on the upper section of the pagoda is the result of a 16th-century earthquake.

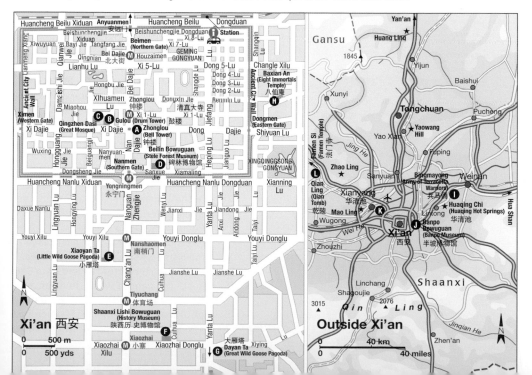

courtyards bear much architectural resemblance to those of a Chinese temple. The surrounding area is one of the most fascinating and diverse parts of Xi'an to explore on foot. Wander down an alley to get a sense of how the Hui live, or try one of the many food stalls selling dishes such as mutton-filled sesame rolls, or Xi'an's famous *yangrou paomo*, a concoction of mutton, noodles and flat bread cooked in a piping-hot broth.

Near **Nanmen** – the city wall's south gate – and in a former Confucian temple is the **Stele Forest Museum** Ⓓ (碑林博物馆; Beilin Bowuguan; daily May–early Oct 8am–6.45pm, rest of year until 6pm or 6.15pm), where 3,000 pieces of valuable stone tablets are preserved. There are exhibits in three main buildings. The first has a chronologically arranged exhibition of ancient Buddhist images from the early period of the Silk Road to the end of the Tang dynasty. The second, the museum's centrepiece, features a "forest" of stele, or around 1,100 stone tablets on which ancient Chinese classical texts – including those of Confucius and Mencius – are engraved.

Xi'an's impressive Xiaoyan Ta (Great Wild Goose Pagoda).

SOUTH OF THE CITY CENTRE

Outside the city walls and about 1km (0.6 mile) south of Nanmen, the 46-metre (151ft) **Xiaoyan Ta** Ⓔ (小雁塔; Little Wild Goose Pagoda; daily 9am–5pm) was built in the early 8th century. Severely damaged during an earthquake eight centuries later and repaired in the late 1970s, it was again damaged in the early 1990s. You can climb up for views over Xi'an.

About 2km (1.2 miles) to the southeast is one of the city's foremost attractions: the **Shaanxi History Museum** Ⓕ (陕西历史博物馆; Shaanxi Lishi Bowuguan; Tue–Sun mid-Nov–mid-Mar 9am–5.30pm, mid-Mar–mid-Nov 8.30am–6pm; free). The museum houses a collection of more than 370,000 historic artefacts displayed in chronological order and offering a clear oversight of the region's history, much of which is core Chinese history. Items range from tools and pottery from Palaeolithic and Neolithic times to bronze cooking vessels from the Shang and Zhou dynasties right on through to Ming- and Qing-dynasty ceramics. Pieces from the nearby Banpo ruins and a select group of terracotta soldiers and horses are also prominently displayed.

A further 1km (0.6 mile) to the southeast is the 64 metre (210-ft) -high, seven-storey **Dayan Ta** Ⓖ (大雁塔; Great Wild Goose Pagoda; daily 8am–5pm), anchoring the southern end of Yanta Lu. One of Xi'an's most recognisable structures, it was built in AD 652, at the beginning of the Tang dynasty, and was used to store Buddhist scriptures brought back to China in AD 645 by the eminent monk Xuan Zang. Xuan, whose adventures are recorded in the Chinese classic *Journey to the West*, had returned from a 15-year pilgrimage to India and spent his last two decades translating the Sanskrit *sutras* into Chinese. The pagoda was built as an add-on to the **Daci'en Si** (大慈恩寺; Temple of Grace; daily 8am–5pm), which had several hundred rooms when it was

established in AD 647 but now consists of only a handful of buildings.

Those planning to visit the sacred mountains of Hua Shan (see page 193) might warm up with a visit to the **Baxian An** 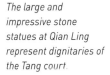 (八仙庵; Eight Immortals Temple; daily 8am–5pm), Xi'an's largest Daoist temple and home to more than 100 monks and nuns. Inside the main hall stands a statue of the Green Dragon (to whose left is the White Tiger); the wall behind is painted with scenes from Daoist legends.

OUTSIDE XI'AN: THE EASTERN TOUR

To the east of Xi'an lie several well-known attractions, some of which are routinely included in day tours organised by hotels and tour agencies. A highlight of any visit to China is Xi'an's most popular site: **the Army of Terracotta Warriors** ❶ (兵马俑; Bingmayong; daily mid-Mar–mid Nov 8.30am–6pm, mid-Nov–mid-Mar 8.30am–5.30pm). This vast treasure, vying with the Great Wall and Forbidden City as China's most famous

monument, lies 30km (20 miles) east of Xi'an and was stumbled upon in 1974 by peasants digging a well. For more on this unmissable sight, see page 202.

On the way back to Xi'an are the **Huaqing Hot Springs** (华清池; Huaqing Chi; daily Mar–Nov 7am–6pm, Dec–Feb 7.30am–6.30pm), in use for over 3,000 years and a favoured retreat for Tang-dynasty nobility. There are baths and pavilions in the park area. During the Tang dynasty, this is where the most famous concubine in China, Yang Guifei, bathed.

The **Banpo Museum** ❶ (半坡博物馆; Banpo Bowuguan; daily Mar–Nov 8am–6pm, Dec–Feb 8am–5.30pm), 10km (6 miles) east of Xi'an, is dedicated to the Neolithic settlement that has been partially excavated near here. Relics, including ceramics, weapons and even infant burial jars from the matriarchal Yangshao culture, are on display here.

THE WESTERN TOUR

Situated around 50km (30 miles) northwest of Xi'an, **Xianyang** ❶ (咸

The large and impressive stone statues at Qian Ling represent dignitaries of the Tang court.

A small section of the Terracotta Army at Bingmayong.

阳) was the capital during the reign of Qin Shi Huangdi, although few traces of the palaces said to have been built here are left. The nine display halls of the **Xianyang Museum** (咸阳博 物馆; Xianyang Bowuguan; Tue–Sun 9am–5.30pm), situated in a former Confucian temple, contains artefacts from the Warring States Period and the Qin and Han dynasties. There is also an impressive collection of 3,000 miniature terracotta horses and soldiers – each about 50cm (20ins) high – from the Han dynasty, and thus slightly newer than the more well-known Qin-dynasty Terracotta Warriors. Unlike many of those sculptures, some of the pieces at the Xianyang Museum have retained their painted-on colour over the years. Given that the admission to the Xianyang Museum is a fraction of the price of a ticket to the Terracotta Warriors, Xianyang is a possible alternative for budget travellers.

Further to the northwest is **Qian Ling** ❶ (乾陵; Qian Tomb; daily Mar–Nov 8am–6pm, Dec–Feb 8.30am–5.30pm), the joint burial place of the Tang emperor Gaozong and his wife, the empress Wu Zetian who succeeded him to the throne, becoming China's only female ruler in the process. The approach to the tomb – itself unopened – is guarded by a "spirit way" of large stone sculptures of animals and dignitaries. A group of 61 decapitated stone sculptures apparently represents foreign dignitaries. Peasants of the time are said to have knocked the sculptures' heads off during a famine, believing the "outsiders" were the cause of the food shortage.

Roughly 115km (70 miles) northwest of Xi'an, **Famen Si** (法门寺; Famen Temple; daily Mar–Nov 8.30am–7pm, Dec–Feb 9am–6pm) is a particularly sacred Buddhist site, for safeguarded there are the alleged remains of Buddha's finger bone – which would be the world's sole remainder of Buddha. In 1981, during restoration work on the crypt that held the Buddhist relics, more than 1,000 long-forgotten sacrificial objects were discovered, now displayed in a museum next to the temple.

The sacred peak of Hua Shan.

ELSEWHERE IN SHAANXI

Westernmost of China's five sacred Daoist peaks, **Hua Shan** ⑭ (华山; Flower Mountain; 2,160 metres/7,090ft) looms 120km (75 miles) east of Xi'an and is one of China's most dramatic holy mountain climbs. As well renowned for its steep ascents and plunging drops as it is for its Daoist mysteries, hiking here can be gruelling and, on occasion, hair-raising. Some sections of steps dissolve into incisions cut from the almost vertical rock faces, with only a chain to hold for support. Courageous wayfarers make nocturnal ascents with torches to arrive before dawn. For the less energetic, a cable car transports visitors to Bei Feng (North Peak), one of the four main summits. A trail along the Canglong Feng (Green Dragon Ridge) connects Bei Feng with Dong Feng (East Peak), Xi Feng (West Peak) and Hua Shan's highest point at Nan Feng (South Peak). If you are hiking, count on a minimum of two hours to reach Bei Feng via the steep path which winds underneath the cable car route. From Bei Feng, if you want to complete a circuit climbing the three other main peaks, factor in another six hours to do so comfortably. Spring and autumn are the best seasons.

A number of hotels operate in the village at the foot of the mountain, and a few basic guesthouses can be found on the mountain itself (useful if the weather worsens or you want to catch the sunrise).

YAN'AN

The time-warped town of **Yan'an** ⑮ (延安), 270km (170 miles) to the north of Xi'an in the arid loess hills of northern Shaanxi, functioned as the Communist Party headquarters in the 1930s and 1940s. It was here that Mao Zedong's epic Long March finally came to an end in October 1935. During the Cultural Revolution and through the 1970s, Yan'an was, and to some extent

remains, a national centre of pilgrimage, in the past as well known to Party officials as the Forbidden City in Beijing. It still attracts large numbers of patriotic domestic tourists.

The main attractions are the three former Communist Party headquarters' sites, each maintained as if the revolutionaries themselves were still living there.

Wangjiaping Revolutionary Headquarters (王家坪革命旧址 Wangjiaping Geming Jiuzhi; daily 8am–6pm) are simple restored barracks where

A reminder of the past in Yan'an.

The hills in and around Yan'an have been terraced and hollowed out for troglodyte houses.

⊘ Fact

Between Zhengzhou and Luoyang are numerous homes burrowed in cliffs of dry loess, which is yellowish and quite soft, and an ideal building material. Though dark inside, these cave houses are naturally warmer in winter and cooler in summer than free-standing houses.

Mao and his top brass lived at various times just a few minutes walk from the **Yan'an Revolutionary Museum** (延安革命纪念馆; Yan'an Geming Jinianguan; daily 8am–5.30pm), which houses more than 2,000 documents and objects from the "golden revolutionary era". There is also a stuffed horse – Mao's own trusted steed. The **Yangjialing Revolutionary Headquarters** (杨家岭革命旧址; Yangjialing Geming Jiuzhi; daily 8am–6pm; free) are 1.5km (1 mile) northwest, including the meeting hall where the first Central Committee meeting was held; banners of Marx, Engels, Lenin and Stalin still hang alongside those of Mao. **Fenghuang-shan Revolutionary Headquarters** (凤凰山革命旧址; daily 8am–6pm), 1km (0.6 mile) southwest and across the river from the museum, contains Mao's wooden bed, desk and latrine.

Perched on a hill in the southeast corner of town is **Bao Ta** (宝塔; daily 6am–8pm), a pagoda which can be climbed for unparalleled views of the town and the cave dwellings that pockmark the surrounding loess hillsides.

Tour groups queue at Longmen Shiku.

HENAN PROVINCE: LUOYANG AND AROUND

A five-hour train journey east of Xi'an, **Luoyang** ⑯ (洛阳) was one of China's greatest ancient capitals, serving as the seat of power for numerous dynasties dating back to the Zhou, who made it their main capital in 770 BC. The city thrived during the Eastern Han dynasty (AD 25–220), as well as the Tang (AD 618–907) and Song (AD 960–1279) periods, before its importance was gradually eclipsed by that of the increasingly prosperous coastal towns. Heavy industrialisation has taken its toll on the modern city, and within its current confines there is little to suggest its former glory. But the environs are covered with long-forgotten burial mounds, and not far outside the city are two of China's most important Buddhist shrines: the time-worn Baima Si and the exquisite rock carvings of the Longmen Shiku. Some visitors also use Luoyang as a base for day trips to nearby Song Shan and the Shaolin Si.

Within the city itself, the most impressive attraction is the **Luoyang**

Museum (洛阳博物馆; Luoyang Bowu-guan; Tue–Sun 9am–4.30pm; free), resembling a huge stone monolith south of the river on Nietai Lu. Opened in 2011, the museum stresses the importance of Luoyang as an ancient capital and boasts some of China's earliest ceremonial bronzeware as well as special collections of jadeware, ceramics and gold and silver artefacts.

Some 13km (8 miles) east of downtown Luoyang is the venerable **Baima Si** (白马寺; White Horse Temple; daily 8.30am–5.30pm), founded in AD 68 and considered China's first Buddhist temple. Now an active monastery, the name of the temple reflects the story of how its two founding monks – both Indians who were found in Afghanistan by special envoys dispatched by the Eastern Han emperor – brought saddlebags of Buddhist scriptures to China on the backs of white horses. The temple was built in the monks' honour, and they lived here and translated the *sutras* from Sanskrit into Chinese. Both monks are interred inside the complex.

THE LONGMEN CAVES

The awe-inspiring **Longmen Shiku** ⑰ (龙门石窟; Dragon Gate Grottoes; daily Feb–Mar and Oct 8am–6pm, Apr–Sept 8am–6.30pm, Nov–Jan 8am–5pm), a Unesco World Heritage Site, are situated 12km (8 miles) south of Luoyang along the banks of the Yi Jiang. An elaborate ensemble of Buddhist statuary in stone, the remarkably varied carvings stretch for about 1km (0.6 mile) on both sides of the Yi and encompass the artistic toil of three dynasties: the latter period of the Northern Wei, the Sui and the Tang. The Turkic Toba, devout Buddhists, first set chisel to stone in AD 493 after moving the capital of their Northern Wei dynasty from Datong to Luoyang. For the next several centuries, grottoes and niches were dug out and decorated with ornate figures and reliefs, most of them sponsored by noblemen of the period.

Martial arts training at Shaolin.

There are said to be more than 2,300 grottoes and niches containing over 40 pagodas, some 2,800 inscriptions and over 100,000 statues and images. Regrettably, many of the most intricate sculptures were stolen by collectors or beheaded around the start of the 20th century, and are now in museums in the West. Another round of destruction took place during the state-sanctioned vandalism of the Cultural Revolution, when finely carved faces were crudely bashed in.

⊘ TRANSPORT

Getting to Henan
Flights: Zhengzhou's Xinzheng Airport, 36km (23 miles) southeast of the city, is reasonably well connected to China's other provincial capitals. There are daily flights to Beijing, Guilin and Shanghai, with less frequent links to Hong Kong and Singapore. **By train and bus:** Straddling the north–south (Beijing–Guangzhou) line and the east–west (Shanghai–Xi'an) line, Zhengzhou is one of China's busiest rail junctions, with daily links to almost all major Chinese cities and tourist destinations – there are several trains each day to Beijing, Shanghai, Taiyuan, Wuhan and Xi'an. There are long-distance buses to cities in surrounding provinces, as well as to Beijing, but given the convenience of trains, these are less popular with tourists.

Getting around Henan
Zhengzhou: There are bullet trains daily to Anyang (1.5 hours), Kaifeng (30 minutes) and a fast train to Luoyang (1 hour 40 minutes). Buses run all day to Dengfeng (30 minutes) and the Shaolin Si (2 hours). **Kaifeng:** There are frequent trains to Zhengzhou (30 minutes or 1 hour) and Luoyang (2.5 hours). Buses leave all day for Anyang (3.5 hours), Luoyang (3 hours) and Zhengzhou (1 hour). **Dengfeng:** Regular buses to Luoyang (1.5 hours) and Zhengzhou (1.5 hours). **Luoyang:** Trains depart all day for Kaifeng (2.5 hours) and Zhengzhou (1 hour 40 minutes), while buses run to Dengfeng.

Shaolin is very popular with tour groups, and has become rather commercialised. Monks offer palm-readings and other fortune-telling services for a modest fee.

Fengxian Si at Longmen Shiku.

arts, **Shaolin Si** ⓲ (少林寺; Monastery of the Mount Shaoshi Forest; daily Mar–Nov 7.30am–6pm, Dec–Feb 8am–5.30pm) is one of China's most famous tourist attractions. Located about 80km (50 miles) southeast of Luoyang and the same distance southwest of Zhengzhou, the monastery can be visited on a day trip from either city, or explored at a more leisurely pace from the nearby town of **Dengfeng** (登封).

Shaolin was first built in the 5th century AD but has been burnt down several times over the ages. Tradition holds that the Indian monk Bodhidharma lived here with the blessing of the emperor and introduced Chan (Zen) Buddhism to the resident Chinese monks. Once a remote and romantic retreat where the wisdom of the ages passed from master to novice, it is now a major tourist area as well as a place of pilgrimage for monks and lay Buddhists alike. A training hall, where many foreign martial arts enthusiasts come to study, has been built next to the monastery. For the typical tourist, however, the highlight of a visit is simply watching the hundreds

The most arresting part of the complex is the **Fengxian Si** (奉先寺: Temple for Worshipping Ancestors), with an exposed 17-metre (56ft) central Buddha statue (complete with 2-metre/6ft ears) surrounded by Bodhisattvas and heavenly guards. Completed in 676 during the reign of the Tang emperor Gaozong, the statue's face is said to be that of his wife, empress Wu Zetian, a powerful Buddhist patron.

SHAOLIN SI

Known worldwide for its pivotal role in the development of Chinese martial

⊙ THE ART OF THE LONGMEN CAVES

As with the Yungang Caves in Shanxi province (see page 174), work on the Longmen Caves was undertaken by the (non-Chinese) Buddhist Tuoba who ruled north China under the Northern Wei dynasty (AD 386–534). When the capital of the Northern Wei was moved from Datong to Luoyang, the stone carvers continued their creations at Longmen. Successive dynasties such as the Sui and Tang added to the worshipful enterprise, with most of the work taking place between the 5th and 8th centuries.

As Buddhist art is carved from stone (rather than wood or metal), much has survived to the present day, despite the sad preponderance of vandalised, headless bodhisattvas. Some of the artwork was originally pigmented, but is now bleached by the elements, although flecks of paint survive on sheltered walls and ceilings.

The effigies number 100,000 in total and are in a variety of sizes: the largest of all measures 17 metres (56ft), the smallest just under 2cm (1 inch). They depict a wide range of Buddhist deities, with the most popular being Avalokiteshvara (Guanyin), and the Maitreya and Amitabha Buddhas, while other carvings depict parables from the life of Sakyamuni. As the carving took place over a long period, a noticeable shift exists from the otherworldly bodhisattvas of the Northern Wei to the more earthly Buddhas of the Tang dynasty.

of tracksuited, shaven-headed young students noisily running through their drills on the dusty fields near the monastery's entrance.

One of Shaolin's greatest treasures is the 18 *arhat* frescoes, painted in 1828, depicting monks in classic fighting poses that today's novices still emulate. In **Qianfo Dian** (千佛殿; Thousand Buddha Hall), the monastery's main hall, depressions in the stone floor serve as reminders of the tough combat exercises performed by the monks.

A short walk to the northwest of the monastery is **Talin** (塔林; Stupa Forest), an eerie resting place for expired monks comprising more than 240 brick-and-stone stupas, each containing the ashes of an accomplished monk. The oldest stupas are from the 9th century AD.

SONG SHAN AND AROUND

The several dozen mountain peaks stretching west from Shaolin Si comprise the holy range of **Song Shan** ⑲ (嵩山), forming the central axis of Daoism's five sacred mountains, as well as being sacred to Buddhists. Nestled in the hills surrounding Dengfeng – a town in the heart of the mountains, about 13km (8 miles) east of Shaolin – are some fascinating historic sights. The **Songyang Shuyuan** (嵩阳书院; Songyang Academy; daily 8am–6.30pm, until 6pm in winter), 3km (2 miles) north of Dengfeng, is one of China's four most influential ancient academies. Originally built in AD 484, during the Northern Wei dynasty, it was completely rebuilt in AD 1035. Among the highlights of the grounds are an enormous Tang-dynasty tablet carved in AD 744 and two giant cypress trees said to date back to 110 BC.

To the northwest of the academy, 3km (2 miles) by road, is the **Songyuesi Ta** (嵩岳寺塔; Songyue Temple Pagoda; daily 8am–6pm), originally constructed in AD 509 and considered China's oldest brick pagoda. About 2km (1.2 miles) before you reach the pagoda is the entrance to the **Taishi Shan Scenic Area** (太室山風景区; Taishi Shan Fengjing Qu; daily 8am–6pm).

To the southeast of Dengfeng, near the town of Gaocheng, is the **Guanxing**

The 13th-century Guanxing Tai observatory near Dengfeng was used to calculate the timing of solstices and other astronomical events.

Longmen Shiku (the Longmen Caves) near Luoyang.

SHAOLIN

Home of the martial arts, Shaolin is now cashing in by opening a commercial centre for training in its esoteric disciplines.

The Shaolin Temple, in the Song Shan range near Luoyang, is the home of most East Asian martial arts. Be it *gongfu*, karate, taekwondo or judo, all are considered to have originated from ancient Chinese fighting techniques.

The origins of Shaolin's martial arts tradition are said to date back to the AD 527 visit of the Indian monk Bodhidharma (Damo). He realised that many of the Buddhist monks were unable to keep up demanding meditation exercises in complete quiet and concentration. Based upon observations of the movements of animals, the monk reputedly developed an exercise he described as a physical training method, which in turn became part of Shaolin boxing *(shaolinquan)*.

Wushu – the art of fighting – is the modern term for Chinese martial arts, whether involving weapons or empty-handed. The mastery of the various techniques once entailed very esoteric knowledge, which would only be passed on within a family or a monastery, or

Shaolin trainees.

from master to pupil. These days, students can enrol in Shaolin Temple-endorsed schools without even stepping foot into China.

For an outsider, the variety of *wushu* styles is rather confusing. Sounding like a recipe for disaster, *zuiquan* (drunken boxing) imitates the stumbling gait and "soft" pliancy of a drunkard. Actually a brilliantly creative and deceptive boxing form, it can be highly effective. *Xingyiquan* (body mind boxing) aims to capture the fighting spirit of 12 animals, while also relying heavily on the use of *qi* energy. *Wuzuquan*, or five ancestors boxing, is a powerful Buddhist fighting art that relies heavily on breathing techniques and the cultivation of power through relaxation.

Taijiquan (tai chi) is a gentler method that aims to repel the opponent without the use of force, and with minimal effort. It is based on the Daoist idea that the principle of softness will ultimately overcome hardness. According to legend, it is also – just like Shaolin boxing – derived from the movements of animals, geared to breaking the momentum of an opponent's attack and letting it disappear into thin air. Originally a method of self-defence, in today's China it is mostly practised by older people for meditation and body-strengthening.

Like *xingyiquan*, *taijiquan* depends on the mastery and application of the life energy *qi*, which can be directed to all parts of the body with the help of mental training. *Qi* must flow and circulate freely in the body. The round movements of *taijiquan* are derived from this – they can be firm or loose, hard or soft, be directed forwards or backwards, but the movement must always be smooth and flowing. Through consistent practice of *taijiquan*, one eventually comes very close to the ideal of Daoism, namely *wuwei* – doing without a purpose.

In a wider sense, *qigong* (breathing technique) is also part of *wushu* and dates back 3,000 years. In *qigong*, techniques for regulating the breathing can bring about concentrated thinking and a state of inner calm.

The public face of the Shaolin Temple since he became abbot in 1999, Shi Yongxin is one of China's most controversial public figures. Dubbed the "CEO monk" he has taken the Shaolin brand worldwide and increased its profitability enormously in the process. His detractors claim he has turned a venerable tradition into little more than a sideshow.

Tai (观星台; Star Observation Platform; daily 8am–5.30pm), an intriguing astronomical observatory which tourism officials claim is the oldest still standing in China. Built in 1276, it was at the centre of a network of 27 such Yuan-dynasty observatories.

One of the Dengfeng area's most impressive attractions is the **Zhongyue Miao** (中岳庙; Central Mountain Monastery; daily 8am–6pm), a spacious Daoist monastery about 2km (1.2 miles) east of the city and accessible by green public bus no. 2. The extensive walled complex, originally founded around 220 BC but having undergone a complete restoration during the Ming dynasty, is an active monastery inhabited by a sizeable population of monks. The sprawling courtyards are filled with ancient cypresses and magnificently carved stelae, exposed to the elements and covered in moss.

ZHENGZHOU

The lively city of **Zhengzhou** ⑳ (郑州), about 80km (50 miles) east of Dengfeng and 20km (13 miles) south of the

Huang He, is the capital of Henan province and an important railway junction straddling the crossroads of China's main east–west (Shanghai–Xi'an) and north–south (Beijing–Guangzhou) lines. There was a fortified settlement here as early as the Shang dynasty, some 3,500 years ago, but all that remains of that period are the high, packed-earth foundations of the **Shang-era walls** located in the southeast of the modern city. Locals of all ages climb to the top for a variety of recreational activities, making it an ideal place to observe daily life.

Another excellent place to people-watch is the **Kong Miao** (孔庙; Confucius Temple; 24 Dong Dajie; daily 8.30am–5pm; free), comprising several halls including the Hall of Great Achievements (Dacheng) decorated with glazed tiles depicting tales from the Three Kingdoms period.

One block further north, at 2 Shangcheng Lu, is the **Chenghuang Miao** (城隍庙; City God Temple; daily 9am–5pm; free), the most intact ancient building in the downtown area. Founded more than

An ancient statue of Confucius at Zhengzhou's Kong Miao (Confucius Temple).

Shaolin's eerie "Stupa Forest" (Talin).

Ⓞ Eat

One of Kaifeng's main attractions – and its unquestionable culinary highlight – is the vibrant **night market** (开封夜市; Kaifeng Yeshi), one of China's biggest. Sprawling from the corner of Gulou and Madao streets, hundreds of mostly Hui Muslim vendors dole out kebabs and noodles; try the *xingren cha* (杏仁茶), a jelly-like porridge sweetened with powdered almonds and a host of berries.

Smile for the camera.

600 years ago, during the Ming dynasty, its buildings have undergone a restoration and the walls of the main hall are adorned with murals depicting the city gods of China's biggest urban centres.

Zhengzhou's most educational attraction is the cavernous **Henan Provincial Museum** (河南省博物馆; Henan Sheng Bowuguan; http://english. chnmus.net; Tue–Sun 9am–5pm), which features three floors of well-presented historic artefacts unearthed in the province – those on display are only a small percentage of the museum's total collection, a testament to Henan's archaeological wealth.

KAIFENG

An hour's bus ride east of Zhengzhou, **Kaifeng** ㉑ (开封) is one of China's most enduring ancient capitals, retaining enough historic sites to hint at its former glory yet largely resisting the indiscriminate modern development that now dominates most of its contemporaries. Although a settlement existed here during the Shang dynasty, dating as far back as 1000 BC, it was not until 364 BC that one of the Warring States declared it as a regional capital. Kaifeng served as a capital for six more dynasties, reaching its pinnacle in the Northern Song (AD 960–1127), when it was believed to be one of the world's biggest cities. Little remains of the great Song capital, however. Due to its proximity to the temperamental Huang He, Kaifeng has been devastated by floods dozens of times, and almost everything from that era is buried under several metres of silt.

Still, most of the pounded-earth city wall survives, giving the ancient centre a quaint, compact feel. In Kaifeng's far northeast corner, just inside the city wall, is one of its only Song-period relics: the **Tie Ta** (铁塔; Iron Pagoda; daily 8am–5.30pm), a 13-storey, 56-metre (184ft) brick structure soaring prominently in the middle of **Tie Ta Gongyuan** (铁塔公园; Iron Pagoda Park; daily 7am–7pm). Built in AD 1049, the octagonal tower gets its name from the dark-brown glazed tiles that adorn its exterior, which from a distance looks like cast

Ⓞ KAIFENG'S JEWS

Small enclaves of Jewish people are believed to have settled in northwest China as early as the Han dynasty (206 BC–AD 220), but those who migrated from Central Asia to Kaifeng during the Northern Song dynasty (960–1127) are widely considered the progenitors of China's longest-running Jewish identity. Only a few Kaifeng families still trace their lineage back to Jews and, on a cultural level, these claims are complicated by the fact that Chinese descent is patrilineal, something adopted by Chinese Jews, while traditional Jewish heritage is matrilineal. But while the cultural debate continues, there is little disputing that the city had a notable Jewish presence at one time – a synagogue stood near the town centre until the late 19th century.

iron. Visitors can climb to the top via a narrow, winding stone staircase.

Kaifeng's oldest standing structure is the **Fan Ta** (繁塔; Fan Pagoda; daily 8.30am–5.30pm), three storeys high and decorated with numerous carved Buddha figures in niches. Originally called the **Po Ta**, it is located outside the town wall to the southeast of the railway station.

In the city centre is the **Daxiangguo Si** (大相国寺; Prime Minister's Monastery; Ziyou Lu; daily 8am–6.30pm), first built in AD 555 and for centuries an important Buddhist centre. The main draw is a magnificent gold-leaf coated statue of a bodhisattva boasting a thousand arms. Most of the present buildings date back to 1766. The unassuming **Yanqing Guan** (延庆观; Yanqing Temple; 53 Guanqian Jie; daily 8.30am–6.30pm) is a Daoist sanctuary with only two halls; the first, the Jade Emperor Pavilion, is notable for its undecorated, high-domed ceiling. Also worth a visit is the **Shanshangan Huiguan** (陕山甘会馆; Shanshangan Guild Hall; 85 Xufu Jie; daily 8am–6pm), an extravagantly decorated Qing-dynasty compound built by an association of merchants from Shanxi, Shaanxi and Gansu provinces to serve as a lodging and networking centre for visiting traders.

ANYANG

About 200km (125 miles) northeast of Zhengzhou, near the Hebei border, is the town of **Anyang** ㉒ (安阳), which marks the location of Yin – the ancient Shang-dynasty (1700–1100 BC) capital. Referred to in ancient Chinese annals, Yin was long forgotten until excavations in the 20th century yielded evidence of the vanished city. Visitors can see the remains of the settlement at the **Yin Ruins Museum** (殷墟博物院; Yinxu Bowuguan; daily Mar–Oct 8am–6.30pm, Oct–Mar 8am–6pm), which has an excellent display of oracle bones unearthed at the site. The bones, mostly tortoise belly shells and ox shoulder

blades, bear the primitive inscriptions upon which the Chinese writing system is based. There is also a new annex housing the intact remains of six chariots – complete with attached horse skeletons – excavated from nearby tombs.

In Anyang's old town is the curious **Wenfeng Ta** (文峰塔; Wenfeng Pagoda; daily 8am–5pm), which – unlike most pagodas – is narrower at the base and gets wider towards the top. The tight squeeze up steep stone steps to the roof is worth it for the city views.

A relic from a more recent era, the **Hongqi Yunhe** (红旗运河; Red Flag Canal) draws visitors to **Linzhou** (林洲), 70km (45 miles) west of Anyang in the Taihuang Mountains. The canal, a testament to the ideological single-mindedness of the period, was engineered by hand during the Cultural Revolution.

Tie Ta (Iron Pagoda) at Kaifeng.

An offshoot of the Grand Canal in Anhui province.

📷 THE TERRACOTTA WARRIORS

Vying with the Great Wall for the title of China's most famous historical sight, this amazing ancient army was only discovered in the 1970s.

Located some 30km (20 miles) to the east of Xi'an, this singularly spectacular sight is just part of a grand mausoleum built by the emperor Qin Shi Huangdi in the 3rd century BC. Although the place is packed with tour groups of every nationality on any given day, and battalions of hawkers vie for your attention outside, it is well worth the effort to persevere through the crowds and linger awhile to admire the magnificent displays. Note that the signs prohibiting flash photography are routinely ignored by everyone, including the staff.

The site comprises three large vaults which have been surmounted with hangar-like structures: between them they house well over 8,000 terracotta warriors and regular new finds add to the total. The main vault contains over a thousand figures, which can be viewed at close quarters from raised walk-ways, while at the rear lie the forlorn fragments of toppled and headless soldiers. The second and third vaults are smaller in size but the figures they contain feature a wider variety of poses. A spectacular pair of half-sized chariots, complete with terracotta horses, are on display in the small museum by the main entrance. This was discovered in 1980 and is similar to carriages used by Qin Shi Huangdi.

Most people will get more out of their visit by taking a guided tour or hiring an audio guide (both are available in English). There is also an informative film that screens in the on-site theatre.

In the main vault, the figures are arranged in typical battle formation with 11 columns comprised of officers, soldiers holding spears and swords (many of them authentic weapons), and others steering horse-drawn chariots. The soldiers are wearing long battle tunics: a few small traces of pigment indicate that the terracotta army was once painted in shades of green, yellow and purple.

Each soldier's head has been individually modelled with unique facial expressions.

Each figure is about 1.8 metres (5ft 10 inches) tall.

The Great Necropolis

Excavation work at the Bingmayong site has continued since its original discovery in 1974. According to historic surveys, a splendid necropolis depicting the whole of China in miniature is centred underneath Qin Shi Huangdi's tomb, its ceiling purportedly studded with pearls depicting the night sky. It is thought that mercury may have been pumped in mechanically to create images of flowing rivers (trial digs have revealed a high mercury content in the soil). The entire complex may cover an area of up to 56 sq km (22 sq miles), but in order to excavate fully, 12 villages and half a dozen factories in the area would have to be relocated.

Qin Shi Huangdi, China's first great emperor and unifier of the country in 221 BC.

Emperor Qin Shi Huangdi, ruler from 247 to 210 BC and the man to whom this extraordinary site owes its existence, bears all the hallmarks of a ruthless megalomaniac. Not only did he surround his tomb with thousands of life-sized statues of his personal army – a project that involved seven hundred thousand workers over 36 years – he is also thought to have buried alive thousands of Confucian scholars. It is possible that the emperor was so superstitious and fearful that he had the necropolis built as a decoy and is, in fact, buried somewhere else.

Not all of the warriors have been restored.

The area surrounding this premium tourist site is crowded with souvenir stalls. Some (particularly within the site itself) are of reasonable quality, but beware pushy vendors – as well as overpriced food stalls.

The discovery of the terracotta warriors has done wonders for the regional economy. Huge numbers of tourists visit each year and the souvenir industry is a significant local employer. Ongoing excavations continue to reveal more buried warriors.

ANCIENT TREASURES FROM THE ROYAL TOMBS

The royal tombs of ancient China offer a fascinating glimpse of the life, wealth and beliefs of the early emperors and rulers.

Almost all our knowledge of ancient China comes from the artefacts found in the tombs of princes and warriors. As early as 3000 BC, neolithic caves were elaborately carved and filled, but it was during the ascendancy of the Shang kings, around 1200 BC, that they were the most dazzling. The dynasty had capitals at Anyang and Zhengzhou, and nothing was spared in the attempt to help Shang royalty reach the afterlife. Sacrifices were on an epic scale. Some 700,000 people laboured to build the tomb of the first emperor, and many of those who worked on the tomb were killed. Others simply died in the process. Courtiers and concubines were slaughtered in the death chambers, and both horses and charioteers perished in order to accompany their master (or mistress) into the underworld. Bureaucrats devoted their careers to overseeing the inventories of the tombs, which they prepared in great detail to present to the officials of the underworld, including deeds to prove the deceased owned the land he or she had been buried on.

The Shang tombs were constructed during the Bronze Age, and have yielded some remarkable bronze items, many of them showing vivid imagination and skill. Perhaps the most dramatic attire of the deceased was the jade suit. The mineral is very hard and could not be carved – but had to be worn down to make the small rectangular squares that were then linked by gold or silver thread to fit the body. Jade suits were used from around 140 BC to AD 220; around 40 have so far been discovered.

This bird-shaped, bronze wine vessel dates from the 12th century BC.

The Elephant Zun, a Shang-dynasty (13th-century BC) container for storing wine, on display at the Shanghai Museum.

A vessel for food offerings, from the tomb of Lady Fu Hao, a warrior queen of around 1200 BC. Her tomb near Anyang contained 250 ritual bronzes.

Mystery figure of Sanxingdui

This life-size figure was discovered when two huge ancient burial pits were accidentally stumbled upon in Guanghan, Sichuan province, in 1986. Barefoot and dressed in robes, it has massive hands that seem to be designed to hold something. It may represent a king or a priest, but there is no clue as to its identity.

The find dates from the 12th century BC and it caused historians to re-think the way Chinese civilisation began. Up until the discovery, it was widely held that only the middle Huang He (Yellow River) valley supported civilisation at that time. The pits, known as the Sanxingdui site, also contained a treasure trove of charred elephants' tusks, bronzes, and jade blades unknown elsewhere, but no human remains. Fifteen years later, another site containing similar artefacts was discovered at Jinsha, only 50km (31 miles) away from Sanxingdui. Historians are still trying to decipher more about these ancient and little-known cultures, known as the Ba and Shu.

The mystery figure of Sanxindui.

The jade funeral suit of princess Tou Wan from the Western Han dynasty (2nd century BC).

A ritual object featuring two bulls and a tiger.

One of a number of bronze heads covered with gold foil found at Sanxindui, from around 1200 BC. All the facial features are emphasised.

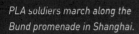
PLA soldiers march along the Bund promenade in Shanghai.

THE CENTRE

Linked by the mighty Chang Jiang (Yangzi River), China's green and densely populated heartlands are full of interest.

Hangzhou's West Lake.

The fertile land of central China, particularly the area around the eastern seaboard – "the land of rice and fish" – has long been the most prosperous and productive part of the country. Plentiful rainfall and mild winters make ideal conditions for rice cultivation, a labour intensive form of agriculture that has made the region home to the highest rural population densities in the world. Many of the important events that have shaped modern China over the past 200 years have taken place here.

The great commercial centre of Shanghai, China's largest city, is its cornerstone for the 21st century: a glittering, high-rise, wealth-generating metropolis which is attracting migrant workers, entrepreneurs and business leaders from across China and the world. With China's best hotels, nightlife and shopping, some excellent museums, historic sights aplenty and a mesmerising skyline, it has a lot to offer tourists too.

Close to Shanghai is the Grand Canal, the ancient conduit that linked north and south China, with picturesque cities and towns – Suzhou and Wuxi, among others – along its banks. Nanjing, upriver along the Chang Jiang, is a gracious, green city with deep layers of history. To the south, Hangzhou was once one of China's most important urban centres, marking as it did the southern terminus of the Grand Canal. The city's West Lake is considered by many Chinese to be the most beautiful place in the country.

The iconic Pearl Oriental TV Tower, Shanghai.

Far off to the west, the Chang Jiang (Yangzi) surges through Chongqing, another boom town, from where cruise boats and ferries depart regularly for the famous Three Gorges – still awe-inspiring despite the effects of the gigantic, and now completed, Three Gorges Dam. Boats continue downstream to the city of Yichang, with a few journeying onwards to Wuhan, capital of Hubei province. Both are within reach of scenic gems, including Shennongjia Forest Reserve and Huang Shan – in Anhui province – one of China's most idyllic mountains.

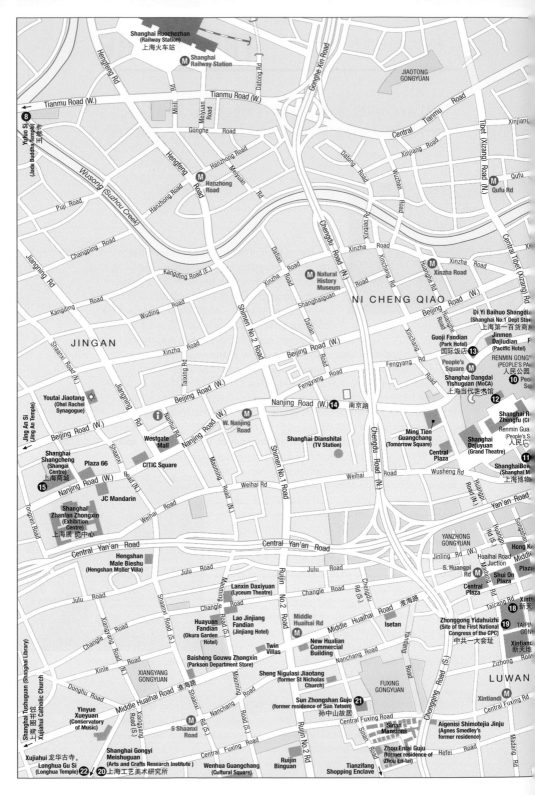

Shanghai Huochezhan
(Railway Station)
上海火车站

M Shanghai
Railway Station

JIAOTONG
GONGYUAN

Hengfeng Rd

Datong Rd

Gonghe Xin Road

Tibet (Xizang) Road (N.)

Central Tibet (Xizang)

Tianmu Road (W.)

Tianmu Road (W.)

Central Tianmu Road

Xinjiang

8 Yufo Si
(Jade Buddha Temple)
玉佛寺

Minli

Meiyuan Road

Gonghe Road

Xinjiang Road

Wuzhen Road

Qufu

M Qufu Rd

Hengfeng Road

Hanzhong Road

Meiyuan Rd

M Hanzhong Road

Datong Road

Perbury Road

Wusong (Suzhou Creek)

Puji Road

Hanzhong Road

Xinchang Rd

Chengdu Road (N.)

Changping Road

Kangding Road (E.)

Dalian Road

Xinzha Road

Xinchang Rd

Huangpi Road (N.)

Xinzha

M Xinzha Road

Jiangning Rd

Wuding Road

Dalian

Xinzha

Shanghaiguan

M Natural
History
Museum

NI CHENG QIAO

Beijing Road (W.)

Huangpi

Di Yi Baihuo Shangdia
(Shanghai No.1 Dept Stor
上海第一百货商

JINGAN

Kangding

Shaanxi Road (N.)

Taixing Rd

Xinzha Rd

Beijing Road (W.)

Fengyang Road

Fengyang Road

Xinchang Rd

Guoji Fandian
(Park Hotel)
国际饭店 13

Jinmen
Dajiudian
(Pacific Hotel)

RENMIN GONG
(PEOPLE'S PA
人民公园

People's
Square M

10 Peo
Sq

Jing An Si (Jing An Temple)

Youtai Jiaotang
(Ohel Rachel
Synagogue)

Beijing Road (W.)

Jiangning Road

Nanjing Road (W.) 14 南京路

Nanmu Rd

Chengdu Road (N.)

Shanghai Dangdai
Yishuguan (MoCA)
上海当代艺术馆

12

Shanghai R
Zhengfu (Ci

i

M W. Nanjing
Road

Shanghai Dianshitai
(TV Station)

Ming Tien
Guangchang
(Tomorrow Square)

Renmin Gua
(People's S
人民

11

Westgate
Mall

CITIC Square

Maoming Road (N.)

Shimen No.1 Road

Central
Plaza

Shanghai
Dajuyuan
(Grand Theatre)

Shanghai
Shangcheng
(Shangai
Centre)
上海商城 15

Plaza 66

Shaanxi Road (N.)

Nanjing Road (W.)

Weihai Rd

Weihai Road

Wusheng Rd

ShanghaiBow
(Shanghi M
上海博物

Huangpi Road (N.)

Yan'an Road

Songshan Rd

JC Mandarin

Shanghai
Zhanlan Zhongxin
(Exhibition
Centre)
上海展览中心

Tongren Road

Central Yan'an Road

Central Yan'an Road

YANZHONG
GONGYUAN

Jinling Rd

Huaihai Road
Juction

Hong K

S. Huangpi
Rd

Maoming Rd

Middle

Shui On
Plaza

Hengshan
Male Bieshu
(Hengshan Moller Villa)

Julu Road

Julu Road

Rujin Road

Julu Road

Changle Road

Chengdu Rd (S.)

Central
Plaza

Lanxin Daxiyuan
(Lyceum Theatre)

Xintia
新天

18

Julu Road

Shaanxi Road (S.)

Changle Road

Maoming Road (S.)

Changle Road

Middle Huaihai Road 淮海路

Taicang Rd

Huayuan
Fandian
(Okura Garden
Hotel)

Lao Jinjiang
Fandian
(Jinjiang Hotel)

Middle
Huaihai Rd

M

Isetan

Zhonggong Yidahuizhi
(Site of the First National
Congress of the CPC)
中共一大会址

19

TAIPIN
GON

Xiangyang Road (N.)

Baisheng Gouwu Zhongxin
(Parkson Department Store)

Twin
Villas

New Hualian
Commercial
Building

Nanchang Road

Yandang

Xintianc
新天t

Xinle

Xiangyang Road (S.)

Shaanxi Road (S.)

Nanchang Road

XIANGYANG
GONGYUAN

Donghu Road

Sheng Nigulasi Jiaotang
(former St Nicholas
Church)

FUXING
GONGYUAN

Chongqing Road (S.)

Zizhong

Road

LUWAN

Xintiandi M

Shanghai Tushuguan (Shanghai Library)
上海图书馆

Xujiahui Catholic Church

Yinyue
Xueyuan
(Conservatory
of Music)

Maoming Road (S.)

S Shaanxi
Road

M

Sun Zhongshan Guju
(former residence of Sun Yatsen)
孙中山故居

21

Sinan
Mansions

Central Fuxing Road

Aigenisi Shimotejia Jinju
(Agnes Smedley's
former residence)

Ruijin No.2 Rd

Madang Rd

Hefei

Xujiahui 龙华古寺,
Longhua Gu Si
(Longhua Temple) 22

Shanghai Gongyi
Meishuguan
(Arts and Crafts Research Institute)
上海工艺美术研究所 20

Wenhua Guangchang
(Cultural Square)

Ruijin
Binguan

Central Fuxing Road

Zhou Enlai Guju
(former residence of
Zhou En-lai)

Tianzifang
Shopping Enclave

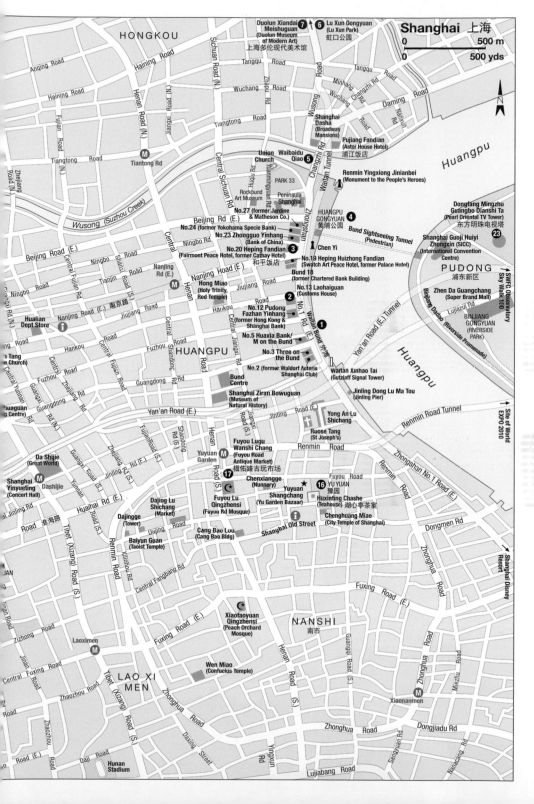

HONGKOU

Duolun Xiandai Meishuguan
(Duolun Museum of Modern Art)
上海多伦现代美术馆 **7**

6 Lu Xun Gongyuan
(Lu Xun Park)
虹口公园

Shanghai 上海

0 — 500 m
0 — 500 yds

N

Anqing Road

Haining Road

Haining Road

Sichuan Road (N.)

Tanggu Road

Tanggu Rd

Minhang Rd

Changzhi Rd

Daming Road

Nanxun Rd

Fujian Road (N.)

Zhapu Road

Wuchang Road

Wuchang Road

Huangpu

Henan Road (N.)

Tiantong Road

Tiantong Road

Zhejiang Road (N.)

Tiantong Rd M

Tiangtong Road

Central Sichuan Road

Wusong Road

Changzhi Rd

Shanghai Dasha
(Broadway Mansions)

Pujiang Fandian
(Astor House Hotel)
浦江饭店

Union Church

Waibaidu Qiao **5**

Wusong (Suzhou Creek)

Central

Beijing Rd (E.)

Rockbund Art Museum

PARK 33

Peninsula Shanghai

No.27 (former Jardine & Matheson Co.)

Renmin Yingxiong Jinianbei
(Monument to the People's Heroes)

Dongfang Mingzhu Guangbo Dianshi Ta
(Pearl Oriental TV Tower)
东方明珠电视塔

Beijing Road (E.)

Ningbo Rd (E.)

Central Fujian Rd

Shanxi Road

Henan Road

Beijing Road (E.)

Ningbo Road

No.24 (former Yokohama Specie Bank)
No.23 Zhongguo Yinhang
(Bank of China)
No.20 Heping Fandian
(Fairmont Peace Hotel, former Cathay Hotel)
和平饭店

3

HUANGPU GONGYUAN
黄浦公园 **4**

Chen Yi

No.19 Heping Huizhong Fandian
(Swatch Art Peace Hotel, former Palace Hotel)

Bund Sightseeing Tunnel
(Pedestrian)

PUDONG
浦东新区

Shanghai Guoji Huiyi Zhongxin (SICC)
(International Convention Centre)
23

Nanjing Road 南京路

Nanjing Rd (E.)

Tianjin Rd

Hankou Road

Jiujiang Road

Hong Miao
(Holy Trinity, Red Temple)

Bund 18
(former Chartered Bank Building)

No.13 Laohaiguan
(Customs House)

Zhen Da Guangchang
(Super Brand Mall)

SWFC Observatory Sky Walk 100

Hualian Dept Store

Nanjing Road (E.)

Jiujiang Road

Hankou

2

No.12 Pudong Fazhan Yinhang
(former Hong Kong & Shanghai Bank)

No.5 Huaxia Bank/ M on the Bund

No.3 Three on the Bund

HUANGPU

Fuzhou Road

Guangdong Rd

No.2 (former Waldorf Astoria Shanghai Club)

1

Yan'an Road (E.) Tunnel

Binjiang Dadao (Riverside Promenade)

Lujiazui Rd

Lujiazui Rd

BINJIANG GONGYUAN
(RIVERSIDE PARK)

Huangpu

Fuzhou Rd

Guangdong Road

Yan'an Road (E.)

Bund Centre

Shanghai Ziran Bowuguan
(Museum of Natural History)

Wartan Xinhao Tai
(Gutzlaff Signal Tower)

Jinling Dong Lu Ma Tou
(Jinling Pier)

Renmin Road Tunnel

Site of World EXPO 2010

Jinting Road (E.)

Yan'an Road (E.)

Yong An Lu Shichang

Ruose Tang
(St Joseph's)

Renmin Road

Zhongshan No.1 Road (E.)

Zhongshan No.1 Road (E.)

Da Shijie
(Great World)

Shanghai Yinyueting
(Concert Hall)

Dashijie M

Fuyou Lugu Wanshi Chang
(Fuyou Road Antique Market)
褔佑路古玩市场

Yuyuan Garden M

17

Chenxianggge
(Nunnery)

Fuyou Road

Dajingge
(Tower)

Dajing Lu Shichang
(Market)

Fuyou Lu Qingzhensi
(Fuyou Rd Mosque)

Yuyuan Shangchang
(Yu Garden Bazaar)

★

16 YU YUAN
豫园

Huxinting Chashe
(Teahouse) 湖心亭茶室

Dongmen Rd

Baiyun Guan
(Taoist Temple)

Dajing Road

Cang Bao Lou
(Cang Bao Bldg)

Chenghuang Miao
(City Temple of Shanghai)

Shanghai Old Street

Zhonghua Rd

Shanghai Disney Resort

Huaihai Rd (S.)

Tibet (Xizang) Road (S.)

Xinbu Rd

Central Fangbang Road (S.)

Fuxing Road (E.)

Zhonghua Road

Laoximen M

Xiaofaoyuan Qingzhensi
(Peach Orchard Mosque)

NANSHI
南市

Fuxing Road (E.)

Henan Road (S.)

Wen Miao
(Confucius Temple)

Guangqi Road (S.)

LAO XI MEN

Zhonghua Road

Daxing Street

Xiaonanmen M

Zhaozhou Rd

Mizhu Rd

Zizhong Road

Jinan Road

Central Fuxing Road

Zhaozhou Road

Zhonghua Road

Yingxun Rd

Dongjiadu Rd

Hunan Stadium

Daji Road

Lujiabang Road

Zhonghua Road

Sanyuan Rd

Nanmacang Rd

The Shanghai World Financial Centre (left) and Jin Mao Tower, currently the 9th- and 21st-tallest buildings in the world.

SHANGHAI

Eyed with envy by the rest of China, the rising star of stylish Shanghai – Paris of the East back in the glitzy colonial days – seems set to put even Hong Kong in the shade.

In all of China, in all the world really, there is no other city like **Shanghai** (上海). This huge, sprawling beast of a metropolis has risen from the mud and silt of the Yangzi Delta, pushed aside its rivals and emerged as one of the liveliest and most exciting cities on the planet.

Shanghai has a reputation as a money-mad place, headlong and greedy in its single-minded pursuit of wealth, caring for nothing but the almighty red-backed Rmb. But this is only partly true; the dollar, the euro, and the yen are equally beloved, as are all the other foreign currencies that have driven the city's get-rich-quick mentality.

For better or for worse, modern Shanghai derives most of its energy from the ceaseless flow of money that swirls around the city, luring investment and talent from around the globe. Each year, more than US$20 billion in foreign cash flows into the city, where it is injected into the metropolis like a super-steroid, swelling the skyline with cutting-edge skyscrapers and modern mega-malls that sprout like bamboo shoots after a spring rain. Swirled together, these ingredients – the cash, the business zeal and the influx of people – have created a new world "fusion city" that is unequalled by anything else in China – or Asia.

At street level too, Shanghai pushes the envelope of the possible. Every week another new nightclub pops into existence, hipper than its month-old rivals. On the restaurant scene, it's the same: no celebrity chef can be without a Shanghai flagship, while the siren song of modern Shanghai pulls in the deep-pocketed financiers, entrepreneurs, superstar designers and large numbers of lower-ranking foreigners who make up the supporting cast.

It also, of course, attracts migrants from all over China. Labourers from the provinces are busy building the city, while earnest college students, young

Main Attractions

The Bund
Nanjing Road
People's Park
Shanghai Museum
Yu Garden and Bazaar
Former French
   Concession
Shanghai Disney Resort

Map on page 210

Commuting to work.

⊙ Tip

In 2003, as part of Shanghai's bold new plan to be an international city, the Chinese (pinyin) word for street, "Lu", was replaced with the English "Road". What was previously called Nanjing Dong Lu, for example, is now Nanjing Road (East). The Chinese characters remain unchanged.

professionals and managers-on-the-go arrive from provincial capitals, adding their own unique brand of ambition to the ever-throbbing, ever-changing metropolis.

BRAVE NEW WORLD

Meanwhile, the city government – which enjoys provincial-level authority – has fuelled the growth by launching a vast number of ambitious infrastructure ventures. Glittering new projects are announced, or begun, or completed, on an almost weekly basis.

The city is huge: the estimated population of the municipality reached 24 million in 2016, and the built-up area now covers an area close to 3,000 sq km (1,158 sq miles). The population density is among the highest in the world.

Administratively, Shanghai is a metropolis without a province, made up of surrounding rural districts and a dozen city districts. Its provincial-level authority has given it enormous power to remake itself, and it has done just that, driving elevated highways through the congested sections of the Old City,

and building the subway lines and bridges and tunnels and other infrastructure that are helping to ease the crowding and traffic.

Shanghai's hosting of the World Expo in 2010 – the largest and longest in history, lasting six months and attracting over 70 million visitors – proved to be a boon for its infrastructure, not to mention its standing as a truly global city. The city underwent a complete transformation ahead of Expo, expanding its metro system into the longest in the world, opening countless new hotels, reshaping the Bund and touching up building facades on almost every city centre street. All that was aside from the 5-sq-km (2-sq-mile) Expo site itself, where iconic structures (most notably the red crown-like China Pavilion which stood above everything else) lined both sides of the Huangpu River. It is estimated that at least $55 billion was spent on Expo-related development – most Shanghainese will tell you it was well worth it.

Shanghai's future-focused energy is evident as soon as you arrive. The

The Shanghai cityscape is at its best after dark.

gateway **Pudong International Airport** (浦东国际机场), connected to the city by the world's fastest train, is building a third terminal, a fourth runway was completed in 2015 and there is a fifth also scheduled to be constructed. Hongqiao Airport, which handles mostly domestic flights, unveiled an ultra-modern Terminal 2 in 2010, which forms part of the Hongqiao Transport Hub, conveniently integrating with city metro lines, nationwide high-speed trains and a long-distance bus station. A massive cruise ship terminal was also unveiled in 2010 on the banks of the **Huangpu River** (黄浦江) north of the Bund, and more ferry docks are popping up on both the Huangpu River and its tributary, Suzhou Creek, as the city looks at better utilising its well-placed waterways for public transport.

Constant crowds are one of the most evident aspects of Shanghai. Every street corner, every last subway station, eatery and ticket queue, teems with people. Most of the time, however, the crowds are managed with extreme efficiency. Go with the flow, and you'll be fine. Do watch the chaotic traffic though – usually right of way goes to whoever is fastest, so never expect that cars or bikes will slow down for you, even at pedestrian crossings and green walking lights.

Like the Hong Kong Chinese, the residents of Shanghai have had longer to absorb the commercial instincts of the West, and they are considered some of China's most worldly, fashionable and open people. Like most Chinese, they are essentially regional, and speak a dialect that nobody else can fully understand, eat their own cuisine, and generally consider themselves to be light years ahead of everyone else in the country.

Now the most expensive city in China, Shanghai's higher living standards, pulsating nightlife and cosmopolitan air can make even Beijing seem dowdy in comparison. This is truly the Chinese vision for the 21st century.

PRESERVING THE PAST

Perhaps unexpectedly given the trends in modern China, once you move away from the commercial thoroughfares of

1930s posters.

⊙ TRANSPORT

Getting around Shanghai

From the airport: The MAGLEV train whisks passengers from Pudong International Airport to a relatively remote eastern suburb, from where a taxi or the subway continue to downtown Pudong and Puxi.

Buses: Shanghai's buses are often slow and crowded, but for point-to-point travel they can still be useful, especially for short distances.

Metro: Fast and reliable, the Shanghai "*di tie*" is the world's longest metro network with 588km (365 miles) of track and 14 lines as of 2017, meaning that you're never far from an underground station. Stored-value cards, which can also be used for taxis, buses, ferries and the MAGLEV, can be bought and topped up in stations and convenience stores.

Taxis: Taxis are cheap and plentiful, however they can be difficult to hail during rush hours and when it rains. Drivers are generally reliable, and pick-ups can be arranged in advance by telephone: DaZhong Taxi 96822; JinJiang Taxi 96961.

Ferries: Regular pedestrian ferries cross the Huangpu River between Puxi and Pudong from several docks south of the Bund, and the trip across the busy river is cheap and enjoyable.

A BRIEF HISTORY OF SHANGHAI

Not content with its meteoric rise from fishing village to commercial hub of China, Shanghai is now poised to become a global financial capital.

Once upon a time, in fact just two centuries ago, Shanghai was nothing more than a silty corner of the Yangzi Delta. The city has no ancient history: while its neighbours Suzhou, Hangzhou and Nanjing took turns as the glittering capitals of China's imperial dynasties, Shanghai was nothing more than a drab gathering of farming huts and fishing villages.

Yet its location meant that it was a city waiting to happen, and happen it did, as successive waves of commerce crashed onto the muddy shores of the Huangpu River, each one bringing with it a new wave of streets and buildings and people and culture.

The first wave of development was modest: a few farmers and fishermen, and a handful of traders, settled on the banks of the Huangpu. In time, they erected a small village, which was immediately attacked, many

The Jin Mao Tower.

times, by Japanese pirates. In response, the residents built a city wall, which surrounded the old city centre until 1912, just south of the Bund in a circular area defined by Renmin and Zhonghua roads.

The next wave of development was a big one: in the aftermath of the Opium Wars of the 1840s, foreign concessions were established, and eventually occupied much of what is now central Shanghai, except for the old walled Chinese city. The British, French and Americans brought modern business to Shanghai: rule of law, customs houses, post offices, court rooms, electricity and the like, and for the next century, the city boomed.

In the latter half of the 1800s, attracted by the money-making opportunities in the foreign concessions, the Chinese flooded in. The city rapidly became the place to be – a growing metropolis with the liveliest culture, the most opulent dance halls, the largest volume of business, the tallest buildings. In time-honoured fashion, the foreigners cared more for commerce than morality, and licentiousness also thrived: opium dens, prostitution and gambling, inevitably accompanied by gangsters.

RADICAL HOTBED

With the emergence of the Chinese Republic after 1912, new ideas flooded into the city, generating radicalism – another Shanghai tradition. The Communist Party was founded in the city in 1921. The 1920s and 30s, considered something of a golden age, saw the city boom still further – many of the familiar building on the Bund date this period. Shanghai had become a brash, cosmopolitan metropolis – seedy yet glamorous, obsessed with making money. Organised crime was everywhere.

The Japanese invasion, from 1937, spelt the beginning of the end, although it remained restricted to the Chinese parts of the city until the end of 1941 when the international community capitulated. After the Communist victory in 1949, Shanghai became a grey, sober city. Its renaissance began, slowly at first, in the 1980s, as the Chinese government started to allow commerce, and sparked by the reawakened entrepreneurial zeal of the Shanghainese, and by inflows of foreign cash, another wave of commerce, the biggest yet, flooded into Shanghai.

Nanjing and Huaihai roads or Pudong, Shanghai retains a significant amount of its former character. The old concession neighbourhoods, and the surrounding areas, are relatively quiet and peaceful, pleasant oases of cosy lane houses, plane trees and hidden villas surrounded by plantation-style lawns and gardens.

That's because Shanghai is not only about the new. The city had its salad days in an era of glorious architecture – the fabulous Art Deco era of the 1920s and 1930s. Back then, the world's top architects built hundreds of Art Deco classics in the city, from big hotels and breweries and warehouses to tiny apartments and out-of-the-way offices. Today, many of these buildings have been lovingly renovated, and they provide some of the classiest, calmest and most beautiful spaces in Asia. Others sit neglected, covered with wires and grime and satellite dishes, ageing but still graceful, waiting for the inbound flood of finance to give them a facelift.

The continued existence of these gentle giants is not entirely due to chance. The powers-that-be in Shanghai – government and investors – have taken a second look at the older parts of the city, and preservation efforts have gained momentum in the past few years as the commercial potential of the city's classic buildings has been rediscovered. And in Shanghai, as always, money talks.

That is the future of Shanghai: new millennium bells and whistles, state-of-the-art restaurants boasting celebrity chefs, design-heavy nightclubs, and some of the grandest infrastructure projects on earth, but also stately welcoming streets, peaceful old buildings and quieter, attractive neighbourhoods. As a blueprint for the future, this is a combination that is hard to beat.

ON THE WATERFRONT: THE BUND

Once the throbbing centre of commercial Shanghai, the **Bund** ❶ (外滩; Waitan) has been born again as a high-end hub of gourmet dining, glitzy nightlife, luxury shopping and expensive hotels. Stretching for 1km (0.6 mile) along the western bank of the Huangpu

> **⊘ Tip**
>
> Taking a river cruise is a highlight for many visitors to Shanghai. Tours vary from the hour-long Yangpu Bridge round trip to a full 3-hour excursion to the mouth of the Chang Jiang (Yangzi). Most boats depart from Shiliupu Wharf on the Bund.

Looking north along the Bund before the new tunnel was completed.

⊘ Tip

All the prime buildings in Shanghai have guards, many of whom will deny entrance at first. Smile, be polite, conceal cameras, and tell them you'd like to "*kan yi kan*", or look around, and they'll usually let you in.

River, the curious term "Bund" comes from Anglo-Indian, meaning embankment. Built by the British after the 1840–42 Sino-British Opium War – when China was forced to open up Shanghai's port and the riverfront became part of the British Concession (later renamed the International Settlement) – the grandiose neoclassical and Art Deco former financial and trade headquarters earned the Bund its 1920s nickname as the "Wall Street of Asia".

Many of these stately buildings were requisitioned by the Communist Party for its own use after 1949, and had fallen into disrepair by the end of the 20th century. Thankfully, Shanghai's riverfront was given a multi-million dollar makeover ahead of the 2010 World Expo. Several traffic lanes were re-routed underground, the riverside boardwalk was broadened and new public spaces were created. The iconic heritage facades were sandblasted and are beautifully illuminated at night. The party has well and truly returned to the Bund.

Facing the Bund buildings, the riverside **promenade** is almost always packed with people. This walkway is ultra-popular with Chinese tourists, and no trip to Shanghai is considered complete without a souvenir snap with Pudong in the background.

With its superb views of glittering Pudong, and its wealth of fine old buildings, the Bund is home to a swag of Shanghai's finest restaurants and nightlife destinations. For sweeping panoramas of the Bund and Pudong, New Heights (No.3), M on the Bund (No.5), Bar Rouge (No.18) and Shook! (No.19) all offer spectacular riverfront terraces serving well-mixed cocktails and bites.

Two of the Bund's most extraordinary buildings are the former Hongkong & Shanghai Bank (HSBC) headquarters at No.12 and **Customs House ❷** at No.13. The latter, built in 1927, is marked by an impressive clock tower modelled on London's Big Ben that tolls a Chinese tune on the hour. The former HSBC building, with its distinctive dome and impressive interior, was completed in 1923 by British architects Palmer and Turner. Their brief was a builder's dream: spare no

Suzhou Creek, with Broadway Mansions in the background.

expense and dominate the Bund. At night this building glows like a jewel, and by day it showcases a domed lobby encircled by magnificent mosaics.

Another notable Bund building is the former Yokohama Specie Bank, just north of the Bank of China: its dark doors open into a spacious gilded lobby filled with timeless details. And north of Yokohama Bank is the Yangtze Insurance Building, which leans toward Yokohama Bank like a talkative drunk, and like a drunk, it leans more with each passing year. Nor is Yokohama Bank the only leaning building in Shanghai; the city is built on silt, and subsidence is a problem that still challenges modern builders.

Where Nanjing Road meets the Bund is the **Fairmont Peace Hotel** ❸ (和平饭店; Heping Fandian), known as the Cathay Hotel in the old days and one of Shanghai's most treasured heritage buildings. A stunning example of Art Deco architecture with its Egyptian motifs, graceful vertical lines and signature peaked green roof, it is one of the most famous structures in China. After a much-needed three-year renovation, the hotel has been restored to its former glory. It joins the Waldorf Astoria Shanghai in the neoclassical former Shanghai Club (Bund 2) as the waterfront's most luxurious hotels.

At the northern end of the Bund, the former British Consulate has been transformed into a stunning state guesthouse. Although the buildings are off-limits, the grounds are a public park so feel free to enter past the stern-looking guards at the front gate to explore this peaceful enclave, home to several century-old trees. Opposite, the small **Huangpu Park** ❹ (黄浦公园; Huangpu Gongyuan) is less charming but filled with history. The riverside park was the original British Public Gardens dating from 1868. A drab concrete Monument to the People's Heroes and the small **Bund History Museum** (外滩历史博物馆; Waitan

Lishi Bowuguan; Mon–Fri 9am–4pm; free) are situated within the park.

The gentrification of the Bund has also spread to neighbouring streets. Running parallel to the Bund at its northern head, the **Rockbund** is an urban renaissance project under the guidance of British architect David Chipperfield. Almost a dozen early 20th-century mansions sporting dramatic Art Deco and Renaissance-style facades are being transformed into luxury residences, offices, shops, restaurants and museums. The **Rockbund Art Museum** and **Bund History Museum** (外滩历史博物馆; Waitan Lishi Bowuguan; Mon–Fri 9am–4pm; free); (上海外滩美术馆; Shanghai Waitan Meishuguan; www.rockbundartmuseum.org; Tue–Sun 10am–6pm) opened in 2010.

The **South Bund**, with its interesting mix of heritage mansions and dockside warehouses, is also undergoing a renaissance and is home to industrial-chic hotel the Waterhouse at South Bund, a man-made 'beach' on the riverfront and countless upcoming lifestyle projects.

Shanghai has China's best nightlife.

Art Deco interior at the Peace Hotel.

NORTH TO HONGKOU

North of the Bund, across **Suzhou Creek** (苏州河; Wusong Jiang), is **Hongkou** (虹口), a rapidly gentrifying riverfront neighbourhood. The famous old **Waibaidu Bridge ❺** across Suzhou Creek was towed downriver for renovation and reinstalled in 2010. The beloved dual-span iron bridge was well due for reinforcement – when it was first constructed in 1908 it was only intended to last for 40 years. A bridge over this point, at the confluence of Suzhou Creek and Huangpu River, was first built by the British in 1863 connecting the British and (unofficial) American concessions (these later merged into the International Settlement). From 1937, the bridge defined the border with the Japanese-occupied territory north of the Suzhou Creek.

Hongkou is now also home to a cruise ship terminal and shopping complex completed in 2010. This is the docking point for many of the huge cruise liners that are increasingly making Shanghai a port of call on their grand Asian tours. Luxury hotels are also cropping up in this area.

Shoppers on Nanjing East Road.

Despite all the development, this is one of those parts of Shanghai that has retained some of its old Chinese charm. As in much of the Old City and the former international and French settlements, laundry is draped from balconies on bamboo canes, and in the side streets, elderly people sit outside on stools to chat, chop vegetables, play cards or guard the bedding airing out in the street.

Hongkou is an important historical neighbourhood too. It was home in the 1930s to a large population of Jewish refugees as, until 1941, China was one of the last countries open to immigrants, requiring neither entry visa nor proof of financial means. Parts of the old Jewish Ghetto still exist and the **Shanghai Jewish Refugees Museum** (上海犹太难民纪念馆; Shanghai Youtai Nanmin Jinianguan; daily 9am–4.30pm; free), located in the old Ohel Moshe Synagogue on Changyang Road, offers fascinating insights into the Shanghai Jewish story.

A key building in Hongkou is the venerable **Pujiang Fandian** (Astor House

Ø ART DISTRICT

Some inner-city neighbourhoods are dotted with art galleries, but 50 Moganshan Road in the north of the city (west of Shanghai Railway Station) has emerged as the cutting-edge gallery district – an area of remodelled warehouses with a treasure trove of galleries. A secondary art enclave has emerged at ShanghART Gallery Shanghai (West Bund, Building 10, 2555 Longteng Avenue, Xuhui District; www.shanghartgallery.com; Tue–Sun 11am–6pm; free). In modern Shanghai, two broad types of art predominate. One is traditional: women with fans, men on bicycles and lush landscapes. The other is political pop art, which has become hot property with global collectors. These works display overt messages about Chinese society, images of Mao and the military and such, and are often rendered in multimedia.

Hotel; 浦江饭店; http://astorhousehotel. com). This lovely old hotel has been slated for full renovation but presently exists in a glorious time-warp; visitors can stroll the atmospheric teak-lined corridors and historic halls. Some of the high-ceilinged rooms have been updated with modern comforts, while others offer budget/mid-range accommodation.

Various cruises on both the Huangpu River and Suzhou Creek offer views of the rapidly changing cityscape along the banks of the city's two main waterways. We recommend the Huangpu River cruises for best views of the Bund and jaw-dropping crane-action at the world's busiest container port.

At the edge of the northern part of Sichuan Road is **Lu Xun Park** ❻ (虹口公园; Hongkou Gongyuan), one of the prettiest parks in Shanghai. Within the park there is a museum and the grave of Lu Xun, China's most famous 20th-century writer. Well worth visiting is the writer's simply furnished **former home** (鲁迅故居; Lu Xun Guju; daily 9am–4pm), where he lived from 1933 until his death in 1936.

A short stroll from Lu Xun Park is the pedestrianised **Duolun Street** (多伦路). This lane, filled with colonial-era houses, was the former stamping ground of Shanghai native Lu Xun and several other important Shanghai literary figures. It has since been transformed into a tourist getaway filled with bookstores, boutiques and cafés, as well as statues of its former residents of note.

A key attraction is the **Shanghai Duolun Museum of Modern Art** ❼ (上海多伦现代美术馆; Shanghai Duolun Xiandai Meishuguan; www.duolunmoma. org; Tue–Sun 10am–6pm). This is a good venue for the display of cutting-edge Asian art. Just down the road is the **Old Film Café** (老电影咖啡馆; Lao Dian Ying Kafeiguan; daily 9.30am–midnight), where they show old Chinese and Russian films from the 1920s and 30s, in an old-fashioned setting with espresso and chocolate cake.

West of the Shanghai Railway Station, on the south side of Suzhou Creek

A display in the Urban Planning Museum.

Chinese chess in People's Park.

on Anyuan Road, is **Yufuo Si** ❽ (玉佛寺; Jade Buddha Temple; daily 8am–4.30pm), famous for its two Buddha statues made of white jade, brought to China from Burma (Myanmar) in 1882. The statues arrived in Shanghai in 1918, when the temple was completed. One effigy depicts the Sleeping Buddha, representing his entry into nirvana, but the other white-jade statue of the Seated Buddha – 2 metres (6ft 7ins) tall, decorated with jewels and weighing 1,000 kg (2,200 lbs) – is the more magnificent.

NANJING ROAD AND PEOPLE'S SQUARE

Shanghai's key commercial street is **Nanjing Road** (南京路), which leads west from the Bund into the heart of the city. The stretch between Henan Road and Xizang Road is a pedestrian-only thoroughfare, one of the main focal points of the city – always filled with sightseers, tourists and shoppers. Shanghai is China's premier shopping city, and this is apparent after just a short stroll here: the amount of merchandise on sale is staggering, be it clothes, electronic goods, touristy tat, specialist items such as traditional theatre props, musical instruments or art. Old state-owned food stores and the aged **No.1 Department Store** ❾ (上海第一百货商店; Di Yi Baihuo Shangdian) rub shoulders with the glitzy commercialism of boutique malls, an Apple store and five-star hotels.

Beyond Xizang Road is the large open space of **People's Park** ❿ (人民公园; Renmin Gongyuan). Once a part of a horse-racing course during the city's glory days, it is now a refreshing green space. The park is split into northern and southern halves by **People's Square** (人民广场; Renmin Guangchang), which is considered the heart of Shanghai. The park and square feature three museums, a glamorous theatre and an underground shopping mall, along with the Stalinist-looking Shanghai City Hall building.

The main highlight is the **Shanghai Museum** ⓫ (上海博物馆; Shanghai Bowuguan; www.shanghaimuseum.net; daily 9am–5pm; free), in the southern part of the park. This facility, opened in 1996, offers an outstanding collection of Chinese culture in a modern setting. Its 10 galleries house fine exhibits of paintings, bronzes, sculpture, ceramics, calligraphy, jade, Ming- and Qing-dynasty furniture, coins, seals and minority art. The bronze collection is one of the best in the world and the ceramics are superb, although its paintings collection is somewhat below par because many artworks fell victim to the vandalism of the Cultural Revolution. Information is well presented in English, and the audio guide is excellent.

In the middle of People's Square is the **Shanghai Urban Planning Centre** (上海城市规划中心; Shanghai Chengshi Guihua Guan; www.supec.org; Tue–Sun 9am–5pm), featuring an entertainingly huge 3-D scale model of the city, which helps to make some sense of the scale of the recent building frenzy. ⓬

The Shanghai Museum.

Nearby, on the opposite side of the park is the former Shanghai Race Club – a striking classical building. Atop the building, with superb views of People's Park, is Kathleen's 5 restaurant and bar. After the former Shanghai Art Museum, now the China Art Museum, moved from the building in 2012, there are plans to relocate the Shanghai Municipal History Museum here, as it currently lacks its own seat and occupies the base of the Pearl Oriental TV Tower. The **Museum of Contemporary Art** ⓬ (上海当代艺术馆; MoCA; www.mocashanghai.org; daily 10am–6pm) is set in the former park greenhouse and features large-scale modern art and design exhibitions. The Arabian-style Barbarossa Lounge (which also has an ambient alfresco rooftop) is a good stop for a post-museums drink.

People's Square is also home to two marquee performance venues. **The Shanghai Grand Theatre** (上海大剧院; Shanghai Daiyuan), is a modern interpretation of a classical Chinese pavilion, staging dance, theatre and musical performances from around the world. The pretty **Shanghai Concert Hall** (上海音乐厅; Shanghai Yinyueting) built in 1930 was moved 66 metres (217ft) to its current location in 2004. The stunning 1,200-seat concert hall is regarded as one of Asia's premier classical concert venues.

A couple of noteworthy buildings flank the park. On the corner of Xizang and Hankou roads is the small, red-brick **Mu'en Tang** (沐恩堂; former Moore Memorial Church), worth investigating to get a feel for Christian architecture in Shanghai. North of the park on Nanjing Road West is the **Park Hotel** ⓭ (国际饭店; Guoji Fandian), designed by legendary Czech architect Ladislaus Hudec. The Park's striking glazed-brick exterior is intact, and so are the simple straight lines of its Art Deco design, featuring four narrow strips that rise to the roof, buttressing the tower and highlighting its vertical features. In any other city in Asia, the Park would be an architectural superstar, but in Shanghai it is just one of many dozens of buildings of similar size, beauty and pedigree.

Tip

Pickpocketing is a problem in Shanghai, especially on buses, in the subway, and in busy tourist areas like the Bund. Bike theft is also endemic, so lock bikes and zip pockets.

The China Art Museum opened in 2012.

NANJING ROAD WEST AND JING AN

A few hundred metres further west, Nanjing Road East morphs into **Nanjing Road West ⑭**, an ultra-upscale shopping street that is home to the city's fanciest malls, all of them packed with famous designer brands, whose multi-digit price tags are even more exorbitant than elsewhere due to China's 30 percent retail tax on luxury goods. This is the **Jing An District**, Shanghai's most expensive shopping mecca: look for Plaza 66 and Citic Square, among the city's priciest malls.

Still further west on Nanjing Road West is the **Shanghai Centre ⑮** (上海商城; Shanghai Shangcheng; www.shanghaicentre.com). This busy complex houses the Portman RitzCarlton Hotel, two residential towers, a pair of multinational office buildings, and a shopping area that includes major airline offices, and Western stores and chain restaurants such as the Pizza Marzano, Element Fresh, Din Tai Fung and Starbucks. Across the street from the Portman is the Soviet-built **Shanghai Exhibition Centre** (上海展览中心; Shanghai Zhanlan Zhongxin) – look for the 1950s-style Red Star atop the building – while further west, past more upscale malls and department stores, is the Buddhist-Daoist **Jing An Si** (静安寺; Jing An Temple). The city's richest temple has recently added a gold-tiled roof and Tibetan style stupa.

NANSHI: THE OLD CITY

The edge of the **Old City**, formerly known as **Nanshi** (南市), begins where Henan Road intercepts Renmin Road. Combined with Zhonghua Road, this defines its circular limit. The city walls paralleled this small ring road until 1912, when they were knocked down and the moats were filled in. During the concession era, the Old City remained under Chinese law and administration, while much of the rest of central Shanghai was administered by foreign powers. Most of the residents in these old back alleys were Chinese, and eventually the area became notorious as a gangster-and-opium slum. Today, the vices are gone, but a few of the tiny lanes, crowded but quaint

Part of the old city wall in Nanshi, the old city.

neighbourhoods, and small houses still exist. Tourist-wise, the key features of this part of Shanghai are the Yu Garden and the surrounding shopping streets, known collectively as Yuyuan Bazaar.

One of Shanghai's best-known sights, the Ming-dynasty **Yu Garden** ⑯ (豫园; Yuyuan; daily Mar–Oct 8.30am– 5.30pm, Nov–Feb until 5pm) is a classical Chinese garden with rockeries, pools, paths and pagodas, similar to Suzhou's famous gardens. The traditional rock-and-tree landscape is filled with artificial hills, carp ponds, dragon-lined walls, and pavilions connected by zigzagging bridges.

In the centre of Yuyuan Bazaar is **Huxinting Teahouse** (湖心亭茶室; Huxinting Chashe), the city's oldest teahouse, which sits in the middle of a small bottle-green pond, with a famous nine-corner bridge that connects it to Yu Garden proper. Dating from Qing times, the second floor serves some of the best – and priciest – tea in town. Despite the crowds, this is a pleasant spot that manages to preserve some of the flavour of Old China.

Fuelled by the constant flow of tourists, the area around Yuyuan has become an ever-expanding bazaar. The complex, with its red walls and upturned tile roofs, has been a marketplace and social centre since the 18th century, and it is replete with curios and tourist souvenirs, as well as numerous food vendors. There is a pattern to shopping at Yuyuan: typical souvenirs like fans, pearls, silk pyjamas, Terracotta Warrior statues and Mao memorabilia are lined up along the main streets, while tucked away inside the courtyards and buildings are stalls that sell a variety of goods, such as beaded necklaces, Chinese medicines, children's toys, jewellery, clothes and so on – and on. It's a hotchpotch of a place – the words "fake" and "tacky" spring to mind – but it can also be fun and rewarding. And it looks wonderful in the early evening, when the red lanterns lining the streets are

lit, and the roofs of the faux-Ming buildings are outlined with fairy lights.

Just west of Yuyuan at Henan Road is the animated **Fuyou Road Antique Market** ⑰ (福佑路古玩市场; Fuyou Lugu Wanshi Chang), which sits inside an old factory. Hawkers come here as early as 4am to set up their stalls. The tiny lane bustles with people by mid-morning, by which time the best goods are usually sold.

XINTIANDI

Due west of Nanshi, and south of People's Park, is **Xintiandi** ⑱ (新天地), an upscale restaurant, bar and shopping

Shopping at Yuyuan bazaar.

Huxinting Teahouse.

Upmarket boutique in the Xintiandi area.

The home of one-time prime minister, Zhou Enlai, in the former French Concession.

district. Covering a two-square-block area, Xintiandi features elements of Shanghai's famous *shikumen* (stone gate) lane houses. The grey-brick alleys, courtyards and terraces were re-imagined by American architect Ben Wood in 2002, pioneering a new model of urban regeneration that has since been replicated around the country. No matter that little of it is original – for first-timers and strangers to the city, Xintiandi gathers together a variety of very pleasant bars and eateries, upscale shopping and hotels, in a pleasant, car-free area that conjures up a sense of the grey-brick lanes of times past. More adventurous souls can venture further into the surrounding streets for a glimpse of the few remaining genuine *shikumen* lane houses.

Xintiandi is also home to the site of the **First National Congress of the Communist Party of China** ❶❾ (中共 一大会址; Zhonggong Yidahuizhi; daily 9am–5pm; free). You can see the room where delegates held the first clandestine gathering of the Party in July 1921. It remains in its original form, complete with a table

set for 13 people, while waxworks of top party officials are also on view.

HUAIHAI ROAD AND THE FORMER FRENCH CONCESSION

Leading west from Xintiandi is **Huaihai Road** (淮海路), Shanghai's other famous shopping thoroughfare. The recently regenerated malls clustered around the intersection of Huaihai Road and Huangpi Road are filled with luxury brand boutiques, while further west, before the junction of Maoming Road, the Twin Villas are identical heritage mansions home to uber-exclusive shopping and the private KEE Club. They are hidden behind a row of street-front shophouses, so look out for the stylish gate and earpiece-wearing butlers.

Huaihai Road leads directly west into the quieter neighbourhoods of the old French Concession, one of the city's most charming areas. The pleasant tree-lined blocks are dotted with villas, terraced houses and other old buildings of various origin and use, including a scattering of beautiful 19th- and early-20th-century apartment houses. Most are semi-hidden from pedestrians, but these are the surprises that make these leafy streets such a delight. Here, an iron gate opens into a stately old villa or into the courtyard of an Art Deco apartment, and there, a small opening leads to a thriving neighbourhood of venerable detached houses or into a compound of graceful but run-down old mansions.

The old houses are of particular interest: these are East-West hybrids that incorporate traditional English elements with Chinese concepts of feng shui. The *shikumen* houses are larger than the new-style lane houses, with bigger gardens and wraparound courtyards featuring the signature stone gates. Most houses have tiny rooms for servants and for ancestral altars, both hallmarks of Chinese interior design. Many of the houses face south, as dictated by feng shui, with the gardens and

biggest rooms always on the south. It is not uncommon, especially among the spider-web streets of Xuhui District, to see entire rows of houses set at crazy angles from the streets, so they can achieve a southerly aspect.

An excellent example of colonial architecture – just one of many – is the **Shanghai Arts and Crafts Research Institute** ⑳ (上海工艺美术研书馆; Shanghai Gongyi Meishuguan; daily 9am–4pm). In this venerable old French mansion on Fenyang Road, visitors can watch artisans at work and purchase a variety of traditional Chinese handicrafts. Back on Huaihai Road is the **Shanghai Library** (上海 图书馆; Shanghai Tushuguan; daily 9am–5pm), one of the largest in the world. Opened in 1996, the library features up-to-date information technology and holds a total of 12 million books. Many foreign consulates are located in the vicinity, and the surrounding neigbourhoods are perfect for leisurely exploration on foot.

Two heritage sites to check out along Sinan Road are the **Sun Yatsen Residence** ㉑ (孙中山故居; Sun Zhongshan Guju; daily 9am–4.30pm) on Xiangshan Road at Sinan Road and the **Zhou Enlai Residence** (周恩来故居; Zhou Enlai Guju; daily 9am–5pm; free), once the home of the former premier, around the corner on Sinan Road. Just steps away you will find Fuxing Park, which was known as French Park when it opened in 1909 (on Bastille Day).

At the end of Sinan Road, Sinan Mansions is a redevelopment of several villa blocks into trendy dining and drinking establishments. In the rabbit-warren alleys between Sinan Road and Taikang Road, Tianzifang is an atmospheric shopping enclave filled with local designer boutiques, stylish souvenir shops and alfresco cafés. A must for shopping enthusiasts.

LONGHUA AND XUJIAHUI

In the west of the city, on the road with the same name, is **Longhua Temple** ㉒ (龙华古寺; Longhua Gu Si), a temple and pagoda built in AD 242 and since destroyed and rebuilt several times. The temple site consists of seven halls that are again being used for religious

Golden Buddha statues at Longhua Temple.

Huaihai Road is one of the city's major shopping thoroughfares.

The Space Needle in Pudong's Century Park.

Xujiahui Catholic Cathedral.

purposes. Adjoining the temple, the Longhua Hotel was designed especially for Buddhist travellers and includes a vegetarian restaurant, although it welcomes all visitors.

Next door, the **Longhua Martyrs Memorial Cemetery** covers 200,000 sq metres (239,200 sq yds) of manicured parklands dotted with giant concrete socialist-realist statues of Communist revolutionary heroes. So peaceful and pleasant is the site that it is hard to imagine that it lies on a 1920s execution ground where Communist soldiers were imprisoned and slain by the Kuomintang government.

To the northwest is **Xujiahui Catholic Cathedral**, an impressive French Gothic building dating from 1846. **Xujiahui** (徐家汇) is a bustling, mall-filled area of mid-range brands popular with teenagers and local shoppers.

PUDONG

Across the river from the Bund, on the eastern banks, is the remarkable **Pudong Xinqu** (浦东新区), or the Pudong New Area. Twenty years ago,

Pudong (literally, east of the Huangpu River) was a rambling collection of warehouses, farms and small houses. Then in 1992 a plan was hatched that would turn Pudong into a global financial centre that would rival or even eclipse Hong Kong. The New Area is scattered over a whopping 1,210 sq km (467 sq miles) of land that contains a foreign trade zone, a high-tech zone, an export zone, a biotech zone, a tourist zone, a financial zone – you get the picture.

A striking counterpoint to the heritage Bund, Pudong's thrusting skyscrapers represent Shanghai's high-reaching global ambitions. The area's glass towers and wide, orderly streets are a complete contrast to the bustling, atmospheric neighbourhoods of Puxi.

For travellers, Pudong's highlight is generally futuristic architecture. A trio of the world's tallest towers dominate the Pudong riverside: the 88-level Jinmao Tower opened in 1999; the 101-floor Shanghai World Financial Centre unveiled in 2008 and the 121-storey Shanghai Tower, currently the tallest

⊘ SHANGHAI'S SATELLITE CITIES

Far from the eyes of tourists, nine architectural experiments have been underway in the outskirts of Shanghai since 2001. This was the satellite city plan, or One City Nine Towns, wherein nine giant new residential "villages", based upon European patterns and designed by top-flight foreign architects, were to be constructed in the remote suburbs.

The German town of Anting (安亭德国小镇), for example, designed by Albert Speer, includes winding streets, tiny courtyards, medieval plazas, and village-square fountains, and was meant to house 50,000 people. Similarly, Thames Town (泰晤士小镇) includes space for pubs, a town square, a village-style church and Olde England style shops. The closest one to Shanghai – just 20 minutes by car – is Pujiang (新浦江城), Italian town, which features Shanghainese-style lane houses and villas for 20,000 people.

As of 2016, six towns have been constructed: the Spanish, Italian, German, British, Dutch and Scandinavian towns. These architectural experiments, however, have failed to attract new residents and to act as thriving suburban hotspots as was hoped. Instead, they have become deserted ghost towns, which currently serve only as popular wedding photography locations for Chinese newlyweds.

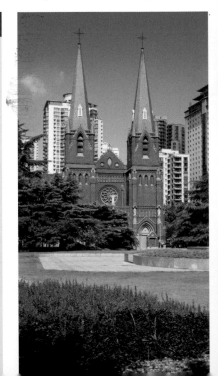

building in China and the 2nd tallest building in the world, was completed in 2015. Those looking for sky-high views over Shanghai can head up to the **SWFC Observatory's Sky Walk 100** (观光天阁100; Guanguang Tiange 100; daily 8am–11pm; www.swfc-observatory. com). The 55 metre (180-ft) -long glass corridor stretches across the trapezoidal gap on the 100th floor, with transparent inset floor panels allowing visitors to peer 474 metres (1,555ft) down to the city below.

A more controversial piece of Pudong architecture is the **Pearl Oriental TV Tower** ㉓ (东方 明珠电视塔; Dongfan Mingzhu Guangbo Dianshi Ta). This was China's tallest skyscraper when it was completed in 1994 and its stack of 11 magenta balls (or 'pearls') has become a Shanghai icon. The base of the tower houses the **Shanghai Municipal History Museum** (www.history museum.sh.cn; daily 8am–9.30pm), while the surrounding area is also home to an aquarium, shopping malls and a pleasant riverfront park that features coffee shops, small restaurants, waterfront walks and wonderful views of the Bund.

Deeper into Pudong you'll find the centrepiece of the **2010 World Expo**, the bright-red China Pavilion with its huge traditional roof. As of 2012, the building houses the **China Art Museum** (中华艺术宫; Zhonghua Yishu Gong; Tue–Sun 10am–6pm; free) which moved here from the Shanghai Race Club. The new museum, showcasing an impressive collection of art and photography, is ten times bigger than its predecessor and is currently one of the biggest art museums in China. It can be easily reached by metro Line 8. Also, on the former Expo site, at a former power station, is the Power Station of Art (上海当代艺术博物馆, PSA, Tue–Sun 11am–7pm; free), China's first state-run contemporary art museum. It opened in 2012 and is home to the Shanghai Biennale.

There is also the Mercedes-Benz Arena, a spaceship-like concert hall on the former Expo site; the orchid-like Oriental Arts Centre, and the Himalayas Arts Centre, whose feng shui-inspired structure is home to an art museum, theatre, underground retail plaza and the Jumeirah hotel.

SHANGHAI DISNEY RESORT

In 2016, **Shanghai Disney Resort** (川沙新镇; www.shanghaidisneyresort.com; daily 9am–7pm), the second Disneyland in China (after Hong Kong Disneyland), opened in Pudong's southeastern area. The resort currently comprises Shanghai Disneyland Park, recreational facilities, two hotels and a lake, but two more themed parks are scheduled to be constructed. When fully complete, the site will cover 390 hectares (963 acres) and will be three times the size of Hong Kong Disneyland. Shanghai Disney Resort is partly owned by The Walt Disney Company and partly by the Shanghai government. To get there, take metro Line 11 and get off at Disney Resort Station.

Tip

Take one of the old ferry boats across the Huangpu River to Pudong – they leave just south of the Bund – and return on the shuttle train through the bizarre Bund Sightseeing Tunnel (daily May–Oct 8am–10.30pm, Nov–Apr until 10pm). The latter is enlivened by surreal lighting displays, cut-out figures and scenes projected onto the walls – all to the accompaniment of a slightly disturbing soundtrack.

The view from the Jin Mao tower.

NANJING, JIANGSU AND THE GRAND CANAL

The old southern capital of Nanjing is one of China's most habitable and pleasant centres, while Suzhou and other cities along the ancient Grand Canal are full of interest and atmosphere.

It is perhaps the greatest tourism slogan of all time: "Above is Paradise, below are Hangzhou and Suzhou." Then, as if that praise from Yuan-dynasty poet Yang Chaoying were not enough, along came Marco Polo, who supposedly visited Jiangnan (the rich delta area south of the Yangzi) in 1276. Polo piled further compliments on the area. Its cities, he wrote, "are the finest and most splendid in the world", and, thumbing through his 13th-century thesaurus, he went on to call them "great and noble, beautiful, magnificent and delightful," along with other flowery phrases too numerous to mention.

These celebrated lines may have amplified the appeal of the Jiangnan region, but even so, and even today, its cities and towns stand apart from the drab factories and dull architecture that typify much of eastern China. The bridges, canals and gardens that so impressed Marco Polo and the Yuan-era poet are still the area's signature highlights, and are among the most charming sights in China.

Cut by waterways and characterised by beguiling water towns, Jiangsu province has a prime location on China's prosperous eastern seaboard. Traditionally called "the land of fish and rice", the area is bisected by the mighty **Chang Jiang** (长江), or

A building at Nanjing University.

Yangzi River, which flows into the East China Sea north of Shanghai and is fed by a web of watercourses in its lower reaches.

The historic silk town of Suzhou is one of China's major sights – famed for its dreamy canal setting and classical gardens. And if Suzhou's charms whet your appetite, you will be drawn to the historic architecture of the other Grand Canal cities and towns – Wuxi, Tongli, Yangzhou, Hangzhou and many others. Meanwhile, the huge lake Tai Hu is ringed with sights, including

Maps on pages 233, 240, 244

Ding Shan, home of the distinctive Yixing pottery. And Nanjing, from the park-like setting of its famous university to the forested Zijin Shan (Purple Mountains) in the east, has a relaxed atmosphere that few modern Chinese cities can match.

NANJING

Nanjing (南京) **❶** is one of China's more attractive big cities and subtly different from the other urban areas of the Yangzi Delta. Like Hangzhou and Suzhou, it is a former capital and has a rich history, but it is also a university town, home to some of China's top colleges.

With a population of 7 million – relatively small in Chinese city terms – Nanjing's current investment and building boom was slower to start than its neighbours but is now in full swing. And although new developments – like the Zifeng Tower, one of China's tallest at 450 metres (1,476ft), and the rising Nanjing World Trade Centre – symbolise Nanjing's big city ambitions, it is also establishing itself as a centre for architecture and the arts, while preserving the historical sites that remember its colourful, and at times brutal, 2,500-year past.

Nanjing can easily be reached by train, boat or plane, and regular express trains zip across from Shanghai in just 75 minutes. It is also one of the few stops on the Beijing–Shanghai bullet train line. Arrival from the north is via the great **Yangzi Bridge** **Ⓐ** (南京 长江大桥; Changjiang Daqiao; closed for renovation until early 2019), which opened in 1968 and has been a symbol of Chinese independence and national pride ever since. When relations between the former Soviet Union and China were severed in 1960, the Chinese constructed the bridge – which had been a Soviet-funded project until then – with their own design and resources. Its construction paved the way for numerous ambitious infrastructure projects that are so beloved by modern China. A stroll around the **Great Bridge Park** (大桥 公园; Daqiao Gongyuan; daily 7.30am–6.30pm) alongside the structure affords excellent views.

Walking along Nanjing's ancient city walls by Xuanwu Hu.

A LONG HISTORY

The history of Nanjing dates back to the beginning of the Warring States Period (403–221 BC). Between the 3rd and 6th centuries AD, Nanjing was the capital of the Southern dynasties at a time when non-Chinese were in command in northern China. After various natural disasters and a peasant rebellion, the new Sui dynasty moved the imperial capital to Xi'an (AD 589) and destroyed Nanjing, along with almost all of its cultural and historical relics.

Nanjing regained national importance at the beginning of the Ming dynasty, when its first emperor, Hongwu (aka Zhu Yuanzhang), set up the seat of government here in the Southern Capital – a literal translation of the name Nanjing – until it was transferred to Beijing in 1421. The well-preserved **city wall** dates from this period. This tremendous fortification had a circumference of over 30km (19 miles) and an average height of 12 metres (39ft). Several of the gates still stand today, including **Zhonghuamen** Ⓑ (中华门) in the south of the city (a

good reference point for navigating Nanjing), and **Zhongshanmen** Ⓒ (中山门) in the eastern part of the wall.

XINJIEKOU AND MOCHOU HU

In the city centre at **Xinjiekou** Ⓓ (新街口) a bronze statue of Sun Yatsen, considered the founding father of modern China, stands over a bustling commercial area, filled with luxury-brand boutiques and global coffee chains. This is also a junction of lines 1 and 2 on the Nanjing city metro. Line 1 zig-zags roughly north-south and Line 2 travels from northeast to southwest. The city's metro system currently comprises six lines.

Opposite the Presidential Palace, facing Daxinggong City Square, the **Jiangsu Provincial Art Museum** (江苏省美术馆; Jiangsu Sheng Meishuguan; 333 Changjiang Lu; Tue–Sun 9am–5pm; free) is another recently instated example of striking contemporary architecture, clad in natural travertine stone with a glass roof. It houses mostly traditional exhibits and hosts the Nanjing biennale. Nearby is

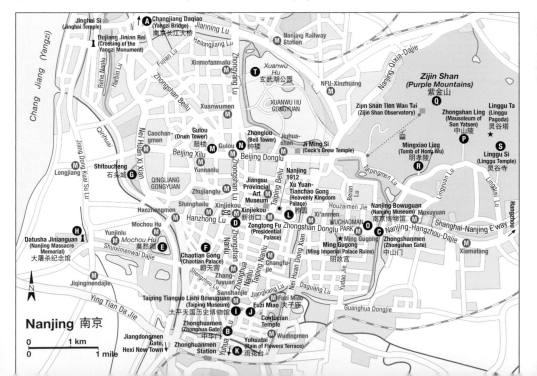

Gulou, Nanjing's Drum Tower, dates from the 14th century, when the city was the largest in the world with an estimated population in excess of 450,000.

Nanjing 1912, a popular entertainment enclave packed with restaurants, bars and cafés, often likened to Xintiandi in Shanghai.

To the southwest of Xinjiekou is **Mochou Hu ⓔ** (莫愁湖), a lake named after the Mochou (Lady Without Sorrows), who is said to have lived here in the 5th century. The **Chaotian Gong ⓕ** (朝天宫; Chaotian Palace; daily 9am–6pm) nearby dates back to the Song dynasty (960–1279), a period known for Confucian revivalism. The palace is one of the area's best-preserved Confucian temples. A reminder of the temple's beginnings is the gate of Ling Xing (Spirit Star), a remnant of the Song dynasty and entrance to the complex. Immediately ahead is a maze of merchants selling bric-a-brac, antiques and magazines, some from the Cultural Revolution. Operas performed in the Jiangsu provincial tradition are held within the main courtyard. The three halls at the back of the complex contain fossilised human, buffalo and deer bones from the Neolithic period, as well as artefacts from the Ming and Qing dynasties.

Shitoucheng ⓖ (石头城), a partially preserved wall to the north of Mochou, is a reminder of Nanjing's turbulent history. There is a secluded, wooded walk that follows the path of the wall, and sections of the original stone wall are still clearly visible.

In the same area of town, close to the gate of **Jiangdongmen** (江东门), is the **Memorial to the Nanjing Massacre ⓗ** (大屠杀纪念馆; Datusha Jinianguan; www.travelchinaguide.com; Tue–Sun 8.30am–4.30pm; free), a sombre reminder of the horrors of the Japanese invasion. Inside is a quiet exhibition of photographs, maps and eye-witness accounts that document the arrival of Japanese troops in December 1937, the rapes, burning and looting of houses and historical relics, and the slaughter of some 300,000 Chinese that followed. Most silencing of all is a viewing hall overlooking a mass grave, one of the many *wan ren keng* (pit of ten thousand corpses) that the Japanese left behind.

SOUTH OF XINJIEKOU

In the southern part of the city, near Zhonghuamen gate, is a Ming-style garden residence housing the **Taiping Museum ⓘ** (太平天国历史博物馆; Taiping Tianguo Lishi Bowuguan; daily 8am–5pm). The turbulent rise and fall of the quasi-Christian "Kingdom of Heaven", popularly known as the Taiping Rebellion, is well documented here in both Mandarin and English. Led by Hong Xiuquan, the Taiping captured Nanjing in 1853, making it the capital of their domain. The city was retaken by Qing troops in 1864 and Hong's magnificent temple was levelled. Cannons, guns, swords and other weapons are displayed alongside photographs and paintings depicting the rebellion. In the official history, Hong's unique take on Christianity – he believed he was the

---

⊘ THE TAIPING REBELLION

The Taiping Rebellion (1850–64), responsible for up to 20 million deaths, is a chapter saturated in blood. Led by the Hakka (Kejia) Hong Xiuquan, a failed civil service candidate who was convinced he was the son of the Christian God, the Taiping exploded out of south China in their campaign to exterminate the Manchu, overlords of the Qing dynasty.

Fired by evangelical zeal and a powerful sense of destiny, the Taiping swept through the provinces of Guangxi, Hunan, Hubei, Anhui and Jiangsu, taking Nanjing in 1853 and transforming it into the capital of their Heavenly Kingdom. Further expeditions against the Manchu in east and north China were abortive, however, and divisions appeared among the upper ranks of the Taiping faithful. Nanjing fell to Qing forces (bolstered by Western military training) in 1864, shortly after Hong Xiuquan's death.

With their radical egalitarian social framework and ethical edicts (for example, the outlawing of foot-binding and opium use), the fanatical Taiping are fêted by the Chinese Communist Party as revolutionary visionaries. On the other hand, the 1999 outlawing of the quasi-Buddhist/Daoist Falun Gong movement also exposed the Chinese Communist Party's ever-present dread of alleged religious mutiny against their monopoly on power. This paranoia is one way the Taiping Rebellion has left its mark on modern China.

younger brother of Jesus – has been erased, and he has been reinvented as a reformist fighter trying to overthrow the decaying Qing dynasty.

Two blocks to the west of the Taiping Museum is a lively market area known as **Fuzi Miao** ❶ (夫子庙). A carnival atmosphere presides over this labyrinth of alleyways and small squares filled with souvenir and antique shops, and street stalls selling food. At its heart is the site of a Confucian temple and ancient study centre, dating back 1,500 years. The temple and surrounding buildings were razed and rebuilt numerous times. The present buildings are Qing-dynasty renovations and recent additions built in the traditional Qing style.

South of Zhonghuamen gate is **Yuhuatai** ❿ (雨花台; Rain of Flowers Terrace; daily 6am–8pm), where in the 4th century, according to legend, the Buddha made flowers rain from the sky. Today there is a memorial in the park to the Communists and their supporters who died in 1927 at the hands of Nationalist troops. And if Zhongshan

Lu with its right-angle turns at junctions seems confusing, there is a reason. From the docks on the Chang Jiang to the mausoleum, this is the route taken by the funeral entourage of Sun Yatsen (also called Sun Zhongshan) and is named after him.

The **Hexi New Town** to the southwest is being developed as a new CBD and is the site of several of Nanjing's most ambitious modern developments. Here you'll find the **Nanjing Olympic Sports Centre**, which hosted the 2014 Summer Youth Olympics, and the multi-tower **Nanjing World Trade Centre**, scheduled for completion in 2019, which will contain a five-star hotel, high-end offices and residences, plus a shopping complex, entertainment and dining.

NORTH AND EAST OF XINJIEKOU

Xu Yuan ❶ (煦园), 15 minutes' walk northeast of Xinjiekou on Changjiang Lu, is a pleasant, recreated Ming-dynasty garden, home to the **Tianchao Gong** (天朝宫; Palace of the Heavenly Kingdom; daily 9am–5pm), once occupied by Taiping leader Hong Xiuquan.

Fuzi Miao, Nanjing's oldest Confucius temple.

Xinjiekou, the bustling heart of modern Nanjing.

The tombs at Mingxiao Ling are a reminder that Nanjing was the national capital during the early Ming period (1368–1417).

Further northwest stand two reminders of the nascent Ming dynasty, **Gulou** (鼓楼), the Drum Tower, and **Zhonglou** (钟楼), the Bell Tower (both daily 8am–midnight). Drum and bell towers were common in all important imperial cities. The Drum Tower – whose purpose was to call the watch and warn the city of attack (the drums within it would signal the start and finish of the night watches along the city walls) – was completed in 1382, just 14 years into the reign of the first Ming emperor. The Bell Tower, completed six years later, was ceremonial.

The lively streets surrounding the leafy campus of Nanjing University are filled with student cafés, eateries and bookstores. In the eastern part of the city, next to Zhongshanmen gate, is the **Nanjing Museum** (南京博物馆; Nanjing Bowuguan; www.njmuseum.com; daily 9am–5pm). It has an extensive collection of ceramics, jade, lacquerware, textiles, bronzes, porcelain and stone figures from Nanjing and elsewhere in Jiangsu province. The collection covers 5,000 years of history, with many pieces dating from Neolithic times. The most important exhibit is a 2,000-year-old shroud from the Eastern Han dynasty (AD 25–220), made from 2,600 green jade rectangles sewn together with silver wire. The facilities are state-of-the-art, and well labelled in English.

Nanjing itself is like a living museum where each piece reveals another chapter in China's history. Southwest of the Nanjing Museum lie scattered the remains of the **Ming Imperial Palace** (明故宫; Ming Gugong) in **Wuchaomen Park** (午朝门公园). Erected by the first emperor of the Ming dynasty but reduced by war to a few scattered vestiges, some marble bridges and the ancient **Wumen** (午门) gate survive.

SUN YATSEN'S MAUSOLEUM

For most Chinese, the **Sun Yatsen Mausoleum** (中山陵; Zhongshan Ling; daily 8.30am–5pm; free) is Nanjing's main attraction. Known as the father of modern China, Sun helped found the Chinese Republic in 1911, and wrote many political treatises, which remain

✪ TRANSPORT

Getting to Nanjing/Jiansu

Flights: Nanjing Lukou International Airport has overseas and numerous domestic connections, and is a quick 29km (18-mile) trip, on an expressway, from downtown Nanjing. Wuxi Shuofang Airport is a thriving regional hub, well connected with the rest of the country. It is close to both Wuxi and Suzhou.

By train and bus: Trains from Shanghai, Beijing and elsewhere in China are cheap and plentiful, and bus services are frequent and often comfortable, depending upon the class.

Getting around Nanjing/Jiansu

Nanjing: Trains are the best way to travel from Shanghai. The China High-speed Rail (CHR) trains are clean, fast and comfortable, and the trip from Shanghai to Nanjing now takes just over one hour.

Suzhou and Wuxi: Trains are again the best option from Shanghai, and the CHR trains reach Suzhou in under 30 minutes. Suzhou station is north of the centre. From Hangzhou, buses or cars take a more direct route to Nanjing, however a bullet train will get you there in comfort in just over two hours.

required reading in schools. Hailing from Guangdong province, Sun wanted his final resting place to be here, amid the lovely **Zijin Shan** ❶ (紫金山; Purple Mountains). His desire was carried out four years after his death when the mausoleum was completed in 1929. The size of this monument is staggering, covering 8 hectares (20 acres). At the end of the tree-lined avenue begins a climb of 392 granite steps leading up to the blue-tiled memorial hall. There are a few places to rest (alternatively take a sedan chair) and enjoy the view of Nanjing along the way.

OTHER SIGHTS AROUND NANJING

Central to Nanjing's newly forming identity as a national capital for contemporary design is the **Sifang Parkland** (formerly Contemporary International Practical Exhibition of Architecture). This privately financed project – costs are estimated at some US$280 million – is located in the Laoshan National Forest Park about 19km (12 miles) west of downtown. Its centrepiece is the strikingly abstract **Sifang Art Museum** (www.sifangartmuseum.org; Wed–Sun 10am–5pm), designed by US architect Steven Holl and boasting a large collection of Chinese and international contemporary art. The park also features a convention centre designed by Irata Isozaki and 20 villas individually designed by prominent global architects, including Chinese provocateur Ai Weiwei.

A quiet stretch along Suzhou's extensive network of canals.

Shixiang Lu (Stone Statue Road) at Mingxiao Ling.

⊙ Fact

Until relatively recently, it took several hours to drive from Shanghai to Suzhou; today, it takes less than an hour to drive, and a trip on the bullet train takes less than 30 minutes. Note that there are four main stations in Suzhou, with different bullet trains stopping at different stations – so check your ticket carefully.

Ruins to the northeast of Nanjing, near Zijin Shan, offer a glimpse of the era of the Ming dynasty (1368–1644). Years before his death, the first Ming emperor, Hong Wu (1327–98), built his tomb known as **Mingxiao Ling ®** (明孝陵; daily 6.30am–5pm). Unfortunately, it was plundered during the Taiping uprising in 1864, and only the yellow walls of the main structure remain. A "sacred path", known as the Shixiang Lu (Stone Statue Road) survives, and is lined with elegant stone carvings – soldiers on one side and animals, both real and mythical, on the other. Pause for a moment and admire the rich detail and evocative shapes and faces of these monumental works.

To the east of the tomb in Linggu (Valley of the Souls) is **Linggu Si ®** (灵谷寺; daily 7am–6.30pm), a temple built at the end of the 14th century. Only the temple site of Wuliang Dian, which has been restored several times and built entirely from stone and without any wooden rafters, remains of the former large structure. Behind Wuliang Dian is the 60

Suzhou canal boats.

metre (200-ft) -high **Linggu Ta** (灵谷塔), a pagoda built in 1929 in memory of the victims of the war between the warlords and Nationalists. There is a magnificent view of the surrounding landscape from the top floor. On the mountain stands an observatory, which has a museum containing astronomical instruments, old and new. The chair lift to the observatory provides a splendid view of the city, and is one of the lesser-known highlights of a visit to Nanjing.

The extensive park around **Xuanwu Hu ❶** (玄武湖公园), a lake in the north of Nanjing, offers pavilions and small islands linked to the shore by dams and curved bridges. Understated in its beauty, it is a pleasant retreat. It is possible to walk along much of the well-preserved stretch of city wall that extends along the southern and western shore of the lake.

SUZHOU

If a tourist could see just one of China's smaller cities, a strong argument could be made for **Suzhou ❷** (苏州). It has

abundant history, and much of it is well preserved; the centre area is filled with gardens, pagodas, silk works, waterways and ancient moats, while the Grand Canal itself slices through the middle of town. It is built around a lattice-work of 24 canals, home to small intimate garden spots tucked away behind houses and hidden between narrow streets.

In many ways, this small city captures the essence of modern China, typifying the tug-of-war between old and new that is taking place across the country. The tourist-friendly sections of Suzhou are only a small part of the whole; most of those sections are in the Old City, while surrounding them are a pair of high-powered industrial zones that are squeezing the downtown area from both sides.

To the east is the Suzhou Industrial Park (SIP), a flourishing 180-sq-km (70-sq-mile) factory land that has also spawned a thriving tourism industry of shopping streets and restaurant strips, most notably the **Jinji Hu** (金鸡湖; Jinji Lake) area. The

SIP was launched in the 1990s as a China–Singapore joint venture, but the local government borrowed the idea and launched an industrial park of its own, to the west of downtown. This is the Suzhou National High-Tech Industrial Zone, and while not as popular as the original SIP park, it is currently a construction-strewn playground for developers.

As much as any Chinese provincial city, Suzhou has benefited from the

Shops in Suzhou.

Zhouzheng Yuan, the Humble Administrator's Garden, Suzhou.

nation's new wealth. The main shopping street, pedestrianised and prosperous **Guanqian Jie**, is lined with clothing and shoe shops and fast-food restaurants. **Rainbow Walk** and **Li Gong Di** (李公堤) are both pedestrian-friendly strips filled with dozens of upscale bars and restaurants, many of them branches of popular Shanghai venues. They are, however, somewhat off the tourist trail, being a 20–30-minute taxi ride east of the city centre.

Across Jinji Hu, and visible from both Rainbow Walk and Li Gong Di, sits the Rmb 170 million (US$25 million) **Suzhou Science and Cultural Arts Centre** (苏州科技文化艺术中心), designed by French architect Paul Andreu. This swooping, soaring, metallic piece of modern architecture is the home of the annual Golden Rooster awards, nicknamed the Chinese Oscars. In addition, Suzhou has golf courses, an upmarket marina bobbing with expensive yachts, and entire neighbourhoods filled with modish bars and restaurants, just like those in Shanghai.

Successful though modern Suzhou is, its high-voltage economy is really only a reawakening of its traditional merchant heritage. Historically this has almost always been a rich city, a trading centre, a place of political prestige, and a popular domestic tourist destination.

It has a long and ostentatious history. Suzhou was the capital of the state of Wu during the Warring States Period (403–221 BC), albeit for a few years only, before flourishing as a trading and silk centre – especially from the early 6th century, when it was linked to other parts of eastern and northern China by the Grand Canal. The economy was at its prosperous peak during the Ming and Qing dynasties, when large numbers of officials, scholars and artists settled here, and local traders rapidly grew rich. This wealth was largely invested in some 287 beautiful gardens, of which 68 are still open to the public.

Its political supremacy may have long been hijacked by Shanghai to the east, but Suzhou retains its commerce

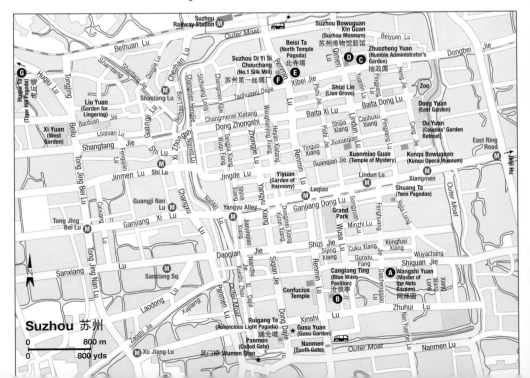

Suzhou 苏州

and culture, and its historical relics have also been well preserved, and are a pleasure to visit.

SUZHOU'S GARDENS

The principles of Chinese garden construction – creating an illusion of the universe in a small space, and achieving a year-round seasonal balance of plants – are apparent throughout Suzhou. Water trickles between twisted, rocky crags; small islands are connected by canals and zigzag bridges; winding paths lead to tiny garden spaces with fountains, carefully manicured plants and fish ponds. A walk through the small alleys in the town, along the canals and through the gardens has a special charm in the misty mornings, when the tourists haven't yet arrived.

Wangshi Yuan Ⓐ (网师园; Master of the Nets Garden) is a delightful and compact garden that dates from the Southern Song period. Famous for its peony blooms in spring, the focus of the garden is its central pool around which cluster charming pavilions and walkways. A small slice of the Master of the Nets Garden has been recreated at the Metropolitan Museum of Art in New York, where it is called Ming Garden.

Also in the vicinity, the **Canglang Ting Ⓑ** (沧浪亭; Blue Wave Pavilion) is a beautifully arranged garden laid out next to a canal. Unlike the carefully manicured gardens elsewhere in Suzhou, the Blue Wave features a profusion of lush, untamed vegetation. The Panmen scenic area by the moat in the southwest of town is well worth exploring for its stretch of city wall, the delightful arched **Wumen Qiao** (吴门桥; Wumen Bridge) and the impressively restored **Ruiguang Ta** (瑞光塔; Ruiguang Pagoda).

The queen of Suzhou gardens, and one of the finest in all of China, is the wonderful **Zhuozheng Yuan Ⓒ** (拙政园; Humble Administrator's Garden), which covers an area of 4 hectares

(10 acres). Wang Xiancheng, a retired court official, had it built in 1513 on the spot where the poet Lu Guimeng lived during the Tang dynasty. The name is something of a mistranslation: Zhuo really means silly or foolish, and is a reference that Wang made to himself, a high-ranking official who fell foul of the emperor and lost his lofty position.

His loss was Suzhou's gain, because Wang then built the Humble Administrator's Garden, a carefully balanced blend of vegetation, water and rocks. Each element of the garden has a layer of meaning: there are seasonal pagodas, where lotus, osmanthus, plum and bamboo bloom or leaf in different seasons, to provide year-round visual pleasure. There are paths with plum and phoenix tiles; to alternate steps on the tiles brings good fortune, according to the rules of Chinese wordplay. There is another area where Hong Xiuquan, the leader of the Taiping rebellion, set up temporary headquarters here, in the Dragon Head building. And those are only a few of the garden's attractions.

> **Ⓞ Tip**
>
> Most of the gardens, temples and pagodas in and around Suzhou are open between 8am and 5 or 5.30pm, and charge a nominal fee.

Fishpond at the Suzhou Museum.

A side canal in Zhouzhuang.

Zhouzhuang, one of the most attractive of the so-called "water towns".

whose family is from Suzhou, the building displays many of his signature design features, such as squares, rectangles and pyramids, plus abundant use of natural light. It also uses Chinese elements such as a garden, a classical footbridge, moon-gate doors, and a traditional rock wall, along with replications of the whitewashed plaster walls and dark clay tiles that are the signature features of Old Suzhou.

The area around the Suzhou Museum and Zhouzheng Yuan garden is as good a place as any to arrange a **boat trip** on the city's picturesque waterways. These trips can be arranged from several areas on the rectangular main canal, the broad waterway that embraces the Old Town like a moat. None of the boats are much of a bargain, but the bigger vessels work out less expensive if you don't mind waiting for them to fill up with tourists. The smaller boats, however, can explore the smaller waterways, so depending upon your budget, that's the choice. Most trips will last an hour or so.

SUZHOU MUSEUM

Near the Humble Administrator's Garden is the **Suzhou Museum** ⓓ (苏州博物馆新馆; Suzhou Bowuguan Xin Guan), which opened in late 2006 (www.szmuseum.com; Tue–Sun 9am–5pm; free). Designed by the famous Chinese-American architect I.M. Pei,

OTHER SIGHTS IN SUZHOU

Further west is **Beisi Ta**  (北寺塔; North Temple Pagoda). The present octagonal pagoda dates from the Southern Song period, although two restorations occurred in the second half of the 17th century. A splendid view of Suzhou can be seen from the top of the 76 metre (250 ft) -high, nine-storey tower, and there is a teahouse with refreshments behind the pagoda.

Another highlight is the **Suzhou No. 1 Silk Mill**  (苏州第一丝绸厂; Suzhou Di Yi Si Chouchang; www.1st-silk.com; daily 9am–5.30pm; free), where tourists can see how ancient Suzhou's most sought-after luxury is made. This is no museum, but a real factory, and from mulberry leaves to worms, to cocoons, to thread, and on to the well-stocked gift shop, it ably guides visitors through the history of silk production in China. A key step is when the silkworm cocoons are steamed, then washed, and then the silk thread is pulled. The thread can sometimes measure almost 100 metres (110 yds) in length, and several threads are spun together into a rich, durable yarn. Many people in the area cultivate silkworms, usually as a profitable sideline.

On the western edge of the town, in the street of the same name, is **Liu Yuan** (留园; Garden for Lingering). It is aptly named: getting lost in the garden's many nooks and crannies is a pleasure. Liu Yuan is a good example of a southern Chinese garden of the Qing era (1644–1911).

Tiger Hill Pagoda  (虎丘塔; Huqui Ta), in the far northwest of town, is one of Suzhou's finest attractions. And yes, it is leaning: at the top, the pagoda is 2.34 metres (7ft 8ins) out of kilter, and it has twice been stabilised: once during the Ming Dynasty, and a second time (unusually for the period) in 1961. The Ming effort was remarkable – it is the uppermost layer that straddles the top of the pagoda and sits off-centre, in an effort to rebalance the 48-metre (157ft) structure. The pagoda was finished in 961, and is made entirely of brick, a rarity in Chinese construction. Tiger Hill Pagoda is quite unusual, because unlike many of China's

Tip

The popularity of Shanghai's hip Xintiandi area has inspired a host of imitators, and Suzhou has two. One is called Xintiandi, but it is a little-visited amusement park rather than a bar-and-restaurant strip. A worthier imitator is Ligongdi: it has the same upmarket restaurants as the real Xintiandi, and the same smattering of faux history, with imitation Ming- and Qing-dynasty arched bridges, pagodas and cobbled paths.

older sites, it has not been completely rebuilt, and the wonderful structure, aged and graceful, still evokes a strong sense of ancient China. The pagoda sits atop a much older site: the tomb of the original Duke of Wu, the founder of a small kingdom, who was buried here 2,400 years ago in a rocky cleft beneath the pagoda.

THE WATER TOWNS

The border between Jiangsu and Zhejiang provinces is sprinkled with water towns – small villages that thrived on the silk, tea, ceramic and rice trades – and six of them have been selected as Unesco World Heritage Sites. Those six – Luzhi, Nanxun, Tongli, Wuzhen, Xitang and Zhouzhuang – were once linked to Beijing by the Grand Canal, the watery highway that opened them up to global commerce (see page 245).

While differing in subtle details, the six water towns have certain features in common. They all thrived during the same era, the Ming and Qing dynasties, and they all provide

the same tantalising glimpses of old China, with their cobbled paths, graceful arched bridges, labyrinthine canal networks and exquisite tiled roofs. Most are easily accessed from Shanghai and/or Suzhou.

Zhouzhuang ❸ (周庄), only an hour and a half by car from Shanghai, is small – just 400 sq metres (4,300 sq ft) – but it packs a lot of history into just a few blocks. Among the highlights are the houses of the rich. Zhang's House, built in the early 14th century, is a sprawling mansion with six courtyards, 70 rooms filled with antiques, and a canal running through the courtyards. Tucked in the rear is a sun-dappled patio, with a stone table carved into a chessboard.

Tongli ❹ (同里) is 20 minutes from Zhouzhuang by car, and two hours by boat. It is larger than Zhouzhuang, with wider canals, broader pavements and more trees. The pace is slower, and it feels less crowded and more lived in. The **Garden of Seclusion and Meditation** (退思园; Tui Si Yuan) – a classic Chinese garden – is one of the

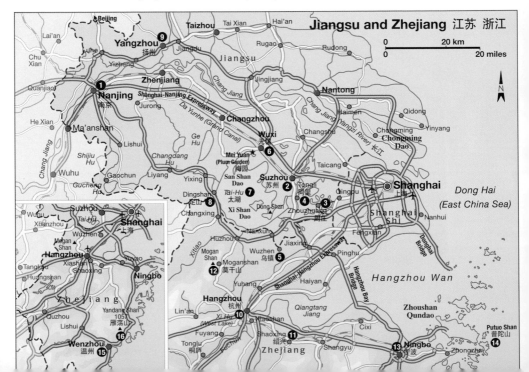

highlights, and so are the canal-side tables at one of the local teahouses. Here, tourists can enjoy the aromatic herbal flavours of the local *longjing* tea, watch trained cormorants dive into the canal for fish, and listen as the evocative music of an *er hu* (a stringed instrument) floats along the cobbled streets. As night falls, red lanterns glow and ripple, reflected in the serene water of the canals.

Wuzhen ❺ (乌镇), once the richest of the water towns, is two hours' drive south from Tongli. A wide canal bisects the centre of town and joins the Grand Canal itself, still a major commercial artery. A branch of the Grand Canal serves as the town's main street, and the houses have back doors that open straight onto the water. Wuzhen is famous for traditional crafts; some shops make wooden barrels and some spin cotton into cloth, while others make silk fans, rice wine, cotton slippers and brass buckles. In Wuzhen, all these products are made the old-fashioned way, just as they were 10 centuries ago.

WUXI AND TAI HU

Wuxi ❻ (无锡), easily reached by train from either Suzhou (15 minutes) or Nanjing (60 minutes), or by boat from Hangzhou on the Grand Canal in about 13 hours, has a history that goes back more than 2,000 years. But the city's importance grew with the completion of the canal, and its wealth was achieved, as in the whole region, through agriculture, trade and silk production. The Grand Canal flows right through the centre of town, underneath elegant arched bridges.

Tai Hu ❼ (太湖), China's third-largest lake, covers 2,420 sq km (934 sq miles) – although it is just 2.5 metres (8ft) deep, on average – and is peppered with 48 islands. The romantic landscape in green and blue, veiled with fine mist, has made this lake the subject of many poems. Not surprisingly, residents have a more pragmatic view of the lake: it provides them with fish, shrimp and hairy crabs, and they breed ducks and geese, as well as grow lotus and water chestnuts on it. The distinctive rock found in all Chinese

On the water in Zhouzhuang.

⊙ THE GRAND CANAL

Most people know about the Great Wall, but far fewer have even heard of ancient China's other great engineering feat: the Grand Canal (大运河; Da Yunhe).

When the canal reached its peak during the Yuan dynasty, it was the longest man-made canal in the world, stretching 1,800km (1,100 miles) between Beijing and Hangzhou, and joining together the Yangzi and the Huang He (Yellow River). But the canal's importance went beyond its sheer length: it shifted China's centre of gravity from north to south, and it helped forge an empire. The rice-producing Jiangnan (south of the Yangzi) area became more important than the wheat-producing north, and a mass migration to the south began. The silks, teas and ceramics of Jiangnan also lured south.

At the end of the 13th century, the waterway extended across the provinces of Zhejiang and Jiangsu, and connected four major river systems. Even today, a steady flow of ships and barges plough its muddy waters and it still forms an unbroken transport route between Hangzhou and the Yangzi, and as far north as Jining. Pleasure boats are restricted to small stretches of the canal, to make way for commercial traffic. Some ferries ply the canal, but they run only during the night. Now, as then, transport is the main function of the Grand Canal.

classical gardens comes from Tai Hu, and was an important family business in the past.

Tour groups tend to muster in numbers at the two main sights on Tai Hu outside Wuxi. Spring is the peak season at **Mei Yuan** (梅园; Plum Garden) overlooking the lake, when its many thousands of plum trees are in blossom. **Yuantou Zhu** (鼋头渚; Turtle Head Islet), a peninsula poking into the lake, is popular for its walks, pavilions and amusement parks. From Yuantou Zhu you can hop on a boat to the island of **San Shan** (三山岛; Three Hills). Finally, the attractive and unspoilt outcrop of **Dong Shan** (East Hill) projects into Tai Hu east of the island of Xi Shan (West Hill) and is easily reached from Suzhou.

Yixing County (宜兴县), on the western shore of Tai Hu, has a reputation for its ceramics – and in particular its teapots. Production is centred on the town of **Dingshan** ❽ (定山). Unglazed *Zisha* (purple sand) Yixing teapots absorb the flavour of the tea, and seasoned, well-used pots simply require the addition of boiling water – or so they say. The Ceramics Exhibition Centre allows you to appreciate the full range of Yixing's ceramic production and its historical importance.

YANGZHOU

Just over an hour by train from Nanjing, **Yangzhou** ❾ (扬州) dates back to the 5th century BC; it found prosperity in its prime position on the southern section of the Grand Canal. A salt monopoly further filled the coffers of this pretty canal town, but the Taiping rebels brought considerable destruction in the mid-19th century. **Daming Si** (大明寺; Daming Temple) in the northwest of town dates back to the 5th century AD, although it was razed by the Taiping and later rebuilt. The temple is chiefly notable for its Jian Zhen Hall, dedicated to a monk who failed five times to reach Japan to promote Buddhism, eventually succeeding on his sixth endeavour. Yangzhou's major scenic area is **Shouxihu Gongyuan** (瘦西湖公园; Shouxihu Park), looping south from Daming Si and marked by its **Wuting Qiao** (五亭桥; Five Pavilion Bridge).

Weaving silk on a traditional loom.

◎ SILK AND SILK CULTIVATION

Nobody knows when the first Chinese person decided to steam the cocoon of a silkworm, unroll it, and spin the resulting strands into one of the finest, softest, and most comfortable fabrics ever invented. According to legend, it happened some 5,000 years ago, when a princess accidentally dropped a cocoon into her tea, unravelled the thread, and hey presto! China had its most famous export.

Silk is made from the cocoons of mulberry silkworms, which thrive in the moist climate of the Yangzi Delta. The delicate worms need plenty of care: dust, rats and temperature changes can kill them. Silk-making remains labour-intensive: the cocoons are steamed to melt the resinous coating and kill the worm, then dipped in hot water to locate the end of the silk strand. Each strand is woven together with about 10 others and the resulting thread made into cloth.

That cloth – strong and durable, with an elegant soft lustre – has been in demand since the day the princess dropped the cocoon. Medieval Europeans, dressed in scratchy wool, couldn't get enough of it. The Silk Road became the most famous trade route in history, and even today, China still produces and exports most of the world's silk. The Suzhou Silk Museum (Tue–Sun 9am–5pm) exhibits timeless garments and offers an insight into silk's labour-intensive manufacturing processes.

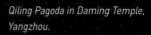

A shoal of carp in Hangzhou's West Lake.

HANGZHOU AND ZHEJIANG

Extolled by Marco Polo as the world's most beautiful and magnificent city, Hangzhou is one of China's six ancient capitals and famed for its spellbinding lake scenery.

One of the wealthiest provinces in China, **Zhejiang** (浙江), with its famous capital city of Hangzhou, spans a region whose geography ranges from canals, rivers and flat, fertile land in the north to hilly interiors and rugged seashores in the south and east. The long and fragmented coastline has several ports, such as industrious Ningbo and Wenzhou, that have played a decisive role in the area's historic prosperity.

Hangzhou is located in the north of the province at the lower end of the Grand Canal (see page 245), and is one of China's most visited destinations. Its most cherished sight is the celebrated West Lake (Xi Hu), but the area is also renowned for picturesque temples, pagodas, wetlands and tea villages. Nearby Shaoxing is a photogenic canal town.

Offshore, and reached by regular ferries from Hangzhou, Ningbo and Shanghai, is the sacred Buddhist island of Putuo Shan, with temples, panoramic sea views, sandy beaches, and Buddhist pilgrims from throughout China.

HANGZHOU

A fortified and prosperous town during the Tang period (618–907),

Pavilion in the grounds of the Xiling Seal Engravings Society on Gushan Island, West Lake.

Hangzhou ❿ (杭州) benefited greatly from its position at the southern end of the Grand Canal. At the beginning of the 12th century, the Chinese court was defeated in a battle against tribes from its northern borders, and fled south. In 1138, the newly formed empire of the Southern Song dynasty took the city as its temporary residence. The town flourished, with officials, writers and scholars moving there as the dynasty blossomed. During the Southern Song dynasty, Chinese culture reached a dramatic

Main Attractions
West Lake (Xi Hu)
Lingyin Si Monastery
Moganshan
Putuo Shan

Maps on pages 244, 252

⊙ Tip

A gentle bicycle ride around West Lake is one of the best ways to enjoy China's most famous waterfront. There are free public bicycles parked at kiosks around the lake, though you need to register first with a passport and deposit. Incidentally, West Lake is the only National Scenic Area in China that is free of charge.

Tai chi in the morning mist, Dragon Well Tea Park.

climax, and artworks from this era, particularly the richly detailed brush paintings, are considered to be among the finest works of art ever produced.

Hangzhou was the subject of poems even earlier than that, under the Tang dynasty, such as in the work of the poet Bai Juyi (772–846), who became governor of the town and had a dam built at West Lake that still bears his name. During the Southern Song period the city's population increased from less than half a million to more than one million, making Hangzhou one of the largest cities in the world at the time. It was nearly wiped out in the second half of the 19th century, when Taiping rebels swarmed through, destroying much of its antiquity. Modernisation has also taken a toll, as the city walls and gates have disappeared, and the numerous old canals have been filled in and paved over.

Today, as in the past, Hangzhou is an important administrative centre in the middle of one of China's most prosperous regions. Its products include silk and *longjing cha* (dragon well tea), and

its pharmaceutical industry and academy of arts are well known throughout China. The population is now over 7 million.

Hangzhou is a very pleasant city to explore, though the areas around West Lake and other tourist sites get very busy at weekends and holidays. Spread out over a large area, it can be difficult to hail a taxi at peak times – consider hiring a driver to ferry you between sites, or hop on one of the free red public bicycles parked at kiosks around the city. Cycling is a great way to see the lake and travel through the tree-shaded streets.

It is said that every Chinese city has a **West Lake** (西湖; Xi Hu). In fact, although there are around 30 West Lakes in China, the one in Hangzhou is by far the most famous. The eastern shore is close to the town, while forested mountains, often shrouded in mist, surround the other shores, lending the landscape a romantic allure.

The lake grew in stages: first in the early 800s with the Bai dyke, and then in 1090, when the famous poet and

administrator Su Dongpo gathered thousands of labourers and dug out and extended the lake, a process that was repeated during the Ming dynasty. The most recent stage – a major one – was finished in 2003, when 80 hectares (200 acres) of lake were added on the western end. The **West Lake Museum**  (西湖美术馆; Xi Hu Bowuguan) has some rare cultural relics and documents on display, all concerning the lake, and some displays about its history and importance.

In the north part of West Lake, the pagoda at **Baochu** Ⓑ (宝俶塔) stands tall against the sky, a symbol of the city. It was originally built in 968, then later destroyed and rebuilt several times. The present pagoda dates from 1933 and is 45 metres (150ft) high. On the northwestern shore, the **Mausoleum of Yue Fei** Ⓒ (岳坟和岳庙; Yue Fen He Yuemiao) commemorates the Southern Song dynasty general who resisted the northern invaders, but, in time-honoured Chinese tradition, was falsely charged, executed and later exonerated. By night, movie director Zhang Yimou's *Impression West Lake* brings lake legends to life in a dancing neon pageant that floats across the northwestern corner of the lake.

In the west of the town, at the end of Lingyin Lu and easily reached by bus, is the beautifully situated **Lingyin Si** Ⓓ (灵隐寺; Monastery of the Hidden Souls; http://en.lingyinsi.org; daily 7am–6pm). The Buddhist Indian Hui Li, who thought the peak resembled part of the Gradhrakuta Mountain in India, founded the monastery in AD 326. Since the second half of the 10th century, the rock walls of the mountain have been carved with about 300 Buddhist sculptures and inscriptions. The most popular figure is at the foot of the mountain: the fat-bellied Buddha from the Song period, one of the most touched and photographed figures anywhere; it is believed to bring good luck. Up to 3,000 monks once lived in

the 18 pavilions and 75 temple halls on the mountain peak.

Beyond these figures is the monastery, one of the most famous Buddhist sites in all of China. Behind the entrance gate to the temple and two stone columns inscribed with Buddhist texts is **Tianwang Dian** (天王殿; Hall of Heavenly Kings), where another statue

Hangzhou's Lingyin Si is one of China's most famous and picturesque Buddhist monasteries. The pillars are painted black instead of the red normally associated with Chinese Buddhism.

☉ TRANSPORT

Getting to Hangzhou/Zhejiang

Flights: Hangzhou Xiaoshan International Airport is one of the busiest airports in China. The airport is 30km (19 miles) from the city centre, and will soon be connected via the new Hangzhou metro (the first metro line started operations in 2012), as well as regular buses.

By train and bus: Hangzhou is well connected by rail and bus to many cities in China, with multiple trains to and from Shanghai every hour.

Getting around Hangzhou/Zhejiang

Hangzhou: The bullet trains connect Hangzhou to Shanghai in just 49 minutes.

Moganshan: The best way to reach Moganshan is by car. Hangzhou is the closest train station on the high-speed line. You can take a bus from there to Wukang or a taxi directly to the mountain top.

Ningbo: The awesome Hangzhou Bay Bridge, which opened to the public in 2008 and was the longest cross-ocean bridge in the world at the time of its construction, has cut two hours from the travel time between Shanghai and Ningbo and other cities in southeastern Zhejiang province. A high-speed rail line reduces journey times further still.

of the Maitreya Buddha can be seen, guarded by the two Heavenly Kings standing at its side. The gilded statue of the Buddha Sakyamuni, which is more than 20 metres (66ft) high and made of precious camphor wood, is in Daxiongbao Dian (Precious Hall of the Great Heroes).

MODERN HANGZHOU

In Hangzhou, as in the rest of China, the old coexists with the new, side by side. And Hangzhou, as one of the wealthiest cities in China, certainly has its share of the new.

Expansive infrastructure and leisure projects are underway citywide. The 350kmh (218mph) bullet trains have cut travel time between Shanghai and Hangzhou to just 45 minutes. These connect with cross-city metro lines. As of 2017, three lines are operational and a further seven lines are planned to be launched by 2020. Meanwhile, **Xiaoshan Airport** is establishing itself as a budget airline hub encouraging visitors from across Asia, and a few European destinations, to fly directly to Hangzhou – and then stay awhile.

Xihu Tiandi ⓔ, by the same developers as Shanghai's Xintiandi, is an atmospheric enclave of grey-brick restaurants, stone paths and gardens, right beside West Lake. This area is home to a collection of upmarket bars and restaurants, both Chinese and international. A few steps away, Hubin Lu promenade bristles with luxury

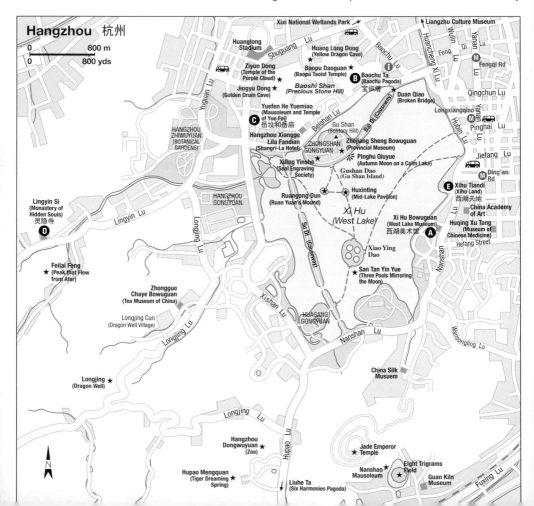

brand boutiques, while Nanshan Lu along the eastern bank and Shuguang Lu to the northwest are lively bar and nightlife strips.

Twenty minutes by taxi west of the city centre, the **Xixi National Wetlands Park** (西溪国家湿地公园; Xixi Guojia Shidi Gongyuan) offers more watery beauty, Covering 11.5 sq km (4.4 sq miles) of winding waterways and marshlands, the sodden area was first cultivated in the Han dynasty and designated as China's first national wetlands park in 2005. Scenes from Feng Xiaogang's 2008 movie *Fei Cheng Wu Rao* were shot here, and thousands of visitors now visit annually to tour the bucolic landscapes by paddleboat.

OUTSIDE HANGZHOU

To the west of Hangzhou, atop a steeply winding road, is the village of **Longjing** (龙井村), where Hangzhou's most famous export, *Longjing cha* (Dragon Well) tea has traditionally been produced. In this picturesque, if somewhat touristy, village you can pick your own leaves from the terraced fields while

local farmers dry the harvest in huge roadside woks.

An excursion to one of the surrounding villages, such as **Meijiawu** (梅家坞), about 20 minutes by car to the south of Hangzhou, offers a more authentic tea-picking experience. The trip through the lovely landscape with its famous bamboo groves can be made by bicycle, hired in town.

Dragon Well Tea Park in Longjing village near Hangzhou, home of the prized longjing tea.

Buddhist carvings at Feilai Feng caves.

A 45-minute bus-ride northwest of the city centre will take you to the **Liangzhu Culture Museum** (良渚文化博物馆; Liangzhu Wenhua Bowuguan; Tue–Sun 9am–5pm; free), in Liangzhu New Town, which showcases 5,000-year-old Liangzhu relics in a visually arresting David Chipperfield-designed museum. Why is this world-class museum in the grim suburbs of Hangzhou, you may ask? Because it sits right over the prehistoric archaeological site where the Liangzhu culture originated and the relics were found.

Heading west from town, Hangzhou Bay becomes the **Qiantang River** (钱塘江), which is called the Fuchun further upstream. By whatever name, the river is famous for its tidal bore, a surging wave of brown foamy water that roars up the river each day. The tide flows with extra vigour during the full moons of autumn, but very high tides can also be seen on about the 15th to 18th days of every lunar month, often around midday.

Further upriver is **Tonglu** (桐庐), home to the rather remarkable **Jiangnan**

Suspended Temple (江南悬空寺; Jiang Nan Xuan Kong Si), built into a cliff face and supported by a series of pillars, which also support pathways and houses, all hugging the side of the cliff for dear life. Still further upriver is **Qiandaohu** (千岛湖; Thousand Island Lake), a popular place for boat trips.

ELSEWHERE IN ZHEJIANG

Shaoxing ⓫ (绍兴), 60km (37 miles) southeast of Hangzhou, is easily reached by train or bus. Famous throughout China for its culinary rice wine, the picturesque canal town is also notable as the birthplace of Lu Xun, the great modern writer. His **Former Residence** (鲁迅故居; Lu Xun Guju) and the **Lu Xun Memorial Hall** (鲁迅纪念馆; Lu Xun Jinianguan) both daily 9am–4pm) stand on Lu Xun street in the south of the city. The best way to appreciate Shaoxing's charms is to amble alongside the town's canals. The **Bazi Qiao** (八字桥; Eight Character Bridge) is a historic 13th-century bridge named after its resemblance to the character *ba* (eight).

MOGANSHAN

In the blessed green hills some 60km (38 miles) to the north of Hangzhou lies **Moganshan** ⓬ (莫干山), a cool, bamboo-clad oasis that draws weekend visitors from Shanghai and Hangzhou. Modern-day residents of Shanghai and Hangzhou are not the first to notice the airy charms of Moganshan, however. In the early 20th century, Shanghai's upper crust flocked to the mountain, where they built a variety of villas, plantations, clubs and other playgrounds, all made from the signature local stone. This was perhaps the closest thing in China to a colonial India-style hill station.

The notorious gangster Du Yuesheng also resided here, and the Guomindang likewise had a penchant for the hill resort. Later still, Communist bigwigs (including Mao) holidayed on the lush slopes. By the 1930s the

A tea plantation in the hills south of Hangzhou.

area was dotted with more than 150 Western-style stone buildings along with churches and other colonial paraphernalia; many old villas remain and some operate as hotels. There is a Mao Museum – Mao slept here – and White Cloud Castle, where Chiang Kaishek honeymooned with Soong Meiling, and later met Zhou Enlai. Just for fun, compare the displays dedicated to Zhou with the ones dedicated to Chiang.

Some of the older buildings are in disrepair, and there they sit, patient structures in various stages of decay, which add enormously to the appeal of Moganshan. Even today, Moganshan is chiefly famous for three highlights: stylish old villas, soft white clouds and wild green bamboo. The mountain is laced with stone paths, steps and walkways, and hiking is mostly about serendipity: turn here, and find an old mansion or a quiet pond; turn there, and find a restful pagoda with fine views of the foothills. One exception is the **Sword Pond Waterfall** (剑池瀑布; Jianchi Pubu), a deep gorge sliced in the vertical rock and filled with ponds

and patios, which is Moganshan's must-see attraction.

North of Hangzhou, close to the shores of Tai Hu and the town of Wuzhen, **Nanxun** (南浔) was known as the "the town of wealth" in the Ming and Qing dynasties. The town retains a gracious air in its watercolour vistas and web of canals that meander past 18th- and 19th-century villas, built by silk and salt merchants, and quaint village eateries. Attractions include Xiaolian Garden and Jiaye Tang Hall Library.

NINGBO AND PUTUO SHAN

Ningbo ⑬ (宁波), at the confluence of the Yuyao and Yong rivers, established itself as a prosperous trading port in Tang times, and later became China's most important port under the Ming. The city attracted both the Portuguese and the British, who established it as a treaty port in 1843. Its commercial importance was later comprehensively usurped by Shanghai, and these days tourists largely pass through en route to Putuo Shan offshore. Over Xinjiang Bridge and

Photo opportunity on Putuo Shan, sacred island of Guanyin. The island becomes very crowded on Buddhist feast days.

south of the ferry terminal, the 17th-century **Portuguese Catholic Church** is a well-preserved relic of the 19th-century European presence.

The easternmost of China's four sacred Buddhist mountains, **Putuo Shan** 

The easternmost of China's four sacred Buddhist mountains, **Putuo Shan** ⑭ (普陀山) is more of an island than a peak, but is a sacred domain nonetheless, and the island's holy ambience is enhanced by its isolation from the mainland. The reigning deity on this island is Guanyin, the Buddhist Goddess of Compassion, who is celebrated in several temples, the most famous of which is the **Puji Chansi** (普济禅寺; Puji Temple; daily 5.30am–6pm). **Fayu Si** (法雨寺; daily 5.30am–6pm), a substantial temple at the foot of Foding Shan, has a splendid thousand-arm Guanyin statue and a marvellous mountain backdrop. Visible from afar, a vast, bronze-plated effigy of the goddess – the 33 metre (108-ft) -high Nanhai (South Sea) Guanyin – rises up brilliantly on the southern tip of the island. Dotted with hotels, Putuo Shan can be reached by ferry from Ningbo in two hours (it can also be reached direct from Shanghai and from Hangzhou).

SOUTHERN ZHEJIANG

Pop into a Chinese restaurant in Paris or Venice and the owners and staff are very likely to come from **Wenzhou** ⑮ (温州). The citizens of this port city, at the southern end of the ragged Zhejiang coastline, have a great tradition of exodus from China to Europe. Those that return from abroad throw their weight behind the free-market bedlam that has gripped the city. There are not many sights in town per se, with the pleasant park on **Jiangxin Dao** (江心岛; Jiangxin Island) the main tourist diversion. Two churches (one 18th-century, the other 19th-century) survive in the city centre.

Some 80km (50 miles) from Wenzhou, the mountainous region of **Yandang Shan** ⑯ (雁荡山) is a stirring expanse of towering cliffs and peaks. The most famous sight is the dramatic 190-metre (625ft) **Dalongqiu Pubu** (大龙湫瀑布; Big Dragon Pool Waterfall), one of the highest falls in China.

Temple in the cliff of Wenzhou Yandang mountain.

Dramatic scenery at Xiao Sanxia
(Three Little Gorges).

CHANG JIANG (YANGZI) REGION

Better-known to Westerners as the Yangzi, the Chang Jiang slices through central China for 6,300km (3,900 miles), forcing its way through the dramatic Three Gorges to the plains beyond.

The longest river in China (and the third-longest in the world) is called, appropriately enough, the **Chang Jiang** (长江) – Long River. Foreigners mistakenly refer to it as the **Yangzi** (扬子; sometimes spelt Yangtze); for the Chinese this term denotes the lower course from Wuhan to the sea. Meandering eastwards for some 6,300km (3,900 miles), this mighty river – which traditionally divides China's north and south – begins life on the slopes of Geladandong, the main peak of the Tanggula Shan range in remote Qinghai province. Its course ends just north of Shanghai, where a 13km (8-mile)-wide mouth empties into Dong Hai, the East China Sea. Along the way, the river flows across nine provinces, with 700 main tributaries draining an area of nearly 2 million sq km (772,000 sq miles) – almost 20 percent of China's total geographic area, one-quarter of the country's arable land and supporting over one sixth of the world's population.

From the delta just north of Shanghai the river is navigable by ocean-going vessels as far as Wuhan, nearly 1,000km (620 miles) upstream. Its murky brown waters flow through many of China's important industrialised areas, not to mention centres of silk-weaving, embroidery, lacquer work and carving. This lower stretch of the river is also known as the Yangzi, its local name changing twice more upriver. When the early colonial powers arrived, they applied this name to the entire river.

One of the most ambitious engineering projects ever undertaken, the main body of the Three Gorges Dam was completed in 2006 and its final turbine hooked up to the grid in 2012. Luxury cruise liners and tourist boats ply the river in excursions that some regard as a China highlight.

Main Attractions
Chongqing
Shibaozhai
Yueyang
Hubei Provincial Museum, Wuhan
Shennongjia Forest Reserve
Wudang Shan
Huang Shan

Maps on pages
260, 264, 268

A local farmer with a heavy load, Three Gorges area.

CHONGQING

The vast city of **Chongqing** ❶ (重庆) is the launching point for boat cruises which journey some 700km (435 miles) down the Chang Jiang, but more notably in recent years it has earned itself the dubious distinction of having become the world's most populous municipality. The population was measured at 30 million people in 2016 (the core city houses around 8.5 million).

Chongqing sits at the confluence of two rivers, where the Jialing joins the Chang Jiang, a strategic location that has always guaranteed its place as an important trading centre. The location of the original core of Chongqing, on a rocky promontory hugging the river, is rare among Chinese cities; the steepness of its streets means that the few cyclists on the roads are spandex-clad.

During World War II and the Japanese occupation of large parts of the country, the Guomindang government under Chiang Kaishek retreated to Chongqing (then known in the West as Chungking) and this part of history is reflected in many of the city's points of interest.

WHAT TO SEE IN CHONGQING

The area around **Jiefang Bei** (解放碑; Liberation Square) is the heart of the city, and although much has been transformed into a pedestrian shopping centre, there are still some narrow, winding backstreets to explore. Steep steps lead from the tip of the peninsula down to the riverbanks. At the tip of the peninsula is a small pavilion, **Chaotianmen** (朝天门; Door Facing Heaven), and near this is the entrance to one of the city's two cable cars (索道), which carry commuters across the river and offer excellent views of this megacity.

The small Buddhist temple **Luohan Si** (罗汉寺; Arhat Temple) is noted for a breathtaking collection of 500 painted terracotta *arhat* sculptures in its main hall. **Hongya Dong** (洪崖洞) is an old-style building jutting out from the side of the cliff. It is noteworthy as a city landmark and also for the numerous inexpensive shops, eateries and the Starbucks it houses.

The **Great Hall of the People** (人民 大会堂; Renmin Dahuitang) is a sprawling, classically inspired building

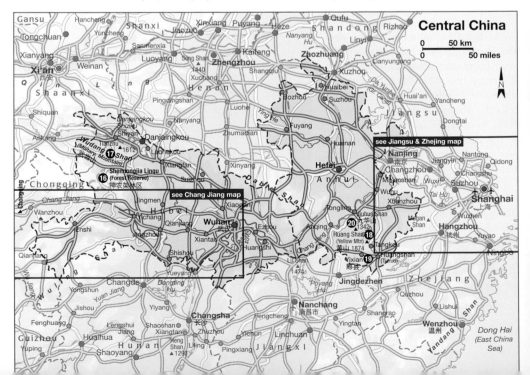

constructed in 1951, and the architectural symbol of Chongqing. The adjoining **People's Square** (人民广场; Renmin Guangchang) is a popular spot for locals to dance in the evenings.

Among Chongqing's war-related attractions is the **former residence of Song Qingling** (宋庆龄旧居; Song Qingling Jiuju), wife of Sun Yatsen. She lived in this German colonial-era residence for the duration of the war of resistance against Japan.

On clear evenings there are good views across the city from **Pipa Shan** (琵琶山), about 2km (1.2 miles) west of Jiefangbei. Further west into the suburbs, **Hongyan** (红岩; Red Crag Village; daily 8.30am–5.30pm) was the site of important negotiations between Mao Zedong and Chiang Kaishek, an attempt to achieve an alliance to oppose the Japanese that ultimately resulted in failure.

DAZU

Before hopping on the ferry to drift through the Three Gorges, take time to visit the well-preserved Tang and Song grottoes at **Dazu ❷** (大足), 100km (60 miles) west of Chongqing. Five of these spots are designated Unesco World Heritage sites. The predominantly Buddhist statuary (Confucian ideals also get a say) is divided into two reliquaries. At **Bei Shan** (北山; daily 8.30am–6pm), a short taxi ride north of Dazu's main street, around 1,000 carvings are segregated into numerous caves, including the noteworthy niche number 155, featuring the Peacock King. **Baoding Shan** (宝顶山; daily 8.30am–6pm), 16km (10 miles) northeast of Dazu, has the more impressive artwork, its highlight being a 30-metre (100ft) reclining Buddha (wofo) in niche number 11.

CHONGQING TO YICHANG

Fengdu ❸ (丰都), traditionally known as the Ghost or Devil Town for its celebrated demon statues housed in temples, is a likely cruise stop from Chongqing. Mount Mingshan's demon temples, which date back to the Tang dynasty (618–907), can be accessed by cable car or boat.

Around 80km (50 miles) further downstream is **Shibaozhai ❹** (石宝寨; Stone

Modern Chongqing looms above the Chang Jiang.

Kite-flying on the river bank at Yichang.

Cruising through the Xiao Sanxia (Three Little Gorges).

Treasure Fortress), a regular stop on the cruise boat itineraries. During the reign of Emperor Qianlong (1735–96), a temple was erected on top of a rock rising up 30 metres (100ft) from the river's edge. According to legend, there was a small hole in the temple wall from which enough rice trickled to feed the monks, thus the name, Stone Treasure. Because the ascent to the temple was tiring, a pagoda-shaped pavilion was built against the rock in the early 1800s,

its 12 storeys reaching as far as the temple and still affording easy access to it by means of wooden staircases within. The next large town downriver, **Wanzhou** ⑤ (万州), is a long-established trading port on the Chang Jiang. Most of the old city is now submerged and a new town has been built to the north of the traditional waterfront centre. **Baidi Cheng** ⑥ (白帝城; City of the White Emperor), now resembling a fortified island, is where the Three Gorges begin. Legend has it that a ruler of the Eastern Han dynasty (AD 25–220) saw a plume of white smoke in the shape of a dragon emerge from a well outside his palace; considering it a good omen, he henceforth called himself the White Emperor. In the main hall of the local temple, Baidi Miao, are the figures of two army generals of Shu from the Three Kingdoms (221–263) period, Liu Bei and Zhuge Liang (whose exploits are related in the classic tale *Romance of the Three Kingdoms*).

SANXIA (THREE GORGES)

The entire length of **Sanxia** (三峡), the Three Gorges, is about 190km (120

miles). From west to east the individual gorges are Qutang Xia, Wu Xia and Xiling Xia. Although it is only 8km (5 miles) long and the shortest of the three, **Qutang Xia** ❼ (瞿塘峡) is probably the most fascinating. Perpendicular walls rise up from the river, pinching the gorge to a width of 100 metres (330ft) and making navigation through the one-way passage tedious.

Before Wu Xia is the town of **Wushan** (巫山), where the Daning He joins the Chang Jiang. Upstream along this tributary are the beautiful **Xiao Sanxia** ❽ (小三峡; Three Little Gorges); the journey involves transferring to smaller vessels at Wushan dock. The exquisite scenery, still impressive despite the rise in water levels, is regarded by many as the highlight of a Chang Jiang cruise. At one point it is possible to spot wooden coffins tucked into a tiny ledge high up on a mountain. These coffins are said to belong to the Ba people, a lost culture from the Bronze Age that was absorbed by the Qin dynasty. The Ba placed the coffins containing their dead in tiny crevices on remote mountain tops.

Back on the Chang Jiang, the 45km (28-mile) -long **Wu Xia** ❾ (巫峡; Witches' Gorge) is relatively calm despite its name. The gorge, surrounded by 12 vertiginous peaks, is steeped in legend; in this case, troublesome dragons have been turned to stone by the goddess Yaoji.

The boat then passes **Zigui** on the northern bank, home of the famous poet Qu Yuan (330–295 BC), who, according to legend, drowned himself in despair over the occupation of his home state by the armies of the Qin empire (the Chinese world still celebrates the Dragon Boat Festival in his honour). The 1,400-year-old town is now underwater, but the temple-cum-memorial hall dedicated to Qu Yuan has not been affected.

The mouth of the Xiangxi (Fragrant River) on the northern bank, its green waters contrasting starkly with the brown Chang Jiang, signals the start of **Xiling Xia** ❿ (西陵峡). The last, longest, and traditionally the most dangerous of the Three Gorges, Xiling stretches for 66km (41 miles) and is itself made up

⊙ Tip

Yangzi ferries and cruise boats are moored at Chongqing's Chaotianmen Docks, on the tip of the main peninsula. There is a ticket office for ferries at the end of Shaanxi Lu by the docks as well as numerous agencies selling cruises, but it is better to use the more reputable agents in town, such as CITS. Unpredictable water conditions mean that cruise schedules are often altered on a daily basis. For more information see page 445.

⊙ TRANSPORT

Getting to Chongqing

Flights: There are frequent flights from most major cities in China.

By train and bus: There are daily trains to Chongqing from cities all over China including Chengdu (2 hours), Beijing (27 hours), Wuhan (15 hours), Yichang (10 hours), Xi'an (11 hours) and Guiyang (9 hours). Buses are a better bet for travel to Yichang.

Boat Trips on the Chang Jiang: Cruise boats, hydrofoils and regular passenger ferries depart daily from the Chaotianmen docks in Chongqing. Most are bound for Yichang (13 hours by hydrofoil, 48 hours by ferry), although a few continue on to Wuhan.

Getting to Hubei

Flights: Wuhan's Tianhe International Airport is one of the busiest in central China, with regular service to most mainland destinations. Internationally, there are daily flights to Hong Kong and weekly connections to Bangkok, Taipei, Macau and Seoul.

By train and bus: Wuhan is very well connected by rail, the

station for high-speed trains is known simply as Wuhan station, the two others are denoted with their districts – Wuchang and Hankou. There are several long-distance bus stations servicing destinations as far afield as Jiujiang, Nanchang, Nanjing and Shanghai.

Getting around Hubei

Wuhan: There are daily fast trains to Wudang Shan (7 hours), while buses run regularly throughout the day to Xiangfan (4.5 hours), from where you can catch onward buses to Wudang Shan. There are numerous daily buses to Yichang (4 hours).

Yichang: Frequent buses run to Wuhan (4 hours) and north to Xiangfan (3 hours), from where there are regular buses to Wudang Shan. There are also daily trains to Xiangyang (4 hours) and Wudang Shan (6 hours). Public ferries run to Wushan and Chongqing.

Shennongjia: For foreigners, the only legal route is from the south, making Yichang the main transit point (see above).

Wudang Shan: There are trains to Wuhan (7 hours) as well as daily connections to Xiangyang (2.5 hours). Buses run daily to Wuhan (6.5 hours) via Xiangyang (2 hours).

of several smaller gorges. The peculiar shape of Niugan Mafei Xia (Horse-Lung and Ox-Liver Gorge) lent it its exotic name. Behind this is the 120 metre (400-ft) -long abyss of Qingtan (Blue Cliff). From the south, the river is overlooked by Huangling Miao (Yellow Hill Temple), whose main hall dates back to the Han dynasty.

The Three Gorges Dam is located at **Sandouping** ⑪ (三斗坪), a 10km (6-mile) stretch in the centre of Xiling Gorge, 35km (20 miles) west of Yichang. Most cruise boats will stop here to allow passengers to take in the immensity of the construction. A minibus ride can take you to the dam's three viewing areas to marvel at the ambitious project and raging jets of water forced through the release gates.

Yichang ⑫ (宜昌) is now a large and crowded city, as many people from the surrounding areas who were displaced by the construction of the Three Gorges Dam have relocated here. A fast highway now connects it with Wuhan, and few cruise boats and passenger ferries continue downstream from here.

Yichang is also an excellent staging point for trips further into **Hubei** (湖北) province, such as the Shennongjia Forest Reserve and Wudang Shan.

DOWNSTREAM FROM YICHANG

If you are continuing downriver from Yichang, you are likely to stop at **Shashi** ⑬ (沙市), 220km (140 miles) west of Wuhan. A 10km (6-mile) bus journey from the long-distance bus station drops you at the ancient town of **Jingzhou**, with its impressive Ming-dynasty city wall and **museum** (www.jzmsm.org; Tue–Sun 9.30am–4pm; free) where the fully preserved 2,000-year-old corpse of a Western Han-dynasty official can be seen.

The last stop downriver before Wuhan is the town of **Yueyang** ⑭ (岳阳) in Hunan province, situated at the point where the Chang Jiang meets Dongting Hu lake. The lakeside waterfront is attractive, but the best-known sight is **Yueyang Lou** (岳阳楼; Yueyang Tower; daily May–Sept 7am–6.30pm, Oct–Apr 7.30am–6pm), one of the region's most famous pavilion towers.

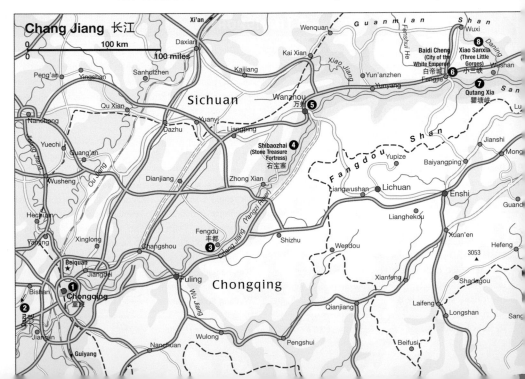

Numerous songs have been composed about it since the Tang dynasty (618–907), although the restored building dates from the late 19th century. The tower is flanked on both sides by two pavilions, Xianmeiting (Plum Blossom of the Immortal Pavilion) and Sanzuiting (Three Drunks Pavilion).

WUHAN

The industrial and commercial city of **Wuhan** ⑮ (武汉), roughly halfway between Chongqing and Shanghai at the confluence of the Chang and Han rivers, is a major entrepôt through which many visitors to central China are likely to pass. A massive metropolis with more than 9 million inhabitants, Wuhan is actually an amalgam of three formerly distinct settlements: Wuchang, Hankou and Hanyang, all now municipalities in their own right, each spilling out from the banks of the rivers that divide them. Taking advantage of their privileged positions along the Chang Jiang as well as major rail and road networks, the cities together comprise one of the country's most important economic centres.

Wuhan is also historically significant, perhaps most noteworthy for being the linchpin of the 1911 revolution that eventually brought down China's last imperial dynasty.

COLONIAL REMINDERS

Of the three modern districts, **Hankou** Ⓐ (汉口) – on the Chang Jiang's northwest bank and north of the Han Jiang – is the most convenient for tourists, with efficient transport, abundant accommodation and a good variety of eating and nightlife options. It also has the greatest concentration of visible history, with an entire quarter of well-preserved colonial European architecture emanating from the waterfront – grandiose remnants of its role as a treaty port in the latter half of the 19th century. Though the former colonial sector encompasses several streets stemming northwest from the erstwhile Bund, or waterfront promenade (now named Yanjiang Dadao), the most complete segment is along the pedestrian-only **Jianghan Lu** (江汉路), now an immensely popular thoroughfare lined with a variety of trendy shops

A vendor selling bamboo cages for keeping crickets as pets or pugilists. The tradition of cricket fighting, and associated gambling on the outcome, goes back at least as far as the Song dynasty. There are regular cricket-fighting events all over China; punters study the insect's form (fighting records are kept) and other attributes to make a qualified bet.

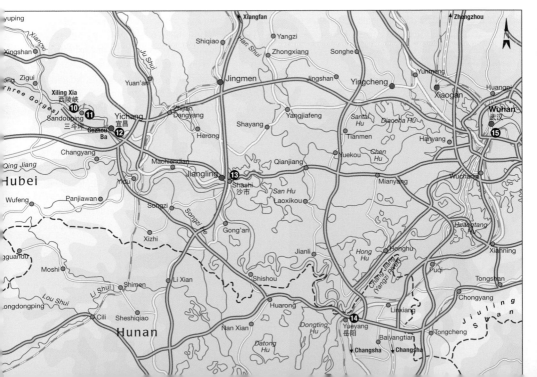

THE GREAT DAM OF CHINA

The long-awaited Three Gorges Dam is now complete, harnessing the power of the Chang Jiang for China's ever-increasing energy needs.

In a land that conceived the Great Wall, China's current leaders are continuing a long tradition of marshalling manpower and resources into colossal and audacious projects. But few can rival central China's great dam: its incredible ambition to supply 10 percent of the nation's electricity, its sheer size of 1,045 square kilometres (403 sq miles) of water and the epic human impact of an estimated 1.4 million people relocated. In 2016, the largest ship elevator in the world, capable of lifting vessels of up to 3,000 tonnes, was inaugurated at the dam.

First visualised by Sun Yatsen in 1919 for its huge power-generating capability, the scheme was shelved for four decades until championed by Mao Zedong in the late 1950s. The disastrous economic consequences of the Great Leap Forward followed by the chaos of the Cultural Revolution again mothballed the project. Strongly advocated by former Premier Li Peng, the National People's Congress ratified construction of the dam in 1992.

The locks and bridge at Sandouping.

The Chinese Communist Party loves grandiose schemes. But the dam is more than a symbol of political power, and the ambitious endeavour has several pragmatic aims. Supporters argue that the devastating floods that have plagued the Chang Jiang region will be controlled, river-shipping tonnage will increase and the dam will generate cheap, clean energy for a power-hungry growing economy.

But the scheme has had many critics, who have argued that as well as destroying many sites of archaeological interest and damaging areas of scenic beauty, the dam's exorbitant costs – that spiralled to a final US$59 billion – would not represent an efficient way to generate power. Numerous landslides have already been recorded in the area, there are fears that substantial silting might lead to flooding downstream and rival forms of power production, such as increasingly efficient solar-power technology, could render the dam obsolete.

Although allegations in some quarters that the dam had somehow triggered the Sichuan earthquake in 2008 have been widely dismissed (the dam was 700km/435 miles from the epicentre), the wisdom of building the world's largest hydro-electric project in an earthquake zone continues to be questioned.

The knock-on effects of such a large project are almost impossible to measure, and some experts suspect the dam's lowering of groundwater levels played a role in the devastating drought that affected millions of hectares of farmland downstream in 2011, regarded as the worst in 50 years. The environmental impacts of the dam include water pollution. Though the upstream municipality of Chongqing has improved its wastewater processing, the huge reservoir behind the dam has inevitably become polluted as cities and industries continue to discharge waste into its stagnant water.

China's escalating energy consumption means the dam now provides less than 3 percent of the nation's needs. Hydropower is still considered a key aspect of China's renewable energy targets, however, and plans for more major dams on the Chang Jiang are being mooted.

The Three Gorges Dam might one day be regarded as a great lesson in hydropower management. It could just as easily be seen as China's worst environmental blunder.

occupying the ground floors of giant European-style stone buildings.

WUCHANG

Wuchang (武昌), on the Chang Jiang's southeast side and accessible via the Great Chang Jiang Bridge or regular public ferries from Hankou, was an ancient port and administrative centre and, as such, has several historic sights. Most prominent of these is the 50-metre (164ft) **Huanghe Lou** ❸ (黄鹤楼; Yellow Crane Tower; daily Apr–Oct 7am–6.30pm, Nov–Mar 7.30am–5.30pm), the grandest of the many towers along the Chang Jiang. Overlooking the city from atop **She Shan** ❷ (蛇山; Snake Hill), the tower – which can be climbed via internal staircases to the top floor – commands sweeping views of the river and its urban environs. The original tower was first built in AD 223, but after it burnt to the ground in 1884 a new one was constructed on a larger scale a few hundred metres/yards away. Much of Snake Hill is covered with recently built classical-style Chinese buildings, including the shopfronts selling souvenirs along Ming Qing Jie, just inside the entrance to the complex.

Just east of here is the captivating **Changchun Guan** ❹ (长春观; Changchun Temple; daily 7.30am–5pm), a multi-faceted Daoist temple compound with an annexed vegetarian restaurant that serves delicious mock meats and vegetable dishes. The temple's many halls are usually filled with incense-wagging worshippers, and resident Daoist monks regularly perform elaborate rituals, while others practise martial arts in the attached training area.

A further 1km (0.6 mile) to the southeast is the **Hong Ge** ❺ (红阁; Red Chamber; Tue–Sun 8.30am–5.30pm), a colonial-style red-brick building which served as the headquarters of the Hubei Military Government leading up to the 1911 Wuchang Uprising. The structure now houses a museum showcasing the rooms filled with period furnishings and maps, as well as the military government's conference hall, dominated by a giant portrait of Sun Yatsen behind the stage. A bronze statue of the leader stands just outside the entrance.

HUBEI PROVINCIAL MUSEUM AND GUIYUAN SI

On Wuchang's far eastern fringe is **Dong Hu** ❻ (东湖; East Lake), an expansive watery network situated within a huge park, which makes for a pleasant retreat from Wuhan's suffocating summer heat. Nearby to the north is the **Hubei Provincial Museum** ❼ (湖北省博物馆; Hubei Sheng Bowuguan; www.hbww.org; Tue–Sun 9am–5pm), dedicated primarily to antiquities excavated from the tomb of Marquis Yi, who died in 433 BC during the Warring States Period. The exhibition is impressive and informative, with an extensive collection of well-preserved funerary objects displayed in an intuitive fashion and bolstered by English-language multimedia presentations. One of the highlights

Daoist ceremony at Wuhan's Changchun Guan Temple.

The Shennong Emperor Shrine at Shennongjia, dedicated to the mythical Xia-dynasty emperor (c.3000 BC). Also known as the Yan Emperor, he is credited with inventing agriculture in China as well as cataloguing hundreds of medicinal herbs.

Buddhist monastery and a magnet for worshippers and tourists alike. To Chinese Buddhists, the monastery is renowned for preserving a complete, 7,000-volume set of ancient scriptures in its Sutra Collection Pavilion, which contains a graceful statue of the Sakyamuni Buddha carved in a Southeast Asian style from a single piece of Burmese white jade. More visually striking is the Hall of Arhats, built in 1850 and holding an intriguing collection of 500 life-sized clay sculptures of *arhats*, or pupils of Buddha, each with his own persona and in a different pose.

AWAY FROM THE RIVER

Further inland, Hubei province has some spectacular scenery, the most rugged of which lies within the **Shennongjia Forest Reserve** ⑯ [神农架林区; Shennongjia Linqu; daily Apr–Oct 6.30am–5.30pm, Nov–Mar 7am–5.30pm], in the far northwest of the province about 200km (125 miles) from Yichang. The wild, mountainous preserve – the highest peak reaches 3,053 metres (10,016ft) – has for centuries

is a complete set of 64 bronze bells unearthed from the tomb, each of them still possessing perfect pitch and tone. Though the ancient bells themselves have only been played twice, concerts are regularly held in the museum auditorium using a duplicate set.

In Wuhan's third district, **Hanyang** [汉阳], on the Chang Jiang's northwest bank and south of the Han River, is the **Guiyuan Si** ⑭ [归元寺; Guiyuan Temple; daily Apr–Oct 7.30am–5.30pm, Nov–Mar 8am–5pm], the city's biggest

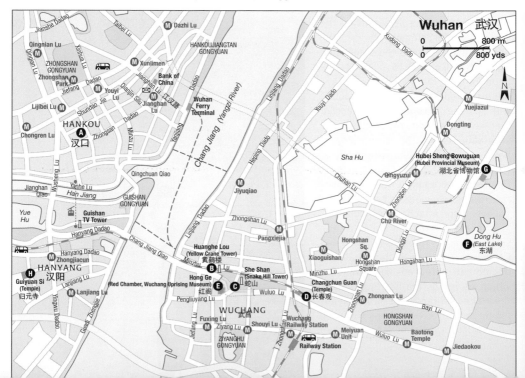

been reputed for its rich diversity of flora, and is named after the mythical Xia emperor Shennong, who according to legend combed its mountains in search of medicinal plants. In the 20th century, the area has become known for alleged sightings of the Chinese "wild man" *(ye ren)*, a giant, red-haired ape-like creature akin to the yeti or bigfoot. Though visitors are unlikely to run across the Ye Ren, those making their way to **Xiaolong Tan** (小龙潭) – in the heart of the reserve – may be fortunate enough to spot a family of endangered golden monkeys.

The reserve is accessed via **Muyu Zhen** (木鱼镇), a small tourist village about 16km (10 miles) south of the entrance with several hotels and restaurants. It is possible to reach Muyu Zhen by a single morning public bus from Yichang, but a more convenient option would be to book a two- or three-day, all-inclusive tour with CITS in Yichang. Many parts of the reserve, including Shennongjia town, are considered militarily sensitive and are off-limits to foreigners.

HUBEI'S FAR NORTHWEST: WUDANG SHAN

Tucked away in Hubei's far northwest are the multiple peaks of **Wudang Shan** ⑰ (武当山; Military Mountain; daily), a misty, mountainous area of major importance to Daoists and martial artists alike. The tree-shaded mountainsides have for centuries been cloaked in Daoist temples, many of which have recently been restored amid a revival in the area's popularity. But Wudang Shan is best known as the birthplace of a fighting style known as Wudang boxing, developed in these mountains by revered Song-dynasty monk Zhang Sanfeng and considered the essential precursor to tai chi. As such, it is respected among martial artists as much as Henan province's more famous Shaolin Si, and fighters from all over the world come here to pay their respects to Zhang. For the average visitor, however, the main attraction is the chance to climb Tianzhu Peak, at 1,612 metres (5,249ft) the area's highest. The path to the top passes by numerous temples and

Guiyuan Si, Wuhan.

Tip

Reaching Huang Shan is easy. Buses trundle to Tangkou at the foot of the mountain from Hefei, Nanjing, Shanghai and Hangzhou, while trains stop at Huang Shan City (aka Tunxi), 70km (43 miles) southeast, from where buses depart to the mountain. There are numerous hotels in Tangkou, or you can stay in lodgings on the trail to the peak and the summit itself. Pack warm clothing and a waterproof for the ascent, along with water and food.

A sea of clouds beneath the summit of Huang Shan.

shrines, but the most atmospheric are those inside the citadel at the top – especially the **Jindian** (金殿; Golden Hall; daily 8am–6pm), which adorns the highest point and yields arresting views of the clouds sweeping through the pointed peaks below.

ANHUI

Anhui (安徽) province may be one of eastern China's poorest, but it lays claim to one of its foremost destinations and scenic wonders. It is to **Huang Shan** ⑱ (黄山; Yellow Mountain) – the mist-wreathed mountain immortalised in countless Chinese paintings – that travellers to Anhui naturally gravitate. Rising up south of the Chang Jiang, it may not be one of China's most sacred mountains, but merits a mandatory stop for its breathtaking mountain scenery. Along with Tai Shan in Shandong province, this is a mountain that all Chinese aspire to climb. It's a tough climb to the summit and the constant mob of tourists is trying, but in favourable weather the views can be mesmerising, with twisted pines, blooms of mist and sunlight-dappled bamboo.

Legions of travellers congregate on the summit area to witness the famed Huang Shan sunrise. The hiking trail up the mountain is divided into the eastern steps and the western steps. The eastern route (7.5km/4.5 miles) is shorter than the 15km (9-mile) western route, but the only soft option is the cable car (or porter). A popular strategy is to ascend by the eastern steps and then descend by the western steps. But this is a mammoth undertaking and heavy on the joints. Many Chinese tourists alleviate the pain of the ascent and descent by availing themselves of one of the three cable cars that now ascend the flanks of the mountain.

Huang Shan City (黄山市), still often called by its former name Tunxi (屯溪) by locals, is worth some time for its beautiful surrounding paddy fields. The well-known Lao Jie (Old Street) is a pedestrian commercial street with shops in the style of Song, Ming and Qing dynasties.

The region around **Yixian** ⑲ (黟县), 60km (38 miles) northwest of Huang Shan City, is very attractive with small hamlets that are bastions of traditional Chinese architecture. The three villages of Xidi, Hongcun and Nanping (the latter was the setting for Zhang Yimou's classic film *Judou*) can be reached by taxi from Yixian town.

For those who find climbing Huang Shan a ridge too far, sacred **Jiuhua Shan** ⑳ (九华山; 1,342 metres/4,403ft) makes for a less exhausting ascent. The temple-covered mountain, around 80km (47 miles) northwest of Huang Shan City, is one of China's four sacred Buddhist peaks (see page 272). Jiuhua Shan may not be quite as scenic as Huang Shan, but makes up for this by being far less crowded. Hotels and restaurants can be found in the village of Jiuhua Shan Town on the mountain and a cable car is at hand for those whose stamina has deserted them.

In the traditional village of Hongcun.

CHINA'S SACRED PEAKS

If you want leg-stretching exercise, wonderful scenery, views and temple architecture, reach for the heights of China's sacred peaks.

One of the best ways to get a feeling for China's enduring spirituality is to follow in the footsteps of the pilgrims and ascend one of its sacred peaks.

There are a total of nine holy mountains (five Daoist and four Buddhist) scattered across the land. The Daoist peaks include Tai Shan in Shandong province – probably the world's most climbed mountain. Perhaps the most dramatic, however, is Hua Shan in Shaanxi province, with its hair-raising ascents. The other Daoist peaks are Song Shan in Henan province, which attracts huge crowds, largely because the Shaolin Temple lies on its slopes, Heng Shan (beiyue) in Shanxi province and Heng Shan (nanyue) in Hunan province further south.

China's Buddhist peaks largely began as Daoist preserves, before becoming associated with the followers of Buddha (fo). Perhaps the best known, Emei Shan in Sichuan province, inspires devotion in its legions of pilgrims. Putuo Shan, on a small island off the east coast, is also a major pilgrimage destination. Buddhist Jiuhua Shan in Anhui province may be overshadowed by nearby Huang Shan, China's most famous (non-sacred) mountain, but that makes it far less touristy. Noted for its dramatic scenery and fine temple architecture, Wutai Shan in Shanxi province is governed by Wenshu (Manjusri), the god of wisdom.

Climbing China's sacred mountains is considered a rite of worship, but you won't need crampons or ice axes as stone steps and guardrails line the route.

The precipitous paths up the slopes of Hua Shan are bedecked with red ribbons and engraved padlocks. Young couples attach the padlock to the guardrail and then throw the key into the mists below to ensure a long and happy marriage.

Zhurong Daoist Temple on the icy 1,290-metre (4,232ft) summit of Heng Shan, Hunan province.

A heavy load: building materials on China's sacred mountains have to be hauled up their steep slopes by hand.

Pavilion on the peak of Heng Shan in Shanxi province.

Mountains of mystery

To primitive man, the mountains were secret places, sources of cosmic energy inhabited by gods and spirits. Poets such as Qu Yuan celebrated the twilight world of witches and immortals that populated the slopes of China's mountainous realm. These were places rife with superstition, magic and the unknown. Animists worshipped mountains such as Tai Shan even before the Daoists claimed it as their own.

The mountain is represented in the Yijing (I-Ching; Book of Changes) by the trigram *ken*, meaning Keeping Still. It is a place where life and death meet, a place of stillness, meditation and internal awareness.

China's Confucian tradition, dealing as it did with the world of man, temporal ritual and human relations, had no place here – hence the absence of sacred Confucian mountains.

Sacred they may be, but these peaceful peaks have become hostage to the tourist economy. Cable cars whisk those with little time or desire for contemplation up to the summit for a quick look at the view, and litter and noise can be a problem.

An image of the bodhisattva Dizang, saviour of damned souls and ruling deity on the Buddhist mountain of Jiuhua Shan. Jin Qiaojue, a Korean monk who died here in the 8th century, was said to have been a reincarnation of Dizang.

China's sacred mountains have huge conservation as well as spiritual value: they are covered in dense forests which support a range of wildlife. Various species of monkey – including the rare golden monkey (jinsi hou) – can occasionally be seen on some of the central peaks, such as Wudang Shan.

The gravity-defying Xuankong Si on Heng Shan contains 40 halls, fashioned from caves in the rock and covered with wooden facades supported on poles.

The western Hunan town of Fenghuang gives a flavour of old China.

THE SOUTH

Historically the most innovative and entrepreneurial region of the country, the southern provinces are at the heart of the Chinese economic boom.

Flower seller.

It was in the south of China, particularly along parts of the southern coast, where Deng Xiaoping's economic modernisation programme germinated, took root and prospered. Over two decades on, and the main focus of this innovation – the Pearl River Delta around the city of Shenzhen – is well established as the country's most prosperous neighbourhood, although Shanghai and its hinterland are catching up fast.

The idea of commerce is hardly an extraordinary notion in southern China. Guangzhou, China's third-largest city, was already an international port in the 9th century, and by the 1500s, when the Portuguese arrived in a showy flotilla, the area had replaced the Silk Road as the trade route of choice into China. Southeast China's other port of note lacks the historical depth of Guangzhou, but has long had a remarkable entrepreneurial zeal. As a British colony, Hong Kong became the definitive capitalist free-market, no-holds-barred trading centre. Having weathered a serious economic crisis following its return to China in 1997, it remains a fascinating and unique travel destination.

Off the coast of western Guangdong is the large island of Hainan, with China's southernmost beaches – fringed by palms and bathed in year-round warmth – now being aggressively marketed to tourists. Further east along the coast, thriving Fujian province has, more than anywhere else in China, looked out across the sea to make a living; together with Guangdong, this is the major source of

Wulingyuan Scenic Reserve.

the Chinese diaspora. The old European enclave of Amoy, now called Xiamen, is one of China's most engaging cities, with its enchanting island of Gulangyu decked out in colonial era architecture and laced with lazy walks.

Inland are the provinces of Hunan and Jiangxi running north to the Chang Jiang (Yangzi River), off most tourist itineraries but encompassing some fabulous scenery (Wulingyuan, Heng Shan and Lu Shan to name but three examples) and a scattering of charming old towns – none more so than Fenghuang, photogenically perched on the banks of the Tuo River.

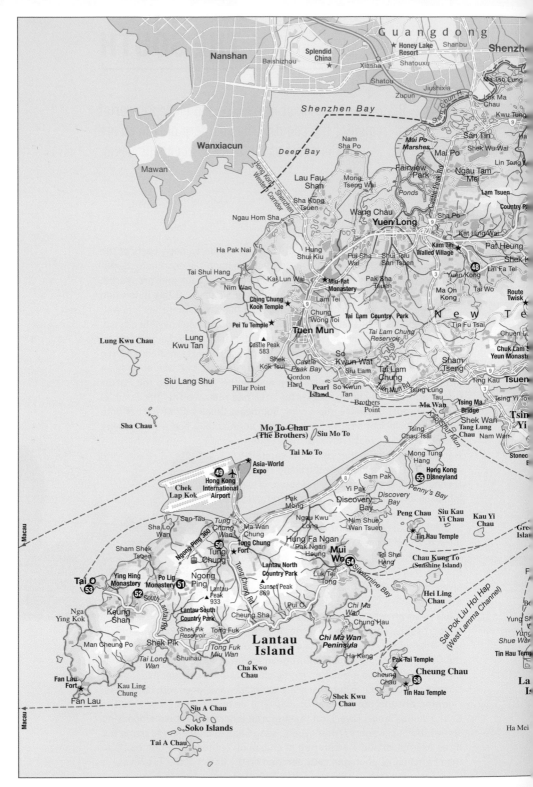

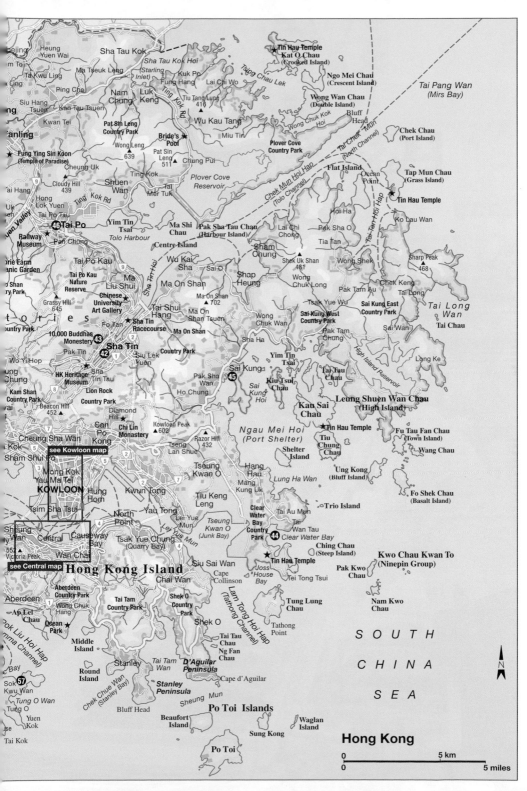

Hong Kong

SOUTH CHINA SEA

5 km

5 miles

Fresh produce for sale in Kowloon.

HONG KONG

Taken from China during the Qing dynasty, Hong Kong – having returned to Chinese sovereignty – is as colourful, vibrant and appealing as ever.

The entry point into China for many tourists, Hong Kong makes a memorable introduction to the Chinese world. Glamorous, hectic, exciting and spectacular, with fabulous food, nightlife and shopping, this is a place like no other.

Archaeological evidence shows this part of the southern Chinese coast has been inhabited since the Stone Age. Han Chinese people began settling here in the Song dynasty (960–1279), but it remained a relatively obscure corner of Guangdong province until British opium merchants recognised the advantages of "annexing" 45 sq km (17 sq miles) of the best deep-water harbour in the region. Despite Lord Palmerston's famously contemptuous valuation – "a barren island with hardly a house upon it" – the colony quickly became a vital trading link between Europe and China, and by the time the British were compelled to hand it back to the motherland it had grown into one of the richest cities in the world.

ORIENTATION

Since the return to China on 1 July 1997, Hong Kong has been a Special Administrative Region (SAR) with its own laws and administration. It can be divided into four parts: Hong Kong Island, Kowloon, the New Territories and the numerous outlying islands.

A Hakka woman in the New Territories.

Hong Kong Island, its skyscrapers set against a spectacular mountain backdrop, is dominated by grand financial institutions, enormous, impressively futuristic buildings. It is also home to some of the SAR's oldest Chinese communities, beautiful walks and, on the southern side, some good beaches.

Across Victoria Harbour – just three minutes by the Mass Transit Railway, eight minutes by the venerable Star Ferry and less than 10 minutes by car through the three tunnels – the Kowloon Peninsula was ceded to the British

⊘ Main Attractions

The Star Ferry
Central District
The Peak
Tsim Sha Tsui
Sai Kung Country Park
Disneyland

**Maps on pages
278, 282, 290**

The iconic green-and-white Star Ferry is old-fashioned, functional and reliable. A trip across the harbour between Central and Tsim Sha Tsui gives wonderful views of the skyline. Fares are very low – splash out an extra 50 cents to sit on the upper deck. The crossing takes seven or eight minutes (6.30am–11.30pm).

in 1860, for better defence of the harbour. Most tourists see only its southern tip – the Tsim Sha Tsui District and its many hotels, bars and shopping centres. To the north past the Yau Ma Tei and Mong Kok districts, Boundary Street marks the demarcation line between the old colony, granted to the British "in perpetuity", and the New Territories, which were leased in 1898 for a 99-year period. Surprisingly for a place known for its crowded urban areas, large areas of the New Territories, which include over 230 outlying islands, are almost devoid of people,

and the empty, hilly countryside makes a pleasant antidote to the frenetic pace of life in the city.

HONG KONG ISLAND: CENTRAL DISTRICT

Central – still occasionally marked on maps as "Victoria", and Chung Wan in Cantonese – is Hong Kong's business and financial hub, at the heart of the incredible cliff face of high-rise buildings that extends along the north shore of Hong Kong Island. Squeezed between the harbour and the precipitous slopes of Victoria Peak, this is where the money is, the financial powerhouses, the glamorous high-end shopping malls, overlooked by the multi-millionaires' mansions on the Peak. And in the midst of all the glitz, there are still strong elements of former days, with wayside hawkers dangling novelties and knock-offs, incense sticks smouldering by tiny shrines, and delivery boys pedalling serenely through red lights with a cargo of fresh meat balanced in their bike's cast-iron basket. It all adds up to one of

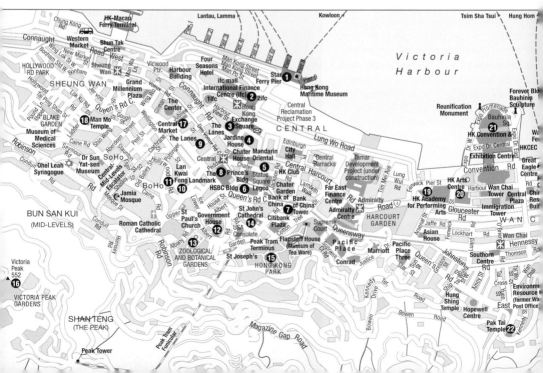

the most fascinating areas of modern Hong Kong.

The best place to begin a tour is at the **Star Ferry Pier** ❶. The green-and-white Star Ferries have been shunting passengers across the harbour between Hong Kong Island and Kowloon since 1898, although the terminal relocated in 2006. Just to the west is the gigantic **International Finance Centre Two (IFC-2)** ❷. Hong Kong's second tallest building, it stands at a whopping 420 metres (1,378ft), is capped by a mass of curving spires, and dominates the famous harbour view. In 2013 the **Hong Kong Maritime Museum** (www.hkmaritimemuseum.org; Mon–Fri 9.30–5.30pm, Sat–Sun 10am–7pm) opened at Central Ferry Pier 8, having relocated from Stanley.

Walkways connect the Star Ferry Pier and IFC to the rest of Central via **Exchange Square** ❸, home of the Hong Kong Stock Exchange and featuring a collection of sculptures by Henry Moore and Ju Ming in the adjacent plaza. Head east along the walkway to **Jardine House** ❹, whose distinctive 1,700-plus round windows have inspired the nickname "House of a Thousand Orifices". Opened in 1973, it was for many years the tallest building in Hong Kong.

Back on street level and inland from the General Post Office, an underpass will take you to **Statue Square** ❺, on either side of Chater Road. On Sundays, throngs of Filipina maids gather here on their day off in a festive, chaotic outdoor party. The 140,000 Philippine nationals, most of whom work here as maids, now form by far the single largest foreign community living in Hong Kong.

This part of Central is the financial district, home to the headquarters of several major banks. Two of these are housed in iconic buildings: facing Statue Square is Norman Foster's US$1 billion **Hongkong & Shanghai Bank Building (HSBC Main Building)** ❻, the most expensive structure in the world when it was completed in 1985. Further east the sharp angles of the gleaming 368-metre (1,209ft) **Bank of China Tower** ❼, designed by Chinese-American architect I.M. Pei, point directly at the other banks, which

Merchandise for sale on Hollywood Road

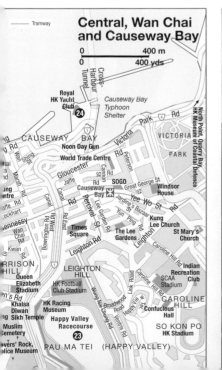

Central, Wan Chai and Causeway Bay

Tramway

0   400 m
0   400 yds

Cross-Harbour Tunnel

Royal HK Yacht Club ㉔
Causeway Bay Typhoon Shelter
Park
Rd
North Point, Quarry Bay, HK Museum of Coastal Defence

CAUSEWAY BAY
Noon Day Gun
World Trade Centre
Victoria
VICTORIA PARK
Peterson

Gloucester
Jaffe Rd
Cannon St
Paterson

Jaffe Rd
SOGO
Causeway Bay ⚓
Great George St
Windsor House

Percival St
Jardine's Bazaar
Yee Wo St
Rd

Lee Garden Rd
Yun Ping Rd
Kung Lee Church

Times Square
The Lee Gardens
Leighton
St Mary's Church

Leighton Rd
Caroline Hill Rd

HARRISON HILL
LEIGHTON HILL
Indian Recreation Club
SCAA Stadium

Queen Elizabeth Stadium
HK Football Club Stadium
CAROLINE HILL

Khalsa Diwan
HK Racing Museum
Confucius Hall

Muslim Cemetery
Happy Valley Racecourse ㉓
SO KON PO HK Stadium

Lovers' Rock, Police Museum
PAU MA TEI (HAPPY VALLEY)

⊙ Tip

To get the most out of a walking tour of Central, visit on a weekday during working hours, as (Lan Kwai Fong/SoHo apart) this is not one of Hong Kong's after-hours locations – unlike Tsim Sha Tsui and Causeway Bay, many shops close by 7pm. Shops are open on Saturdays, but the energised atmosphere of the working week is lacking. Sundays are quiet, with shops shut, although the weekly Filipina get-together is in full swing.

makes for bad (or good, depending which side you're on) feng shui.

The former Supreme Court Building, now the **Legislative Council (Legco) Building**, is a rare survivor of classical architecture in among all the steel, glass and concrete.

DES VOEUX AND QUEENS ROADS

Heading inland from the Star Ferry/IFC on the elevated pedestrian walkways you will cross over the main east–west highway, Connaught Road, before reaching **Des Voeux Road**. The tram stop here, at the junction with Pedder Street, is one of Central's most photographed spots, a blur of traffic and people. Across the street, **The Landmark ⑧** is a prestigious shopping mall dedicated to luxury brands. Five floors surround a vast atrium, around which walkways connect with neighbouring buildings such as **Chater House** and **Prince's Building**, flaunting a further abundance of marble and relentlessly upmarket shops.

The next east–west road away from the harbour, **Queen's Road Central**,

A Western District tailor's workshop.

marked the waterfront before land reclamation began in the 1850s. Running between its shops and emporia and those of Des Voeux Road are two narrow alleyways, **Li Yuen Street East** and **Li Yuen Street West** – also known as **The Lanes ⑨**, lined with stalls and outlets selling clothing, fabrics and counterfeit designer fashion accessories. The atmosphere is a complete contrast to the smart high-rises on the larger avenues nearby, and bargaining is still expected.

LAN KWAI FONG AND BEYOND

Behind Queen's Road Central the terrain rises steeply. D'Aguilar Street leads up to **Lan Kwai Fong ⑩**, which together with neighbouring SoHo is a prime nightlife area. Modern cuisine, bars, clubs, English pubs and tiny snack shops bring in the crowds, and late-night revellers can get everything from pizza to sushi in the wee hours. At weekends many bars stay open until 5am or later.

At the top of Lan Kwai Fong, winding Wyndham Street is becoming an extension of the trendy bar zone, leading on

to **Hollywood Road** ⑪, packed with shops selling top-dollar antiques. Beyond is **SoHo** (SOuth of HOllywood), accessed via the handy Central–Mid-Levels Escalator. What began as a handful of restaurants and cafés on **Staunton** and **Elgin streets** has spread like a rash, with a diverse mix of bars, cafés, restaurants, clubs, boutiques and designer shops spreading along Wyndham Street and NoHo (North of Hollywood Road) to Gough Street and west to Sheung Wan along Bridges and Tai Ping Shan streets

COLONIAL RELICS

The higher up one gets on the Island, the more desirable the property and the higher the rents – a pattern established in the early colonial years, when the upper slopes were considered less prone to malarial mosquitoes.

Just above Lan Kwai Fong on Upper Albert Road, the rarefied air is immediately apparent at **Government House** ⑫, grand home of the former colonial leaders of Hong Kong and now the official residence of the Chief Executive.

The mansion dates from the 1850s but during World War II was remodelled by the Japanese, who added a tower with a vague Shinto look. There is a clear view of the building through the wrought-iron gates, which are opened to the public only a couple of times a year, usually in spring and autumn (no set dates).

Opposite Government House are the **Zoological and Botanical Gardens** ⑬

Hong Kong residents live cheek by jowl.

The view south to Shek O from the Dragon's Back, Hong Kong Island.

⊘ TRANSPORT

Getting around Hong Kong

Hong Kong has an excellent public transport system. If you are staying more than a day or so, buy a stored-value Octopus card. The **Mass Transit Railway** (MTR) is an extensive subway system linking the north shore of Hong Kong Island with Kowloon, Lantau and the New Territories, and extended to the south shore of Hong Kong Island in December 2016. **Trams** are extremely useful for travelling along the north shore of Hong Kong Island. **Bus** services are good but less useful for tourists, except for the routes down to the south coast of Hong Kong Island. Taxis are cheap and plentiful. The outlying islands are linked to Central by frequent **ferries** (see margin tip page 296).

Hollywood Road is the place to look for antiques.

The view from the Peak.

(www.lcsd.gov.hk; daily 6am–7pm; free), a lush tropical area housing a small assortment of wildlife. It opened in 1864 and still retains elements of its original Victorian gentility, with the added Eastern spirituality of elderly Chinese performing their tai chi exercises each morning. From here it is just a short stroll to the Victorian Gothic **St John's Cathedral** ⓮, consecrated in 1849 and the city's oldest Anglican church. In nearby **Hong Kong Park** ⓯, **Flagstaff House** is another example of bespoke architecture. It is home to the **Museum of Tea Ware** (http://hk.art. museum/; Wed–Mon 10am–6pm; free) and completed in 1846. The building – of more interest than the museum – is reputedly Hong Kong's oldest surviving colonial structure.

THE PEAK

Make your way along to the **Peak Tram terminus** on Garden Road to ascend Hong Kong's most notable natural landmark, properly though rarely called **Victoria Peak** ⓰ (Shan Teng in Cantonese). "The Peak" is the residential aspiration of most of the population. The upper tram terminus at the **Peak Tower** is shaped like a wok, and is for many people one of the ugliest buildings in Hong Kong. Of course, the main reason for coming up here is to marvel at some of the world's finest vistas. Many find the night-time views even more incredible, a vast glittering swathe of electric light, most spectacular immediately below in Central and Wan Chai as the buildings attempt to outdo each other in their eye-catching displays. The **viewing platform** has been raised 30 metres (100ft) to the top of the "wok" for a 360-degree panorama. Attractions inside the tower include Hong Kong's own **Madame Tussaud's** waxworks (www.madametussauds. com.hk; daily 10am–10pm). The area around the Peak Tower is in fact Victoria Gap, whereas the summit of Victoria Peak itself (552 metres/1,811ft) lies to the west.

WESTERN DISTRICT

Located, as the name suggests, just to the west of Central, much of this area

is worlds apart from the ultra-modern financial district, offering instead a glimpse of the more traditionally Chinese Hong Kong – despite a surge of recent development. Western is known as a last refuge of the Hong Kong Chinese artisan, unseen by most visitors, where there are mahjong-makers, herbalists and craftsmen. The area begins at Possession Street and sprawls west to Kennedy Town, but its atmosphere begins to emerge around the purpose-built **Central Market** ⑰, the starting point for the Central–Mid-Levels Escalator. Up the hill, on the western stretch of Hollywood Road, **Man Mo Temple** ⑱ (www.discoverhongkong.com; daily 8am–6pm) is still one of Hong Kong's most atmospheric temples, dimly lit and thick with incense smoke.

WAN CHAI AND CAUSEWAY BAY

To the east of Central, Wan Chai and Causeway Bay are among the territory's most crowded and active districts, revealing the authentic flavour of modern Hong Kong. Despite its reputation,

Wan Chai has lost much of its former risqué character, although there's still a lively bar and restaurant scene. **Causeway Bay** is one of Hong Kong's premier shopping districts. The tram line (which was on the waterfront when it was built at the beginning of the 20th century) runs right the way through these districts, and provides cheap and convenient transportation.

Close to the Wan Chai waterfront are the **Academy for Performing Arts** ⑲ and the **Hong Kong Arts Centre** ⑳,

Betting on the horses contributes around 12 percent of Hong Kong's annual tax revenues. As well as Wednesday nights at Happy Valley, there are weekend (daytime) races at Sha Tin in the New Territories which attract even larger crowds.

two of the most popular venues for theatrical and cultural performances in Hong Kong. Right on the harbour is the futuristic **Hong Kong Convention and Exhibition Centre** , which underwent a HK$4.8 billion extension in order to serve as the venue for the formal handover ceremony in 1997. Elevated walkways lead south from the convention centre to **Lockhart Road**, a lively neighbourhood of bars and restaurants: in recent years, more bars and restaurants have been springing up on Johnston Road, Queen's Road East and Amoy Street. Queen's Road East traces Wan Chai's original waterfront, and is home to the Hung Shing (Tai Wong) Temple (1860) and the old Wan Chai Post Office (1912), recalling an earlier era, while the picturesque **Pak Tai Temple** is nearby in Stone Nullah Lane.

Inland is **Happy Valley** , home of the Hong Kong Jockey Club's Happy Valley Racecourse. During the September–July racing season, it attracts over 50,000 punters on Wednesday race nights. The **Hong Kong Racing Museum** (daily noon–7pm, until 9pm on race days; free) is at the Happy Valley Stand, providing a background to Hong Kong's obsession with racing. Opposite are the Colonial and Parsi cemeteries.

Causeway Bay actually was a bay until the 1950s, when it disappeared into a land-reclamation project. The present-day "bay" is occupied by the **Royal Hong Kong Yacht Club** on Kellett Island (which also was once a real island before land reclamation), and the Typhoon Shelter.

THE SOUTH SIDE

In contrast to the intensely built-up northern part of the island, the southern coast is lined with beaches and countryside. **Aberdeen** has a character unlike any other town in Hong Kong, and is famous for its bustling harbour, a natural typhoon shelter crowded with fishing boats, houseboats, pleasure junks and tiny sampans, rounded off by a rather theatrical floating seafood restaurant.

A short bus or taxi ride away is **Ocean Park** (www.oceanpark.com.hk; daily, times vary so check online), a fun theme park with a spectacular cable-car ride overlooking the South China Sea, a 3,000-seat marine-mammal theatre, the world's largest reef aquarium and numerous adventure rides. The MTR's South Island Line was extended as far as Ocean Park in December 2016.

The beach at **Repulse Bay**, widened to several times its original size, can get extremely crowded at weekends. Nearby **Stanley** was the site of the largest indigenous settlement in Hong Kong when the British first set foot here in 1841. The main attraction is **Stanley Market**, which draws thousands in search of the perfect souvenir or clothing bargain.

Around the coast from Stanley, in the southeast corner of the island, **Shek O** is one of its most laid-back villages. It

A Chinese Opera performance at the Arts Centre in Wan Chai.

is best known for adjacent **Big Wave Bay**, the haunt of Hong Kong surfers.

KOWLOON

The Kowloon Peninsula is in many ways very different from the glittering island across the harbour, more down to earth and more Chinese. Yet, somewhat paradoxically, Tsim Sha Tsui – its southern tip – is the location of the majority of Hong Kong's tourist hotels. Nathan Road is host to the quintessential Hong Kong image of gaudy neon signs and hundreds of small electronics shops. Save for the waterfront views, it is not an especially attractive place. But few can deny the electricity that charges life here, especially at night.

Lacking the steep mountainsides that hem in the north shore of Hong Kong Island, Kowloon sprawls. Until Kai Tak Airport closed in the late 1990s, regulations restricted its buildings to a modest height. Now they shoot skywards as never before: the city's tallest building, the 484m (1,588ft) **International Commerce Centre** (ICC), was completed in 2011 on reclaimed land west of Tsim Sha Tsui.

TSIM SHA TSUI

Kowloon Peninsula starts at **Tsim Sha Tsui**. The waterfront promenade from the **Star Ferry Pier** 25 to Tsim Sha Tsui East offers spectacular views of the harbour and Hong Kong Island. The **Railway Clock Tower** 26, erected in 1915 next to the ferry terminal, is the final vestige of the historic Kowloon-Canton railway station, the Asian terminus of the old *Orient Express* to London.

From the Star Ferry Pier eastward along the harbour, a **waterfront promenade** provides a great vantage point for viewing the north shore of Hong Kong Island. At 8pm each night the promenade is the place to be for watching the Symphony of Lights, the world's largest sound and light show, which lights up the glittering skyline more than ever. The promenade itself – dubbed the **Avenue of Stars** 27 – is decorated with tributes to the famous and less so of Hong Kong and Chinese cinema, with Hollywood-style stars set in the pavement.

Floating restaurant in Aberdeen harbour.

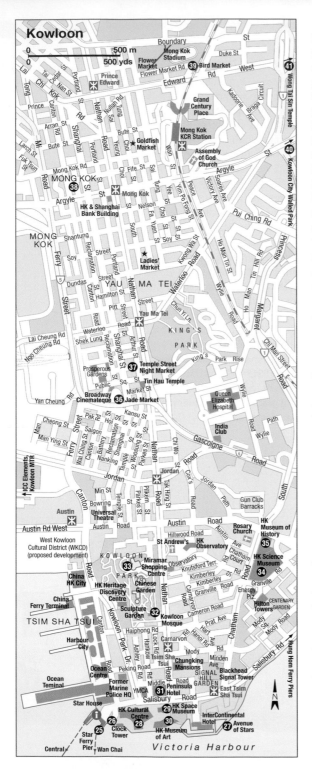

Kowloon

Next to the Clock Tower, the **Hong Kong Cultural Centre** 28 is a minimalist structure with an impressive concave roof spoilt by ugly tiles. It caused a great deal of controversy in 1984, as it was designed without windows on the prime harbour site. The Centre stages local and international opera, classical music, theatre and dance. The complex abuts the igloo-like **Hong Kong Space Museum** 29 (www.lcsd.gov.hk; Mon, Wed–Fri 1–9pm, Sat–Sun 10am–9pm; exhibition halls reopening 2017), with IMAX movies on space travel and exhibitions of Chinese astronomical inventions. The **Hong Kong Museum of Art** 30 (http://hk.art.museum/; closed for major renovation until 2019) is the main art museum of Hong Kong.

Across Salisbury Road is the venerable **Peninsula Hotel** 31, built in 1928, where people used to stay before boarding the *Orient Express*.

At the bottom of **Nathan Road** – the start of Hong Kong's famous Golden Mile tourist belt – hundreds of small shops lie tightly crammed together: tailors' shops, jewellers and electronics stores. Less than a kilometre (about half a mile) north on Nathan Road, in the southeastern corner of Kowloon Park, are the four minarets and large white marble dome of **Kowloon Mosque** 32. The pleasant expanse of **Kowloon Park** 33 lies beyond.

From the mosque, streets lined with discount clothing stores lead eastward to Chatham Road. **Carnarvon** and **Kimberley** roads are both stuffed with clothing and electronics shops, while nearby **Knutsford Terrace** hosts numerous bars and restaurants. On the other side of Chatham Road, **Tsim Sha Tsui East** is home to two of the best museums in Hong Kong. The **Hong Kong Science Museum** 34 (http://hk.science.museum; Mon–Wed, Fri 10am–9pm, Sat–Sun 10am–9pm; free on Wed), aimed at younger visitors, displays more than 500 scientific and technological interactive exhibits.

Just opposite is the **Hong Kong Museum of History** ❸❺ (http://hk. history.museum/; Mon, Wed–Fri 10am–6pm, Sat–Sun 10am–7pm), charting the 6,000-year story of Hong Kong from Neolithic times right up to the handover.

YAU MA TEI AND MONG KOK

Continue north on Nathan Road, and left onto Kansu Street, to the **Jade Market** ❸❻ (Mon–Sat 10am–4pm), packed with stalls selling ornaments and jewellery. Dealers offer jade in every sculptable form – from large blocks of the raw material to tiny, ornately carved chips. Remember that not everything on offer is genuine.

North from here is **Yau Ma Tei**. Shanghai Street continues north into an area once famous for its temples, but now renowned for the **Temple Street night market** ❸❼ that lights up after dusk. Palmists, physiognomists, and a fortune-teller whose trained bird selects slips of paper to predict the future, vie to reveal your destiny. This area has numerous open-air restaurants, where oysters, prawns, clams, lobsters and fish are laid out on beds of ice to tempt diners.

Mong Kok ❸❽ is one of the most crowded, noisy and lively districts in the territory. In the early days of British rule, *gweilos* (foreign devils) seldom ventured past Yau Ma Tei, and even today, despite a certain amount of gentrification around the edges (notably at Langham Place), Mong Kok is notorious for Triads, illegal gambling dens and sleaze. It is also known for several colourful street markets: the **Ladies Market** (www.ladies-market. hk; around noon–10.30pm), selling a mixture of clothes and souvenirs, the **Goldfish Market** (www.goldfish-market.hk; around 10am–10pm), and the factory outlet shops on Fa Yuen Street, offering fashion bargains galore. Further north is Hong Kong's premier **Flower Market** (www.flower-market.hk; 9.30am–7.30pm), at the end of which you will find the Yuen Po Street **Bird Market** ❸❾ (www.bird-garden.hk; 7am–8pm), with hundreds of songbirds and beautiful birdcages for sale.

> **◔ Tip**
>
> The Chinese are generally relaxed about tourists visiting temples, but it's polite to bear in mind some rules of etiquette regarding photography. There is usually a sign to indicate if taking photographs of the interior is banned, but, nonetheless, it is considered disrespectful to take pictures of people worshipping unless you have their permission.

Kowloon by night.

ACROSS BOUNDARY STREET

Just to the north of these markets is Boundary Street, the old demarcation between British Hong Kong and the New Territories, leased to Britain for 99 years in 1898. The area between Boundary Street and Lion Rock (the mountain that hems in Kowloon from the north) is known as **New Kowloon**.

Near the eastern end of this thoroughfare, and close to the old airport, is the **Kowloon City Walled Park** ⓴. The infamous Walled City was a small area of the New Territories excluded from British control due to a legal loophole. The area deteriorated into a semi-lawless enclave which was left to its own governance. After World War II, low-rise blocks built without authority and lacking proper foundations sprang up on the site, resulting in a multi-storey squatter area with unauthorised electricity and water supplies. In 1987, with China's consent, 35,000 residents were resettled in housing estates, and the entire block was razed to the ground. The park that replaced it, modelled on the Jiangnan garden style of the early Qing dynasty, has exhibits on the Walled City.

Due north, one of Kowloon's most colourful and popular places of worship, the **Wong Tai Sin Temple** ⓵ (daily 7am–5.30pm; donation expected) on Lung Cheung Road, sits opposite an MTR station bearing the same name. The temple hosts a row of fortune-tellers who can divine your future via the I Ching (Yijing) and other arcane Chinese oracles. East of Wong Tai Sin Temple and near Diamond Hill MTR station is the **Chi Lin Nunnery** (Thu–Tue 9am–4.30pm, garden until 7pm; donation expected), a reconstructed Buddhist temple complex.

THE NEW TERRITORIES

The buffer between the urban area of Kowloon and the boundary with Shenzhen and Guangdong province, the New Territories are an odd mixture. Nobody is ploughing with water buffalo any longer, but there are corners where time seems to have not so much stood still as gone into reverse. Conversely,

Offerings at Wong Tai Sin Temple.

other areas are as modern as any-where else in Hong Kong, notably the New Towns such as Sha Tin and Yuen Long. There is scenic beauty aplenty, with calm beaches to seek out and lofty mountains to hike.

Sha Tin ㊷ is one of Hong Kong's largest New Towns, with massive housing projects occupying what was once an area of rice paddies. The **Ten Thousand Buddhas Monastery** ㊸ (daily 9am–5.30pm; free) is reached by climbing 431 steps up the hillside above the Sha Tin railway station. There are 12,800 small Buddha statues on the walls of a main altar room, and huge, fierce-looking guardian deities protect the temple. Further up the hill is another series of temples.

In Tai Wai, south of Sha Tin, is the impressive **Hong Kong Heritage Museum** (www.heritagemuseum.gov.hk/; Mon, Wed–Fri 10am–6pm, Sat–Sun 10am–7pm; permanent exhibitions free) displaying a range of cultural exhibits relating to the former colony.

East of Sha Tin lies the New Territories' most attractive area. In summer,

Clear Water Bay ㊹ is dotted with revellers on corporate junks, and the beach is jam-packed with sunbath-ers. Branching off Clear Water Bay Road, the highway leads down to **Sai Kung** ㊺, a seaside town known for its Chinese seafood restaurants, and a kicking-off point for exploring the natural beauty of **Sai Kung Country Park**. While the fringes of the town have fallen prey to development, Sai Kung still remains very much a fish-ing community. The most interesting part of the town is hidden behind the Tin Hau temple, off Yi Chun Street. A

Bamboo chim sticks at Wong Tai Sin Temple are used for fortune-telling. People shake the container until a single chim falls out. Each has a number that is later interpreted, for a fee, by a fortune-teller at one of the rented stalls

The steps leading to the Ten Thousand Buddhas Monastery, Sha Tin.

maze of narrow alleyways leads past traditional herbalists and noodle shops interspersed with ordinary family homes.

To the north is **Tai Po** ⓐ, meaning "buying place". Once a small market community, this is now a booming new town. Two sites worth visiting here are the 19th-century Man Mo Temple and the Hong Kong Railway Museum (www.heritagemuseum.gov.hk/; Wed–Mon 10am–6pm; free).

The western side of the Kowloon Peninsula has been reshaped by huge land-reclamation and construction projects that have redrawn the map, most notably for the road and rail links that connect to Hong Kong International Airport on Lantau Island. **Tsuen Wan** ⓐ is another new town, although the Chinese presence seems to have begun about the 2nd century AD. A historical remnant in the centre of town is the **Sam Tung Uk Museum** (www.lcsd.gov.hk; Wed–Mon 10am–6pm; free) a 200-year-old walled Hakka village complete with period furniture. Just northeast of Tsuen Wan, the main hall

View across Clearwater Bay.

of the multi-faith **Yuen Yuen Institute** is modelled on the Temple of Heaven (Tiantan) in Beijing.

In **Tuen Mun**, east of 583-metre (1,900ft) **Castle Peak** and adjacent to the Ching Chung light-rail station, is the huge **Ching Chung Koon** temple, which serves as a repository for many Chinese art treasures, including 200 year-old lanterns and a jade seal over 1,000 years old. The library, which holds 4,000 books, documents Daoist history. In the far northwest of the SAR is the **Hong Kong Wetland Park** (www.wetlandpark.gov.hk; Wed–Mon 10am–5pm), which contains extensive wetland habitats. Access to birdwatching hides is provided via an extensive network of boardwalks.

Just outside **Yuen Long** ⓐ are the walled villages of **Kam Tin**. The most popular for visitors is the Kat Hing Wai village, which stands rather incongruously across the road from a supermarket. There are 400 people living here, all with the same surname: Tang. Built in the 1600s, it is a fortified village with walls 6 metres (20ft) thick, guardhouses on its four corners, slits for the arrows used in fighting off attackers, and a moat. The authenticity of the village may seem spoilt by some of the commercialism; inside, one street is lined with vendors' outlets.

THE OUTLYING ISLANDS: LANTAU

Hong Kong's international airport opened in 1998 off Lantau's northern coast on a tiny island called **Chek Lap Kok** ⓐ, with reclaimed land connecting it to Lantau. While this part of the island has undergone considerable development, together with the northeast (Disneyland), much of Lantau – with twice the area of Hong Kong Island – has escaped the worst excesses of development for now, and most of the island remains rural.

On the northern side of Lantau, pay a visit to **Tung Chung** ⓐ, an old

fortress near a bay that curves around the pointed southern tip of little Chek Lap Kok island. On a hill overlooking this harbour is the old fort, constructed in 1817. Its thick ramparts are still standing, as are six old cannons dating from the 19th century which guarded the town and bay from smugglers and pirates.

Up on the mountainous central spine is the island's best-known attraction, the brightly painted red, orange and gold **Po Lin Monastery** ❺❶ (daily 9am–6pm; free), where the world's largest outdoor bronze statue of Buddha (24 metres/79ft high) was consecrated in 1993. The huge statue is a popular tourist attraction, but also a major site of pilgrimage for Buddhists. The monastery also has a large and popular vegetarian restaurant. A cable car, **Ngong Ping 360** (www.np360.com.hk; reopening mid-2017), links Tung Chung with the monastery, offering stunning panoramic views. West of Po Lin, in the direction of Tung Chung on Lantau's north coast, is an excellent walking path that traverses mountain

Alice in Disneyland.

ridges and small canyons en route to Lantau's **Yin Hing Monastery** ❺❷, a haven rich with traditional Buddhist paintings and statues.

Offshore from Lantau's principal town, **Tai O** ❺❸, on the west coast, the island's Tanka "boat people" have built rickety homes on stilts over parts of a creek, where waters rise during tide changes. Efforts to entice them into new government-built flats have proved largely unsuccessful.

Lantau is also popular for its many long, smooth and often empty

Po Lin Monastery, Lantau.

> **⊙ Tip**

Ferries run from the Outlying Districts ferry piers in Central to Silvermine Bay (Mui Wo) on **Lantau** approximately every 30–50 minutes throughout the day on weekdays, and every 40–60 minutes at weekends. To **Cheung Chau** departures are every 30 minutes daily. **Lamma** ferries run at 20–60-minute intervals to Yung Shue Wan, less often to Sok Kwu Wan.

beaches. The finest are on the southeast coastline that arcs from Cheung Sha south of Silvermine Bay to Tong Fuk. The most popular and crowded beach (easiest to reach, but with poor-quality water) is **Silvermine Bay Beach** ❹. Take a ferry to Mui Wo, where you can catch buses and taxis to South Lantau Road. Keen hikers can cover most of Lantau's sights on the 70km (43-mile) **Lantau Trail**, a wild trail across the island that begins and terminates at Mui Wo.

HONG KONG DISNEYLAND

After years of wrangling over costs and various delays, **Hong Kong Disneyland** ❺ (www.hongkongdisneyland.com; daily from 10.30am, closing hours vary so check online) opened in 2005 in Lantau's northeastern corner. Partly owned by the government, the theme park has proved a major draw for visitors from mainland China. To get there, take the MTR Tung Chung line from Hong Kong Island or Kowloon to Sunny Bay station, then cross the platform for the three-minute ride to the

Victorian-themed Disneyland Resort station. The trains are brightly coloured with Mickey Mouse-shaped windows.

The 126-hectare (310-acre) theme park features four themed "lands" similar (but smaller) to those at other Disneyland parks, and has been built with an emphasis designed to make it more relevant to Asians.

LAMMA

The third-largest of the outlying islands, and less well known both to visitors and to locals, is **Lamma**, associated with some of the earliest settlements in Hong Kong. Although just over 13 sq km (5 sq miles) in size and home to a prominent power station, Lamma is rich in grassy hills and beautiful bays and is renowned for its seafood restaurants. There are no high-rise buildings and no roads. The town of **Yung Shue Wan** ❻, at the north end of Lamma, is one of two ferry gateways to the island (Sok Kwu Wan is the other). The village, popular with expatriates and Chinese keen to get away from the crowds of the city, has

Hung Shing Ye beach, Lamma.

streets lined with small restaurants and bars. Yung Shue Wan's Tin Hau Temple is dedicated to the Queen of Heaven and the Goddess of the Sea. The 100-year-old temple is guarded by a pair of stone lions. Inside, behind a red spirit stand (to deflect evil spirits) is the main shrine with images of the beaded, veiled Tin Hau.

A well-maintained concrete pathway runs much of the length of the island to Yung Shue Wan's sister village of **Sok Kwu Wan** 57, about an hour to an hour and a half away. Heading south, the path passes the haphazard housing of the village outskirts, fields and trees until it reaches **Hung Shing Ye**, a pleasant beach. The route then leads steeply up and down across hills and valleys, treating hikers to sweeping views out across the sea and back to the apartment buildings of Aberdeen and the south side of Hong Kong Island. Sok Kwu Wan is famous for its seafood restaurants – most visitors stop here for a meal before catching the ferry back to Central.

CHEUNG CHAU

Cheung Chau 58 island is much smaller than Lamma, and is urbanised in a charming "Old China" way. This dumbbell-shaped isle, with hills at either end and a village nestled in the middle, is so narrow at its narrowest point that you can walk from Cheung Chau Harbour on its west side to Tung Wan Harbour on the east in just a few minutes. Cheung Chau is a fishing island, its curving harbour filled with boats of all sizes, shapes and colours, including Chinese junks and sampans. They compete for space with the ubiquitous *kaido*, the small boats used as motorised water taxis. The colourful **Pak Tai Temple**, around 300 metres/yds north of the pier, is the island's most interesting shrine.

Cheung Chau is famous for its four-day **Bun Festival**, which usually takes place in May and is one of Hong Kong's

most colourful events. It originated many years ago after the discovery of a nest of skeletons, believed to be the remains of people killed by pirates. The island was subsequently plagued by a series of misfortunes; to placate the restless spirits of the victims, offerings were made once a year. During the festival, giant bamboo towers covered with edible buns are erected in the courtyard of Pak Tai Temple, while colourfully clad "floating children" are hoisted up on stilts and paraded through the crowds.

The Cheung Chau Bun Festival originated when offerings – including buns – were made to the restless spirits of people killed by marauding pirates.

A holiday atmosphere on Cheung Chau.

MACAU

Following in the steps of Hong Kong, Macau has become a Special Administrative Region of China. Its Portuguese colonial ambience and rapidly expanded resort status offer a unique experience in China.

In 1557 the Portuguese established the first European colony on Chinese soil in Macau, almost 300 years before the British claimed Hong Kong. For much of its recent history this was a sleepy outpost, playing second fiddle to its high-profile neighbour on the opposite shore of the Pearl River. But things have changed quickly since Lisbon returned the enclave to China in 1999. Macau is being developed into a leisure destination with luxurious Vegas-style resort and casino complexes, luring ever greater numbers of tourists, particularly from mainland China.

Yet away from all the glitz, glamour and mega-developments the old Macau survives – graceful old buildings redolent of southern Europe, overlooking cobbled streets shaded by ancient banyan trees. Drive from the gargantuan Venetian Macau on the Cotai strip to Coloane village for lunch in one of the restaurants on the square, and you could be on the Iberian peninsula rather than in the heart of the Orient.

THE HISTORIC CENTRE

The obvious place to start any foray into this old city is the **Largo do Senado** ① (Senate Square), Macau's largest piazza, paved with a bold wave-pattern mosaic.

Across the main road (Almeida Ribeiro) is the **Leal Senado** ② (Loyal Senate; Tue–Sun 9am–9pm) building, regarded by most as the best example of Portuguese architecture in Macau. At the northern end of the square is **São Domingos** ③ (St Dominic's), on the site of a chapel established here in 1597 by Spanish Dominicans newly arrived from Mexico. The current yellow-walled church dates from the 17th century. The white building on the eastern side of the square is **Santa Casa da Misericórdia** ④ (Holy House of Mercy).

○ **Main Attractions**

São Paulo facade
Fortaleza do Monte
Museum of Macau
Guia Fortress and
  Lighthouse
Coloane Village

Map on page 300

On the battlements of Monte Fort.

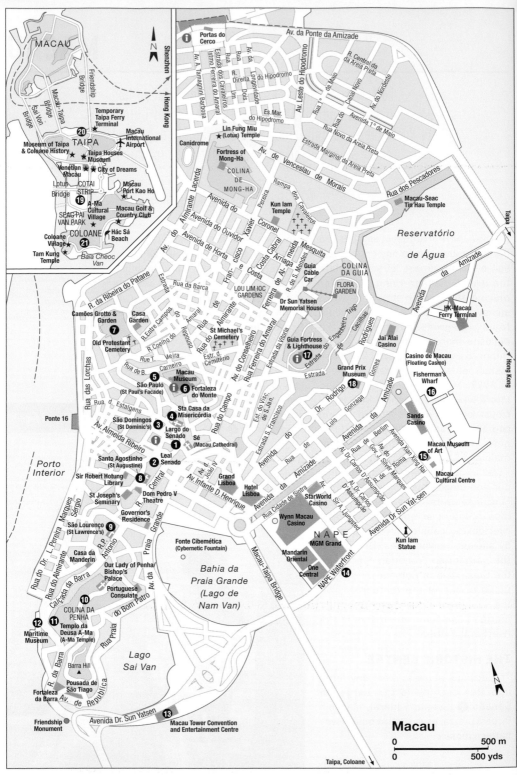

MACAU

Shenzhen

Hong Kong

Taipa

Hong Kong

Taipa, Coloane

Macau

0   500 m

0   500 yds

From São Domingos follow the pavement north along one of Macau's main shopping streets before turning uphill to the ruins of **São Paulo** ❺ (St Paul's; open access). The site must have bad feng shui. After the first church on the site was destroyed by fire in 1601, Japanese Christians (fleeing persecution in Nagasaki) crafted the classical facade between 1620 and 1627. In 1835 another fire destroyed São Paulo, the adjacent college and a library. In 1904, efforts were made to rebuild the church, but little progress was achieved. Nonetheless, it remains Macau's most enduring icon.

Overlooking São Paulo are the massive stone walls of the **Fortaleza do Monte** ❻ (Tue–Sun 7am–7pm; free), often simply called Monte Fort, built in the early 1600s. When Dutch ships attacked and invaded Macau in 1622, the half-completed fortress was defended by 150 clerics and African slaves. A lucky cannon shot hit the powder magazine of the Dutch fleet's flagship and saved the

city. The **Museum of Macau** (www.macaumuseum.gov.mo; Tue–Sun 10am–6pm; free on 15th of every month) on the site of the fortress has well-captioned exhibits that chart the history of the enclave.

A short stroll to the west will take you to picturesque **Camões Grotto** ❼, where Luís de Camões, the celebrated Portuguese soldier-poet, is said to have composed part of the national epic, *Os Lusíadas* (The Lusiads).

SOUTH TO BARRA

Several Unesco World Heritage sites lie along an easy-to-follow route from Largo do Senado to the southern tip of the Macau Peninsula. Among several notable buildings around the Largo de Santo Agostinho square is the Baroque-style **Santo Agostinho** ❽ (St Augustine's). Further south on Rua de São Lourenço is

Sao Domingos church.

Largo do Senado square.

For more details see page 446.

⊘ TRANSPORT

Getting to Macau

Macau's airport is linked to several Asian cities and cities across China. Jetfoils operate every 15 minutes (7am–midnight) from the Shun Tak Centre on Hong Kong Island. Journey time is around 1 hour. For more details see page 446. For those in a hurry, helicopter flights from the Shun Tak Centre depart every 30 minutes (9am–10.30pm). Journey time is 15–20 minutes.

Getting around Macau

The city streets are notoriously congested these days, and taxis can be hard to come by. It is hardly worth bothering with buses.

Traditional load carrier.

The Skywalk at the Macau Tower.

Penha. The chapel and Bishop's Palace next door were important centres of Roman Catholic missionary work. Heading down to the foot of Barra Hill to Largo do Barra is **Temple da A-Ma** ⑪ (daily 7am–6pm), the oldest temple in the territory, said to date back 600 years to the Ming dynasty. It is dedicated to Tin Hau, the patron goddess of fishermen and called A-Ma in Macau. Close by is the **Maritime Museum** ⑫ (http://en.macaotourism.gov.mo; Wed–Mon 10am–6pm), tracing the history of shipping in the South China Sea.

NEW MACAU

The 338-metre (1,110ft) **Macau Tower** ⑬ features an observation deck (www.macautower.com.mo; Mon–Fri 10am–9pm, Sat–Sun 9am–9pm) with 360-degree views of Macau; a look through its glass floors is not recommended for vertigo sufferers. Thrill-seekers can "skywalk" around the edge of the clear handrail-free platform, climb all the way to the top of the mast or even leap off in a controlled bungee jump.

the elegant pale-yellow church of **São Lourenço** ⑨ (St Lawrence's), raised up above street level and surrounded by a small garden.

Take a detour up **Colina da Penha** ⑩ (Penha Hill) for sweeping views and to visit the Chapel of Our Lady of

Across Nam Van Lake (also called the Baia da Praia Grande), a series of brash casinos are the glistening landmarks of Macau's burgeoning skyline. The copper-coloured **Wynn Macau**, the gold-and-silver **MGM Grand**, the 34-storey **StarWorld Casino** and the golden **Sands Macau** symbolise the new breed of Vegas-style gambling palaces for which Macau is becoming famous. Bounded on the north by the Avenida da Amizade, the rectangle of reclaimed land on which they sit is known as the **NAPE**.

In addition to the casinos, the area is also home to a growing number of small restaurants, cafés and bars. The **NAPE waterfront** ⓮ is marked by the bronze statue of Kun Iam, designed and crafted by Portuguese artist Christina Reiria. The **Macau Cultural Centre** is located at the far end of the NAPE and has two auditoria that host a regular programme of performances. Next door, the **Macau Museum of Art** ⓯ has spacious art galleries over five floors (www.mam.gov.mo; Tue–Sun 10am–7pm; free),

which houses a permanent collection of over 3,000 works of Shiwan ceramics, calligraphy and art from Macau and China.

Further east towards the ferry terminal, an artificial volcano marks the entrance of the **Fisherman's Wharf** ⓰ entertainment area.

NORTH TO THE BORDER

The hill of **Colina da Guia**, the highest point in Macau, rears up in front of the Hong Kong ferry terminal and is home to the **Guia Fortress and Lighthouse** ⓱ (open daily; free), a 17th-century Western-style construction. A cable car links the hilltop with a pleasant small park and aviary at **Flora Garden** below (daily 6am–8.30pm; free).

Every year, in the last weekend of November the streets of Macau are taken over by the Macau Formula 3 Grand Prix and the Macau Motorcycle

Kun Iam statue.

Guia Lighthouse offers a splendid view across Macau.

Grand Prix. Learn more about the "Guia Race" history of these exciting road races at the **Grand Prix Museum** ⑱ (http://en.macaotourism.gov.mo; Wed–Mon 10am–6pm, free) at 431 Rua Luis Gonzaga Gomes in the basement of the Tourism Activities Centre. Next door, the **Wine Museum** (http://en.macaotourism.gov.mo; Wed–Mon 10am–6pm, free) tells the story of Portuguese wines and their role in Portuguese culture.

At the northern end of Macau is the modern border gate between the Special Administrative Region and the city of Zhuhai in mainland China.

TAIPA AND COLOANE

What were until recently the two outlying islands of Taipa and Coloane are now melded together by the **Cotai strip** ⑲, 620 hectares (1,550 acres) of reclaimed land either side of the 1.3km (0.8-mile) road that used to link the two. Cotai is the focus for Macau's drive to become Asia's leisure capital, and home to the colossal **Venetian casino** – complete with a vast hotel,

The Venetian, casino resort extraordinaire.

shops, gondolas and a campanile – as well as other mega-resorts.

In **Taipa Village** ⑳ a few bits and pieces of Old Macau survive. The **Taipa Houses Museum** (http://en.macaotourism.gov.mo; Tue–Sun 10am–7pm; free) consists of five beautifully restored houses, while local history and developments are explained in the three-storey, mint-green **Museum of Taipa and Coloane History** (http://en.macaotourism.gov.mo; Tue–Sun 10am–6pm; free).

The relatively quiet island of **Coloane** ㉑ is a retreat from Macau's new-found bustle, traffic and casinos. Peaceful **Coloane Village** lies in the southwest of the island, its petite Portuguese-style village square alive with restaurant tables and festivities at weekends and holidays. It's a great place to sit with some Portuguese wine and Macanese food and watch the world go by. The village backstreets have a few furniture shops, cafés and the odd temple.

Over on the quiet eastern side of Coloane is **Hac Sa Beach**, famous for its black sand and Fernando's restaurant.

⊘ MACAU'S CASINOS

Macau's premier entertainment rumbles to the rattle of the roulette ball with the speed of a croupier shuffling a deck of cards. Gambling – or gaming as the industry would have it – is Macau's principal revenue-earner, fleecing the pockets of millions of Chinese and other nationalities every year, but equally sending a few on their way with riches beyond the dreams of avarice. With over 30 casinos open and plenty more on the way, "Asia's Las Vegas" has overtaken the original in terms of gaming revenue.

The casinos fall into two groups: the older, relatively low-rent establishments, owned by local gazillionaire Stanley Ho and epitomised by the original Lisboa; and the often spectacular new breed of Vegas-style palaces and resorts such as the Sands, Wynn, Grand Lisboa and Venetian, which have been taking over since the law was changed in 2002 to allow foreign investment and ownership into the lucrative business.

China's newly flush punters are streaming in. Revenues have grown enormously over the past few years, and Macau became the world's no. 1 gambling destination in 2010, a status it continues to hold as of 2017.

The extraordinary Grand Lisboa Hotel.

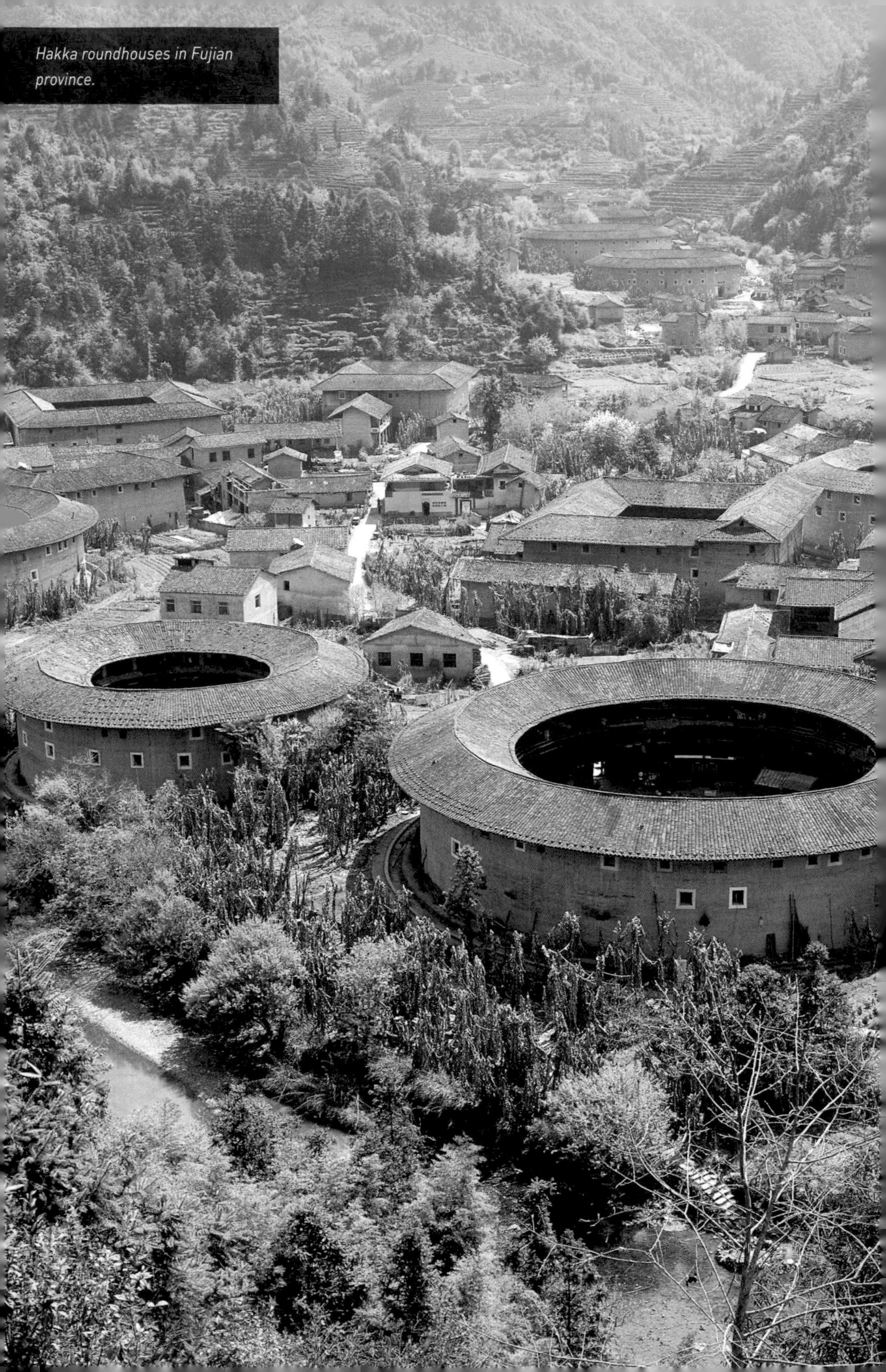

Hakka roundhouses in Fujian province.

GUANGDONG, HAINAN ISLAND AND FUJIAN

Many of the West's important historical encounters with China occurred down south; today the region remains dynamic, outward-looking and almost as removed from Beijing's influence as it was thousands of years ago.

The southern provinces of **Guangdong** (广东), **Hainan** (海南) and **Fujian** (福建) are – particularly in their coastal areas – among the wealthiest and most forward-thinking in China, with a tradition of looking out across the South China Sea to the tropical regions beyond for trade and settlement. Indeed most overseas Chinese *(huaqiao)* hail from these parts, and what the Western world knows as "Chinese" food is almost without exception the distinctive cuisine of Guangdong. The region is also decisively set apart from the Chinese heartland by language: Cantonese and Fujianese are dialects with a rich linguistic heritage, and most southerners are more at ease speaking their mother tongue than they are the national language, Mandarin. Even on a physical level, locals differ markedly from their northern relations, who are typically taller, stockier and fairer-skinned.

In recent times Shenzhen and the Pearl River Delta have developed at breakneck speed to become China's largest manufacturing zone, pulling in migrant workers by the million from the poorer hinterland. Meanwhile, Hainan Island has been busily promoting itself as China's very own tropical beach paradise.

GUANGZHOU

The provincial capital of Guangdong, **Guangzhou** ❶ (广州; Canton) has long

Guangzhou is one of China's wealthiest cities.

been at the core of China's economic reforms. Close to the mouth of the Zhu Jiang (Pearl River), the city is thought to have been founded in 214 BC as an encampment by the armies of the Qin emperor Qin Shi Huangdi. By the Tang period (AD 618–907), it was already an international port, and it was the first Chinese city to come into contact with European maritime power after a Portuguese flotilla arrived in 1514. These pioneers were, of course, followed by the British and a chain of events that would eventually lead to the Opium

☉ Main Attractions

Shamian Island, Guangzhou
Zhaoqing
Chaozhou
Hainan Island Beaches
Gulangyu Island, Xiamen
Maritime Museum, Quanzhou
Hakka Roundhouses, Fujian

⊙ Maps on pages 308, 316, 322

Jogging in Yuexiu Park in central Guangzhou, the city's largest open space.

business and trade: it is still one of the richest cities in China and continues to expand with bold new engineering projects like the Zhu Jiang New City, home of the Guangdong Museum (www.gdmuseum.com; Tue–Sun 9am–5pm) and the Zaha Hadid-designed Guangzhou Opera House.

More than 13 million people live in the main urban area as of 2016, with a total of over 57 million in the Pearl River Delta Mega City.

SHAMIAN ISLAND AND OLD GUANGZHOU

In the southwest of the city, the island of **Shamian** Ⓐ (沙面岛; Shamian Dao) is a preserved relic of the colonial past and the most picturesque spot in the city. Originally a sandbar on the north bank of the Zhu Jiang (珠江; Pearl River) before it was reclaimed and expanded, the small island – just 1km by 0.5km (0.6 mile by 0.3 mile) – was divided in 1859 into several foreign concessions, primarily French and British. At night-time, Chinese were kept off the island by iron gates and narrow bridges.

Wars and the opening of China to foreign trade. Over the years, close contact with overseas Chinese ensured the continuation of Guangzhou's openness to the world and a desire for reform. This, in turn, would eventually spawn revolutionary zeal.

Mao earmarked Guangzhou as China's principal international port. While the rest of China was isolated from the world, Guangzhou did business with the West at the biennial Canton Fair, which runs to this day. In the post-Mao era, the city has remained a centre for

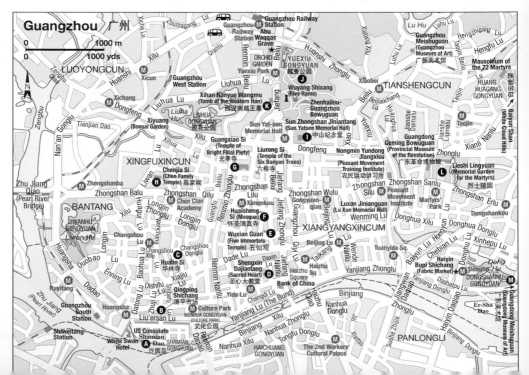

Rather than feeling like an artificial enclave for tourists, Shamian is a thriving community, with century-old mansions forming an attractive backdrop, and antique cannons pointing out over the river as a reminder of more turbulent times. The more significant buildings sport plaques outlining their antecedents, while statues are dotted about depicting rickshaw pullers, tradesmen and – rather daringly – a trio of women from down the ages, the most recent of whom wears tight shorts and gabs on her mobile phone.

Shamian is possibly the only part of this ever-changing city that feels genuinely timeless. The only significant change to the island in recent decades came in 1983 when the jarring, 34-storey White Swan Hotel was built, along with an elevated driveway. Despite the architecture being at odds with the surroundings, its presence scarcely affects Shamian's true character. **Shamian Gongyuan** (沙面 公园; Shamian Park), a few steps from the White Swan, is chock-a-block with people most hours of the day, performing tai chi, ballroom dancing, kicking feathered quoits back and forth, playing mah-jong and generally revelling in their own mini-island resort.

Opposite Shamian on Qingping Lu is **Qingping Shichang ⓑ** (清平市场), a market occupying the side alleys north of Liu'ersan Lu. This district has flourished since the economic reforms of 1978 and, always busy with shoppers, has a carnival feel. It was one of the first places to develop under China's gradual adoption of market economics, and for years it was a capitalist oddity. Qingping was once notorious for selling every imaginable animal for sustenance, including dogs, cats, owls and a variety of insects. Now, however, many stalls have moved inside and the exotic animals have all but disappeared in various beautification and hygiene campaigns.

The immediate area is notable for its old world ambience and pre-revolution architecture, although you need to get off the main roads and head into the side streets to find most of the market stalls and musty old antique

⊙ Tip

Every month, thousands of migrant workers pour into Guangzhou looking for work – often unsuccessfully. As a result, you may encounter more crime, such as pickpocketing, here than elsewhere in China. Be especially careful near the train station and on the metro.

Shamian Island elegance.

⊘ Tip

For some much-needed fresh air, peace and quiet, make the easy half-day trip north of Guangzhou to the White Cloud Hills (白云山; Baiyun Shan), whose highest point reaches almost 400 metres (1,300ft). The area is only around 8km (5 miles) from the city centre, and you can get there either by taxi or on bus No. 24 from the south side of Renmin Park by Gongyuan Qian metro station – journey time around 30 minutes.

shops selling jewellery, timepieces, Mao paraphernalia and antique porcelain reproductions. Just north are the pedestrianised shopping streets of Dishipu, Xiajia Lu and Shangjiulu (collectively referred to as "Shangxiajiu"). A little further on, spilling out either side of Changshou Lu, is Guangzhou's most famous jade market.

Xiajiu Lu leads north to the famous three-storey Guangzhou Restaurant. Founded in 1935, it's the city's oldest. Behind it, located in a narrow side alley named Shangxia Jie, is **Hualin Si** Ⓒ (华林寺; daily 8am–5pm; free). This temple is said to have been founded by an Indian monk in 526, although the existing buildings date from the Qing period. There are 500 statues of *luohan* – pupils of the Buddha – in the main hall.

ALONG THE WATERFRONT

Beside the bridge that connects the eastern end of Shamian with the mainland is **Renmin Daqiao** (人民大桥), the oldest steel bridge across the Zhu Jiang, built in 1933. About 100 metres (110 yds) to the east is a memorial to the Chinese

Incense offerings at Guangxiao Temple.

demonstrators who died in a hail of bullets fired by foreign troops guarding the foreign quarters in the mid-1920s. Stretching further east from here is the so-called Guangzhou "Bund", a moderately elegant strip of 19th-century waterside buildings which shares more than just a name with its more famous Shanghai namesake. Here, on Yanjiang Xilu, are some of the city's trendiest restaurants, bars and clubs. Just to the north are the 50-metre (165ft) double towers of **Sacred Heart Church** Ⓓ (圣心大教堂; Shengxin Dajiaotang), the Catholic cathedral. Completed in 1888, it was left to decay after 1949 but following restoration in the 1980s it now holds services under the auspices of the Patriotic Catholic Church – which finally received papal approval in 2007 after long-running disputes between Beijing and the Vatican.

NORTH TO ZHONGSHAN LU

About 500 metres (550 yds) north, the Daoist **Wuxian Guan** Ⓔ (五仙观; Five Immortals Temple or Temple of Five Genies; daily 9am–noon, 1.30–5pm) dates back to the 14th century and marks the place where the mythical five rams (who founded Guangzhou, according to legend) appeared. A 5-ton Ming-dynasty bronze bell in the tower at the rear remains silent; its ringing is traditionally associated with catastrophe for the city.

South of Zhongshan Lu in Guangta Lu, one can spot the onion dome of **Huaisheng Si** Ⓕ (怀圣清真寺), a 7th-century mosque founded by a trader who was said to be an uncle of the Prophet Mohammed. Arab traders were frequent visitors to China at that time, so the legend may contain some truth, although it does not give sufficient evidence for an exact date of the mosque's origins. The 25-metre (82ft) minaret, **Guang Ta** (Naked Pagoda), rises up among Guangzhou's high-rise skyline, and the mosque – the buildings of which are of recent construction

– acts as a cultural centre for the city's sizeable Muslim community.

THREE TEMPLES

To the north of Zhongshan Lu, a narrow street leads to **Liurong Si** (六榕寺; Temple of the Six Banyan Trees; daily 9am–5.20pm), and within its grounds is **Hua Ta** (Flower Pagoda), built in 1097 and a symbol of the city. The ageing, shaded pagoda appears to be nine storeys high, each level with doorways and encircling balconies, but in fact it contains 17 levels. There is a good view from the top.

A few minutes' walk to the northwest is **Guangxiao Si** (光孝寺; Temple of Bright Filial Piety; daily 6.30am–5pm), a Buddhist temple preserved during the Cultural Revolution on orders from Premier Zhou Enlai. Local legend has it that the temple is older than the town, dating from around AD 400. Some of the present buildings were, however, built after big fires in 1269, 1629 and 1832. At the entrance is a brightly painted laughing Buddha (Milefo), and in the main courtyard, a huge bronze incense burner fills the air. The main hall is noted for its impressive ceiling of red-lacquered timbers, and the back courtyard contains some of the oldest iron pagodas in China. The Indian monk Bodhidharma, founder of Chan (Zen) Buddhism and Shaolin boxing, visited the temple.

Restored after the Cultural Revolution, **Chenjia Si** (陈家祠; Chen Family Temple; daily 8.30am–5.30pm) dates from 1894 and lies further west, near the intersection of Zhongshan Qi Lu and Kangwang Zhonglu. It has six courtyards and a classic layout, with the rooftops and walls decorated with wooden and stone friezes. The largest frieze stretches 28 metres (92ft) across the roof of the central hall and depicts scenes from the epic *Romance of Three Kingdoms*, with thousands of intricate figures against a backdrop of ornate houses, flourishing gates and pagodas. Families with the name Chen, one of the most common in Guangdong province, donated money to build the temple.

NORTH OF DONGFENG LU

After the overthrow of the Qing dynasty in 1911, Guangzhou became the centre

The Five Rams sculpture in Yuexiu Park recalls a legend in which five heavenly creatures flew over the city to save the people from famine.

The Sun Yatsen Memorial Hall.

of the movement led by Sun Yatsen and the headquarters of the Guomindang (Nationalists), the first modern political party in China. Sun Yatsen is still revered today as the founder of modern China, and to the northeast of the intersection of Jiefang Lu and Dongfeng Lu, the blue roof tiles of the **Sun Yatsen Memorial Hall ①** (中山纪念堂; Sun Zhongshan Jiniantang; www.travelchinaguide.com; daily 8am–6pm) stand out strikingly within the setting of a formal garden. The hall, built after Sun's death in 1925 and completed in 1931, houses a large theatre and lecture hall that can seat several thousand people. Guangzhou's largest park, **Yuexiu Gongyuan ①** (越秀公园), due north, is attractively landscaped with artificial lakes, hills, rock sculptures and lush greenery showcasing the province's subtropical flora. It is dominated by **Zhenhailou** (镇海楼; Tower Overlooking the Sea), built as a memorial to the seven great sea journeys undertaken by the eunuch Admiral Zheng He. Between 1405 and 1433, Zheng travelled to east Africa, the

The Martyrs' Memorial Garden.

Persian Gulf and Java. With the sea in fact too far off to see, today the tower houses the **Municipal Museum** (广州市博物馆; Guangzhou Shi Bowuguan; www.guangzhoumuseum.cn; daily 9am–5pm), with relics relating to the city.

Nearby is the **Sun Yatsen Monument** (孙中山纪念碑; Sun Zhongshan Jinian Bei), built of marble and granite and sitting on a hill above Sun Yatsen Hall. Climb to the top for a great view of the city. Yuexiu Park also features some recreational facilities, including a golf driving range, bowling alley and swimming pool.

Opposite the park to the west on Jiefang Bei Lu is the **Xihan Nanyue Wangmu ⓚ** (西汉南越王墓; Tomb of the Western Han; daily 9am–5.30pm), the burial site of the Emperor Wen Di, who ruled the Nanyue kingdom, a vast swathe of southern China and what is now northern Vietnam from 137 to 122 BC, discovered when bulldozers were clearing the ground to build new apartments in the 1980s. The museum houses the skeletons of the emperor and 15 courtiers, including concubines, guards, cooks and a musician, who were buried alive with him. One part of the museum recreates the setting of the tomb so that visitors can walk downstairs into the actual chambers, though the highlight is the exhibition building, slightly up the hill, where thousands of funerary objects are displayed, including the suit of jade in which the emperor was buried.

EASTERN DISTRICTS

In the eastern part of the city, on Zhongshan Lu, is the former Confucius Temple, which lost its religious function during the "bourgeois revolution" in 1912. In 1924, the **Peasant Movement Training Institute** (农民运动讲习所; Nongmin Yundong Jiangxisu) opened here, and in effect became the first school of the Chinese Communist Party. During a period of cooperation between the Guomindang and Communists,

Mao Zedong and other prominent party members worked and taught at the Institute: Mao's quarters can be viewed. This is where he developed his theory of peasant revolution.

After the collapse of a workers' uprising in 1927, the Communists were forced to retreat for a time from the cities. A park and memorial, **Lieshi Lingyuan** ❶ (烈士陵园; Memorial Garden for the Martyrs), was created in 1957 in memory of the uprising and its 6,000 victims.

Further east, on Ersha Island, is the **Guangdong Museum of Art** Ⓜ (广东美术馆; Guangdong Meishuguan; 38 Yanyu Road; www.gdmoa.org; Tue–Sun 9am–5pm; free). Its dozen exhibition halls display some of the more avant-garde examples of Chinese art, with frequent exhibitions of work by local students as well as special events celebrating artists from overseas. There is also an outdoor sculpture area.

SHENZHEN AND THE PEARL RIVER DELTA

Shenzhen ❷ (深圳) is a frenetic Special Economic Zone (SEZ) on the border with Hong Kong. For the typical overseas tourist venturing into mainland China for a day or two from Hong Kong, it provides a decidedly unrepresentative, but fascinating, glimpse of "the other side". Shenzhen leads tourists to bargain shopping, wild nightlife and no less than five US-style theme parks.

Shenzhen is a sprawling city that resembles Disneyland-meets-New York City as its skyline looms on the horizon approached from Hong Kong. Bounded by its eponymous river to the south (marking the border with Hong Kong), it has spread from its historic centre in the Luohu District across every inch of land up to the border with Hong Kong, and north into the hilly green hinterland. But Shenzhen is a migrant city, with little left in the way of traditional Cantonese culture. It has prospered as a financial centre – one of the nation's stock markets operates here – and as a base for foreign investors. Hong Kong money, from factory capital to sponsored second wives, turns many of the local wheels.

If you are coming up from Hong Kong on the train, you will arrive at **Luohu**

Downtown Shenzhen.

(罗湖; Lo Wu when transliterated from the Cantonese). After disembarking at Lo Wu station in Hong Kong, it's simply a case of walking across the border (indoors) to emerge into a large concrete plaza on the Chinese side, after sweating through often long queues of buses and easily flustered immigration officers. The **Lo Wu Commercial City** (罗湖商业城; Luohu Shangye Cheng) is to your right. This is one of Shenzhen's largest – and cheapest – retail centres, selling a vast array of electronics, leather goods, jewellery and a medley of other merchandise that is packed layer upon layer.

Opposite is the railway station, with frequent trains to Guangzhou and various Pearl River Delta destinations, and the metro, which can whisk you north to the downtown area (around 2km/1.2 miles away), on to Futian District – a major nightlife and shopping area – and beyond, to the cluster of theme parks around 15km (9 miles) west of town.

The most popular of these parks is **Window of the World** (世界之窗; Shijie Zhichuang; daily 9am–10pm, until 10.30pm during public holidays), a sort of global Lilliput which showcases scale models of everything from Thai palaces to Japanese teahouses – to say nothing of the Eiffel Tower.

Nearby, **Splendid China** (锦绣中华; Jinxiu Zhonghua; daily 10am–6pm) is a good option for anyone without the time to travel the entire country. For here are the Terracotta Warriors, the Great Wall, the Old Summer Palace, the Forbidden City and much more besides, all replicated in miniature, spread over 30 hectares (75 acres) and achievable in a couple of hours. The adjacent **China Folk Culture Village** (民俗文化村; Minsu Wenhua Cun; daily 10am–9pm) recreates the homes and lifestyles of the country's ethnic minorities.

The ubiquitous Overseas Chinese Town (OCT) development company opened its most ambitious project in 2007, the **OCT East** (东部华侨城; Dongbu Huaqiao Cheng) scenic spot that encompasses several specific theme parks. Set around a man-made lake in eastern Shenzhen's hills, the 890-hectare (2,225-acre) site has been crafted as a facsimile of Interlaken, Switzerland, complete with ski chalets, mineral baths and Chinese "Fräuleins" in braids. It's an impressive, albeit slightly plastic, reproduction. To the south are Shenzhen's two best **beaches**, **Dameisha** (大梅沙; free) and **Xiaomeisha** (小梅沙). The sandy strands and resort developments give visitors a glimpse into the quick rise of China's often crowded, chaotic beach culture.

AROUND THE DELTA

While international trade is all the rage in the Pearl River Delta, early attempts by Western traders to introduce opium to China in the 19th century met with stiff official resistance, commemorated at both a park and a museum in the town of **Humen** (虎门), north of Shenzhen's airport. It was here that Commissioner Lin Zexu contaminated several thousand chests of opium with quicklime in 1839, then deposited the

⊘ THE RISE OF THE PEARL RIVER DELTA

Building on its glorious trading history, the Pearl River Delta (PRD) was the first part of China to be prised open in the reforms of the 1980s and it has revelled in economic success ever since. Huge industrial estates now dominate areas where, a generation ago, there were only paddy fields and fish ponds.

The statistics are arresting: the PRD's thousands of factories generate a GDP of US$1 trillion following double-digit percent increases since the 1980s and 8.6 percent in 2015. The delta contributed that year to around 9.1 percent of the entire Chinese economy. It attracts almost half of the total foreign investment in China; and it is the world leader in light manufacturing – churning out vast quantities of high-tech electronics, garments, footwear and toys. A population of less than 1 million about 30 years ago stood at an estimated 57 million in 2016.

Today, the region's supremacy is being challenged by the growth of manufacturing centres such as Chongqing and other parts of China the government wants to develop. Rising wages on the back of worker complaints about exploitation have raised the costs of business in the delta, sending some factory investors to cheaper frontiers such as Vietnam. Workers, for their part, are heading back to rural villages to work, creating a Pearl River Delta labour shortage.

haul in the so-called opium pits on the shore to the south of town. The British retaliated, sparking the First Opium War. Much is made (and rightly so) of the immorality of foreign merchants in the **Opium War Museum** (鸦片战争博物馆; Yapan Zhanzheng Bowuguan; www.ypzz.cn; Apr–Oct 8.30am–5.30pm, Nov–Mar until 5pm) in Zhixin Park. On the coast 5km (3 miles) south of Humen town, the original **opium pits** and the **fortress of Shajiao** (沙角炮台; Shajiao Potai) are worth a visit (8am–5pm).

Some 25km (16 miles) southwest of central Guangzhou, **Foshan** (佛山; Buddha Mountain) is famous for its venerable **Zu Miao** (祖庙; Ancestral Temple; daily 8.30am–7pm). Dating back to the 11th century, the Zu Miao's main effigy is a 3-ton statue of Beidi (Pak Tai in Cantonese), a Daoist deity in charge of the waters whom the locals sought to venerate in this flood-prone region. Note the distinctive ceramic figures on the roof tiles made in the adjacent town of **Shiwan** (石湾; Stone Bay), one of China's leading ceramic centres and home to the **Nanfeng Ancient Kiln** (南风古灶; Nanfeng Guzao; daily 8am–5pm), two early-Ming-dynasty kilns which have remained in constant use for around six centuries.

Heading south towards Zhuhai and Macau, the countryside is less developed. **Shunde** (顺德) is home to **Qinghui Yuan** (清晖园; Qinghui Garden; daily mid-Mar–mid-Oct 8am–6pm, mid-Oct–mid-Mar 8am–5.30pm), a classical Chinese garden with a series of fish ponds, bamboo groves and fanciful engravings.

Zhongshan ❸ (中山) is one of the more attractive cities in the region, and has become popular with Hong Kongers as a weekend retreat. Its central district is partly landscaped, and pedestrians can walk past the city's older houses. The nearby village of **Cuiheng** (翠亨村), where Sun Yatsen was born in 1866, lies to the southeast. The man most frequently described as the Father of Modern China spent only part

of his childhood here, and the original house was demolished in 1913. However, it has since been reconstructed and turned into the **Dr Sun Yatsen Residence Memorial Museum** (孙中山故居; Sun Zhongshan Guju; Cuiheng Dadao; daily 9am–5pm), standing as a suitable testament to his life as well as an illuminating depiction of rural existence in pre-revolutionary days.

ELSEWHERE IN GUANGDONG

One of Guangdong's more agreeable cities and a favourite destination for Hong Kongers and mainland tourists, **Zhaoqing ❹** (肇庆) sits on the Xi Jiang River, 110km (68 miles) west of Guangzhou. The town is famous for its **Qixing Yan** (七星岩; Seven Star Crags), a range of limestone peaks that rise from a man-made lake in the north of town. Extravagant comparisons with Guilin are inaccurate, but the crags are picturesque in the right light conditions and set in pleasant surroundings.

The Ming-dynasty **Chongxi Ta** (崇禧塔; Chongxi Pagoda; daily 8am–5pm) affords long views over the river to the

Originally intended as fortifications for villages, Kaiping's diaolou watch-towers evolved into showpieces of wealth and style, as locals who had made their fortunes overseas returned home. Many display Western European, Greek and even Arabic influences in their architectural details.

Star Lake, Zhaoqing.

south and across to two further pagodas rising up on the opposite bank. It's also possible to walk on the pleasingly unrestored sections of the Song-dynasty city wall. Access is off either side of Renmin Nanlu, close to the river. The forested reserve of **Dinghu Shan** (鼎湖山), 20km (12 miles) to the northeast, is a lovely range of pathways, temples, woodland, waterfalls, streams and pools.

South from Zhaoqing, **Kaiping** ❺ (开平) is famous for its *diaolou* towers. These multi-storeyed defensive village houses, built from the early 17th century to the 1930s, display an ornate fusion of Chinese and Western architectural styles. The remaining *diaolou* – more than 1,800 in all – are scattered over a wide area, some hidden beside duck ponds in the backstreets of Kaiping, but most in the villages around the city. Twenty of the most outstanding examples were collectively given Unesco World Heritage listing in 2007, but the area still receives relatively few foreign visitors.

EASTERN GUANGDONG

This corner of Guangdong is historically one of the main centres of emigration from China, and contains three of its best-known cities – Shantou, Chaozhou and Meizhou. The last two are traditional homelands to their respective ethnic groups – the Chiu Chow (Teochew) and the Hakkas.

Nearing the border with Fujian province and one of China's original SEZs,

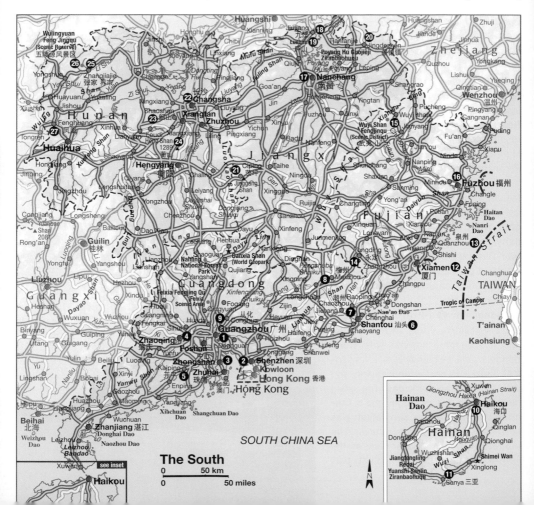

The South

Shantou ⑥ (汕头) is a port city that was opened to foreign trade after the Second Opium War. The crumbling colonial quarter on the knob of land poking into the harbour is a fascinating – albeit slightly melancholy – area, where locals reside amid decaying European architecture. **Shipaotai** (石炮台公园; Stone Fort Park) preserves a moated fortification built in 1879 for coastal defence. The fort is squat and solid, its 5 metre (16-ft) -thick outer wall made of a surprising blend of granite, glutinous rice, brown sugar and crushed seashells. Atmospheric arched tunnels run around its base, with chambers on either side. Enter the circular central courtyard to see the wave-like steps which allowed cannons to be rolled up to the battlements. A total of 18 cannons face the harbour. Nearby is the marvellously restored **Tianhou Gong** (天后宫; Tianhou Temple), dedicated to the Queen of Heaven.

Chaozhou ⑦ (潮州), 40km (25 miles) north of Shantou, is a historic trading town, its attractive centre full of narrow lanes and a section of Ming-dynasty wall bordering the Han Jiang river. The Guanyin Pavilion, inside the expansive Tang-dynasty temple **Kaiyuan Si** (开元寺; daily 7.30am–5.30pm), is notable for its arrangement of Guanyin effigies representing the various earthly manifestations of the goddess. The temple complex features some ancient stonework and several venerable old trees. Directly east from the square in front of the temple you'll find a long section of the **Old City Wall**, the largest remaining in Guangdong. The nearest opening is **Guangji Gate** (广济门; Guangji Men); you can climb steps here to reach a three-storey watchtower on top of the wall. Opposite, the **Guangji Bridge** (广济桥; Guangji Qiao), a medieval trading link between Guangdong and Fujian, stretches across the wide Han Jiang.

Further inland, and bisected by a loop of the Mei Jiang, is the small city of **Meizhou** ⑧ (梅州), considered the home of the Hakka people (although the ancient origins of this migratory ethnic group are likely to have been in central China). Hakkas have spread all over China and are found in overseas Chinese communities worldwide; around 95 percent of these are from the Meizhou area.

NORTHERN GUANGDONG

Forming part of a near-continuous line of hills that stretch right across southern China and relatively unknown to tourists, the northern parts of Guangdong are a world away from the booming coastlands.

The **Feixia Scenic Area** (飞霞风景区; Feixia Fengjing Qu) is an attractive riverside site of hills and temples an hour by bus north of the town of Qingyuan. Two to three hours northeast of Guangzhou by bus is the town of **Conghua** ⑨ (从化), home to **Conghua Hot Springs** (从化温泉; Conghua Wenquan), a well-known destination famous for lychees and popular for its clean air and serene setting.

The city of Shaoguan is the access point for the **Nanling National Forest Park** (南岭国家森林公园) and the

Craggy scenery in northern Guangdong.

Gathering seaweed on the Fujian coast.

Chebaling National Nature Reserve (车八岭国家 自然保护区), where the last remaining South China tigers may just survive. Around 50km (30 miles) northeast of Shaoguan, **Danxia Shan** (丹霞山; Danxia Shan World Geopark; daily) is an area of high eroded peaks of red sandstone, sculpted by time and water into a variety of odd shapes.

HAINAN ISLAND

Historically and geographically out on a limb, for centuries shunned as a miserable place of exile battered by typhoons, **Hainan Island** (海南岛) has come into its own as a tropical resort destination with Chinese characteristics. It basks in year-round warmth, and there are plenty of palm-fringed beaches on which to take advantage of that fact, particularly in the south around Sanya – the only stretches of sand in China really worth packing a beach towel for.

The island's capital, **Haikou** ⑩ (海口), is a pleasant city, with an unmistakably laid-back ambience. The Old Quarter in the north of the city centre is attractive, and features a promenade extending along Changdi Lu past clipped lawns and the banks of the Haidian River.

The real reason to come to Hainan, though, is to voyage down to the surf and sun at the island's southern extremity. These days most people fly straight to Sanya, the southern hub, but if you are travelling from Haikou along the east-coast highway, places of interest en route include some fine beaches around the village of **Qinglan** (清澜), and Hainan's surfing centre at **Shimei Wan** (石梅湾; Shimei Bay) near the town of Xinglong – also home to the beautiful **Xinglong Tropical Botanical Garden** (兴隆热带植物园; Xinglong Redai Zhiwuguan).

SANYA AND THE BEACHES

Sanya ⑪ (三亚) itself was originally one of several fishing villages on the southern tip of Hainan, and fishing docks still occupy a focal point at the town's hub. The Sanya River divides the town from north to south, with the original settlement lying to the west. It's all pleasantly relaxed; shabbiness now rubs shoulders with a form of gentrification – several good restaurants have opened

Beach scene near Sanya.

and there is a trend for upmarket tea-houses. As China's main beach resort, it is very popular with domestic tourists, as well as visiting Russians.

The rocky **Luhuitou** (鹿回头) Peninsula, immediately south of Sanya, is dominated by a giant sculpture depicting the legend of a hunter and a deer. The statue is located in a hill park in the north of the peninsula, with superb views of Sanya City, Dadonghai Bay and other nearby beaches available from the highest point.

Five minutes southeast of the city centre by road, or a 45-minute walk, lies the long fine-sand bay of **Dadonghai** (大东海). The whole of its beachfront has been developed, with mostly high-end hotels and villa resorts. Off the main drag, side streets are wall-to-wall with seafood restaurants, beachwear and souvenir knick-knack shops; it's all fairly laid-back, with little hard sales pressure.

Palm-tree shade is a little scarce, although it's possible to rent chairs and tables under parasols. The water is clean, but deceptive currents mean that it's not suitable for children or weaker swimmers.

Yalong Wan (亚龙湾; Yalong Bay), 20km (12 miles) to the east, is a gorgeous 7km (4.5-mile) strip of pale, powdery sand; warm sunshine throughout the winter high season attracts crowds of domestic tourists as well as large numbers of Russian sunseekers, and activities include scuba diving, deep-sea fishing and paragliding. Further proof, if it were needed, that Yalong Bay represents one of China's most successful gentrification operations is the raft of internationally managed resorts – Marriott, Sheraton and Hilton included – that line the seafront. Backpackers beware.

Hainan's island culture is best typified by the livelihood of its minority Li and Miao peoples. Several Li and Miao villages can be reached around the town of **Wuzhishan** (五指山市; also called Tongza and Tongshi) in the highlands north of Sanya, which has a very interesting **Minority Nationalities Museum** (民族博物馆; Minzu Bowuguan; closed for reconstruction) dedicated to the culture of the Li and

⊘ TRANSPORT

Getting to Hainan
Haikou and Sanya airports are both well connected with mainland cities, Hong Kong, and Macau. Hainan's railway links with the mainland rail network via the ferry, which the train itself actually boards. There are direct services from Sanya to Guangzhou (3 daily, 15 hours). Sleeper buses run between Haikou and Guangzhou (daily, 12 hours).

Getting around Hainan
Haikou: Trains to Sanya via Dongfang take around 2 hours, with 24 services daily. Buses to Sanya take 3 hours.
Sanya: Trains and buses to Haikou take approximately 2 and 3 hours respectively. Wenchang is 3½ hours away by bus, or 90 minutes by train. Minibuses ply the routes between the south-coast resorts.
Tongzhi: There are plenty of buses to Haikou (3 hours) and Sanya (1.5–2 hrs).

Getting to Fujian
Fuzhou and Xiamen are the main airports. Overlanding from Guangdong is easier by bus, as rail links are slow (14 hours Guangzhou–Xiamen). Rail is better between Fujian and Jiangxi or Hunan.

Getting around Fujian
There are no train services between Xiamen, Quanzhou and Fuzhou.
Xiamen: Trains to Yongding (2 fast trains daily, 3 hrs), Wuyishan (3 daily, 13 hrs) and Nanchang (4 daily, 17 hours). Frequent buses to Fuzhou (3 hours), Quanzhou (2 hours) and Yongding (5 hrs).
Fuzhou: Trains to Wuyishan (6 daily, 5.5 hours) and Nanchang (11 daily, 12–13 hours). Frequent buses to Xiamen (3 hours), Quanzhou (2 hrs), Wuyishan (6–8 hours).
Quanzhou: There are frequent buses to Xiamen and Fuzhou (both 2 hours), as well as Yongding and Wuyishan.

◉ Tip

At the terminal just north of Zhongshan Lu, ferries cross the narrow channel to Gulangyu every 10–15 minutes from 5.45am until 9pm, and then every 20–30 minutes until 12.30am. The journey time is 5–7 minutes. It's also possible to take a 30-minute boat tour that circles Gulangyu, before dropping you off on the island.

the Miao. The **Jianfeng Ling Primeval Forest Reserve** (尖峰岭热带原始森林自然保护区; Jiangfengling Redai Yuanshi Senlin Ziranbaohuqu), 110km (68 miles) northwest of Sanya, is a striking mountainous area that has been successfully reforested and welcomes visitors.

FUJIAN PROVINCE

Historically linked to Taiwan by proximity and a common tongue (minnanhua), Fujian province has, like its neighbouring provinces of Guangdong and Zhejiang, spearheaded the emigration of Chinese overseas. Thanks to Taiwanese investment and an expedient maritime footing, it is one of China's wealthiest provinces. Seldom visited by foreign tourists because its low but hard-to-cross mountains present transport barriers, it offers enough history, scenery, folk traditions and other attractions to rank alongside some of the country's more lauded destinations. On a gloomier note, the province is permanently earmarked as an ideal launch pad for any (however unlikely) mainland invasion of Taiwan, and officials in Taipei fear that it bristles with missiles. The islands of Kinmen and Matsu, in the waters just offshore from Xiamen and Fuzhou, remain in Taiwanese hands. But with Taiwan-China ties improving since 2008, moneyed Fujianese tourists now visit Taiwan en masse, and the two sides have set up a busy ferry link between Kinmen and the Fujian metropolis of Xiamen.

XIAMEN

One of China's most engaging cities, the port of **Xiamen** ⑫ (厦门) has an attractive old centre and an utterly beguiling offshore haven, the island of Gulangyu. Formerly known in the west as Amoy, it became wealthy during the expansive maritime trading years of the Ming dynasty. The port was opened to foreign trade after the Opium War, and the offshore island of Gulangyu became a foreign enclave, complete with the full array of colonial trappings. Much of the island's architecture, spread over small hills above a swimming beach, still looks more European than Chinese. In 1980, Xiamen joined the likes of Shenzhen in becoming a Special Economic

Elds deer in the highlands of central Hainan.

Zone, and its economy thrived amid a raft of economic incentives and tax-relief measures. It continues to attract a disproportionate number of economic migrants and is today one of southern China's wealthiest and most tastefully developed cities.

Xiamen is an island, linked to mainland Fujian by a 5km (3-mile) causeway. The **Old Town** Ⓐ is focused around the lower (western) end of Zhongshan Lu, and is a pleasant place to wander around. On Siming Nanlu, about 2km (1.2 miles) south, lies the **Overseas Chinese Museum** Ⓑ (华侨博物馆; Huaqiao Bowuguan; Tue–Sun 9.30am–4.30pm) its outstanding collection of pottery and bronzes gathered with the help of donations from members of the huge overseas Fujianese community. There is also a section on the diaspora itself.

Xiamen's most famous temple is **Nan-putuo Si** Ⓒ (南普陀寺; daily 8am–8pm), north of the university in the southeast of town. The Tianwang Dian (Heavenly King Hall) at the entrance is home to the Bodhisattva Milefo, Weituo and the awesome Four Heavenly Kings. The name of the temple echoes Putuo Shan (see page 256) and, unsurprisingly, effigies of the goddess Guanyin are in abundance.

Along the shore south of the temple is the **Huli Shan Fort** Ⓓ (胡里山炮台; Huli Shan Paotai), a gun emplacement established on a hill. The impressive cannons, originally imported from Germany in 1891 to defend Xiamen against pirate attacks, were used a few decades later to sink a Japanese battleship and are still in place on the firing platform.

GULANGYU ISLAND

Occupied by colonial powers until World War II, the island of **Gulangyu** Ⓔ (鼓浪屿) is Xiamen's main attraction, a laid-back, hilly retreat accessed by ferry from the city, and a museum piece of colonial architecture. Peace and quiet is a big part of the appeal – there are no cars, motorbikes or even bicycles allowed, although electric trains now trundle slowly along the pleasant leafy lanes. The island measures just 2 sq km (0.75 sq mile) in area, so even if you get lost (most people do), it's easy to retrace your steps.

Nanputuo Temple, Xiamen.

Close to the pier, in the main restaurant and shopping area and rather at odds with the rest of Gulangyu, is **Xiamen Undersea World ℉** (海底世界; Haidi Shijie; 8am–6pm), a well-equipped aquarium. Turn left from the pier to reach the huge **Koxinga statue** (郑成功铜像) at the easternmost point of the island. Xiamen became a hive of anti-Manchu resistance after the Qing took control of China in 1644. Led by Koxinga (Zheng Chenggong), the Ming rebels fought a losing war against the northern invaders. Koxinga is claimed by politicians on both sides of the thorny Taiwan question. To the Chinese, he's unambiguously presented as a great military patriot, partly for his reclamation of Taiwan from Dutch colonialists. However, his fierce Ming loyalties saw him flee to Taiwan and establish his own kingdom in opposition to the new Qing court. Accordingly, some view him as a forefather of Taiwanese separatism.

Continue walking along the coast to reach one of the most picturesque places on Gulangyu, the **Shuzhuang Garden ⑥** (菽庄花园; Shuzhuang Huayuan; daily 7.30am–5.30pm) in the southeast, with its zigzag bridge that enables you to believe that you "walk on water" at high tide. Beyond the garden, the pleasant sandy and swimmable beach extends along much of the island's southern coast.

The leafy sanctuary at Shuzhuang was the pet project of Lin Er Jia, who is believed to have brought the first piano to Gulangyu, starting a musical tradition that continues to this day – the island has its own concert hall, where the Xiamen Philharmonic Orchestra occasionally gives performances. With the absence of any vehicles it is still possible to hear the tinkling scales and trills that still cascade out of many an open window around the island. The **Piano Museum** (鼓浪屿钢琴博物馆; Gangqin Bowuguan; daily 8.15am–6pm) at Shuzhuang Garden includes numerous antique pianos from Austria, Germany, France, the UK and the US.

Sunlight Rock ℍ (日光岩; Riguang Yan; daily 8am–7pm), a favourite photo opportunity and the highest point on the island at 93 metres (305ft), is to the

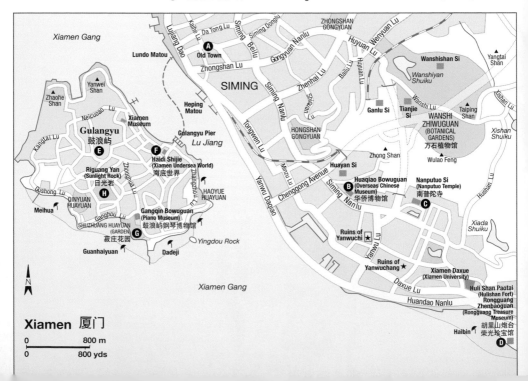

Xiamen 厦门

0   800 m

0   800 yds

north. The charge includes a cable-car ride to the summit. Just below it, within the same park, is the **Koxinga Memorial Hall** (郑成功纪 念馆; Zhengchenggong Jinianguan; daily 8am–5pm; admission included with Sunlight Rock), with a mixture of 17th-century artefacts and a large dose of Taiwan-related propaganda.

Some of the most interesting buildings on Gulangyu are situated in the area immediately uphill from the main ferry pier – on Fujian Lu, Lujiao Lu and Longtou Lu (the latter is also a good bet for restaurants). A little further west, the **Xiamen Museum** (厦门博物馆; Xiamen Bowuguan; 43 Guxin Lu; daily 8.30am–5pm) has reopened. The museum's cupolas are visible from most points on the island.

QUANZHOU AND THE SOUTHWEST

A thousand years ago **Quanzhou** ⑱ (泉州) was arguably the world's most significant port, with a lucrative position at the centre of the maritime silk trade. It prospered enormously during the Song and Yuan dynasties, when it was visited by Marco Polo (the port was known as Zaytoun then) and played host to thousands of Arab merchants, many of whom made fortunes introducing Chinese inventions such as gunpowder and printing to the West. The port fell into irreversible decline following the restrictions on maritime trade imposed by the Ming emperors in the 15th century. Yet it has retained its heritage remarkably well by Chinese standards, and all new buildings must follow height and design standards to keep them in harmony with the past.

The **Ashab Mosque** (清净寺; Qingzhen Si; daily 8am–5.30pm) on Tumen Jie dates from 1009, and its presence stands as testimony to Quanzhou's heyday as a cosmopolitan city, home to many thousands of Muslim traders. It is said to be the only mosque in Han (ie eastern) China built along traditional Islamic, rather than Chinese, lines. English language signs help to bring alive the past for the (rather rare) foreign visitor.

Islam was not the only foreign religion to reach Quanzhou, as you soon realise on the ground floor of the **Maritime Museum** (海外交通史博物馆, Haiwai Jiaotongshi Bowuguan;

A bird's-eye view across Gulangyu Island.

A Hakka roundhouse is a remarkable sight.

daily 9am–6pm, until 5.30pm in winter) on the northeast side of town. Nestorian crosses, carved fragments from Hindu temples, stones bearing the star of David, Arabic inscriptions and even remnants of a 7th-century Manichean shrine compete for attention in this fascinating display. On the upper floor you will find a masterly survey of China's seafaring history and a sizeable display devoted to the remarkable expeditions of Admiral Zheng He. Imaginative layout and lively exhibits make this one of China's best museums, fully worthy of its Unesco sponsorship. All labels are translated into English.

Kaiyuan Si (开元寺; Kaiyuan Temple; daily 8am–5pm) is Quanzhou's largest Buddhist temple, and one of China's most beautiful. The temple dates back to the late 7th century, but its two pagodas were later additions, constructed in the 13th century. They have managed to survive largely as they are built of stone, not wood.

Yongding ⑭ (永定) in southwest Fujian near the border with Guangdong is unremarkable in itself, but there is an unusual attraction northeast of town. A large Hakka earthen roundhouse called Zhenchenglou is located north of the village of Hukeng.

WUYI SHAN

In the isolated northwestern corner of Fujian, **Wuyi Shan ⑮** (武夷山) is a Unesco World Heritage Site with towering peaks and dense forest cradling a rich and unique ecosystem. Several trails head into the peaks, and this is prime hiking territory. However, despite the remote location, a nearby airport facilitates the passage of a huge number of Chinese tour groups, and a fairly unappealing new town has sprung up to cater to their needs. Wuyi Shan has an unfortunate reputation as one of China's foremost tourist traps. The price hikes and aggressive vendors can mar what is, otherwise, one of the most spectacular parts of southern China. Spring or autumn is the best time to visit to avoid the crowds (winters are cold and often wet).

The entrance to the reserve is just 10km (6 miles) southwest of Wuyishan City, and there are frequent minibuses

between the two. These take you to the resort area around the confluence of the Chongyang Stream and Jiuqu River (Nine Bend Stream).

Most visitors climb up to some of the most famous vantage points and strange rock formations. The Heavenly Tour Peak, Tiger Roaring Rock, Thread of Sky, Water Curtain Cave and King Peak will occupy a couple of half-days. The extraordinary "hanging coffins", mostly made from whole trees, are wedged in caves high up on cliff faces. Carbon dating has revealed that they are more than 3,000 years old, but no one has yet explained how or why they were installed in such seemingly inaccessible locations.

Rain or shine, the raft trip down **Nine Bend Stream** (九曲溪; Jiuqu River; Jiuqu Xi) is an essential part of the Wuyi experience. Throughout the 80-minute trip you are likely to be regaled by tales of the curious rock formations and anecdotes about celebrities who have taken the trip.

FUZHOU

The provincial capital, **Fuzhou** ⑯ (福

州), is of limited interest. It's a clean and well-maintained sort of place, but there is little in the way of sights.

Directly behind the Mao statue is the modest **Jade Hill** (玉山; Yu Shan), and on its western flank stands the 10th-century **Bai Ta** (白塔; White Pagoda), commanding views over the city. Further west, beyond the major shopping thoroughfare of Bayiqi Zhonglu, is **Wu Shan** (乌山; Black Hill), crowned with the corresponding **Wu Ta** (乌塔; Black Pagoda), an ancient granite structure dating back to the 8th century.

Xichang Temple (西昌寺; Xichang Si) is the city's largest and oldest temple, dating back to pre-Tang times, although it has been much restored in recent times thanks to donations from prosperous overseas residents. Situated off Gongye Lu some 1.5km (1 mile) west of the centre near the Min River, the buildings epitomise Fujian style at its most flamboyant.

To the east of the city are the wooded slopes of **Gu Shan** (鼓山). Horrendously crowded at weekends, it makes for a pleasant escape at other times.

Pagoda at Quanzhou.

⊘ TULOU: HAKKA ROUNDHOUSES

The Hakka (*kejia* in Mandarin; literally "guest people") are a Chinese people whose distinctive earthen houses – *tulou* – can be found in the borderland counties where Guangdong, Jiangxi and Fujian provinces meet. Communal entities, tulou are fortified against marauding bandits and generally made of compacted earth, bamboo, wood and stone. They contain many rooms on several storeys, so that several families can live together. The small, self-contained design is a common characteristic of Hakka dwellings (eg the Hakka walled villages at Kam Tin in Hong Kong's New Territories). *Tulou* come in a variety of styles, and can be circular, triangular, rectangular, octagonal or other shapes. The extraordinary round earth houses range in size from the small scale (around 12 rooms) to the large (up to 72 rooms). Most are three storeys high, but the largest have up to five storeys. Some *tulou* stand independently, while others cluster into groups. The tulou located in Hukeng near Yongding in southwest Fujian include the circular Zhenchenglou and a Five Phoenix House (Wufenglou), among others. Five Phoenix buildings tended to belong to Hakka officials and are more palatial than typical *tulou*.

THE SOUTHERN INTERIOR

Best-known in China for their revolutionary past and fiery cuisine, these relatively poor inland provinces contain some sublime scenery and historic towns.

Map on page 316

The subtropical provinces of Jiangxi and Hunan are on few tourist itineraries, although their associations with Mao and the early years of the Chinese Communist Party ensure that a steady stream of Chinese tour groups continues to flock to places such as Shaoshan and Jinggangshan. Nonetheless, there is plenty to see here, not least some pockets of beautiful scenery, and a scattering of attractive towns and villages to discover and explore – notably Fenghuang, in western Hunan.

JIANGXI PROVINCE

Jiangxi (江西) province is one of China's most neglected areas, a forgotten backwater through much of Chinese history. This landlocked province, south of the Yangzi, found a modicum of importance after the Grand Canal was constructed in the 7th century AD in neighbouring Zhejiang. Suddenly Jiangxi found itself on part of a complex trading route that linked prosperous Guangdong with northern China. However, its star faded with the advent of coastal shipping which made it quickly overshadowed by the more prosperous provinces to the south and east. The 20th century saw Jiangxi mired in conflict, initially between competing warlords and then caught up in the Communist–Nationalist civil war. In recent years it has been playing catch-up with its coastal neighbours.

NANCHANG

Jiangxi's capital, **Nanchang** ⑰ (南昌), until recent years known primarily for it role in Chinese communism's history, is now at the forefront of another revolution: the rapid economic upsurge of China's so-called "second-tier" cities, many of them capitals of interior provinces that are now benefiting from the spread of investment inland from the more developed coastal areas such as Guangdong and Fujian.

The limestone crags at Wulingyuan.

The premier historic site in town is the impressive nine-storey **Tengwang Pavilion** (滕王阁; Tengwang Ge; 7 Yanjiang Bei Lu; May–mid-Oct 7.30am–6pm, mid-Oct–Apr 8am–5.30pm), which towers majestically over the Gan Jiang River. At night, a multicoloured array of lights brings its graceful flying eaves to life. It is surrounded by a garden of elegant pavilions and gently weeping willows.

Around 2km (1.2 miles) to the east off Minde Lu, Nanchang's main commercial and nightlife thoroughfare, is **Zhu De's Former Residence**, (朱德旧居; Zhu De Jiuju; 2 Huayuanjiao Jie; daily 8.30am–6pm; free). Together with Mao and Zhou Enlai, Zhu De led 30,000 Communist troops in the abortive 1 August 1927 rebellion against the Nationalist forces. Despite its calamitous failure, the uprising is considered the first major conflict of the Chinese Civil War and, as such, 1 August (bayi) has come to be celebrated as the anniversary of the People's Liberation Army's formation. The **1 August Uprising Museum** (八一纪念馆; Bayi Jinianguan; 380 Zhongshan Lu; Tue–Sun 8am–5pm), situated a short distance to the south on Zhongshan Lu, covers the events more fully, but the grandest tribute to the uprising is without doubt **1 August Square** (八一广场; Bayi Guangchang), China's largest public square after Beijing's Tiananmen.

ELSEWHERE IN JIANGXI

Tucked between the Yangzi's southern bank and the northern fringe of Poyang Lake is the rambling port of **Jiujiang** ⑱ (九江), a compact town with a scenic walkway offering the chance to stroll along the Yangzi. Clubs and brothels hidden by day rule the scene after dark.

In addition to being a crucial overflow reservoir when the Yangzi bursts its banks, the lake of **Poyang Hu** (鄱阳湖) provides a wetland habitat for several endangered species of waterfowl.

The large **Poyang Lake National Nature Reserve** (鄱阳湖国家级自然保护区; Poyang Hu Guojieji Ziranbaohuqu), situated around the village of **Wucheng**, is considered by many birdwatchers to be one of Asia's supreme avian spectacles, attracting six species of crane each winter.

Rising up west of Poyang Hu (Poyang Lake) in the north of Jiangxi, **Lushan** ⑲ (庐山; 6am–6pm) offers respite from the steamy summers along the central plains. It was singled out as a retreat for missionary and expatriate families in the 19th century, and their European-style stone dwellings, later occupied by Nationalists and Communists alike, survive; some now operate as charming hotels. The resort is surrounded by sometimes dramatic mountain scenery, and there are numerous hiking trails. Tourists from throughout China journey up the winding roads from Nanchang to gaze at waterfalls and towering cliffs.

Jingdezhen ⑳ (景德镇), in the northeast of the province, is a historic kiln town and the manufacturing base of

Handicrafts made from forest nuts, Fenghuang.

celebrated Jingdezhen porcelain. Several museums detail the history of the town, which fashioned imperial porcelain and overseas export ware, and pottery factories and workshops are open to the public.

Celebrated as the cradle of the Chinese Revolution, the rugged mountains of **Jinggangshan** (井冈山), along Jiangxi's southwestern border with Hunan province, provided essential shelter for the embryonic Chinese Red Army divisions during fierce fighting with the Nationalists in the late 1920s and early 1930s. The village of **Ciping** ㉑ (茨坪) served as a base for Mao Zedong and Zhu De after they united their divisions to form the Fourth Red Army in 1927.

Given Jiangxi's hinterland position in China, it has been able to preserve some of its older towns from the reconstruction drives common along the coast. In addition to Jindgdezhen, a complex of 16 villages known as **Wuyuan** (婺源) in the northeast of the province draws visitors to its old southern-style architecture in the lush, wooded flatlands below Lushan. Many of the homes stand with their original white walls and carved, black roof tiles.

The area, known for education, has produced more than 3,000 locally written or edited books. A Confucian master and early railway engineer known throughout China came from Wuyuan. The region also grows succulent green tea leaves and affords vistas of cloud-covered mountains overlooking fields of yellow flowers planted along a river. In the autumn, fiery red leaves alter some of the scenery. Wuyuan divides up into the east, west and north scenic spots, each with distinct preserved villages or natural views. Two older villages appear on a list of proposed sites for Unesco world cultural heritage status. Wuyuan also claims to shelter the world's largest wintering habitat for wild mandarin ducks as well as one of the highest waterfalls in the country. Adding to the area's status, the villages here produce a type of ink stone with a name best translated as "black dragon tail".

☉ TRANSPORT

Getting to Jianxi

By train and bus: Nanchang has rail connections with Fujian and Hunan, and with Wuhan, Nanjing and Shanghai, further north. Buses run from Changsha, Wuhan, Shanghai, Xiamen, Guangzhou and other cities. An airport north of the city has flights to/from Nanchang, Lushan and Jiujiang.

Getting around Jianxi

Nanchang: The fastest trains to Jiujiang (12 daily) take 2.5 hours, while buses take 2 hours. Trains and buses to Jingdezhen (several daily) both take 4 hours. There are frequent buses to Lushan (1.5 hours), and 3 daily to Jingganshan (5–8 hours).

Jiujiang: Trains to Nanchang (12 daily) take 2.5 hours. There are frequent buses to Lushan (1 hour), and hourly to Jingdezhen (2 hours).

Lushan: There are buses every 40 minutes or so from Nanchang (1.5 hours). Similarly frequent buses run from Jiujiang (1 hour).

Getting to Hunan

By train and bus: Hunan lies on the main Guangzhou–Beijing line, and rail connections with Guangdong, and north to Wuhan, Nanjing and Shanghai, are frequent. Buses run to Guangzhou, Wuhan and other cities.

Getting around Hunan

Changsha: There are frequent buses to Shaoshan (2 hours), regular trains to Zhangjiajie (7 daily, 6 hours; note that some take much longer) and also trains to Shaoshan (1 daily, 3 hours).

Yueyang: There are frequent trains and buses to Changsha (1.5–2 hours) and one daily bus to Zhangjiajie (7 hours).

Shaoshan: There are frequent buses to Changsha (2–3 hours). One train per day departs for Changsha (3 hours).

Zhangjiajie: Buses depart for Fenghuang (2 daily, 4 hours). There are trains to Changsha (7 daily, 6 hours).

Fenghuang: There are regular buses to Jishou (1 hour) and Haihua (2 hours). Jishou and Haihua are both well connected by train with Changsha (8–9 hours).

HUNAN PROVINCE

The large province of **Hunan** (湖南) is famed for its cuisine, a fiery brew of chilli and spices, and as the birthplace of Mao Zedong. This is one of China's main rice-growing regions, and the landscape is dominated by paddy fields, but there are some scenic mountain areas, too, including Heng Shan and the reserve of Wulingyuan.

CHANGSHA

Located on the main Guangzhou–Beijing rail line, the provincial capital, **Changsha ㉒** (长沙), is by far the largest city in Hunan, with a population of over 7 million. While at first sight it is not the most enticing of places, further investigation reveals a city with a fair amount to offer.

The **Hunan Provincial Museum** (湖南省博物馆; Hunansheng Bowuguan; 50 Dongfeng Lu; closed for renovation until the end of 2017) stands out as the main sight in the city. The first settlements in the Changsha area date back 5,000 years, and the gigantic concrete museum housing more than 110,000 artefacts is rightly famous for

its 2,100-year-old Western Han tombs, corpses and coffins, as well as Shang- and Zhou-era bronzes discovered in the region.

Also of interest is **Clearwater Pool** (清水潭; Qingshui Tang; daily 8.30am–5pm) on Bayi Lu. The site contains the first Chinese Communist Party provincial headquarters, established by Mao in 1921, as well as a house where the future leader lived for two years.

Nature lovers can hop on a city bus to **Juzi Zhoutou** (橘子洲头), a flat island in the middle of the Xiangjiang (湘江) river that invites strolls among the tangerine *(juzi)* trees that give this park its name. And just outside the urban reaches, hikers will find trails and pavilions in the jungles of **Yuelu Hill Park** (岳麓山风景区).

MAO'S HOMELAND

Mao's childhood home in **Shaoshan ㉓** (韶山), 90km (55 miles) southwest of Changsha, is a place of pilgrimage for students of the Communist Revolution and Maoist iconography. The intensity with which Mao is still venerated

Socialist Realist art on sale in Fenghuang.

Mao befriends the peasants in this Socialist Realist painting.

⊙ Tip

The main trails on Heng Shan are well endowed with vendors and food stalls, so bringing your own supplies is not necessary – although it's always advisable to carry water. In winter, the hike should only be attempted with proper planning and, preferably, with prior experience on mountains. This is one of the few places in southern China where you can rely on seeing snow.

Bowing to the Chairman in Shaosan's Bronze Square.

here is a throwback to an earlier time, and a phenomenon in itself (see box). Nothing can prepare you for the old-world propaganda and tack that lies in store in this otherwise peaceful area of Hunanese countryside – something of an eye-opener in China's fast-changing society.

The mud-walled **Former Residence** (毛泽东故居; Mao Zedong Guju; daily 9am–5pm; free), where Mao was born on 26 December 1893 and brought up with his two brothers, is surprisingly large. Inside are detailed descriptions in both Chinese and English of every section of the house, including the rooms of his brothers Mao Zemin and Mao Zetan, who both died fighting for the Communist cause.

In the middle of the village is the **Bronze Square**, where, in something reminiscent of Turkmenistan or North Korea, tour groups line up to bow. Across from the Mao statue is the **Museum of Comrade Mao** (毛泽东纪_念馆; Mao Zedong Jinianguan; 9am–5pm; free), which presents visitors with a timeline of the life of the

Great Helmsman. Next to this is **Mao's Ancestral Temple** (毛氏宗祠; Maoshi Zongci; daily 9am–5pm), which traces the family ancestry back to a Ming patriot who fought the Mongols.

HENG SHAN

Hunan's religious dimension is provided by the southernmost of the Daoist sacred mountains, **Heng Shan ㉔** (衡山), 120km (75 miles) south of the provincial capital, Changsha. The mountain, the highest part of a range that stretches from Hengyang northwards all the way to Changsha, is accessed on foot from the town of **Nanyue** (南岳), rising just to the north: allow around five hours to reach Wishing Harmony Peak (Zhurong Feng), the highest point, and another three hours to descend back to Nanyue; in all it's a full day's hike. Alternatively, there are frequent minibuses which travel all the way to the summit, or a cable car to the top of an adjacent peak from approximately halfway up.

Frequently misty, the route up the 1,290-metre (4,232ft) mountain passes

several temples, including the Nanyue Damiao at the start of the climb, and the nearby Zhusheng Si; at the peak is the Zhurong Dian (Zhurong Hall).

THE FAR NORTHWEST

Prosperous **Zhangjiajie City** ㉕ (张家界市; Zhangjiajie Shi) is the regional hub of the far northwest of Hunan, and lies some 33km (21 miles) south of the fabulous scenery at Wulingyuan. A short taxi ride south of Zhangjiajie City brings you to what is purported to be the world's longest **cable-car** run (daily 8am–5.30pm), which climbs the spectacular face of **Tianmen Shan** (天门山) – a vertiginous panorama of rock shards festooned in forest and often shrouded in mist. The cable car runs for a distance of 7.5km (4.5 miles), rising 1,300 metres (4,260ft) in elevation. A fascinating way to enjoy the mountain landscapes is to walk along one of three glass skywalks on Tianmen Shan which, however, are definitely not for the faint-hearted.

A one-hour bus ride from Zhangjiajie City (last bus at 6.30pm) lies **Zhangjiajie**

Village (张家界村; Zhangjiajie Cun), the most popular springboard for exploring principal **Wulingyuan Scenic Reserve** ㉖ (五陵源风景区; Wulingyuan Feng Jingqu). From this entrance there is a stunning 5.7km (3.5-mile) stroll along the valley floor among vertical karst peaks, as well as a handful of trails which climb the steep valley walls. Another climbing option is the **Bailong Lift**. Tacked onto

There is a sizeable population of rhesus monkeys at Wulingyuan.

Fenghuang has become popular with Chinese tourists in recent years.

⊘ **Fact**

Fenghuang's tourist facilities have developed quickly but are still relatively modest – although quantity is not a problem: there are plenty of cheap restaurants and guesthouses.

a sheer cliff face, it's cited in the *Guinness Book of World Records* as being the largest outdoor elevator in the world. It whisks guests up 326 metres (1,070 ft) in under two minutes and provides jaw-dropping views.

Wulingyuan Reserve protects a magnificent landscape, with mature forests, crystal-clear lakes, limpid streams and, rising above all, 3,100 precipitous quartzite sandstone crags. The area shelters over 3,000 plant species, including more than 500 species of tree, and some rare animals – including a few clouded leopards, various monkeys, and 1-metre (3ft) long giant salamanders. Unfortunately, it is often flooded with noisy tour groups, and parts of the park are littered with their rubbish. The entrance ticket is also one of the most expensive in China. Another problem is the highly volatile weather, which often leaves the peaks smothered in clouds and mist.

FENGHUANG

In the far west of Hunan, close to the border with Guizhou, is the ancient riverside town of **Fenghuang** ㉗ (凤凰), home to Miao and Tujia ethnic minorities. The Tuo River runs through the old district (the town dates back to 248 BC), surrounded by the red sandstone city walls and grand old gateways, while Ming- and Qing-style architecture lines up along the elegant intersecting stone-paved streets. It all adds up to one of the most attractive places in China, and in recent years Fenghuang has woken up to its tourist potential.

The focus for tourism is pedestrianised **Dongzheng Jie** (东正街), which runs from the centrepiece covered bridge of Hongqiao, past the 18th-century **Dongmenlou** (东门楼; East Gate Tower) and into the thicket of low-rise buildings southwest of the river. The Tuo River is straddled by several bridges, and its depth is sufficiently shallow to allow two sets of **stepping stones**, opposite where Wenxing Jie meets the riverside city walls, to provide an alternative means of crossing. It's possible to take a short riverboat ride; otherwise, try the restaurants and craft shopping.

Fenghuang.

⊘ THE CULT OF MAO

The cult of Mao was a pervasive, propaganda-fuelled phenomenon that etched the leader as a deity in the minds of most Chinese. In the 1960s his image was everywhere, dominating didactic posters emblazoned in red. Popularity and iron fists allowed Mao to arrest intellectuals who questioned his rule and deflect blame for the great famine of 1961. Workers and students alike wore badges with his portrait, and after the 1966 publication of *Quotations from Chairman Mao* – the "Little Red Book" – his words were on the lips of students and soldiers. Mao's increasing paranoia encouraged him to harness the power at his disposal to launch the disastrous Cultural Revolution in 1966.

Following his widely mourned death in 1976, the power of the personality cult rapidly waned. But today the Chairman's image is China's most prevalent, adorning banknotes, staring down from classroom walls and swinging from taxi-drivers' rear-view mirrors. Chinese people often admit they have forgiven Mao's costly, deadly mistakes of the 1950s and 1960s, preferring to revere him now as the man who united a once fractious China into the strong nation that endures today. Despite espousing scorn for traditional superstitions during his lifetime, Mao is regarded as "lucky". Anyone who visits his hometown of Shaoshan can see up close how old habits die hard.

RED TOURISM

History-seeking tourists are making a long march across China's sites of communist glory and revolutionary fervour.

Relatively few of China's burgeoning middle class are old enough to remember the disasters of the Great Leap Forward (1958–61) and the Cultural Revolution (1966–76), let alone the Civil War that ended with Communist victory in 1949. Instead, they learnt about revolution from their parents and grandparents, without fully experiencing its travails. As China has prospered, curiosity about the revolutionary past has grown alongside the disposable incomes that fuel China's domestic tourism boom. The result is red tourism – a burgeoning industry that is exploiting sites associated with the Chinese Communist Revolution to win over the hearts, minds and wallets of the people.

The boom is not just a case of the central government indulging in wild glorification of its past victories – dozens of remote mountain villages are transforming themselves into major attractions where tourists can dress up in scratchy army uniforms, sing revolutionary songs and feel a step closer to the heroes of liberation. Like much of the kitschy "Maomorabilia" and Cultural Revolution tat on sale around China it's often difficult to detect much historical gravitas amid all the fun and the festivity. A resort near Huang Shan, Anhui Province, even went a step too far in 2011 by organising short-lived activities in which visitors dressed up as invading Japanese soldiers to "capture" female villagers. But for many Chinese who have seen idealism washed away in a tide of money since the opening and reform policy, learning the history of their country is a sobering reflection on the suffering that led to the eventual comforts of modern life.

The epicentre of revolutionary tourism is in Yan'an (see page 193), the endpoint of the Long March and the birthplace of the Communist revolution. Red culture in Yan'an now forms the backbone of the local economy, drawing in an estimated 20 million tourists in 2015. Inevitably, there is a good deal of propaganda here too – Chinese officials rarely shy away from using history as a tool to prove the legitimacy of Communist rule.

MAO: FROM CRADLE TO GRAVE

Beijing's Chairman Mao Mausoleum and Great Hall of the People are must-sees for would-be red tourists. More enjoyable, perhaps are the rousing performances of communist song-and-dance routines at the extraordinary East is Red restaurant in the capital.

Visit Mao's birthplace at Shaoshan in Hunan province for a chance to see both Mao Zedong's Childhood Home and the nearby Museum of Comrade Mao – the best place to witness the quasi-religious fervour that the Great Helmsman still commands. The "Cradle of the Revolution", Jinggangshan in Jiangxi province, is where Mao Zedong and General Zhude launched the Long March in 1927 and has several historic sites.

The Luding Bridge in western China's Sichuan province is an ideal spot to learn a few tales of wartime heroism. Finish up at The Zunyi Conference Site and Long March Museum at Zunyi in Guizhou and you will likely feel you have experienced enough of the circuitous journey that Mao and his Communist forces made to usher in a new China.

Mao paraphernalia comes in all shapes and sizes.

📷 CHINESE WILDLIFE

China is the world's third-largest country and its varied habitats endow it with a bountiful biodiversity.

China's vast territory encompasses practically every climate and habitat on earth, from frigid Siberian taiga to tropical rainforest. Central and southern China's location at the boundary of the temperate and tropical zones ensures that there is also an abundance of endemic species, with 17 percent of mammals and 36 percent of reptiles found nowhere else on earth. However, centuries of population pressure compounded by rapid economic growth and a cavalier attitude towards the natural bounty (particularly during the Mao years) has put the landscape under intense pressure, destroying many habitats and threatening the survival of numerous species. The demand for animal parts from the Chinese medicine trade (see page 91) and the local penchant for eating anything that moves have also contributed to the decline. Some progress has been made to preserve the country's biological diversity, but the challenge remains enormous.

Much of China is mountainous, and it is in the remote montane forests that some of the most spectacular wildlife survives. Western Sichuan is home to the giant panda, and its smaller relative, the red panda. Snow leopards prowl at higher elevations throughout the Himalayan zone. Further south, a few clouded leopards, black bears and golden takin remain in the wilder parts of Yunnan, while its tropical south still shelters wild elephants. The Siberian tiger is endangered in the far northeast and the South China tiger is considered extinct in the wild. A handful of South China tigers may remain in the forests of northern Guangdong; the larger, paler Manchurian tiger is endangered in the far northeast. The wide open spaces of western China are home to herds of Tibetan antelope and wild Bactrian camels. Numerous species of monkey thrive in southern and southwestern areas, including the rare golden monkey.

Other star species include the giant salamander and Chinese alligator. Birdwatchers are drawn to China's lakes and wetlands, stopping off points for cranes on their migration between Siberia and tropical Asia.

A snow leopard. A few thousand of these magnificent creatures live in rocky habitats at altitudes of 3,000–6,000 metres (10,000–20,000ft) throughout the Himalaya and Tian Shan.

Less well known than their black-and-white cousins, red pandas thrive in the sub-Himalayan forests of Yunnan and Sichuan.

Tibetan macaques are common on Emei Shan in Sichuan province.

The endangered status of the giant panda is only in part due to man's impact on the environment; their principal food is the arrow bamboo, which periodically dies off across large swathes of forest, leaving the pandas having to make do with an alternative, omnivorous diet. Some weaker individuals cannot cope with the change and starve to death.

Conservation

China's State Environmental Protection Administration works hand in hand with international agencies such as the WWF, the Wildlife Conservation Society, Wetland International and the National Geographic Society in a bid to protect species such as the giant panda (xiongmao), the giant salamander (wawayu) and the golden, or snub-nosed, monkey (jinsi hou). Some nature reserves are also Unesco World Heritage Sites, a status that brings in much-needed investment and useful experience in management. Since the establishment of Dinghu Shan Nature Reserve in Guangdong province in 1956, China has created over 2,700 nature reserves, and almost 15 percent of China's land is now protected.

China is also party to the Convention on Biological Diversity, the Convention on International Trade in Endangered Species (CITES) and other international conventions protecting the environment. But lack of experienced personnel and under-investment in nature reserves and other conservation schemes remain serious problems. There is still a great need for increased scientific research on specific conservation issues and exploratory surveys to catalogue wildlife populations and locations.

Blood pheasants live in the forests of northwestern Yunnan. Together with their close relatives, the tragopans, they are some of the most spectacular of Chinese birds.

Tibetan antelope (chiru in Tibetan) are under threat from poachers who can make big profits from the animals' fine wool. Population numbers are thought to remain over 70,000, however, so it is not classified as an endangered species.

Er Hai lake in western Guizhou is a major draw for birdwatchers.

Fishermen on the Li River near Yangshuo.

The Jade Dragon Snow Mountain from Lijiang.

THE SOUTHWEST

From Guilin to Chengdu, tropical Xishuangbanna to snowy Himalayan peaks, there is a huge amount to see in China's fascinating southwestern corner.

The giant Buddha at Leshan.

The southwest is many travellers' favourite part of China, and it isn't hard to understand why. In terms of scenery and cultural diversity, this region is hard to beat, and exploring its riches gives a greater sense of adventure, a more complete "travel experience". Many parts of the southwest lie outside the mainstream Han Chinese world, and therefore look and feel quite different from the rest of China.

Guangxi is less known for its cultural aspects than for its incredible scenery. The Li River winds its way lazily through an astonishing landscape around the city of Guilin, familiar to anyone who has set eyes on a classical Chinese scroll painting. To the north, a scenic route leads via the stunning Longsheng rice terraces to Guizhou, one of the poorest parts of China, populated by a colourful array of minority groups, with exotic architecture and festivals. The landscape across much of the province is wild and mountainous and travel is often rough, with poor accommodation and terrible roads, but can be extremely rewarding for the hardy.

Miao festival dancers in Guizhou province.

The large province of Sichuan, famous for its spicy food, is split between the densely populated east and south, centred around the pleasant city of Chengdu, and the wild mountains and forests of the largely Tibetan west and north, which provide a habitat for pandas and an array of other wildlife. The holy Buddhist mountain of Emei Shan and the stupendous Buddha statue at Leshan, south of Chengdu, are further attractions.

Finally, much of southern Yunnan feels more like Laos or Thailand than China, with elaborate Buddhist temples, jungles and minority peoples. Beyond the pleasant provincial capital, Kunming, the land rises to the easternmost ridges of the Himalayas. Here you will find the magical cities of Dali and Lijiang, both set against dramatic mountains and within easy reach of some of the best trekking in China. The far northwest around Zhongdian is culturally part of Tibet, and marketed as "Shangri-la" to tourists seeking adventure.

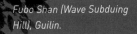

GUANGXI AND GUIZHOU

The provinces of Guangxi and Guizhou are endowed with extraordinary limestone landscapes, spectacular rice terraces and a colourful array of minority peoples.

"The river is like a green silk belt, and the hills are like turquoise jade hairpins." So wrote the Tang-dynasty scholar and writer Han Yu (768–94), becoming the first prominent voice to immortalise the landscape around Guilin in **Guangxi** (广西; the full name is Guangxi Zhuang Autonomous Region). Nowadays, tourists swarm from all over the world to sample the magical scenery. Together with Beijing, Shanghai and Xi'an, Guilin is one of China's foremost destinations.

The Guilin area owes its exquisite beauty to geological disruptions over 300 million years ago. Limestone formations pushed through an ancient seabed, then the wind and rain eroded the hills and peaks into innumerable shapes, leaving behind labyrinthine caves and grottoes within them. With some peaks rounded and some sharply pointed, perpendicular cliffs and trees that sprout from the cracks to bend skyward, this is a dreamlike landscape, familiar to anyone who has looked at a Chinese scroll painting, and which has long lured travellers to the area.

China's southwest is also where Han uniformity runs up abruptly against a constellation of non-Han ethnic tribes. The largest ethnic minority in China, the Zhuang comprise about one-third of Guangxi's 46 million inhabitants, dominating its western half. Another 5

Miao mother and child in Langde Shan village, near Kaili, Guizhou.

percent belong to 10 other minorities, such as the Yao, Miao, Dong and Yi, living primarily in the western and northern mountains of Guangxi. Longsheng, with its immaculate terraced slopes, and the famous covered wooden bridge at Sanjiang in northern Guangxi, are testament to the industrious, rustic existence of these tribes that is so distinct from the prevailing Han culture.

Guizhou (贵州) province to the north is also home to a particularly colourful patchwork of ethnic groups, notably in the picturesque southeastern region

⦿ Main Attractions

Yuzi Paradise
Yangshuo and
  Surroundings
Longsheng Rice Terraces
Villages, Guizhou
Zhenyuan
Huangguoshu Falls

⦿ Maps on pages
342, 350

Guilin, a perennial favourite of tour groups, has excellent transport links with cities across China.

around Kaili. There are some beautiful old villages here, and if you are lucky enough to witness one of the numerous festivals (see page 354) then any travel hardship in accessing this remote area will have been worthwhile.

GUILIN AND THE LI RIVER

The tourist hub for the amazing limestone region of Guangxi, **Guilin ①** (桂林) literally means "cassia tree forest", named after the local cassia or osmanthus trees, whose scent wafts through the city in autumn. Historical records put Guilin's founding at 214 BC, during the reign of Qin Shi Huangdi, the first emperor of a united China, when he ordered the construction of the Ling Canal to connect the central plain of China with the south and with Southeast Asia, via the Yangzi, Li and Zhu rivers. The canal, one of the world's longest, still exists and can be easily seen at Xing'an, 65km (40 miles) northwest of Guilin.

Guilin has been a significant political and cultural centre since the Tang dynasty (618–907), but its golden years arrived during the Ming dynasty (1368–1644), after Zhu Shouqian, the son of the founding Ming emperor who was appointed ruler of this part of China, set up his court in Guilin.

Being so far from Beijing, Guilin and Guangxi have a tradition of sheltering refugees. In 1647, the fleeing Ming court established a temporary residence here in their flight from the Manchus. Three

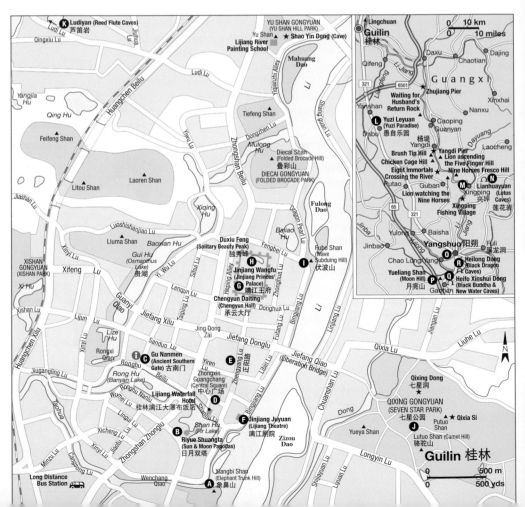

centuries later, as the Japanese army swept into China, hundreds of thousands of northerners sought safety in Guilin. In 1949, it was one of the last Guomindang strongholds to fall to the Communists.

At first glance there is little to see of Guilin's rich history – almost the entire city was razed by the Japanese army in 1944. When it was rebuilt, there was little to distinguish it from any other mid-sized Chinese city – apart from the unusual sight of limestone peaks in the city centre. As one of China's premier tourist sights, the city is typically swamped with visitors, but Guilin remains attractive. Parks and osmanthus trees mottle the urban landscape, and a few limestone peaks, such as Xiangbi Shan (Elephant Trunk Hill) and Fubo Shan, rise above the buildings. The Li Jiang River cuts through the town, and many small restaurants offer river cuisine, such as fish, eel, frog, turtle, snail, shrimp and snake.

CITY SIGHTS

Guilin's landmark **Xiangbi Shan** Ⓐ (象 鼻山; Elephant Trunk Hill; daily) is a good place to start a walk around the city. Located slightly south of the centre on the riverbank, the hill distinctly resembles a limestone elephant. If you have the energy, climb the 200-metre (650ft) hill and catch your breath inside the Puxian Pagoda, which was built more than 500 years ago.

At night the colourful lights of the 40-metre (130ft) **Riyue Shuangta** Ⓑ (日 月双塔; Sun and Moon pagodas; daily) cast glittering gold and silver reflections on Shan Hu (Fir Lake), just to the north of Xiangbi Shan.

To the northwest, beside an 800-year-old banyan tree on the northern bank of the Rong Hu Lake, is an authentic remnant of the Old City. The **Gu Nanmen** Ⓒ (古南门; Ancient Southern Gate), was built during the Tang dynasty and expanded in Ming times, when Guilin became the provincial capital. It was once part of the city walls, so the oldest part of the gate is a modest stone tunnel. A Ming-style single-storey building now sits on top of the wall. From here the lakeside promenade turns westward, and then north, along Yiwu Lu

Gold Buddha at Qixing Gongyuan (Seven Star Park), Guilin.

Ⓞ TRANSPORT

Getting to Guanxi

By air: Guilin and Nanning are well connected with cities across China as well as to Hong Kong.

By train and bus: Guangxi lies on the Beijing–Hanoi railway, with other long-distance routes between Guangzhou and Yunnan crossing the province. Guilin is a major rail hub. Sleeper buses run to Guilin (and Yangshuo) from Guangzhou, Shenzhen, Changsha and other cities.

Getting around Guanxi

Guilin: There are regular bus services to Yangshuo (1–1.5 hours, every 20 minutes), Longsheng (1.5 hours, hourly) and Nanning (4–4.5 hours, every 15 minutes). There are trains to Nanning (10 daily, 5–6 hours,).

Yangshuo: There are frequent minibuses to Guilin (1–1.5 hours). The nearest railway station is at Guilin.

Longsheng: Buses depart every 15 minutes to Guilin and take 1.5 hours. Guilin is the nearest railway station.

Pingxiang (Vietnam border): There are bus services to local towns, and trains to Nanning (3 daily, 3.5 hours).

It may be mainly for the benefit of tourists these days, but using cormorant to catch fish has a long history in this part of China.

Riyue Shuanta (the Sun and Moon pagodas) in Guilin.

following the banks of Baoxian Hu, the former moat that forms the western border of the Old City and runs parallel with the Li River.

Further north, as you enter the middle section of the city's grid layout, the lakeside fairy lights give way to neon lights, and Guilin is suddenly indistinguishable from any medium-sized Chinese city. The main hub of activity is the area around **Central Square** ⓓ (中心广场; Zhongxin Guangchang), built in 1999 south of the intersection of Jiefang Lu and the city's other main

thoroughfare, Zhongshan Lu. In this downtown area department stores, stalls and restaurants are open until late. Between Central Square and the Li River, pedestrianised **Zhengyang Lu** ⓔ (正阳路) runs south from Jiefang Lu to Nanhuan Lu. Popularly referred to as "walking street", this area is geared towards tourists, with a selection of restaurants, bars, galleries and fairly kitsch souvenir stalls.

On the waterfront thoroughfare, Binjiang Lu, the **Lijiang Theatre** ⓕ (漓江剧院; Ljiang Juyuan) has a changing programme of evening shows that often feature Guangxi's minorities. Evening boat trips along the city's restored waterways, and other tours, can be booked at the numerous agents along Binjiang Lu, or through hotel tour desks.

The most historic area of Guilin is the **Jingjiang Princes' Palace** ⓖ (靖江王府; Jingjiang Wangfu; daily May–mid-Oct 7.30am–6.30pm, mid-Oct–mid-Dec and Mar–Apr 7.30am–6pm, mid-Dec–Feb 8am–6pm), a short stroll north of the city centre. Its walls, gates and halls follow the classic lines of a Ming-dynasty city. Tour guides will always stress that it was built 34 years before the larger Forbidden City, but unlike Beijing's palace, most of what you see today has been reconstructed in the last 20 years.

First built in 1372 as the palace of Zhu Shouqian, the palace was home to the next 12 generations of Jingjiang princes until the end of the dynasty in 1644. When the Ming court fled south, they tried to establish a Southern Ming dynasty from here, but in 1650 the Manchus drove them out of Guilin and the city was destroyed.

Parts of the original city walls are still in place, and some original stone carvings and balustrades have been recovered and restored. The main palace in the centre of the complex, **Chengyun Hall** (承云大厅; Chengyun Daiting), houses a small exhibition about the 14 princes who lived here down the centuries.

Guilin's ancient city within a city has its very own karst mountain inside its walls. **Duxiu Feng**  (独秀峰; Solitary Beauty Peak) rises up above the Ming buildings, and climbing the 300 or so steps to the pagoda at the top rewards you with the delightful view enjoyed by princes and poets over the centuries. At the western foot of the peak is the entrance to **Pingshiku** (平石窟; Peace Grotto), a network of caves and passages where the princes once worshipped their ancestors.

To the east lies **Fubo Shan** ❶ (伏波山; Wave Subduing Hill; daily Apr–Nov 7am–6pm, Dec–Mar 6am–6.30pm). A short, steep climb up the steps takes you to a small viewing platform on the summit, from where you can see the hills of **Diecai Shan** (叠彩山; Folded Brocade Hill; daily Apr–Nov 6am–6.30pm, Dec–Mar 7am–6pm), which at 220 metres (720ft) in height are the tallest in the city and so called because when this group of hills catch the changing daylight they are said to resemble piles of folded fabric.

Across the Li River from the city centre and reached via Liberation Bridge (Jiefang Qiao) lie the scenic peaks of **Qixing Gongyuan** ❶ (七星公园; Seven Star Park; daily Mar–Nov 6am–7.30pm, Dec–Feb 6.30am–7pm). The park within which they are set allows you to sample all the city's natural attractions in one manageable 40-hectare (100-acre) site. It is a pleasant mix of landscaping, caves and temples set amid the seven peaks, which lie in the shape of the Big Dipper constellation.

The **Ludiyan** complex ❶ (芦笛岩; Reed Flute Caves; daily Apr–Nov 7.30am–6pm, Dec–Mar 8am–5.30pm) is located about 7km (4 miles) northwest of the city centre and is considered to be the most dramatic of Guilin's cave systems.

SOUTH OF GUILIN

The extraordinary beauty of the countryside south of Guilin is no secret, and a steady stream of riverboats make the scenic journey along the Li River between Guilin and Yangshuo. The landscape in this region is dominated by the outlandish limestone pinnacles rising sheer from the otherwise flat

Waterfall at Qixing Gongyuan (Seven Star Park).

園; Yuzi Leyuan; daily 8.30am–7pm). Large contemporary sculptures are spread over 60 hectares (150 acres) in a landscape of winding paths, lakes, modern architecture and the odd karst outcrop. It's a fascinating place to explore for a few hours.

If you opt to travel between Guilin and Yangshuo by road, it is also possible to join a boat at **Xingping** for a short river trip. From Yangshuo, there are local buses every 20 minutes for the one-hour journey to Xingping, which was the main town in the area 400 years ago. Surrounded by seven peaks on the east side of the river, it is worth allowing some time to stroll through the oldest part of Xingping, where traditional houses line narrow, unpaved footpaths.

Three km (2 miles) outside Xingping are the caves of **Lianhuayan** (莲花 岩; Lotus Caves; daily). The entrance includes a guide, who will turn on the multicoloured lights within the 600-metre (2,000ft) underground passageway and point out a multitude of hard-to-discern animal shapes.

A summer rainstorm in Yangshuo. Northern Guangxi is one of the rainiest parts of the country.

terrain of paddy fields. Farmhands in conical hats work the rice terraces, while on the river villagers fish from bamboo rafts using trained cormorants. This is the classic Chinese landscape familiar from so many scroll paintings, and for many visitors, this region represents a quintessential taste of China.

On the road to Yangshuo, 30km (18 miles) south of Guilin, the mountains make an inspired setting for the sculpture park at **Yuzi Paradise** (愚自乐

Li River scenery, Yangshuo.

YANGSHUO

The town of **Yangshuo** ❶ (阳朔) lies amid stupendous scenery on the west bank of the Li, 60km (37 miles) downstream from Guilin. It has long enjoyed a prime position on the backpacker trail, although these days it is crammed with foreign and domestic tourists of all budgets, and fills up even more in the afternoons when visitors disembark from the Guilin boats.

Despite all this, Yangshuo somehow manages to retain a riverside country town feel, and for most tourists remains one of the most enjoyable destinations in all of China. The great appeal is the opportunity it provides to slow down, bike or hike and explore the Chinese countryside that is otherwise only glimpsed from trains and buses. It is certainly one of the easiest places in China to spend time. There is a good selection of reasonably priced accommodation in the town, a wide choice of clean, inexpensive restaurants with foreigner-friendly food, cheap beer and excellent Yunnan coffee.

Xi Jie (西街; West Street) is the centre of the tourist scene. Most visitors arrive either at **Yangshuo Quay** (阳朔码头) at the bottom of the street, or at the bus station on the corner of Diecui Lu and Pantao Lu. Chengzhong Lu has a few pavement cafés and small guesthouses, and there are more hotels along Binjiang Lu, some with great river views.

AROUND YANGSHUO

Try to hire a bike in town and pedal out into the countryside. Electric scooter hire presents a less strenuous alternative to cycling and is as easy to arrange. The 10km (6-mile) journey to **Yueliang Shan** ❷ (月亮山; Moon Hill), southwest of town, is fabulous and highly recommended; the view from the summit of the hill (a reasonably tough clamber) is spellbinding.

Nearby are two popular cave complexes that rely less on coloured lights for effect and more upon the visitor's sense of adventure. The **Heifo Xinshui Dong** ❸ (黑佛新水洞; Black Buddha New Water Caves; daily) were discovered in 1991, and the 1.5- or 3-hour tours will involve some scrambling along ladders and wading through

⊘ Tip

Yangshuo's small army of mainly female bicycle guides can usually be found around the bike-hire shops and cafés on Xi Jie, dressed smartly in polo shirts and trousers. Most speak good English and will charge around Rmb40 per hour or Rmb200 per day to act as your guide. If you want to go further than Yulong River, hiring a guide will ensure you don't get lost and will definitely enhance your day out.

Cruise vessels on the Li River.

◎ Shop

Shopping can easily consume many hours in Yangshuo, with shops selling a vast range of souvenirs, minority handicrafts, embroidery, textiles, art and jewellery. Surprisingly, urban offerings include Asian-inspired interior design, CDs and DVDs. Yangshuo's clothes shops offer everything from tie-dye and minority batiks to branded sports shoes and designer clothing, including one or two shops with particularly quirky and surprisingly witty T-shirt designs.

mud. About 3km (4 miles) down the road, the **Heilong Dong** ⓡ (黑龙洞; Black Dragon Caves; daily) can be explored by boat or by kayak if you arrange your tour with a guide or agent in Yangshuo in advance.

Yangshuo has become one of China's foremost adventure sport capitals in recent years. Rock climbing, boating and ballooning trips can all be organised from operators in town. All three pursuits offer spectacular new perspectives on the landscapes around Yangshuo. Rafting around **Yulong Qiao** (玉龙桥; Jade Dragon Bridge) is a particular highlight.

If you are staying overnight in Yangshuo, don't miss the amazing **Impression Liu Sanjie** show (印象刘三姐; Yinxiang Liu Sanjie; daily). This beautifully choreographed musical extravaganza, orchestrated by film director and producer of Beijing's 2008 Olympic opening ceremony, Zhang Yimou, takes place nightly in an open-air venue on the Li River, close to Yangshuo, with the karst peaks providing an inimitable backdrop to the performance.

NORTH TO THE GUIZHOU BORDER

To the northwest of Guilin and nearing the border with Guizhou province are the counties of **Longsheng** (龙胜) and **Sanjiang** (三江). This region's traditional architecture, terraced hills and ethnic costumes (the Miao and some Yao groups are famous for their embroidery skills) make it an excellent introduction to southwest China's minorities. **Longsheng** ❷, although unspectacular itself, is the access point to an enchanting surrounding landscape. To the southeast of town is the region's most famous attraction, **Longji Titian** (龙脊梯田; Dragon's Backbone Terraces), the evocative name given to a series of steep hills layered with rice terraces. The effect is extraordinary, and highly photogenic. Basic accommodation can be found in Ping'an, a small Zhuang village positioned amid the terraces and within range of other minority villages.

Sanjiang ❸ (三江), the scruffy capital of the Sanjiang Dong Autonomous County 165km (100 miles) northwest of Guilin, is of no particular interest in

◎ LI RIVER BOAT TRIPS

A boat trip on the Li River is a highlight of a trip to China. The most popular journey is to sail the 80km (50 miles) from Guilin down to Yangshuo, through the heart of the incredible karst scenery which has made the region famous. For most of the year, boats leave from the tourist port at Zhujiang Pier, 20km (12 miles) south of central Guilin; tickets include transport to the pier from the city centre. Shorter trips are also possible, as well as trips starting in Yangshuo and Xingping.

The cruise passes the endlessly fascinating limestone spires that shoot up from the flat plains. It's a relaxing way to take in the peaks and catch a glimpse of life along the riverbank. En route, guides will intermittently point out the names that the poets have bestowed on the peaks: Waiting for Husband's Return; Lion Ascending the Five Finger Hill; Chicken Cage Hill; Eight Immortals Crossing the River. As you approach the town of Xingping, fellow passengers will pull out Rmb 20 notes to compare the real thing with the peaks that appear on the back of the note. The journey takes three to five hours, depending on the water level, with lunch and transport back to Guilin by bus included in the (hefty) ticket price.

itself; the reason to visit is the wooden **Chengyang Wind-and-Rain Bridge** (程阳风雨桥; Chengyang Fengyuqiao; 8.30am–5pm) 18km (11 miles) north of town. There are over 100 such bridges in the county, but the Chengyang bridge is celebrated as the finest – 78 metres (255ft) long and 20 metres (66ft) high, it straddles the Linxi River and was completed by the Dong people in 1916 with such precision that it did not require the use of a single nail. Simple accommodation and restaurants are available on the other side of the river in Chengyang itself, and several other minority villages dot the area.

SOUTHERN GUANGXI

As one approaches the southern coastal areas of Guangxi, the landscape assumes a more tropical feel. Guangxi's capital of **Nanning** ④ (南宁), southwest of Guilin, is an affluent metropolis of over 1 million people. Among its attractions are the **Provincial Museum** (省博物馆; Sheng Bowuguan; Tue–Sun 9am–5pm), with its fine bronze drum collection, and the adjoining cultural centre, where architectural examples from the Dong, Miao, Yao and Zhuang minorities have been recreated in an open-air museum. Just 5km (3 miles) southeast of the city, in Qingxiu Park, stands the highest pagoda in Guangxi.

The port of **Beihai** ⑤ (北海) on the south coast still sports 19th-century European buildings that recall its history as a treaty port (the best examples are near the waterfront); the town is also known for its beaches. **Silver Beach** (北海银滩; Beihai Yintan) is a pleasant enough stretch of sand, although it does get very crowded at times. Be aware that the water is not especially clean.

Some 200km (125 miles) southwest of Nanning en route to the Vietnamese border, the country town of **Ningming** ⑥ (宁明) is the jumping-off point for a boat trip along the scenic **Zuo River** (左江). With its sources just inside northern Vietnam, the Zuo provides an opportunity for a much quieter river experience than the Lijiang. Tourism here has yet to be developed to

The Dragon's Backbone Terraces at Longsheng.

Cable-cars on Qianling Shan, Guiyang.

a stage even remotely comparable to Guilin or Yangshuo, and visitors will be rewarded with beautiful karst scenery and traditional Zhuang villages.

Spectacular **Detian Falls** (德天大瀑布; Detian Da Pubu; daily), a four- to five-hour drive west from Nanning, is the world's fourth largest transnational waterfall. Spanning some 200 metres (650ft) along the Sino-Vietnamese border, the best time to visit (but also the most crowded) is the summer months when water levels are at their highest. Cascading 50 metres (165ft) through a three-tier rock formation, the falls are set against a stunning backdrop of karst mountains, rice paddies, and thick jungle vegetation. The falls can be visited as a day-trip from Nanning, but for those eager to stay longer, a number of hotels have sprung up along the riverside in recent years.

It's worth visiting the **Friendship Pass** (友谊关; Youyiguan) on the Vietnamese border 30 minutes south of Pingxiang by taxi or pedicab, even if you're not crossing into Vietnam. Graced by two imposing landmarks

– a colonial French customs house and a ceremonial Chinese gateway – the crossing straddles a narrow pass between tall, misty mountains. Cracked stone steps lead up to vantage points on either side. Inside the French-era building, faded photographs show Mao Zedong trading jokes with Ho Chi Minh; friendship hasn't always been in great supply – within 15 years the two neighbours were at war with each other.

GUIZHOU PROVINCE

Guizhou (贵州), one of China's poorest provinces (by GDP per capita measurements in 2015, it was ranked 25th out of all Chinese provinces and regions), is a little-known backwater that rewards exploration. Situated on the eastern section of the Yunnan-Guizhou plateau, its hilly landscape is both tricky to cultivate and soaked with persistent rain, but this authentic slice of the Chinese countryside is populated by an intriguing ethnic patchwork of minorities (including Dong, Miao, Buyi, Sui, Hui and Zhuang, plus picturesquely named sub-groups such as the Small Flowery

Miao and the Long-Horned Miao. High in the west, Guizhou drops off sharply towards the east; there is an area of limestone karst scenery in the south central region.

Although the Han Chinese have penetrated the province for over two millennia, infertile land and tribal resistance to Han rule traditionally made the province an insignificant region of the Chinese empire, until a large influx of Chinese arrived during the Qing dynasty. Guizhou is perhaps most often associated in the Chinese mind with both rural poverty and *maotai*, a potent and high-priced liquor fermented from sorghum, considered the *ne plus ultra* of Chinese *baijiu* ("white spirit").

GUIYANG

Guizhou's modest capital, **Guiyang ❼** (贵阳), right in the centre of the province, has little to entice visitors, and largely acts as a transit point. The **Provincial Museum** (贵州省博物馆; Tue–Sun 9–4.30pm; free) on Beijing Lu has displays relating to the province's ethnic tribes, and Qianling Shan Park to

the west is a pleasant, wooded area of hills topped by the attractive Buddhist **Hongfu Si** (弘福寺; Hongfu Temple; accessed by steps or cable car).

EASTERN GUIZHOU: THE MIAO AND DONG AREAS

Many tourists come to Guizhou with one target in mind: the tribal reaches in the province's east and the Miao and Dong Autonomous Prefecture, an area home to a fascinating variety of minority groups.

Just across the border from Guangxi, the far southeast of the province is home to the Dong minority, known for their construction of wooden towers and bridges, and indigo-dyed clothing, also seen over the border in Guangxi province at Sanjiang. The town of **Zhaoxing ❽** (肇兴), the Dong's main centre, is utterly entrancing, with five impressive drum towers and five wind-and-rain bridges. Almost all other buildings in the town are of traditional wooden three-storey design.

The regional capital, **Kaili ❾** (凯里), connected to Guiyang by train and

The covered wind-and-rain bridges in some of the Dong minority villages of southern Guizhou and northern Guangxi are a striking sight.

Huangguoshu Falls in full flow.

A Guiyang temple.

encircled by minority hamlets reachable by minibus, is a functional base equipped with hotels, banks, restaurants and internet cafés. Ask at your hotel in Kaili or at CITS in the Yingpanpo Binguan (Yingpanpo Hotel) for maps and details of the local festivals and markets in surrounding villages – it's best to coincide your exploration with festival dates if possible; tours can also be arranged at CITS. The lovely Miao hamlets of **Matang** (麻塘), **Chong'an** (重安) and **Shibing** (施秉) to the north and **Xijiang** (西江) to the southeast are among the many intriguing settlements spread across the hilly countryside around Kaili.

Zhenyuan ❿ (镇远) is ranged photogenically along the deep, green valley of the Wuyang River a short train journey (1 hour 30 minutes) northeast of Kaili. Its **Heilong Dong** (黑龙洞; Black Dragon Cave; daily) is in fact a collection of Buddhist and Daoist temples and pavilions that cling to the rock face on the opposite side of the river from the historic Old Town. The complex, dating from 1530, gives

good views of **Zhusheng Qiao** (竹生桥; Zhusheng Bridge) on which sits **Kuixing Lou** (魁星楼; Kuixing Pavilion). Beside the bridge, on the edge of the Old Town, a steep climb up a paved path provides even better views. At the top, the old city walls seem to offer less protection than the karst mountains on which they were built. Following a path to the left and then down the hill leads to the small temple of **Sigong Si**, from where a descent back into the town is possible. The Han Dragon Boat racing festival (on the fifth day of the fifth lunar month) is the town's major festival.

For more water-based activities a cruise along the **Wuyang River** (舞阳河; Wuyang He) is recommended. They can be arranged at the large town of **Shibing** (施秉), 40km (19 miles) west of Zhenyuan.

Tongren, near the border with Hunan to the east, is the access point to the mountain and forest reserve of **Fanjing Shan** ⓫ (梵净山; daily), renowned for its diverse fauna and flora. Home to several rare species including the golden, or snub-nosed, monkey *(jinsi hou)* and the giant salamander *(wawa yu)*, the preserve also sustains a huge array of trees and medicinal plants. At 2,494 metres (8,180ft), the climb up to the summit is hardly a stroll (allow at least a day up and a day down), and climbers should be prepared for chilly weather in the upper reaches. For those with less time or desire for strenuous exercise, the cable car will cover the distance on your behalf, albeit for a hefty charge. Fanjing Shan, literally "Buddhist Pure Mountain", doubles as a Buddhist mountain; a monastery near the summit can offer basic accommodation so you can stay overnight and catch the sunrise.

ZUNYI AND THE NORTH

Zunyi ⓬ (遵义) would be an undistinguished industrial blob 165km (102 miles) north of Guiyang were it not

⊙ TRANSPORT

Getting to Guizhou

By air: Guiyang airport has regular connections with most large cities in China.

By train and bus: There are several daily trains between Guiyang and Kunming (10–12 hours), Guilin (2 daily, 17 hours), Changsha (5 daily, 13 hours), Chongqing (10 daily, 9–11 hours), Chengdu (7 daily, 11–20 hours) and Guangzhou (5 daily, 22 hours). There is one daily bus to/from Guilin, taking around 10 hours.

Getting around Guizhou

On the whole, it is better to take buses rather than trains in Guizhou.

Guiyang: There are frequent buses to Anshun (1.5 hours), Kaili and Zunyi (both 2.5 hours). Trains to Kaili take 2.5 hours, to Zunyi 3 hours and to Anshun 1.5 hours.

Kaili: Frequent buses to Guiyang take 2.5 hours, and there are erratic bus services to surrounding villages. Trains to Guiyang take 2.5 hours.

Zunyi: Buses to Anshun (3 daily, 3.5 hrs) and Guiyang (every half hour, 2.5 hrs).

lauded by Communist Party cadres for its historic revolutionary credentials. Dragging itself into Zunyi in January 1935 halfway along the Long March, the Communist army held a meeting here that paved the way for Mao Zedong to assume control of the Chinese Communist Party (CCP), and approved his strategy of promoting rural revolt among the peasantry. The event is memorialised at the **Zunyi Conference Site** (遵义会议址; Zunyi Huiyizhi; daily 9am–5pm), laid out with 1930s period furnishings, while the **Long March Museum** (长征博物馆; Changzheng Bowuguan; daily 9am–5pm) brings you up to speed on the circuitous route followed by the weary army.

Around six hours by bus northwest of Zunyi, the small town of **Chishui** ⓭ (赤水) is set in an impressively remote region of subtropical forest on the Guizhou-Sichuan border. The **Shizhangdong Pubu** (十丈洞大瀑布; Shizhangdong Falls; daily) 40km (25 miles) south of town is uncluttered by tourism and makes for an enjoyable escape; trails through Sidonggou,

closer to town, open up the remarkable landscape to exploration.

WESTERN GUIZHOU

In a karst region 100km (60 miles) southwest of Guiyang, the unkempt town of Anshun is primarily a place from which to reach the Huangguoshu waterfalls and the Longgong Caves, although the hilltop Mingdynasty **Xixiu Shan Ta** (西秀山白塔; Xixiu Mountain Pagoda) is worth a mention. Minibuses regularly depart Anshun for the region's major attraction, **Huangguoshu Pubu** ⓮ (黄果树瀑布; Huangguoshu Waterfalls; daily 8am–5pm), 45km (28 miles) to the southwest; en route, many tours also take in the flooded **Longgong Dong** (龙宫洞; Longgong Caves), where boats tour China's longest underground river. Huangguoshu is but one of many falls in the area, but is the most impressive (and most commercialised). Watch the water crashing into Rhino Pool and its consequent huge bloom of spray or access the tunnel behind the curtain of water. Time a trip to the 68-metre

Mao befriends the peasants, Zunyi Conference Hall Revolutionary Museum.

Rural life in much of Guizhou has changed very little.

Birdwatchers flock to Caohai Hu to catch the winter migratory period, when a plentiful array of rare birds, including black-necked cranes, stop over here.

A Miao lusheng festival.

(223ft) falls during the summer rainy season, when the floodwaters are at their most forceful. Accommodation options exist in the park.

Around 90km (55 miles) northwest of Anshun, in an area of striking limestone scenery, the karst cave network of **Zhijin Dong** (织金洞; Zhijin Caves; daily 8.30am–5.30pm) is famed for its scale, extending into the hillside for several kilometres.

Located a 15-minute stroll from the town of **Weining** (威宁县) in the far west of the province, and accessible by bus and train from Guiyang, **Caohai Lake ⑮** (草海; daily; free) – literally 'Grass Sea' – is a migratory stopover for a number of rare and endangered bird species. Black-necked and red-crowned cranes, white storks, and the white-tailed sea eagle, are all drawn to the lake's waters in spring and late autumn. Having twice been drained (during both the Great Leap Forward and Cultural Revolution) in failed attempts to convert the land to agricultural use, in 1992 the Chinese government finally recognised the natural value of the lake's ecosystem by awarding it national nature reserve status. For a charge, visitors to the lake can hop into a punt-style boat for a closer look at the water.

For travellers planning to go from Guizhou onwards to Yunnan, a stop-off at the dramatic **Maling He Xiagu** (马岭河峡谷; Maling River Gorge; daily 8am–6pm), close to the small city of Xingyi is a must. The gorge runs along a 15km (9-mile) stretch of the river, and the banks on either side rise vertically up to 100 metres (330ft) in places. What makes the gorge most spectacular are the tributaries flowing into the river straight off the sides of the canyon, creating a chain of beautiful waterfalls. Rafting along a decent stretch of the river is possible, though those expecting white water will be disappointed. Some 6km (4 miles) to the south of Xingyi is **Wanfenglin** (万峰林; Forest of Ten Thousand Peaks; daily), an area of roughly 2,000 sq km (770 sq miles) of stunning karst peaks, whose scenery will be familiar to anyone who has visited Guilin.

⊘ MIAO FESTIVALS

The Miao are famous for their festivals, with hundreds taking place around Guizhou during the course of a year. The most famous are the *lusheng* **festivals**, at which young girls don their traditional costumes and dance to the music of the *lusheng* pipes (long reed pipes made from bamboo). These festivities mainly occur from October to April, particularly in January and February when agricultural work is at a minimum. Often accompanied by bullfights, they are held at a designated site called a "flower ground", which could be anything from the local basketball court to a picturesque natural setting, and are real community events: the gatherings are traditionally an opportunity for young people to find suitable marriage partners – the Miao call this "fishing".

A more ritualised courtship takes place from the 15th to 17th days of the third lunar month at the **Sister's Meal festival**, with the symbolic exchange of sticky rice and other gifts between prospective partners. It is centred around the Miao villages of Shidong and Taijiang to the northeast of Kaili. Shidong is also the best place to catch the **Miao Dragon Boat festival**, commemorating the slaying of a dragon that once terrorised the local population, while **Miao New Year** takes place over a five-day period around the end of the 10th lunar month.

The Dragon Palace Park is famous for its eye-catching karst landscapes.

THE MINORITIES OF SOUTHWEST CHINA

The minority groups of southwestern China, with their magnificent costumes and exuberant festivals, have retained their identity and traditions into the present day.

The swathe of southern China from western Hunan province through Guizhou, parts of Guangxi and much of Yunnan is home to a sizeable concentration of minority peoples, remnants of a larger population that has been displaced by the Han Chinese over the course of many centuries and retreated to remote highland regions (a trend accelerated by persecution following the rebellions of the 19th century). This isolation has created a strong sense of identity and tradition, which makes a visit to a minority village – particularly at festival time – an interesting experience.

The largest minority group is the Zhuang of Guangxi and eastern Yunnan, although they are more integrated into mainstream Chinese life than the other main groups – the Miao (numbering over 8 million, most of whom are concentrated in Guizhou), the Yi (Yunnan), Dong (southern Guizhou), Dai (southern Yunnan), Bai (Dali region) and Naxi (Lijiang region). There are dozens of smaller groups scattered around the region.

All China's minority populations are now guaranteed freedom to retain their language and customs by the Chinese constitution. That isn't to say that they are on an equal footing with the Han, although this is perhaps less to do with discrimination than the fact that it is difficult for these tradition-bound communities to break the cycle of rural poverty. (See also The Chinese, page 37. For more on Miao festivals in Guizhou province, see page 354).

A Khampa horseman from the remote plateaux of eastern Tibet.

The well-known Naxi orchestra in Lijiang performs music dating back to the Song Dynasty. The Naxi people of northwestern Yunnan are a matriarchal society and one of the few southwestern minorities to have a written script.

The elaborate headgear of the "Long Horned" Miao.

Minority costume

The Miao and other minority groups, such as the Dong, are known for their colourful festivals – a time when the community comes together, with the people (mainly the women) resplendent in traditional costume. Most striking of all are the remarkable silver headdresses worn by Miao girls at the *lusheng* festivals. There are several Miao subgroups, each of which has its own distinctive costume. The Small Flowery Miao specialise in

Miao festival dancing.

extravagant bouffant hairdos, while the Long-Horned Miao tie their hair around wooden horns projecting from the sides of the head. The Dong wear splendid indigo-dyed garments. These forms of dress are not merely ornamental; they are an assertion of a cultural identity distinct from mainstream China and the relentless consumerism that continually erodes the minorities' way of life.

Bai music and dance festival, Dali.

Bai dancers at the foot of the Three Pagodas in Dali. As well as being skilled architects, the Bai people are known for their dance, music and lacquer work. White is their preferred colour for clothes, and their name means "white people".

Miao men playing lusheng pipes at festival time. The dyeing and weaving of their indigo robes is an important cottage industry.

The gigantic Buddha at Leshan.

SICHUAN

Hidden behind a ring of mountains, Sichuan is famous for its fiery cuisine and the world's biggest Buddha. The remote western forests provide a refuge for the endangered giant panda.

Isolated from the rest of China by a series of mountain ranges, **Sichuan** (四川) is the country's fourth-most populous province. Most of its 81 million people are crowded into some of the world's highest rural population densities in the flatlands of the Red Basin, south and east of the provincial capital, Chengdu. A large chunk of what was eastern Sichuan was cleaved off the province in 1997 to form Chongqing Shi; this area is detailed in the Chang Jiang chapter. Sichuan is famous for its cuisine, often spelled "Szechuan" or "Szechwan" in the West.

Sichuan has a long history. The two kingdoms of Shu and Ba date back to the 9th century BC, and were part of present-day Sichuan under the first emperor of a united China, Qin Shi Huangdi. The character for Shu survives as the official abbreviation for Sichuan. Around AD 1000, during the Northern Song dynasty, four districts were created to facilitate administration. They were called Chuan Xia Si Lu (four districts of Chuanxia), and were later abbreviated to the modern name Sichuan.

Today, Sichuan is one of inland China's richest provinces, but its economy and infrastructure took a serious setback in 2008, when on 12 May, a magnitude 8.0 earthquake struck the town of Wenchuan, 80km (50 miles) northwest of Chengdu. The quake was estimated to have killed more than 69,000 people in Sichuan and

surrounding provinces, with a further 18,000 listed as missing. Although the shaking was reportedly felt as far away as Thailand and Shanghai, the city of Chengdu came through the ordeal with no major buildings collapsed. The worst affected areas were the remote northwest parts of Sichuan, which see next to no foreign tourist traffic.

THE LAY OF THE LAND

The heart of Sichuan is the fertile Red Basin, surrounded by mountains to the north, south, east and west, with a

Main Attractions
Giant Panda Breeding and Research Base
Emei Shan
Jiuzhaigou Nature Reserve
Hailuogou Glacier

Maps on pages, 361, 362

Synchronised tai chi in a Chengdu park.

⊘ Tip

Chengdu is renowned, perhaps more than any other Chinese city, for its teahouses, which have long served as places to socialise, discuss issues of the day, and conduct business transactions. Today, the city's teahouses are bustling, with hawkers offering patrons shoe shines, massages, and ear cleanings. Some older teahouses hold performances; the Yuelai Teahouse (悦来茶馆; 54 Huaxing Jie) dates back to 1905 and hosts daily folk and Sichuan opera performances.

A Chinese bulbul atop a pillar, Wenshu Yuan, Chengdu.

climate very favourable to agriculture: this is one of China's major rice-growing areas, and the warm summers, mild winters and high humidity allow cultivation throughout the year. Even during the cold months of January and February, the markets are filled with fresh fruit and vegetables.

In complete contrast, the western half of Sichuan is wild and mountainous. The expansive forests are rich in fir and deciduous trees, and shelter rare wildlife. This is the home of the giant panda, forced into ever higher mountain regions by human encroachment, and threatened with extinction despite great efforts to save the species.

The mountain areas are home to 15 recognised ethnic groups, including a sizeable Tibetan population: much of western Sichuan lies within the traditional Tibetan lands of Kham. Police presence is noticeable in many of the Tibetan regions, including in the Tibetan quarters within Chengdu. Various incidents testifying to the friction between Tibetans and Han Chinese

have occurred in the past years, including a rash of cases of Tibetan monks setting themselves on fire in reaction to Chinese authorities.

CHENGDU

Sichuan's easy-going capital, **Chengdu** ❶ (成都), lies on the western edge of the Red Basin. The city, which is more than 2,000 years old, now has a population of around 5.2 million in the city proper, and over 14 million in greater Chengdu, making it China's fourth most populous city. In contrast to some other Chinese urban centres, and despite raging redevelopment, it has managed to preserve an atmosphere that evokes a sense of history.

As the centre of the kingdom of Shu, Chengdu was already the political, economic and cultural centre of western Sichuan by 400 BC. During the Five Dynasties period (AD 907–60) numerous hibiscus trees were planted on the city walls, beginning a tradition of tree-planting that has continued over the centuries and resulted in the city having particularly attractive parks.

⊘ TRANSPORT

Getting to Sichuan

Flights: There are domestic flights to Chengdu from all major cities in China. Jiuzhaigou and Panzhihua are the most useful airports.

By train and bus: Chengdu is a major transport hub, with extensive rail and bus links to cities throughout China. Rail connections include Lhasa (44 hours), Kunming (19 hours), Beijing (28 hours), Guangzhou (30 hours), Xi'an (13 hours), Guilin (27 hours) and Shanghai (28 hours).

Getting around Sichuan

Chengdu: There are frequent buses to Emei Shan (3 hours), Dujiangyan (1.5 hours), Leshan (3 hours), Jiuzhaigou (10 hours), Songpan (8 hours), Kangding (6 hours), Yibin (4 hours), Zigong (4 hours), and Ya'an (2 hours). A high-speed train connects Chengdu to Dujiangyan (30 minutes) and Qingcheng Shan (40 minutes). There are regular trains to Emei Shan (2–3 hours), Panzhihua (13 hours) and Xichang (9 hours). Jiuzhaigou is most easily reached by a daily flight from Chengdu. **Emei Shan:** There are frequent buses to Chengdu (3 hours) and Ya'an (1 hour), while trains connect Emei with Chengdu (2–3 hours), Panzhihua (10 hours) and Xichang (7 hours). **Leshan:** Buses depart for Chengdu (3 hours), Emei Shan (30 minutes), Yibin (4 hours) and Zigong (3.5 hours). **Yibin:** There are buses to Chengdu (4 hours), Zigong (1 hour) and Gongxian (2.5 hours).

Built on flat terrain, Chengdu is relatively easy to explore on foot or by bicycle, although the city's growing motor vehicle traffic is making it increasingly difficult to do so. It has almost a southern aspect, with pleasantly colourful old streets lined by scores of small, traditional shops and restaurants, and walkways that remain crowded until late with traders, buyers and people just out for a stroll. The commercial centre is concentrated around Dongfeng Lu and Dong Dajie, southeast of the large Mao statue and Tianfu Square subway station.

One could eat one's way through the region's countless specialities by visiting the snack bars or **teahouses** (chadian), which often have free performances of Sichuan opera or other instrumental pieces to entertain guests as they sip their jasmine tea. These teahouses are popular gaming hangouts, particularly for older men playing weiqi (played with black-and-white stones on a 19 by 19 line board), or Chinese chess. To sample this thriving teahouse culture, take a walk around **People's**

Tianfu Square in downtown Chengdu.

Park Ⓐ (人民公园; Renmin Gongyuan), a short distance west of Tianfu Square. For some visitors, particularly during the hot summer months, the sprawling park leaves lasting impressions of the city, with its crowds at leisure, sipping tea in wicker chairs, playing cards and Chinese chess, and as evening approaches perhaps practising ballroom dancing en masse.

Kuanzhai Xiangzi (宽窄巷子; Kuanzhai Alley), around five minutes' walk northwest of Renmin Park, has been

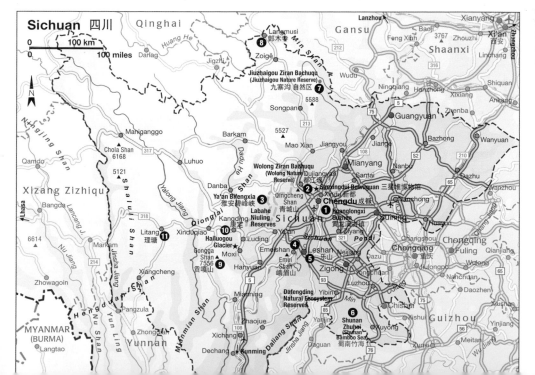

Relics, including a series of wells, from the Tang dynasty at Du Fu Caotang (Du Fu's Thatched Cottage).

restored as a pedestrianised shopping, dining, and nightlife street featuring Qing-era architectural styles.

TEMPLES AND OTHER SIGHTS

Chengdu has several attractive temple complexes. **Wuhou Si** Ⓑ (武侯祠; Temple of the Duke of Wu; daily 8am–6pm), southwest of the city centre, was built by the king of the Cheng empire in the last years of the Western Jin period (AD 265–316), and named after the Three Kingdoms military strategist Zhuge Liang. The temple site as seen today was rebuilt in the Kangxi era of the Qing dynasty, in the late 1600s. There are more than 40 sculptures of famous personalities from the Shu and Han periods, as well as numerous memorial stones, scrolls and sacral implements.

To the south of the temple is the Tibetan part of town, with its own distinct atmosphere and some interesting shops.

Further out towards the western suburbs is an attractive park containing **Du Fu Caotang** Ⓒ (杜甫草堂; Du Fu's Thatched Cottage; daily May–Oct 8am–6.30pm, Nov–Apr until 6pm). Du Fu (see page 92) who lived in the 8th century and is possibly China's most famous classical poet, fled an official post in Chang'an (now Xi'an) and sought refuge in Chengdu with his family. He built a straw hut on the property of a helpful friend, and lived there for three years in very modest circumstances. He wrote more than 240 of his popular poems here. The memorial to Du Fu has been renovated or rebuilt several times during the subsequent dynasties, and even today there is an active Chengdu Du Fu study society.

Another temple of note is the nearby **Qingyang Gong** Ⓓ (青羊宫; Green Goat Temple), a fascinating complex dedicated to Laozi, the founder of Daoism. You can compare its more sober mysteries with the **Wenshu Yuan** Ⓔ (文殊院; Wenshu Temple), in the north of town halfway between the Mao statue and the railway station; this is Chengdu's largest and busiest Buddhist temple.

It is worth visiting the **Sichuan Provincial Museum**  (四川省博物馆; Tue–Sun 9am–5pm; free), near Du Fu's Thatched Cottage, which is the most comprehensive collection of Sichuan's bronze, porcelain, textiles, calligraphy, sculpture and other archaeological finds on display in Chengdu.

SOUTHEAST OF THE CENTRE

Wangjianglou ⑥ (望江楼; River Viewing Pavilion Park; daily; free) stands on the southern bank of the Jin Jiang River, in the southeastern part of Chengdu. It was built during the Qing dynasty in memory of Xue Tao (AD 768–831), a famous Tang-dynasty poet. Today, this area is a public park with several towers and pavilions. The Chongli Pavilion, which is 30 metres (100ft) tall and has four floors, is particularly noticeable because of its striking ornaments, green-glazed tiles and red-lacquered columns. More than 100 varieties of bamboo, including such rare varieties as spotted and square bamboo, have been planted here in honour of Xue Tao, who is thought to have loved the plant.

Very close to the pavilion, heading back in the direction of the city centre, the **Sichuan University Museum** (四川大学博物馆; Sichuan Daxue Bowuguan; http://scudm.scu.edu.cn; daily 9am–5pm) is worth a visit for its eclectic collection of Sichuan-related artefacts, some of them Tibetan.

PANDA CENTRE

Head northeast of town for 6km (4 miles) to the **Giant Panda Breeding Research Facility** (成都大熊猫繁育研究基地; Chengdu Daxiongmao Fanyu Yanjiujidi; www.panda.org.cn; daily 7.30am–6pm), far preferable to the city zoo as a natural environment for both the giant and lesser (red) pandas. There are more than a dozen pandas living here, and the centre includes excellent exhibits and a museum.

The museum in particular makes the facility worth visiting, as much as a glimpse of the pandas themselves. Covering an area of some 7,000 sq metres (75,000 sq ft), the base hired US experts to help develop bilingual interactive exhibits that explain how the

Tip

The area around Wenshu Yuan is one of the most enjoyable parts of Chengdu for exploring on foot, with a network of renovated alleyways lined with an array of traditional shops. As well as the famous teahouse within the temple grounds, there is a sprawling teahouse area immediately to the east.

The area around Chengdu's Wenshu Yuan.

Giant pandas at Chengdu Zoo.

panda lives, its habitats and the efforts that are being made to protect the species from human encroachment.

OUTSIDE CHENGDU

There are several places of interest easily reached by bus from Chengdu. Some 18km (11 miles) north of the city, in the town of **Xindu** (新都), is the Buddhist monastery **Baoguang Si** (宝光寺; Precious Light Monastery; daily 8am–5.30pm). It is thought to have been founded during the Eastern Han

Emei Shan.

dynasty, providing housing for more than 3,000 monks in the 10th and 11th centuries. The oldest structure is the 30 metre (100-ft) -tall Sheli Pagoda; the 500 well-preserved Qing Luohan *(arhat)* effigies are impressive.

Qingcheng Shan (青城山), 64km (40 miles) west of Chengdu, is a Daoist peak providing excellent hiking opportunities in a mountainous landscape of temples, caves and lakes. To the north is **Qingcheng Hou Shan** (青城候山), a further expanse of rambling walks and trails. There is a steep but not too strenuous hike to the summit, where it's possible to shelter in temple tea gardens and take in the views.

It is worthwhile making the effort to visit the **Sanxingdui Museum** (三星堆博物馆; www.sxd.cn; daily 8.30am–6pm (gallery 1) and 8.30am–6.30pm (gallery 2), a mysterious collection of archaeological discoveries 40km (25 miles) north of Chengdu. A farmer digging a ditch in 1929 unearthed the first of the finds here, but later systematic digging revealed a host of ancient relics dating back 3,000 years and more, some of them looking more Mayan than anything else that belongs to ancient Chinese history. The official explanation is that they belong to the ancient Shu civilisation of Sichuan, isolated from the central Yellow River plains where Chinese culture was long thought to have evolved. But the artefacts remain something of an enigma, and further ongoing digs elsewhere in the region suggest that a non-Han Chinese civilisation may have flourished in the region thousands of years ago.

Dujiangyan ❷ 〔都江堰〕, on the upper course of Min Jiang and 55km (34 miles) northwest of Chengdu, is a town famous its 2,000-year-old irrigation project. Built between 306 and 251 BC, the network of water channels was capable of irrigating an area of 200,000 hectares (500,000 acres). Today, the farmland is still supplied with water from the system, although capacity has been considerably enlarged by the addition of dams and pumping stations. A 3-metre (10ft) 1,900-year-old stone statue of Li Bing, the original builder, stands in Fulongguan (Pavilion of the Dragon's Defeat), while the Daoist Erwang Miao (Two Kings Temple) was built in his honour. Dujiangyan was close to the epicentre of the 2008 earthquake, but the irrigation system has survived.

The **Giant Panda Preservation Research Centre at the Ya'an Bifengxia Base** ❸ 〔保护大熊猫研究中心雅安碧峰基地; Baohu Daxiongmao Yanjiu Zhongxin Ya'an Bifengxia Jidi〕 is home to the pandas that were relocated from Wolong after the latter was badly damaged in the 2008 earthquake. More than 100 Giant Pandas live at the site, which is presented as a more natural environment than the Chengdu Panda Base.

Around 40km (25 miles) south of Chengdu and easily reached by bus, **Huanglongxi** 〔黄龙西〕 is a well-preserved old riverside town, its winding streets lined with ramshackle shops and temples dedicated to Guanyin.

EMEI SHAN

Daoists began erecting temples around the mountain of **Emei Shan** 〔峨眉山〕 in the 2nd century AD, but as Buddhism gained popularity from the 6th century onwards, the mountain became a sacred place of Buddhism. It has been a major pilgrimage centre for centuries, and although buses and cable cars now ascend the heights, the old-fashioned method of walking up is well worth the effort. Beautiful scenery abounds, and the protected forests shelter rare animal and bird species, as well as an abundance of butterflies.

The Emei mountain range lies to the southwest of the Red Basin some 160km (100 miles) from Chengdu. **Emeishan** ❹ town, 7km (4 miles) from the start of the trail, can be reached either by bus or train (around two hours from Chengdu; it's possible to get off the Kunming–Chengdu train here). There are minibuses between the town and the main access point to the beginning of the trail at **Baoguo Si** 〔报国寺〕, a 16th-century monastery around which there is a range of

Tibetan macaques are common on Emei Shan. Note they can be aggressive if provoked.

Pilgrims at Baoguo Si, a major departure point for the ascent of Emei Shan.

up to **Jieyin Dian** (接引殿), a pavilion at an altitude of 2,670 metres (8,760ft). From here the summit can be accessed by a cable car, or via a two-hour hike. Just below the summit is **Jinding Si** (金顶寺; Golden Peak Temple), with a 20-metre (66ft) bronze hall.

The peak of Emei Shan is a lofty 3,099 metres (10,167ft), and in favourable weather conditions a remarkable natural phenomenon can be experienced here. If the sun is in the right position, an observer's shadow is cast onto the clouds below the peak, and an aura of pastel rainbow colours forms around the silhouette (one can also see this phenomenon from an aeroplane above the clouds). Buddhist pilgrims interpret this as a special sign, and in the past, some would throw themselves from the peak into their shadow, imagining that this led directly to the longed-for nirvana.

Most hikers choose to descend the mountain on a different route, while others take the easy option: bus or cable car up and hike back down. The trail from Jieyin Dian pavilion runs

accommodation, making it a convenient base for day trips up the mountain. The temple is set on a slope and comprises four halls, built one above the other. There are also various exhibition halls with artefacts, calligraphy and paintings.

Steps lead all the way from Baoguo Si to the summit, although many people start the hike from Wannian Si, 500 metres (1,640ft) further up and reached by cable car from Jingshui village (itself reached by bus from Baoguo Si). Alternatively, buses wind

Wannian Si on Emei Shan.

down to **Xixiang Chi** (洗象池; Elephant Bathing Pool), a relatively large temple built against a rock, offering a lovely view of the surroundings. According to legend, this is where the elephant of Bodhisattva Samantabhadra (Puxian; the patron deity of Emei Shan) took his bath. Below this point, the descent divides into a relatively steep but shorter path to Wannian Si or a longer route to Qingyinge.

Further along the Wannian Si path is a small gorge, **Yixiantian** (一线天; Thread of Sky), through which winds a stream lined with lush vegetation. **Wannian Si** (万年寺; Temple of Eternity) stands at the lower end of the steeper path. It was built in the 4th century and once consisted of seven halls, but today only one 16-metre (52ft) high hall remains. The square structure, with a domed roof and made of bricks without rafters, is typical of Ming-dynasty architecture. It contains a bronze figure dating back to around 920 of Samantabhadra on a white elephant,.

According to some of the many folk tales relating to the mountain, this Bodhisattva came to Emei Shan riding on the white elephant. The northern and southern paths join again at Qingyinge (Pavilion of Pure Sound), where the two streams Black Dragon and White Dragon also join – the source of the pure sounds. The pavilion is now a rest house that also serves meals.

LESHAN

Around 50km (30 miles) east of Emei Shan, the town of **Leshan** ❺ (乐山) is famed for its colossal 71-metre (233ft) seated statue of Buddha (dafo). The large-scale restoration work has done much to improve the appearance of the statue, which had suffered from centuries of erosion and, more recently, pollution. The giant figure overlooks the confluence of two rivers, the Dadu He and Min He, and despite the simple artistic rendering, is astonishing in scale. Believing the effigy would protect boats on the river, the monk Haitong began work on the Herculean task in 713; it took 90 years to complete. Equipped with a sophisticated elaborate drainage system to combat

Sage advice on the slippery slopes of Emei Shan.

Buddhas at Wuyou Si, just south of the Big Buddha.

The intense blue of Jiuzhaigou's lakes is caused by calcium deposits.

Thousand Buddha Cave, Wuyou Si, Emei Shan.

weathering of the sandstone, *dafo*'s heights can be scaled along steps in the rock. There are several temples in the hills around, linked by paths through the woods.

THE BAMBOO SEA

In the southeastern corner of Sichuan, close to the border with Guizhou, is the remarkable **Shunan Bamboo Sea** ❻ (蜀南竹海; Shunan Zhuhai). Often used as a film set, its vast forests of 12-metre (40ft) bamboo are accessed by an extensive network of paths, It's a very out-of-the-way place – easiest access is from the city of **Yibin**, 75km (47 miles) away.

NORTH AND WEST SICHUAN

The rugged mountains of Sichuan's northwestern half begin immediately to the west and north of Chengdu. This is a wild, remote area with fabulous scenery, including some of China's largest remaining forests, much of it lying within the historic boundaries of Tibet. The mountainous terrain makes access to many areas extremely difficult.

JIUZHAIGOU AND NORTHERN SICHUAN

In the northwest of Sichuan close to the border with Gansu province, about 500km (300 miles) from Chengdu, **Jiuzhaigou Nature Reserve** ❼ (九寨沟 自然区) is a natural wonderland. The park was opened in 1978, and abounds with lush montane forests, grassy steppes, fantastically clear blue lakes, rivers and waterfalls, all framed with high mountains and peaks covered with eternal snow. The Tibetan people in the region have a legend about the creation of Jiuzhaigou. An immortal called Dage and a fairy called Wunuosemo lived deep in the mountains and fell in love. One day, Dage gave Wunuosemo a mirror as a present, which he had polished to a high shine with the wind and the clouds. Unfortunately, she dropped the mirror and it broke into pieces, which transformed into the 108 lakes of the Jiuzhaigou.

Many travellers spend a few days horse-trekking in the hills around the town of **Songpan** (松潘). The town itself is nothing special (although its old stone gates remain), but the treks can be exhilarating, passing mountain lakes and waterfalls. Guides operate from Songpan, and finding them is no problem.

Continuing on towards Gansu province, on the route between Chengdu and Xiahe, is the remote village of **Langmusi** ❽ (郎木寺), with its population of Tibetans, Goloks and Hui Muslims as well as Han Chinese. Surrounded by dramatic grassy mountains, Langmusi has the feel of an untouched traditional Tibetan village, and is becoming popular with tourists. This is an excellent area for hiking, and is one of the few places outside Tibet where visitors can witness a traditional Tibetan sky burial (although remember to keep a respectful distance and avoid photography if you see such a burial). From Langmusi the rough roads continue across expansive grasslands to the beautiful Labrang Monastery at Xiahe (see page 418).

THE ROAD TO TIBET

Travelling through mountainous western Sichuan is fascinating, and the region itself becomes more markedly Tibetan in character the further west you penetrate. At the time of writing, however, crossing into Tibet through western Sichuan via roadways remains officially illegal. This is as much to do with the dangers presented by the treacherous road conditions as political sensitivities. Visitors to the **Hailuogou Glacier** (海螺沟) can stop at the nearby town of **Luding** (泸定) to see the Luding Bridge, famous for a Communist victory over Guomindang troops on the Long March. More spectacular, though, is the glacier itself and the breathtaking mountain scenery on **Gongga Shan** ❾ (贡嘎山; 7,556 metres/24,790ft). You can hire guides from the nearby village of Moxi (accessible by road from both Leshan and Emeishan) for return treks up to the glacier, which take around three days.

The Tibetan presence becomes stronger at **Kangding** ❿ (康定; 2,560 metres/8,400ft), capital of Ganzi Tibetan Autonomous Prefecture, which is effectively a border zone between Han Chinese and Tibetan Sichuan, with a sprinkling of Qiang and Yi minorities. There is little to do in this town, which resounds to the sound of a raging river that intersects it, except lounge in the town square with the locals or take a cable car to a mountain monastery overlooking it, but Kangding's remoteness will be appealing to some.

For Yunnan-bound travellers, the route from high and remote **Litang** ⓫ (理塘; 4,000 metres/13,100ft), home to a Tibetan monastery, south through Xiangcheng takes you to Zhongdian (see page 383) – now popularly known as Shangri-la. This in one of China's most scenic road journeys, and it is not as time-consuming as many people seem to imagine. Litang to Xiangcheng is around five hours by bus – weather permitting – while the road from Litang down to Zhongdian, enjoying wonderful mountain views en route, is around eight hours.

> **Tip**
>
> The old Panda Reserve at Wolong was badly damaged in the 2008 earthquake and closed. In 2012, however, a new panda centre was built. 74 pandas have since been transferred there and in 2016 the centre started to receive visitors.

Damage from the 2008 Sichuan earthquake.

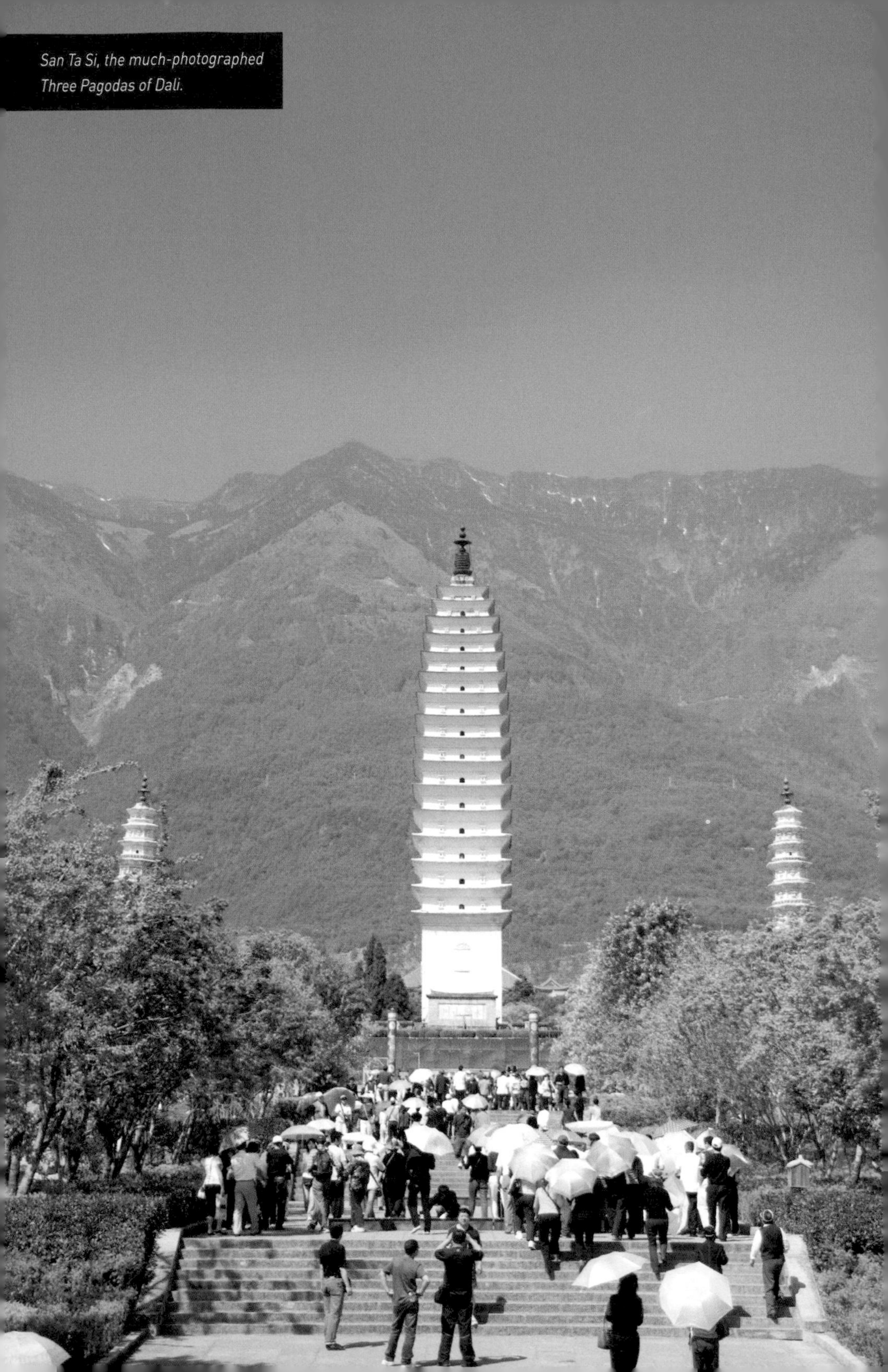

San Ta Si, the much-photographed Three Pagodas of Dali.

YUNNAN

With Myanmar, Laos and Vietnam on one side and Tibet on the other, culturally diverse and ethnically rich Yunnan is one of China's most fascinating regions.

China's southwestern province of **Yunnan** (云南) lies at the threshold of Southeast Asia, and no place in China offers the traveller as much diversity, both geographical and cultural. From the tropical south to the Himalayan northwest, there is an abundance of interest in the form of ancient cities, colourful minorities and wonderful scenery. Yunnan is also one of the few parts of the country where travel is possible and enjoyable throughout the year.

HISTORY

Historically isolated at the furthest edge of the empire, Chinese troops first marched into Yunnan in the 4th century BC. When political reversals cut them off from their homeland, they stayed on and created the Kingdom of Dian, near present-day Kunming. The Han dynasty (206 BC–AD 220) later tried to reassert control over Dian to protect newly established posts on the southern Silk Road, but overall Chinese control of Yunnan remained intermittent, and by the Tang dynasty (618–907) the area was divided into several small princedoms. The prince of one of these made the long journey to Chang'an (Xi'an). When the Tang emperor asked from where he came, the prince replied he was from far away to the south, beyond the clouds of rainy southern Sichuan. So the emperor

Bai women in Dali.

named the prince's homeland Yunnan, or South of the Clouds.

In the 8th century one of the princes seized power in central Yunnan and founded the Nanzhao Kingdom, which fought a century-long, three-sided war with Tibet and China for control of the southwest. Yunnan remained beyond China's jurisdiction until Kublai Khan conquered Nanzhao's successor, the Kingdom of Dali, in 1253. Even as the Han Chinese finally became a majority of the population, rulers and officials of the imperial court continued to

Main Attractions

Kunming Muslim Quarter
Qiongzhu Si
Western Hills
Stone Forest
Yuanyang Rice Terraces
Dali and Surroundings
Lijiang and Surroundings
Tiger Leaping Gorge
Lugu Lake
Zhongdian

Maps on pages,
374, 376,
378, 382

A street market in Kunming. The best places to look for souvenirs are the shops along Jingxing Jie and Zhengyi Lu.

regard Yunnan as wild, dangerous and culturally deprived – in other words, the perfect place to send malcontents and political troublemakers to start life over as pioneers on the frontier.

THE LAND

The heart of the province lies on the Yunnan-Guizhou Plateau, at an average altitude of 2,000 metres (6,500ft). Mountains comprise a significant part of the landscape, with the ranges in the sub-Himalayan northwest the highest. The northern half of Yunnan has temperate-zone flora and fauna, with clearly marked seasons that guarantee spring flowers and bright autumn colours. In the lower-lying south, tropical vegetation dominates: year-round temperatures here are higher than anywhere else in China.

Some of the greatest rivers in Asia pass through Yunnan on their journey south and east from the Tibetan Plateau. The Chang Jiang (the Yangzi, known as the Jinsha Jiang in Yunnan) weaves its way across the north, while the Yuan Jiang (Red River), Nu Jiang (Salween) and Lancang Jiang (Mekong) all flow southwards before crossing into Vietnam, Myanmar and Laos respectively.

Yunnan is home to 25 recognised minority nationalities. Their lifestyles and local ecosystems vary almost as much as their colourful costumes. Altogether they form one-third of Yunnan's population.

KUNMING

Yunnan's capital, **Kunming** ❶ (昆明), sits at 1,900 metres (6,200ft) above sea level off the northern shore of Dian Chi Lake. In recent years the city has undergone rapid development as a business and logistics hub for China's burgeoning economic links with Southeast Asia. The traditional architecture in most of the older neighbourhoods has disappeared as a result, though in comparison with other large Chinese cities Kunming still retains quite a laidback atmosphere. The altitude makes the climate pleasantly cool in the summer months, and winter days are sunny and mild. There are also some beautiful walks and temples in the nearby hills.

Kunming did not become an important centre until the Yuan dynasty (1271–1368), when the Mongols made it the provincial capital, replacing Dali. Nonetheless, the city's most ancient landmarks, the two 13-tier pagodas

⊘ TRANSPORT

Getting to Yunnan

Kunming is an important regional centre and is connected with most cities in China, as well as to airports in Thailand, Hong Kong, South Korea, Singapore, Malaysia, and Dubai. Dali, Lijiang and Jinghong also benefit from good air connections. There are trains linking Kunming with Beijing, Shanghai, Chengdu, Xi'an, Guilin and Guangzhou.

Getting around Yunnan

Kunming: Buses to Hekou run twice daily (6 hours) and to Yuanyang three times daily (3–4 hours). The Stone Forest is 1 hour away by bus.

Dali: There are 2 or 3 daily flights between Dali and Kunming. Overnight trains from Kunming take 7–8 hours, frequent buses 4–5 hours. Frequent buses to Lijiang take 3 hours, to Ruili 8–9 hours.

Lijiang: There are several daily flights to/from Kunming (and elsewhere in China), and buses to Dali (3 hours) and Zhongdian (4 hours). Overnight trains from Kunming take 9 hours, of which there are two a day.

Jinghong: There are about 20 flights per day between Kunming and Jinghong. Sleeper buses to/from Kunming depart every 30 minutes (4–8pm), journey time 9 hours. Jinghong to Dali by bus takes 14 hours and Ruili 22 hours.

Xisi Ta **A** (西寺塔; West Pagoda; open access) and **Dongsi Ta B** (东寺塔; East Pagoda; under renovation) in the southeast quarter date back earlier to the Tang dynasty.

Head directly north from Xisi Ta and you'll pass through what was once the city's traditional **Muslim quarter**. Two large mosques – **Yongning Qingzhen Si** and **Shuncheng Qingzhen Si** – and a number of Hui restaurants are the most visible remnants of this community.

Continue north to reach the heart of what was once the Old Quarter. The **Yunnan Provincial Museum G** (云南 省博物馆; Yunnansheng Bowuguan; Tue–Sun 9am–5pm; free) on Wuyi Lu has an extensive collection of local bronzeware and exhibitions on Yunnan's minority cultures.

Yuantong Si D (圆通寺; Yuantong Temple; daily 8am–5.30pm), in the northern part of town, has been Kunming's most important Buddhist temple for more than 1,000 years. It was greatly expanded in the 14th century to encompass today's ornamental gardens. A short walk west from here

lies **Cui Hu E** (翠湖; Green Lake), with ornate boats on the water and bright pavilions on its shores. The grounds form the city's major park, occupied every morning with Chinese tai chi enthusiasts and joggers, as well as those practising their ballroom dancing. Yunnan University is located nearby; youthful crowds are catered for at the shopping and dining precinct of **Wenhua Xiang F** (文化巷) and Wenlin Jie. Weekends are particularly lively, and when the weather is fine many of the cafés, restaurants and bars set up tables and chairs alfresco.

Kunming's most arresting historical attraction is **Tanhua Si G** (昙华 寺; Tanhau Temple; daily 8am–5pm), a lofty pagoda located approximately 3km (2 miles) east of the city centre down Renmin Lu. An active Buddhist place of worship dating back to 1634, it is named after a species of magnolia tree that grows in its front courtyard – another popular spot for communal exercises. A climb to the seventh floor provides splendid views across the city.

The Stone Forest.

OUTSIDE KUNMING

With the beautiful Western Hills (Xi Shan) and Dianchi Lake right on its doorstep, there are numerous possibilities for day trips from Kunming.

Qiongzhu Si Ⓗ (筇竹寺; Bamboo Temple; daily 8.30am–5pm) lies 13km (8 miles) northwest of the city. It is a famous hall of 500 idiosyncratic 19th-century statues of the *luohan* (Buddhist saints and disciples), each uniquely sculpted to embody a Buddhist virtue. The surreal, grimacing figures surf amid a foaming frenzy of sea monsters, or reach upwards with super-extended limbs.

Heilongtan Ⓘ (黑龙潭; Black Dragon Pool; daily 7.30am–8pm), 11km (7 miles) north of the city, is more conventional. It is flanked by a Ming-era Daoist temple, and the nearby botanical garden has a collection of camellias, rhododendrons and azaleas.

Atop Phoenix Song Mountain, 7km (4 miles) northeast of Kunming, stands **Jin Dian** (金殿; Golden Temple; daily 7.30am–6pm), which is actually furnished with walls, columns, rafters and altars made of bronze – about 300 tons of it – rather than gold. A cable car links with the **World Horticultural Garden** (世博园; Shiboguan; daily 9am–5pm), with masses of colourful local blooms, rare species of tree, a tea plantation, some peculiar topiary and a themed area relating to ethnic minorities.

The **Western Hills** Ⓙ (西山; Xishan), which rise to 2,350 metres (7,700ft) west of Kunming and Dianchi Lake, have three temples of note, though the crowds can be overwhelming, particularly during Chinese holidays.

The hike to the temples provides some great viewing opportunities across **Lake Dianchi** Ⓚ (滇池湖). At 340 sq km (130 sq miles), this is one of the largest freshwater lakes in China, extending for 40km (25 miles) end to end. Instead of signing up for a tour from Kunming, consider taking a taxi to **Huating Si** (华亭寺; Huating Temple; daily 8.30am–5pm) at the base of the hills and then hiking uphill from there. The original structure at Huating is thought to date back to the 1300s, but it has been through several reconstructions since.

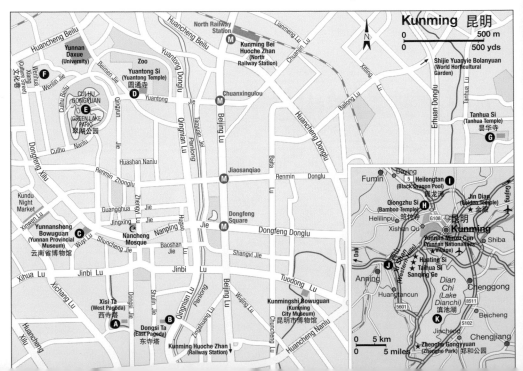

Some of the statuary here is notable, with impressively large gilded Buddhas in the main hall.

From Huating, a forest path snakes upwards to the Chan Buddhist **Taihua Si** (泰华寺; Taihua Temple; daily 8am–6pm), although the way is easier to find by the road. The Taihua complex features a pond and a pavilion for viewing Lake Dianchi, making it a perfect place to rest for a while, before continuing up more than 1,000 steps to **Sanqing Ge** (三清阁), a Daoist temple with tremendous views.

There is a chairlift and a shuttle-bus service to the highest lookout point at **Dragon Gate** (龙门; Longmen). The walk afterwards involves negotiating your way through a series of vertiginous corridors and grottoes that were chipped from the cliff face by Qing-dynasty monks – if you are claustrophobic, scared of heights or don't like crowds, it is best avoided.

The chairlift also rattles downhill to the lakeside **Yunnan Nationalities Village** (云南民族村; Yunnan Minzu Cun; daily 8am–7pm), featuring all 25 of Yunnan's minorities in traditional dress, dancing and singing. Most foreign visitors find it tacky, though it is a staple on the Chinese tour-bus circuit.

THE STONE FOREST

Some 126km (78 miles) southeast of Kunming and reached by frequent minibuses is the region's most famous tourist attraction, the **Stone Forest** ❷ (石林; Shilin; daily 8am–6pm). So famous, in fact, that many visitors complain that the "forest" of bizarre limestone rock formations has become a circus, with cheek-by-jowl crowds, designated walking trails and Sani minority tour guides and souvenir-sellers hiding behind every rock. To a certain extent, this is true. The crowds can be maddening, but the otherworldly rocks – some of which tower more than 30 metres (100ft) high – are still a sight to behold, particularly early in the morning and late in the afternoon.

Around 10km (6 miles) to the north is the **Black Stone Forest** (乃古石林; Naigu Shilin), somewhat less spectacular – but with far fewer tourists.

Pedestrianised Zhengyi Lu, downtown Kunming

The recently built temple behind Dali's Three Pagodas, with the snow-flecked Cang Shan Mountains in the distance.

SOUTH TO VIETNAM

Thanks to recent improvements to Yunnan's network of highways, travel times by bus from Kunming south to the Vietnamese border have been halved to only six hours. However, if you have time on your hands it's worth breaking up the trip with overnight stays at Jianshui and Yuanyang. The route passes through the old city of **Tonghai** ❸ (通海) at the southern end of the central Yunnan lakes region, with its 2,000-year-old **Xiu Shan Park** (秀山公园; Xiu Shan Gongyuan). A half-hour bus ride away

is **Xinmen** village (薪门). More than 750 years ago one rampaging Kublai Khan passed through this settlement and founded a garrison whose Mongol descendants are still much in evidence.

The ancient city of **Jianshui** ❹ (建水), a further 80km (50 miles) south of Tonghai, is one of the best-preserved cities in southeastern Yunnan, famous for its old walls. From here, the road to Vietnam heads east, then southeast, taking a few hours by bus. It's a picturesque journey.

Another scenic road from Jianshui runs south to **Yuanyang** ❺ (元阳) along vertiginous ridges and mountains of rice terraces, with villages perched on the lofty slopes. Continuing on to **Luchun** (绿春) brings some of the very best scenery in all of southern Yunnan, with a series of awesome landscapes of terraced paddy fields rivalling those in northern Guangxi and attracting large numbers of photographers.

DALI

Dali ❻ (大理) is an ancient walled city some 400km (250 miles) west of Kunming, and one of the most picturesque

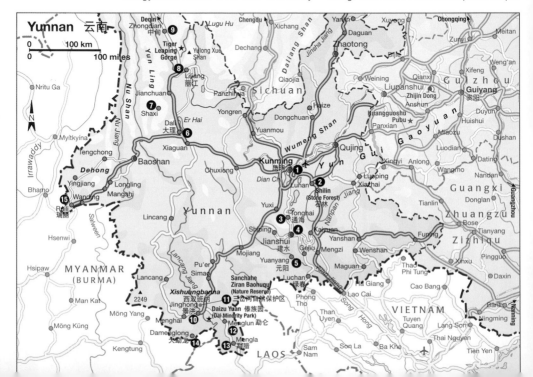

destinations in all of China. Mountain scenery, the beauty of Er Hai Lake, a mild climate and the presence of the traditionally garbed Bai people and their Yi neighbours all combine to make Dali a favourite stop for foreigners as well as Chinese tourists – and there is a good range of accommodation, shops and restaurants to cater to their needs. Note that the old town lies some 18km (12 miles) north of "new Dali" (Xiaguan) – an endless source of confusion among travellers (see margin).

The ancient town is a legacy of the Nanzhao Kingdom, which began to coalesce in the 5th and 6th centuries AD. Yunnan's centre of power shifted west from Kunming during this period to a collection of six *zhao*, or kingdoms. At the height of its power in the 8th century, Nanzhao extended north into Sichuan, west into Burma (Myanmar) and south into Vietnam. Internecine conflict brought its swift demise two centuries later.

CITY SIGHTS

It is possible to get a glimpse of some Nanzhao historical treasures at the small **Dali Museum** Ⓐ (大理博物馆; Dali Bowuguan; daily 8–11.30am and 2–5.30pm) on Cangping Lu. The museum was also the headquarters of Du Wenxiu, an ethnic Hui Muslim who led the Panthay Rebellion (1856–73) against the Qing dynasty and was executed for his efforts.

The nearby **South Gate** Ⓑ (南门; Tonghaimen; also called Nanmen) is the best-preserved section of the old city walls. The gate is largely a reconstruction, as the original walls were badly damaged in the Panthay Rebellion, and restoration efforts did not begin until the 1990s.

All four city gates and the walls that link them are worth a look; the walls themselves feature a total of 45 battlements, while the **North Gate** Ⓒ (北门; Anyuanmen, also called Beimen) has some surviving woodcarvings. Not far from the South Gate, straddling **Fuxing Lu** (复兴路) – now a very busy tourist street, chock-a-block with souvenir shops – is the Qing-dynasty **Wuhualou** (五华楼), or Tower of Five Glories.

Tip

Confusingly, there are two Dalis. The old walled town, where almost all foreign visitors stay, is known as Dali Gucheng (大理古城; Dali old city), while the newer, larger Dali, around 20 minutes south of the old city by road, is usually marked on maps as Xiaguan (下关), but sometimes as just Dali and sometimes as Dali Shi (Dali City). Whatever it is called, it's a less than charming urban sprawl. Most buses from Kunming and Lijiang terminate at Xiaguan rather than Dali Gucheng, but taxis are available for the final leg at around Rmb30.

Dali's Tonghaimen (South Gate).

Further north along Fuxing Lu is **Yu'er Park ⓓ** (玉耳公园), a tranquil garden. Two blocks on and to the left, on Pingdeng Lu (Equality Street) is a small **Catholic church**, a legacy of early – and largely unproductive – proselytising efforts by missionaries bent on converting the Buddhist Bai.

Dali's most spectacular and famous attraction is the San Ta Si, more commonly known as the **Three Pagodas ⓔ** (三塔寺; www.travelchinaguide.com; daily 8am–7pm), which are around 1km (0.6 mile) north of town. Well over 1,000 years old, the exact date of construction of the fluted towers is uncertain, but they are known to be of Nanzhao provenance. The central tower (Qianxunta) is 69 metres (230ft) tall and has 16 tiers, while its two flanking structures have 10 tiers and stand at 43 metres (141ft). The pagodas were restored in 1979, after miraculously surviving earthquakes and the vicissitudes of nature for centuries, although the Chongsheng Monastery (崇圣寺) they once stood guard over is long gone. It has been replaced by a new and sprawling monastery complex of the same name that draws tour-bus crowds of Chinese daily.

Although the Three Pagodas are the picture-postcard scene most associated with Dali, there are a couple of other Nanzhao-era pagodas still standing. West of the South Gate is the **Lone Pagoda** (一塔寺; Yita Si), another 16-tiered tower. Further south, **Futu Pagoda** (蛇骨塔; Shegu Ta) also goes by the name of the Snake Bone Pagoda – which recalls the legend of a local hero who died in battle with a huge python that once preyed on the inhabitants of Dali.

AROUND DALI

Dali's most obviously compelling natural attraction is **Er Hai ⓕ** (洱海), or "Ear Sea", a 250-sq-km (100-sq-mile) lake, named after the lake outline's apparent resemblance to an ear. On the kind of sunny day that is commonplace during Dali's pleasant spring and autumn months, the lake is a profound shade of aquamarine, and when the weather turns colder it is crowned

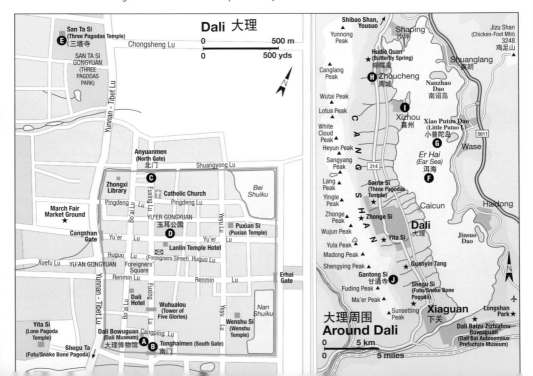

from the far side by the snow-frosted peaks of the Cang Shan mountains.

Not so long ago, the only boats that traversed the Er Hai were fishing vessels and small ferries plying the waters in coordination with local market days in nearby villages. Times have changed, and most of the lake traffic today can be accounted for by sightseeing boats (for details on boat trips, see margin).

Over on the eastern shore of the lake is the picturesque Bai village of **Wase**, and just offshore is **Little Putuo Island**  (小普陀岛; Xiao Putuo Dao), which derives its name from the mythical mountain home of Guanyin, the Chinese goddess of compassion. There is a small statue of the goddess – who is said to guard the lake's waters – in a temple on the crown of the island.

A few kilometres north is the fishing village of **Shuanglang** (爽朗), which has perhaps the best views of the lake and the mountains on the far side. In recent years the village has seen a number of its traditional residences tastefully converted into cafés and guesthouses, and Shuanglang is benefiting from its newfound reputation as a laidback alternative to Dali. **Nanzhao Island** (南诏岛; Nanzhao Dao) is a tacky adjunct to the Er Hai boat cruises, and best avoided.

Rounding the northern tip of the lake, the road passes **Hudie Quan** (蝴蝶泉; Butterfly Spring), once a charming pond shaded by an acacia tree and locally famed for its butterflies – now an obligatory stop on the tour-bus lake circuit, and awash with souvenir stalls.

Nearby **Zhoucheng**  (周城), a more authentic Bai village that looks much as Dali did three decades ago, is a far more enticing prospect. The women still sport traditional red vests and bonnet-like headwear, and the buildings are also traditional – mostly in *sanfang*, or courtyard style, with upturned eaves, and fronted by cobbled streets. Continuing in the direction of Dali, the road passes **Xizhou**  (喜州), another traditional Bai village, and a renowned southern

Silk Road trading town during the Ming dynasty. A stop in Xizhou is not complete without trying one of the town's famous wheat pancakes, which are cooked in both sweet and savoury varieties.

The beautiful **Cang Shan mountains** (苍山) flank the western side of Er Hai Lake, providing a splendid backdrop to the Dali area. The Nanzhao-era temple of **Gantong Si**  (甘通寺) is the chief attraction, accessed via an 11km (7-mile) trail. The site is very picturesque, with tremendous views, although only one hall remains of what was once a huge 36-hall Buddhist place of worship.

Situated off the beaten-track some three hours' drive north of Dali is the delightful ancient Bai town of **Shaxi**  (沙溪古镇), once an important trading post on the merchant route between Tibet and China. The rhythm of life in Shaxi moves at a completely different pace from Yunnan's better-known tourist towns and offers visitors a chance to escape the throngs and tacky souvenir shops. The market square – its flagstones worn to a shimmering smoothness by centuries of footsteps

Bai festival, Dali.

– is well preserved, though the mule caravans and traders for whom it was built are now long gone. Set in a wide, fertile valley flanked by lush hills, the countryside surrounding Shaxi also affords opportunities for cycling, hiking, and strolls along the banks of the pretty Heihui River (黑惠江).

LIJIANG AND THE NORTHWEST

The diversity and scenery for which Yunnan is famous reaches its high point in the northwest, both in terms of culture and – literally – in terms of geography. The Naxi and Tibetan "minorities" form the majority in these parts, and have recorded their significant cultural and historical achievements in their own written languages. The landscapes are magnificent: the southeastern-most corner of the Tibetan Plateau extends into the area, and the surrounding Himalayan peaks reach altitudes of over 6,000 metres (22,000ft).

The prime draw is the beguiling town of **Lijiang** ❽ (丽江). With its backdrop of snow-capped mountains, rich local culture, twisting cobblestone lanes and vaulted stone footbridges crossing rushing canals of clear water, it's not hard to see why it has become China's No. 1 tourist attraction, and improved infrastructure (including an airport) has ensured that it can cope. As appealingly old-world as Lijiang is, however, bear in mind it is actually an expanded recreation of the original Old Town, most of which was levelled by an earthquake in 1996. Tourist numbers have grown exponentially over recent years (16 million visitors per year), which has unfortunately lent the town a rowdy, theme-park atmosphere.

The settlement here has flourished for centuries as a caravan stop for those travelling to and from Tibet. It was Kublai Khan who gave the town its name ("beautiful river") when his troops passed through here in 1253, and the Khan also introduced Chinese music to the Naxi, initiating a unique musical tradition which still flourishes today.

THE OLD TOWN

Tourists flock to the 750-year-old Naxi district of Lijiang, known as **Dayan** (大

Lijiang's old town is one of the largest and best preserved in China.

研). The most logical place to begin a walking tour is on its northern edge at **Yu He Square** Ⓐ (Yu He Guangchang), noted for its large waterwheels. Head south from here and take Xin Yi Jie, which runs to the east of Dong Da Jie (the main drag). This smaller street crosses Wuyi Jie, which climbs into the more tranquil eastern section of the Old City. Tiny food shops and small groceries are built into the fronts of the old Naxi homes, with carved wooden doors leading into central courtyards of intricate tile work. Massive wooden posts frame the scene, and stairways wind to the lattice-work balconies.

To complete the 3-km (2-mile) circuit, turn right onto Wen Hua Xiang and walk through a quiet residential neighbourhood before turning right onto Chongren Xiang, then right again onto Qi Yi Jie. The second street on the left, Guangyi Jie, leads to the entrance of the **Mu Family Mansion** Ⓑ (木府; Mufu; www.travelchina guide.com; 8.30am–5.30pm) a re-creation of a Ming-style palace commemorating the rule of the Mu family, who governed Lijiang in the name of the Yuan, Ming and Qing emperors from 1254 until 1723. This series of six large pavilions in a walled compound was financed by the World Bank and constructed soon after the earthquake in 1996.

While the recent changes to overcome Lijiang are undeniable, they have strengthened a Naxi cultural revival which flourishes in the arts, particularly music. The 23 Tang-dynasty songs which Kublai Khan bequeathed to the Naxi were lost elsewhere in China but have survived here. Performances of this music, augmented with original Naxi folk music, take place at the **Naxi Orchestra Hall** Ⓒ (纳西音乐厅; Naxi Yinle Ting; daily 8pm), opposite the Dongba Palace on Dong Da Jie.

A short walk north of the square, following the stream, is the **Black Dragon Pool Park** Ⓓ (黑龙潭公园; Heilongtan Gongyuan; 7.30am–9.30pm). This park, where willow and chestnut trees line

pathways which meander around a small lake, is home to some architectural treasures, notably the **Five Phoenix Hall** Ⓔ (五凤楼; Wufeng Lou), built in the 17th century and recently moved here from the Fuguousi Temple outside Lijiang. It is one of the best places in town to admire the view of Yulongxue Shan (Jade Dragon Snow mountain), whose jagged snowy profile is reflected in the water of the lake.

Outside the rear gate of the park is the **Dongba Culture Museum** (东巴文化博物馆; Dongba Wenhua Bo Wu Guan; daily

Lijiang's Naxi orchestra preserves a unique musical tradition.

Lijiang's old market square (Sifang Jie).

8am–5pm), with collections of the ritual clothing and accoutrements used by the Naxi shamans, as well as a collection of painted scrolls and manuscripts written in their pictographic script.

AROUND LIJIANG

A 6km (4-mile) drive north of Lijiang Old Town is the beautiful ancient town of **Shuhe** (東河古鎮; Shuhe Guzhen), which was once an important market town on the tea trading routes leading to Tibet. Somewhat smaller and quieter than Lijiang's old town, Shuhe's stream-lined streets and alleys make for a pleasant morning or afternoon stroll, or as a charming place to stay.

The high plains (2,400 metres/7,850ft) around Lijiang are dominated by the **Jade Dragon Snow Mountain ❶** (玉龙雪山; Yulongxue Shan), 5,596 metres (18,359ft) in altitude and the best-known massif in the province. First climbed in the 1960s, its 13 peaks are mantled with permanent snow. Yulongxue Shan is home to half of Yunnan's 13,000 plant species, including 400 species of tree and one-third of China's known

medicinal herbs and plants. Its many ravines, creeks, cliffs and meadows all have Naxi names and are settings for the myths and legends of these people, who have made the plain their homeland for 1,000 years. Still heavily forested, the mountain bursts into bloom every spring when the camellias, rhododendrons and azaleas start flowering. Herders take their cattle, goats, sheep and yaks to graze on its slopes.

For closer views of the mountain, travellers can travel north to **Baishuitai** (白水台), or White Water Creek. From here, take a pony ride or cable car up the steep slope to Yunshanping, a delightful meadow at 3,300 metres (10,830ft). Further north, the 5,400 metre (17,720-ft) -high Haba peak towers beside Yulongxue Shan. The 16km (10-mile) narrow valley between the two massifs, cut by the surging waters of the Jinsha Jiang, is **Tiger Leaping Gorge ❼** (虎跳峡; Hutiaoxia), so named because at its narrowest point a fleeing tiger is supposed to have escaped a hunter by leaping across the 30-metre (100ft) gap to safety.

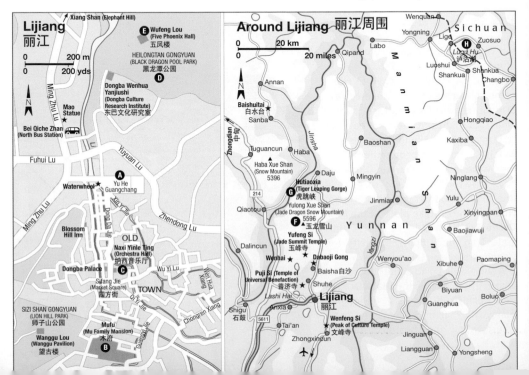

NORTH TO LUGU LAKE

On the border between Yunnan and Sichuan, 240km (145 miles) by road from Lijiang, **Lugu Lake** ❿ (泸沽湖; Lugu Hu) is a beautiful body of water dotted with small islands and surrounded by mountains. Log cabins are the dominant architecture to be found along the shore. The countryside around is home to the Yi minority, easily recognisable by the women's long tri-coloured skirts and large black hats.

The Mosuo people, who live in the area of Lugu Lake and Yongning Basin, have a true matrilineal society. Property and land passes from mother to daughter, and all children remain permanently attached to their mother's household.

THE FAR NORTHWEST

The road into northwest Yunnan climbs up onto the edge of the Tibetan Plateau, at 3,500 metres (11,500ft). **Zhongdian** ❾ (中甸), 200km (120 miles) north of Lijiang, exhibits all the traits of Tibetan culture: barley cultivation, yaks, lamas and active monasteries, butter tea and prayer flags. As a marketing gimmick,

it has, however, been re-branded by the tourism authorities as **Shangri-la** (香格里拉; see box).

The **Old Town** – which, like Lijiang, has mostly been built in recent years – is located on the southern edge of Zhongdian, and is full of restaurants and cafés, souvenir emporia and rustic guesthouses. Muddy alleys have become cobbled lanes, and Tibetan folk dancing takes place around a central square in the evenings, with visitors enthusiastically joining the circle. On a hill behind the Old Town, a 23-metre (70ft) **golden prayer wheel** is pushed by locals, launching their prayers heavenwards. Besides the spiritual benefits, the spot offers a fine view over the old town.

About 5km (3 miles) north of town, in the village of **Songzanlin** (松赞林), lies **Songzanlin Monastery**, (松赞林寺; Sumtseling Gompa in Tibetan; daily 8.30am–5.30pm), a sprawling monastery of the Gelugpa (Yellow Hat) sect. The monastery was first built in 1679, during the reign of the fifth Dalai Lama, and at the peak of its importance was said to be home to 2,000 monks. The

A few wild elephants still survive in the forests of Xishuangbanna.

The waterwheels on Yue He Square of Lijiang's old town. Lijiang was built around an extensive canal system, which supplied drinking water.

prayer halls represent some excellent examples of Tibetan religious architecture and contain within them some beautifully rendered statuary, woodcarvings, and paintings. Nicknamed "The Little Potala" by many Chinese tourists, the complex as a whole is best viewed from the shores of the lake which stands just before the main gate of the monastery.

The road from Zhongdian to **Deqin** (德钦) consists of 190km (115 miles) of fantastic mountain scenery. Reaching altitudes of 4,000 metres (13,200ft), with sharp curves and precipitous drops, it is an incredible engineering feat and an unforgettable journey. Midway along the route, close to the town of **Benzilan** (奔子栏), is the spectacular "first bend" of the Jinsha Jiang, after which the road ascends the beautiful Baima Snow Mountain range. Upon descending towards Deqin, visitors are rewarded with breathtaking views of **Meili Mountain** (梅里雪山; Meili Xueshan; Kawa Karpo in Tibetan), one of Tibet's sacred mountains, and at 6,740 metres (22,113ft), Yunnan's highest.

The hike through Tiger Leaping Gorge is a popular expedition, and there are numerous guesthouses en route. In the rainy season from July to August hiking can be dangerous due to landslides.

XISHUANGBANNA

Down in Yunnan's deep south is China's little slice of Southeast Asia, a tropical nugget cushioned between Laos and Myanmar (Burma). The region is known as **Xishuangbanna** (西双版纳), a name derived from the Thai *Sip Sawng Panna*, meaning 12 rice-growing districts, and is populated by 14 minorities. The most populous group is the Dai, who speak a language closely related to Thai and account for around one-third of the autonomous prefecture's 830,000-strong population. Most of the Dai are Theravada Buddhists, and their exotically shaped pagodas add to the overall sense of being in Southeast Asia rather than China, further compounded by the palm trees, year-round heat and, in a few areas, tracts of tropical jungle. There are even a few wild elephants.

JINGHONG AND AROUND

Once a sleepy town lining the Mekong River (known locally as the Lancang Jiang), the regional capital **Jinghong** ⓾ (景洪) is today a rapidly expanding city of close to half a million inhabitants.

The main reason to visit is to explore the surrounding minority villages (bike trips are a good option), but the city itself is not without appeal.

The **Tropical Flower and Plants Garden** (热带花卉园; Redai Huahuiyuan; also known as the Botanical Gardens; daily 7.30am–6pm) off Jinghong Xilu has more than 1,000 examples of Xishuangbanna's native flora. About 1km (0.6 mile) southwest of the centre is the **National Minorities Park** (勐巴拉纳 西公园; Mengbalanaxi Gongyuan; daily 7am–9pm), which is avoided by most foreign tourists due to its somewhat ersatz daily song-and-dance performances. Nonetheless, the lush park makes a very pleasant setting.

The **Jinsha Night Market** (金沙夜 市 场; Jinsha Yeshichang), underneath the Xishuanbanna Bridge, is a lively place in the evenings, with numerous food stalls and even an outdoor massage area. Just north of Manting Park is **Wat Manting** (曼听佛寺; Manting Fosi), Xishuangbanna's largest Buddhist monastery. Red and gold predominate colour-wise in this giant temple, with traditional Thai-style sloping roofs and large dragon statues protecting the entrance.

Travelling out of town, you will encounter minority villages everywhere, some within walking distance. Exploring on your own can be fun, but hiring a guide to visit a Dai village will provide a more intimate glimpse of village life, as most of the guides (check first) speak Dai. Guides can be hired in Jinghong at the Mei Mei Café or the Forest Café.

Better-known locally as Wild Elephant Valley, the **Sanchahe Nature Reserve** ⑪ (三岔河自然保护区; Sanchahe Ziran Baohuqu), some 50km (30 miles) north of Jinghong, is one of Xishuangbanna's most popular attractions – 359 hectares (887 acres) of tropical rainforest, with a cable-car ride, herds of wild elephants, a small zoo and some touristy performing elephant shows. One of the highlights is the cable-car trip over the jungle, which lasts for around 40 minutes.

Ganlanba (橄榄坝; also known as Menghan) is a nondescript town on the Mekong around an hour southeast of Jinghong. It is situated in the heart

Tibetan prayer flags near Zhongdian.

☉ SHANGRI-LA

In 2001 the State Council, a lofty arm of the Chinese bureaucracy, announced that new research had proven that James Hilton's 1933 novel *Lost Horizon*, set in a remote and idyllic Himalayan valley, was in fact based on the area surrounding the town of Zhongdian. They declared that the area was now known officially as Shangri-la, and a campaign of tourist promotion followed. In fact, Hilton never saw the Himalayas, and the name of his hidden valley is probably based on the Tibetan word *shambala*, meaning paradise.

Nonetheless, this bold re-branding exercise, aided by an airport with direct flights to Beijing and Shanghai, and the creation of a new "Old Town", has proved to be a dramatic success. Tourist arrivals have increased tenfold, and the cobblestone streets of the "Old Town" are filled with shops and guesthouses, catering to the newly arriving masses.

After years of repression, the local Tibetans are encouraged to revel in their culture and religion, and despite some initial misgivings, the local people generally consider an increase in tourism to be less of a threat than the alternatives of mining and logging.

of a fertile plain that has long been an important agricultural zone for the Dai people. The chief attraction is the **Dai Minority Park** (傣族园; Daizu Yuan; 24 hours). The mornings are peaceful, and it is possible to walk around the five villages undisturbed. In the afternoon the place is flooded with crowds of tourists on golf carts, and the daily shows of singing and dancing and water-splashing are in full swing. The largest of the temples in the cultural village – **Chunman Dafo Si** (春满大佛寺) – is well worth a visit, as it has been renovated in fine style, with a gold-leaf stupa. In each of the five villages are guesthouses, offering an inexpensive opportunity to overnight and dine with a local Dai family.

Menglun ⑫ (勐仑), 90km (55 miles) east of Jinghong, is home to the splendid **Tropical Botanical Gardens** (热带植物园; Redai Zhiwuyuan) down by the Luosuo River (http://en.xtbg.ac.cn; daily 7.30am–6.30pm). The largest garden of its kind in all China, it features more than 3,000 examples of the local flora labelled in both Chinese and Latin.

The route south to **Mengla** ⑬ (勐腊) traverses one of the wilder parts of Xishuangbanna, an area which has retained plenty of its forest cover. A quiet road runs north from Mengla through picturesque forested scenery to Yaoqu; some 25km (16 miles) along the way is the **Bupan Aerial Walkway** (补蛙望天 树空中索道; Bupan Wangtianshu Kongzhong Suodao), strung between the trees approximately 40 metres (130ft) above the ground, allowing for close-up views of the forest canopy.

A road heads west from Jinghong to the small town of **Damenglong** ⑭ (大勐龙), close to the Burmese border – the 70km (43 miles) taking anywhere from three to five hours by bus or car. The chief attraction in the vicinity is the **Bamboo Shoot Pagoda** (曼飞龙笋塔; Manfeilong Sun Ta), nestled beside Manfeilong village about 30 minutes' walk from downtown Damenglong. Founded in 1204, and the most famous stupa in Xishuangbanna, it is said to commemorate a visit to the region by the Sakyamuni Buddha, and an oversize footprint in a niche on the stupa is said to be his.

THE FAR WEST (DEHONG)

The Dehong region lies to the west of Xishuangbanna and is most easily accessed by road from Dali. The lively town of **Ruili** ⑮ (瑞丽), a short hop from Myanmar, enjoys a multi-ethnic, borderland frisson that comes from thriving trade (much of it illegal). It may be seedy, but it's a different world (especially at night) from the political conformities in Beijing. The main attraction for Chinese tourists is the sprawling **Jade Market** (珠宝街; Zhubao Jie) – said to be among the busiest in the world, and no place to spend money unless you really know your jade. Bicycles are available for hire inexpensively in the city centre, and it is possible to cycle out to several Dai Buddhist temples.

The small border town of **Wanding** (畹町), to the east on the Shweli River, is the official access point (over the bridge) to Myanmar.

A Dai Buddhist temple in a village near Menghai, Xishuangbanna.

NEW INFRASTRUCTURE

Massive investment in ambitious road and rail projects has opened up far-flung regions of China to tourism, not always to the benefit of smaller heritage sites.

For a developing country, it's hard not to be impressed by the modernity of China's transport network. Whether you touch down by Beijing international airport's striking Terminal 3, one of the largest in the world; hop on a high-speed train that serves even remote and minor towns, or take a taxi along the ever-expanding city-encircling ring roads, you can't help but be awed at the sheer movement of people that powers China's economy.

These huge projects help link up an enormous, scattered population and employ millions of potentially restless migrant workers. And for those who complain about being relocated amid the clouds of construction dust, few have the time or necessity to listen.

Of course, some of the first customers to try out a new transport link are tourists. As disposable incomes have risen enormously in recent years, leisure travel has become a relatively new form of entertainment and China has plenty of famous sites and diverse regions to explore. A year after the Qinghai–Tibet Railway opened for business in 2006, visitor numbers jumped 40 percent to around 2.5 million. High-speed bullet trains have also created the possibility for a larger number of day trips. The Shanghai–Hangzhou high-speed railway has cut around an hour off a single journey between the two cities, particularly useful for a population with few chances to travel other than on weekends.

China's network of expressways (gaosu gonglu) is relatively new. Started in 1988, it expanded to 123,000km (73,000 miles) of multi-laned roads by 2015. All this tarmac is being well-used as private car ownership is rocketing – over 170 million vehicles were on China's roads in 2015, up 15 percent from a year earlier.

Along with an increase in tourists exploring the country is the cash they carry with them. Although the communist spirit dictates that China's great lakes and mountains belong to the people, the pricing of entry tickets to famous sites is in the hands of local governments. Entry to Jiuzhaigou, a scenic valley in Sichuan province much criticised for over-tourism, is currently Rmb 220 in peak season, considerably more than the daily wage of the average worker. And while Chinese people take a new-found interest in their country's historical sites, local governments often have a less than subtle approach to renovation and cultural protection. World Heritage regulations are often flouted, old buildings knocked down and replaced by ersatz counterparts and local people pushed out by wealthy investors.

The World Heritage-listed old town of Lijiang in Yunnan province is an example of an ancient spot that has been exploited for maximum financial return. Though it passed 800 years in relative obscurity, the city, with a total population of just over a million, now attracts around 16 million tourists a year. Many locals fear the charm of the place has been lost.

Sustainable tourism has become a new buzzword in China's travel industry, but much work needs to be done to convince tourist operators of the existence of benefits beyond a quick buck.

Lijiang is now accessed by air and vastly improved roads.

CHINESE FESTIVALS

Traditional festivals in China have always served as a means of honouring the past. Many are specifically associated with ancestral worship.

Most festivals in China are celebrated according to the Chinese lunar calendar: the first day of the lunar month is determined by when the moon is at its thinnest. These lunar months, of course, don't coincide with those of the Western calendar, so these festivals fall on different dates each year.

The biggest Chinese festival is the Spring Festival, or Lunar New Year, which falls in either January or February. Forget travelling and forget sightseeing during the Lunar New Year – the whole country comes to a standstill. Among the other better-known traditional Chinese festivals, the Qingming Festival on the 12th day of the third lunar month, in April, is an occasion to pay tribute to one's forebears. This festival is marked by visits to the graves of ancestors. Tombs are cleaned, spirit money burnt, and food offered in honour of the departed.

The Dragon Boat Festival, on the fifth day of the fifth lunar month (June or July), commemorates the poet and loyal minister Qu Yuan, who in 278 BC drowned himself in despair and protest over his country's future. It is typically celebrated more in southern China and especially in Hong Kong, where dragon-boat races are held with much international fanfare, and celebrants eat *zongzi*, glutinous rice wrapped in lotus leaf.

The Mid-Autumn Festival, also known as the Moon Festival and occurring on the 15th day of the 8th lunar month (September or October), is celebrated today primarily by the eating of mooncakes. During the Yuan dynasty (1279–1368), when China was occupied by the Mongols from the north, the Han Chinese often communicated with each other by hiding messages inside mooncakes.

The Miao minority of Guizhou province have an extensive festival calendar.

Elaborately decorated dragon boats race to the beat of loud drums. The frantic paddling represents the desperate actions of Qu Yuan's friends as they try to save him from drowning.

Beautifully decorated mooncakes for the Mid-Autumn Festival. Fillings vary but are usually a rich mixture of sugar, egg yolk and bean paste; they are best when accompanied by Chinese tea.

Bringing in the Lunar New Year

The Chinese celebrate their new year according to the lunar calendar, the actual date in the Gregorian calendar falling in January or February.

In China, this festival is more popularly known as chun jie, or Spring Festival. It is by far the biggest and most important of Chinese festivals marking the beginning of a new year coupled to one of twelve zodiac animals.

Celebrations, which begin on the eve of the new year with a family reunion dinner, typically last four days. Forget travelling during this time as chunyun – the Spring Festival travel rush – sees hundreds of millions of students and workers clog up transport networks in an attempt to reunite with their families.

Tradition holds that the *cai shen* (fortune god) leaves for the heavens on new year's eve to give a report of a family's actions during the past year. He returns on the fifth day of the new year to bestow fortune, so many stores and businesses will reopen on the fifth day. *Hong bao* (red packets, known as *lai see* in Cantonese) filled with money are usually given to the young and old as people visit their relatives and friends to usher in the new.

Nowadays, the festive parades, dragon dances and fireworks are more common in the countryside and in Chinatowns around the world than in large cities in China. In Beijing, people celebrate by attending *miao hui* (temple gatherings), which are really social gatherings in a large park.

A wall hanging depicts the Chinese zodiac.

The Spring Festival dragon dance in Hong Kong: the dragon is held aloft by a group of performers, who walk in set patterns so that it appears to be flying.

Dragon lanterns at the Mid-Autumn Festival in Shanghai.

Red lanterns at Chinese New Year.

Camel caravan in the desert near Dunhuang.

A mountain pasture in southern Tibet with a pyramid of prayer flags.

THE WEST

The vast expanses of western China, from the Roof of the World to the Silk Road oases of Xinjiang, encompass some of the most extreme terrain on earth.

Tibetan monks.

China's breathtaking western region, comprising Tibet, Qinghai, Gansu and Xinjiang, occupies a mind-boggling swathe of remote territory inhabited by a variety of peoples and cultures. This region lies at the edges of Chinese consciousness and on the road less travelled, and the sheer physical distances involved are daunting – the city of Kashi (Kashgar) is closer to Baghdad than it is to Beijing.

Tibet (*Xizang* in Chinese) comes to us with high expectations – fabulously remote, exotic and otherworldly. Chinese political control and a huge influx of Han migrants has changed the character and appearance of Lhasa and other towns, a process by the completion of the railway linking Lhasa with the rest of China, but Tibet's unique landscape and high altitude environment still exercise a powerful hold on the imagination, and the idiosyncratic religious culture still casts an undeniable spell. To the north, and culturally part of Tibet, Qinghai is an immense swathe of mountain and desert largely devoid of people.

Lhasa's Potala Palace

Emerging from the city of Xi'an, the legendary Silk Road soon passes into Gansu, the province that bridges the gap between classical Han China and the remote west. Lanzhou, its capital, has the feel of a frontier town, an enticing glimpse of what is to come. Labrang Monastery at Xiahe, to the south, is one of the most magical places in China, and the best place to see Tibetan culture outside Tibet itself, while in the far west are the magnificent Mogao Caves.

From Gansu the route leads westwards to Xinjiang before dividing into two strands, one north and one south of the formidable Taklamakan Desert. This trade link from China to the shadowy barbarian lands beyond brought wealth and worldliness to the remote oasis towns. Xinjiang, once known as Chinese Turkestan, is a gigantic expanse of glaciered mountains, waterless basins and intoxicating emptiness. Highlights include the wonderfully atmospheric desert cities of Turpan and Kashi (Kashgar), and – in contrast to the rest of the region – the lush mountains to the east of Ürümqi.

Mother and child in Lhasa.

TIBET AND QINGHAI

Visiting the fabled Roof of the World remains one of the great travel adventures of our times. Modernisation and change are inevitable, but the vivid Tibetan culture survives, albeit in a diminished state.

Known as **Xizang** (西藏) in Chinese, Tibet has, for the most part, long been hidden from the rest of the world, isolated and impenetrable beyond the world's highest mountains. For centuries, this mysterious land was the dream of innumerable explorers and adventurers. The mystery and allure remain, and since opening to tourism in the 1980s, the Land of Snows has been the goal of both backpackers and well-heeled travellers intent on seeing the top of the world. To the north of Tibet is **Qinghai** (青海), a vast, empty stretch of wilderness, much of which lies within the boundaries of the ancient Tibetan lands of Amdo.

Visiting Tibet is a unique and unforgettable travel adventure, even if the erosion of the traditional culture in the face of a huge influx of Han Chinese is a cause for sadness. Lhasa has rapidly become a modern Chinese city, with garish new office blocks and apartments replacing the older Tibetan buildings. Some of the monasteries are almost empty. The railway link to Golmud in Qinghai province opened in 2006 (see page 405) and can only accelerate these changes. Yet this is still one of those rare places that inspires a feeling of wonder. The extreme altitude makes the air sparkle with clarity; the dramatic mountains cast deep shadows across colossal camel-coloured

Prayer flags on a remote mountain pass

landscapes; the strange, gloomy temples, their exotic deities dimly lit by pungent yak-butter lamps, seem to belong to another world.

A BRIEF HISTORY

Ethnologists believe that the Tibetan people are descended from a nomadic race who migrated southeast from Central Asia. The first named king of Tibet, Nyatri Tsenpo, was the first of a long line who practised the shamanist Bon religion. In the 7th century, Songtsen Gampo created a powerful military

Main Attractions
Potala Palace
The Jokhang
Norbulingka
Samye Monastery
Gyantse
Tashilhunpo Monastery, Shigatse
Everest Base Camp
Mount Kailash

Maps on pages 396, 400

⊙ Tip

Lhasa's altitude is around 3,680 metres (12,070ft), and some of the highway routes to the city reach 5,000 metres (16,400ft). Until Tibet became part of China it was the world's highest capital (La Paz in Bolivia is officially 3,631 metres/11,913ft above sea level). Some tourists experience symptoms of acute mountain sickness (AMS) – headaches, nausea and vomiting, and dizziness. Acclimatisation normally takes two to three days – avoid physical exertion during this time.

state, conquering a vast territory, and even threatening the Chinese capital as well as India and Nepal to the south. Songtsen Gampo's Chinese and Nepalese wives brought Buddhism to Tibet, which flourished until the 9th century, when the pro-Bon Langdarma came to power. Tibet then broke up into numerous small vassals. Influenced by the Indian scholar Atisha, Buddhism was gradually revived, and in the 1100s, the abbots of the larger monasteries became powerful enough to challenge the worldly rulers. In 1207, the first Mongol armies invaded Tibet, and later Kublai Khan gave secular powers to the powerful abbots of the Sakya Monastery.

In the 1300s and 1400s, the great reformer Tsongkhapa (1357–1416) further revived Buddhism and established new monasteries that became centres of both religious and secular power. He founded the Gelugpa (Virtue) sect – known as the Yellow Hat sect after the colour of the monks' hats – which was to become the dominant religious and secular power. Indeed, its highest representatives became the Dalai Lama and the Panchen Lama, incarnations of the highest gods of Tibet. The Great Fifth Dalai Lama founded the theocracy of the Yellow Church, supported by the Mongol Khan Gusri, who benevolently governed the Tibetan kings and followers of Tibet's ancient Bon religion.

Chinese rule over Tibet began in the 18th century. In 1720, the Qing emperor Kangxi chased the Dsungar invaders out of Tibet and took control. Chinese functionaries, so-called Ambane, headed the local government. Finally, in the late 19th century, the British began to penetrate into Tibet, and the country quickly became a centre of great-power conflicts. In addition to the British, the Chinese and Tsarist Russians also made claims on the country. China, torn by war and revolution in the early 1900s, lost control of Tibet until 1950, a year after the Communists came to power, when the Chinese army invaded and took control.

Hopes for meaningful autonomy were quickly crushed. In 1959, a Tibetan uprising was brutally repressed before the Cultural Revolution of the

late 1960s and early 1970s resulted in vigorous suppression of religious life. Conditions improved after Mao's death in 1976, and the first tourists were allowed in from the early 1980s. But while Beijing continually states that the Tibetans are happy and grateful for the benefits brought by their rule, there continues to be periodic anti-Chinese outbursts. Violent demonstrations occurred in the late 1980s and into the 1990s, and the spring of 2008 saw the entire region – including Tibetan areas of Gansu, Qinghai and Sichuan – explode in violence that led to a bloody crackdown on Tibetan dissidents and temporary restrictions on tourism. Four Tibetans were executed for their involvement in the unrest.

Tibet is governed by a People's Government, whose chairman is subordinate to the branch secretary of the Chinese Communist Party. This causes ongoing tension as the latter is invariably Han Chinese rather than Tibetan. The sense of political subordination is compounded by economic inequality, cultural repression and what are seen

to be disproportionate responses to political protest.

LHASA AND THE TIBETAN HEARTLANDS

The only sizeable city in Tibet, and centre of Tibetan Buddhism, **Lhasa ❶** (拉萨) lies at a dizzying altitude of 3,680 metres (12,070ft) on the banks of the **Lhasa He** (Kyichu) and a tributary of Yarlung Tsangpo Jiang. While its name conjures up lofty and romantic images, Lhasa has increasingly assumed the cast of a Chinese city, with ugly concrete buildings, polluting traffic, and

Enter a Tibetan monastery or temple and you will immediately notice the unusual odour produced by the butter lamps.

The Potala Palace.

Lhasa's Jokhang Temple, the city's holiest shrine.

even satellite links to the Shanghai Stock Exchange.

THE DALAI LAMA'S RESIDENCE

Crowned by golden roofs visible from far and wide, the **Potala Palace** Ⓐ (布达 拉宫; Budala Gong; daily 8.40am–5pm) is a huge, dramatic building, symbol of Tibet and residence of the Dalai Lamas from its completion in the 1640s until 1959.

The section known as the White Palace (Potrange Karpo) was built first; the smaller Red Palace (Potrang Marpo), which houses almost all the items of interest, was completed 50 years later. The entire palace covers an area of almost 400 metres (1,300ft) from east to west, and 350 metres (1,150ft) from north to south. The 13 floors hold almost 1,000 rooms, with ceilings supported by more than 15,000 columns.

Within the Red Palace are the great ceremonial halls, 35 small chapels, four meditation halls, and eight vaults for deceased Dalai Lamas. The most splendid and valuable vault is for the fifth Dalai Lama, decorated with 4 tons of gold, and innumerable diamonds, turquoise, corals and pearls. In the northeastern part of the palace is the chapel of Avalokiteshvara, considered the oldest part of the structure and said to have been preserved from the original palace of King Songtsen Gampo. The chapel contains a statue of the king with his Chinese wife, Wen Cheng, and his Nepalese wife, Bhrikuti. There is a tremendous view down into the valley and the Old City from the roof of the Red Palace.

TIBET'S HOLIEST TEMPLE

Holiest of all Tibetan religious sites, the **Jokhang** Ⓑ (大昭寺; Dazhao Si; daily 7am–noon and 3–6.30pm) is at the epicentre of the Tibetan world and the heart of Lhasa, the destination for devout pilgrims from across the land. The pilgrims constantly prostrate themselves in the dust outside the temple; others continuously turn their prayer wheels and chant mantras.

⦿ TRANSPORT

Getting to Tibet

Flights: Lhasa's Gongkar airport, 90km (55 miles) southwest of the city, has daily flights to/from Chengdu as well as several connections weekly with Xi'an, Xining, Kathmandu, Kunming, Chongqing and Zhongdian.

By train and bus: Express trains run to Lhasa via Golmud daily from several cities including Beijing (47 hours). Buses operate between Lhasa and Kathmandu and Golmud.

Getting around Tibet

Lhasa: There are regular minibuses from Lhasa to destinations outside the city, including the Drepung and Sera monasteries. There are at least a dozen buses daily between Lhasa and Shigatse (6 hours), from where there are onward buses to Gyantse (1.5 hours). For most other destinations in Tibet, it will be necessary to hire a Land Cruiser and driver through a Lhasa-based travel agency, which will also arrange all the required permits.

Tibet Travel Permits

At the time of writing, all foreigners require a Tibet Travel Permit issued by the Tibet Tourism Bureau (TTB) in Lhasa. To get the permit you must already have a Chinese visa, and apply not more than one week in advance of your arrival. Applications should be made via a travel agent and require you to email a scan of your passport and also your Chinese visa.

Permits will only be issued to groups in which there are four or more travellers of the same nationality. You must enter and leave Tibet on the same day, and travel on the same itinerary. Permits will not be issued to individuals and at politically sensitive times may not be issued at all.

If you wish to travel to restricted areas (including Mt Everest, Mt Kailash, Lake Manasorovar and the Rongbuk Monastery) you will also require an Alien's Travel Permit (also known as a PSB Permit). This is available on arrival in Lhasa from the People's Security Bureau (PSB). You must take your original passport and Tibet Travel Permit, not copies, and allow several hours for your permit to be processed. The cost is Rmb 50 per person. It is possible for a travel agent to attend the PSB office on your behalf.

Enter the incense-filled interior by walking through a prayer hall supported by red columns. The main building, built on a square mandala foundation, dates all the way back to the 7th century, when it was built as a shrine for a Buddha statue that the Chinese princess Wen Cheng brought to Lhasa as a wedding gift from the Chinese emperor. This Buddha, called Jobo in Tibetan, gave the temple its name: Jokhang, the hall of the Jobo Buddha. Four gilded roofs mark the holiest halls: the chapels of the Jobo Buddha, Avalokiteshvara and Maitreya, and the chapel of Songtsen Gampo.

The golden Jobo statue is richly decorated with jewels and usually covered with brocade and silk bands. At the feet of the Buddha, lamps made of heavy silver and filled with yak oil burn continually. It is not certain whether the statue is actually the original from the 7th century, since other artefacts were destroyed during the Cultural Revolution and later replaced with copies.

From the roof of the Jokhang is a view of Potala Palace and of the Barkhor Ⓒ (八角街; Bajiao Jie), the sacred ritual path that surrounds the site, crowded with pilgrims and traders. There used to be a longer ritual path, the Lingkhor, which surrounded the town, but it has been broken up by new buildings.

At the entrance of the Jokhang temple, along the Barkhor, a willow tree planted in 1985 marks the spot where, in 641, a Chinese princess originally planted another willow as a friendship symbol. A floor tile in front of the temple entrance has an inscription of a Tibetan-Chinese friendship treaty, from 821.

North of the Barkhor is **Ramoche** Ⓓ (小昭寺; Xiaozhao Si; daily 9am–5pm), probably the oldest monastery in Lhasa. It is said to have been constructed in the first half of the 7th century and served as a shrine for a statue brought to Tibet by the Nepalese wife of King Songtsen Gampo. Later, after the arrival of the Chinese princess Wen Cheng, the Jobo Buddha was housed here before it was transferred to the Jokhang.

Pilgrims pray in front of the Jokhang Temple, Lhasa.

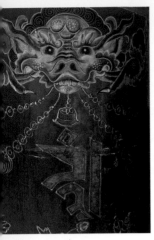

Tibetan temples are liberally adorned with images of protector deities, fearsome creatures who protect people's souls from straying off the path to enlightenment.

THE DALAI LAMA'S SUMMER RESIDENCE

About 7km (4 miles) west of the city centre and set in pleasant grounds, the **Norbulingka** Ⓔ (罗布林卡; Luobulinka; daily 9am–noon, 5–6pm) was built on the orders of the seventh Dalai Lama in the second half of the 18th century. Since then, it has served as a summer residence for the Dalai Lama. The New Summer Palace, which was built for the 14th Dalai Lama and completed in 1956, is the best-preserved of the whole site. On the top floor of the building, which is decorated with numerous wall murals, is an audience hall with paintings from the history of the Tibetan people. Also open are the meditation room and bedroom of the Dalai Lama.

THE BIG THREE

Three great monasteries near Lhasa are considered to be important centres of the Yellow Hat sect and pillars of the theocratic state: Sera, Drepung and Ganden.

Just 5km (3 miles) north of Lhasa, at the foot of the chain of mountains dominating the Lhasa Valley, **Sera Monastery** ❷ (色拉寺; Sela Si; daily 9am–noon, 2–4pm) was built in 1419 by a pupil of Tsongkhapa, at a place where his great master had spent many years studying and meditating in a small hut. During its most active period, almost 5,000 monks lived here, and it had a brilliant reputation because of its famous academy. Today, Sera is home to around 300 monks.

En route to Drepung Monastery and 10km (6 miles) west of central Lhasa is the small **Nechung Monastery** (乃穷寺; Naiqiong Si), which used to house the Tibetan state oracle. Both monks and lay people could become oracle priests. Before important state decisions, the oracle was consulted after the priests had put themselves into a trance. The last oracle priest went into exile in India with the Dalai Lama.

Drepung Monastery ❸ (哲蚌寺; Zhebang Si; daily 9am–5pm), built in 1416, was for a long time the political headquarters of the Yellow Hat sect.

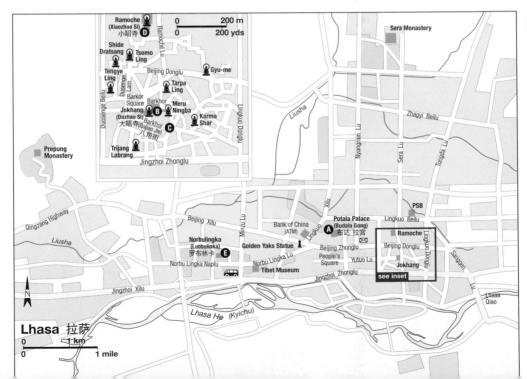

Lhasa 拉萨

The predecessors of the Great Fifth Dalai Lama lived here before moving to the Potala. The tomb stupa of the second, third and fourth Dalai Lamas are housed in Drepung. Probably the largest monastery in the world at the height of its power, nearly 10,000 monks are said to have lived within its walls. The lower part of the site is occupied by hermitages for the monks, along with numerous storerooms. Further up are prayer halls and *dukhang*, which contain valuable statues and documents.

The third big monastery of the Gelugpa sect is **Ganden** ❹ (甘丹寺; Ganden Si; daily 9am–noon, 2–4pm), 40km (25 miles) northeast of Lhasa. The monastery, which was founded in 1409 by Tsongkhapa, is one of the most sacred places of Tibetan Buddhism. It once housed 5,000 monks, making the almost total destruction of the site during the Cultural Revolution even more tragic. Hardly any of the monastery's treasures were preserved, and the buildings were torn down to their foundations. Only in 1985 was the reconstruction of the monastery finally completed, and that was limited to the most important buildings, including the mausoleum of Tsongkhapa, recognisable from a distance by its red walls. Since then, several hundred monks have returned.

THE YARLUNG VALLEY

A two-hour bus ride east from Gonggar Airport south of Lhasa is **Tsedang** ❺ (泽当; Zedang). From here, one can undertake excursions to the Yarlung Valley and the Tibetan kings' graves, and to the ancient monasteries of Samye and Mindroling. The town of Tsedang is said to have been built on the spot where Bodhisattva Avalokiteshvara (worshipped in China as Guanyin) descended from heaven in the shape of a monkey and, with the help of a female demon, produced the first Tibetan.

Some 7km (4 miles) south of Tsedang is **Trandruk Monastery** (also called Khrabrug), one of the first Buddhist monasteries in Tibet and said to have been built under the rule of King Songtsen Gampo. After the Cultural Revolution, the site was used as a farm.

Yumbulakhang monastery towers over the Yarlung Valley southeast of Lhasa.

A further 5km (3 miles) south into the Yarlung Valley heartlands is the ancient and spectacular site of **Yumbulakhang** (雍布拉康; daily 8am–6pm), which looks as if it grew out of the peak of a hill. Home of the Yarlung kings (AD 627–842), it is thought to have dated from a much earlier period, possibly around 130 BC and the first Tibetan king, Nyatri Tsenpo. Sadly, it was reduced to ruins in the Cultural Revolutiuon and most of what stands today is a 1980s reconstruction. There is a superb view across the valley below, whose fields have been cultivated for over two millennia.

In the neighbouring valley to the southwest is **Chongye**, burial place of Yarlung kings, although the tombs are only discernible as small mounds of earth. The biggest mound, which has a small temple built upon it, is claimed to be the burial ground of Songtsen Gampo.

SAMYE MONASTERY

Gyantse is one of the best-preserved Tibetan towns.

Tibet's oldest monastery, **Samye** ❻ (桑木耶寺; Sangmuye Si; daily 9am–12.30pm, 3–4pm) makes a fascinating trip from Tsedang. Part of the appeal is the ferry across the Yarlung Tsangpo River from a point 35km (20 miles) west of Tsedang; on the opposite bank, a lorry carries travellers to the monastery in about 30 minutes.

Samye was founded by the Indian teacher Padmasambhava around AD 770. Considered to be the founder of Tibetan Buddhism, he is said to have succeeded in winning over the demon gods of the Bon religion – many of the demon gods in Tibetan monasteries refer back to such Bon gods. The site has been built on a mandala foundation and reflects the cosmic view of Tibetan religion. The main temple stands in the centre and symbolises the mythical Buddhist peak of Mount Meru, while four smaller chapels were erected on the four cardinal points of the compass.

About 60km (37 miles) west of Tsedang is **Mindroling Monastery** ❼ (敏珠林寺; Minzhulin Si; daily 9am–6pm), which can also be visited on an excursion to or from Lhasa. Built in 1676, it is a monastery of Nyingma, the oldest order founded by Padmasambhava.

THE ROAD TO NEPAL

The journey from Lhasa, via Gyantse and Shigatse to the high Himalayas and then over the border into Nepal is a bona fide travel adventure, taking in some of Tibet's grandest scenery and its largest monasteries.

Between Lhasa and Shigatse there are two options, northern and southern, but the latter is far more interesting. This route winds along the banks of the Yarlung Tsangpo before climbing up to the 4,800-metre (15,750ft) pass of **Kampa La**. Looking south from here are the turquoise waters of **Lake Yamdrok** (羊卓雍错; Yangzhuo Yongcuo), around whose shores the road continues for about 30km (19 miles). From the opposite shore, a hairpin road hewn into the steep mountain face leads up to the next pass, the 5,000-metre (16,400ft) **Karo La**.

GYANTSE

West of Lake Yamdrok the route passes small villages, fertile valleys, cattle herds and many yaks. **Gyantse ❽** (江孜; Jiangzi), which lies by the northern bank of the Nyangchu River, 265km (165 miles) southwest of Lhasa, is the third-largest of the old Tibetan towns. Its location on the route to India, Sikkim and Bhutan made it one of the most important trading centres. In 1910, an English diplomat compared the market of Gyantse – where one could buy Scotch whisky and Swiss watches, among other things – with Oxford Street in London. The **dzong**, a fortification on a hill visible from some distance away, was attacked and pointlessly destroyed in 1904 by Colonel Younghusband's military expedition from British India.

The main Tibetan structure in Gyantse is **Palkhor Chode Monastery** (白居寺; Baiju Si; Mon–Sat 9am–noon, 3–5pm). The circular site, enclosed by a wall, once housed several monasteries belonging to different sects. The 32-metre (105ft) **Kumbum** dagoba in the centre of the complex is a unique example of Tibetan architectural skill. Built in the shape of a three-dimensional mandala, it symbolises Mount Meru; the central structure at the tip

Tashilhunpo, home of the Panchen Lama, is at the centre of an ongoing controversy. After the 10th Panchen Lama died in 1989, the Chinese authorities invited the Dalai Lama to help in the search for his successor, but then disagreed with his choice and installed their own child. The Tibetans' successor is currently detained in Beijing.

The railway to Tibet.

is a chapel for the original Buddha. Again, there are four chapels at the four cardinal points of the compass. Other shrines are located on the four floors. The path to the centre is thus a symbol of the spiritual path of salvation. The stupa was erected in the first half of the 17th century.

SHIGATSE

Shigatse ❾ (日喀则; Rikaze; also spelled Xigaze), 360km (224 miles) west of Lhasa on the southern bank of Yarlung Tsangpo, is Tibet's second city and the seat of the Panchen Lama, the second head of Tibetan Buddhism. In ancient Tibet, this was the provincial capital of Tsang. The Great Fifth Dalai Lama bestowed the title of Panchen Lama on his teacher from Tashilhunpo Monastery. While the Dalai Lama is said to be an incarnation of the Tibetan deity Avalokiteshvara, the Panchen Lama is worshipped as the reincarnation of the Buddha Amithaba, and is therefore higher up in the heavenly hierarchy. This latent conflict of hierarchy was constantly manipulated by the

Russians, British and Chinese in their colonial rivalries.

The residence of the Panchen Lama, **Tashilhunpo Monastery** (扎什伦布寺; Zhashilunbu Si; daily 9am–noon, 2–5pm) is one of the most impressive religious centres in Tibet. The site dates from the 15th century but was substantially expanded during the 17th and 18th centuries. Nearly 4,000 monks once lived here; today, there are around 600. The most important building is without doubt the **Maitreya Temple**, a chapel built in 1914 by the ninth Panchen Lama. A 26-metre (85ft) -tall golden statue of Maitreya, the Buddha of the Future, is housed in the redstone building.

The memorial of the fourth Panchen Lama is also worth seeing. Erected in 1662, it is decorated with 85kg (187 lbs) of gold, 15 tons of silver and innumerable precious stones. The gilded roofs of the chapels for the deceased Panchen Lamas tower over the entire site. On feast days, huge *thangkas* (scroll banners) are hung. To the west of the town, in a large park, is the palace of the

seventh Panchen Lama. The Panchen Lama controversy (see margin) has made the resident monks somewhat wary of tourist visits.

SAKYA

About 145km (90 miles) southwest of Shigatse is **Sakya ⑩** (萨迦; Sajia), reached via a road that crosses two mountain passes – on most days you can see Mount Everest from here. The **monastery** (daily 9am–noon, 4–6pm) at Sakya has a special place in Tibetan history. Its foundation in 1073 saw the creation of a new order, the Sakyapa school. Since 1247, when the Mongol Khan Göden made the abbot Pandita of Sakya vice-king of Tibet, the Sakya Trizin, an incarnation of the Bodhisattva Manjusri, ruled over most of the region to the west of Shigatse.

The Sakya Monastery buildings are striking because of their dark-grey colour and the white horizontal stripes under the roof, as well as the red vertical stripes on the corners. While the southern monastery was left alone during the violence of the Cultural Revolution, the northern monastery was almost completely destroyed. Some buildings have since been rebuilt.

WORLD-RECORD HEIGHTS

Heading on Highway 318 towards Nepal, southwest of Lhatse and about halfway between Shekar and Dingri, the road branches directly south into the **Mount Everest** (珠穆朗玛峰; Qomolangma) region, from where ascents of the world's highest peak are staged each year. From late spring to early autumn it is possible to visit the **Everest Base Camp** and the nearby **Rongbuk Monastery** (绒布寺), at 4,980 metres (16,339ft) the highest monastic dwelling on earth. Only 200 metres (650ft) lower in elevation than the base camp itself, the monastery often affords monumental views across the Rongbuk Valley onto the north face of Everest, towering far above all else, its snow-crowned summit catching the first and last light of every day. The monastery was founded in 1902, though ascetics had already inhabited the mountain area for a few hundred

⊘ RAILWAY ON THE ROOF OF THE WORLD

To hasten Tibet's development, China built the world's highest railway linking Lhasa with the Chinese rail network. China said the 1,142km (710-mile) rail line, which opened ahead of schedule in July 2006, would bring unprecedented economic opportunities to a perennially poor region, but critics maintained that the central government would use it to strengthen its political grip on the Tibetan people. The reality is a little of the former, and rather more of the latter.

The railway has allowed for a dramatic increase in tourist numbers to Tibet, both foreign and domestic Chinese. The train carriages are pressurised and feature individual oxygen tubes that can be inserted into passengers' noses in the event that altitude symptoms are felt. Beijing hailed it as an engineering marvel, the latest in a long line of colossal Chinese construction projects – roughly half of the line has been built on permafrost, with bridges spanning the most unstable sections of frozen ground. In areas prone to melting, cooling pipes have been embedded into the ground to ensure it remains frozen and to stabilise the tracks. The project cost about Rmb 26 billion (US$3.2 billion).

At its highest point, the Tanggula Pass, the tracks climb to 5,072 metres (16,640ft), making it the world's highest rail crossing. The chosen route has caused concern over its potential impact on the fragile environment of this area, but Beijing has pushed aside these worries, stating that the railway avoids certain nature reserves. The train also passes through an earthquake zone, raising other safety issues.

Other critics worried that the railway would lead to increased settlement of Tibet by Han Chinese, further swamping Tibetan culture and mirroring the transformation of parts of Xinjiang. Their concerns have been realised.

There are daily trains between Lhasa and Beijing, taking around 47 hours (2 nights) and every other day between Lhasa and Xi'an (around 30 hours), Shanghai (around 49 hours) and Guangzhou (around 52 hours), with the latter within easy reach of Hong Kong.

mountain than can typically be had from the base camp on the southern, Nepalese side. During the usual climbing seasons in late spring and early autumn, the camp is filled with brightly coloured tents sheltering the climbing parties ahead of their ascents. In recent years, and partially thanks to the improved road conditions, visitor numbers here have increased markedly, leading to a slight improvement in tourist amenities while also negatively impacting on the once-pristine environment. In warmer months, there are spartan tent guesthouses offering an ample supply of blankets to stave off the nightly chill, but the minimal food available is basic and extortionately priced.

ON TO NEPAL

Back on the Friendship Highway and about 50km (31 miles) south from the Everest turn-off is the Tibetan village of **Dingri** (定日), a convenient stopover on the road to Nepal that boasts sweeping views across the dusty plains to Everest and

Apart from a handful of major routes, most Tibetan roads are unsurfaced, making a four-wheel-drive vehicle essential.

Tibetan pilgrims prostrate themselves en route to the Jokhang temple in Lhasa while reciting mantras.

years – the hillsides around the complex are dotted with caves once used for meditation. There is a bare-bones guesthouse with mostly dorm-style accommodation nearby, and it is also possible to camp here if you have your own tent.

About 8km (5 miles) further south is **Everest Base Camp** (珠峰大本营; Zhufeng Dabenying), which lies at 5,180 metres (16,995ft) and consistently yields superior views of the

neighbouring mountains such as Cho Oyu, Shishapangma and Gyachung Kang – all among the world's fifteen tallest peaks. The best vantage point is from the derelict ruins of the fort on the hill overlooking the main village, from where a host of other ruins – the result of a devastating 18thcentury invasion by Nepalese Gurkhas – can be seen scattered across the arid landscape. Dingri has a couple of modest hotels and guesthouses as well as a few tiny restaurants.

Heading southwest, the road gradually climbs for the next 80km (50 miles), topping out at the exposed passes of Lalung La (5,050 metres/16,568ft) and Thong La (5,120 metres/16,798ft), both offering unfettered vistas of the Himalayas, and especially the mighty peak of Shishapangma. The road then switches back tightly on the descent to the village of **Nyalam** (聂拉木), and with the elevation loss comes a gradual increase in vegetation as well as temperature. From here, it's another 35km (22 miles) of switchbacks to the border town of

Zhangmu (樟木), a curiously sordid amalgam of Chinese, Tibetan and Nepalese influences near the border crossing, and the 9km (6 miles) of no-man's land to Kodari, on the Nepalese side.

THE WILD WEST

The inhospitable high country of **Western Tibet** is one of the world's most isolated places, its barren, sparsely populated plains and windswept mountain passes making the Tsangpo River (Brahmaputra) Valley region through which the Friendship Highway winds seem positively benign in comparison. While much of eastern and southern Tibet is identified with monks and monasteries, the far-flung western territories are known for their unadulterated wilderness, lands where the endless vistas are punctuated only by raging melt-water torrents and the occasional soot-stained canvas of a

Yaks are the main domesticated animal in Tibet.

Zhangmu, on the border with Nepal.

nomad's tent. But for all its remoteness and inaccessibility, the wild west is considered by Tibetans to be an extraordinarily sacred place, with holy lakes and mountains that easily rival the importance of man-made monuments such as the Jokhang and Potala in the Tibetan psyche. And though travel through this area is challenging at the best of times, the few visitors who dedicate the time and effort to getting here invariably find it a transforming experience.

The most scenic and rewarding artery through the west is the so-called "southern route", via lonely Highway 219, which extends northwest from the fork just after Lhatse on the Lhasa–Nepal route. This road, which runs in an arc parallel with the Himalayas, is crossed by freezing rivers throughout most of each summer, making for slow progress. The main goals for most visitors to this area – foreign or Tibetan – are the adjacent holy sites of Lake Manasarovar and Mount Kailash, near the sources of Asia's greatest rivers.

The blue waters of Lake Manasarovar.

THREE HOLY PILGRIMAGE SITES

Some 900km (560 miles) northwest of Lhatse, well past the tiny settlements of Saga and Zhongba, lies **Lake Manasarovar** ⓫ (瑪旁雍错; Mapang Yongcuo; Mapham Yutso in Tibetan), at an average elevation of 4,550 metres (14,928ft) the world's highest freshwater lake. Celebrated as the holiest of all lakes by both Tibetan Buddhists and Hindus, it is an important place of pilgrimage for adherents of both faiths. For Tibetan devotees, the four-day, 88km (55-mile) clockwise circuit around the lake is considered sacred, and during warmer months pilgrims come to pay their respects at the handful of temples and monasteries along its shores. For their part, groups of Indian Hindus come here each year to purify themselves by bathing in and drinking from the lake's icy waters, which are frozen throughout the winter months. Hindu mythology holds that the lake was first conceived in the mind of Lord Brahma, and it is also revered because some of the subcontinent's

major rivers – such as the Brahma-putra, the Indus, the Ghaghara and the Sutlej – originate near here.

The area's most famous attraction is **Mount Kailash** ⑫ (冈仁波齐峰; Gangrenboqi Feng; Kang Rinpoche in Tibetan), the legendary Trans-Hima-layan hump that is considered holy by Hindus, Jains, Tibetan Buddhists and Bon believers. Dominating the skyline about 30km (19 miles) north of Lake Manasarovar, Kailash has drawn wor-shippers for thousands of years – it is believed that circumambulating it will bring good fortune, and thousands of pilgrims arrive each year to complete the circuit, or *kora*, that winds for 58km (36 miles) through a series of river val-leys at the mountain's base. Hindus and Tantric Buddhists navigate the route in a clockwise fashion, while Jains and Bon adherents circle it anticlockwise; Westerners tend to walk in a clockwise direction in deference to the Tibetan Buddhist majority here. Some pilgrims attempt to complete the entire course in one long day, while others – mostly Tibetan Buddhists – cover the distance by performing the requisite sequence of body-length prostrations, a physi-cally demanding process that usually takes several days. As the watershed of the major rivers feeding South Asia, Kailash is believed to have geomantic energy, and climbing on the mountain itself is considered strictly taboo. The route is accessed via the small town of **Darchen** (塔青, Taqing), which has a guesthouse, a store with food supplies and a Swiss-established medical clinic.

About 70km (44 miles) north of Darchen is another popular point of pilgrimage, the **Tirthapuri Hot Springs** (札达不若温泉, Zhadaburuo Wenquan), where pilgrims come to soak their feet in the shallow pools, often after com-pleting the circuits just to the south. Near the springs is a small temple built around a cave where Padmasambhava and his Tibetan consort Yeshe Tsogyel are said to have meditated – inside is a pair of granite stones with indentations believed to be their footprints. The springs are about 6km (4 miles) south-west from the turn-off at Montser.

REMAINS OF GUGE: TOLING AND TSAPARANG

Further north are all that remains of the 10th-century kingdom of **Guge**, then located near the main Indo-Tibetan trade routes of the day and largely responsible for bringing Bud-dhism to the heart of Tibet. The tem-ples and religious buildings of the monastery at **Tholing** ⑬ (托林寺; Tuolin Si), most of them built from 1014–25, are considered to be the fin-est surviving examples of the Guge style of Buddhist art, which incorpo-rated Indian, Tibetan and Nepalese influences. In the complex are monks' quarters, halls containing well-pre-served murals and an impressive row of 108 earthen pagodas. The turn-off is 131km (81 miles) north of Tirthapuri at Namru, from where it is a further 144km (90 miles) over a mountain-ous road to Tholing; the final descent

Mount Kailash, sacred peak for Buddhists, Hindus and Jains.

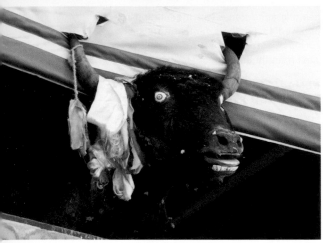

A yak's head is adorned with prayer flags at a temple entrance.

Roads through the old Tibetan mountains, Qinghai province.

yields intoxicating views of the ruins scattered across the valley, framed by the snow-capped peaks of the north Indian Himalayas.

The sprawling ruins of the citadel at **Tsaparang** (阿里土林; Ali Tulin), where the later Guge kings moved their capital, lie 26km (16 miles) west of Toling. Prior to its decline, Tsaparang was a thriving religious and commercial centre, located near the crossroads of several Silk Road trade routes.

QINGHAI PROVINCE

Bordered by Tibet, Xinjiang, Gansu and Sichuan and occupying the northeastern fringe of the Tibetan Plateau at an average altitude of 4,000 metres (13,100ft), **Qinghai** (青海) is one of China's least visited and poorest provinces, a place for which the term "back of beyond" is unusually apt. Named after the huge Qinghai Hu (Green Sea Lake), the province is a swathe of mountains and plateaux and home to several hardy minority groups, including Hui, Tibetans, Mongols and Kazakhs. Geographically part of Tibet and historically a distant region that for centuries solely supported nomadic herdsmen – mostly Tibetans and Muslims – it was taken over by the Communists in 1949 and later found fame as a far-flung gulag where intellectuals and political prisoners were carted off for re-education through forced labour. Qinghai has been one of the last provinces to benefit from the government's drive to develop China's western reaches, but in recent years there has been increased investment in its main

⊙ TRANSPORT

Getting to Qinghai
Flights: Xining is the only sizeable airport, with flights to Beijing, Shanghai, Lhasa and Ürümqi.
By train: There are several trains that run daily between Xining and Lanzhou (3 to 4 hours), Xi'an (12 hours), and 1 daily to Beijing (25 hours).

Getting around Qinghai
There are several trains operating daily between Xining and Golmud (17 hours), as well as flights.

Frequent buses run between Xining and Ta'er Si with a journey time of around 30 minutes.

Although there are public buses from Xining, you will find that Qinghai Lake is best reached on an organised tour, who will provide transport.

cities of Xining and Golmud, and tourist numbers are on the rise, although most of these only make brief stopovers on their way into Tibet proper.

XINING

The gateway to the province is its capital and largest city, **Xining** ⑭ (西宁), which principally serves as an access point to the chief attractions of Ta'er Si and Qinghai Hu but also has some historically significant sights of its own. The **Dongguan Great Mosque** (东关清真大寺; Dongguan Qingzhen Dasi; daily 8am–8pm), in the downtown area on Dongguan Dajie, features an intriguing blend of Arabic and Chinese architectural styles, with green-tiled domed towers flanked by Chinese-style archways. Its sprawling inner courtyard can get packed out with worshippers during prayer times. Just north of the city is the **Beishan Si** (北山寺; North Mountain Temple; daily 8am–5pm), originally a series of Buddhist grottoes carved into the cliff face during the Northern Wei dynasty but now functioning mostly as a Daoist place of worship. After climbing a lengthy set of steep steps to the base of the cliff, some of the 18 grottoes can be accessed by interconnecting wooden walkways embedded into the rock.

BIRTHPLACE OF TSONGKHAPA

The sizeable **Ta'er Si** (塔尔寺; Kumbum Monastery; daily 8am–5pm), 25km (15 miles) southeast of Xining, is one of the most important Tibetan religious centres outside of the Tibetan heartlands. Construction began in 1560 to mark the birthplace of Tsongkhapa, but many of its once-exquisite halls bore the brunt of legalised vandalism from Red Guards during the Cultural Revolution. Extensive restoration work has resulted in the complex returning to fully functioning monastic life, with several hundred resident monks. The entrance ticket provides access to nine temples, the most renowned of

which is the Hall of Butter Sculpture, replete with reliefs fashioned from yak butter portraying Tibetan myth and Buddhist parables.

CHINA'S LARGEST LAKE

The immense **Qinghai Hu** ⑮ (青海湖; Green Sea Lake; originally called by its Mongolian name Kokonor) is China's biggest lake, covering an area greater than 4,500 sq km (2,800 sq miles). Famous for its birdlife, it forms part of the **Qinghai Lake Natural Protection Zone**, which limits visitors to two main viewing areas (daily 9am–5pm). The lake's eastern fringe is only about 150km (90 miles) west of Xining, but to see any concentration of birds you will need transport to the northwest side; CITS in Xining offers one-day bus tours that often ply the lake's entire perimeter. Alternatively, casual observers can see the lake from the bus or train while travelling between Xining and Golmud.

Qinghai Lake is a spring and summer stopover for countless migratory birds en route to or from the Siberian Arctic, including various species of cranes, geese, gulls and swans. The "Bird Islands" at its northwest corner offer the best vantage points.

Ta'er Si Monastery near Xining, birthplace of Tsongkhapa.

THE SILK ROAD: CHINA'S ANCIENT LINK WITH THE WEST

Conduit for religious and scientific ideas as well as merchandise, the Silk Road has shaped Chinese culture.

The ancient Silk Road flourished for much of the first millennium AD, reaching its prime during the Tang dynasty. From the 15th century, land trade between China and the Middle East was beginning to wither away, superseded by new maritime routes between Europe and Asia, and by the 18th century, the Silk Road had largely ceased to function.

In its heyday, it was more than simply a conduit for silk and other trade goods. As well as the merchants, there were invaders, travellers, pilgrims and missionaries using the road and, crucially, spreading their ideas. The scientific knowledge, inventions, religions, philosophies and even the food that passed along the route transformed isolated regions into an interdependent global community. This made it the first and perhaps the most important of all information superhighways, helping to lay the foundations of our modern world – and instrumental in shaping Chinese culture and society.

From Chang'an (modern day Xi'an), the Silk Road headed westwards into the Hexi corridor – westernmost outpost of the Chinese empire – to reach the fortress town of Jiayuguan, and on to the oasis town of Dunhuang before splitting into a northern and a southern route which relinked at Kashi (Kashgar) on the threshold of Central Asia.

A 13th-century illustrated manuscript of Turkish origin depicts a Silk Road bazaar. From left to right are a jeweller, a herbalist, a butcher and a baker.

The Silk Road extended for approximately 8,000km (5,000 miles). Silk would normally take several months, even years, to reach the Mediterranean from the orchards of eastern Cathay.

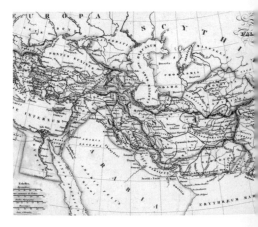

As with all trade routes, the Silk Road acted as a conduit for ideas – religious and cultural exchanges between east and west, north and south. Buddhism, for instance, reached China from India via Afghanistan. This unusual Buddha image – it is in Greek garb – from northern Pakistan illustrates the point.

On the Karakoram Highway.

Modern Silk Road travel

The break up of the Soviet Union and the opening of the Ürümqi–Almaty railway in the 1990s ushered in a new era for Silk Road travel, at least in terms of tourism. These days it is possible to travel without undue difficulty (by train or air-conditioned bus) from the cities of Xinjiang to their counterparts across the Tien Shan in Central Asia: Tashkent, Samarkand and Bukhara, all in Uzbekistan, can be reached as long as your papers are in order. Note that onward visas should be arranged either in your home country or from Beijing – they are not generally available at borders.

There are overland crossings between Xinjiang and Kazakhstan at Korgas and Tacheng, as well as a rail link at Alashankou to Druzba and on to Almaty in Kazakhstan. Two roads lead to Kyrgyzstan, the relatively easy Irkeshtam Pass to Osh and the less-frequented Torugart Pass to Naryn and Bishkek. Private transport must be used at the latter as foreigners are not permitted to cross in public buses. The Karakoram Highway leads to Baltit (Hunza), Gilgit and Islamabad in Pakistan. It is open from May to the end of October, though early snowfall and landslides frequently close sections of the road.

There are fascinating possibilities further north, too, across the Altai region from the far north of Xinjiang, then by train north to Siberia through some of Central Asia's lushest scenery.

The classic fable Journey to the West describes the travels of the Buddhist monk Xuan Zang. The Silk Road was instrumental in the spread of Buddhism – and Islam – into China from other parts of Asia.

Bactrian camels are the traditional means of transport along the Silk Road, their hardiness essential for travel in a desolate wilderness like the Taklamakan Desert.

Silkworm on a mulberry leaf.

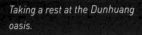
Taking a rest at the Dunhuang oasis.

THE SILK ROAD

For centuries the main conduit of commerce and culture between China, Central Asia and Europe, the Silk Road passed through the heart of what is now China's fascinating northwestern region.

China's vast northwestern region, known in earlier times as Chinese Turkestan, is accessible to travellers along the classic Silk Road. In AD 200, this transcontinental route linked the Roman empire in the west with the imperial court of China, while foreign traders who belonged to neither of the two old empires conducted trade along the route.

Before the discovery of the sea route from Europe to India in the 16th century, the Silk Road was the most important connection between the East and West. It experienced its last great era during the 13th century, when the entire route from China to the Mediterranean lay within the Mongol empire. This ancient trade route began in the old capital of Xi'an (then called Chang'an), reached the Huang He (Yellow River) at Lanzhou, then headed westwards through deserts and mountains before dividing into two routes at the oasis of Dunhuang.

The northern route went via Hami, another oasis, before running to the south of the Bogda Shan range to the oasis of Turpan. It then reached Ürümqi, ascended several mountain passes through the Tian Shan range to Korla, and on to Kashi (Kashgar) from where it continued west into Central Asia. The southern route led from Dunhuang to Khotan, Yarkand and Kashi,

Uighurs in Ürümqi.

holding a course between the river oases on the northern slopes of Kunlun Shan and the formidable Taklamakan Desert. For more on the Silk Road, see page 412.

EASTERN GANSU: LANZHOU

Lanzhou ❶ (兰州) is the largest city and provincial capital of Gansu (甘肃) province. Due to its strategic location astride the Huang He (Yellow River), set in a long and narrow defile dominating all traffic between central China and the northwest, it has long been a vital garrison

Main Attractions

Labrang Monastery, Xiahe
Jiayuguan
Mogao Caves, Dunhuang
Turpan
Tian Chi (Heaven Lake)
Kashi
Karakoram Highway

Maps on pages
417, 430

town that has expanded rapidly in recent decades to a major city of more than 3 million people. With an economy based on heavy industry and petrochemicals, Lanzhou suffers from appalling pollution and isn't the most obviously appealing city. Yet it is a very cosmopolitan place, with a noticeable Hui Muslim presence and a strong flavour of Central Asia.

As well as good hotels and restaurants, Lanzhou has a few attractions to appeal to visitors, including the fast-flowing Huang He, already a major river though still some 1,500km (900 miles) from the East China Sea. Take the cable car across the chocolate-coloured, loess-rich waters up to **Baita Shan** (白塔山; White Pagoda Hill; daily 6.30am–8.30pm; charge), where fine views across the city can be enjoyed together with a cold drink and a snack.

Close to the cable-car station, by the river bank and facing symbolically westwards towards Central Asia, stand the **Journey to the West Statues** (西游记; Xiyouji) featuring the celebrated Buddhist monk Xuan Zang and his legendary companions, Monkey, Pigsy

and Sandy (see page 93). Xuan Zang visited Khotan on his historic journeys across China, which are immortalised in this famous literary work. Nearby is **Waterwheel Park** (水车园; Shuicheyuan; daily 8am–6pm), where two giant reconstructed waterwheels turn in the powerful current. Introduced as an irrigation technique from Yunnan in the 16th century, these two wheels are all that remains of an estimated 250 used in the area in the early 20th century.

Also in the same downtown area, the **Daoist Baiyun Guan** (白云观; White Cloud Temple; daily 7am–6.30pm) offers a tranquil and attractive retreat from the city bustle. Close to the West train station, the **Gansu Provincial Museum** (甘肃省博物馆; Gansu Sheng Bowuguan; www.gansumuseum.com; Tue–Sun 9am–5pm) is definitely worth visiting for its unsurpassed collection of Silk Road artefacts including, most famously, the "Flying Horse of Gansu" discovered at Wuwei in 1968, and a 2nd-century silver plate showing Dionysus, the Greek God of Wine, found near Lanzhou but clearly originating

The Huang He (Yellow River) flows through the middle of Lanzhou.

far to the west and carried overland to China during the early Silk Road era.

AROUND LANZHOU

Linxia (临夏), formerly known as Hezhou, is a little-visited but prosperous trading town on a southern spur of the Silk Road leading to the Tibetan Plateau and Lhasa. Nowadays a city of 300,000, it is home to an Islamic majority population comprising Chinese-speaking Hui Muslims, Mongol-speaking Dongxiang Muslims and Turkic-speaking Salar Muslims who are believed to have originally migrated from distant Uzbekistan.

The town is an important Sufi centre for Muslim mystics (recognisable by their six-cornered hats), as well as a cultural meeting point for Han Chinese, Hui Muslims, Tibetan Buddhists and Dongxiang Mongols. There's not a great deal in the way of sights, but it's a convenient place to stay overnight if travelling between Lanzhou and Xiahe. There are several good hotels, and it's easy to find cheap and delicious Muslim food – *lamien* noodles, lamb and

beef kebabs, toasted *bing* flat breads and the like – at the night market on central **Nationalities Square** (民族广场; Minzu Guangchang).

The **Maijishan Caves** (麦积山石窟; Maiji District; daily 8am–5pm) in Tianshui, 290km (180 miles) southeast of Lanzhou are exceptionally striking. Dating from the Later Qin era (AD 384–417), more than 190 cave shrines are cut into the face of the Maijishan (or Wheat Stack Mountain). It is likely that

Statues in Lanzhou depict Xuan Zang and his companions on their Journey to the West.

Prayer wheels at Labrang Monastery.

Labrang Monastery, Xiahe.

the caves started out as a local site for ancestor worship but were then inhabited by Buddhist monks some time after AD 420.

Inside the caves are some 7,200 Buddhist sculptures, which are predominantly made from clay, though there are also a small number of statues made from imported sandstone that must have been winched up the cliff face and into position. The most common arrangement of statues is a central Buddha (typically Amitābha, important in the Mahayana sect) accompanied by a large number of Bodhisattvas and attendants. Some of the statues show the influence of Gandharan art, particularly in the depiction of clothing and hair, attesting to the exchange of artistic ideas between Afghanistan and China at this time.

The caves have been heavily restored, first during the Sung Dynasty and, more recently, by the archaeologists who excavated them in the 1950s. Take a torch to best appreciate the details in the darker caves.

Another spectacular cave site within reach of Lanzhou is **Bingling Si** (炳灵寺; Thousand Buddha Caves; daily July–Nov), located 80km (50 miles) west of the city, which comprise Buddhist grottoes carved into a 60-metre (200ft) cliff face. The caves are decorated with Buddhist sculptures, frescoes and statues. Most celebrated is the striking 27 metre (89-ft) -high statue of Maitreya, the future Buddha. Entry into the more interesting caves is expensive and getting to Bingling Si on one's own can be a hassle, but local travel agencies run day trips that involve travel by both bus and boat.

XIAHE

Highly recommended is a trip to **Xiahe ❷** (夏河), a dusty town 280km (175 miles) to the southwest of Lanzhou, reached by direct bus (6 hours) or by changing buses at Linxia. Here, attached to and effectively supported by the predominantly Tibetan town of Xiahe, stands the awe-inspiring **Labrang Monastery** (拉卜楞寺; Labuleng Si; daily 8am–6pm). The

surrounding grasslands and mountains where one can hike amid Tibetan nomads are another powerful draw.

Labrang Monastery is the second-largest of the six major Gelug "Yellow Hat" monasteries in Tibetan Buddhism, and a major pilgrimage centre attracting Tibetans from as far afield as Lhasa and even Dharamsala – the Dalai Lama is a member of the Yellow Hat order, though of course he cannot visit, at least for the present. It is a major centre of learning, containing six academic institutes and 10,000 books of Tibetan scripture, as well as important Buddhist cultural relics.

Established in 1709, Labrang once held as many as 4,000 monks, though the monastery suffered grievously during the Cultural Revolution. Today numbers of monks are once again approaching 2,000, the temple buildings have been largely restored, and crowds of Tibetan pilgrims throng the prayer-wheel corridors in their colourful clothing. In an interesting – if ironic – sign of the changing times, increasing numbers of Han Chinese visitors come to worship at the temple, some even painfully completing the full 6-km (4-mile) pilgrimage circuit (kora), constantly prostrating themselves full length as they go.

The monastery complex is large and completely dominates the western part of town. The white or ochre walls and gilded roofs are predominantly Tibetan in style, though the occasional Chinese dragon also graces some eaves. In all there are 18 halls, six colleges, the **Gongtang Ta** (贡唐塔), a magnificent golden stupa bearing gilded bas-reliefs of the Goddess Tara, and miles – literally – of covered prayer-wheel corridors.

The modern town of Xiahe, where some surprisingly good restaurants are to be found, lies to the east. It's here that the Han Chinese and Hui Muslims have their shops. In a commercial endeavour that clearly indicates the pragmatism of local Muslims, many Hui shopkeepers and pedlars make a good living by selling all kinds of religious paraphernalia, including Buddha images and prayer wheels, to visiting Tibetan Buddhists. Accommodation can be found in the Tibetan area west of the monastery as well as in the newer town.

From Xiahe a fascinating overland route runs southwards across high-altitude grasslands into Sichuan, passing through the Tibetan towns of Langmusi, Zoige and Songpan (see page 368) before eventually reaching Chengdu.

NINGXIA

To the northeast of Lanzhou is the diminutive **Ningxia Hui Autonomous Region** (宁夏回族自治区；Ningxia Huizu Zizhiqu), China's second-smallest province and home to a large population of Hui, Chinese Muslims descended from Middle Eastern traders who arrived in China along the Silk Road. The Hui constitute around 30 percent of the population of Ningxia.

Situated close to the Huang He, the source of irrigation that sustains the

> ⊘ **Fact**
>
> Most of the people of Gansu speak a dialect of Mandarin Chinese. In outlying areas, Tibetan, Mongol, Kazakh and Salar – the last a Turkic language – are also spoken, but Mandarin, also called Putonghua or "common speech", is understood by just about everyone.

⊘ TRANSPORT

Getting to the region

Lanzhou and Ürümqi are the main transport hubs, with frequent trains and flights from Beijing, Xi'an, Guangzhou and Shanghai. Ürümqi is also linked by air with Tashkent and other Central Asian cities, and by train to Almaty.

Getting around the region

Lanzhou: Trains going west stop at Jiayuguan (11 hours), Liuyuan/Dunhuang (14 hours), Daheyan/Turpan (22 hours) and Ürümqi (24 hours). There are 3 direct buses daily from Lanzhou to Xiahe (6 hours); more frequent buses travel via Linxia.

Dunhuang: Train departures from Dunhuang include Jiayuguan (6 hours), Lanzhou (11 hours), Turpan (11 hours), Ürümqi (14 hours), Xi'an (24 hours) and Yinchuan (18 hours).

Ürümqi: There are flights to Lanzhou and Kashi; there are also daily train departures to these cities (25 and 23 hours respectively), though domestic flights have become so cheap that these are rarely used. Trains also leave daily for Kuqa (14 hours). Buses go to Turpan, Kuqa and Kashi.

Turpan: Buses to the nearest train station (Daheyan) run every 30 minutes. There are buses to Ürümqi (5 hours), Kuqa (15 hours) and Kashi (26 hours).

Kashi: There are bus connections between Kashi and Ürümqi (24 hours), Turpan and Taxkorgan (6 hours).

region, **Yinchuan** (银川) was formerly the capital of the non-Chinese Xi Xia dynasty, obliterated by Genghis Khan. The **Ningxia Museum** (宁夏博物馆; Ningxia Bowuguan; Tue–Sun 9am–4.30pm; free) on Jinning Nan Jie has wide-ranging displays on the Xi Xia dynasty and Hui culture. In the courtyard stands **Xi Ta** (西塔; West Pagoda; same hours), which you can climb for views over town.

The land around Yinchuan is rich in interest, with the fascinating **Xi Xia Wangling** (西夏王陵; Western Xia Tombs; daily 8am–6pm) just 20km (12 miles) to the west. Near **Qingtongxia**, 80km (50 miles) south, the 108 Dagobas (青铜峡 一百零八塔; Qingtongxia Yibailingba Ta; daily 8am–6pm) are an otherworldly collection of stupas arranged in rows. The town of **Zhongwei** (中卫) in the west of the region is famed for its multi-faith Gao Miao (Gao Temple), originally constructed in the 15th century. The Huang He can be visited at **Shapotou** (沙坡头), and fragments of the Great Wall snake to the north along the fringes of the Tengger Desert.

WESTERN GANSU

From Lanzhou, Gansu province extends northwestwards in a great arc to the border with Xinjiang. The varied loess landscape and the diverse desert moods make the overland journey between Lanzhou and Jiuquan, an ancient crossroads and garrison town, truly extraordinary. In the south, the distant snow-covered peaks of Qilian Shan flank the railway line. The train reaches a flat, 800km (500-mile) long corridor when it arrives at the old administrative and garrison town of **Wuwei** (武威). The famous "Flying Horse", an Eastern Han-period bronze statue, was excavated nearby in 1969.

The next point of interest, **Zhangye** (张掖), lies 140km (87 miles) to the west. Founded in 121 BC as a garrison town, its most notable sight is China's longest reclining Buddha, a supine 35 metres (115ft), housed in the **Dafo Si** (大佛寺; Big Buddha Temple; daily 8am–6pm). Zhangye's wooden pagoda (Mu Ta) dates from the Tang period (its first six floors are made of brick), and there is also a fine 16th-century *Gulou* (Drum Tower) in the geographical centre of the city.

Jiuquan ❸ (酒泉), a thriving industrial town 200km (125 miles) further west, was founded in 111 BC as a garrison outpost. Between 127 and 102 BC, the Han emperors relocated nearly a million peasant families here, including at least 700,000 victims of a devastating flood in Shandong. Today, the Old Town Quarter around the drum and bell towers is changing: small alleys are being torn down and modern buildings erected. The town's more recent attraction is the **Silk Route Museum** (酒泉丝绸之路博物馆; daily), which opened in 2009 and is spread out across an enormous sprawling site. The museum houses over 35,000 artefacts including well-preserved frescoes from the Wei Jin tomb, fossils, Buddhist temple carvings and a large selection of jade figurines.

Xiahe, which has grown up around Labrang Monastery, is one of the largest Tibetan cultural centres outside of Tibet proper (Xizang province).

Out in the Gobi desert, at Jiuquan Satellite Launch Center, China's ambitious commercial space programme launches Long March rockets into the heavens.

JIAYUGUAN

Some 30km (20 miles) further on is **Jiayuguan ④** (嘉峪关), a historic fortress town close to the western end of the Great Wall – almost 5,000km (3,100 miles) from Beijing – built to guard the pass between the Qilian Shan and Hei Shan mountain ranges.

Completed in 1372, just four years after the rise of the Ming dynasty, the fort (daily summer 8.30am–8pm, winter until 6pm) was historically the last bastion of imperial China. Beyond it lay the barbarian lands. The structure comprises a square inner courtyard enclosed by walls and two gates. On top of the 10-metre (33ft) high, 640-metre (2,100ft) long wall are 17-metre (56ft) high watchtowers from the late Ming and the early Qing periods. The wall was first restored around 1507, again during the Qing period, and

again in recent years for the benefit of tourists. The structure, which dominates the landscape and is particularly impressive when approached from the west, can also be viewed from a distance on the train bound for Liuyuan.

A monument with the inscription "Strongest Fort of the World" has stood outside the western gate since 1809, while at the southern entrance is an elevated pavilion-like stage: dignitaries used to watch plays from the pavilion opposite on the right-hand side. Within the complex is the **Great Wall Museum** (entrance included with fort admission).

Some 8 km (5 miles) northwest of the fort is the last section of wall, known as the Overhanging Great Wall, most of which has been restored in recent years. There are sweeping views of the landscape from its battlements.

Weijin Bihua Mu (魏晋壁画墓), eight tombs from the Wei (AD 220–65) and the Jin (AD 265–420) dynasties, are 20km (12 miles) to the northeast of Jiayuguan. They contain wall murals with scenes from daily life, but only one of the eight tombs is open to visitors.

Jiayuguan fort with the forbidding Qilian Shan mountains in the background.

Consequently, few foreign tourists make it out here.

DUNHUANG

The town of **Dunhuang** ❺ (敦煌), in an irrigated cotton-producing oasis, is on many people's itineraries as it is the base for visiting the magnificent Mogao Caves. The 2006 opening of a branch line connecting with the main Lanzhou–Xinjiang railway has made it far more accessible.

About 40km (25 miles) before Dunhuang, near the road, is a well-preserved watchtower dating from 1730, an example of the type of communications used at that time. By daylight, flag signals were given from the top platform; at night, fire signals lit the skies. After crossing the drained plain of Shule He, remnants of the Great Wall from the Eastern Han period are visible.

Between cotton fields and threshing areas at the edge of the town, **Baima Ta** (敦煌白马塔; White Horse Dagoba) is reminiscent of Beijing's White Dagoba. Baima Ta is where the white horse of the famous travelling Indian monk

The Mingsha Shan near Dunhuang.

Kumarajiva (AD 344–431) is said to have died. The **Dunhuang Xian Bowuguan** (敦煌县博物馆; County Museum; Tue–Sun May–Sept 8.30am–6.30pm, Oct–Apr 9am–6pm; free) has some local finds, visual displays and models of the oasis, reflecting the historic significance of this settlement, as well as a few manuscripts from the Mogao Caves.

MOGAO CAVES

The most important attraction in northwest Gansu and the main reason most Silk Road travellers and Buddhist pilgrims visit Dunhuang, are the **Mogao Caves** (莫高窟; Mogao Ku; daily May–Oct 8am–6pm, Nov–Apr 9am–5.30pm). Located about 25km (16 miles) southeast of the town centre and readily accessible by taxi or minibus, the caves were cut into the soft rock face of the **Mingsha Hills** (鸣沙山; Mingsha Shan) over a period of more than 1,000 years, from the 3rd to the 14th centuries. They represent China's most extensive collection of Buddhist statuary, paintings and manuscripts, though many of the original materials are now in

foreign museum collections, especially in Europe and Japan. Mingsha Shan itself is a mountain range of pure sand, imposingly etched against a cloudless blue sky. Watching the sunset from the top is an unforgettable experience.

Having suffered many depredations at the hands of robbers, warlords, iconoclastic Muslims and Red Guards over the years (but none so damaging to the Mogao Caves, at least, as their late 19th–early 20th-century discovery by archaeologist-explorers like Aurel Stein and Paul Pelliot), the cave complex is now extremely well cared for. Visitors cannot enter without a guide, photography is strictly forbidden, and generally the only illumination available will be the guide's torch – to prevent the murals fading over time.

Almost 500 caves survive, set back against and cut into the cliff face, and connected by a series of ramps and walkways. Not all the caves are open to the public – even accompanied by an obligatory guide – and it may be necessary to make special arrangements (and payment) with the Mogao authorities to explore further such off-limits grottoes. An estimated 45,000 sq metres (484,000 sq ft) of murals and more than 2,000 painted stucco figures can be seen, though it would take considerable dedication and several days to try to visit all of them.

The years of darkness have kept the generally pastel colours fairly bright, and it is a wonderful experience, even to the lay person with limited knowledge of Buddhist art, to wander through the caves as the torchlight reveals image after image derived, variously and distinctively, from South Asian, Gandharan, Turkic, Tibetan and Chinese traditions. A well-presented museum in front of the caves features examples of the astonishing number of scripts found on manuscripts and other documents preserved at the caves, including writings not just in Chinese and Sanskrit, Tocharian and Tibetan languages, but also in various Turkic dialects, Persian and even Hebrew.

The grottoes show an uninterrupted history of Chinese painting, particularly of landscapes, over a period of nearly 1,000 years. One of the most beautiful caves (no. 323) shows an Indian Buddha statue made from sandalwood being presented to the reigning emperor. Most impressive is a 35-metre (115ft) high statue of Maitreya Buddha carved into the cliff face.

WEST TO XINJIANG

China's Central Asian backyard, the autonomous region of **Xinjiang** (新疆) is a huge expanse of desert and mountains bordered to the north by Mongolia, to the south by Tibet and to the west by the ex-Soviet republics of Kazakhstan, Kyrgyzstan and Tajikistan. It is predominantly Islamic, with the Muslim Uighur people accounting for approximately 45 percent of the total population. The proportion of Han Chinese, however, has increased from 8 percent in 1940 to almost 50 percent today, with migrants lured by financial incentives offered by

Tip

To get to the Mogao Caves you can take a regular bus, minibus or taxi for the 30-minute journey. From the centre of Dunhuang it's easy enough to find transport. Once you reach the caves you are obliged to join a guided tour to see a selection of the caves – there is no alternative.

Entrance to the Mogao Caves.

the government. As in Tibet and Inner Mongolia, the Han are concentrated in the larger cities; smaller oases and nomadic areas are still dominated by Uighurs and Kazakhs.

Economic deprivation and a sense of political and social subordination to the Han have resulted in ongoing calls for separatism among the Uighur population. Tension between the two communities regularly erupts into violence and subsequent repression, most severely in summer 2009 when an Uighur mob rioted and killed 200 people and were then subject to retaliatory attacks from the Han.

TURPAN

One of the most rewarding cities in the region is **Turpan** ❻ (吐鲁番; Tulufan), a remote Silk Road oasis and the first place of significance reached on the route west from Gansu. It is 11 hours by train from Dunhuang and and a half hours by bus from Ürümqi, although access is not straightforward as the nearest railway station is at Daheyan, 60km (37 miles) from the town.

Turpan's Emin Mosque and Minaret.

Turpan is atmospheric, although only a handful of old buildings have been preserved. **Sugong Ta** (苏公塔; Emin Minaret), built with clay bricks in 1777 and finished in 1788, and the sparsely furnished mosque next to it are the symbols of the town, and have been designated a historical monument. Sugong Ta's 72 steps leading to the top are closed to visitors. The mosque, the largest in Turpan, can hold up to 3,000 people and is used only during important Muslim festivals.

In an ancient and fantastic underground irrigation system – the Karez wells – snowmelt from the mountains is channelled to the oasis over long distances underground (to prevent the water from evaporating) using the force of gravity. The subterranean canal system is over 3,000km (1,860 miles) long.

Turpan Museum (吐鲁番博物馆; Tulufan Bowuguan; daily 10am–7pm; free) on Gaochang Lu is worth visiting. The second largest museum in Xinjiang, it houses an intriguing collection of funerary goods, mummies, silks and painted figurines excavated at the nearby Astana Tombs some 40km (25 miles) to the east.

To the northeast of town, **Putao Gou** (葡萄沟; Grape Valley; daily) is the most celebrated of Turpan's extensive vineyards and a must on every tour-group itinerary. Turpan has been cultivating grapes for almost two millennia, and today more than 100 varieties are grown, accounting for around 90 percent of China's seedless grape produce. In times past, the most valued variety of grape, known as *manaizi* or "mare's nipple" grapes, formed part of Turpan's tribute to the Chinese court at Xi'an and later Beijing. Today the grape harvest contributes substantially to the wealth of the oasis and its people, and vines are cultivated just about everywhere they can be grown, for fruit, wine and indeed shade. To celebrate this bounty, an annual Turpan Grape Festival is held each August–September at the end of the harvest.

AROUND TURPAN

Turpan lies within the **Turpan Basin** (吐鲁番盆地; Tulufan Pendi), some 150km (93 miles) long from east to west and, at 150 metres (490ft) below sea level, second in the low-altitude stakes only to the Dead Sea in Israel. The exact low point is Aydingkol Hu (Moonlight Lake), a salt lake in the basin that is drying up and is 154 metres (500ft) below sea level. In summer, the temperature here can rise to 47°C (117°F).

Stretching 100km (60 miles) to the east, the **Huoyan Shan** (火焰山; Flaming Mountains) are a range of bare sandstone mountains rising up to 1,800 metres (5,900ft), which achieved fame in the novel *The Journey to the West*.

Some 45km (28 miles) to the southeast of Turpan is the ruined city of **Gaochang** (高昌), the ancient Karachotcha or Khocho. Founded as a garrison under the Han emperor Wudi (140–86 BC), during its heyday the town had 30,000 inhabitants, over 3,000 monks and more than 40 Buddhist monasteries. Today, one can see the division of the town into a centre with sacred buildings and suburbs with bazaars and housing estates.

The **Astana Ancient Tombs** (阿斯塔那古墓; Asitana Gumu), 6km (4 miles) to the northwest, are a burial ground for Gaochang's dead. There are over 500 tombs, although only three are open to visitors, and with many archaeological remains having been carted off to museums, few visitors make the effort to visit.

To the north of Gaochang is the ancient cave monastery of **Bezeklik** ❼ (柏孜克里千佛洞; Bozikeli Qian Fo Dong; daily 8am–4pm). The trip through the canyon leading to Bezeklik begins

Bactrian camels, a mainstay of Silk Road transport, have been domesticated for around 2,500 years. They can survive for five days without water, carry heavy loads and move surprisingly quickly. They also produce milk and wool, and their dung can be used as fuel for fires.

A vine-covered arbor, Turpan.

at a watchtower dating from the Qing period (around 1770), located opposite the cave monastery site Samgin (Murtuq), used from around 450 to the 1200s. The caves of Bezeklik – there are around 80, of which only five can be visited – have been carved into the cliff face some 80 metres (260ft) above the western bank of the river.

The plunder of valuable paintings by German and British archaeologists damaged the pictorial representation of the Buddha and Bodhisattva (redemption deities) in several caves. After 1860, Islamic fanatics destroyed most of the facial depictions, a legacy of destruction that continued with the Cultural Revolution in the late 1960s. What remains in the caves is underwhelming, but the caves themselves are still an impressive sight, and the setting is superb.

About 30km (19 miles) southeast of Bezeklik and 70km (43 miles) east of Turpan, near the eastern rim of the Turpan Basin, the traditional Uighur village of **Tuyoq** (吐峪沟; Tuyugou; daily) offers a fascinating opportunity to visit a remote and traditional Uighur community set in a narrow valley in the southern flanks of the Flaming Mountains. There is only one road into the village, and tourists have to pay a fee to enter.

There are numerous caves set high into the steep mountainside above the village, but they are all but inaccessible, and such artistic treasures as they once held have mainly either been destroyed or dispersed to museums in China and Europe. Yet the appeal of Tuyoq is less these caves than the village's idyllic setting and bucolic charm. Mud-brick houses and courtyards surrounded by lush grapevines cluster in the valley around the green-and-white mosque, while a locally revered shrine surmounted by a green dome, the Tomb of the Seven Sleepers, dominates the hillside above the settlement. The local Uighur people, amiable but shy, do not permit non-Muslims to enter either the shrine or the dusty cemetery that abuts it.

Predating even Gaochang is the ruined city of **Jiaohe Gucheng** (交河故

The ruined city of Gaochang.

城), which in the past was called Yariko or Yarkhoto. Lying 10km (6 miles) to the west of Turpan, it was founded in the Han period and served as the centre of a kingdom until the 5th century. Jiaohe lies on a plateau on a sharp curve of a river – a natural fortification. Civil wars and lack of water at the time of Mongol rule in the early 13th century brought the town to ruins. The central sacred site and the remnants of Buddhist monasteries and stupas in the northwest, which are most prominent among the ruins, are still well preserved. The remains of underground dwellings, which offered protection from the summer heat and the arctic winter, are of special interest.

ÜRÜMQI

The road from Turpan to Ürümqi leads westwards across the lunar-like Turpan depression before reaching the Baiyang He, a pass which leads to a completely different landscape. The route travels along the richly forested valley of the **Baiyang He** (White Poplar River) and then through pastures along the northern slope of Tian Shan before arriving in Ürümqi (186km/116 miles from Turpan).

The capital of Xinjiang autonomous region, **Ürümqi ❽** (乌鲁木齐; Wulu-muqi) is a large city 186km (116 miles) west of Turpan and 900 metres (2,900ft) above sea level. It has the dubious honour of being the world's most continental city – situated further from the sea than any other. Over 80 percent of its 2.8 million population are Han Chinese. The city has little ethnic character, and industrial proliferation has resulted in high levels of pollution, particularly in the freezing winter.

The **Xinjiang Sheng Bowuguan** (新疆省博物馆; Regional Museum; Tue–Sun mid-Apr–mid-Oct 10am–6pm, mid-Oct–mid-Apr 10.30am–6pm; free) is worth a visit. Apart from significant archaeological finds, it also exhibits life-sized models of the houses and tools of the nationalities in the region. The highlight, however, is the display of some 3,000-year-old mummies of European, Kashmiri and East Asian ancestry found in Xinjiang (one

Hami is famous for its deliciously sweet melons (Hami Gua).

The sands of the Taklamakan Desert.

academic even postulates a Celtic connection after an analysis of the weave and dye of their clothing).

HEAVENLY MOUNTAINS

Definitely worthy of exploration is the breathtaking **Tian Chi** ❾ (天池; Lake of Heaven), some 110km (68 miles) east of Ürümqi on the slopes of Tian Shan (天山), at the foot of the high Bodga range. The road between Ürümqi and Tianchi passes through some ravishing scenery. The lake has a developed tourist arrival area, but trails and walks into the surrounding hills get you away from the hubbub. It's a great idea to stay the night here: some travellers intend to visit for a couple of days and end up staying for weeks in lakeside yurts where local Kazakh families dwell.

SILK ROUTES TO KASHI

The long journey from Ürümqi and Turpan west to Kashi (Kashgar) was historically one of the most treacherous on the Silk Road, a brutal stretch of desert infested with bandits and plagued either by intense heat or extreme cold. There were in fact two principal routes: a northern road, from Korla to Kashi via Kuqa and Aksu; and a southern, starting from Dunhuang and running along the northern edge of the Kunlun Shan via Khotan and Yarkand. Both routes pass along the edges of the formidable Taklamakan Desert (whose name is popularly mistranslated into "he who goes in does not come out"). As elsewhere on the Silk Road, the predominant theme is barren landscapes punctuated by the irrigated fields and poplar trees of the occasional oasis.

Korla ❿ (库尔勒; Kuerle) is an important transport hub and something of a boomtown, with a high proportion of Han Chinese. **Kuqa** (库车; Kuche) was formerly an important staging post on the Silk Road. The area around this Uighur town is rich in ancient pre-Islamic city ruins; to the west are the **Kezier Qianfodong** (克孜尔千佛洞; Kizil 1,000 Buddha Caves), although only a few are open to tourists. A relatively short distance west, the industrial city of **Aksu** (阿克苏) is

Tian Chi (Heaven Lake).

of limited interest, although it makes a good stopping point en route to Kashi, with a good range of hotels and restaurants.

The southern route has long descended into obscurity, but at one time the settlements along its barren length were thriving centres of commerce. The most significant was **Khotan ⑪** (和闐; Hotan/Hetian), centre of an early Buddhist empire in the 3rd century BC, when the eldest son of the Indian emperor Asoka is said to have settled there. The city was for a time one of the greatest on the Silk Road, famed for its jade and its carpets, and is claimed to have been the first place outside Han China to have cultivated silk. There is little of the Old City remaining, but it remains an atmospheric place, largely Uighur in identity.

A long trawl further west, **Yarkand ⑫** (莎車; Shache) has retained a picturesque charm and is one of the least modernised cities in China.

KASHI (KASHGAR)

On the Tumen River in the middle of an irrigation oasis that nurtures cotton and other crops, **Kashi ⑬** (喀什; Kashgar) lies closer to Islamabad, Delhi, Kabul, Tehran and even Baghdad than it does to Beijing, with the borders of Kyrgyzstan, Tajikistan, Afghanistan and Pakistan close by.

One of the most famous of all the Silk Road towns, today Kashi is changing fast. Once ringed by crenellated walls and staunchly Uighur, it is becoming increasingly Chinese, as waves of settlers from the east follow the railway (completed in 1999) from Turpan and Ürümqi to seek their fortune in China's "Wild West". Large parts of the Old City have been demolished in recent years, although the authorities have now belatedly recognised that what remains of the **Old Town** (老城; Altyn Shahr/Laocheng; daily) is a valuable tourist asset and should be preserved.

Old Kashgar is best seen to the west of **Id Gah Square** (艾提朵尔广场; Aitikaer Guangchang) – where parts of the ancient city wall are still extant to the west of Seman Lu; another section of the Old Town has been preserved to the east of Id Gah Square and is now actively promoted as a tourist attraction. The square itself is teeming with snack bars, teahouses, craft shops, workshops and numerous small stores selling everything from flowers to cameras. There has also been a proliferation of modern shopping centres blaring out loud Uighur music.

Id Gah Mosque ⓐ (艾提朵 尔清真寺; Aitika Qingzhensi) has been renovated many times and is China's largest mosque, able to hold 6,000 worshippers. Although paint is peeling off its central dome and two flanking minarets, the building, dating from 1442, still dominates its surroundings. Behind the gate are tree-lined squares for prayer. Some 100 metres (330ft) behind is the Great Prayer Hall, open only for Friday prayer. The steps in front of the side walls are a popular meeting place,

Uighur schoolgirls in Kashi.

Silk fabric at the Sunday Market in Kashi.

particularly for the elderly. On religious feast days, up to 50,000 worshippers come for Friday prayer.

To the north of the mosque and square runs an extremely lively bazaar street of barber shops, book and fur traders, blacksmiths, bakers, tailors and, directly by the mosque, dentists. The covered bazaar has just about anything for sale.

The most important weekly event is the *basha*, or **Sunday market** Ⓑ (Xingqiri Shichang or Yekshenba Bazaar), still held by the banks of the Tumen River. Tens of thousands of visitors and buyers and sellers come to this market from all around, giving it a cosmopolitan atmosphere.

Another major Uighur site is the **Tomb of Yusup Has** Ⓒ (哈斯哈 吉南 墓; Hasihaji Nanmu; daily 8am–6pm; charge for non-Muslims), around 2km (1.5 miles) southeast of Id Gah Square. Yusup Has was the author of the Uighur text *Qutatu Bilik* or *Benefical Lore*, one of the greatest works of Uighur literature, and together with Mahmud Kashgari remains among the

most respected and revered of Uighur intellectuals.

About 5km (3 miles) northeast of town is **Xiangfei Mu** (香妃墓), the Abakh Hoja mausoleum, dating back to the 16th century and renovated in 1980 and again in 1997. All the buildings of the mausoleum are examples of traditional Uighur architecture. Abakh Hoja (Aba Hezhuo), who died in 1695, was an outstanding political and Muslim religious leader in Kashi. His sarcophagus, one of 57 in the mausoleum that houses his descendants, lies on an elevated pedestal in the centre of the central building's main hall, which is reminiscent of a mosque (but not facing Mecca), and is flanked by a slightly leaning minaret. In the near left corner is the sarcophagus of Xiangfei (Fragrant Concubine), the daughter of the last Hoja, Ali Hoja, and the great-granddaughter of Abakh Hoja, and source of the mausoleum's popular name. According to legend, Xiangfei is said to have refused to sleep with the emperor Qianlong, who had abducted and taken her to Beijing

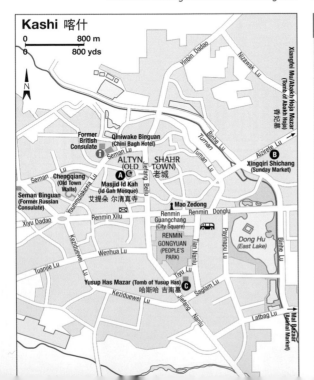

Kashi 喀什

⊙ THE GREAT GAME

During the late 19th and early 20th centuries, Kashi was at the very centre of the "Great Game". Both the British and the Russians maintained consulates in this remote but strategically significant oasis. The diplomatic representatives of these two great powers lived and competed with each other in this distant locale, plotting and planning each other's downfall while at the same time meeting for dinner and drinks on a regular basis; driven to friendship by isolation, while at the same time serving the interests of their masters in London and Moscow. The **former British Consulate**, known as Chini Bagh or "Chinese Garden", is located behind the Chini Bagh Hotel (Qiniwake Binguan) on Seman Lu, while the **former Russian Consulate** survives at the Seman Binguan, also on Seman Lu.

after the repression of a rebellion here in 1758. Since she would not consummate the relationship, she was forced to commit suicide by the empress dowager, the emperor's mother. Her body was taken back to Kashi in a carriage, the remnants of which are exhibited in the small mosque.

AROUND KASHI

About 35km (21 miles) northeast of town lie the remains of **Ha Noi Ancient City** (罕诺依故城; Hanuoyi Gucheng) and **Mor Pagoda** (莫尔佛塔; Muer Fota), both dating from the pre-Islamic period when Buddhism flourished in Xinjiang, and contemporaneous with other abandoned cities in the Taklamakan Desert such as Niya and Karahoja. Thought to have flourished between the 7th and 12th centuries AD, there's little enough to see nowadays, though the well-preserved remains of the Mor Pagoda are clearly indicative of the Buddhist civilisation that once flourished here.

More interesting (and harder to get to) is the natural phenomenon known as **"Shipton's Arch"** (天洞; Tiandong). Remote, unique and astonishing – yet only 40km (25 miles) from downtown Kashgar – this is considered to be by far the largest natural rock arch anywhere in the world. Discovered by British mountaineer and Kashgar-based diplomat Eric Shipton (1907–77), it is located in the heart of the remote canyons of the inaccessible Kara Tagh or Black Mountains. Known in Turkic as Tushuk Tash or "Pierced Rock", and in Chinese as Tiandong or "Heavenly Gap", its location was completely forgotten in the troubled years following the Chinese Communist seizure of power in 1949, and the arch was only rediscovered (and permanently located using GPS technology) by a National Geographic expedition in 2000.

The **Mausoleum of Mahmud al Kashgari** (马哈茂德陵墓; Mahamaode Lingmu; 1008–1105) was built outside Kashi. The building, which is about 45km (28 miles) away along the road to Pakistan, towers over a mosque once destroyed in an earthquake. Mahmud

The shores of Karakul Lake surrounded by the High Pamirs.

came from the house of the ruling Karachanid family and was one of the most important scholars of his time. Exiled from Xinjiang after the clan's overthrow in 1058, he returned to Kashi shortly before his death.

About 20km (12 miles) north of Kashi, the Buddhist **Sanxian Dong** (三先洞; Caves of the Three Immortals), on a sheer rock face by the Qiakmak River, are not only less interesting than those of Bezeklik or Dunhuang, but are relatively inaccessible and not worth the effort.

Further to the southwest, 200km (125 miles) from Kashi at the beginning of the high peaks of the Pamir range, is **Karakul Lake** (卡拉库尔湖; Kalakuer Hu). The ice-covered peaks of Muztagata (7,546 metres/24,755ft) and Kongur (7,719 metres/25,324ft), the second- and third-highest peaks in the Pamirs, can be seen from Kashi on clear days.

TAXKORGAN

The Karakoram Highway.

About 250km (155 miles) south of Kashi on the **Karakoram Highway** en route to Pakistan is **Taxkorgan** ⑭ (塔什库尔干; Tashikuergan), 3,600 metres (11,800ft) above sea level and the last outpost in China before the Pakistan border. The town is the capital of an autonomous district of the same name. A majority of Tajik people live here. According to accounts by Ptolemy (around AD 140), traders from East and West used to trade goods in this area.

Continuing south from Taxkorgan leads to Pakistan's **Karakoram range** (喀拉昆仑山; Kalakunlun Shan), whose awesome craggy peaks contrast markedly with the more rounded Pamirs. The 750km (460-mile) long track across the 4,700-metre (15,420ft) high **Khunjerab Pass** (红其拉甫山口; Hongqilafu Shankou) ⑮ is sometimes difficult due to weather or sometimes to sectarian unrest. About 270km (170 miles) south of the pass is the nearest airport in Pakistan, at Gilgit. Along the road are numerous wall murals, engravings and sculptures from the era of the Silk Road, and the scenery en route is some of the most dramatic on earth.

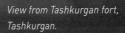

The Long Corridor at the
Summer Palace, Beijing.

CHINA

TRAVEL TIPS

TRANSPORT

On arrival

On arrival you will have to fill in a form with details of your health, and an entry card, on which you fill in details about the length of your stay in China. It will be put with your passport.

There are exchange bureaux at the arrival halls of airports, railway stations and ports where you can change money. The Chinese airlines provide buses that for a modest fare will take travellers from the airport, which is often a long way outside the city, to the airline offices in town.

You can also find taxis to your hotel, but be wary of people offering taxis away from taxi ranks. Before setting off in a taxi, agree on a price for the journey, or ensure that the driver agrees to use the meter.

By air

The following airports handle international flights:

Beijing

Beijing's Capital Airport, 25km (16 miles) from the centre, connects the city to all parts of China and to the world's major cities (http://en.bcia.com.cn; hotline: 010-96158). The journey into the city centre takes 30–60 minutes depending on traffic. Airport shuttle (Rmb 15–30) operates regularly to downtown Beijing, and many hotels offer car or minibus services.

Plentiful taxis are on hand, with security guards to ensure licensed drivers accept all passengers.

The Airport Line of Beijing's subway connects Terminals 2 and 3 with Dongzhimen (interchange for lines 2 and 13) and Sanyuanqiao (interchange for line 10).

Chengdu

Chengdu's Shuangliu Airport is 20km (12 miles) south the city centre (tel: 028-8520 5555). Several shuttle buses run from outside the departure hall to the downtown Chengdu stopping at various points along the way (Rmb 10). A taxi costs around Rmb 50 into the city centre. Beware of numerous touts luring travellers into unlicensed taxis.

Chongqing

Chongqing's Jiangbei Airport is 25km (16 miles) north of the city (tel: 023-966 666). Airport Express buses leave from Terminal 2 to the city centre. The airport is connected to Line 3 of the metro links the airport with the city centre. Metered taxis from the airport to town cost around Rmb 50.

International routes available into Chongqing include Macau, Nagoya, Seoul, Singapore and Bangkok.

Guangzhou

Guangzhou's Baiyun International Airport (tel: 020-3606-69995; www.baiyunairport.com) is 28km (17 miles) north of town and handles flights from various Asian cities as well as Los Angeles, Honolulu, Melbourne, Sydney, Amsterdam, Frankfurt, Paris and Addis Ababa. The airport is connected to Guangzhou subway system's Line 3, which terminates at Tianhe Coach Terminal. An interchange station with Line 2 leads conveniently to Guangzhou Railway Station and Guangzhou Railway Station South.

Shuttle buses connect the city with the airport (45 minutes), leaving from immediately outside both the domestic and international arrivals terminals every 20 minutes. Buy bus tickets for Rmb 15–30 after boarding. A taxi to or from the airport will cost around Rmb 150. Passengers must pay any road or bridge tolls.

Guilin

Liangjiang International Airport (tel: 0773-284 5359) is 28km (17 miles) from Guilin. It has direct flights from Hong Kong, Korea and Malaysia. The airport shuttle bus connects with flight arrivals and takes passengers to the Minhang Dasha building and train station on Shanghai Road in Guilin at a cost of around Rmb 20. The taxi fare will be around Rmb 150.

Hainan Island

Direct flights operate between the resort of Sanya and Hong Kong, as well as to most major domestic cities. There are also flights between the provincial capital Haikou and Singapore and Hong Kong.

Hong Kong

Hong Kong is a major international air-traffic hub for the region, so there is no shortage of flights. Flight time between London and Hong Kong is 10–12 hours.

Hong Kong's international airport (www.hongkongairport.com; tel: 852-2181 8888) is at Chek Lap Kok, a small island to the north of Lantau Island and about 30km (20 miles) from the main downtown area.

The Airport Express (AEL) is a comfortable train service that runs every 10 minutes and takes 24 minutes into town, offering the most convenient and cost-effective way (HK$90–100) to get to and from the airport (the journey by road via taxi or bus takes around 40 minutes and costs about HK$250 to Kowloon; HK$300 to Hong Kong Island).

There are numerous buses linking the airport to the city and to destinations in Guangdong. The Airbus services (prefixed "A") run at regular intervals from 6am to midnight and cost around HK$35 to Tsim Sha Tsui and $40 to Central. Slower commuter buses are prefixed "E", and there are shuttle buses ("S") to Tung

Chung MTR station. There are also direct ferry services from the airport to Macau and Shenzhen.

Kunming and Jinghong

Kunming's Changshui International Airport, 25km (16 miles) from the city centre, is connected with Hong Kong, Bangkok, Chiang Mai, Kuala Lumpur, Seoul, Singapore, Vientiane and Yangon (Rangoon). The taxi fare to most of the city's hotels is about Rmb 50.

Macau

Macau International Airport is located on the east side of Taipa Island, and is linked by bridges to the downtown area. It generally takes less than 30 minutes to get from the airport to anywhere in Macau.

For transport to and from the airport there are authorised taxis and the regular AP1 bus, which serves major hotels, the ferry terminal and the border gate.

There are regularly scheduled flights between Macau and several cities in Asia, including Bangkok, Kuala Lumpur and Singapore.

Shanghai

Shanghai is one of China's main transport hubs, connected to a number of foreign destinations and almost all domestic locations. Most domestic and some international flights use the old airport at Hongqiao (http:// en.shairport.com; hotline: 021-96990), about 15km (9 miles) west of the city centre. The international airport in Pudong (http://en.shairport.com; hotline: 021-96990) is 45km (28 miles) east of the city centre. It has two terminals and the number of destinations served is steadily increasing.

From Hongqiao Airport it takes 30 minutes to the city. Hongqiao Terminal 2 connects directly to the Hongqiao Transport Hub, integrating with the city-wide metro system (Lines 2 and 10; about 30 minutes to People's Square), plus high-speed trains to Beijing, Nanjing, Hangzhou and beyond, and a long-distance bus terminal. Terminal 1 is accessible via metro line 10 only. Most hotels have shuttle buses. Otherwise, plenty of taxis are available right outside both terminals. Don't hire drivers who tout their services at the terminal entrances; their cars don't have meters and they will try to charge you exorbitant rates. To get into the city, most drivers use the expressway that connects to the ring road.

From Pudong a taxi will take approximately an hour (reckon on Rmb 150–200) to the city. Between Terminal 1 and 2 of Pudong Airport there are stations for both the Maglev and the metro. The high-speed Maglev train can rocket you at 431kmh (268mph) to Longyang Road Station (in the Pudong suburbs) in just 8 minutes. Trains run daily between 6.45am and 9.40pm at 15–20-minute intervals. A one-way ticket costs Rmb 50 (Rmb 40 with a same-day airline ticket). From the metro station you can take Line 2 to People's Square (approximately 25 minutes) and onward to Hongqiao Airport. The Line 2 metro actually connects Pudong and Hongqiao airports on an east–west route across the city, however the full trip takes almost 2 hours.

There are also multiple airport bus lines departing from both Terminals 1 and 2 of both airports. Airport Shuttle No. 1 connects Hongqiao and Pudong airports. The trip takes around 1 hour.

Shenzhen

Shenzhen Bao'an International Airport (www.szairport.com; tel: 0755-2345 6789) is one of China's busiest and handles flights to/from Bangkok, Ho Chi Minh City, Kuala Lumpur, Nagoya, New York, Seoul, Singapore, Taipei and Tokyo.

The airport is 35km (20 miles) west of downtown Shenzhen. Hotel (and other) shuttle buses take around 30 minutes from the Hong Kong land border, and also go to Hong Kong Airport. There is also a direct ferry link to Hong Kong Airport.

Line One of the city's metro opened an airport station in 2010, taking passengers to the city centre and the Hong Kong crossing at Luohu.

The main hall at the Southern Railway Station, Shanghai.

Ürümqi

The airport (www.xjairport.com; tel: 0991-380 1453) is 17km (11 miles) north of the city. Airport shuttle buses take passengers to the town centre for Rmb 15. China Southern customers can take a free shuttle bus to Southern Airlines Pearl International Hotel.

A taxi from the airport will cost around Rmb 40, or you can take bus No. 51, No. 27 or No. 535.

Ürümqi is connected via international flights to Almaty (Kazakhstan), Bishkek (Kyrgyzstan), Islamabad (Pakistan), Novosibirsk, Moscow (Russia), Tashkent (Uzbekistan) and Tehran (Iran).

Xiamen and Fuzhou

Xiamen's international airport (tel: 086-5929 6363) handles international flights to/from Bangkok, Jakarta, Kuala Lumpur, Manila, Niigata, Osaka, Penang, Seoul, Singapore, Taipei and Tokyo. Xiamen's airport is a 10-minute taxi hop from the city.

Fuzhou has a smaller airport, connected to Bangkok, Kuala Lumpur, Osaka and Singapore.

Xi'an

Xianyang airport (www.xxia.com; tel: 086-0299 6788) is about 40km (25 miles) northwest of Xi'an. Most major hotels offer limousine or bus transfers, which have to be arranged ahead of time. Shuttle buses depart from the airport's Terminal 1 from

There are plenty of internal flights all over China.

early morning until the last flight's arrival to the Melody Hotel (86 Xi Dajie) just to the west of the Bell Tower, to Xi'an railway station, and to several other destinations (Rmb 25).

A taxi into the city will cost around Rmb 130, but you may have to bargain hard as overcharging is common. The trip takes about 50 minutes.

Xi'an's airport connects it to most of the big cities in China, as well as to Nagoya and Hiroshima in Japan.

Airline offices

Beijing

Air Canada, Room C201, Lufthansa Centre, 50 Liangmaqiao Lu, www.air-canada.com, tel: 010-6468-2001.
Air China, Room 105, B Heqiao Building, 8 Guanghua Road, www.air china.com.cn, tel: 95583, 400-810 0999.
Air France, Beijing's Capital Airport, www.airfrance.com, tel: 400-880 8808.
Austrian Airlines, Unit C604, Kempinski Hotel, 50 Liangmaqiao Lu, www.austrian.com, tel: 010-6464 5999.
British Airways, Room 1910, 19th Floor, China World Office 1, 1 Jiaguomenwai Avenue, www.britishairways.com, tel: 400-650 0073.
Cathay Dragon, 28/F, East Tower, Twin Towers, B-12 Jiangguomenwai Dajie, www.dragonair.com, tel: 400-888 6628.
Cathay Pacific, 28/F, East Tower, Twin Towers, B-12 Jiangguomenwai Dajie, www.cathaypacific.com, tel: 400-888 6628.

China Eastern Airlines, 12 Xinyuanli Zhong Jie, Chaoyang District, www.flychinaeastern.com, tel: 010-95530.
Finnair, Room 204, Scitech Tower, 22 Jianguomenwai Dajie, www.finnair.com; tel: 010-6512 7180.
Japan Airlines, www.jal.com, tel: 400-888 5301.
KLM, www.klm.com, tel: 400-880 8222.
Korean Air, 901-3, Hyundai Motor Building, 38 Xiaoyun Lu, www.koreanair.com, tel: 400-658 8888, 010-8453 8137.
Lufthansa, www.lufthansa.com, tel: 4008 868 868.
Qantas, www.qantas.com, tel: 021-6145 0188.
Singapore Airlines, Unit 4303, Beijing Yin Tai Center Tower C, 2 Jian Guo Men Wai Avenue, www.singapore air.com, tel: 010-6505 2233.
Swiss International Airlines, S101 Lufthansa Centre, 50 Liangmaqiao Lu, www.swiss.com, tel: 010-8454 0180.
Thai Airways, Units 303–4, Level 3 Tower W3, Oriental Plaza, 1 East Chang'anjie, www.thaiairways.com, tel: 010-8515 0088.
United Airlines, www.united.com, tel: 400 883 4288.

Hong Kong

Air Canada, Hong Kong International Airport, www.aircanada.com, tel: 852-2867 8111.
Air China, Room 1906-1910, China Resources Building, 26 Harbour Road, Wanchai, www.airchina.hk, tel: 852-3970 9000.
Air France, Hong Kong International Airport, tel: 852-2501 9498.
Air New Zealand, Hong Kong International Airport, www.airnewzealand.com.hk, tel: 852-2862 8988.
American Airlines, Hong Kong International Airport, www.aa.com, tel: 852-3057 9197.
British Airways, www.britishairways.com, tel: 852-3071 5083.
Cathay Dragon, 7/F, The Cameron, 33 Cameron Road, Tsim Sha Tsui Kowloon, tel: 852-2747-3333.
Cathay Pacific, 7/F, The Cameron, 33 Cameron Road, Tsim Sha Tsui Kowloon, tel: 852-2747 3333.
KLM www.klm.com, tel: 852-2808 2168.
Lufthansa, www.lufthansa.com, tel: 4008 868 868.
Qantas, www.qantas.com, tel: 852 2298 8111
Singapore Airlines, 17/F, United Centre, 95 Queensway, Admiralty, www.singaporeair.com, tel: 852-2520 2233.
Virgin Atlantic Airways, 18/F, Alexandra House, 15–20 Chater Road,

⊘ Plane tickets

Domestic plane tickets (usually very easy to obtain) are generally sold as one-way tickets, with return fares simply being twice the one-way fare. Ask for discounts, which are generally available from travel agents and airline offices.

Central, www.virgin-atlantic.com, tel: 852-2532 3030.

Shanghai

Air Canada, Room 3901, 1468 Nanjing Road (W), www.aircanada.com, tel: 010-6468-2001.

Air China, 199, YingBin San Rd, Hongqiao International Airport, www.air.china.com.cn, tel: 95583, 400-810 0999.

Air France, Shanghai Pudong Airport, Terminal 1, tel: 400-880 8808.

All Nippon Airways, Room 201, Longemont Yes Tower, 369 Kaixuan Road, www.ana.co.jp, tel: 400-882 8888.

British Airways, Floor 11, Sea of Clouds, 118 Qing Hai Road, tel: 021-6375 8385.

Cathay Dragon, Room 1605-1608, 1788 Nanjing Road (W), www.dragon air.com, tel: 400-888 6628.

Cathay Pacific, Room 1605-1608, 1788 Nanjing Road (W), www.cathay pacific.com, tel: 400-888 6628.

China Eastern Airlines, 258 Weihai Road, www.flychinaeastern.com, tel: 021-95530.

Delta Airlines, Unit 2105-2106, Park Place Plaza, 1601 Nanjing Road (W), www.delta.com, tel: 400-1202 364.

Japan Airlines, www.jal.co.jp, tel: 400-888 5301.

Lufthansa, www.lufthansa.com, tel: 4008 868 868.

Qantas, www.qantas.com, tel: 021-6145 0188.

Shanghai Airlines, 212 Jiangning Road, tel: 021-6255 8888.

Singapore Airlines, Room 1106–1110, Plaza 66, 1266 Nanjing Road (W), tel: 021-6288 7999.

United Airlines, www.united.com, tel: 400 883 4288 .

Virgin Atlantic, Suite 3221, Central Plaza, 381 Huaihai Road (Middle), www.virgin-atlantic.com, tel: 021-5353 4600.

Overland routes

Several of China's international borders are open for crossing by rail or road. Some frontiers, such as those with India and Bhutan, are restricted areas.

Kazakhstan

There is a daily bus service and a twice-weekly train service (around 30 hours) between Ürümqi and Almaty in Kazakhstan (you will need to obtain a visa in advance). A faster train is expected to connect Ürümqi and Almaty from June 2017.

Kyrgyzstan

It is possible to travel to Kashi from Bishkek in Kyrgyzstan over the Torugut Pass providing you have your own transport. Foreigners are not permitted to cross the border by bus.

Laos

From Laos, travellers can enter Mengla County in southern Yunnan at Boten in Luang Nam Tha province. It's possible to obtain a visa at the border. There are also passenger boats along the Mekong River between Jinghong and Chiang Saen in Thailand and buses between Jinghong and Luang Namtha in Laos.

Mongolia

It is possible to travel by train between China and Mongolia. There are also buses, but they tend to be slower and far less convenient than the rail links. (For details on trains between Moscow and Beijing which pass through Mongolia, see below.)

Myanmar (Burma)

A border crossing with Myanmar (Burma) opened in 1996, but the Burmese discourage foreigners from using it.

Nepal

You can generally cross the border between Tibet and Nepal at Zhangmu/ Kodari, but since the devastating Nepal earthquake of April 2015, the border has been closed to foreigners with no information on when it'll reopen). It's possible to travel by road between Kathmandu and Lhasa, but it requires considerable time, not only for travel, but for bureaucracy as well. You cannot obtain a Chinese visa at the border, and the most convenient approach is to join a tour to Lhasa in Kathmandu. Independent travellers should note that transport on the Nepal side is good, but scarce on the Tibetan side. Most travellers must plan on a vehicle hire/share to Lhasa.

Pakistan

It is possible to travel the Karakorum Highway between Islamabad and Kashi. Officially the border is open between April and October, though even those dates are weather-dependent: both snowfall and landslides regularly close the road. During this time, there are daily buses, weather permitting, between Taxkorgan and Kashi (5 hours). Note that immigration is at Taxkorgan, not at the top of the pass.

Russia/Mongolia

The 5- or 6-day odyssey on the Trans-Mongolian/Trans-Manchurian railways between Moscow and Beijing is one of the world's classic rail journeys. If arriving from Europe via the Trans-Manchurian or Trans-Mongolian railways (often called the Trans-Siberian, which in fact goes to Siberia's Pacific Coast, not China), all the same health and customs procedures apply as if arriving via an international flight.

There is a choice of two routes. The Chinese train – which is better-equipped and maintained – takes 5 days via Ulan Bator (Ulaanbaatar) through Mongolia, entering China via Erlian. The Russian train, which goes through Manchuria (Dongbei), takes a day longer, and enters China at Manzhouli. Both leave once a week from Moscow.

Depending on the type of train, there are two or three classes. Food on board is not included in the ticket price. If you want to interrupt the train journey in Russia for longer than 24 hours, you need a tourist visa and will have to produce proof that you have a hotel booking.

Vietnam

A twice-weekly train service connects Hanoi and Beijing (40 hours), via the so-called "Friendship Gate" between Pingxiang in China's Guangxi province and Dong Dang in Vietnam. It is also possible to cross the border here on foot and connect with bus routes on either side. The train stops at a number of cities in China, including Nanning, Changsha and Guilin.

You can also cross the border on foot at Hekou in the southeast of Yunnan province. A new railway line between Kunming and Hekou was inaugurated in 2014 and now four trains link the cities daily; buses plying the route are also plentiful.

Neither Vietnamese nor Chinese visas are available at these border posts – you will need to obtain a Chinese visa in advance from the embassy in Hanoi.

By sea

Japan

Several ships sail each week between Shanghai and Osaka, Japan, and a less regular service exists to Kobe. There is also a weekly boat between Kobe and Tianjin/Tanggu; trips take two days and can be booked through CITS.

South Korea

A ferry service is available from Inchon, South Korea, to Weihai, Qingdao, Tianjin and Dalian. The voyage between Inchon and Weihai takes about 18 hours, departing thrice weekly. Between Inchon and Qingdao the journey takes 15 hours, departing three times weekly. Between Inchon and Tianjin takes nearly 24 hours, operating every five days. Ferries between Dalian and Inchon sail three times weekly and take around 18 hours; tickets can be booked through CITS.

GETTING AROUND

Orientation

All main cities can be reached by plane, train and buses. The road network has been improved in recent years, even in the remote northern provinces, and in many places buses offer a quicker alternative to trains.

Road names

Street names are determined by the traditional chequerboard of Chinese urban design. The most important traffic arteries are divided into sectors and laid out in a grid typically based upon the compass points.

Suffixes are added to the primary name to indicate north (*bei*), south (*nan*), east (*dong*) or west (*xi*), and, additionally, to indicate the middle (*zhong*) section. A major urban highway is likely to be labelled *da dao'* (avenue) or *lu* (road). Slightly smaller roads may be known as *jie* (street). A small lane is *nong* or *xiang*.

In 2003 Shanghai changed all of its pinyin street names into English.

Lu became Road, and the suffixes *zhong, nan, bei, dong* and *xi* became Centre, South, North, East and West respectively. These appear in all listings in this book.

Domestic travel

Air

All of China's major cities are connected by domestic flights and the Chinese government is investing huge amounts of money to improve existing airports and add many new ones. Buying a return ticket on some routes is difficult, except to cities such as Beijing and Shanghai. For shorter journeys within China, the train is generally more enjoyable than travelling by plane, and there is a far lower chance of delays.

Air China (tel: 400-810 0999, global sales hotline) flies to more than 200 destinations within China; other major domestic airlines are China Eastern Airlines (hotline: 95530) and China Southern Airlines (domestic hotline: 4006695539-1-1020-412 3120), both of which operate on around 120 domestic routes.

For domestic departures you need to check in about 30 minutes before the flight, although Shanghai demands arrival one hour in advance.

Beijing, Shanghai and Hong Kong are the major transport hubs. Additional details are listed below.

Chengdu

Chengdu Shangliu Airport is the busiest airport in western China. All of China's major airlines operate out of Chengdu, making it possible to fly to almost any city in China, as well as 20 international destinations, including Amsterdam, Bangkok, Kuala Lumpur and Vancouver.

Chongqing

Chongqing's Jiangbei Airport is an important hub for Air China, Sichuan Airlines and Chongqing Airlines, offering frequent connections with several international destinations, and every major city in China and many minor ones.

Guangzhou

Domestic flights operate between Guangzhou and major cities in China. Tickets for internal flights are sold at the offices of the Chinese carriers and also at the China Southern Airlines main office at 181

Huanshi Donglu (tel: 020-95539), near the main train station.

Guilin

As the tourism hub of Guangxi province, Guilin has flights to almost every major city, including two flights a day to Hong Kong and at least six to Guangzhou and Beijing. The airport is about 28km (17 miles) from the city centre and there's a shuttle bus to the downtown area.

Kashi (Kashgar)

The airport is 11km (7 miles) north of the city. There is a regular bus service between the airport and the town costing Rmb 10. China Southern Airlines and Hainan Airlines have daily flights between Kashi and Ürümqi, and seats are not usually difficult to come by.

Kunming

Kunming is one of the home bases for China Eastern Airlines and for Lucky Air, which between them operate flights to destinations around Yunnan province, notably Dali, Mangshi (now known as Pu'er), Lijiang, Shangri-La, and Jinghong in Xishuangbanna.

Lanzhou

Lanzhou Airport is inconveniently located some 70km (43 miles) north of town. There are three Airport Express Shuttle bus lines going to Lanzhou (Rmb 30). Air China office is at 638 Donggang West Road 46 (tel: 0931-879 2902).

Taxi drivers charge between Rmb 150–200 for the trip, and bargaining is expected. Travellers with early-morning flights may want to spend the night before at one of hotels which are very close to the airport, such as the Kaida's Western Hotel (tel: 931-816 1555).

Lhasa (Tibet)

Gongar Airport (tel: 0891-6182220), with flights to a number of major Chinese cities, is over 60km (38 miles) from Lhasa. The bus ride (Rmb 30) takes about 2 hours.

Travelling hard-seat class.

Macau

There are regular scheduled flights between Macau and numerous cities in China.

Nanchang

The capital of Jiangxi is growing fast, as is its role as a transport hub. There are daily flights to Beijing, Guangzhou, Shanghai and Shenzhen, and several flights a week to other mainland cities.

⊙ Rail journey times

The distance and approximate travelling time from Beijing. (D) = bullet train:

Beijing to/Distance in miles (km)/Time (hours)
Chengdu/**1,273 (2,048)**/*25*
Chongqing/**1,586 (2,552)**/*24*
Datong/**249 (400)**/*6*
Dalian/**770 (1,239)**/*10*
Guangzhou/**1,437 (2,313)**/*10 (D)*
Guilin/**1,326 (2,134)**/*22*
Hangzhou/**1,026 (1,651)**/*6.5*
Harbin/**862 (1,388)**/*9 (D)*
Hohhot/**423 (680)**/*10.5*
Kunming/**1,975 (3,179)**/*38*
Lanzhou/**1,169 (1,882)**/*17*
Lhasa/**2,525 (4,064)**/*43*
Luoyang/**509 (819)**/*8*
Nanjing/**719 (1,157)**/*9.5*
Qingdao/**551 (887)**/*6 (D)*
Shanghai/**908 (1,462)**/*10 (D)*
Suzhou/**855 (1,376)**/*8.5*
Taiyuan/**319 (514)**/*8.5*
Ürümqi/**2,345 (3,774)**/*40*
Wuhan/**764 (1,229)**/*9 (D)*
Wuxi/**829 (1,334)**/*10.5*
Xi'an/**724 (1,165)**/*9 (D)*

Nanjing

Nanjing Lukou International Airport is about 35km (22 miles) from downtown Nanjing (tel: 025-5248 0315).

Shanghai

Most domestic flights use Shanghai's old airport at Hongqiao about 15km (9 miles) west of the city centre. Some domestic flights also leave from Pudong International Airport, approximately 45km (28 miles) east of the centre. For enquiries and ticket bookings at either airport, dial the Shanghai Airports hotline, tel: 021-96990.

Ürümqi

Within Xinjiang, there are flights from Ürümqi to Yining, Tacheng, Kelamayi (Karamai), Kashi (Kashgar), Akesu (Aksu), Hetian (Hotan), Kuche (Kuqa), Kuerle (Korla), Qiemo (Jumo) and Aletai (Altai). Ürümqi is connected via domestic flights to Beijing, Shanghai, Guangzhou, Changsha, Chengdu, Guilin, Xi'an, Zhengzhou, Tianjin, Fuzhou, Lanzhou and Chongqing.

Xi'an

Airlines flying to Xi'an daily include Air China, China Eastern Airlines, Hainan Airlines and Shanghai Airlines.

Chinese railways

The Chinese rail network comprises almost 121,000km (more than 75,000 miles), of which 65,000km (40,000 miles) are electrified. Average train speed is not very high, although increasing rapidly due to modernisation and investment programmes.

The D trains are high-speed bullet trains, which are much quicker but up to 50 percent more expensive than T express trains.

Tickets and Reservations

Demand for train tickets is usually high, so, wherever you want to travel to, it is advisable to buy your ticket as soon as reservations open. This varies between types of train and destinations. The usual maximum advance period is 10 days, but may be as long as 20 days for Z trains (high-speed long-distance trains), or as short as three days for local services. During the main travel season (Chinese New Year, and the 1 May and 1 October holiday periods it becomes nearly impossible to buy tickets to and from major cities.

There are special ticket counters for foreigners at railway stations. The price also depends on both the class and the speed of the train; there are slow trains, fast trains, express trains and inter-city trains. Reservations can be made at ticket offices downtown, through travel agencies or at your hotel, and this is the easiest option in many places, particularly if you want to travel at short notice. When boarding a train, allow plenty of time, as finding the platform and your allocated coach can be tricky.

In Hong Kong, tickets can be purchased through travel agents, hotels, CITS offices or at the Intercity Passenger Services Centre at Hung Hom railway station (daily 6.30am–8pm; tel: 852-2947 7888). In provincial cities, large hotels and the CITS office (for a list of these, see page 458) can help get train tickets.

Berth and seating options

There is no first or second class on classic Chinese trains, but four categories or classes: *ruanwo* or soft-sleeper, *ruanzuo* or soft-seat, *yingwo* or hard-sleeper, and *yingzuo* or hard-seat. The soft-seat class is usually only available for short journeys.

The new high-speed trains (category C, D and G) have the first and second class, both with soft seats. Seats in second class are very compact while first class seats are much larger. G-category high-speed trains also have a premium business class.

Long-distance trains normally only have soft-sleeper or

hard-sleeper facilities. The soft-sleeper class has four-bed compartments with soft beds, and is recommended, particularly for long journeys. The hard-sleeper class has open, six-bed compartments. The beds are not really hard, but are cramped and not very comfortable. While you can reserve a place for the first three classes (you always buy a ticket with a place number), this is not always essential for the hard-seat category.

There is always boiled water available on the trains. There are washrooms in the soft-sleeper and hard-sleeper classes. The toilets, regardless of which class, are usually not very hygienic, and it is a good idea to bring your own toilet paper. There are dining cars on long-distance trains.

Beijing

Beijing has three main railway stations: Beijing Zhan (Beijing Station), Beijing Xi Zhan (Beijing West Station) and Beijing Nan Zhan (South Station). Beijing Station is centrally located and connected to the subway system. The west station is out in the southwestern suburbs and less easily accessible. The South Station is connected to subway line 4 and provides super-fast bullet trains that reach nearby Tianjin in just 30 minutes. A few trains to other parts of China run from the city's three smaller stations.

It is possible to buy rail tickets through a travel agency, but it's cheaper to use the foreigners' booking office inside the railway station

itself. Most convenient are the many ticket agencies around town – look out for small shops marked with trains and planes on their signage.

Chongqing

Chongqing is connected via direct trains to Beijing (24 hours), Shanghai (27 hours), Chengdu (2.5 hours), Kunming (19 hours), Guangzhou (21 hours), Zhengzhou (17 hours), Yangzhou (32 hours), Wuchang (5 hours), Guiyang (9 hours), Nanning (22 hours) and more. Sleeper tickets can be bought at hotels and ticket agencies. Chongqing has Chongqing Station (重庆站) and a North Station (重庆北) the designated station will be printed on the ticket. Both stations are located along the Line 3 light rail.

Chengdu

Chengdu has three railway stations; the North and East stations are mostly used for passenger traffic while the South station is primarily a freight hub, although passenger trains departing for Xichang stop here. Tickets can be booked at the railway stations, but it's usually more convenient to book them at ticketing agents around the city (for example, at 1 Nijiaqiao Lu, just around the corner from Renmin Nan Lu). The North and South stations are connected to the city by subway, while the East station is connected only by bus. Trains depart daily to every major city in the country, including the train that runs along the world's highest railway to Lhasa. Very comfortable bullet trains depart hourly

to Chongqing (2 hours), Qingcheng Shan (40 minutes) and Dujiangyan (50 minutes).

Guangzhou

Trains arrive in Guangzhou either at the central Guangzhou railway station (Guangzhou Huoche Zhan) or at Guangzhou East railway station (Guangzhou Dong Zhan) in Tianhe in the city's eastern reaches. There are trains to and from most large cities in China, though all Hong Kong-bound trains depart from Guangzhou East.

In Guangzhou, most hotels and the CTS office can help get train tickets. There is approximately one departure every 10 minutes on the express trains between Shenzhen and Guangzhou. Travelling times range from 36 minutes to more than 2 hours.

Guilin

Guilin has two railway stations: the South station in the city centre and North station, inconveniently out in the suburbs. There are services to all main cities in China, and trains between Beijing and Vietnam pass through twice a week.

Hong Kong

Hung Hom station (tel: 852-2947 7888) in Kowloon has 12 departures a day to Guangzhou (see above), with a journey time of just under 2 hours. There is also a daily train to Foshan (just over 2 hours). Tickets can be bought through travel agents, hotels, CTS offices or at the station. A much cheaper alternative, or if

Long-distance road travel has vastly improved in recent years.

tickets to Guangzhou are sold out, is to take the MTR to the border terminus of Lo Wu (a 40-minute journey, with three departures an hour from 5.30am to 11pm), walk across the border to Shenzhen station and take a train from there.

Kunming

The main (Nanyao) railway station is just 4km (2.5 miles) from the city centre, with connections to all major cities in China.

Lanzhou

From Lanzhou, there are long-distance trains to Beijing, Shanghai, Xining, Ürümqi, Xi'an, Chengdu, Golmud and Lhasa (Tibet). Going west to Ürümqi (24 hours), trains stop at Jiayuguan (10 hours), Liuyuan, the train station serving Dunhuang (14 hours), and Daheyan, the station serving Turpan (22 hours).

Sleepers can be hard to come by if you try to reserve them yourself at the station. You would do better to go to a travel agency or through your hotel.

Lhasa (Tibet)

In 2006 the Qinghai–Tibet rail line became the highest railway in the world (topping the Andean former title-holder). The line is not without controversy, with concerns over its effects on the ecology of the Himalayas and the cultural integrity of the Tibet Autonomous Region. Nevertheless, it is a stunning feat of engineering and offers a breathtaking trip – both scenically and literally, since an extra oxygen supply has to be provided. The nearly 41-hour journey from Beijing to Lhasa (www.china tibettrain.com) covers 3,757km (2,35235 miles) and attains an altitude of more than 5,000 metres (16,650ft). Ticket prices range from Rmb 360 for a hard seat to Rmb 720 for a hard sleeper, Rmb 1,144 for a soft sleeper. Tourist trains offer sleeping carriages, full dining services and observation cars. Trains run daily from the following stations: Beijing West (tel: 010-9510 5105), Shanghai (tel: 021-9510 5105), Chengdu (tel: 028-9510 5105), Lanzhou (tel: 0931-9510 5105), Chongqing (tel: 023-9510 5105) and Xining (tel: 0971-9510 5105). Various stops are made along the way.

Shanghai

There are four main railway stations in Shanghai: Shanghai Railway

Station in the city's north, Shanghai South Railway Station to the south, Shanghai West Railway Station in the west and Shanghai Hongqiao Railway Station also in the west. The latter is the main station for high-speed bullet trains to Beijing, Hangzhou, Suzhou, Nanjing and other cities across the country.

Shanghai Railway Station and Shanghai South Railway Station are both reachable on metro line 1. Shanghai Hongqiao Railway Station is on lines 2 and 10, and Shanghai West Railway Station – on line 11. There are several high-speed trains a day to Suzhou (25 minutes), Hangzhou (45 minutes), Nanjing (75 minutes) and other nearby destinations. The bullet trains to Beijing have cut the trip to the Chinese capital to around 5 hours. There are multiple daily departures and the trains are very comfortable, with plenty of leg room and power sockets for computers. The express train to Hong Kong runs every day and takes 18 hours.

Train tickets can be purchased at railway stations, or at any of the official outlets that are scattered throughout town, with blue-and-white signs that say, in English: Booking Office for Train Tickets. Alternatively, you can buy tickets through CITS or any other travel agency, or at a number of hotels, for a small surcharge.

Ürümqi

The railway station is located at the southwestern end of town. From Ürümqi, domestic trains head east and south to Beijing, Shanghai, Zhengzhou, Chengdu and Xi'an, all of which stop at Lanzhou. Heading further west, a stretch of track links Ürümqi with Kashgar, via Kuqa, and the trip takes around 23 hours.

Between Ürümqi and Lanzhou, the stops include Daheyan (Turpan railway station), Hami, Liuyuan (serving Dunhuang) and Jiayuguan. As with rail travel out of Lanzhou, sleepers are difficult to come by.

Xi'an

There are trains from Xi'an to many large cities in China, including Beijing (9 hours by bullet train), Shanghai (14–19 hours), Guangzhou (21 hours), Chengdu (13 hours), Hefei, Wuhan, Qingdao, Lanzou and Ürümqi (27 hours). In Xi'an most hotels, travel agencies and CITS can help get train tickets. Xi'an has three stations, Xi'an Station, Xi'an North Station, which is along the Subway Line 2, and Xi'an South Station.

Xining

The railway station is on the eastern edge of the city, across the Huangshui River. It's about 3km (2 miles) into the city centre from here – take bus 2 or 28. There are rail links to major cities in eastern China.

Long-distance buses

Overland buses are the most important means of transport in many parts of China, especially where there is no railway line. In most towns and settlements there are main bus stations for overland buses. Although some rural bus journeys can be slow, China's enormously improved highway infrastructure makes major routes fast and reasonably safe. High-speed (gaosu) buses stick to the expressways and don't make regular stops to pick up passengers en route. There are regular breaks during bus journeys; on journeys lasting several days you will usually find simple restaurants and overnight accommodation near the bus stations. Some buses have numbered seats, but it is not usually necessary to book a ticket or seat in advance. Modern buses with air conditioning operate in tourist areas.

Beijing

Long-distance buses connect Beijing with many cities, including Tianjin, Chengde, Beidaihe, Taiyuan and Hohhot. On some routes buses are faster, but generally less comfortable, than trains.

Sleeper buses operate on longer routes. Buses are recommended for relatively short journeys to places such as Tianjin (2 hours) or Chengde (4 hours). Beijing's main long-distance bus stations are at Dongzhimen (for the northeast), Deshengmen (for Chengde), Zhaogongkou and Haihutun (for Tianjin and various cities in southern Hebei province).

Chengdu

Chengdu has numerous long-distance bus stations, and which one you use will depend on where you want to go; generally, choose the one that's located closest to your destination. Some of the busiest stations are Xinnanmen (city central), Wuguiqiao (southeast), Beimen (north central), and Jinsha (northwest). Buses are good for short trips within Sichuan that aren't accessible by train, such as the old towns in Luodai, Ping'le, Anren and Huanglongxi, and for other cities such as Zigong and Mianyang if the trains are all booked.

Chongqing

There are buses connecting Chongqing to many cities in Sichuan province, including Emei, Dazu, Leshan, Shazhou, Yibin and Neijiang, as well as other cities within the Chongqing municipality. The Caiyuanba long-distance bus station is next to the Chongqing Railway Station.

Guangzhou

The southern China transit hub, with 11 long-distance bus stations, can get travellers on the road to cities almost anywhere in Guangdong province as well as to Shanghai, Chongqing, the Guangxi region and the provinces of Fujian, Hainan, Hubei, Hunan, Jiangsu, Sichuan and Zhejiang. Major depots include the Guangzhou Provincial Long-Distance Bus Station at 145–149 West Huanshi Road and the Guangzhou Tianhe Long Distance Bus Station at 633 Yanling Road.

Guilin

The tourism hub of Guangxi province, Guilin is served by frequent and inexpensive buses to destinations within the province. Of Guilin's three bus stations, the main one is on Zhongshan Nan Lu.

Kashi (Kashgar)

The long-distance bus station is on Tiannan Lu, just south of Renmin Lu. There are daily buses from Kashi to Korla, Kuqa, Aksu, Hotan, Daheyan, Ürümqi and Yengisar.

Kunming

Kunming has four major bus stations, located in the north, south, east and west of the city, each of which serves destinations in their respective direction. Most useful for travellers, the West Bus Station, at the intersection of Chunyu Lu and Yining Lu, serves Dali, Lijiang, and Shangri-La. The South Bus Station, on Caiyun Bei Lu, serves Jinghong, Jianshui, and the borders with Laos and Vietnam.

Lanzhou

Travelling east from Lanzhou, there are long-distance buses going to Xi'an, Yinchuan and Guyuan. The long-distance bus station serving points east is on Pingliang Lu between Minzhu Lu and Jiuda Lu. Going west, buses serve Linxia, Xiahe and Hezuo.

The west bus station is at the western edge of town on Xijin Donglu. There are several buses a day serving Linxia and Hezuo, but only one direct bus to Xiahe, in the early morning. If you miss that service, you can always take one of the many buses going to Linxia, and change there for one of the many minibuses going to Xiahe.

Foreigners travelling in southern Gansu are required to buy travel insurance (even if they have their own travel insurance), and are not usually allowed to board the bus without it. You can purchase insurance at PICC, at travel agencies or directly at the bus stations.

Lhasa

The long-distance bus station is at the junction of Jinzhuzhong and Minzu roads. Services ply the Sichuan and Qinghai highways and destinations include Golmud, Lanzhou, Chengdu, Tongmai and Chongqing.

Nanchang

In Jiangxi, the regular, well-maintained buses provide the best means of transport within the province. This is particularly true on the modern high-speed expressways, where buses outperform trains in both speed and ease of buying tickets.

Shanghai

It's generally more convenient and comfortable to travel between Chinese cities via train rather than bus, although the city is connected to surrounding provinces by modern highways that have made travel immeasurably easier. Coaches to many destinations in Zhejiang, Jiangsu, Anhui, Shandong and other surrounding provinces depart from the Hongqiao Long-Distance Bus Station, attached to Hongqiao Railway Station. There are also regular departures from Shanghai South Long-Distance Bus Station and Shanghai North Railway Station. The Shanghai Tour Bus Centre at 2409 Zhongshan No. 2 (S) Road has daily buses to nearby tourism destinations, including Zhujiajiao, Tongli, Zhouzhuang and Wuzhen. Tickets are available at the Bus Centre.

Tianjin

Most long-distance buses terminate at the main railway station north of the river, some 2km (1.2 miles) from the city centre.

Ürümqi

Ürümqi is the hub of bus travel throughout Xinjiang, though trying to figure out which station to leave from can be confusing, and buying tickets at the wrong station can incur additional charges. For most destinations in Xinjiang, buses leave from the long-distance bus station on Heilongjiang Lu. For Turpan, buses leave from the Urumqi–Turpan bus station, near Erdaoqiao Market at the southern end of town. Buses to Turpan take around 3 hours on the expressway.

Buses to Kashi leave from the long-distance bus station on Heilongjiang Lu or from the Nanjiao bus station in the south of Ürümqi. They leave regularly and take around 30 hours. Luxury express sleeper coaches are also available. Be aware beforehand that if you get a sleeper seat, you are confined to the same position for the whole ride. Foreign women travelling alone have reported being harassed on these bus trips.

Buses to Tianchi depart midmorning from the north gate of People's Park (Renmin Gongyuan) west of the Hongshan intersection and return in the late afternoon. The journey to Tianchi takes around 2–3 hours. Unlike in Gansu, it is not necessary to purchase PICC travel insurance when travelling in Xinjiang.

Xi'an

There are long-distance buses connecting Xi'an with Zhengzhou, Yichang and Luoyang, as well as to Yan'an, Lanzhou, Hanzhong and Huashan. The long-distance bus station is near the railway station in the northeastern corner of the Old City, and tourist buses bound for many of the nearby attractions such as the Terracotta Warriors depart from here.

Xining

The city's long-distance bus station is across the river from the railway station. Bus routes include Lanzhou, Golmud, Tongren, Zhangye and Maduo. Foreigners are not permitted to take the Lhasa bus from here.

Water transport

With a few exceptions, passenger transport on China's extensive river network has given way to commercial shipping. However, there are regular ferry and boat connections between the large coastal cities in China. The same is true for some

⊘ Individual travel

There are three ways of travelling in China for the individual traveller. The most comfortable, and of course, most expensive way is to book a full package tour through a travel agent. Everything is pre-booked and the traveller can choose a tailor-made route. The same is the case for sightseeing: a guide from a China travel agency is available in each town and will help put together and arrange a sightseeing programme.

The second possibility is booking a mini-package tour. The agent pre-books the flights, accommodation with breakfast, transfers and transport of luggage in China, while the traveller is responsible for organising sightseeing. The traveller is met at the airport or railway station on arrival at each town and taken to the hotel. Each hotel has a travel-agency counter, where you can discuss your plans for sightseeing and have them arranged for a fee.

The mini-package option is a good idea. The most essential bookings have been made (to make them yourself requires a lot of time and strong nerves), and with thorough preparation, you have a good chance of getting to know China beyond the usual tourist routes. You should get a definite booking with an experienced travel agent at least three months before departure.

Then there is completely independent travel, without any pre-booking. You'll have to arrange your own air and train tickets at each place you visit. Unless you speak Chinese, you will probably find it easiest to do this through a travel agency, where it is more likely you will find English-speaking staff. At airports and stations, you will often find that information about destinations is given in pinyin, but off the beaten track it will usually be in Chinese characters only.

Last-minute plans can often fall through: you may have to wait several days for your railway or air ticket, or abandon your chosen destination and choose a different one. Reserve air or rail tickets as soon as you arrive; your hotel can do this for you, for a small commission. This can be very useful for hard-to-obtain tickets.

Travel agencies will book hotels for a small fee, but are geared towards the expensive ones.

of the big rivers, particularly the Chang Jiang (Yangzi; see below) and the Zhu Jiang (Pearl River), but not the Huang He (Yellow River). Services on the Grand Canal are limited, although boats still run from Hangzhou in Zhejiang province to Suzhou and Wuxi in Jiangsu province. Information on routes and timetable are available from travel agents or shipping agencies.

Chongqing and the Three Gorges

This is China's most popular river trip. The most spectacular scenery on the Chang Jiang (Yangzi) is to be found downstream from Chongqing as far as Yichang (only a few boats go as far as Wuhan, and beyond). This stretch takes anything from 11 hours on a hydrofoil to 2 or 3 days on a cruise ship. There are also boats departing daily from Wuhan going upstream to Chongqing; this journey takes around 3 days. From Yichang it is possible to board boats in either direction.

Since the construction of the Three Gorges Dam the water level on the Chang Jiang has risen by some 175 metres (575ft), which has made the landscape a little less dramatic.

When planning a river trip, there are two main things to bear in mind: when to go and the type of vessel. High season is May–October and for travel during this time you will need to reserve well in advance. The river is very busy at this time, so you may prefer to go off-season, for a more peaceful experience.

It is important to know exactly the kind of boat you are buying a ticket for. There are three basic types of vessels plying the Chang Jiang: hydrofoils, passenger boats/Chinese cruise ships, and international cruise ships. There is no standard classification for categories of accommodation on the boats, so make sure you understand exactly what, for example, "first class" means before you pay for it.

Hydrofoils are the fastest way to travel along the river, but you obviously cannot savour the scenery or stop along the way.

Passenger boats and Chinese cruise ships ferry everything from passengers to cargo. These usually have cabins ranging from first class (two bunks in a room with private shower) to fourth class (communal bunking). Passengers are left to fend for themselves at mealtimes, and hygiene and sanitation are poor. These boats may suit those on a tight budget, but are devoid of all amenities, and only stop at towns, not tourist sights, along the way.

Tickets for these boats can be purchased at Chaotianmen Docks, but it is far easier to book through a hotel in town (which generally have English-speaking staff), or at one of the agencies around town (which generally do not).

Luxury **international cruise ships** are the preferred option for most tourists. But even here, there can be a great deal of difference in facilities and quality, so be clear about the kind of ship you're booking yourself on. Trips booked from outside China are often much more expensive than booking a comparable ship through a local travel agent, but the former often provide added amenities, ranging from casinos to daily movies to mah-jong lessons. Cruise ships make stops along the river at sites of interest; entrance fees to these may be included in the price of your ticket.

Hainan

Ferries to Haikou's Xiuying and Xingang ports operate from the Guangdong cities of Haian, Xuwen, and Zhanjiang.

Hong Kong

There is a wide choice of services on ferries and fast hydrofoils between Hong Kong and many Guangdong cities – including Guangzhou (2 hours by hydrofoil), Shekou (near Shenzhen Airport), Zhongshan and Zhuhai. Longer-distance routes to Xiamen and Shanghai are no longer running. Most departures are from the China Ferry Terminal at the China Hong Kong City Building, Canton Road, Tsim Sha Tsui.

Travellers heading to Macau will find a variety of rapid craft speeding throughout the day and night from the Hong Kong Macau Ferry Terminal in the Shun Tak Centre, Sheung Wan, on Hong Kong Island. Jetfoils and catamarans make the journey in around an hour (but allow longer for queues at immigration in Macau). There are also (much less frequent) services from Hong Kong Airport, and between Macau and various cities in Guangdong province.

It is possible to go straight from Hong Kong to Taipa on Cotai Water Jet (tel: 852-2859 1588), which depart for the Taipa Ferry Terminal roughly every 30 minutes from 7am–11.30pm, from the Shun Tak Centre on Hong Kong Island.

A variety of ferry companies manage these routes. For information on ferry schedules from Hong Kong, call 852-2859 3333 or 2736 1387/ 2516 9581.

Shanghai

Shanghai is connected to ports elsewhere in China. Vessels also travel up the Chang Jiang (Yangzi) to destinations along the river, including Nanjing, Wuhan and Chongqing. Daily ferries to the popular island of Putuo Shan depart from Wusong Port at 7.30pm for the overnight trip, or fast boats depart from Luchao Port (purchase ticket and depart by bus from Shanghai Huangpu Tourist Station, 1588 Waima Road). Tickets to all destinations can be booked at the foreigner ticket booth at the Ferry Ticket Booking Office, 1 Jinling Road (E), tel: 021-5657 5500. Tickets can also be purchased at the Shiliupu Wharf ticket office, from where boats to most domestic destinations depart. The wharf is situated on the Huangpu River on Zhongshan Road (C), just south of the Bund.

The Su Zhou Hao ferry sails between Shanghai and Osaka in Japan. The 2-day crossing departs weekly from the Shanghai Port International Cruise Terminal (tel: 021-6181 8000; 500 Dongdaming Road). Tickets available from the Shanghai International Ferry Company (tel: 021-6537 5111; www. shanghai-ferry.co.jp).

City transport

The visitor can choose between taxis, buses or bicycles for transport in the cities. In Beijing, Hong Kong, Guangzhou, Tianjin, Shanghai and Shenzhen there are also underground metro systems.

Taxis are certainly the most comfortable form of transport, and drivers will agree a fixed rate for longer journeys and excursions, with prices usually starting at around Rmb 300– 400. In smaller cities this can be bargained down considerably. Taxis are plentiful in all cities, and if you don't speak the language, it is a good idea to carry details of your destination written in Chinese.

Buses in Chinese towns are almost always overcrowded. The fare depends on distance, and should be paid to the conductor. Buses are not easy for foreigners to use, as information is almost exclusively in Chinese script. In some cities such as Beijing, there are also minibuses for certain routes; these carry a maximum of 16 people. They are a bit more expensive, but will stop at any point you want along the route. Drivers pack in as many people as they can, and you may end up standing or sitting next to the driver.

You can hire **bicycles** practically everywhere in China, either at hotels or at bike-hire shops. However, with the recent huge increase in road traffic, cycling is less pleasant than it once was: Beijing has retained its cycle lanes, but in some cities – notably Shanghai – travelling on two wheels is decidedly hazardous.

Rental rates should be around Rmb 5 per hour and up to Rmb 40 per day. Shop around, as these can vary widely. You will usually be required to leave a deposit of up to Rmb 500 and some form of ID. Ask for a receipt, try to avoid leaving your passport, and make sure you have checked your bicycle's brakes, gears and tyre pressure before renting. You must use the designated parking areas, where your bike will be kept safe for a small fee. Cycle helmets can be hard to find, and night-time cycling can be hazardous due to a lack of cycle lights.

Touring by bicycle

Riding a bike comes into its own when exploring an area of natural beauty. The area around Yangshuo in Guangxi is fantastic for cycling – the extraordinary karst landscape (the terrain between the peaks is actually flat) is just minutes by bike from the town centre, along quiet roads and trails.

A – Z

A

Accommodation

Choosing a hotel

China's large cities have numerous modern hotels, most of them at the high end of the market, including many of world-class calibre. Many belong to international hotel chains, and their prices are in line with the West. Tour groups usually stay in well-appointed tourist hotels.

Finding rooms at hotels in the middle and lower price ranges can be difficult, particularly during Chinese New Year (a week or two in January or February), and during the May and October holiday periods, when hotels are often completely full.

Worth mentioning are a few well-preserved hotels built by the colonial powers in a few cities. These include the Peace Hotel (Heping Fandian) in Shanghai, the Astor (Lishunde Dafandian) in Tianjin and the Raffles Beijing Hotel (Beijing Fandian) in the nation's capital.

In some of the more far-flung provinces, you may still come across some hotels that will not allow foreigners – usually because of rules imposed by Chinese agencies or the local police, who often determine where foreigners may stay. This is not a problem in the main tourist areas.

Websites www.ctrip.com and www. elong.net can be used to book hotels in advance, though the best prices can often be achieved by bargaining for a room in person at the front desk – particularly during low season or for longer stays.

Rates at all but the cheapest hotels are subject to 10–15 percent service surcharge.

Guesthouses

Individual travellers may be able to find cheap lodgings in guesthouses in smaller towns off the tourist track. They usually have rooms with two or more beds, or dormitories, shower and washing facilities.

Other accommodation

It is difficult for foreigners to find accommodation outside of hotels and guesthouses, although some universities and institutes have guesthouses where foreign visitors can find good, cheap lodging. Youth hostels in China can be viewed, and sometimes booked, online at www.hihostels.com.

Admission charges

Admission charges vary from Rmb 10 for a state run museum to Rmb 100 or so for larger theme parks and around Rmb 200 for some nature parks. Most temples charge only a few kuai.

B

Budgeting for your trip

In a vast country such as this prices, will vary considerably, not only between city and countryside but also between provinces. You might need as little as US$50 a day in, say, Yunnan province, to cover accommodation, meals, attractions and transport, but in Hong Kong you could pay four times that amount just for your hotel. Allowing for a reasonably good standard of accommodation away from the city hotspots, you would need around US$120 a day. Transport and food are very reasonably priced everywhere (see also Admission charges, above).

C

Climate

China is a huge country, covering 35 degrees of latitude, with a great variety of climates. It is generally warm and humid in southeastern and central China, but the west, the north and northeast are quite dry. Most of China has a summer rainy season and a winter dry season. The best times for travelling are generally spring (Apr/May) and autumn (Sept/Oct).

Northern China, north of the Chang Jiang (Yangzi River), has cold, dry winters – particularly cold in the northeast where temperatures remain well below freezing for months on end. Summers are warm or hot with variable humidity and some torrential rain. Beijing and Xi'an can be affected by sand blowing in from the Gobi Desert in spring.

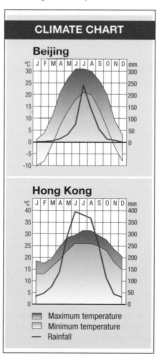

CLIMATE CHART

Beijing

Hong Kong

Maximum temperature
Minimum temperature
— Rainfall

⊘ Typhoons

July to October is typhoon season in southern China. In Hong Kong, storm warnings are graded as 1, 3, 8, 9 and 10 – 1 signalling a mild possibility, 10 indicating a head-on, life-threatening storm. Never underestimate a typhoon.

In **Central China** summers are hot and humid, with a lot of rain. In low-lying regions around the Yangzi and along the coasts, winters are fairly mild but often damp (Shanghai is often grey and cool from December to March). The cities of Chongqing, Wuhan and Nanjing are notorious for their summer heat and humidity.

Most of **Southern China** has a subtropical climate, with long, hot summers and short, cool winters. There are spells of heavy rain in the summer, and typhoons can affect the coasts between July and September. Upland areas inland tend to get a lot of rain throughout the year and can be cold in winter. The exception is Yunnan, which has warmer, drier winters. Southern Yunnan (Xishuangbanna) and Hainan island have true tropical climates with year-round warmth.

In **Western China**, the Tibet-Qinghai Plateau has moderately warm summers, while winters can get very cold; there is little rainfall throughout the year. Most of Xinjiang is arid and fiercely hot in summer (Turpan is the hottest of all), frigid in winter. Northern areas are less hot in summer.

What to wear

In the summer months, take light cotton clothes that are easily washed and not too delicate. Something warm is useful, even in the hottest season, as the air conditioning in hotels and shopping malls is often vigorous. Footwear should be comfortable and strong.

Most Chinese wear ordinary clothes to evening performances at the Beijing Opera, the theatre or the circus. It is best to follow this custom, especially at some of the venues in rural areas: the floor is often of compressed mud, making high-heeled shoes an unwise option. In contrast, urban discos and clubs call for more formal dress.

Rainwear is useful, especially during the summer months. China's rainy season is from May to August.

Children

The Chinese are very fond of children, so travelling with a family in China can be a great pleasure. Facilities are mostly good. If you have toddlers or babies, note that disposable nappies and baby food in jars are available in all of the larger cities, but plan to pick up sufficient supplies for trips to more remote areas. Children travel at reduced cost on trains and planes, and some hotels will allow one or two children under 12 to stay in their parents' room for no extra charge. Larger hotels usually offer some form of childcare, but expect to pay a fee.

Disabled travellers

Only in recent years have the needs of disabled people received attention in China. Regulations regarding rooms and other facilities for the disabled must be met by new hotels. In general, though, towns, institutions, public transport and sights offer little accessibility.

Travelling in a group for the disabled certainly reduces these problems considerably. The China National Tourist Offices and CITS (see page 458) have information about special trips for the disabled.

E

Electricity

Electricity in China is 220 volts, 50 cycles AC. Don't forget to take an international adaptor, to accommodate different-style plugs. If travelling away from tourist centres, it is worth taking battery-operated equipment.

Embassies and consulates

Beijing

Australia, 21 Dongzhimenwai Dajie, Chaoyang District, tel: 010-5140 4111.
Canada, 19 Dongzhimenwai Dajie, Chaoyang District, tel: 010-5139 4000.
Ireland, 3 Ritan Donglu, tel: 010-6532 2691.
New Zealand, 3 Sanlitun Dongsan, Chaoyang District, tel: 010-8531 2700.
South Africa, 5 Dongzhimenwai Dajie, Chaoyang District, tel:

010-6532 7323.
United Kingdom, 11 Guanghua Lu, Jianguomenwai, tel: 010-5192 4000.
United States, 55 Anjialou Lu, Chaoyang District, tel: 010-8531 3000.

Shanghai

Australia, 22/F, CITIC Square, 1168 Nanjing Road (W), tel: 021-2215 5200.
Canada, 8/F, Shanghai Centre, 1788 Nanjing Road (W), tel: 021-3279 2800.
New Zealand, 2801-2802A & 2806B-2810, 5 Corporate Avenue, 150 Hu Bin Road, tel: 021-5407 5858.
South Africa, Room 2706, The Bund Center, 220 Yan'an Road (E), tel: 021-5359 4977.
United Kingdom, The British Centre, 17/F Garden Square, 968 West Beijing Road, tel: 021-3279 2000.
United States, 1469 Huaihai Road ©, tel: 021-6433 6880.

Hong Kong

Australia, 23/F, Harbour Ctr, 25 Harbour Road, Wan Chai, tel: 852-2827 8881.
Canada, 5/F, Tower Three, Exchange Square, 8 Connaught Place, Central, tel: 852-2810 4321.
New Zealand, Rm 6501, Central Plaza, 18 Harbour Road, Wan Chai, tel: 852-2877 4488.
South Africa, Rm 1906-8, 19/F, Central Plaza, 18 Harbour Road, Wan Chai, tel: 852-3926 4300.
United Kingdom, 1 Supreme Court Road, Admiralty, tel: 852-2901 3000.
United States, 26 Garden Road, Central, tel: 852-2523 9011.

Emergencies

Security and crime

There is still less crime in China than in many other countries but, as vigorous crime crackdowns by the government (in the form of thousands of executions per year) attest,

⊘ Important numbers

Police: 110
Fire: 119
Ambulance: 120
Local directory assistance: 114
Domestic directory assistance: 116
International directory assistance (English): 114
Time: 117
Weather: 12121
For emergency services in Hong Kong, tel: 999. In Macau, tel: 919.

☺ Overseas Chinese embassies

Australia, 15 Coronation Drive, Yarralumla, ACT 2600, Canberra, tel: (61-2) 6228 3999; http://au.china-embassy.org
Canada, 515 St Patrick Street, Ottawa, Ontario KIN 5H3, tel: (1-613) 789 3434; http://ca.china-embassy.org
New Zealand, 2–6 Glenmore Street, Wellington, tel: (64-4) 472 1382; www.chinaembassy.org.nz

South Africa, 972 Pretorius Street, Arcadia 0083, Pretoria, tel: (27-12) 4316 5001, www.chinese-embassy.org.za
United Kingdom, 31 Portland Place, London W1B 1QD, tel: (44-20) 7299 4049; www.chinese-embassy.org.uk
United States, 2201 Wisconsin Avenue NW, Washington DC 20007, tel: (1-202) 337 1956; www.china-embassy.org

crime is an increasing problem.

Take the same precautions applicable anywhere, on the street and with valuables in hotels and on public transport. Pickpockets and bag-slashers can be a problem, especially on crowded trains and buses, and in stations. Because of the influx of poor migrant workers, cities such as Guangzhou tend to have more crime than elsewhere, and muggings have been reported in some areas, notably Shenzhen. Still, one needn't worry in most towns and cities. Women should dress discreetly and avoid going out alone at night, though generally they are safer in China than in many other parts of the world. It is a good idea to carry the telephone number of your hotel concierge on a piece of paper, or loaded into a mobile phone, as few police officers speak English.

Scams are a perennial problem at major tourist areas. The infamous teahouse scam begins with a friendly stranger inviting a tourist to enjoy some traditional tea and conversation and ends with him/her being presented with an enormous bill. Bar street touts can often be heard hawking the pleasures of the "lady-bar". The curious discover this is a bar with some form of female company and a great deal of extortion. Unscrupulous taxi drivers will try to pass off counterfeit currency on passengers. Some visitors have reported drivers handing back an Rmb 100 note fare on the grounds of it being counterfeit only to discover later that the driver had switched a real note for a fake one. Always carrying small change solves this problem.

The **Public Security Bureau** (Gongan Ju) is the ever-present police force responsible for everything – chasing murderers, quenching dissent, issuing visa extensions. They are usually friendly towards foreigners, even if the rules that they

are strictly enforcing seem illogical at times. Also, with serious travel-related disputes – for example, with taxi drivers or hotels – they are usually able to resolve the problem. To stay in their good books, don't be caught trying to travel in restricted areas or on an expired visa. Throughout China, visitors who are not staying in hotels must register with the local Public Security Bureau. (See page 458 for contact details.)

Luggage

Luggage should be sturdy and lockable – sometimes a requirement for transport. Avoid taking shiny designer luggage, which is an obvious target for thieves.

Entry regulations

Visas and passports

All foreigners must acquire an entry visa before arrival in China, although those visiting Hong Kong or Macau only do not usually require one. Visa regulations change with great frequency and independent agents sometimes know best how to work around the rules.

If you are part of a group, the tour operator will often obtain the visas; group visas will usually be issued for groups of at least 10, and the guide accompanying your group will keep them. Individual travellers can apply at any Chinese embassy. The procedure is straightforward, taking about a week, depending on current regulations and on your own country's rules for visiting Chinese citizens. A 30-day single-entry visa is usually issued. Your passport must be valid for six months after the expiry date of the entry visa.

It used to be much quicker and easier to obtain or renew visas in Hong Kong than elsewhere in China, but the difference is less marked these days.

If your visa expires while you are in China, it can be extended by the local Public Security Bureau. However, make sure you visit them before it expires, because fines for overstaying can be steep, and it may be a long and frustrating process getting the stamp you need.

Holders of passports of 51 countries, including Australia, Canada, Ireland, New Zealand, the United Kingdom and the United States, do not require a visa for a 72- or 144-hour stay in selected areas of China if they arrive in one of 18 cities (including Shanghai, Beijng, Chengdu and Guangzhou) with valid passports and visas for their onward destination countries and hold return tickets for this trip with confirmed seats.

Nowadays, most of the country is open to foreigners, except some border areas and military zones. A permit is still required for Tibet.

Customs

On arrival, each traveller must complete a health declaration form.

Tourists can freely import two bottles of wine or spirits and 400 cigarettes, as well as foreign currency and valuables for personal use without restrictions. The import of weapons, ammunition, drugs and pornographic literature is prohibited.

On departure, antiques such as porcelain, paintings, calligraphy, carvings and old books must carry the red lacquer seal of an official antique shop. Otherwise, they can be confiscated by the customs officials without compensation.

Festivals

Holidays such as **National Day** and **International Labour Day** are fixed on the modern calendar, but most traditional festivals and events are determined by the lunar calendar, which means the date varies slightly from year to year. The following calendar of events highlights the major national festivals, but each region has its own special days and events (see also page 388).

January/February

The most important festival time is the **Lunar New Year**, or **Spring Festival**, which usually falls in late

January or early February. Public buildings are festooned with coloured lights, people from all over China travel to reunite with family and friends, debts are settled, and food is consumed – lots of it. In recent years, a more relaxed atmosphere has brought the revival of old Spring Festival traditions, such as giving *hong bao* – small red envelopes containing money – to children and young adults. Temple fairs feature martial-arts demonstrations, stand-up comedy, home-made toys and, of course, food. One slightly less traditional activity that has become common during this time is shopping. As with the post-Christmas period in the West, the week following Spring Festival sees the streets of every town and city heaving with pedestrians looking for a bargain.

Northerners, who have amazing resilience to the bitter winters, partake with gusto in ice-sculpting competitions and winter swimming. The time and duration of the festivals depend on the weather. Both Longqing, outside Beijing, and Harbin, in Heilongjiang, are noted for their ice-sculpture festivals.

April

On the 12th day of the third lunar month, at the beginning of April, the Chinese honour their deceased ancestors by observing **Qingming**, sometimes referred to as the "grave-sweeping" day. It is much less impressive nowadays, as people are cremated instead of being buried. Qingming is a time for remembering ancestors and for age-old ritualistic ceremonies, but also for revelling on a warm spring day. Qingming was made a one-day public holiday in 2008, and it's become common for workers and students to head home to mark the occasion.

May/June

International Labour Day on 1 May has once again reverted to being a single one-day holiday after several years spent as one of China's three "Golden Week" holidays. Following hot on its heels is **Youth Day**, a commemoration of the May 4 Movement of 1919, reflected by large editorials and government hoopla in the official press.

International Children's Day is celebrated in earnest on 1 June by letting classes out early and treating children to outings at public parks.

⊘ Travelling during festivals

If you wish to see or take part in any of the major Chinese festivals, you will need to travel to your destination well in advance, particularly for the Lunar New Year, 1 May and 1 October holidays. At these times of year, many attractions become impossibly overcrowded and tickets on any form of transport are extremely difficult to obtain, as millions of people hit the road for family reunions.

The fifth day of the fifth lunar month (usually in June) brings the **Dragon Boat Festival**, with dragon-boat races in many cities. It commemorates the memory of Qu Yuan (340–278 BC), a poet in the days of the Kingdom of Chu, who, rather than submit to political pressure, drowned himself in the Miluo River, in Hunan. To prevent the fish from eating his body, the people threw glutinous rice cakes *(zongzi)* into the river. Nowadays, *zongzi* are eaten to mark the occasion.

July/August

1 July is the **Anniversary of the Communist Party**, which was founded in Shanghai in 1921. This means very little to the average citizen, but is plenty of fun for high-level party members.

1 August is the **Anniversary of the People's Liberation Army**. Inaugurated in 1927 and formerly marked by enormous parades, it is now celebrated mainly in the media.

September/October

The timing of the **Mid-Autumn Festival** depends on when the moon reaches its fullest, usually around mid-September. The shops do great business in "mooncakes" – pastries filled with gooey sesame paste, red-bean and walnut filling. *Tang yuan*, glutinous rice-flour balls with sweet fillings in sugar syrup, and *yue bing*, a cake baked specifically for this occasion, are also eaten. In the tradition of poets, this is the time to drink a bit of wine and toast the moon. It is now a one-day public holiday (see page 456 for a full list of public holidays).

Late September is normally the time when Chinese communities celebrate the memory of **Confucius**.

1 October is the PRC's birthday, **National Day**, celebrated with a one-week public holiday. Government buildings, road intersections and hotels are decked out in lights, and flower arrangements and Sun Yatsen's portrait are displayed in Tiananmen Square. Tens of thousands turn out on the square for picture-taking and general merry-making.

November/December

November and December are quiet months in China, but **Christmas** is gaining momentum as a consumer celebration. Christian churches hold special services that draw thousands of spectators. In Beijing, for example, it is fashionable to exchange greetings cards and presents, while Santa Claus makes the odd shop appearance.

Local festivals for deities

Various deities in the Chinese Daoist and Buddhist pantheon are honoured in festivals across China. Some are local concerns, but three of the most widespread are the birthdays of Confucius (28 September), Guanyin (19th day of the 2nd lunar month) and Tin Hau (23rd day of the 3rd lunar month).

Other religious festivals

Islam

In Xinjiang and other predominantly Muslim areas, two main festivals are celebrated: **Id al-Fitr** (Turkish: Bayram, the "Festival of the Breaking the Fast"), held at the end of Ramadan, and **Id al-Adha** (Turkish: Kurban, the "Festival of the Sacrifice", held to mark the culmination of the Hajj pilgrimage to Mecca. Ramadan – observed by many Muslims in China – is easier on the non-Muslim visitor than it would be, for example, in Iran

⊘ Hong Kong holidays

In Hong Kong, the Christian **Good Friday** and **Easter Monday** are public holidays, as are **Christmas** and **Boxing Day**. There are also days off for the Chinese ancestor-worshipping festivals of **Qingming** (April) and **Chung Yeung** (October), as well as **Buddha's Birthday** (May) and **sar Establishment Day** (1 July).

or Saudi Arabia, as Han Chinese restaurants remain open everywhere.

Tibetan Buddhism

Labrang Monastery, at Xiahe in Gansu province, is one of the six great monasteries of the Tibetan Yellow Hat sect, and is the most important Tibetan monastery in China outside the Tibetan Autonomous region. Major festivals are held here each year involving merit-making, *sutra*-chanting and devil-dancing. The most important of all, **Monlan** or "Great Prayer", falls sometime in February or March, with pilgrims dressed in their finest clothes visiting from all over the Tibetan-speaking world.

Gay travellers

Between the establishment of the People's Republic in 1949 and economic liberalisation in the 1990s, homosexuality was considered a psychological illness and severely circumscribed. China, though, has a long tradition of gay sexuality – known as the "way of the cut sleeve" in traditional literature – and in the past two decades gay people of both sexes have increasingly reasserted their presence and rights, especially in go-ahead cities such as Shanghai, Beijing and Guangzhou. Don't expect a scintillating gay scene elsewhere, however.

H

Health and medical services

The most frequently reported health problem in Eastern Asia is diarrhoea. The best prevention is to ensure maximum hygiene while travelling, especially in restaurants and roadside snack bars. Never eat raw, uncooked, or partially cooked food, including salads, other than in the top hotels. Animal or human excrement is still frequently used as fertiliser, so bacteria on uncooked vegetables can easily be ingested. Also suggested if travelling outside of a tour group: acquire chopsticks and a tin bowl with a lid for train journeys and meals in small roadside restaurants. Drink only boiled or bottled water, even though the tap water is drinkable in

some places, and reduce exposure to insects as far as possible.

Adjustment to a different climate and different food frequently leads to minor colds or digestive problems. Keep well hydrated in the heat and humidity.

Tibet, the northwest, and the tropical province of Yunnan make particularly high demands on the body. Heart disease and high blood pressure can both lead to serious problems in Tibet because of high altitude. Temperatures are high and conditions dry along the Silk Road.

If planning to visit areas outside of Beijing, Shanghai, Guangzhou and Hong Kong, you should take out emergency evacuation insurance.

The largest emergency evacuation company is International sos Assistance (for Beijing, tel: 010-6462 9100; for Hong Kong, tel: 852-2528 9900; for Shanghai, tel: 021-5298 9538; www.internationalsos.com) which has clinics in many major cities.

Insect-transmitted illnesses

Malaria

Transmitted to humans by mosquitoes, which are most active from dusk to dawn.
Symptoms: fever and flu-like symptoms, chills, aches and tiredness. Up to one year after returning home, travellers should consult a physician for any kind of flu-like illness.
Risk: little or no risk in urban areas and popular tourist destinations; there is no risk in provinces bordering Mongolia or in Heilongjiang, Ningxia, Qinghai, Hong Kong or Macau. The highest risk exists in rural areas not visited by most travellers. In these areas, transmission is most common from May to December; in the south, transmission occurs year-round. Whether taking preventative drugs or not, travellers in risk areas should avoid being bitten by mosquitoes: use mosquito repellents, wear long-sleeved shirts and long trousers and ask at your hotel for a mosquito net or an electronic mosquito repellent device (*quwenqi*) or coil (*wenxiang*).

Taking drugs to prevent malaria is recommended only for travellers to rural areas and those who expect to have outdoor exposure during evening hours. Deciding which medicine to take is not easy. Consult medical authorities or a physician in travel medicine for advice before you travel.

☉ Emergency evacuation

International SOS, 16/F, 633 King's Road, North Point, Hong Kong, tel: 852-2528 9998, alarm tel: 852-2528 9900.
International SOS Clinic/Raffles Medical Beijing, Suite 105, Wing 1, Kunsha Building, 16 Xinyuanli, Chaoyang District, Beijing, tel: 010-6462 9112; alarm tel: 010-6462 9100.

Dengue fever

Primarily an urban viral infection transmitted by mosquitoes in or around human habitations. The mosquitoes are typically at their most active around dawn and dusk.
Symptoms: sudden onset of high fever, severe headaches, joint and muscle pain, and a rash, which shows up 3–4 days after the fever.
Risk: occurs in parts of southern China and Taiwan. The risk is minimal for most travellers. Those who have lived several years in high-risk areas are more susceptible than short-term visitors. There is no vaccine or specific treatment available.

Japanese encephalitis

A mosquito-borne viral disease prevalent in rural areas, often in rice-growing areas.
Symptoms: none, or headache, fever and other flu-like symptoms. Serious complications can lead to a swelling of the brain (encephalitis).
Risk: low or minimal risk. Occurs in rural China and Korea; very rarely in Hong Kong and Taiwan. Mosquitoes bite in the late afternoon and early evening. Transmission is usually during the rainy season. There is no specific drug for treatment, but there is a preventative vaccine, which should be considered for those who plan visits of four weeks or more to rural areas.

Contamination

Hepatitis A

A viral infection of the liver transmitted by faecal-contaminated food or drink, or through direct person-to-person contact.
Symptoms: fatigue, fever, loss of appetite, nausea, dark urine and/or jaundice, vomiting, aches. There is currently no specific treatment for Hepatitis A, although an effective vaccine is available and highly

recommended, especially for those who plan to travel repeatedly or at length in China. Immune globulin is recommended only for short-term protection.

Hepatitis B

All countries in Asia, including China, report high levels of infection. Hepatitis B is a viral infection of the liver transmitted through the exchange of blood or blood-derived fluids, or through sexual activity with an infected person. Unscreened blood and unsterilised needles, or contact with potentially infected people with open skin lesions, are sources of infection. Inoculations for this type of hepatitis should be started six months prior to travel.

Typhoid fever

A bacterial infection transmitted by contaminated food and/or water, or directly between people. Travellers to East Asia are susceptible to typhoid fever, particularly in rural areas.
Symptoms: fever, headaches, tiredness, loss of appetite and constipation. Be cautious in selecting food and water. Drinking bottled or boiled water and eating only well-cooked food lowers the risk of infection. Typhoid fever is treated with antibiotics. Vaccination is recommended for travellers off the tourist routes, especially if staying for six weeks or more. Available vaccines protect 70–90 percent of users.

Cholera

An acute intestinal infection caused by bacteria, most often through contaminated water or food. The risk is virtually non-existent in China.
Symptoms: abrupt onset of watery diarrhoea, dehydration, vomiting and muscle cramps. Medical care must be sought quickly when cholera is suspected. The available vaccine is not recommended for most travellers.

Schistosomiasis (bilharzia)

An infection from a flatworm larvae that penetrates the skin, including unbroken skin.
Risk: schistosomiasis is found in some areas of China, including rivers and lakes of southeastern and eastern China, especially along the Chang Jiang (Yangzi River) and tributaries. The risk comes from bathing, wading or swimming in contaminated fresh water.
There is no easy way to identify

infested water. If exposed, immediate and vigorous drying with a towel or rubbing alcohol on the exposed areas can reduce risk. Water treated with chlorine or iodine is virtually safe; salt water poses no risk.

Medical services

There is a big difference in China between urban and rural medical services. If travelling in the countryside, there may be no appropriate medical services beyond primary healthcare, which is good in China. Some hospitals in cities have special sections for foreigners where English is spoken. Medicines are often quite expensive. Pharmacies in China often sell medicines over the counter that are prescription only in Western countries.

Many of the large hotels have their own doctors. Payment must be made on the spot for treatment, medicine and transport. If planning to visit areas outside Beijing, Shanghai, Guangzhou and Hong Kong, consider emergency evacuation insurance.

International SOS, 16/F, 633 King's Road, North Point, Hong Kong, tel: 852-2528 9998; alarm tel: 852-2528 9900.

Beijing

Emergency/evacuation
International SOS Clinic/Raffles Medical Beijing, Suite 105, Wing 1, Kunsha Building, 16 Xinyuanli, Chaoyang District, tel: 010-6462 9112; 24-hour alarm tel: 010-6462 9100.

Emergency/general
The best hospitals for foreigners are the **China-Japan Friendship Hospital**, Heping Donglu, Chaoyang District, tel: 010-8420 5121, http://english.zryhyy.com.cn; and the **Beijing Friendship Hospital**, 95 Yong'an Lu, Xuanwu District, tel: 010-6301 6616, www.bfh.com.cn.
More expensive, but the best place for treatment of serious illness, is the private **Beijing United Family Hospital**, 2 Jiangtai Lu (close to Lido Hotel), 24-hour service centre tel: 400 891 9191, 24-hour emergency hotline tel: 010-5927 7120, http://beijing.ufh.com.cn. All staff speak excellent English.

Chengdu
Global Doctor, Room 9-11, Lippo Tower, 62 Kehua North Rd, tel: 028-8528 3660, www.globaldoctor.com.au.

Chongqing
Global Doctor, Room 701, Business Tower, Hilton Chongqing, 139 Zhongshan San Lu, Yuzhong District, tel: 023-8903 8837, www.globaldoctor.com.au.

Fujian
Fujian Provincial Hospital, 134 Dong Dajie, Fuzhou, tel: 0591-8755 7768.
City Medical Consultancy, 123 Xidi Villa, Hubin Beilu, Xiamen City, tel: 0592-532 3168, www.citymedicalxiamen.com (24 hours).

Guangzhou

Emergencies
Global Doctor, Building D, Tianyu Garden, 136 Linhe Zhong Rd, tel: 020-3890 6699, www.globaldoctor.com.au.
Sun Yatsen Memorial Hospital, 107 Yanjiang Xilu, tel: 020-8133 2199, www.syshospital.com.
Guangzhou Can-Am International Medical Centre, 5/F, Garden Hotel, 368 Huangshi Dong Lu, tel: 020-8386 6988 (24-hour hotline), www.canamhealthcare.com.

Guilin
Guilin No.1 People's Hospital (Guilin Shi Renmin Yiyuan), 12 Wenming Lu, tel: 0773-282 5116.

Hangzhou

Chinese Medicine Hospitals
Hangzhou Hospital of Traditional Chinese Medicine, 453 Tiyuchang Lu, tel: 0571-8582 7888, www.hztcm.net.

Western Medicine Hospitals
Sir Run Run Shaw Hospital, International Clinic, 5/F, Tower 3, 3 Qingchun (E) Lu, Hangzhou, tel: 0571-8600 6118, www.srrsh-english.com.
Anchorhealth (International Medical Centre of Zhejiang Hospital), 2/F, Out-Patient Bldg, Zhejiang Hospital, 12 Lingyin Lu, Hangzhou, tel: 0571-8807 2705.

Hong Kong
Though many Chinese people still prefer traditional cures for minor ills, modern Western practices dominate, and most doctors did much of their training overseas. There are also numerous expatriate doctors and dentists.

Hospitals
No Hong Kong hospital is cheap, but all have good specialists and facilities.

⊘ Avoiding illness

To reduce the risk of infection on your travels:
   Reduce exposure to insects.
   Ensure decent quality of food and water.
   Be aware of potential diseases in the regions that you visit.
   Avoid high-risk activities linked with HIV/Aids, such as drug-taking using suspect needles and unprotected sex.

The most notable hospitals are:
Central Medical Practice, 1501 Prince's Bldg, Central, tel: 852-2521 2567.
Hong Kong Adventist Hospital, 40 Stubbs Road, Happy Valley, tel: 852-3651 8888. Operates an expat-staff outpatient department Sun–Fri noon, and also has a **dental clinic** with 24-hour emergency service, www.hkah.org.hk.
Prince of Wales Hospital, 30–32 Ngan Shing St, Sha Tin, New Territories, tel: 852-2632 2211, www3.ha.org.hk/pwh.
Queen Elizabeth Hospital, 30 Gascoigne Rd, Kowloon, tel: 852-3506 8888, www3.ha.org.hk/qeh.
Queen Mary Hospital, 102 Pokfulam Rd, Hong Kong, tel: 852-2255 3838, www3.ha.org.hk/qmh.

Clinics

Clinics are an economical alternative. **Anderson & Partners**, tel: 852-2608 9700 and **Vio & Partners**, tel: 852-2590 2222 have clinics on both sides of the harbour.

Kaifeng

Kaifeng No. 1 People's Hospital, 85 Hedao Lu, tel: 0378-666 5120.

Kashi (Kashgar)

People's Hospital, 66 Qitajichang Lu, tel: 0998-297 0222.

Kunming

First Affiliated Hospital of Kunming Medical University, 295 Xichang Lu, tel: 0871-6532 4888.
Yunnan First People's Hospital, 157 Jinbi Lu, tel: 0871-6363 9921.
Richland International Hospital, Beijing Lu extension, Shangdu Guoji Xiaoqu, tel: 0871-6574 1988.

Lanzhou

Gansu Province People's Hospital, 169 Donggang Xi Lu, tel: 0931-8281 973.

Lhasa

Number One People's Hospital, 18 Linkuo Beilu, tel: 0891-6323 302.

Macau

Kiang Wu Hospital, Estrada Coelho do Amaral, tel: 853-2837 1333.
S. Januário Hospital, Estrada do Visconde de S. Januário. Tel: 853-2831 3731.

Nanchang

Nanchang No. 1 Hospital, 128 Xiangshan Beilu, tel: 0791-8886 2309, www.nc1y.com.

Nanjing

Nanjing Drum Tower Hospital, 321 Zhongshan Lu, tel: 025-8330 4616.

Qingdao

Qingdao Municipal Hospital, East complex, 5 Donghai Lu, tel: 0532-8593 7690.

Shanghai

**Emergency/evacuation
International SOS 24-Hour Service**, tel: 021-5298 9538.

**Emergency/general
Shanghai East International Medical Centre**, 150 Jimo Rd, Pudong, 24-hour hotline tel: 021-5879 9999, 150-0019 0899, www.seimc.com.cn.
Huashan Hospital, 15/F, Foreigners' Clinic, 12 Ürümqi Rd ©, tel: 021-6248 3986, www.sh-hwmc.com.cn.
Parkway Health, Rm 203–4, Shanghai Centre, 1376 Nanjing Rd (W), tel: 021-6445 5999, www.parkwayhealth.cn.

Shenzhen

Shenzhen People's Hospital, 1017 Dongmen Bei Lu, tel: 0755-2553 3018.

Ürümqi

Xinjiang People's Hospital, 91 Tianchi Lu, tel: 0991-856 2222.
Ürümqi Chinese Medical Hospital, 116 Huanghe Lu, tel: 0991-584 5674.

Xi'an

Xi'an Gaoxin Hospital, 26 Tuanjie Nanlu, Yanta District, tel: 029-8833 0120.
Shaanxi Province People's Hospital, 256 Youyi Xilu, tel: 029-8525 1331.

Zhengzhou

First Affiliated Hospital of Zhengzhou University, Daxue Lu, tel: 0371-6691 3345.

I

Internet

While hotel business centres generally charge several Rmb per minutes for internet use, the ubiquitous internet cafés elsewhere charge Rmb 3–5 per hour. These places may ask for your passport number, but generally will accept any nine-digit number you provide them with. Wi-fi networks are spreading out across China, and most hotels and hostels offer free access, as do many cafes and restaurants (just ask for the password). Starbucks, McDonald's and several other chains offer free WiFi when you key in a local mobile phone number. Most places have a slow connection.

   Internet censorship can be frustrating and you'll need a VPN (virtual private network) to get around blocked sites. Freegate can be downloaded and used for free and works about 50 percent of the time.

M

Media

An English-language newspaper, the *China Daily*, is published every day. It is informative but toes the party line. It is often obtainable from the big hotels for free. Same-day editions are available only in large cities; elsewhere, it'll probably be several days late. *Global Times* is similar, but in a tabloid format.

   In Shanghai, the English-language *Shanghai Daily* (www.shanghaidaily.com) is published every day and iDEALShangai (www.idealshanghai.com) is a brand launched in 2012, offering English-language lifestyle information on Shanghai and the neighbouring cities. There are plenty of free listing magazines, including *That's*, *City Weekend* and Talk in both Beijing and Shanghai. Many other cities in China have their own English-language listings magazines and websites as well, and these are often the most updated source of information. *Time Out* magazine is published in Beijing, Shanghai and Hong Kong and can be picked up in supermarkets and cafés that attract foreign customers.

Throughout China, large hotels sell foreign language newspapers and journals, including the *International Herald Tribune*, *The Times*, *Asian Wall Street Journal*, *Time*, *Newsweek* and many more. Foreign online newspapers are not generally blocked, except for the BBC online news in Chinese.

Money matters

The Chinese currency is called **renminbi** (people's currency) and is often abbreviated **Rmb** The basic unit is the **yuan** (colloquially, **kuai**). Ten **jiao** (colloquially, **mao**) make one yuan; ten **fen** make one jiao. Thus, 100 fen make one yuan. Notes are currently issued for 1, 2, 5, 10, 20, 50 and 100 yuan. Coins come in 1 yuan, 5 jiao, 1 jiao and 5 fen.

Hong Kong and Macau have retained their separate currencies, the Hong Kong dollar (HKD) and pataca (MOP), respectively. The former is pegged to the US dollar at a rate of between 7.75 and 7.85; the pataca is pegged to the Hong Kong dollar. Hong Kong dollars are also widely accepted in Guangzhou and Shenzhen, but if you are staying more than a day in mainland China it is worth changing your money to Chinese currency.

Major currencies are accepted in banks and hotels. Global network-connected ATM machines (Cirrus, Plus) can be found in major cities and tourist towns – try branches of the Bank of China, major hotels and department stores. **Citibank** also has a presence in Beijing, Shanghai and Guangzhou, and its ATMs usually accept lots of different cards.

Many places frequented by foreigners take the usual **credit cards** such as American Express, Visa, Diners Club and MasterCard. Don't expect to use them much outside of the major cities, however. Train and bus tickets must be purchased in cash, but plane tickets can be bought with credit cards.

When you change money, you get a receipt that allows you to change Rmb back to foreign currency within six months. Otherwise you are restricted to exchanging US$500 worth of foreign currency into Rmb per day at the Bank of China. Chinese locals are permitted to exchange more.

Tipping

It was once illegal to accept tips in mainland China. Moreover, for a long time, tipping was considered patronising. However, tourism has changed attitudes in areas such as Guangzhou and Shanghai, and it has become the custom for travel groups to give a tip to Chinese travel guides and bus drivers. If you are travelling with a group, ask the guide, who is responsible for the "official" contacts of the group, whether a tip is appropriate and, if so, how much.

Tipping is still uncommon in most restaurants and hotels, although it is accepted in the top-class ones. As part of the ritual any gift or tip will, at first, be firmly rejected.

Hong Kong and Macau

Tipping is customary in Hong Kong bars, restaurants and hotels. Though a 10 percent service charge is often added to restaurant bills, a further 5 percent is usually added, to go direct to the staff. Taxi drivers do not expect to be tipped, but rounding up the fare to the nearest dollar or two is appreciated. In Macau, Shenzhen and Guangzhou tipping is increasingly common practice.

Nightlife

Bars, discos and karaoke

Nightlife is increasingly a feature of modern China, especially in Beijing, Shanghai and Guangzhou. In southern Chinese towns, there tends to be more life at night than in the north of the country, with restaurants, bars and cafés generally remaining open until midnight or even later.

In the larger cities, many bars and pubs have opened in recent years, and are now meeting places for affluent young professionals. Also common are karaoke bars. The Japanese-style singalong swept China in the 1990s, increasing the planet's off-key harmonies considerably. Most are easily recognised by the letters "OK" among the characters for their names. Some of these are pricey, with the clientele being rich businessmen, and some are fronts for prostitution; such hostess-style bars are illegal, and can fleece customers, so beware. Stick to major chains such as Partyworld.

Discos are popular throughout China. Many hotels have their own, frequented by well-off local youths and open until the early hours. Some of the newer hotels are also developing the lobby bar-lounge concept.

Check the monthly English-language magazines in Beijing, Shanghai, Guangzhou, Chengdu and other large cities for the latest listings on nightclubs around town. These cater to the large expat communities and are excellent sources of information.

Opening hours

Shops are open every day, including public holidays – the one major exception being at Chinese New Year. Opening hours are usually from 8.30 or 9am to 8pm, but may extend to 10pm in places. Stalls in major shopping malls may stay open later than others. Government offices and banks are usually open Mon–Fri, from 8.30 or 9am, and close at 5, 5.30 or 6pm, with a lunch break from noon to 1.30pm. Many banks, notably the Bank of China, are now open seven days a week from 8am to 6pm. Times are approximate; allow for local variations.

⊘ Import and export

Most antiques that date from before 1911 may not be legally exported. Those that can be taken out of China must carry a small red seal or have one affixed by the Cultural Relics Bureau. All other antiques are the property of the Peoples' Republic of China and, without the seal, will be confiscated without compensation. Beware of fakes: factories producing "antiques" (and the seal) are thriving.

Foreign currency can be freely imported and exported, the only restriction being that you may not export more foreign currency than you imported, except with a special permit.

You should not export, or even buy in the first place, objects made from wild animals, especially ivory. The majority of Western countries ban the import of ivory objects, and will confiscate them without compensation.

Outdoor pursuits

Spectator sports

The Olympic Games

The 2008 Olympics in Beijing was a huge success for the Chinese government, both in terms of enhancing China's image abroad and of promoting sports among its own people, combined with a US$43 billion investment in world-class sporting facilities. The country's athletes excel in swimming, diving, gymnastics badminton and weightlifting, winning 38 gold medals at the London 2012 Olympics and 26 at the Rio 2016 Olympics.

Football

Soccer is a hugely popular spectator sport in China, although relatively few people play it. *Bamboo Goalposts* provides an entertaining account of British football journalist Rowan Simon's efforts to establish the game at grass-roots level despite the many obstacles.

Participant sports

Golf

Golf is booming in China. It is extremely popular with well-heeled businessmen, their expat friends and the burgeoning middle classes. There are about 500 courses in the country, mainly in the south, with many more planned (a controversial issue, given the pressure on land resources in the country). An estimated 1 million Chinese people play golf, although it is still considered an elite sport, out of reach for most of the population. The most famous course is probably **Mission Hills** (www.missionhillsgroup. com), north of Shenzhen, ranked in 2004 in the Guinness World Records Book as the world's largest, with 216 holes. This course, credited with giving birth to golf in China, has hosted events such as the World Cup of Golf and The Asian Amateur Championship.

Hiking

Hong Kong is good for hiking, with the ridge walk along the spine of Hong Kong Island and numerous trails in the New Territories and outlying islands. On the mainland, the holy Daoist and Buddhist mountains such as Emei Shan in Sichuan and Tai Shan in Shandong make for fabulous hikes. Heng Shan in Hunan is another highlight, but avoid weekends and holidays as it is very popular with tour groups. The Wulingyuan area of Hunan is also very scenic, as are the Wuyi Shan mountains of Fujian. The dramatic karst scenery of Guangxi province surrounding Guilin (excluding individual climbs such as the ascent of Moon Hill) is more usually explored by cyclists or rock-climbers. Guizhou is recommended for hikes between villages in the province's east and south. In the northeast, the Changbai Shan close to the North Korean border is a more remote hiking area, while in Xinjiang the area around Tianchi (Heaven Lake) near Ürümqi is simply beautiful. The wilds of western Sichuan and Tibet will appeal to the more adventurous hiker and require proper preparation and equipment.

In **Yunnan**, tropical Xishuangbanna also offers village treks as well as more hardcore jungle treks; these are best organised through tour operators in Jinghong. The **Cangshan Mountains** west of Dali and **Tiger Leaping Gorge** near Lijiang are also excellent hiking country. Tours can be arranged through hotels and guesthouses, but it is possible to explore the area independently.

Running

China is cashing in on the craze for running, with Beijing currently holding three marathons a year. The cost of registration is often bolstered with tour packages that include transport, accommodation and even additional outings. The Hong Kong Marathon (February or March) is a challenging race, though nothing compared to the gruelling Beijing Great Wall Marathon (May). The Xiamen International Marathon (January) is attracting increasing attention from abroad and is known for its scenic seaside course. Being part of a crowd of runners setting off from Tiananmen Square in the Beijing Marathon (October) is also an experience.

Other activities

Adventure sports

In **Guangxi** province, Yangshuo is a good base from which to try out a wealth of outdoor activities amid some stunning landscapes. Cycling can be followed by rafting down the Li River, or combined with a hike accompanied by tour guides. Bikes, tandems and mountain bikes can all be hired in the town. Bamboo rafting and kayaking are offered by various companies. Rock-climbing over the limestone crags is a popular pastime. Caving around Yangshuo can be arranged by a travel agent or with a freelance guide. Hot-air balloon flights are operated by Guilin Yangshuo Flying Balloon Club – a wonderful way to enjoy the landscape.

Cycling tours

With their spectacular sceneries, variety of landscapes and minority villages, Sichuan and Yunnan provinces are the most popular areas for cycling tours. Although locals are generally hospitable, the police may be highly suspicious of foreign travellers away from major tourist areas and road safety is a serious issue so using an experienced tour leader is recommended. Odyssey Cycling (www.odysseycycling.com) has been operating for over 20 years and offers various cycling tours, mostly in southern China. For cycling tours throughout China, travelogues and comprehensive information on cycling see Bike China (www.bikechina. com). Bike Asia (www.bikeasia.com) runs a few tours, including to Tibet.

Skiing

Opened in 2000, Huaibei International Ski Resort at Jiugukou Natural Scenic Area, 70 km (43 miles) from Beijing, has more experience dealing with safety issues and providing professional teaching than some fly-by-night operators. Its slopes also offer views of the Great Wall.

Watersports

In **Guangdong,** watersport facilities are available at the Xiaomeisha resort to the east of Shenzhen. In **Fujian**, you can try whitewater rafting, trekking and kayaking in Wuyishan. **Hainan Island's** warm, white-sand beaches have facilities for scuba diving, fishing and paragliding. Surfing is also possible on some of the beaches within an hour's drive of Sanya, though much of the island's wave potential is still uncharted.

Photography

Taking photographs of or filming military installations is prohibited. As in other countries, some museums, palaces or temples will not allow photographs to be taken, or will charge a fee. At other times, photography is allowed, but without using a flash.

No special permit is necessary for a movie camera, as long as it is clearly not for professional use.

Postal/courier services

Domestic mail delivery is exceedingly fast and cheap in China, and it puts most Western postal services to shame. Within some cities, there is often same-day delivery; between large cities, delivery is usually overnight. International mail, too, is efficient.

Express mail (EMS) is available to the majority of international destinations, as are private international courier services. Note that large parcels must be packed and sealed at the post office.

For general delivery or *poste restante* services, you should visit the central post office. Card members can also use American Express offices for receiving mail.

Courier services

Beijing
DHL: tel: 800 810 8000, www.cn.dhl.com.
Fedex: tel: 800 988 1888, 400 886 1888, www.fedex.com.

TNT: tel: 800-820 9868, www.tnt.com.cn.
UPS: tel: 800-820 8388, www.ups.com.

Public holidays

Traditional festivals, such as the Spring Festival (Lunar New Year), follow the lunar calendar and thus dates vary annually (within a four-week range). Important official holidays follow the Gregorian calendar. This calendar does not apply to Hong Kong or Macau.

1 January: New Year's Day
January/February: variable. Lunar New Year (Spring Festival)
4 or 5 April: Tomb Sweeping Day (Qingming Festival)
1 May: International Labour Day
May/June: Dragon Boat Festival
September: Mid-Autumn Festival
1 October: National Day
Lunar New Year and **1–7 October** are also week-long public holidays for the majority of Chinese. Most shops are open on holidays. Long school/university holidays in China are taken over Lunar New Year and between 1 August and 30 September.

Don't plan on travel or border crossings during holidays unless reservations have been made and confirmed a long time in advance. It is especially wise not to make any travel plans during Lunar New Year, when everyone is travelling to their hometown.

In Hong Kong, the Christian Good Friday, Easter Monday and Christmas Day are public holidays, and there are several other holidays.

Public toilets

Except for Hong Kong, where facilities are generally clean and well-maintained, public toilets in China are best avoided. Squat toilets are the norm, privacy cannot always be counted upon, toilet paper is rarely provided and standards of hygiene and sanitation are generally low. Some international fast-food chains provide Western-style facilities, but by far the most pleasant option is to head for a good hotel.

Religious services

Officially, the People's Republic encourages atheism. However, there

are Buddhist and Daoist temples and places of worship throughout the country, as well as mosques in the Muslim areas and in all large cities, which have regular prayers at the prescribed times. Catholic and Protestant churches can also be found in most big cities.

Shopping

Mainland China today is awash with quality goods, and they can be found in any major city in any of the countless department stores that litter the downtown areas. Typically "Chinese" goods such as silk, jade and porcelain are of a better quality in Hong Kong than elsewhere in China, but not necessarily cheaper. Away from the sleek, air-conditioned shopping malls, it is worth looking in the smaller towns or in the places where ethnic minorities live for local products, which will be difficult to find anywhere else in China. The most usual articles on offer are craft objects for everyday use or specially worked or embroidered garments.

Shoppers are also tempted by low prices for everyday items and clothing. Be warned that low prices are often matched by low quality, and that pirated DVDs and fake "designer" labels are on sale in many places.

Bargaining

Generally speaking, bargaining is acceptable (and expected) in free markets and souvenir stands but not in state-operated stores and modern shops. In busy tourist areas, foreigners are constantly overcharged for both goods and services, so haggling is an essential strategy for buying goods at a reasonable price.

It's advisable to check prices first at state-operated stores, such as the Friendship Store, before buying a similar item in a hotel shop or on the free market. And in the free market, bargain, and be stubborn – but friendly – if interested in an item. Avoid drawn-out haggling just for the sport.

Bargaining usually begins with the shopkeeper suggesting a price and the buyer responding with a lower one. In Beijing, the starting price might be 50 percent higher

⏀ Domestic area codes

Add 0 to the codes below if dialling from within China:

Beijing 10
Chengdu 28
Chongqing 23
Guangzhou 20
Guilin 773
Hangzhou 571
Harbin 451
Kashi 998
Kunming 871
Luoyang 379
Nanjing 25
Sanya 898
Shanghai 21
Shenyang 24
Shenzhen 755
Suzhou 512
Qingdao 532
Tianjin 22
Ürümqi 991
Wuhan 27
Xi'an 29
Xiamen 592
Zhengzhou 371

The international dialling code for Hong Kong is 852; for Macau it is 853; these are used when dialling from elsewhere in China.

than the price that shopkeepers will eventually accept. In areas that attract large number of foreign shoppers, the starting figure might be many times higher than the final price. Look for missing buttons, stains and other flaws, keep smiling, and don't be afraid to walk away if you find the price unacceptable.

In Hong Kong the once common practice of bargaining for goods is a dying art. Price differences are usually so marginal that it is hardly worth it, and it is a complete waste of time in department stores and modern shops. Elsewhere, shopkeepers who are not used to bargaining will probably react rather impatiently to your efforts. However, you might get a better deal by paying in cash rather than a credit card. Small, family-run shops might be more amenable to bargaining. In markets you should certainly attempt to use your bargaining skills, but even here it is highly unlikely that you'll be able to reduce the asking price by more than about 10 to 20 percent.

Where to Shop

Department stores: In every town there is a department store selling products for everyday use, from toothpaste to bicycles. However, the quality of clothing fabric (synthetic), the cut and the sizes are usually disappointing.

Some big department stores are state-owned institutions, but there are many privately owned small shops where you will often find products from Hong Kong, including higher-quality clothing. There are many luxury shopping malls in China, where you can find designer labels and a wealth of choice. Oriental Plaza in Beijing is a vast, glittering mall where consumers can spend the entire day shopping. Shoppers will likewise be spoilt for choice in the large cities of Shanghai, Guangzhou and Shenzhen.

Friendship Stores: Though something of an anomaly in the frenetic modern Chinese marketplace, state-run Friendship Stores still offer a reasonable selection of wares for export. Visitors will probably be mainly interested in their silk fabrics, crafts, traditional paper cuttings (cheap and easy to pack), jade carvings, kites and chopsticks, and the generally good range of books and magazines. Some large Friendship Stores have a delivery section that will send purchases to your home country. Shops and department stores generally open around 9am and close as late as 10pm.

Markets: Food items such as fruit, vegetables, fish and meat are sold

⏀ Dialling codes

Country codes: China: 86; **Hong Kong:** 852; **Macau:** 853
Direct-dial international calls: dial 00, then the country code and telephone number.
Home country direct-dial: dial 108, then the country's international area code. For example, to call Britain, dial 108-44, then the domestic area code and number. For the United States and Canada, dial 108-1 (NB in Hong Kong, this is Directory Assistance number).
AT&T: 108-11 (from Hong Kong: 800 96 1111)
MCI: 108-12 (from Hong Kong: 800 96 1121)
Sprint: 108-13 (from Hong Kong: 800 96 1877)

at markets. In the free markets, where prices are more flexible, and sometimes higher (offsetting better quality and availability), you may also find wicker baskets, metalwork and clothes, and even tailors. Well worth looking out for are antiques/curio markets where you can sift through a cornucopia of memorabilia and knick-knacks. Perhaps the best-known of these is Panjiayuan Market in Beijing (see below), but many other cities and towns (eg Tianjin) have their own antiques markets. Be on your guard against being fleeced.

Student travellers

There are no special rules for foreign students in China. Taking an ISIC card may get you discounts at sights, however, so take one along with you.

Telecommunications

Telephones

Domestic long-distance calls are cheap; international calls are expensive. Local calls in China from hotels are usually free of charge. International calls made from hotels typically have high surcharges added to China's already high IDD rates. IP (Internet Phone) cards are the cheapest way to phone abroad; these can be purchased at newsstands and hotels in large cities. You call a local number, enter a PIN code and then the number you wish to dial abroad. Calls are typically much cheaper than standard phone cards and can be used for long-distance calls within China as well.

Like many nations expanding their domestic telephone networks, China's telephone numbers can change at short notice. If you hear a peculiar ringing sound on the line and can't get through, the number may have changed.

Hong Kong is known for having one of the most advanced telecommunications systems in the world. It also has one of the highest rates of mobile phone penetration. Mobile phones can be rented at Hong Kong International Airport. To avoid roaming charges on your own mobile, pick up a prepaid SIM card, widely

⊙ Time zone

All of China is officially on Beijing time: GMT +8 hours, EST +16 hours. There is no daylight-saving time. In the far west of China (Xinjiang), an unofficial time zone exists which is, sensibly, 2 hours behind Beijing time. Be warned that this can cause confusion.

available in telephone company shops and convenience stores.

An "unlocked" mobile phone brought from outside China can be fitted with a Chinese SIM card in one of the many mobile phone shops dotted around cities and towns. SIM cards go from about Rmb 50 upwards – the most expensive cards merely have a more convenient or "lucky" number. Top-up cards, chongzhika, can be bought at face value for Rmb 50 or 100.

U

Useful addresses

Public Security Bureaux

Beijing: (deals with customs/visa matters only) 2 Andingmen Dongda-jie, tel: 010-8402 0101 (main), 010-8401 5292 (visa enquiries). Mon–Sat 8.30am–5pm.
Chengdu: 391 Shuncheng Dadao, tel: 028-8640 7067.
Chongqing: 555 Huangnipang Huanglong Lu, Yubei District, tel: 023-6396 1944. Mon–Fri 9am–noon, 1.30–5pm.
Guangzhou: 155 Jiefang Nanlu, tel: 020-9611 0110.
Guilin: 16 Shijian Yuan Lu, tel: 0773-582 9930.
Hangzhou: 35 Huaguang Lu, tel: 0571-8728 0185.
Kaifeng: 86 Zhongshan Lu, tel: 0378-315 5561.

⊙ Visitor hotlines

Beijing Tourism Hotline: tel: 12301
Shanghai Tourism Hotline: tel: 962020
Shanghai Call Centre:
tel: 962288
Guangzhou: tel: 020-8666 6666 (24 hours)

Kashi (Kashgar): 111 Yunmulakexia Lu or 67 Renmin Donglu, tel: 0998-282 2048.
Kunming: 411 Beijing Lu, tel: 0871-301 7878.
Lanzhou: 482 Wu Du Lu, tel: 0931-871 8611. Mon–Fri 8–11.30am, 2.30–5.30pm.
Luoyang: 1 Tiyuchang Lu, tel: 0379-394 8257.
Nanjing: 1 Honggongci, tel: 025-8442 0004.
Nanning: 4 Xi Er Li, Xiuling Lu, tel: 0771-289 1264. Mon–Fri 9am–4.30pm.
Qingdao: 272 Ningxia Lu, tel: 0532-8579 2555.
Shanghai: 1500 Minsheng Rd, Pudong, tel: 021-2895 1900. Mon–Sat 9am–4.30pm.
Shenzhen: Shenzhen Municipal Public Security Bureau Building, 4018 Jiefang Road, tel: 0755-8446 4679.
Tai'an: Corner of Dongyue Lu and Qingnian Lu, tel: 0538-827 5264.
Ürümqi: 29 Nan Hu Dong Lu, Shuimo District, tel: 0991-491 8456. Mon–Fri 10am–1.30pm, 3.30–6pm.
Xi'an: 58 Xidajie, tel: 029-8727 5934.
Zhengzhou: 110 Erqi Lu, tel: 0371-6962 0359.

China National Tourism Offices

Australia, 234-242 George Street, Sydney, NSW 2000, tel: 02-9252 9838, www.cnto.org.au.
Canada, 480 University Avenue, Suite 806, Toronto, Ontario M5G 1V2, tel: 1-416 599 6636, www.tourismchina-ca.com
United Kingdom, 71 Warwick Road, London, SW5 9HB, tel: 020-7373 0888, www.cnto.org.uk

⊙ Weights and measures

Both the local and international standards for weights and measures are used in China:
feet/chi/metre
3.28/03.00/1.00
1.09/01.00/0.33
1.00/00.91/0.31
acre/mu/hectare
2.47/15.00/1.00
0.16/01.00/0.07
1.00/03.22/1.61
pound/jin/kilo
2.20/02.00/1.00
1.10/01.00/0.50
1.00/00.91/0.45
gallon/sheng/litre
0.22/1.00/1.00
1.00/4.55/4.55

United States, 370 Lexington Avenue, Suite 912, New York, NY 10017, tel: 1-212-760 8218, www.cnto.org

CITS American Express Offices
www.citsamericanexpress.com
Beijing, 7F-8F, Yiqing building, 36 GuangQu Road, Beijing, tel: 010-8715 5000.
Guangzhou, 2th floor, East Tower, Fortune Plaza, 116, East Ti Yu Road, Guangzhou, tel: 020-8519 1000.
Shanghai, 7th floor, Central Place, 16 Henan Road, Shanghai, tel: 021-2306 7000.

W

What to bring

Nowadays, if you are travelling to the major cities of Shanghai, Beijing or Guangzhou, you will probably be able to find most basic items, and then some. However, if you plan to spend much time travelling out-side of the main centres and in the countryside, then it's worth bringing your own gear: hotel shops will have a limited choice of Western goods, but in small towns and rural areas, items such as tampons and deo-dorant are still difficult to find. It's always a good idea to bring your own medication.

It is prudent to bring a set of well-fitting earplugs as travel and even accommodation can be extremely noisy in China. Westerners may have difficulty finding suitably sized clothes, so be sure to bring adequate clothing if you are tall or well built.

An electrical adaptor may be useful, too; many of the older hotels have sockets which require a three-pin plug and hotels often only have a limited number of adaptors available.

Women travellers

China has long been considered a very safe travel destination with a low rate of violent crime and sexual harassment. There have been cases of foreign women being attacked or threatened however, usually when walking along on or near a bar street at night alone, taking an unlicensed or unregulated taxi and in certain nightclubs where local thugs enjoy impunity.

LANGUAGE

GENERAL

The use of English is steadily increasing in China, but on the whole you will still find it difficult to meet people away from the big hotels and business and tourist centres who speak any English, never mind German or French. Group travellers generally have translators with them in case of communication problems. But if you are travelling on your own, it is worth taking a dictionary and learning some standard Chinese (known in the West as Mandarin Chinese and in China as *putonghua*, meaning common language).

Over a billion people in China, and many other Chinese in Southeast Asia and North America, speak Mandarin Chinese. Yet within China itself the situation is complicated by the fact that in many parts of the country – particularly in the south – a dialect form of the language is spoken which bears little relation to Mandarin. The Cantonese spoken in Hong Kong and Guangzhou is one such dialect, and is almost completely incomprehensible to Mandarin speakers. A native of Guangzhou or Hong Kong cannot understand someone from Beijing or vice versa. The different dialects have the same grammar and vocabulary; it's the pronunciation that differs, as well as the use of seven tones (see below) instead of the usual four, which makes Cantonese particularly difficult for Westerners to master. Other regional dialects include Fujianese and Shanghainese.

The mutual incomprehension is, however, eased by the fact that the Chinese character script remains the same for all dialects and can be understood by all literate Chinese. People can understand each other by simply writing the symbols.

Minority languages include Tibetan, Mongolian and Uighur, although many people in these areas have at least some knowledge of Mandarin Chinese.

LANGUAGE AND WRITING

Written Chinese is a language of characters with each character representing one syllable. There are in total more than 47,000 characters, though modern Chinese uses only a fraction of these. For a daily newspaper, between 3,000 and 4,000 characters are sufficient. Scholars know between 5,000 and 6,000. Many characters used to be quite complicated, but reforms were introduced in the People's Republic in 1949 to simplify the written language. Today, these simplified characters are used throughout mainland China, though in Hong Kong and Taiwan, the complex ones are still used.

Many Chinese words are composed of two or more characters or single-syllable words. For instance, the Chinese word for film is *dianying*, and is made up of the two words: *dian* for electricity and *ying* for shadow. To make reading easier, the pinyin system joins syllables which together form words.

Pinyin

Standard Chinese is based on the pronunciation of the northern dialects, particularly the Beijing dialect. There is an officially approved roman writing of standard Chinese, called Hanyu Pinyin (the phonetic transcription of the language of the Han people). Pinyin is used throughout the People's Republic; many shops and public facilities show names both in symbols and in pinyin.

Most modern dictionaries use the pinyin system. (Taiwan, however, usually uses the older Wade-Giles transliteration system.) This transcription may at first appear confusing: the city of Qingdao, for example, is pronounced *chingdow*. It would definitely be useful to familiarise yourself a little with the pronunciation of pinyin (see below). Even when asking for a place or street name, you need to know how it is pronounced, otherwise you won't be understood. This guide uses the pinyin system throughout for Chinese names and expressions.

NAMES AND FORMS OF ADDRESS

Chinese names usually consist of three, or sometimes two, syllables, each with its own meaning. Traditionally, the first syllable is the family name, the second or two others are personal names. For instance, in Deng Xiaoping, Deng is the family name, Xiaoping the personal name. The same is true for Fu Hao, where Fu is the family name, Hao the personal name.

Until the 1980s, the address *tongzhi* (comrade) was common, but today *xiansheng* and *furen*, the Chinese equivalent of Mr and Mrs, are more usual. A young woman, as well as female staff in hotels and restaurants, can be addressed as *xiaojie* (Miss). Address older men, especially those in important positions, as *xiansheng* or *shifu* (Master).

PRONUNCIATION

The pronunciation of the consonants is similar to English (see below). The i after the consonants ch, c, r, sh, s, z, zh is not pronounced; it indicates that the preceding sound is lengthened.

Pinyin/phonetic/sound
a/a/f**a**r
an/un/r**u**n

ang/ung /l**ung**
ao/ou/l**oud**
b/b/**b**ath
c/ts/ra**ts**
ch/ch/**ch**ange
d/d/**d**ay
e/er/d**ir**t
e (after i, u, y]/a/tr**a**m
ei/ay/m**ay**
en/en/wh**en**
eng/eong/**ng** has a nasal sound
er/or/hono**ur**
f/f/**f**ast
g/g/**g**o
h/ch/lo**ch**
i/ee/k**ee**n
j/j/**j**eep
k/k/ca**k**e
l/l/**l**ittle
m/m/**m**onth
n/n/**n**ame
o/o/b**o**nd
p/p/tra**pp**ed
q/ch/**ch**eer
r/r/**r**ight
s/s/me**ss**
sh/sh/**sh**ade
t/t/**t**on
u/oo/sh**oo**t
u (after j, q, x, y]/as German **ü**/über
w/w/**w**ater
x/sh/as in **sh**eep
y/y/**y**ogi
z/ds/re**ds**
zh/dj/**j**ungle

TONES

It is sometimes said that Chinese is a monosyllabic language. At first sight, this seems to be true, since each character represents a single syllable that generally indicates a specific concept. However, most words are made up of two or three syllables, sometimes more. In the Western sense, spoken Chinese has only 420 single-syllable root words, but tones are used to differentiate these basic sounds, which often makes it very difficult for foreigners to learn the language. For instance, if one pronounces the syllable *mai* with a falling fourth sound (mài) it means to sell; if it is pronounced with a falling-rising third sound, it means to buy.

Mandarin has four tones and a fifth, "neutral" sound: The first tone is spoken high-pitched and even, the second rising, the third falling and then rising, and the fourth sound falling.

first sound *ma*: mother
second sound *má*: **hemp**
third sound *mă*: **horse**
fourth sound *mà*: **to complain**

GRAMMAR

The Chinese sentence structure is simple: subject, predicate, object. The simplest way of forming a question is to add the question particle "ma" to the end of a statement. It is usually not possible to know from a Chinese word whether it is a noun, adjective or another form, singular or plural: it depends on the context.

WORDS AND PHRASES

The following pages contain useful words and phrases translated into pinyin and Chinese characters.
English Pinyin Characters
Hello Nǐ hǎo 你好
How are you? Nǐ hǎo ma? 你好吗?
Thank you Xièxie 谢谢

☺ Styles of calligraphy

In the history of Chinese calligraphy, there are four basic styles of writing. The first is the archaic *xiao zhuan* (small-seal script), established in the Qin dynasty (221–206 BC) and which is meticulous and laborious.

The square *li shu*, with its clear brushstrokes, was established in the Han dynasty and used in official writing. Many of the inscriptions on steles of ancient Chinese classics are done in this style.

Cao shu ("grass" or cursive style), in which brushstrokes are often joined together in one continuous flow, was developed as a quicker and simpler alternative to the more formal scripts. More so than any other style, the flamboyance of *cao shu* is a form of individual expression.

Finally, *kai shu* is a combination of the more formal li shu and the more expressive *cao shu*, and is the basis of today's standard calligraphic script.

Calligraphy is still highly esteemed, practised by housewives and politicians alike. Even the old masters will claim they are but students of this fine art.

Goodbye Zài jiàn 再见
My name is... Wǒ jiào... 我叫...
My last name is... Wǒ xìng... 我姓...
What is your name? Nín jiào shénme míngzi? 你叫什么名字?
What is your last name? Nín guìxìng? ....您贵姓?
I am very happy... Wǒ hěn gāoxìng... 我很高兴
All right Hǎo 好
Not all right Bù hǎo 不好
You're welcome Búkèqi 不客气
Can you speak English? Nín huì shuō Yīngyǔ ma? 您会说英语吗?
Can you speak Chinese? Nín huì shuō Hànyǔ ma? 您会说汉语吗?
I cannot speak Chinese Wǒ bù huì Hànyǔ 我不会汉语
I do not understand Wǒ bù dǒng 我不懂
Do you understand? Nín dǒng ma? 您懂吗?
Please speak a little slower Qǐng nín shuō màn yìdiǎnr 请您说慢一点儿
What is this called? Zhège jiào shénme? ..这个叫什么?
How do you say... ... zěnme shuō? ...怎么说?
Please Qǐng 请 / 谢谢
Never mind Méi guānxi 没关系
Sorry Duìbùqǐ 对不起

Pronouns

Who/who is it? Shéi? 谁?
My/mine Wǒ/wǒde 我 / 我的
You/yours (singular) Nǐ/nǐde 你 / 你的
He/his Tā/tāde 他 / 他的
She/hers Tā/tāde 她 / 她的
We/ours Wǒmen/wǒmende 我们 / 我们的
You/yours (plural) Nǐmen/nǐmende 你们 / 你们的
They/theirs Tāmen/tāmende 他们 / 他们的
You/yours (respectful) Nín/nínde 您 / 您的

Travel

Where is it? zài nǎr? 在那儿?
Do you have it here? Zhèr... yǒu ma? 这儿有...吗?
No/it's not here/there aren't any Méi yǒu 没有
Hotel Fàndiàn/bīnguǎn 饭店 / 宾馆
Restaurant Fànguǎn 饭馆
Bank Yínháng 银行
Post Office Yóujú 邮局
Toilet Cèsuǒ 厕所
Railway station Huǒchē zhàn 火车站
Bus station Qìchē zhàn 汽车站
Embassy Dàshíguǎn 大使馆

Consulate Lǐngshìguǎn 领事馆
Passport Hùzhào 护照
Visa Qiānzhèng 签证
Pharmacy Yàodiàn 药店
Hospital Yīyuàn 医院
Doctor Dàifu/yīshēng 大夫 / 医生
Translate Fānyì 翻译
Bar Jiǔbā 酒吧
Do you have...? Nín yǒu... ma? 你有...吗?
I want/I would like Wǒ yào/wǒ xiǎng yào 我要 / 我想要
I want to buy... Wǒ xiǎng mǎi... 我想买...
Where can I buy it? Nǎr néng mǎi... ma? 哪儿能买吗?
This/that Zhège/nèige 这个 / 那个
Green tea/black tea Lùchá/hóngchá 绿茶 / 红茶
Coffee Kāfēi 咖啡
Cigarette Xiāngyān 香烟
Film (for camera) Jiāojuǎnr 胶卷儿
Camera memory card Cúnchǔ kǎ 存储卡
Ticket Piào 票
Postcard Míngxìnpiàn 明信片
Letter Yì fēng xìn 一封信
Air mail Hángkōng xìn 航空信
Postage stamp Yóupiào 邮票

Shopping

How much? Duōshǎo? 多少?
How much does it cost? Zhège duōshǎo qián? 这个多少钱?
Too expensive, thank you Tài guì le, xièxie ... 太贵了，谢谢
Very expensive Hěn guì 很贵
A little (bit) Yìdiǎnr 一点
Too much/too many Tài duō le 太多了
A lot Duō 多
Few Shǎo 少

Money matters, hotels, transport, communications

Money Qián 钱
Chinese currency Rénmínbì 人民币
One yuan/one kuai (10 jiao) Yì yuán/yī kuài 一元 / 一块
One jiao/one mao (10 fen) Yì jiǎo/yì máo 一角 / 一毛
One fen Yì fēn 一分
Traveller's cheque Lǚxíng zhīpiào 旅行支票
Credit card Xìnyòngkǎ 信用卡
Foreign currency Wàihuìquàn 外汇券
Where can I change money? Zài nǎr kěyǐ huàn qián? 在哪儿可以换钱?
I want to change money Wǒ xiǎng huàn qián 我想换钱
What is the exchange rate? Bǐjià shì duōshǎo? 比价是多少?

We want to stay for one (two/three) nights Wǒmen xiǎng zhù yì (liǎng/sān) tiān 我们想住一（两，三）天
How much is the room per day? Fángjiān duōshǎo qián yì tiān? 房间多少钱一天
Room number Fángjiān hàomǎ 房间号码
Single room Dānrén fángjiān 单人房间
Double room Shuāngrén fángjiān 双人房间
Reception Qiāntai/fúwùtai 前台 / 服务台
Key Yàoshi 钥匙
Clothes Yīfu 衣服
Luggage Xínglǐ 行李
Airport Fēijīchǎng 飞机场
Bus Gōnggòng qìchē 公共汽车
Taxi Chūzū qìchē 出租汽车
Bicycle Zìxíngchē 自行车
Telephone Diànhuà 电话
Long-distance call Chángtú diànhuà 长途电话
International call Guójì diànhuà 国际电话
Telephone number Diànhuà hàomǎ 电话号码
Telegram Diànbào 电报
Computer Diàn nǎo/jìsuànjī 电脑 / 计算机
Check email Chá diànxìn 查电信
Use the internet Shàng wǎng 上网

Time

When? Shénme shíhou? 什么时候?
What time is it now? Xiànzài jǐdiǎn zhōng? 现在几点钟?
How long? Duōcháng shíjiān? 多场时间
One/two/three o'clock Yì diǎn/liǎng diǎn/sān diǎn zhōng 一点 / 两点 / 三点钟
Early morning/morning Zǎoshang/shàngwǔ 早上 / 上午
Midday/afternoon/evening Zhōngwǔ/xiàwǔ/wǎnshang 中午 / 下午 / 晚上
Monday Xīngqīyī 星期一
Tuesday Xīngqīèr 星期二
Wednesday Xīngqīsān 星期三
Thursday Xīngqīsì 星期四
Friday Xīngqīwǔ 星期五
Saturday Xīngqīliù 星期六
Sunday Xīngqītiān/xīngqīrì 星期天 / 日
Weekend Zhōumò 周末
Yesterday/today/tomorrow Zuótiān/jīntiān/míngtiān 昨天 / 今天 / 明天
This week/last week/next week Zhègexīngqī/shàngxīngqī/xiàxīngqī 这个星期 / 上星期 / 下星期
Hour/day/week/month Xiǎoshí/tiān/xīngqī/yuè 小时 / 天 / 星期 / 月
January/February/March Yīyuè/

èryuè/sānyuè 一月 / 二月 / 三月
April/May/June Sìyuè/wǔyuè/liùyuè... 四月 / 五月 / 六月
July/August/September Qīyuè/bāyuè/jiǔyuè 七月 / 八月 / 九月
October/November/December Shíyuè/shíyīyuè/shíèryuè ...十月 / 十一月 / 十二月

Eating out

Restaurant Cāntīng/fànguǎn'r 餐厅 / 饭馆儿
Attendant/waiter Fúwùyuán 服务员
Waitress Xiǎojiě 小姐
Eat Chī fàn 吃饭
Breakfast Zǎofàn 早饭
Lunch Wǔfàn 午饭
Dinner Wǎnfàn 晚饭
Menu Càidān 菜单
Chopsticks Kuàizi 筷子
Knife Dāozi 刀子
Fork Chāzi 叉子
Spoon Sháozi 勺子
Cup/glass Bēizi/bōlíbēi 杯子 / 玻璃杯
Bowl Wǎn 碗
Plate Pán 盘
Paper napkin Cānjīn zhǐ 餐巾纸
I want... Wǒ yào... 我要
I do not want... Wǒ bú yào... 我不要
I did not order this Zhège wǒ méi diǎn 这个我没点
I am a vegetarian Wǒ shì chī sù de rén 我是吃素的人
I do not eat any meat Wǒ suǒyǒude ròu dōu bù chī 我所有的肉都不吃
I do not eat any meat or fish Wǒ suǒyǒude ròu hé yú, dōu bù chī 我所有的肉和鱼都不吃
Please fry it in vegetable oil Qǐng yòng zhíwù yóu chǎo chǎo 请用植物油炒炒
Beer Píjiǔ 啤酒
Red/white wine Hóng/bái pútaojiǔ 红 / 白葡萄酒
Liquor Bái jiǔ 白酒
Mineral water Kuàngquánshuǐ 矿泉水
Soft drinks Yǐnliào 饮料
Cola Kělè 可乐
Tea Cháshuǐ 茶水
Fruit Shuǐguǒ 水果
Bread Miànbāo 面包
Toast Kǎomiànbāo 烤面包
Yoghurt Suān nǎi 酸奶
Fried/boiled egg Chǎo/zhǔ jīdàn 炒 / 煮鸡蛋
Rice Mǐfàn 米饭
Soup Tāng 汤
Stir-fried dishes Chǎo cài 炒菜
Beef/pork/lamb/chicken Niú/zhū/yáng/jī ròu 牛肉 / 猪肉 / 羊肉 / 鸡肉
Fish Yú 鱼
Vegetables Shūcài 蔬菜

Spicy/sweet/sour/salty Là/tián/suān/xián 辣 / 甜 / 酸 / 咸
Hot/cold Rè/liáng 热 / 凉
Can we have the bill, please Qǐng jié zhàng/mǎidān 请结账 / 买单

Specialities

Peking Duck Běijīng kǎoyā 北京烤鸭
Hot pot Huǒ guō 火锅
Phoenix in the Nest Fèng zài wōlǐ ... 凤在窝里
Mandarin fish Tángcù guìyú ...糖醋鳜鱼
Thousand layer cake Qiān céng bǐng 千层饼
Lotus prawns Ôu piàn'r xiārén 藕片虾仁
Home-style cooking Jiā cháng cài 家常菜

Appetisers

Deep-fried peanuts Zhá huāshēngmǐ ...炸花生米
Boiled peanuts Zhǔ huāshēngmǐ ... 煮花生米
Soft beancurd Bàn dòufu 拌豆腐
"Hairy" green beans Máo dòu 毛豆
Cucumber in garlic sauce Pái huánggua 拍黄瓜
Pressed beancurd strips Dòufu sī 豆腐丝
Thousand-year-old eggs Sōnghuā dàn 松花蛋
Smoked beancurd with celery Qíncài dòufu gān'r 芹菜豆腐干

Meat dishes

Aubergine/eggplant fritters stuffed with minced pork Qié hé ...茄盒
Spicy chicken with chillies Làzi jīdīng 辣子鸡丁
Spicy chicken with peanuts gōngbào jīdīng ...宫爆鸡丁
Pork with egg and "tree ear" fungus Mùxù ròu 木须肉
Shredded pork with bamboo shoots Dōngsǔn ròusī 冬笋肉丝
Beef in brown sauce Hóngshāo niúròu ...红烧牛肉

Sizzling "iron plate" beef Tiěbǎn niúròu... 铁板牛肉
Beef with potatoes Tǔdòu niúròu ... 土豆牛肉

Seafood

Prawns with cashew nuts Yāoguǒ xiārén 腰果虾仁
Carp in brown sauce Hóngshāo lǐyú 红烧鲤鱼
Boiled prawns Shuǐzhǔ xiārén 水煮虾仁
Stir-fried prawns Qīngchǎo xiārén 清炒虾仁
Sweet and sour mandarin fish Tángcù guìyú 糖醋鳜鱼
Hot and sour squid Suānlà yóuyú juàn 酸辣鱿鱼卷

Vegetable dishes

Sweetcorn with pine kernels Sōngrén yùmǐ 松仁玉米
Mangetout/snowpeas Hélán dòu 荷兰豆
Spicy "dry" green beans Gānbiān biǎndòu 干煸扁豆
Spicy "fish flavour" aubergine Yúxiāng qiézi 鱼香茄子
Greens with dried mushrooms Xiānggū yóucài 香菇油菜
Spicy beancurd with chilli Málà dòufu 麻辣豆腐
Stir-fried egg and tomato Xīhóngshì chǎo jīdàn 西红柿炒鸡蛋
Fried shredded potato Tǔdòu sī 土豆丝
Clay pot with beancurd soup Shāguō dòufu 沙锅豆腐
Sour cabbage with "glass" noodles Suāncài fěnsī 酸菜粉丝
Potato, aubergine and green pepper Dì sān xiān 地三鲜

Staple food

Steamed bread Mántou 馒头
Cornbread Wōtou 窝头
Fried rice Dàn chǎo fàn 蛋炒饭
Plain rice Bái fàn 白饭
Sizzling rice crust Guōbā 锅巴
Noodles Miàntiáo 面条
Pancakes Bǐng 饼

Soups

Hot and sour soup Suānlà tāng 酸辣汤
Egg and tomato soup Xīhóngshì jīdàn tāng 西红柿鸡蛋汤
Beancurd soup Dòufu tāng 豆腐汤
Lamb and marrow soup Yángròu dōngguā tāng 羊肉冬瓜汤
Fish-head soup Yútóu tāng 鱼头汤

Fast food

Noodles Miàntiáo 面条
Stuffed pasta parcels Jiǎozi 饺子
Meat/vegetable filling Ròu xiàn/sù xiàn 肉馅 / 素馅
Steamed meat buns Bāozi 包子
"Potstickers" (fried jiaozi) Guōtiē 锅贴
Egg pancake Jiān bǐng 煎饼
Wonton soup Húndùn 馄饨
Soy milk Dòu jiāng 豆浆
Deep-fried dough sticks Yóutiáo 油条

Numbers

One Yī 一
Two Èr 二
Three Sān 三
Four Sì 四
Five Wǔ 五
Six Liù 六
Seven Qī 七
Eight Bā 八
Nine Jiǔ 九
Ten Shí 十
Eleven Shíyī 十一
Twelve Shíèr 十二
Twenty Èrshí 二十
Thirty Sānshí 三十
Forty Sìshí 四十
Fifty Wǔshí 五十
Sixty Liùshí 六十
Seventy Qīshí 七十
Eighty Bāshí 八十
Ninety Jiǔshí 九十
One hundred Yìbǎi 一百
One hundred and one Yìbǎi língyī 一百零一
Two hundred Liǎng bǎi 两百
Three hundred Sān bǎi 三百
Four hundred Sì bǎi 四百
Five hundred Wǔ bǎi 五百
One thousand Yìqiān 一千

HISTORY

Behind the Wall (Colin Thubron). Written in the mid-eighties, it is a reminder of what China was then, and – Thubron being as prescient as he is – there are many fascinating insights into the China of today.

China: A New History (John King Fairbank). A definitive general account of China's long history by a doyen of American Sinologists.

The Great Chinese Revolution, 1800– 1985 (John King Fairbank). A concise and thorough summary of two turbulent centuries, by a leading China scholar.

Life along the Silk Road (Susan Whitfield). A fascinating and erudite collection of historical "short stories" based on characters – the merchant, the soldier, the courtesan, etc – chiefly based on first-hand information derived from the archives and murals of Dunhuang.

Mao: The Unknown Story (Jung Chang, Jon Halliday). Thought-provoking and searingly critical appraisal of the Mao era. Essential reading for anyone interested in the evolution of modern China.

Oracle Bones: A Journey Between Past and Present (Peter Hessler). The follow-up to the New Yorker correspondent's 2001 *River Town* interweaves his experience as a journalist in China with explorations of the country's history.

Red Star Over China (Edgar Snow). First-hand account of the birth and early years of Chinese Communism by an American journalist and sympathiser who was a personal friend of Mao Zedong and Zhou Enlai.

The Opium War (Julia Lovell). A rollicking tale of one of the founding myths of the Chinese Communist Party – that continues to shape Sino-British relations.

The Search for Modern China (Jonathan Spence). Definitive history of China from the establishment of the Ming dynasty to the modern day.

Trespassers on the Roof of the World: The Race for Lhasa (Peter Hopkirk). Engaging and painstakingly researched account of the major 19th-century attempts by Westerners to reach this long-forbidden city.

BIOGRAPHY

China Remembers (Li Jia and Calum MacLeod). Vivid personal accounts of China's 20th century, with scene-setting background history.

God's Chinese Son (Jonathan Spence). Spence's masterly grasp of storytelling and historical research makes this an enthralling biography of Hong Xiuquan, leader of the Christian Taiping.

The Good Women of China (Xinran). This collection of short biographical vignettes came from women callers to a new radio show in the years of burgeoning freedom following the Cultural Revolution. Poignant, revealing and informative.

The Hermit of Peking: the Hidden Life of Sir Edmund Backhouse (Hugh Trevor-Roper). Marvellous piece of investigative spadework from the famed historian on the trail of forger and eccentric Wykehamist Edmund Backhouse.

The Man Who Loved China (Simon Winchester). The story of Joseph Needham, the Cambridge professor who devoted 60 years of his life to researching and chronicling the *History of Science and Civilization* in China in more than 20 encylopaedic volumes.

On China (Henry Kissinger). The former American security chief describes more than 50 official trips to China.

The Private Life of Chairman Mao (Dr Li Zhisui). A gossipy, erudite and highly amusing look at the depravities, personal habits and disastrous policies of Chairman Mao, by his Western-educated personal physician.

The Soong Dynasty (Sterling Seagrave). The story of China's most influential family, including Chiang Kaishek, his wife, Soong Mayling, and her brother, T.V. Soong – for a time China's richest man – during the first half of the 20th century.

Wild Swans: Three Daughters of China (Jung Chang). The turbulence of the Cultural Revolution in China as seen through the eyes of three generations of women – grandmother, mother and daughter.

CURRENT AFFAIRS

China Shakes The World (James Kynge). This is primarily a piece of highly readable economics by the *Financial Times'* former Beijing Bureau chief, but it goes far beyond statistics to deliver a superb snapshot of life in 21st-century China.

China Wakes: The Struggle for the Soul of a Rising Power (Nicholas D. Kristof and Sheryl WuDunn). A captivating collection of vignettes from the experiences of these former *New York Times* correspondents.

The China Dream: The Elusive Quest for the Greatest Untapped Market on Earth (Joe Studwell). Salutary observations and cautionary tales for those contemplating doing business in China.

The Chinese (Jasper Becker). Fine analysis of contemporary China and what makes the country tick, from a former correspondent of the *South China Morning Post*.

The Coming Collapse of China (Gordon Chang). Strong on polemic, Chang's book may seem opinionated, but it is backed up by solid research and ultimately convinces.

The Dragon in the Land of Snows: A History of Modern Tibet since 1947 (Tsering Shakya). A painstakingly researched yet highly readable account of modern Tibet – the best yet published.

The Search for a Vanishing Beijing, a Guide to China's Capital through the Ages (M.A. Aldrich). A deeply informed exploration of China's history, legends and culture, as seen through the window of its fast-changing capital city.

The Ugly Chinaman and the Crisis of Chinese Culture (Bo Yang, translated by Don Cohn). A controversial and scathing indictment of many aspects of traditional Chinese culture, which has sparked intense debate in the Chinese-speaking world.

Wild Grass, Three Portraits of Change in Modern China (Ian Johnson). The book tells the stories of three ordinary Chinese people who, in their own small ways, challenge the system.

Wild West China: The Taming of Xinjiang (Christian Tyler). An important book tackling China's Islamic northwestern region and its aspirations for independence.

TRAVEL WRITING

Bamboo Goalposts (Rowan Simons). Highly amusing account of British journalist and football enthusiast's attempts to persuade the Chinese to embrace the beautiful game.

My Life as an Explorer (Sven Hedin, with a prologue and epilogue by Peter Hopkirk). The epic memoirs of the legendary Swedish explorer, adventurer and archaeologist give a fascinating insight into aspects of the Silk Road and Tibet that no longer exist.

News from Tartary (Ian Fleming). Classic travelogue across northwest China and Xinjiang in the 1930s.

Red Dust, a Path Through China (Ma Jian). It begins as a travel-adventure article by a disillusioned Beijing native, but soon evolves into a sweeping appraisal of modern China.

Riding the Iron Rooster: By Train Through China (Paul Theroux). Highly readable and informed account of China on the cusp of opening to the outside world.

The River at the Centre of the World: A Journey up the Yangtze and back in Chinese Time (Simon Winchester). Fascinating account of the author's voyage from the mouth of China's longest river to its source in Tibet, masterfully weaving travel prose with historical narrative.

River Town: Two Years on the Yangtze (Peter Hessler). Hessler's celebrated tale of two years in Fuling on the Yangtze River.

Seven Years in Tibet (Heinrich Harrer). The evocative account of a German national trapped in Tibet by World War II who became friends with the Dalai Lama.

Shadow of the Silk Road (Colin Thubron). Although Thubron follows the Silk Road from Xi'an all the way to its western terminus in Turkey, his account of contemporary Chinese Central Asia in the first half of this book is unsurpassed.

The Travels of Marco Polo (Ronald Latham). Tried and tested English translation of Polo's *Il Milione*, including his travels through 13th-century China.

PHILOSOPHY

Art of War (Sun Tzu, translated by Ralph D. Sawyer). Though there are dozens of English translations of this ancient Chinese military treatise, this is one of the most highly acclaimed.

Bardo Thodol (known in the West as *The Tibetan Book of the Dead*, discovered by Karma Lingpa). The classic text detailing what Tibetans believe the human consciousness experiences in the interim period between death and rebirth.

Daode Jing (Tao Te Ching) (Laozi). Both profound and accessible, the Classic of the Way and its Power is a keystone to understanding Daoist philosophy.

Understanding Confucianism: Origins, Beliefs, Practices, Holy texts, Sacred Places (Jennifer Oldstone-Moore). Learned yet very readable account of the principals of the philosophical system that made traditional China tick and laid the foundations of Chinese culture.

FICTION

A Case of Two Cities, by Qui Xiaolong. One of a series of wonderfully gritty detective novels featuring the gentle and poetic Inspector Chen Cao, and his investigations into the seamy, crime-ridden underworld of modern Shanghai.

The True Story of Ah Q, by Lu Xun. A scathing but engaging look at the deep endemic flaws in the Chinese character, by China's most famous 20th-century novelist.

OTHER INSIGHT GUIDES

Insight Guides cover destinations all over the world, providing information on culture and all the top sights, as well as superb photography.

Other Insight Guides to China include *The Silk Road* (covering all the main sights along the historic route between China and the Mediterranean). The smaller-format City Guides cover *Beijing*, *Shanghai* and *Hong Kong*.

Insight Guides' Explore series offers an itinerary-based approach to destinations, with recommendations from a local expert to make the most of a short stay. Titles in this region include *Shanghai*, *Beijing* and *Hong Kong* as well as *Tokyo*, *Singapore* and *Kuala Lumpur*.

Insight Fleximaps combine clear, detailed cartography with essential travel information. The laminated finish makes the maps durable, weatherproof and easy to fold. Titles covering this region include *Beijing*, *Shanghai*, *Guangzhou*, *Hong Kong*, *Kuala Lumpur*, *Macau*, *Ho Chi Minh City* and *Vietnam, Cambodia & Laos*.

⊘ Send Us Your Thoughts

We do our best to ensure the information in our books is as accurate and up-to-date as possible. The books are updated on a regular basis using local contacts, who painstakingly add, amend and correct as required. However, some details (such as telephone numbers and opening times) are liable to change, and we are ultimately reliant on our readers to put us in the picture.

We welcome your feedback, especially your experience of using the book "on the road". Maybe we recommended a hotel that you liked (or another that you didn't), or you came across a great bar or new attraction we missed.

We will acknowledge all contributions, and we'll offer an Insight Guide to the best letters received.

Please write to us at:
Insight Guides
PO Box 7910
London SE1 1WE
Or email us at:
hello@insightguides.com

CREDITS

INSIGHT GUIDE CREDITS

Distribution
UK, Ireland and Europe
Apa Publications (UK) Ltd;
sales@insightguides.com
United States and Canada
Ingram Publisher Services;
ips@ingramcontent.com
Australia and New Zealand
Woodslane; info@woodslane.com.au
Southeast Asia
Apa Publications (SN) Pte;
singaporeoffice@insightguides.com
Hong Kong, Taiwan and China
Apa Publications (HK) Ltd;
hongkongoffice@insightguides.com
Worldwide
Apa Publications (UK) Ltd;
sales@insightguides.com
Special Sales, Content Licensing and CoPublishing
Insight Guides can be purchased in bulk quantities at discounted prices. We can create special editions, personalised jackets and corporate imprints tailored to your needs. sales@insightguides.com www.insightguides.biz

Printed in Poland by Pozkal

First Edition 1990
Thirteenth Edition 2017

Every effort has been made to provide accurate information in this publication, but changes are inevitable. The publisher cannot be responsible for any resulting loss, inconvenience or injury. We would appreciate it if readers would call our attention to any errors or outdated information. We also welcome your suggestions; please contact us at: hello@insightguides.com

www.insightguides.com

Editor: Sarah Clark
Author: Magdalena Helsztyńska
Head of Production: Rebeka Davies
Update Production: Apa Digital
Picture Editor: Tom Smyth
Cartography: original cartography Berndtson & Berndtson, updated by Carte

CONTRIBUTORS

This 13th edition of our comprehensive guide to China was managed and copyedited by Managing Editor Sarah Clark and thoroughly updated by travel writer Magdalena Helsztyńska.

It builds on the solid foundation of previous editions, which were written by a panel of China experts including David Drakeford, Jane Voodikon, Matt Bowden, Amy Fabris-Shi, Ralph Jennings, Sophie Ibbotson, Max Lovell-Hoare, Brice Minnigh, Ed Peters, Brent Hannon, Andrew Forbes, Graham Bond and Ruth Williams, and were commissioned by former Insight editor, Tom Le Bas.

The book was indexed by Penny Phenix.

ABOUT INSIGHT GUIDES

Insight Guides have more than 45 years' experience of publishing high-quality, visual travel guides. We produce 400 full-colour titles, in both print and digital form, covering more than 200 destinations across the globe, in a variety of formats to meet your different needs.

Insight Guides are written by local authors, whose expertise is evident in the extensive historical and cultural background features. Each destination is carefully researched by regional experts to ensure our guides provide the very latest information. All the reviews in **Insight Guides** are independent; we strive to maintain an impartial view. Our reviews are carefully selected to guide you to the best places to eat, go out and shop, so you can be confident that when we say a place is special, we really mean it.

Legend

City maps

	Freeway/Highway/Motorway
	Divided Highway
	Main Roads
	Minor Roads
	Pedestrian Roads
	Steps
	Footpath
	Railway
	Funicular Railway
	Cable Car
	Tunnel
	City Wall
	Important Building
	Built Up Area
	Other Land
	Transport Hub
	Park
	Pedestrian Area
	Bus Station
	Tourist Information
	Main Post Office
	Cathedral/Church
	Mosque
	Synagogue
	Statue/Monument
	Beach
	Airport

Regional maps

	Freeway/Highway/Motorway (with junction)
	Freeway/Highway/Motorway (under construction)
	Divided Highway
	Main Road
	Secondary Road
	Minor Road
	Track
	Footpath
	International Boundary
	State/Province Boundary
	National Park/Reserve
	Marine Park
	Ferry Route
	Marshland/Swamp
	Glacier / Salt Lake
	Airport/Airfield
	Ancient Site
	Border Control
	Cable Car
	Castle/Castle Ruins
	Cave
	Chateau/Stately Home
	Church/Church Ruins
	Crater
	Lighthouse
	Mountain Peak
	Place of Interest
	Viewpoint

INDEX

N

INSIGHT ● GUIDES

OFF THE SHELF

Since 1970, **INSIGHT GUIDES** has provided a unique perspective on the world's best travel destinations by using specially commissioned photography and illuminating text written by local authors.

Whether you're planning a city break, a walking tour or the journey of a lifetime, our superb range of guidebooks and phrasebooks will inspire you to discover more about your chosen destination.

INSIGHT GUIDES

offer a unique combination of stunning photos, absorbing narrative and detailed maps, providing all the inspiration and information you need.

PHRASEBOOKS & DICTIONARIES

help users to feel at home, when away. Pocket-sized with a free app to download, they go where you do.

CITY GUIDES

pack hundreds of great photos into a smaller format with detailed practical information, so you can navigate the world's top cities with confidence.

EXPLORE GUIDES

feature easy-to-follow walks and itineraries in the world's most exciting destinations, with our choice of the best places to eat and drink along the way.

POCKET GUIDES

combine concise information on where to go and what to do in a handy compact format, ideal on the ground. Includes a full-colour, fold-out map.

EXPERIENCE GUIDES

feature offbeat perspectives and secret gems for experienced travellers, with a collection of over 100 ideas for a memorable stay in a city.

www.insightguides.com

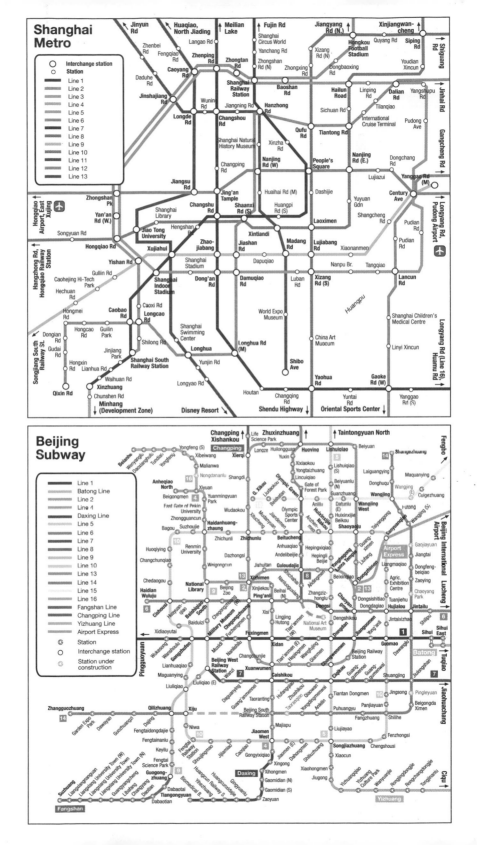